Mastering Adobe Captivate 2019

Fifth Edition

Build cutting edge professional SCORM compliant and interactive eLearning content with Adobe Captivate

Dr. Pooja Jaisingh
Damien Bruyndonckx

BIRMINGHAM - MUMBAI

Mastering Adobe Captivate 2019
Fifth Edition

Commissioning Editor: Amarabha Banerjee
Acquisition Editor: Larissa Pinto
Content Development Editor: Flavian Vaz
Technical Editor: Sachin Sunilkumar
Copy Editor: Safis Editing
Project Coordinator: Pragati Shukla
Proofreader: Safis Editing
Indexer: Rekha Nair
Graphics: Alishon Mendonsa
Production Coordinator: Tom Scaria

First published: August 2012
Second edition: February 2014
Third edition: March 2015
Fourth edition: September 2017
Fifth edition: January 2019

Production reference: 1310119

Published by Packt Publishing Ltd.
Livery Place
35 Livery Street
Birmingham
B3 2PB, UK.

ISBN 978-1-78980-305-1

www.packtpub.com

During the writing of this book, my uncle, Philippe Bruyndonckx, retired after a successful career of more than 45 years as director of a social facility for children and teenagers. I've always been inspired by the dedication, hard work, and enthusiasm of that man. During his retirement speech, he made a bold statement about the importance of these core values.

I dedicate this book to my uncle and to all the men and women who know that, despite the sophistication of technology, eLearning will always remain a craft that requires hard work, dedication, attention to detail and, above all, a true love for those we serve.

– Damien Bruyndonckx

I would like to dedicate this book to my friends and colleagues at Adobe, and thank them for creating an industry-leading eLearning tool and giving us content-creation power. Thank you Tridib, Priyank, Ashish, Shameer, Akshay, Suresh, Krishnan, Sankaram, Nipun, Gourav, Manoj, Shubha, Avranil, Shreya, and all the amazing Captivate engineers. A special thanks to Dr. Allen Partridge for writing the foreword for this book, and for encouraging Damien and me throughout this project.

– Dr. Pooja Jaisingh

`mapt.io`

Mapt is an online digital library that gives you full access to over 5,000 books and videos, as well as industry leading tools to help you plan your personal development and advance your career. For more information, please visit our website.

Why subscribe?

- Spend less time learning and more time coding with practical eBooks and videos from over 4,000 industry professionals

- Improve your learning with Skill Plans built especially for you

- Get a free eBook or video every month

- Mapt is fully searchable

- Copy and paste, print, and bookmark content

Packt.com

Did you know that Packt offers eBook versions of every book published, with PDF and ePub files available? You can upgrade to the eBook version at `www.packt.com` and as a print book customer, you are entitled to a discount on the eBook copy. Get in touch with us at `customercare@packtpub.com` for more details.

At `www.packt.com`, you can also read a collection of free technical articles, sign up for a range of free newsletters, and receive exclusive discounts and offers on Packt books and eBooks.

Foreword

Training in all forms plays a substantial role in the success of organizations and businesses across the globe. Over the past quarter of a century, the impact of training on organizational success has become ever more apparent. Organizations have come to recognize that training impacts virtually all aspects of goal attainment in virtually every type of organization. From recognizing the impact of leadership training in information-driven businesses to identifying the impact of training in businesses that rely on learning to mitigate the effects of high turnover, every successful business today has come to recognize that without effective training, the organization cannot succeed. While training is still delivered in a variety of ways, delivery of most forms of training in online asynchronous formats has the potential to radically reduce the costs of training in the organization. It can potentially magnify the impact and value of that training by offering learning in a modality that provides better opportunities for personalization, repeated and convenient access, as well as careful monitoring and tracking of training outcomes.

The creation of online learning materials that fulfill this promise is the challenge addressed by Adobe Captivate. As a rapid eLearning authoring tool, Adobe Captivate has led the way in creating powerful tools for instructors, instructional designers, developers, and subject matter experts. Captivate is an easy-to-learn and easy-to-use multimedia authoring tool. It provides a host of special tools aimed at facilitating the easy creation of various training experiences, such as scenario-based training, process (step-by-step) training, product training, software/application capture, and video-based training. It supplements these tools with quiz creation and tracking capabilities as well as a variety of pre-built, easy-to-assemble information delivery and content creation tools.

Adobe Captivate has a nearly twenty-year history of leadership in the online course authoring space. During that time, there are a handful of people who have documented and shared some of the most essential strategies, methods, technologies, and pedagogical/andragogical approaches to online learning. Without question, Dr. Pooja Jaisingh and Damien Bruyndonckx have been among the foremost of these experts.

In this, the fifth edition of *Mastering Adobe Captivate 2019*, that extraordinary tradition is both evolved and well maintained. Readers will find the latest information about creating online eLearning with Adobe Captivate 2019, including the use of incredible new features, such as 360 virtual learning, and features that radically expedite the development process, such as the video overlay functions. These enhanced features allow even novice users to rapidly create beautiful, high-performance eLearning that includes automated assessments with extremely little time and effort. This extraordinary overview of Adobe Captivate 2019 provides readers with an easy-to-access and easy-to-comprehend guide to the use of the software.

Allen Partridge

Sr. Manager, eLearning Evangelism Group – Adobe Systems

January 2019

About the authors

Dr. Pooja Jaisingh works as a senior learning evangelist at Adobe for Captivate, Captivate Prime LMS, and Presenter. She has created several award-winning eLearning courses and eBooks, and regularly conducts workshops and webinars on Adobe eLearning tools and services. In her previous roles, she has worked as a teacher trainer, instructional designer, and chief learning geek. She has authored several courses on Adobe Captivate and Captivate Prime for Lynda.com and LinkedIn Learning. Pooja is CPLP and COTP certified. She holds a master's degree in education and economics and a doctorate in educational technology. You can contact her on Twitter, @poojajaisingh, and via her website at www.poojajaisingh.com.

I started my eLearning career reading books authored by Dr. Michael Allen. He completely changed my perspective and gave me wonderful ideas on making eLearning engaging and interesting. Though I met him in person only a few years back, his work in the eLearning field has always inspired me. Thank you Dr. Allen for everything you do!

Authoring a book can be a whirlwind experience. But when you have Damien as a co-author, everything seems to be easy and controlled. I've thoroughly enjoyed co-authoring this book with my dear friend Damien!

I would also like to thank Packt Publishing for bringing this book to life, and our friend Kirsten Rourke for reviewing this book. Your feedback helped us immensely in finessing the content.

Finally, I would like to thank my friends and family for always being there for me through thick and thin. And special thanks to my little princess, Mishti, for bringing joy and happiness into my life!

Damien Bruyndonckx has an interest in teaching that dates back to his original training as an elementary school teacher. He began his career in 1998, teaching French as a foreign language in two elementary public schools in Louisiana, USA. In 2001, he came back to Belgium, his home country, and began to work as an IT trainer. He soon acquired the title of Adobe Certified Instructor on various Adobe products, which allowed him to work for a large number of customers and Adobe-authorized training centers across Europe. In 2009, he went back to teaching at IHECS, a higher education school of communications based in Brussels, where he was asked to implemented eLearning in the curriculum. Thanks to his work at IHECS, Damien became an Adobe Education Leader in November 2011. Today, Damien is the co-owner and the pedagogical director of DiDaXo, a Belgium-based eLearning company. Damien is the author or co-author of the *Mastering Adobe Captivate* series by Packt Publishing. You will find him speaking at various Captivate- and eLearning-related events around the world. He lives in Thuin, Belgium, with his girlfriend and his two children. Damien is a music lover and occasionally works as a sound and lighting technician in the entertainment industry.

The publication of a book like this one always marks the end of a crazy adventure. For the second time, Dr. Pooja Jaisingh was my "partner in crime," and once again, it has been a privilege to work with her.

I also want to thank our friend Kirsten Rourke for reviewing the book. Dear Kirsten, it is always a pleasure to interact with you, in person or remotely. The work done together on this book makes no exception!

Thank you to the Packt Publishing team that has made this book possible. Special thanks to Flavian Vaz for sticking with us throughout the making of this project

Finally, I would like to thank the ones that share my life on a daily basis. Without the support, dedication, encouragement, and love of my sweet Céline, none of this would be possible.

About the reviewer

Kirsten Rourke has worked as a learning and development trainer and consultant for over two decades. She is an eLearning developer, public speaker, and certified technical trainer who owns and operates Rourke Training, which provides instructional design, development, speaking, and training services in partnership with several training vendors.

When not playing video games obsessively or dancing, she divides her time between eLearning development, creating training videos, publishing articles on software, or giving virtual and in-person training. She can be found presenting at industry events, such as DevLearn, at @kirstenrourke on Twitter, or at rourketraining.com.

> *I would like to thank Damien and Pooja for allowing me to join them in the creation of this book. I enjoyed it tremendously. I'd also like to thank my husband, David, for his infinite patience, and Pragati Shukla at Packt Publishing for her coordination skills and ability to herd cats with grace.*

Packt is searching for authors like you

If you're interested in becoming an author for Packt, please visit authors.packtpub.com and apply today. We have worked with thousands of developers and tech professionals, just like you, to help them share their insight with the global tech community. You can make a general application, apply for a specific hot topic that we are recruiting an author for, or submit your own idea.

Table of Contents

Preface

Adobe Captivate is the industry-leading solution for authoring highly interactive eLearning content that can be delivered on any device. With Adobe Captivate, you can capture onscreen action, enhance eLearning projects, insert SCORM- and xAPI-compliant quizzes, optimize content for multiscreen delivery, make videos interactive, create stunning virtual reality training, and publish your work in various formats (including Adobe Flash and HTML5) for easy deployment on virtually any LMS, desktop, or mobile device.

Mastering Adobe Captivate 2019 is a comprehensive step-by-step guide to creating SCORM-compliant eLearning content including demonstrations, simulations, virtual reality projects, and quizzes that can be experienced on any device. The sample projects in this book have been designed to demonstrate virtually every feature of Adobe Captivate, giving you the expertise you need to create and deploy your own professional quality eLearning courses.

Who this book is for

If you are a teacher, instructional designer, eLearning developer, or human resources manager who wants to implement eLearning, then this book is for you. A basic knowledge of your OS is all it takes to create the next generation of responsive eLearning content.

What this book covers

Chapter 1, *Getting Started with Adobe Captivate 2019*, introduces Captivate as an eLearning solution. It takes you through the Captivate interface and presents the sample applications that you will build during the course of the book. At the end of this chapter, you will have a precise idea of what Captivate 2019 is capable of and of the work that will be covered in the rest of the book.

Chapter 2, *Working with Standard Objects*, teaches you how to work with the standard objects of Adobe Captivate. These objects include the Text Caption, the Smart Shape, and the Image objects, among others. Important Captivate workflows are also discussed in this chapter.

Chapter 3, *Working with Multimedia,* covers how to include and edit various types of multimedia elements in your eLearning projects. The tools covered in this chapter include the insertion of animations, as well as video and audio files into the project.

Chapter 4, *Working with the Timeline and Other Useful Tools,* covers various tools and features (such as the Alignment tools and Smart Guides) used to lay the objects out in the physical space of the slide. The use of the Timeline panel to synchronize the components of the project is also discussed in detail.

Chapter 5, *Developing Interactivity,* covers the interactive objects and workflows of Adobe Captivate 2019. These objects include the Drag and Drop interaction, Click Box, Text Entry Box, and Button. The all-new Interactive Video workflow is also covered in this chapter. Adding interactivity to allow you to design branching scenarios is discussed in this chapter as well.

Chapter 6, *Crafting the Graphical Experience with Styles and Themes,* focuses on the aesthetic aspects of your projects. You will learn how to ensure visual consistency both within a project and across projects using Styles, Master Slides, Themes, and Templates.

Chapter 7, *Working with Quizzes,* discusses the powerful Quizzing engine of Captivate. You will import questions into your Captivate project using various techniques, review each question type in Captivate, and integrate them into question pools to generate random quizzes. In the second part of this chapter, you will learn how to report these interactions to a SCORM- or xAPI-compliant LMS to easily track your student's performance.

Chapter 8, *Capturing On-Screen Action,* covers the screen capture engine of Captivate. You will learn how to capture interactive demonstrations and simulations using a wide variety of tools and techniques.

Chapter 9, *Producing a Video Demo,* focuses on producing a video tutorial from start to finish. This includes using the all-new Background Removal feature and all the specifics of that type of project as compared to the regular Captivate projects used in previous chapters.

Chapter 10, *Creating a Responsive Project,* discusses the use of Fluid Boxes to create a Responsive Project. You will learn how to optimize your eLearning content for multiple screens and devices, including the desktop computer, the tablet, and the smartphone.

Chapter 11, *Creating Virtual Reality Projects*, covers the brand new virtual reality features of Adobe Captivate 2019. In this chapter, you will create a virtual reality project, import 360 images into Captivate, add text labels and interactive hotspots on the 360 images, and insert Question Overlay Slides in the 360 experience.

Chapter 12, *Using Captivate with Other Applications*, explores the relationship between Captivate and other Adobe and third-party applications. First, you will convert a PowerPoint presentation into a Captivate project. You will then export some Captivate data to Microsoft Word in order to localize a Captivate project. You will also import an Adobe Photoshop file, edit audio with Adobe Audition, and edit SVGs with Adobe Illustrator.

Chapter 13, *Creating Accessible eLearning*, discusses how and why it is important to make your eLearning courses accessible for people with hearing, visual, and mobility disabilities. You will learn how to add accessibility text, closed captions, keyboard shortcuts, and tabbing order to the slides and objects in your Captivate projects to make them accessible for learners with special needs.

Chapter 14, *Variables and Advanced Actions*, unleashes the full power of Captivate by exploring Variables, Advanced Actions, and the use of JavaScript in Adobe Captivate. These features will help you design and develop highly interactive eLearning content that offers a unique personalized experience to each learner.

Chapter 15, *Finishing Touches and Publishing*, covers the project-wide preferences and the publication of your eLearning content in various formats. First, you will make your projects ready for publishing by modifying project-level options and preferences. One of these options is the Skin, which lets you customize the playback controls and the table of contents of your projects. In the second part of this chapter, you will make your projects available to the outside world by publishing them in various formats, including Adobe Flash, HTML5, video, and PDF.

To get the most out of this book

You need the latest version of Adobe Captivate 2019 (available as a free 30-day trial version on the Adobe website) to complete the exercises in this book. Some exercises require the installation of the Adobe eLearning assets and Text-To-Speech voice agents. Both these packages are part of your Adobe Captivate license and are available for free on the Adobe website. You can download your trial copy of Adobe Captivate 2019 from https://www.adobe.com/be_en/products/captivate/download-trial/try.html

This book assumes a clean install of Adobe Captivate with all the preferences at their default. If needed, you can reset Captivate preferences to default using the following steps:

1. Make sure Adobe Captivate 2019 is not running.
2. Navigate to the folder where Captivate is installed:
   - `C:\Program Files\Adobe\Adobe Captivate 2019 x64` (Windows)
   - `/Applications/Adobe Captivate 2019` (Mac)
3. Navigate to the `utils` directory.
4. Double-click the `CleanPreferencesWin.bat` (Windows) or the `CleanPreferencesMac` (Mac) file.
5. The next time you start Captivate, your preferences should be back to default.

Other requirements are as follows:

- A modern web browser with the latest version of the Flash Player installed
- Microsoft PowerPoint 2013 or higher (optional)
- Microsoft Word 2013 or higher (optional)
- Latest version of Adobe Photoshop CC (optional)
- Latest version of Adobe Audition CC (optional)
- Latest version of Adobe Illustrator CC (optional)

Download the example code files

You can download the example code files for this book from your account at `www.packt.com`. If you purchased this book elsewhere, you can visit `www.packt.com/support` and register to have the files emailed directly to you.

You can download the code files by following these steps:

1. Log in or register at `www.packt.com`.
2. Select the **SUPPORT** tab.
3. Click on **Code Downloads & Errata**.
4. Enter the name of the book in the **Search** box and follow the onscreen instructions.

Once the file is downloaded, please make sure that you unzip or extract the folder using the latest version of:

- WinRAR/7-Zip for Windows
- Zipeg/iZip/UnRarX for Mac
- 7-Zip/PeaZip for Linux

The code bundle for the book is also hosted on GitHub at `https://github.com/PacktPublishing/Mastering-Adobe-Captivate-2019-Fifth-Edition`. In case there's an update to the code, it will be updated on the existing GitHub repository.

We also have other code bundles from our rich catalog of books and videos available at `https://github.com/PacktPublishing/`. Check them out!

Download the color images

We also provide a PDF file that has color images of the screenshots/diagrams used in this book. You can download it here: `https://www.packtpub.com/sites/default/files/downloads/9781789803051_ColorImages.pdf`.

Conventions used

There are a number of text conventions used throughout this book.

`CodeInText`: Indicates code words in text, database table names, folder names, filenames, file extensions, pathnames, dummy URLs, user input, and Twitter handles. Here is an example: "Open the `Chapter01/encoderDemo_800.cptx` file in the exercise folder."

Bold: Indicates a new term, an important word, or words that you see onscreen. For example, words in menus or dialog boxes appear in the text like this. Here is an example: "Click the **Browse** button at the bottom of the **Recent** tab of the Welcome screen."

 Warnings or important notes appear like this.

 Tips and tricks appear like this.

Get in touch

Feedback from our readers is always welcome.

General feedback: If you have questions about any aspect of this book, mention the book title in the subject of your message and email us at customercare@packtpub.com.

Errata: Although we have taken every care to ensure the accuracy of our content, mistakes do happen. If you have found a mistake in this book, we would be grateful if you would report this to us. Please visit www.packt.com/submit-errata, selecting your book, clicking on the Errata Submission Form link, and entering the details.

Piracy: If you come across any illegal copies of our works in any form on the Internet, we would be grateful if you would provide us with the location address or website name. Please contact us at copyright@packt.com with a link to the material.

If you are interested in becoming an author: If there is a topic that you have expertise in and you are interested in either writing or contributing to a book, please visit authors.packtpub.com.

Reviews

Please leave a review. Once you have read and used this book, why not leave a review on the site that you purchased it from? Potential readers can then see and use your unbiased opinion to make purchase decisions, we at Packt can understand what you think about our products, and our authors can see your feedback on their book. Thank you!

For more information about Packt, please visit packt.com.

1
Getting Started with Adobe Captivate 2019

Welcome to *Mastering Adobe Captivate 2019, Fifth Edition*. Since its introduction in 2004, Captivate has been the leading solution for authoring interactive eLearning content. In the beginning, it was a very simple screen-capture utility called FlashCam. In 2002, a company named eHelp acquired FlashCam and turned it into a full-fledged eLearning authoring tool called RoboDemo. In 2004, another company called Macromedia acquired eHelp and changed the name of the product once again. **Macromedia Captivate** was born. A few months later, Adobe acquired Macromedia and, consequently, Macromedia Captivate became **Adobe Captivate**.

As the years passed, Adobe released Captivate 2, 3, and 4, adding tools, objects, and features along the way. One of the most significant events in the Captivate history took place in July 2010, when Adobe released Captivate 5. For that release, Adobe engineers rewrote the code of the application from the ground up. As a result, Captivate 5 was the first version to be available on both macOS and Windows. Version 6 was another milestone for Captivate as it was the first version to offer an HTML5 publishing option. More recently, version 8 has introduced the ability to create Responsive Projects, as well as a brand new user interface. A Responsive Project allows you, the eLearning developer, to automatically adjust the layout of your Captivate projects to fit the various screen sizes of tablet and smartphone devices. This makes mobile learning a whole lot easier by creating content that looks perfect on any device.

At the time of writing, the latest version of Captivate is Adobe Captivate 2019. This version introduces many new features and enhancements, including the ability to create Interactive Videos and an exciting new project type for creating Virtual Reality training courses. Other new features introduced in Captivate 2019 include the ability to test your content on an actual mobile device (a feature called *Live Preview on Devices*) the ability to record your webcam and to change the background of your video (something called the *Chroma Key* effect) as well as other smaller enhancements.

With all this power only one click away, it is easy to overload your projects with lots of complex audiovisual effects and sophisticated interactions that can ultimately drive the learner away from the primary objective of every Captivate course: learning.

While working with Captivate, never forget that Captivate is an eLearning authoring tool. At the most basic level, it simply means that you, the developer, and your audience are united by a very special kind of relationship: a student-teacher relationship. Therefore, from now on–and for the rest of the book–you will not be called *the developer* or *the programmer*, but *the teacher*. The ones who will view your finished applications will not be the *users* or the *visitors*, but will be called *the learners* or *the students*. You will see that this changes everything.

In this chapter, you will learn about the following topics:

- Discovering the available options to install Captivate
- Seeing the general steps of the Captivate production process
- Exploring and customizing the Captivate 2019 interface
- Working with panels and workspaces
- Viewing the completed sample applications you will work with during the course of this book

Getting Captivate

Before you can start working with Captivate, you have to download and install the software. In this section, you will discover the three ways that Adobe makes Captivate available to you.

The Captivate perpetual license

This is the old-fashioned way of obtaining the software. You buy Captivate and get a serial number to activate your installation. The serial number is valid for a specific version of Captivate, and for a specific platform (macOS or Windows) only. Once activated, that version of Captivate is permanently available on your computer. With this option, you get all the functionalities of Captivate, and you can start working on your eLearning projects right away! You also get all the patches and bug fixes for the version you bought. All the step-by-step exercises of this book work flawlessly with the Captivate 2019 perpetual license.

See the Captivate page on the Adobe website at
`http://www.adobe.com/products/captivate.html`.

You can download and use this version of Captivate free of charge for 30 days. This should be more than enough time for you to go through the exercises of this book. However, once the trial period is over, you will not have access to Captivate unless you convert your trial to a licensed version. This can be a perpetual or a subscription license.

Download your Captivate 30-day trial from
`http://www.adobe.com/go/trycaptivate/`.

The Captivate subscription

With this licensing model, you subscribe to Captivate on a monthly basis. This means that you pay a certain amount each month to keep using Captivate. The main benefit of the subscription model is that you automatically get all the updates as they are released. The subscription model is the best way to ensure that you always have access to the latest version of Captivate. Note that the subscription is just another licensing model; the software itself is identical to the perpetual licensing model.

More information on the various Captivate licensing models can be found at
`http://www.adobe.com/products/captivate/buying-guide.html`.

Although the Captivate subscription model is very similar to the way Adobe Creative Cloud works, Captivate is—at the time of writing—*not* a part of the Creative Cloud.

Captivate and the Creative Cloud
If you already have a Creative Cloud subscription, you'll need another subscription for Adobe Captivate.

Captivate in the Technical Communication Suite

The **Technical Communication Suite (TCS)** is yet another bundle of applications from Adobe. It is designed to create technical content, such as help files and user guides. TCS includes applications such as FrameMaker, RoboHelp, Acrobat Professional, and of course, Captivate. The Technical Communication Suite itself is also available under both the perpetual and the subscription licensing model.

 For more information on TCS, visit
http://www.adobe.com/products/technicalcommunicationsuite.html.

A first look at a typical production workflow

Creating content with Captivate is a three-step process, or to be exact, a four-step process. However, only three of the four steps take place in Captivate. That's why we like to refer to the first step as *step zero*!

Step zero – the pre-production phase

This is the only step of the process that does not involve working with the Captivate application. Depending on the project you are planning, it can last from a few minutes to a few months. This step is probably the most important step of the entire process. This is where you create the scenarios and the storyboards. This is where you develop the pedagogical approach that will drive the entire project. What will you teach the students? In what order will you introduce the topics? How and when will you assess the students' knowledge? These are some of the very important questions you should answer before opening Captivate. Step zero is where the teacher's skills fully express themselves.

Scenario-based training

In this series of posts on the Adobe eLearning community portal, Dr. Pooja Jaisingh shares her experience in creating scenario-based training. These posts clearly stress the importance of *step zero*, and give you an initial, high-level approach to the Captivate production process. The first post of the series can be found at `https://elearning.adobe.com/2012/03/my-experience-with-crea ting-a-scenario-based-course-part-1/`.

Step one – creating the slides

At the most basic level, a typical Captivate project is a collection of slides, just like a Microsoft PowerPoint presentation. So, your first task when creating a new Captivate file is probably to create a bunch of slides to work with. There are several ways to do this:

- Captivate has the ability to record any action you perform onscreen. You typically use this ability to create software-related interactive training or simulations. You use your mouse to perform actions on your computer, and behind the scenes, Captivate watches and records any action you do using a sophisticated screen-capture engine based on screenshots. Each of these screenshots becomes a slide in your new Captivate project. Using the screen-capture feature of Captivate is covered in `Chapter 8`, *Capturing Onscreen Action*.

- Very often, though, the Captivate project you are working on has nothing to do with software-related skills. In this case, you don't need to use screen capture to take screenshots. Instead, you create the slides entirely within Captivate. This is the preferred approach for new training materials that don't require screen-capture capabilities.

- A third solution is to import the slides from Microsoft PowerPoint. You typically use this solution to convert existing training material made with PowerPoint into interactive online training modules, but it is not considered best practice for new training material. Importing PowerPoint slides into Captivate is covered in `Chapter 12`, *Using Captivate with Other Applications*.

Step two – the editing phase

This step is the most time-consuming phase of the entire process. This is where your project slowly takes shape to become an actual interactive course module.

In this step, you arrange the final sequence of actions, record narrations, add objects to the slides (such as Text Captions and Buttons), arrange those objects in the Timeline, add title and ending slides, develop the advanced interactions, create the Question Slides for the quiz, configure the quiz reporting options, and so on. At the end of this step, the project should be ready for publication. Sometimes, it can take several rounds of edits until you have a project that is ready to publish.

Note that, for most projects, step one and step two overlap. Unless you use screen capture, there is no clear distinction between step one and step two. It is ok to go back and forth between those two steps when developing your next Captivate project.

Step three – the publishing phase

Step three is where you make your project available to your learners. Captivate allows you to publish your course modules in a wide variety of formats. The two formats that you will use most of the time are the Flash and the HTML5 formats:

- Flash is the historical publishing format of Captivate. Publishing the project in Flash makes the deployment of your eLearning courses very easy; only the Flash Player plugin is needed. The very same Flash Player that is used to read Flash-enabled websites is all you need to play back your published Captivate projects. The major caveat of this publishing format is that it is not supported on mobile devices. This publishing method is fading out today, as Adobe announced the end of the free Flash Player plugin for the year 2020.
- Captivate can also publish your projects in HTML5, which makes the project available on any device, including desktops and laptops, as well as tablets and smartphones. In today's technological landscape, HTML5 has become the preferred format for publishing your online courses for computers and mobile devices.

Note that some features of Captivate are only available either in Flash or in HTML5. For example, Responsive Projects and Virtual Reality Projects can only be published in HTML5, while a Text Animation object can only be published in Flash. It is very important to know the publishing format you will use before starting the development of a new project.

The end of the Flash Player

In July 2017, Adobe made an announcement that they would no longer develop and maintain the Flash Player plugin beyond 2020, and that they encourage content developers to migrate to HTML5. This is not a surprise, but it stresses the important evolution that HTML5 represents for our industry. It also clearly states that Adobe Captivate is bound to end up as an HTML5-only authoring tool at some point in the future. You can see the original Adobe announcement at `https://blogs.adobe.com/conversations/2017/07/adobe-flash-update.html` and the announcement from the Captivate team at `https://elearning.adobe.com/2017/07/flash-the-future-of-interactive-content-for-elearning/`.

Captivate can also publish the project as a standalone application (`.exe` on Windows and `.app` on Macintosh) or as video files that can be easily uploaded to YouTube and viewed on a tablet or smartphone.

Step three will be covered in great detail in `Chapter 15`, *Finishing Touches and Publishing*.

Exploring the Captivate interface

In this book, we will cover the three steps of the process requiring the use of Captivate. You will discover that Captivate has specific tools to handle each of these three steps.

Downloading the sample code

Before you start reading this section, it is important that you download the sample files we refer to throughout this book. You can download the sample files for all Packt Publishing books that you have purchased from your account at `http://www.packtpub.com`. If you purchased this book elsewhere, you can visit `http://www.packtpub.com/support` and register to have the files emailed directly to you.

You will now discover the Adobe Captivate interface using the following steps:

1. Open Captivate.
2. If needed, click the **Recent** tab at the top of the Welcome screen.
3. Click the **Browse** button at the bottom of the **Recent** tab of the Welcome screen.
4. Open the `Chapter01/encoderDemo_800.cptx` file in the exercise folder.

Your screen should look similar to this screenshot:

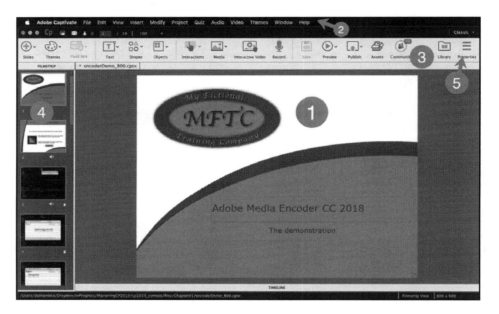

Cleaning the Preferences

The above screenshot assumes that you have not changed any default of Adobe Captivate 2019. If Captivate does not look the same as in the above screenshot, you can clean your preferences and reset everything to default with the `CleanPreferencesMac` (if you are using a Mac) or the `CleanPreferencesWin.bat` (if you are on Windows) script located in the `/utils` folder of your Captivate installation. This process is described in the following blog article by our friend, Kevin Siegel, available at `https://blog.iconlogic.com/weblog/2013/08/adobe-captivate-fastest-cleaned-prefs-in-the-west.html`

The default Captivate screen looks very simple and clean. The main area is covered by the **Stage** (**1**). The Stage is where you lay out the objects that make up each slide of the project. The objects on the Stage will appear in your course. The objects in the Scrap Area (the grey area around the slide) will not be visible when taking the course. This makes the Scrap Area very useful! It is the perfect place to put instructions, reminders, color schemes, etc. that are used by the teacher when creating the course, but that should not be displayed to the student.

At the very top of the screen is the **Menu bar** (**2**). The Menu bar gives you access to a wide range of Captivate features.

Below the Menu bar is the main **Toolbar** of Captivate 2019 (**3**). The Toolbar is primarily used to insert new slides and new objects into the project, but it also contains important tools for operations, such as previewing, publishing, and saving.

 If you have several versions of Captivate installed on your system, a quick look at the Toolbar gives you a hint about which version you are using. If you see the **Interactive Video** icon, it means that you are in Captivate 2019, as that icon is new in Captivate 2019!

On the left side of the screen is the **Filmstrip** (**4**). It shows the sequence of slides in your Captivate project. The primary use of the **Filmstrip** is to let you select the slide(s) you want to work with, but it can also be used to perform basic operations on the slides, such as reordering or deleting slides.

5. At the far right side of the Toolbar, click the **Properties** icon (**5**).

This action reveals the **Properties** inspector. The **Properties** inspector is one of the most important components of Captivate. It is used to control and adjust the properties of the selected object.

6. Click the **Properties** button on the Toolbar again to hide the **Properties** inspector.
7. Click the **Library** icon located just next to the **Properties** icon to open the **Library** panel.

The **Library** is another very important component of Captivate. It maintains a list of all the assets (such as images, audio clips, animations, and so on) included in the current project.

> 8. Click the **Library** button on the Toolbar to close the **Library**.
> 9. Click the **Timeline** button that stretches across the bottom of the screen. This action reveals the **Timeline** panel.

The **Timeline** panel is used to arrange the sequence of objects on the current slide. In short, you use the **Timeline** panel to decide when an object appears on the stage and how long it stays visible. This panel is also used to set up the stacking order of the objects. You will learn more about the **Timeline** in Chapter 4, *Working with the Timeline and Other Useful Tools.*

It is possible to open many panels at the same time.

> 10. Click the **Properties** button on the Toolbar to reopen the **Properties** inspector.

Both the **Timeline** *and* the **Properties** inspector should now be open.

Because the **Properties** inspector, **Library**, and **Timeline** are the most important panels of Captivate, they are only one mouse-click away on the default user interface. However, Captivate contains many other panels that give you access to a myriad of interesting tools. To get the most out of Captivate, you should know how to turn panels on and off.

> 11. Open the **Window** menu.

The **Window** menu displays a list of all the panels that are available in Adobe Captivate. Note the checkmark in front of the **Filmstrip**, **Timeline**, and **Library** entries of the **Window** menu. This reminds you that these panels and icons are currently visible on the interface.

> 12. Click the **Library** menu item of the **Window** menu. This action removes the **Library** icon from the Toolbar.
> 13. Click the **Window | Library** menu item again to reactivate the **Library** icon of the Toolbar and open the **Library** panel.
> 14. Click the **Window | Slide Notes** menu item to open the **Slide Notes** panel.

The **Slide Notes** panel appears at the bottom of the screen next to the **Timeline** panel, as shown in the following screenshot:

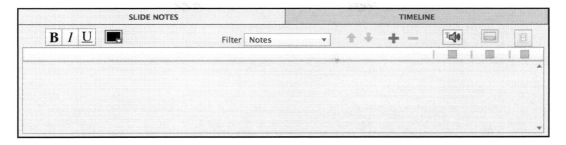

Let's now open one more panel.

15. Use the **Window | HTML5 Tracker** menu item to open the **HTML5 Tracker** panel.

The **HTML5 Tracker** panel lists the features and objects used in the current project that are not supported in HTML5. There should be one unsupported feature listed in the **HTML5 Tracker** panel (because the transitions between slides are not supported in HTML5).

Note that this panel is floating on top of the interface. This is very different from the **Slide Notes** panel you opened earlier that was attached (docked) at the bottom of the interface. Each panel of Captivate is either docked or floating. Also note that in Captivate 2019, it is not possible, by default, to dock a floating panel or undock a docked panel.

The interface is now very different from what it was when you first opened Captivate.

16. Quit Captivate without saving any changes made to the open file.
17. Reopen Captivate.

When Captivate reopens, you should see the **Recent** tab of the Welcome screen by default. There is a thumbnail showing the last open project(s).

18. Double-click the **encoderDemo_800** thumbnail to reopen the project.

When the project reopens, note that the default Captivate interface is displayed, even though many more panels were open when you exited Captivate.

Thanks to these little experiments, you were exposed to some important basic concepts about the Captivate interface. Before moving on, let's summarize what you have learned so far:

- The Captivate interface is composed of panels laid out around the main editing area called the Stage.
- The grey area around the Stage is called the Scrap Area. Objects on the Scrap Area do not show in the online course.
- By default, most of the panels are hidden, making the interface simple and clean.
- The **Properties** inspector, the **Library** panel, and the **Timeline** are the most important and most commonly used components of Captivate. This is why they are easily accessible from the default interface.
- Some panels of Captivate are not immediately available on the default interface. You must use the **Window** menu to show and hide these panels.
- The panels of Captivate are either docked on the interface or floating on top of it.
- When you close and restart Captivate, the interface returns to its default layout.

Using the Advanced Interface Mode

If you are used to other Adobe tools, such as Photoshop, InDesign, or Illustrator, the default behavior of the Captivate interface probably looks very different. Luckily, there is a way to make the Captivate interface behave similarly to the interface of other popular Adobe tools. This is called the **Advanced Interface Mode**:

1. Use the **Adobe Captivate | Preferences** (macOS) or the **Edit | Preferences** (Windows) menu item to open the **Preferences** dialog of Captivate.
2. In the **General Settings** category of the **Preferences**, select the **Enable custom workspaces/panel undocking** option, as shown in the following screenshot:

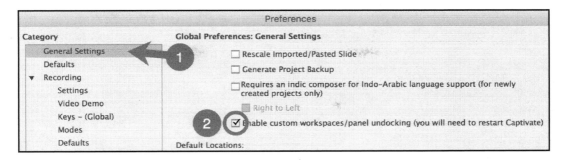

3. Click **OK** to validate the new option and close the **Preferences** dialog.

4. As indicated in the **Preferences** dialog, restart Adobe Captivate to enable the new option (make sure you don't save the eventual changes made to the file).

5. When Captivate restarts, double-click the **encoderDemo_800** thumbnail on the **Recent** tab of the Welcome screen to reopen the project.

When the project reopens, note that the **Properties** and **Library** icons of the Toolbar are no longer displayed.

6. Go to **Window | Properties** to reopen the **Properties** inspector.

7. Use the same procedure to reopen the **Library**, the **Timeline**, and the **Slide Notes** panels.

8. Return to the **Window** menu one more time to activate the **HTML5 Tracker** floating panel.

9. At the bottom of the interface, click the **Timeline** button to reveal the **Timeline** panel.

The interface should now look pretty much the same as when you closed Captivate earlier in this chapter.

10. Restart Captivate one more time without saving the changes made to the project.

11. When Captivate restarts, reopen the project by clicking the **encoderDemo_800** thumbnail on the **Recent** tab of the Welcome screen.

In Advanced Interface Mode, the panel layout is always maintained when you restart Captivate. In the next section, you will take a closer look at those panels. But first, let's first have a quick summary of what has been covered in this section:

- To make the Captivate interface behave like the interface of other common Adobe tools, you must switch to the Advanced Interface Mode.

- To enable the Advanced Interface Mode, select **Enable custom workspaces/panel undocking** in the Preferences dialog of Captivate. It is necessary to close and restart Captivate for this change to take effect.
- In the Advanced Interface Mode, the **Library** and the **Properties** icons of the Toolbar are not displayed. Enabling and disabling panels is done exclusively through the **Window** menu.
- In the Advanced Interface Mode, the workspace is always maintained when you restart Captivate.

Working with panels

You already know that Captivate contains a lot of panels and that those panels can be shown or hidden using the **Window** menu. In the Advanced Interface Mode, the Captivate interface offers even more flexibility. In this section, you will learn how to move the panels and create a unique custom screen:

1. Place your mouse on the black line at the top of the floating **HTML5 Tracker** panel.
2. Drag the panel to the right and drop it on top of the **Properties** and **Library** labels in the top right corner of the screen.

When a panel is moved above a possible docking location, a blue outline appears on the screen. Releasing the mouse at that moment docks the panel at the location highlighted by the blue outline.

This action docks the **HTML5 tracker** panel with the **Properties** inspector and the **Library** panel, as shown in the following screenshot:

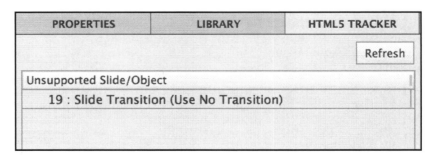

This first action illustrates how to dock the panels that are initially floating on the interface. You will now do the opposite to illustrate that a panel that is initially docked can be turned into a floating panel.

3. Place your mouse on top of the **Library** label on the right side of the screen.
4. Drag the **Library** panel out of the **Library/Properties/HTML5 Tracker** group and drop it on top of the stage.

The **Library** panel is now a floating panel, even though it was docked by default. You have now arranged the panels in a truly unique way. This customized arrangement of your panels is called a **workspace**.

Creating a new workspace

The Advanced Interface Mode of Captivate allows you to apply your own unique (custom) workspaces. Depending on the project you are working on, the size of your computer screen, your working habits, and so on, you might want to have several workspaces and quickly switch between them. In this section, you will first learn how to reset to the default workspace. Then, you will create and save a new custom workspace.

The default workspace you see when you first open Captivate is called the **Classic** workspace, as shown in the top-right corner of your screen:

1. Click the **Classic** button at the top-right corner of the screen.
2. Choose **Reset Classic** in the drop-down menu, as shown in the following screenshot.

After doing this, your Captivate screen reverts to what it looked like when you opened the application at the beginning of this chapter:

The default **Classic** workspace is an excellent starting point for defining a custom workspace.

3. Use the **Window | Timing Properties** menu item to activate the **Timing** inspector on the right side of the screen.

4. Select the **Adobe Media Encode CC 2018** title on the slide and note that the **Timing** inspector updates.

Just like the **Properties** inspector, the **Timing** inspector always shows the properties pertaining to the object you select.

5. Use the **Window | Properties** menu item to activate the **Properties** inspector.

6. Drag the **Properties** inspector out of the **Properties/Timing** group and drop it on top of the **Filmstrip** label on the other side of the screen. This docks the **Properties** inspector with the **Filmstrip**.

After this last action, your screen should look like the following screenshot:

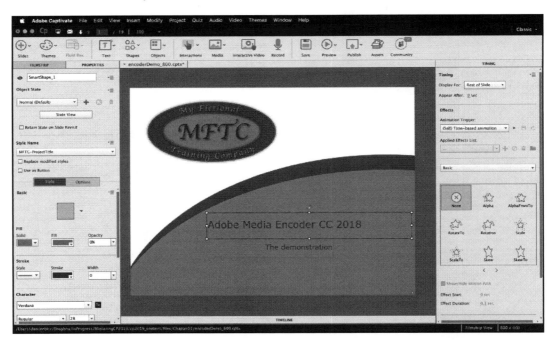

This workspace is very practical when you have to precisely define the timing and apply effects to the selected object. You will now save this panel layout as a new workspace.

7. Click the same **Classic** button you used earlier at the top right corner of the screen.
8. Choose **New Workspace** from the drop-down menu.
9. In the **New Workspace** dialog, name your new workspace Timing and click **OK**.

Note that a **Timing** button now replaces the **Classic** button. You can use this button to switch between the Classic workspace and your own custom Timing workspace!

10. Click the **Timing** button at the top-right corner of the screen.
11. Select the **Classic** workspace in the drop-down menu to reapply the default Classic workspace.
12. Click the **Classic** button and reapply the **Timing** workspace.

This demonstrates how you can quickly switch between your saved workspaces.

Extra credit

You now know all the tools to create custom workspaces. Take some time to experiment with these tools on your own. Try turning panels on and off using the **Window** menu. Explore the other panels of Captivate, such as the **Question Pool** and the **Project Info**. When you feel like you have a great workspace, save it under a name of your choice.

Renaming and deleting custom workspaces

If you ever need to rename or delete a custom workspace, use the following steps:

1. Go to **Window** | **Workspace** | **Manage Workspace**.

Note that the **Window** | **Workspace** menu displays the same items as the workspace switcher button at the top-right corner of the screen.

2. In the **Manage Workspace** dialog, choose the workspace to delete/rename.

Note that the default **Classic** workspace is not listed. This means that this default workspace cannot be renamed or deleted.

3. Click the **Rename** or **Delete** button. In this example, click the **OK** button to close the box without any changes.
4. Open the workspace switcher one more time to reapply the **Classic** workspace before moving on to the next topic.

Updating a workspace

There is no menu item to update an existing workspace. If you want to update an existing workspace, use the **New Workspace** menu item and give the new workspace the same name as the existing workspace you want to update.

Workspaces in normal mode

You can return to the normal interface mode using the following steps:

1. Use the **Adobe Captivate** | **Preferences** (macOS) or **Edit** | **Preferences** (Windows) menu item to reopen the **Preferences** dialog of Captivate.
2. In the **General Settings** category, deselect the **Enable custom workspaces/panel undocking** and click **OK** to validate.
3. Restart Captivate without saving the changes made to the open project.
4. When Captivate reopens, double-click the **encoderDemo_800** thumbnail to reopen the project.

Confirm that the **Properties** and **Library** buttons are back in the top-right corner. This indicates that you are back in normal interface mode.

5. Click the workspace switcher button at the top right corner of your screen. It should currently read **Classic**.

In normal interface mode (that is, when the **Enable custom workspaces/panel undocking** option of the **Preferences** is *not* selected), only the **Classic** workspace can be applied or reset. If you want to use your custom *Timing* workspace again, you first need to return to Advanced Interface Mode, and then restart Captivate.

Before moving on to the next topic, these are the key points to keep in mind when creating custom workspaces:

- It is necessary to set Captivate to Advanced Interface Mode to dock and undock panels and create new workspaces.
- Use the **Window | Workspace | New Workspace** menu item to save the current panel layout as a new workspace. This menu item is also accessible from the workspace switcher at the top right corner of your screen.
- Use the **Window | Workspace | Manage Workspace** menu item to rename or delete your custom workspaces.
- To update an existing workspace, use the **New Workspace** command to give the new workspace the same name as the workspace you want to update.
- The default **Classic** workspace of Captivate cannot be deleted or renamed.
- In normal interface mode, only the default **Classic** workspace is available.

Joining the Captivate community

One of the most recent additions to the Toolbar is the **Community** icon. Clicking this icon opens the Adobe eLearning Community portal inside Captivate.

 The Adobe Community portal is a website that is available at `http://elearning.adobe.com` using a standard web browser.

The Adobe eLearning Community Portal is the best place to find information and to interact with other Captivate users. The eLearning Community Portal features the following:

- Blog posts from members of the community.
- Showcases of Captivate course modules.
- A very active forum where you can ask questions and get answers from some of the most influential and popular Captivate users.
- A wide library of video tutorials.
- An agenda of upcoming events, including webinars hosted by members of the Captivate team or members of the community (including us, the authors of this book!).
- And much more!

Performing activities on the eLearning community (such as answering questions, writing blogs/articles, and so on) gives you an opportunity to score points and enhance your level as a product expert. These points can be turned into a wide variety of exciting incentives, including free Captivate licenses and invitations to live events.

 See the full listing of levels and incentives at `https://elearning.adobe.com/levels/`.

From newbies to legends, there is a place for everyone on the eLearning portal!

Exploring the sample applications

Now that you know a bit more about the Captivate interface, let's take a look at the sample applications you will build in this book. These applications are designed to showcase almost every single feature of Captivate. Use them as a reference if there is something unclear while you are working through the exercises.

Experiencing the Encoder demonstration

The first application that you will explore is a project that uses the screen capture feature of Captivate to create a screenshot-based course module:

1. With the `Chapter01/encoderDemo_800.cptx` file still open, click the **Preview** icon on the Toolbar.
2. From the drop-down list, choose the **Project** item to preview the entire project.

Captivate generates a temporary file and opens it in the floating **Preview** pane. Follow the onscreen instructions to go through the project. This puts you in the same situation as a learner viewing this eLearning content for the first time.

This first sample project is called a **Demonstration**. As the name suggests, a demonstration is used to demonstrate something to the learner. Consequently, the learner is passive and simply watches whatever is going on. In a demonstration, the Mouse object is shown. It moves and clicks automatically. If the learners move their own mouse, it will not affect the content in any way.

This particular demonstration features some of the most popular Captivate objects, including Text Captions, Highlight Boxes, and Smart Shapes. The audio narration was generated by Captivate's Text-To-Speech tool. We have simply typed the narration in the Slide Notes panel, and Captivate turned it into audio files using the voice of a predefined speech agent. You will learn more about audio and Text-To-Speech in `Chapter 3`, *Working with Multimedia*.

Another popular feature in Adobe Captivate is the ability to add Closed Captions to the audio narration. You will learn more about Closed Captions and Accessibility in `Chapter 13`, *Creating Accessible eLearning*.

3. When you reach the end of the project, close the **Preview** pane.
4. Take some time to take a closer look at the **Preview** icon as shown in the following screenshot:

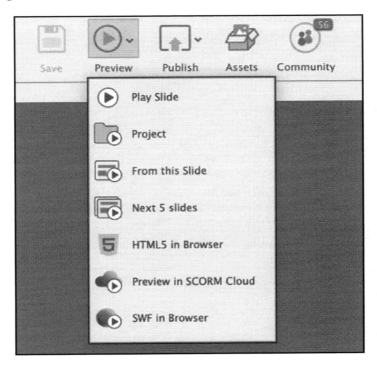

This is one of the icons you'll use the most during this book and when you design your courses. It has seven options that control which part of the project you want to preview, and how you want to preview it. Note that each of these options is associated with a keyboard shortcut that will be different depending on the system you work on (macOS or Windows). Place your mouse on top of each of the items to see the associated keyboard shortcut in a tooltip.

Previewing a Responsive or a Virtual Reality Project

When in a Responsive or in a Virtual Reality Project, the preview options will not behave exactly as described in the following list because those projects can only be published in HTML5. Responsive Projects will be covered in Chapter 10, *Creating a Responsive Project*, and Virtual Reality projects will be covered in Chapter 11, *Creating Virtual Reality Projects*.

Let's now describe the options of the **Preview** icon in more detail:

- **Play Slide**: This option plays the current slide in the Captivate interface. It is the only preview option that does not open the default web browser or a floating preview pane. Because of that, the **Play Slide** option is not able to render all the features of Captivate. Previewing a single slide is a good option to quickly test the timing of the objects.
- **Project**: This option generates a temporary Flash file and plays the entire project in the Preview pane.
- **From this Slide**: This option generates a temporary Flash file. Captivate opens the Preview pane and plays the project from the currently selected slide to the end.
- **Next 5 slides**: This is a great option to quickly test a specific sequence of the project. Captivate opens the Preview pane to play a temporary Flash file containing five slides, starting from the currently selected slide.

You can use the **Defaults** category in Preferences to change the number of slides you want to include in the Preview when using this option. To access the Preferences, use the **Adobe Captivate | Preferences** (macOS) or the **Edit | Preferences** (Windows) menu item.

- **HTML5 in Browser**: Using this preview option, you can see the project in a context very similar to the one that will be used by your learners. It generates the project in the HTML5 format. The project is then played in the default web browser. Note that some features and objects of Captivate are not supported in the HTML5 output. If you plan on publishing your project in HTML5, make sure you use this preview option to ensure that the features, animations, and objects you use in your project are supported in HTML5.

- **Preview in SCORM Cloud**: You can use this preview option to test the reporting features of your course. It generates a temporary HTML5 file of the project and uploads it to SCORM Cloud. When the upload is complete, you can see your project in a special preview pane, along with a log of all communications exchanged between the LMS and your content. You will learn more about SCORM, LMS, Quiz, and reporting in Chapter 7, *Working with Quizzes*. Note that this preview option is the only one that is not associated with a keyboard shortcut.

- **SWF In Browser**: This option is very close to the **HTML5 in Browser** option described above. The only difference is that Captivate publishes the project in Flash (rather than HTML5) before playing it in the default web browser.

Floating and Modal panels

In Captivate, a panel can be floating or docked. When a panel floats, the tools and switches on the other panels are still active. But when the **Preview** panel is open, only the buttons of that panel are active, while the tools of the other panels are no longer active. The **Preview** panel is said to be a *Modal* floating panel because it disables every tool situated on other panels. Also, note that the **Preview** panel cannot be docked.

Experiencing the Encoder simulation

You will now open another sample project. Actually, it is not a real *other* project, but another version of the Encoder demonstration you worked with in the previous section:

1. Use the **File** | **Open** menu item to open the `Chapter01/encoderSim_800.cptx` file situated in the exercises download.
2. Once the file is open, click the **Preview** icon on the Toolbar and choose the **SWF In Browser** option.
3. The project opens in the default web browser and starts playing automatically.

 You may have to adjust the security settings of your web browser in order to allow playing back Flash content. Please, refer to the user guide of your browser for specific instructions.

This project is made of exactly the same slides and assets as the demonstration you saw in the previous section. When the project reaches slide 3, it stops and waits for you to interact with the course. This is the main difference between a demonstration and a simulation.

In Captivate, a **simulation** is a project where the learner is active. In a simulation, the Mouse object is hidden, as learners use their own mouse to click around the screen and progress toward the end of the course. The fact that the students are active implies a new level of complexity; the learners can perform either the correct or the incorrect action.

In each case, the course must react accordingly. This concept is known as **branching**. This means that each student experiences the course module based on their own actions.

4. Follow the onscreen instructions and try to perform the correct actions, as described in the demonstration project of the previous section.
5. If you ever perform the incorrect action, a red **Failure Caption** is displayed on the screen. Failure captions are one of the most basic forms of branching. The caption shows only if the student's answer is incorrect.

6. On slide 11, you will fill the new width of the video file. Type 400 and press *Enter* to continue to the next step.

7. When you are done, close your browser and return to Captivate.

This second sample file features pretty much the same Captivate objects as the demonstration you completed in the previous section. Both typing and mouse actions are replaced by interactive objects. The Mouse is replaced by **Click Boxes** and a **Text Entry Box** replaces the typing object on slide 11. These interactive objects can stop the course and wait for the learner to interact. Using the interactive objects of Captivate will be covered in Chapter 5, *Developing Interactivity*.

Both the Encoder demonstration and simulation are based on the same screenshots. To create these sample courses, the first two steps of the production process described earlier were used:

- In step one (the slide creation step), the actions were performed in the actual Adobe Media Encoder. They were recorded by Captivate behind the scenes.
- In step two (the post-production step), the course was edited in Captivate. Audio and Closed Captions were added, the title and ending slides were created, timing was adjusted, and so on.
- Step three (the publishing step) has not yet been performed on these files.

Experiencing the Encoder Video Demo

Video Demo mode is a special recording mode of Captivate that is used to produce .mp4 video files. These files can be uploaded to online services such as YouTube, Vimeo, or Daily Motion for playback on any device (including the iPad, iPhone, and other internet-enabled mobile devices):

1. Use the **File** | **Open** menu item to open the Chapter01/encoderVideo.cpvc.

First, note that a Video Demo project does not use the same `.cptx` file extension as a regular Captivate project. It uses the `.cpvc` file extension instead. This is the first indication that this project is going to behave differently than the other ones you have worked with so far. In addition to having a specific file extension, Video Demo projects also have their own unique interface, as shown in the following screenshot:

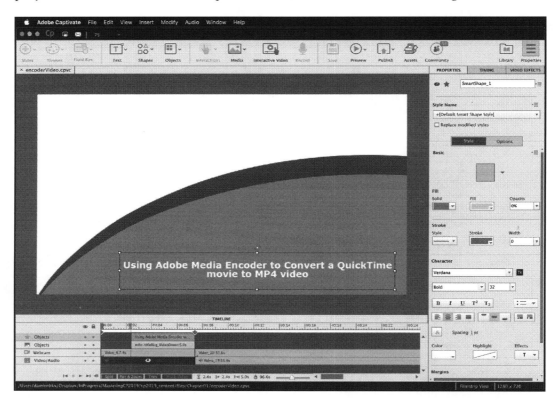

In the preceding screenshot, note the absence of the **Filmstrip** panel. A Video Demo project is not based on slides. Actually, it is a single big video file. So the **Filmstrip** panel makes no sense in a Video Demo project.

In a video file, interactions are not possible. The file can only be experienced from start to finish in the order defined by the teacher. To use instructional design terminology, a video file gives a *linear* experience to the learner, while branch-aware interactive projects provide a *nonlinear* experience where a learner can make choices that change the way the course progresses. Therefore, interactive objects, quizzes, and branching are not available in a Video Demo project.

2. Take some time to inspect the rest of the Video Demo screen. Try to spot the other differences between the regular Captivate interface and Video Demos.

3. When you are ready, click the **Preview** icon. Surprise! Only two options are available in the **Preview** icon!

4. In the **Preview** dropdown, choose the **Project** option.

5. Watch the whole video as if you were viewing it on YouTube!

6. Click the **Edit** button in the bottom-right corner of the screen to return to the Edit mode.

7. Close the file without saving it when done.

You have now experienced the Video Demo you will create in Chapter 9, *Producing a Video Demo.*

Experiencing the take the train sample application

You will now preview the next sample application using the following steps:

1. Use the **File** | **Open** menu item to open the Chapter01/takeTheTrain.cptx file.

2. Once the file is open, click the **Preview** icon on the Toolbar and choose the **HTML5 in Browser** option.

3. View the course in your web browser, as a student would.

This sample application is very different from the projects you worked with so far because it is not based on screenshots or screen recording. The capture tool of Captivate was not used in this example. Instead, all the slides have been carefully crafted in Captivate.

For its audio narration, this project does not use text-to-speech. Instead, the narration was recorded and polished in an external audio application (Adobe Audition, in this case) and imported to the project.

This course is also much more involved than the Encoder examples. Advanced Actions and Variables are used throughout the project to power the dynamic features, such as the name of the student appearing in the title of slide 4. This course also features the certificate interaction at the very end (only if you pass the Quiz!), an Interactive Video is inserted on slide 23 of the project, and it uses the built-in collection of characters to spice up the training with a human touch! But the most impressive feature of this particular project is probably the **Quiz**, one of the most important and most popular tools in Captivate.

The project contains seven Question Slides. Six of these are stored in the **Question Pool**. Each time the project is viewed, three questions are randomly chosen from the Question Pool and displayed to the student. If you want to experiment with this feature, view the sample project a second time. Because we used the Question Pool to generate the questions, you should not be asked the same Quiz questions as when you first experienced the project.

Experiencing a Responsive Project

The next sample course you will see is not part of the download that comes with this book. Instead, you will use one of the sample applications that is included in Captivate. Use the following steps to open it:

1. Close every open file (without saving) and return to the Captivate Welcome screen.
2. Click the **Resources** tab of the Captivate Welcome screen (see **1** on the following screenshot).

As shown in the following screenshot, you can access various sample files and tutorials right from the Welcome Screen of Captivate:

You will now open one of the sample files provided by Adobe.

3. Double-click the thumbnail image on the Welcome Screen to open the `Responsive Learning Sample` project (see 2 in the preceding screenshot).

4. Click **OK** to clear the message telling you that there are lots of unused assets in the Library.

The project you just opened is a **Responsive Project**. This means that it can adapt itself to the screen it is viewed on. Note the extra toolbar at the top of the stage. This extra toolbar lets you switch between different devices in order to check how the project is displayed on screens of different sizes.

5. In the top-left corner of the stage, open the **Custom** drop-down menu.
6. Choose **iPhone 6/7/8** in the list of available devices.

This action resizes the Stage to the size of an iPhone 6 (375 px by 559 px). As shown in the following screenshot, the elements of the current slide are rearranged to fit the new size of the Stage. Some elements (such as the big image that was on the right side of the stage) have even been completely removed to accommodate the reduced screen real estate of a smartphone:

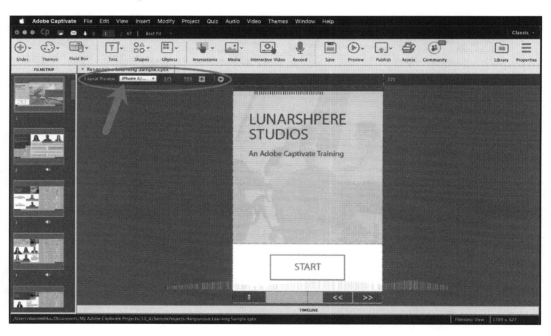

You will now preview this project in a web browser, using the following steps.

7. Click the **Preview** | **Project** icon on the Toolbar.

There are a lot of differences in the way you preview a Responsive Project, compared to the way you preview a non-responsive Captivate project:

- Firstly, the **Preview** icon on the Toolbar contains different options than usual (including the all-new **Live Preview on Devices** feature)
- Secondly, a Responsive Project is always previewed in the default browser installed on your computer and not in the **Preview** pane of Captivate
- Thirdly, in the web browser, there is a slider just above the preview to let you change the size of the Stage as you preview your project

All these changes have a single root cause: a Responsive Project can only be published in HTML5. That's why you need a browser to preview the project.

8. Preview the whole project in the web browser and use the slider above the preview to change the size of the stage (see **1** in the following screenshot). Note how the elements of the various slides of the project are rearranged on the smaller screen sizes.
9. During the preview, also note the very small double arrow icon in the top left corner of the preview (see **2** in the following screenshot). This icon is used to toggle the Table of Contents on and off.
10. When the preview is finished, close the web browser and return to Captivate.

To make this project responsive, we have used Fluid Boxes to define the slide layouts for the different screen sizes. You will learn more about Responsive Projects and Fluid Boxes in `Chapter 10`, *Creating a Responsive Project*.

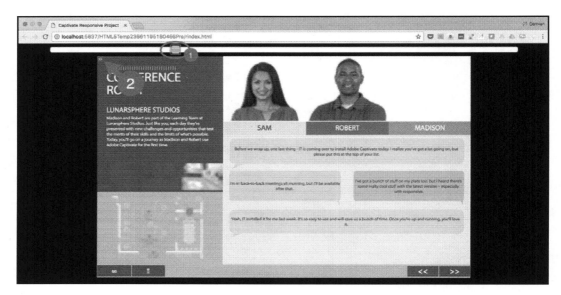

The special previewing features of the Responsive Projects let you test the responsiveness of your project during the development phase, but they have one major disadvantage. Because you preview the project using the default browser of your desktop or laptop computer, you can't experience the course on an actual mobile device.

Previewing a responsive project on your mobile device

New in Captivate 2019 is the ability to preview your project directly on your mobile device. This new feature is called *Live Preview on Devices*. This is the perfect way of ensuring that all the interactive objects you have used in your course module translate well on a touchscreen. Use the following steps to test it out:

The following steps require that you have a Smartphone connected to the same network as the computer you are using to run Captivate. If these conditions are not met, you will not be able to experience that workflow.

1. In the `Responsive Learning Sample.cptx` file, use the **Preview | Live Preview on Devices** icon on the Toolbar.

Captivate publishes a temporary file of the project in HTML5. When done, it opens the default web browser installed on the system and displays a big QR code.

2. Use your Smartphone to scan the QR code that Captivate has generated in your Web Browser.
3. Enjoy your Responsive Project directly on your mobile device!

The Live Preview on Devices feature makes it incredibly easy and convenient to test your Responsive Projects on an actual mobile device!

Experiencing a Virtual Reality project

Adobe Captivate 2019 has introduced a new type of project. Thanks to Virtual Reality (VR) courses, you are able to generate an interactive 360° Virtual Reality environment that will immerse your learners in a specific training situation! VR projects are based on 360° pictures or videos used to recreate an entire environment. You will now experience one such project using the following steps:

1. Open Captivate or close every open file without saving them.
2. Click the **Resources** tab of the Captivate Welcome screen.
3. Double-click the **2019 Release – Virtual Reality** thumbnail.
4. When the project opens in Captivate, use the **Preview | Project** icon on the Toolbar.

Just like Responsive Projects, VR projects can only be published in HTML5. This is the reason why Captivate displays the project in your default web browser once it has finished publishing the preview.

5. When the project is loaded in the browser, click the Play icon to start playing it.
6. After the narrated introduction, use your mouse to drag the background image in any direction you like. Don't hesitate to explore the ceiling and floor as well.

You should notice that the background image moves in the direction you drag it! You are in the very center of an entire 360° space! The black circular buttons are interactive hotspots that have been added to the 360° environment using the tools of Adobe Captivate.

7. Click the hotspot above the sofa. This displays some text in the 360° environment.
8. After a few seconds, the label disappears and you are brought to the second hotspot.
9. Click that second hotspot and continue viewing the project as a student would.
10. Return to Captivate when done.

The new Virtual Reality projects of Adobe Captivate 2019 make it incredibly easy to create immersive trainings in a custom 360° space based on 360° images or videos. Typical topics for such Virtual Reality courses include virtual tours, safety drills, first responder situations, crisis management, and so on. But, of course, the sky is the limit, and your imagination that will ultimately define what Virtual Reality will be used for.

Experiencing Virtual Reality on your mobile device
Similar to Responsive Projects, you can also use the new **Preview | Live Preview on Devices** feature of Adobe Captivate 2019 to preview a VR project on your mobile device. If you have a VR device available, tap the VR icon in the Playbar and put your Smartphone in the VR device to take the VR experience to the next level. Enjoy!

Here is a list of certified VR devices by the Captivate engineering team:

- Cardboard
- Google Daydream
- Galaxy Gear VR
- Oculus Go

Experiencing the Introduction to Fluid Boxes project

This is the last sample project for you to experience before wrapping up this chapter. Use the following steps to open and preview this project:

1. Open the `Chapter01/Introduction to Fluid Boxes.cptx` file.
2. Use the **Preview** | **Project** icon on the Toolbar to preview the entire project in the **Preview** pane of Captivate.

This project has been entirely developed in Microsoft PowerPoint and converted into a Captivate project using Captivate's ability to import PowerPoint slides. You will learn about importing PowerPoint presentations in Captivate in `Chapter 12`, *Using Captivate with Other Applications*.

3. Use the **File** | **Close All** menu item to close every open file. If prompted to save the changes, make sure you do *not* save the changes to these files.

 The filenames on each tab should have asterisks to the left of the name if there are unsaved changes. If there are no asterisks, it means you have saved all the changes.

After viewing these sample applications, you should have a pretty good idea of the tools and general capabilities of Adobe Captivate. Before moving on, let's summarize what you have learned from these sample courses:

- Captivate is able to capture the actions you do on your computer and turn them into slides using a sophisticated capture tool based on screenshots.
- A **demonstration** is a project in which the learner is passive and simply watches the onscreen action.
- A **simulation** is a project in which the user is active.
- Audio and video can be imported to Captivate. The application also features Text-To-Speech and Closed Captioning.
- Question Slides can be created in Captivate. These Question Slides can be stored in Question Pools to create random quizzes. Quiz slides can even be added on top of an Interactive Video or embedded into the 360° space of a VR project.
- Other objects that can be included in a Captivate project include Text Captions, Highlight Boxes, Smart Shapes, Images and more.

- Captivate contains many interactive objects. Some of them are able to stop the course and wait for the user to interact.
- A Video Demo is not based on slides. It is a video file that can be published as a standalone `.mp4` file or uploaded to YouTube or other video applications.
- Video Demo projects use the `.cpvc` file extension and have a specific user interface.
- A Responsive Project is able to adapt itself to the screen on which it is viewed. You can use Fluid Boxes to decide how the elements of the slides of the project should be rearranged on various screen sizes.
- A Virtual Reality (VR) project allows you to recreate an entire 360° environment and to make it interactive using Hotspots and Questions.
- For a truly immersive experience, a VR project supports the VR devices that you can use with your Smartphone.
- Captivate is able to import PowerPoint slides, making it very easy to convert an existing PowerPoint presentation into an interactive Captivate project.

Summary

In this chapter, you were introduced to the four steps of a typical Captivate production process. You toured the application interface and learned how to customize it to fit your needs. Thanks to the Advanced Interface Mode and the Workspace feature, you were able to save your customized interface as a new Workspace and to reapply your custom panel layout anytime you want to.

Finally, you walked through the sample courses that you will develop in this book, giving you a first, high-level overview of the rich set of features of Adobe Captivate 2019.

In the next chapter, you will start crafting the *Take the Train* project and learn about the basic objects of Adobe Captivate.

Meet the community

The title of the book you are reading is *Mastering Adobe Captivate 2019*. To truly *master* a piece of software, we are convinced that you should be introduced to the community that supports it. The Adobe eLearning community portal (`http://elearning.adobe.com`) makes it easy to be part of the community and to get in touch with the most famous Captivate legends. To further help you, at the end of each chapter, you'll find a *Meet the community* section, in which we will introduce you to key members of the community. By the end of this book, you'll have the names, blog addresses, Twitter handles, and so on of some of the most influential members. We hope these resources will jump-start your own Captivate career and your involvement in the community.

At the end of this first chapter, let's meet with David Kelly. David is the executive director of The eLearning Guild. He is the guy that goes on stage at all the big eLearning events organized by the Guild in North America. If you ever participate in one of these events, you won't miss him! David is a hero of the worldwide eLearning community and we are very proud to introduce him to you.

David Kelly

David Kelly is the executive vice president and executive director of The eLearning Guild. David has been a learning and performance consultant and training director for more than 15 years. He is a leading voice for exploring how technology can be used to enhance training, education, learning, and organizational performance. David is an active member of the learning community and can frequently be found speaking at industry events. He has contributed to organizations including ATD, eLearn Magazine, LINGOs, among others. David is also known for his curation efforts, especially related to conferences and events for learning and performance professionals.

Contact details

- Blog: `http://davidkelly.me/`
- Twitter: `@LnDDave`
- Facebook: `https://www.facebook.com/davidkelly.me/`
- LinkedIn: `www.linkedin.com/in/lnddave`
- eLearning Guild: `https://www.elearningguild.com/`

Working with Standard Objects

2

Now that you have a better understanding of the features of Adobe Captivate, it is time to start exploring them in greater detail. In this chapter, you will begin developing the *Take the Train* project you experimented with in the previous chapter.

You will begin by creating a new blank project and applying a custom theme to it, so the project looks the way you want. Later in the book, you will learn how to create themes, but for now, you will simply apply it to the project so you can concentrate on learning how to work with the Standard Objects of Captivate.

Standard Objects are the fundamental building blocks of every Captivate project. They allow you to enrich your courses with Text Captions, shapes, images, and more.

In this chapter, we will cover the following topics:

- Creating a new Captivate file
- Applying a theme to the newly created file
- Adding slides to the project
- Applying Master Slides
- Working with the Properties inspector
- Working with Text Captions
- Inserting various types of images
- Working with shapes
- Applying Text Effects

Throughout this chapter, you will also discover how to modify the object properties. You will see that even though each of those objects is a little different from the others, they all share some common properties and workflows.

But enough talking for now. It's time to start developing your first Captivate project!

Creating a new Captivate project

When starting a new eLearning project, you may be tempted to jump right into Captivate and start adding slides to your course. You learned in `Chapter 1`, *Getting Started with Adobe Captivate,* that it is important to extensively research the topic and design the pedagogical approach of your course before beginning to work in Adobe Captivate. Starting your course without this preparation can waste a lot of your time later on. We cannot stress this enough. Captivate is a tool for teaching things to people. It helps you with the *craft* of teaching, but not with the *art* of teaching.

As this book is designed to teach you how to use Adobe Captivate, we have done all the important research and pre-production work for you. This will allow you to concentrate on the *ins* and *outs* of Captivate itself.

When you open Adobe Captivate 2019 for the first time, the following welcome screen appears:

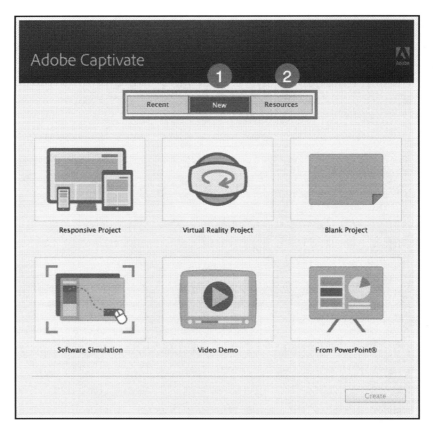

If this is not the first time you're opening Captivate, you will instead see the welcome screen displaying a list of recently opened files. If so, click the **New** tab at the top of the screen (marked **1** in the preceding screenshot) to return to the default welcome screen.

 Clicking the **Resources** tab (marked **2** in the preceding screenshot) takes you to a list of sample files and tutorials that will help you get started with Adobe Captivate.

From the welcome screen, you can create different types of Captivate projects. Be aware that the welcome screen only contains the most common project types. To see a full listing of all the project types supported by Adobe Captivate, open the **File** menu in the top-left corner of the screen. The first two items of the **File** menu contain a comprehensive list of project types:

- The **New Project** menu item lets you create different types of Captivate projects.
- The **Record a New** menu item lets you create a new screen recording project. This is typically used for software simulations and video tutorials.

 The **Device Demo** project type is only available for Mac users. It allows you to record the on-screen action taking place on your iOS device (iPad or iPhone).

The project you will create in this chapter is a typical non-responsive Captivate project based on slides. For such projects, you use the **Blank Project** icon of the welcome screen:

1. Click the **Blank Project** icon of the welcome screen.
2. In the **Canvas** drop-down menu that appears in the bottom-left corner of the welcome screen, choose a size of **1024 x 627** for your new project.
3. Click the **Create** button.

Captivate creates a new project containing a single slide. Your next task is to save the project:

4. Click the **Save** icon on the toolbar to save the project. You can also use the **File | Save** menu item or the *command + S* (macOS) / *Ctrl + S* (Windows) shortcut.

5. Save your file as `Chapter02/takeTheTrain.cptx` within the `sample` files folder you downloaded in the previous chapter.

It is a best practice to save your file immediately after creating it. This ensures your file has a name and exists on your system before you attempt to import other elements into it. You can tell that you've saved your file because the asterisk in the filename's tab disappears. If there is an asterisk present on the filename's tab in the Captivate interface, it means that there have been changes to the file since the last save.

 The `Chapter02/final` folder contains the completed project as it should look at the end of this chapter. If you are confused about any of the exercises in this chapter, use it as a reference.

Choosing the right project size

Choosing the right size for your project is the first critical decision you have to make. And you have to make it right because the size of the project plays a critical role in the quality of the student's experience when viewing the project.

Even though it is possible to resize a Captivate project later, you want to avoid doing that as the resize operation always results in a loss of quality. Here are a few things to keep in mind when choosing the right size for your project:

- Where will the project be viewed? If your Captivate module will be deployed on an intranet site and be viewed mostly on a desktop computer, you can safely create a somewhat larger project. If your project will be viewed mainly on tablet devices or smartphones, you should consider a smaller size, or a responsive project.
- The website where your course will be published probably has its own elements to display (logos, links, footer elements, sidebars, and so on), leaving less space on the screen to display your Captivate module.
- A larger project yields a bigger file size. If your project will be viewed over a fast LAN Ethernet connection, this might not be a big concern. But if the project needs to be transmitted over a slower network connection, you should consider a smaller file size.

Knowing your audience and how they will experience the finished course is important in determining the right size for your project.

In this example, the project size is 1,024 by 627 pixels. This is the default size proposed by Captivate. It is a *general-purpose* size that looks nice on a desktop computer, while accommodating most tablet devices at the same time.

Knowing your device size

If you want to know the characteristics of your device (including its viewport size), browse to `www.mydevice.io`. Just scroll down that page to access a table showing the screen size of the most popular mobile devices. What you are interested in is the CSS width and the CSS height columns of the table, which represent the pixel dimensions of the viewport.

Applying a theme to the project

Now that you've started your `takeTheTrain` project, your next task is to apply a theme. The theme determines the look of the Captivate project. It brings a set of styles and a set of predefined Master Slides to use and reuse throughout your course development.

Captivate includes many predefined themes that you can apply to your projects. While these themes are a great way to jump-start your next project, you will probably design and develop your own customized themes. This is what we have done for this project. Later in this book, you will learn how the custom theme we are using was made. But for now, let's focus on applying it to the project:

1. With the new project open, click the **Themes** icon on the toolbar.
2. Click the **Browse** link in the bottom-left corner of the theme chooser.
3. In the `Chapter02` folder of the exercise files, select the `takeTheTrain_Theme.cptm` file. (Note that a theme uses a `.cptm` file extension, while a regular Captivate project uses a `.cptx` file extension.)
4. Captivate displays a warning message telling you that the current styles will be overridden. Click **Yes** to close the message and apply the custom theme to the project.
5. Save the project when done.

After applying the theme, you notice a big change in how the project looks. This change comes from the Master Slides of the theme that are already at work! You will now take a closer look at the Master Slides included in the theme and choose one for the first slide.

6. Click the **Properties** icon on the right side of the toolbar to open the **Properties** inspector.

7. At the very top of the **Properties** inspector, in the **Master Slide** section, click the drop-down arrow to reveal a list of the available Master Slides. This operation is illustrated in the following screenshot:

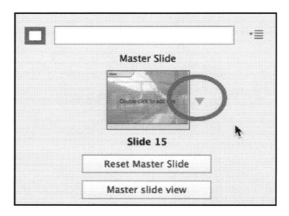

A Master Slide is a predefined layout that you can apply to your Captivate slides. This can dramatically speed up the development of your courses, while maintaining a strong visual consistency within and across your course modules.

You will now apply one of these Master Slides to the first slide of your project.

8. With the list of Master Slides open, click the **title** Master Slide to apply it to the selected slide

The **title** Master Slide is applied to the first slide of your project.

Working with placeholders

The Title Master Slide you just applied to the first slide of the project contains many objects. Some of these, such as the blue circle on the right of the slide, the blue lines stretching across the slide, or the image background, are aesthetic elements. Other objects define the placement and formatting of your content.

These objects are **placeholder** objects. Your next task is to add text in the two placeholders of the slide:

1. Double-click the title placeholder
2. Write `Take the train !` into the placeholder
3. Double-click the subtitle placeholder
4. Write `A guide to the best way of moving around in Belgium !` into the placeholder
5. Click anywhere on the slide or press the *Esc* key to complete your edits

Using Master Slides and placeholders makes it fast and easy to develop your eLearning content. It also ensures that the look and feel of your slides and objects are consistent within the file and across projects.

Adding slides to a project

Now that the first slide of the project is finished, your next task is to add a second slide and apply the appropriate Master Slide:

1. Click the **Slides** icon, which is the first icon on the toolbar
2. Click **Content Slide**
3. In the **Properties** inspector, open the **Master Slide** list
4. Apply the **Title&text** Master Slide to your new slide

The **Title&text** Master Slide has a big rectangle that defines the content area of this slide. It also contains two placeholder objects that you will fill with text using these steps.

5. Double-click the title placeholder
6. Type `Reading the schedule` in the title placeholder
7. Double-click the caption text placeholder
8. Type `Click the Next button to explore the various components of the schedule` into the placeholder
9. Click anywhere on the slide or hit the *Esc* key to finish editing

Your new slide should now look like the following screenshot:

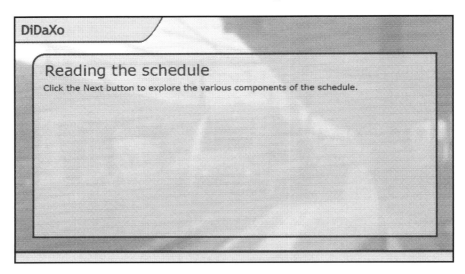

Working with the Properties inspector

The **Properties** inspector is one of the most important and most widely used tools in Captivate. In this section, you will study the **Properties** inspector in more detail. When you first open Adobe Captivate, the **Properties** inspector is hidden by default. To turn it on, perform the following steps:

1. Click several times on the **Properties** icon situated in the top-right corner of the toolbar to toggle the **Properties** inspector on and off.
2. Make sure that the **Properties** inspector is turned off before moving to the next step.
3. In the **Filmstrip**, double-click any slide. This also opens the **Properties** inspector.

In Captivate, double-clicking an object opens the **Properties** inspector and displays the properties for that object. Double-clicking anywhere on the scrap area around the stage is yet another way to open the **Properties** inspector.

The **Properties** and **Library** icons on the Toolbar are used to toggle the corresponding panels on and off. Make sure the **Properties** inspector is visible before moving on with this exercise.

Panels in advanced interface mode
Remember that in advanced interface mode, the **Properties** and **Library** icons are not present on the toolbar. Use the **Window** menu to turn these panels on and off.

The **Properties** inspector is dynamic. This means that its content changes depending on which object is selected. Let's experiment with this.

4. With the **Properties** inspector open, click the first slide thumbnail on the **Filmstrip** to make it the active slide.

5. After clicking slide 1, the **Properties** inspector displays the properties of that slide. For example, you can see that the **title** Master Slide is applied to the currently selected slide:

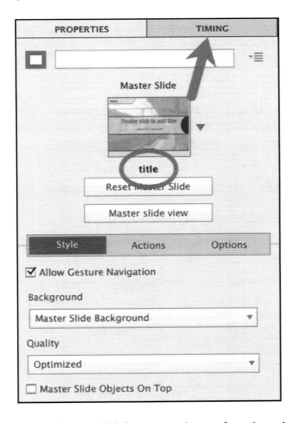

Take some time to examine the available properties and options in the **Properties** inspector.

The **Properties** inspector is actually a group of two panels, namely, the **Properties** and the **Timing** panels.

6. At the very top of the right column, click **Timing** to make it the active panel (see the arrow in the preceding screenshot).
7. Take some time to examine the properties of the **Timing** panel. When you are done, return to the **Properties** inspector.

The **Properties** inspector itself is divided into three different tabs, namely, **Styles**, **Actions**, and **Options**.

8. Take some time to examine the content of each of these tabs.
9. In **Filmstrip**, select the second slide to make it the active slide. The **Properties** inspector now displays the properties of that slide.

The selected slide contains two objects. You will now use the **Properties** inspector to examine the properties of these objects.

10. Click the **Reading the schedule** title to make it the active object.
11. Take another look at the **Properties** inspector. It now displays the properties relevant to the selected object.
12. Don't forget to examine the **Options** tab of the **Properties** inspector, as well as the **Timing** panel. Look at their properties and controls.
13. Click the second text to make it the active object.
14. The **Properties** panel now shows the properties of the second text. When you take another look at the **Style** and **Options** tabs of the **Properties** inspector, you should notice that the displayed properties are not exactly the same as when the title object was selected.
15. Also, examine the **Timing** panel of the selected object and compare it to the Timing panel of the title object.

Even though both the objects of the slide are used to display text, these are two very different objects in Captivate. The title object is called a **Smart Shape**, while the second text is a **Text Caption**. This explains why the controls in the **Properties** inspector are a little different for each of these two objects. The **Options** tab and the **Timing** panel contain the very same options and properties for both objects. Only the **Style** tab of the **Properties** inspector is a little bit different.

To work with the **Properties** inspector, remember the following:

- In normal interface mode, the **Properties** inspector is not displayed by default. Use the **Properties** button on the right side of the toolbar to toggle its visibility on and off. In advanced interface mode, use the **Window** menu.
- You can also double-click any object to open the **Properties** inspector of that particular object. This object can be a slide in **Filmstrip** or any object present on a slide.
- When clicking the **Properties** button on the toolbar, you reveal both the **Properties** inspector and the Timing panel.
- The **Properties** inspector and the **Timing** panel are both *dynamic*. This means that they show the properties relevant to the *active* object. Selecting another object changes the content of these panels.
- The **Properties** inspector is further divided into tabs.
- Usually, the **Style** tab is specific to the selected object. The **Options** tab is usually the same for all objects.

Now that you know how the **Properties** inspector works, you will learn about the basic objects of Captivate.

Exploring the objects of Captivate

Captivate supports more than a dozen objects. In this section, you will learn about standard non-interactive objects of Captivate. Later in this book, more complex objects will be covered.

Working with the Text Caption object

The Text Caption is typically used to display text on the screen. In its most basic form, the Text Caption is a text item that appears and disappears from the screen according to its position on the **Timeline**. On the second slide of your project, the bottom text area is a Text Caption. Let's select it and examine what you can do with it.

There are two editing modes available when working with Text Captions:

- First, you can consider the Text Caption as *an object*. In this case, eight white squares appear around the Text Caption. These white squares are the *handles* used to resize the Text Caption. In this mode, you can move the Text Caption around and resize it, but you cannot edit the text inside the Text Caption.
- To edit the text, you must be in text-editing mode. In text editing mode, the eight white handles disappear and a blinking cursor appears in the Text Caption.

To switch from object mode to text-editing mode, double-click the Text Caption. To switch from text-editing mode back to object mode, use the *Esc* key.

You will now modify the height of the Text Caption on slide 2:

1. Click once on the Text Caption on slide 2. Note that even though there is just one line of text in the Text Caption, it is almost as high as the content area defined on the Master Slide.
2. Reduce the height of the Text Caption by dragging the middle white square at the bottom upward. You will see a double-sided arrow when you are resizing. Make sure the Text Caption is only as high as needed to properly enclose the text.

Creating new Text Captions

The Text Caption you just worked with was created by adding text in a placeholder from the Master Slide. You will now create and modify a brand new Text Caption:

1. Still on slide 2, click the **Text** icon on the toolbar and select the **Text Caption** item.
2. Type `Click Continue when done.` into the new Text Caption.
3. Hit the *Esc* key to leave text-editing mode. The new Text Caption should still be selected.

When adding a new Text Caption, note the following:

- By default, the new Text Caption is inserted in the middle of the slide. In fact, this is the case every time you add any new object on a slide, regardless of it being a Text Caption or anything else.
- By default, the Text Caption is in text editing mode, allowing you to type in text right after inserting the object.

Resizing and moving Text Captions

In Captivate, resizing and moving an object is very easy and can be done in two different ways, namely, using the white handles, or using the **Options** tab of the **Properties** inspector:

1. While still on the second slide of your project, use the resize handles to adjust the Text Caption so that the text you just typed fits into a single line.
2. Open the **Options** tab of the **Properties** inspector.

The **Options** tab contains properties that control the size and position of the selected object. **W** indicates the width of the object, while **H** stands for the height. Both dimensions are expressed in pixels:

3. On the stage, use the white handles to make the Text Caption a bit bigger.
4. Take another look at the **Properties** inspector. The height and width fields of the **Options** tab reflect the new size of the object.

If you want to give your objects a specific size, you can enter the height and width in the **Properties** inspector directly. If the **Constrain proportions** checkbox is selected, Captivate automatically calculates the new height of the object when you modify the width (and vice versa) so that the height/width ratio of the object does not change:

5. With the Text Caption still selected, take a look at the X and Y values in the Options tab of the Properties inspector.
6. Use your mouse to move the Text Caption around the slide.

See how the **X** and **Y** values change as you move the Text Caption. The **X** coordinate is the distance (in pixels) between the left edge of the selected object and the left edge of the slide. The **Y** coordinate is the distance (in pixels) between the top edge of the selected object and the top of the slide. You can manually enter the **X** and **Y** coordinates in the **Options** tab to give the selected object a pixel-precise position on the slide:

7. Use your mouse to move the new Text Caption and place it roughly under the first one.
8. As you do so, notice the vertical and/or horizontal dotted green lines that appear on the stage. Use them to properly position your Text Caption under the first one.

These dotted green lines are called **Smart Guides**. They automatically appear and disappear as you move objects around. Smart Guides help you align the object quickly and precisely.

You can turn the Smart Guide feature on or off by going to the **View | Show Drawing / Smart Guides** menu item. The aforementioned procedure assumes that the Smart Guide feature is turned on, which is the default value.

After this procedure, your slide should look like the following screenshot:

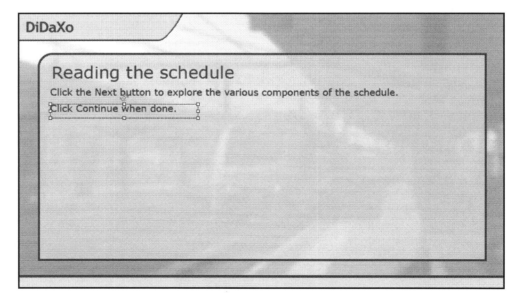

Formatting a Text Caption

You will now examine some of the formatting capabilities of the Text Caption object. To do so, make sure that the Text Caption you just inserted is selected before performing the following steps:

1. If necessary, open the **Properties** inspector by clicking the **Properties** icon on the toolbar.
2. In the **Style** tab of the **Properties** inspector, open the **Caption Type** drop-down list and choose **Adobe Green**.
3. Directly under the **Caption Type** drop-down list, experiment with the five **Callout Type** options.
4. Open the **Caption Type** drop-down list again and choose the **Transparent** item at the top of the list.
5. Experiment with the other properties. For example, change the color of the text, the font family, or the size.
6. When you are done, click the small menu icon just above the **Style Name** drop-down list and choose **Reset Style**, as shown in the following screenshot:

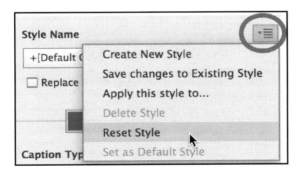

Your last action resets the Text Caption to its default formatting. In Chapter 6, *Crafting the Graphical Experience with Styles and Themes*, you will learn how to create these styles and how to apply them to the other Text Captions of the project.

Before moving on to the next object, let's summarize what you have learned about Text Captions:

- The Text Caption object is used to display text to the learner
- Changing the size or moving an object with the mouse also changes the corresponding values in the **Options** tab of the **Properties** inspector, and vice versa

- Apply a **Caption Type** to the object to quickly format it
- Captivate provides five **Callout Type** options for each **Caption Type**
- Most of the formatting properties of Text Captions can be found in the **Style** tab of the **Properties** inspector

The Text Caption object is very simple to use. In earlier versions of Captivate, it was the only means of displaying text to the learner. In the more recent versions of Captivate, you can also display text using a much more powerful object, called the Smart Shape.

Working with Smart Shapes

Smart Shapes are a predefined collection of shapes, including rectangles, circles, banners, stars, arrows, and many more. Before working with Smart Shapes, let's add another slide to the project using the following steps:

1. In **Filmstrip**, select the first slide of the project
2. Click the **Slides** icon, which is the first icon on the toolbar
3. Click the **Content Slide** icon
4. With the new slide selected, use the **Properties** inspector to apply the **contentBkg** Master Slide to the new slide

Note that Captivate adds a new slide *after* the currently selected slide. In this case, Captivate has added the new slide as slide 2 because slide 1 was selected when you added the new slide. It not possible to insert a slide at the very beginning of a project. To place a slide at the beginning of a project, drag and drop slides in the **Filmstrip** panel.

Drawing a simple Smart Shape

You will now draw a simple rounded rectangle Smart Shape via the following steps:

1. Make sure that you are on the newly-created slide 2.
2. Click the **Shapes** icon on the toolbar. Take some time to examine the list of available shapes.
3. Click the rounded rectangle shape in the **Basic** section of the list of shapes.
4. Click and drag your mouse on the stage to draw a rounded rectangle shape in the top-right corner of the content area of the slide. Resize and move the shape as necessary.

In the top-left corner of the shape, you'll see a yellow handle in addition to the eight white handles that surround the shape. This yellow handle is one of the features that make a Smart Shape...smart. It is used to modify the shape. In this case, the yellow handle will adjust the roundness of the rectangle. Other Smart Shapes might display multiple yellow handles, allowing you to customize multiple aspects of the selected shape. The number of yellow handles actually depends on the shape.

5. Use the yellow handle to adjust the roundness of the rectangle to your taste

Don't worry about the exact positioning and formatting of the rounded rectangle. These elements will be adjusted later.

Formatting Smart Shapes

As you might expect, you use the **Properties** inspector of Captivate to format your Smart Shapes. In this section, you will discover the main formatting properties of the Smart Shapes object via the following steps:

1. On slide 2 of the `Chapter02/takeTheTrain.cptx` project, select the rounded rectangle shape.
2. Look at the **Style** tab of the **Properties** inspector.
3. In the **Fill** section, open the **Solid** drop-down menu.

This menu is one of the many reasons why I love Smart Shapes: because it offers you so many possibilities. Let's review these options one by one:

- **Solid Fill**: This is the default value. It allows you to define a single solid color as the background of your Smart Shape. Simply use the **Fill** property next to the drop-down menu you just opened to choose a color with the color picker.
- **Gradient fill**: This lets you arrange two or more colors in a gradient. This capability is unique to the Smart Shape object. The gradient editor is very similar to the one found in other Adobe applications, such as Photoshop, Illustrator, and InDesign.
- **Image fill**: This lets you choose an image to be used as the background of the Smart Shape.

As you can see, this drop-down menu opens a world of formatting capabilities, making the Smart Shape object the most versatile object of Captivate (and you just opened a single drop-down menu!). Let's dig deeper into the formatting capabilities of the Smart Shape object.

4. In the **Fill** section of the **Style** tab of the **Properties** inspector, open the **Opacity** drop-down menu.
5. Change the **Opacity** value to **10%** and look at your Smart Shape on the stage.
6. Reopen the same drop-down menu and change the **Opacity** value to **100%**.
7. Select the **Opacity** value and type 85 with your keyboard. Don't forget to apply the new value by using the *Enter* key.

The opacity property lets you create objects that are more or less transparent. With a lower value, your Smart Shape is more transparent, letting more of the background image show through the object. With an opacity value of 0, the Smart Shape is fully transparent. With a higher value, your Smart Shape becomes more and more opaque. With a value of 100%, the Smart Shape is completely opaque, and the background image behind the Smart Shape object is completely invisible.

The opacity property is unique to Smart Shapes. A Text Caption can only be completely transparent or completely opaque. This is one of the key differences between a Smart Shape and a Text Caption.

You will now reset the formatting of the selected Smart Shape and add a small border to your rounded rectangle:

8. With the rounded rectangle Smart Shape of slide 2 still selected, click the small menu icon on the right of the **Style Name** label in the **Properties** inspector.
9. Click the **Reset Style** item to return to the default formatting.
10. Now find the **Stroke** section of the **Style** tab of the **Properties** inspector.
11. In the **Style** drop-down menu, make sure you choose a solid border.
12. In the **Stroke** drop-down menu, choose a white stroke.
13. Open the **Width** drop-down menu and choose a width of 3 pixels for your stroke.
14. You should now have a solid white stroke of 3 pixels all around your Smart Shape.

The ability to create highly customizable strokes around a shape is yet another formatting capability that makes the Smart Shape object so powerful. Your slide should now look like the following screenshot:

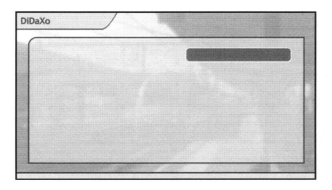

Creating your own Smart Shapes

In addition to predefined shapes, Captivate allows you to draw your own Smart Shapes and save them for later use. In the following exercise, you will experiment with this feature hands-on, via the following steps:

1. In slide 2 of the `Chapter02/takeTheTrain.cptx` project, click the **Shapes** icon on the toolbar to open the Smart Shapes menu.

2. Choose the Polygon tool in the Smart Shapes menu. It is the line that ends with a star at the top of the menu. With the Polygon tool selected, the mouse pointer turns into a crosshair.

3. Click anywhere on the slide where you want the first point of the Polygon to be located.

4. Click a second time at another location to create a second point. Captivate automatically connects the two points with a dotted line.

5. Use the same technique to add other points to the shape.

6. To close the shape, click a second time on the first point you created. Captivate displays a small circle next to the mouse pointer to indicate that the shape can be closed.

You now have your very own custom shape on the slide. Don't worry if the shape is not exactly like the one you intended to create! In the next subsection, you will learn how to modify the shape you just created.

Modifying a custom shape

A Smart Shape is a **vector object** similar to those you can draw with Adobe Illustrator. To create these shapes, designers use the Pen tool of Illustrator to draw Bezier points and Bezier curves. Even though Captivate is not equipped with a full-fledged pen tool, you can, however, access these Bezier points and modify your shape via the following steps:

1. Right-click the shape you created and choose the **Edit Points** item in the contextual menu. This action reveals the points that you defined when you created the polygon.
2. Move those points to modify the shape. You can also move the green handles to modify the curvature of the connecting lines, as shown in the next screenshot.
3. When you are happy with the shape, hit the *Esc* key on your keyboard to leave the point-editing mode and to select the shape.

Note that you can only move the *existing* points or modify their curvature; you cannot add or remove points to or from the shape:

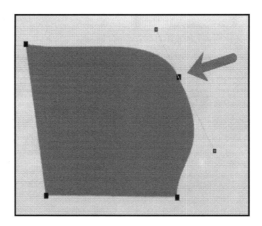

Converting predefined shapes to freeform
Another way to create your own Smart Shapes is to start with a predefined shape and modify it using the very same technique. Simply right-click a Smart Shape and choose the **Convert to freeform** item in the contextual menu to access the Bezier points. Have fun!

Saving a custom shape

Captivate gives you the ability to save your custom shapes and add them to the list of predefined shapes. In this exercise, you will save your custom shape and insert a second instance of it via the following steps:

1. In slide 2 of your project, make sure that your custom shape is selected (with white selection handles around it).
2. Locate the **Custom** section at the very top of the **Style** tab in the **Properties** inspector.
3. Click the icon in the top-right corner of the **Custom** section and choose the **Save Shape** item, as shown in the following screenshot:

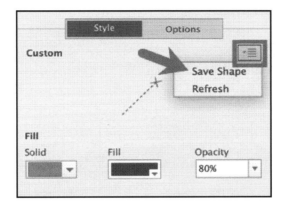

4. Type myShape into the **Rename Item** dialog and click **OK** to save your custom shape.

By saving your custom shape, you make it a part of the collection of predefined shapes, so you can reuse it in the future. Perform the following step to draw a second instance of the same shape.

5. Click the **Shapes** icon on the toolbar to open the Smart Shapes panel.

Note that your new shape is present in the **Recently Used Shapes** section at the top of the drop-down menu. If you did not use that shape recently, it would not be a part of the menu. In that case, here is how you can draw that shape.

6. Choose the Polygon tool (the dotted line that ends with a star).
7. Randomly add a few points to the slide in order to create a new custom shape. The actual shape you come up with is of no importance.
8. Make sure that the new shape is selected, and look at the **Custom** section at the top of the **Style** tab in the **Properties** inspector.
9. Click the little black arrow to reveal a list of additional shapes.
10. Choose your custom shape in the list of additional shapes, as shown in the following screenshot:

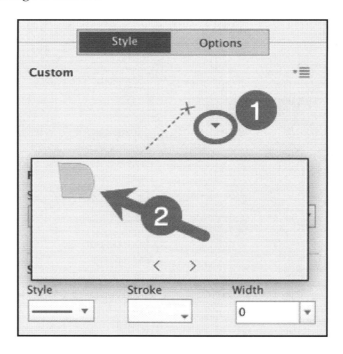

You should now have two instances of your custom shape on the slide. Since these two shapes were added for demonstration purposes only, your next task is to remove them from the slide.

11. Press and hold the *Shift* key and select both your custom shapes. Hit the *Delete* key on your keyboard to remove them from the slide. You can also right-click a shape and use the **Delete** menu item.

12. Save the file when done.

You should now be back to the original situation, with only one rounded rectangle in the top-right corner of the slide.

Adding text inside Smart Shapes

The awesomeness of Smart Shapes does not end here! In this exercise, you will add text inside a Smart Shape. This means that you can create an entire project without ever using Text Captions. You likely will still use Text Captions though, because they are so quick and easy to create. However, most of the time, you will probably only use the transparent Caption Type. For all your other text needs, the Smart Shape object gives you much more power, flexibility, and opportunities to be creative.

On slide 2, select the rounded rectangle Smart Shape:

1. In the **Properties** inspector, the **Style** tab should contain four sections: the **Basic** section at the top, the **Fill** and **Stroke** sections, and a collapsible **Shadow and Reflection** section at the bottom. This is shown in the following screenshot:

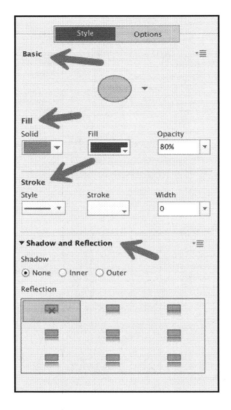

2. Double-click the rounded rectangle. This action brings a blinking cursor in the middle of the shape.
3. Type Liege Guillemins inside the Smart Shape. When done, use the *Esc* key to leave text editing mode and select the shape as an object.
4. Take another look at the **Properties** inspector.

By adding text inside your Smart Shape, the **Character** and the **Margin** sections have been automatically added to the **Style** tab. These two sections are the same as those used to format the text inside a Text Caption, so you have the exact same text formatting capabilities on a Smart Shape as on a Text Caption.

 Liège Guillemins is the main train station of the city of Liège in the eastern part of Belgium. A great place to visit on your next European trip!

Duplicating object

Currently, you have a single rounded rectangle Smart Shape on your slide. However, you need three of those on this slide, and they should all look the same.

Instead of drawing two brand new Smart Shapes, you will build on what you've already created by duplicating the existing rounded rectangle and changing the text. Follow these steps:

1. Select the rounded rectangle Smart Shape.
2. Use the *Ctrl + D* (Windows) or *command + D* (Mac) shortcut to duplicate the existing shape.
3. Double-click the newly created shape and replace the text with `Bruxelles - Midi`.
4. Hit the *Esc* key to leave text-editing mode, while keeping the Smart Shape selected.
5. Repeat the procedure to create a third shape. Write `Oostende` in the third Smart Shape.
6. Arrange your Smart Shapes so that the slide looks like the following screenshot:

 To duplicate an object, you can also drag it with the mouse while holding down the *Ctrl* (Windows) or *command* (Mac) key. This gives you the ability to duplicate an object and to position the copy on the stage in a single action.

Bruxelles-Midi is the main train station of Brussels, the capital city of Belgium, and *Bruxelles* is how you spell Brussels in French. *Oostende* is a city situated at the far west of the country, along the coast.

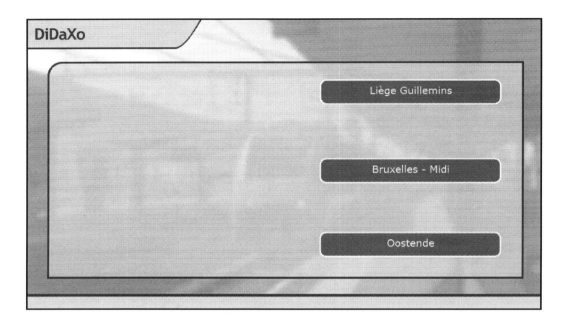

Extra credit – creating additional Smart Shapes

In this extra credit section, you will draw two additional Smart Shapes on your slide. This will give you the opportunity to experiment with another predefined shape. Follow these steps to draw two arrows pointing downward between the rounded rectangles:

- Make sure you are still on the second slide of your new Captivate project.
- Click the **Shapes** icon on the toolbar to open the list of available shapes.
- In the **Arrows** section, click the downward-arrow shape.
- Draw a downward-pointing arrow between the first two rounded rectangles.
- With the new arrow selected, experiment with the yellow square to see how it affects the shape of the arrow.

- When the arrow has the desired shape, move it into place. Use the green dotted Smart Guides to align the objects accurately.
- With the new arrow selected, open the **Style Name** drop-down list of the **Properties** inspector and apply the **shape_As_HB** style to the selected arrow. This style is part of the theme that you applied to your project earlier in this chapter.
- Use the *Ctrl + D* (Windows) / *command + D* (Mac) shortcut to duplicate the arrow.
- Move the second arrow between the second and the third rounded rectangles. Use the green dotted Smart Guides to properly align the shapes.

After these steps, your slide should look like the following screenshot:

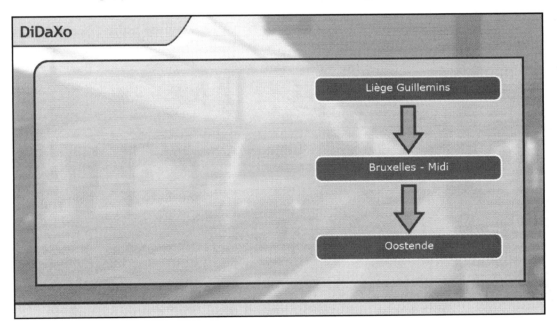

 Remember that Smart Guides can be turned on and off using the **View | Show Drawing / Smart Guides** menu item.

In this section, you learned a lot about Smart Shapes. Before moving on to the next section, let's summarize what was covered in this section:

- Smart Shapes are a collection of predefined shapes that can be manipulated in many ways with the tools of Captivate.
- The collection of Smart Shapes includes rounded rectangles, banners, triangles, arrows, callouts, and more.
- When a Smart Shape object is selected, special yellow handles allow you to modify the Smart Shape.
- Use the **Polygon** tool to draw custom shapes that you can save for reuse.
- Smart Shapes are vector objects similar to those you create with Adobe Illustrator. Use the **Edit Points** or the **Convert to Freeform** menu items to access the Bezier points and curves of your shape.
- The **Fill** of a Smart Shape can be a **Solid Fill**, **Gradient Fill**, or **Image Fill**.
- You can control the **Opacity** of a Smart Shape. An opacity of 0% means that the object is completely transparent, while an opacity of 100% means that the object is completely opaque.
- Text can be added inside a Smart Shape.
- When a Smart Shape contains text, additional text formatting properties are displayed in the **Style** tab of the **Properties** inspector.
- These text formatting properties are the same as those of a Text Caption object.

I must admit that I love Smart Shapes! In `Chapter 5`, *Developing Interactivity*, you will discover even more capabilities of this very flexible Captivate object. For now, let's move on to the next feature of this chapter.

Working with images

Captivate lets you insert various types of images on any slide. Once an image is inserted, you can modify and format it using the image-editing tools of Captivate.

Keep in mind, though, that Captivate is not an image-editing application. To guarantee the best possible results, you should always prepare your images in a dedicated image-editing application, such as Adobe Photoshop or Adobe Illustrator, before inserting the image into Captivate. However, if you don't have access to these programs, you can do basic image editing inside Captivate.

Inserting an image

Your first task of this chapter is to insert an image on a slide.

An image is worth a thousand words

Images play an important role in eLearning, and are a tremendously efficient way to convey meaning without using a single word! In our modern world, where learners are more and more reluctant to read (especially on a screen), this old saying takes on a whole new dimension. The more I progress into eLearning, the more I use images. Another benefit of images is that they don't need to be translated when creating a multilingual course. You can save on translation costs while creating a more efficient and appealing eLearning module!

Adding images to your project is simple to do in Captivate, and is similar to what is found in other applications. Follow these steps to insert an image into a slide:

1. Make sure that you are still on the second slide of your Captivate project
2. Click the **Media | Image** icon on the Toolbar.
3. Navigate to the `Chapter02/` folder of your exercise files and choose the `belgiumRailroadMap.png` file.

The image is inserted in the middle of the slide. Obviously, it is way too big! It needs to be altered so it integrates nicely with the rest of the slide.

4. Make sure that the image is selected on your slide.
5. Use your mouse to change the size of the image by clicking and dragging the white handles. This will most likely distort the image. You can avoid distortion by pressing and holding the *Shift* key on your keyboard while using a corner handle to resize (scale) the image.

In the **Style** tab of the **Properties** inspector, click the **Reset To Original Size** button to restore the image to its original aspect. You will now use the **Options** tab of the **Properties** inspector to resize this picture.

6. Switch to the **Options** tab of the **Properties** inspector.
7. Make sure that the **Constrain proportions** checkbox is selected and change the width of the picture to 480 pixels. Captivate calculates the new height of the image (392 pixels) so that its height/width ratio does not change.
8. Move the image to the left side of the slide, next to the Smart Shapes you created in the previous section.

Your slide should now look like the following screenshot:

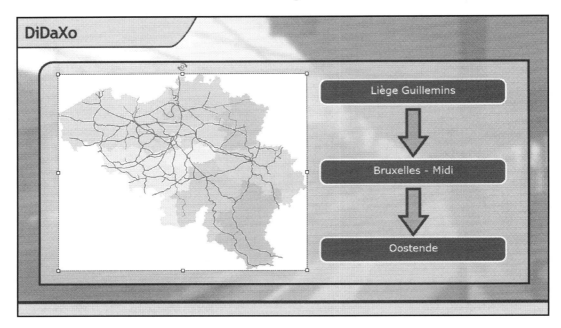

About image types

Captivate lets you insert many different image types in your projects, including `.jpg`, `.gif`, and `.png` images. If you want to know more about these image formats, visit

`http://www.sitepoint.com/gif-jpg-png-whats-difference/`.

Using the image editing tools of Captivate

Now that you have inserted an image in the project, you will explore some of the image editing tools available in Captivate:

1. Make sure that the newly imported image is selected, and take a look at the **Style** tab of the **Properties** inspector.
2. Click the **Edit Image** button.

This action opens a dialog showing the image on the left and a set of control sliders on the right.

3. Move the sliders to see how each affects the image.
4. When done, click the **Reset All** button in the bottom-right corner of the dialog.
5. Take some time to inspect the other controls available in the dialog. Note that the image can also be flipped, resized, and cropped.
6. Click **Cancel** to close the dialog without saving the changes.

These image editing capabilities are a great convenience to fine-tune the images you insert in Captivate. However, let's reiterate the fact that these tools are not meant to replace actual image-editing software, such as Adobe Photoshop or Adobe Illustrator. If you have access to a dedicated image-editing application, it is better to prepare your image in one of those applications before inserting it into Captivate.

Inserting a picture slide

Inserting images into existing slides is one of the many possibilities offered by Captivate. Another nice feature is the ability to create a new slide with an image as the background. In this project, you don't need to use this feature because all the slide layouts you need are included in the theme that you applied to your project earlier in this chapter.

But if you want to use an image as the background of a slide, here is the general process:

1. Use an external image editing application (such as Adobe Photoshop) to prepare an image with the same size as your project.
2. Use the **Insert | Image Slide** menu item and select an image on your computer.
3. A new slide is inserted after the selected slide. This new slide uses your picture as its background.

Even though the use of themes and Master Slides is a much better way of creating reusable slide layouts, the ability to create a new slide based on an image is a nice little feature of Captivate that is worth mentioning.

You will learn more about Master Slides and themes in `Chapter 6,` *Crafting the Graphical Experience with Styles and Themes.*

Inserting Character images

Characters are a collection of images that can be inserted in your Captivate projects. These images represent male and female characters in various postures and expressions. Inserting these in your eLearning projects brings in a human and sometimes humorous touch.

Downloading the eLearning assets
These characters are part of the eLearning assets available with your Captivate license. However, these eLearning assets are not included in the main Captivate installation package. A separate package must be downloaded and installed to use the characters. You can find these extra installers
at `http://www.adobe.com/go/Cp2019_win_assets_installer` (for Windows)
or `http://www.adobe.com/go/Cp2019_mac_assets_installer` (for macOS). Make sure you download and install this additional package before moving on with this section.

You will now create a new slide and insert a Character image using the following steps:

1. In the **Filmstrip**, select the first slide of your project.
2. Click the **Slides** icon on the toolbar to insert a new **Content Slide.**
3. Use the **Properties** inspector to apply the **2Cols Text right** Master Slide to the newly created slide.
4. Click the **Media** icon of the Toolbar.
5. In the **Media** drop-down menu, click **Characters.**

This opens the **My Assets** dialog, as shown in the following screenshot. You can use it to insert various types of assets from various sources into your Captivate projects:

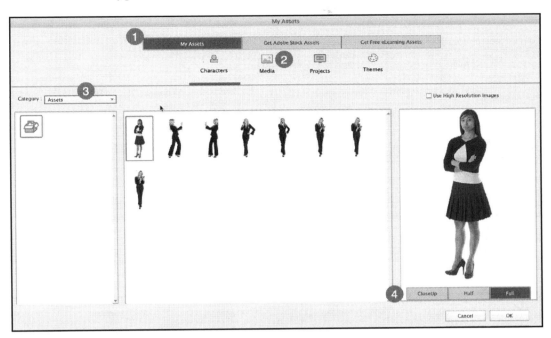

This dialog is one of the treasures of Adobe Captivate. So, before moving on with the exercise, let's spend some time examining its features.

The top row of buttons (marked as 1 in the preceding screenshot) lets you decide where you want to look for assets:

- The **My Assets** button lists the assets that are stored on your computer. These can be assets that are part of the Captivate installation, or assets downloaded after the installation of Captivate using the other features of this dialog. These assets are further arranged and sorted by types. They are accessible through the second row of icons (marked as 2 in the preceding screenshot).

- Use the **Get Adobe Stock Assets** button to download stock images and videos from Adobe Stock. Adobe Stock is a huge online library of stock images and videos. You can use this online library in almost every Adobe application, including Photoshop, Illustrator, Premiere etc, and, of course, in Captivate. Adobe Stock is not included with your Captivate license and requires an extra subscription. More information can be found at `https://stock.adobe.com/`.
- The **Get Free eLearning Assets** button lets you access the online assets library of eLearning Brothers. eLearning Brothers is a company that teamed up with Adobe to offer you a huge library of free assets. Access to this online library is part of your Captivate license. It contains thousands of eLearning assets, including cutout people, templates, themes, interactions, scenarios, and more.

Spend some time browsing these online resources. With the exception of Adobe Stock, all this wonderful content is part of your Captivate license, so don't hesitate to browse the library and use those assets. Once you download an asset from the eLearning Brothers library, you can access it via the **My Assets** button of this dialog box.

In this exercise, you will use an image asset already stored on your computer, so make sure that you return to the **My Assets** button before continuing with this exercise.

6. In the row of buttons, marked as 2 in the preceding screenshot, make sure that you are in the **Characters** assets.
7. Open the **Category** drop-down menu (marked as 3 in the preceding screenshot).
8. Select the **Casual** category.
9. In the left column of the dialog, choose any character of your liking.
10. In the center column, take some time to examine the available poses for the character you selected. When done, select the very first pose at the top of the list.
11. Note that you can choose three different shots for the chosen pose (see 4 in the preceding screenshot.) In this example, choose the **Full** shot.
12. Click **Open** to insert the chosen pose in your slide.

You may have noticed the **Use High Resolution** checkbox just above the character preview in the third column of the **My Assets** dialog. The best practice is to use this checkbox for **CloseUp** or **Half** shots. When using **Full** shot, as it is the case in this example, checking this box is not needed as the image is already optimized for high resolution.

From now on, the newly inserted character behaves just like another image. In fact, it actually *is* a .png image. This means you can move and resize it just like any other image (don't forget to hold down the *Shift* key while resizing the image to prevent image distortion). You can also use the buttons of the **Properties** inspector to further edit this image, as discussed in the previous section.

The **Flip image horizontal** option of the **Image Edit** dialog box is an easy way to double the number of available postures!

Make sure your slide looks like the following screenshot before moving on:

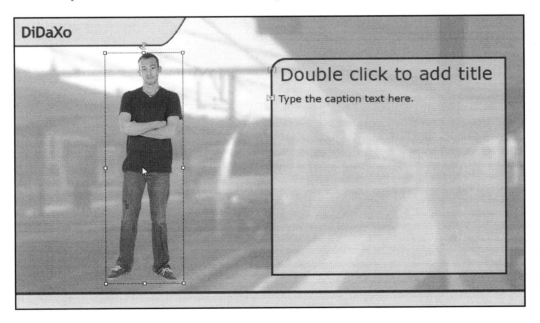

Working with SVG images

The image files you have been working with so far in this section are all *bitmap* images. This means that they contain pixels. Each pixel is a tiny little dot of a certain color, and it is the collection of all these tiny little colored dots that recreates the picture as you see it.

Bitmap images are great, but they have one important limitation. To guarantee the best possible image quality, you must consider that a bitmap image is designed for a specific size. You should use an external application (such as Adobe Photoshop) to generate the image. Ideally, you should not resize the image after you insert it in Captivate.

A bitmap image is composed of a fixed number of pixels. Imagine, for example, an image of 300 pixels in width and 200 pixels in height. This image contains 60,000 pixels (the multiplication of 300 by 200). So, what happens if you enlarge this picture after you insert it in Captivate? Well, you basically ask those 60,000 pixels to cover a bigger area, so there is no other choice than to make each pixel a little bigger. If you enlarge the picture just a tiny bit, this is barely noticeable, but if you want to make a tiny picture much bigger, you start to see each pixel, because you need to enlarge them too much and it makes the image fuzzy. Reducing the size of an image is usually OK, even though the best practice is to give the picture its correct size in a dedicated image-editing application *before* inserting it into Captivate.

SVG stands for Scalable Vector Graphics. SVG images are different, because they do not contain any pixels! Instead, they are made of a collection of shapes defined by mathematical coordinates and formulas (called vectors). The biggest advantage of this approach is that an SVG image is not tied to a specific size. If you resize it, the computer regenerates the image for the new size. It means that an SVG image stays crisp and focused, whatever its size! Let's experiment with this hands-on via the following steps:

1. Return to slide 3 of your Captivate project.
2. Click the **Media** icon on the toolbar and choose the **SVG** option.
3. Browse to the `Chapter02/mapSymbolPin.svg` file and insert it into your slide.

At first sight, this looks just like any other image. Now, let's experiment with the magic of SVG files.

4. Reduce the size of the picture (remember to hold down the *Shift* key to resize it proportionally).

5. Move the pin so that it points to the yellow area in the center of the map of Belgium.

6. Now, place your mouse pointer on top of one of the corner handles of the SVG image you just imported.

7. Hold down the *Shift* key and dramatically enlarge the image, but do not release your mouse button just yet. You should see that the more you enlarge the image, the more it gets pixelated. When the image is dramatically bigger than the original, the deterioration is unacceptable.

8. Release the mouse button and see how the SVG image reacts.

This is where it gets interesting! When you release the mouse button, Captivate recalculates the image for its new size. After a short delay, you will see that the image is again nice and crisp, even though you have enlarged it dramatically! This is illustrated in the following screenshot:

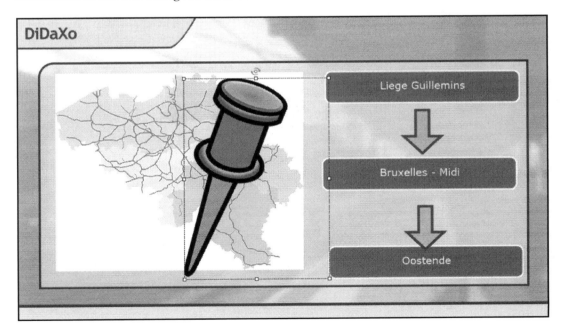

Of course, you don't need the image to be that big, so let's return to a more reasonable size that fits nicely into this slide.

9. Hold down the *Shift* key and resize the SVG image so that it fits on top of the map of Belgium, pointing to the yellow area at the center.

After this short experiment, you should understand the huge advantage of SVG images over bitmap images, especially when developing responsive eLearning content (that is, content that has the ability to adapt itself to any screen size, from large desktop computers to tiny smartphones).

Before moving on to the next section, let's quickly summarize what you learned in this section by comparing SVG files to their bitmap counterparts in the following table:

	SVG images	Bitmap images
File extension	`.svg`	`.png`, `.jpg`, and `.gif`
Contains	Vector shapes and paths used to calculate the picture	A fixed number of pixels
Size	Resolution-independent as the picture is recalculated for each size	Because it contains a fixed number of pixels, a bitmap image is designed for a specific size
Authoring tool	Adobe Illustrator	Adobe Photoshop
Limitation	Cannot reproduce an actual photographic image	Cannot be easily enlarged; usually much bigger file size
Typical use case	Drawings, illustrations, logos, buttons, icons, and other interface elements	Photographic images

In modern-day eLearning, where the demand for responsive content increases by the day, SVG files are just awesome! They can be scaled to any size without losing their quality and the file size is usually much smaller than that of a bitmap file. This makes SVG images easy to transmit to mobile devices over Wi-Fi or 4G data links. You will learn more about responsive eLearning in `Chapter 10`, *Creating a Responsive Project*.

Seeing the content of an SVG file

If you are curious about the inner workings of an SVG file, you can use Windows Explorer (Windows) or the Finder (macOS) to navigate to the SVG file you inserted in the previous exercise. Open it with a text editor, such as Notepad (Windows) or TextEdit (macOS). You should see a bunch of tags, coordinates, and color codes that represent the individual vector shapes and paths that compose the SVG image. But... there is no trace of any pixel in this file!

This concludes your first exploration of images in Adobe Captivate. Before moving on to the next topic, let's summarize what you learned in this section:

- You can easily insert many types of images in Captivate.
- Captivate provides some image-editing capabilities. These are found in the **Image Edit** dialog accessible through the **Image Edit** button situated in the **Style** tab of the **Properties** inspector.
- It is best to prepare the image in an external image-editing application (such as Adobe Photoshop) before inserting it into Captivate.
- If needed, use the **Reset To Original Size** button to change the picture back to its original size.
- Use the **Insert | Image Slide** menu item to create new slides with an image as the background.
- Captivate gives you access to thousands of free and paid assets that you can use within your Captivate course. Use the **Assets** button on the toolbar to access the asset libraries.
- **Characters** are a collection of images (photographs and illustrations) that you can use in your eLearning projects.
- The installation of an extra package is required to use the Characters.
- JPG, PNG, and GIF images are all bitmap images. This means that they contain a fixed number of pixels. This also means that they are designed for a predefined and fixed size.
- SVGs contain vector images that are resolution-independent and very lightweight. This makes them well adapted for responsive projects, but they can also be used in regular (non-responsive) projects.

If you click the **Text** icon on the toolbar, you will find one more non-interactive object that is not covered in this chapter. The **Text Animation** object is a legacy object of Captivate. The only reason this object is still supported in Adobe Captivate 2019 is to ensure backward compatibility with legacy Captivate projects. The Text Animation object is based on Flash technology and is only available when you publish your project in Flash. Remember that Adobe has announced the end of the Flash player for 2020, so this object is likely to disappear in future Captivate versions. You should not use this object in your newer Captivate content.

Working with Text Effects

The Text Effects feature lets you create and apply some sophisticated visual effects to the Text Captions and Smart Shapes containing text. If you are a Photoshop user, you'll be in familiar territory because Captivate's Text Effects feature shares most of its functionalities with the effects of Photoshop.

Follow these steps to experiment with Text Effects:

1. Return to slide 2 of the `Chapter02/takeTheTrain.cptx` file.
2. Double-click the Title placeholder and type `Jan` as the title text.
3. Double-click the Text Caption placeholder and type in the following text (hitting the *Enter* key after each line of text):

   ```
   Nationality : Belgian
   Lives in : Brussels
   Occupation : Student
   Takes the train : Everyday!
   ```

4. Hit the *Esc* key to leave text-editing mode and leave the Text Caption object selected.
5. Reduce the height of the Text Caption so that it takes approximately half the available space.
6. Select the title Smart Shape.

Now that you have some text on the slide, you can start experimenting with Text Effects.

7. With the title **Smart Shape** selected, look at the **Properties** inspector.

8. In the **Character** section of the **Properties** inspector, click the **Effects** icon next to the **Color** and **Highlight** properties.

9. Click any of the effects in the drop-down menu.

10. Repeat the preceding operations to apply other predefined effects and get a feel of what is possible.

11. When you are done, reopen the **Text Effects** menu, and click the **Clear** button to remove the applied effect.

In addition to applying predefined Text Effects, Captivate also lets you create your own custom Text Effects. Let's create one and save it for later use.

12. Make sure the title Smart Shape (containing the text **Jan**) is still selected.

13. Reopen the Text Effects drop-down menu and click the first available + icon. This operation is shown in the following screenshot:

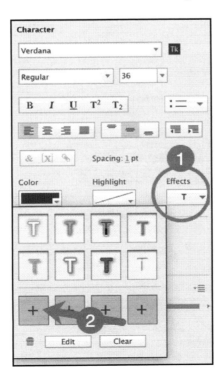

The **Text Effects** window opens. The left side of the window contains nine effects. You can easily turn these effects on and off by clicking their respective checkboxes. The right side of the window displays the options of the effect selected on the left side. Currently, no effect is applied.

14. In the left column of the **Text Effects** window, select the **Drop Shadow** checkbox. A Drop Shadow effect is added to the selected text object. For this example, accept the default settings of the **Drop Shadow** effect.

15. In the left column of the **Text Effects** window, select the **Outer Glow** checkbox. The **Outer Glow** effect is also applied to the Text Caption and the options of the **Outer Glow** effect are displayed on the right side of the **Text Effects** window.

To make your effect more appealing and visible, modify the color of the **Outer Glow** effect.

16. On the right side of the **Text Effects** window, click the **Color** option of the **Outer Glow** effect.

17. In the color picker on the right side of the window, choose any bright green color. The **Text Effects** window should now look like the following screenshot:

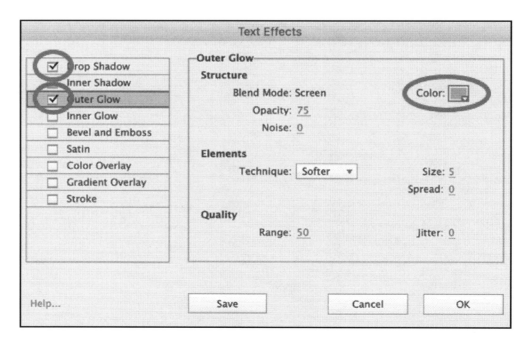

Hey! It looks like you just came up with a very nice effect. Let's save it for future use.

    18.   At the bottom of the **Text Effects** window, click the **Save** button.

The **Text Effects** window closes and your effect is applied to the selected Text Caption. Because you have saved your nice effect, it is easy to apply it to another text object of the project.

    19.   Select the Text Caption object located just below the title on which you applied an effect.

    20.   In the **Properties** inspector, open the **Effects** icon one more time.

    21.   There should be a new predefined effect in the drop-down menu! Apply your new effect to the selected Text Caption.

In this section, you have experimented with Text Effects. You have also created a custom Text Effect and you have saved it for later use. Finally, you have applied the same custom effect to another text object. Note that a Text Effect must be applied to the entire text content. It is not possible to select a portion of the text and apply the effect to the selected portion only. You will now remove those effects and return to the initial situation.

    22.   Select the title Smart Shape containing the text **Jan.**

    23.   In the **Properties** inspector, reopen the **Effects** icon.

    24.   Select the effect you have applied.

    25.   Click the trash can icon to remove your custom effect from the menu.

    26.   Now, click the **Clear** button to remove the effect from the selected object.

    27.   Select the Text Caption object and repeat the preceding action to remove your Text Effect from the Text Caption.

You should now be back to the initial project and your slide should look like the following screenshot:

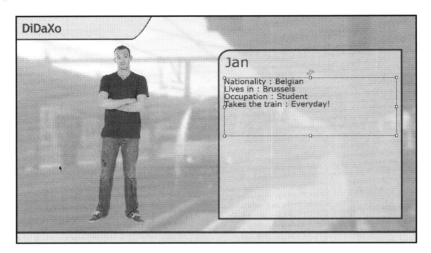

 Text effects applied to objects are not visible in text editing mode. Make sure you select your Text Caption/Smart Shape as an object (that is, there is no blinking cursor in the object and the white resize handles are visible) to see your Text Effect.

Before wrapping up this chapter, let's summarize what you learned about Text Effects:

- There are nine basic Text Effects (such as Drop Shadow and Outer Glow) that can be mixed and combined in order to create complex visual effects.
- Text Effects can be applied to both Text Captions and Smart Shapes (provided that the Smart Shape contains text).
- Custom Text Effects can be saved for reuse later.
- The **Text Effects** window of Captivate looks like the **Effects** window of Photoshop. (Actually, it is the same technology at work behind the scenes!)
- Use the **Effects** icon of the **Properties** inspector to define and apply a Text Effect to the selected Text Caption or Smart Shape.

Summary

In this chapter, you learned a lot about the standard non-interactive objects of Captivate. Although very simple to use, these objects are the fundamental building blocks of every single eLearning project that you will build with Adobe Captivate.

Among the objects you studied in this chapter, one of them stands out. The **Smart Shape** object lets you draw custom or predefined shapes in your project. These shapes can be used in such a wide variety of situations that they can advantageously replace the Text Caption object in most situations.

Another important object is the **Image** object. You have learned that there are two very different types of images. Bitmap images contain a fixed number of pixels and are therefore designed for a predefined size. SVG images contain vector paths and shapes used by the computer to regenerate the picture each time its size changes. SVG images are therefore resolution-independent and very lightweight.

Now, let's be honest. You are not there yet! There is still a lot of work to do before sharing the project with your learners.

In the next chapter, you will build on your new skills and learn about other objects that are used to incorporate multimedia elements into your eLearning content.

Meet the community

In this section, we would like to introduce you to Anita Horsley, one of the most active members of the Captivate community and an awesome Captivate Certified Instructor. She authored the *Fast Track to Adobe Captivate 6* video series by Packt Publishing (see `http://www.packtpub.com/fast-track-to-adobe-captivate-6/video`).

Damien

Anita has been a reviewer for two of my previous Captivate books. We finally met in October 2014 during the Adobe Learning Summit in Las Vegas. I was completely jet-lagged from the trip, but Anita was kind enough to offer me a gigantic cup of coffee!

Pooja

I have had the privilege of co-presenting with Anita at various conferences in the past few years, and she is a delight to work with. She always comes up with fantastic ideas to present content during the sessions. My daughter is very fond of Anita and wants to be a firefighter like Anita one day!

Anita Horsley

During Anita Horsley's tenure as a firefighter, she initiated, developed, and managed the health and safety program. At the Oregon State Fire Marshal, she founded the eLearning track and also implemented and coordinated the eLearning team and internal training. She managed the learning management system and chaired the Oregon State Captivate User Group. She currently works for Connect 4 Education Innovative Services as the Director of Training and Development. She is the founder and President of CALEX Learning Consultants, LLC. In addition to this, she continues to develop and teach Captivate, and often presents at conferences nationally. She authored the video tutorial series *Fast Track To Adobe Captivate 6* by Packt Publishing. She also has a blog named *Crazy About Captivate*, which provides tips and tricks on Adobe Captivate. She holds a Master's in Education, an Adobe Certified Expert in Captivate, and is an Adobe Captivate instructor.

Contact details

- Website: https://c4eis.com/
- Personal website: http://calex-llc.com
- Blog: http://captivatecrazy.blogspot.com
- Twitter: @captivatecrazy
- LinkedIn: http://www.linkedin.com/in/anitahorsley
- Google +: https://plus.google.com/u/0/+CALEXLearningConsultantsLLCCharleston/posts
- Facebook: https://www.facebook.com/CALEXLearningConsultantsLLC

Working with Multimedia 3

In this chapter, you will continue to experiment with the objects and features of Adobe Captivate 2019. You will now focus on the objects and features used to transform your eLearning content into a compelling multimedia experience.

Multimedia means the use of various media and technologies to convey your message to the learner. This includes static text and images (already covered in the previous chapter) as well as audio, video, and animation.

Some of these animated content can be created entirely within Captivate, while other rich content is developed in external applications, such as Adobe Animate CC and Adobe Photoshop CC.

In this chapter, you will cover the following topics:

- Inserting animated GIF and HTML5 animations in your course
- Inserting video files in the project
- Adding sound effects to objects
- Adding background music to the project
- Recording narration to the slides
- Importing external sound files into Captivate
- Editing a sound clip in Captivate
- Generating narration with Text-to-Speech

These are a lot of exciting things to cover, so let's get started by inserting some animations in your course module.

Preparing your work

Before jumping into inserting animation, prepare Captivate and open the project files of this chapter using the following steps:

1. Open (or restart) Captivate.

If you are using the default interface mode (as described in Chapter 1, *Getting Started with Captivate 2019*), restarting Captivate resets your workspace to default. If you are using the Advanced Interface Mode, be aware that the screenshots in this book and the step-by-step instructions were created using the default interface. To switch back to the default interface mode, refer to Chapter 1, *Getting Started with Adobe Captivate 2019*.

2. Use the **File | Open** menu item to open the Chapter03/takeTheTrain.cptx file. You can also use the *Ctrl + O* (Windows) or *command + O* (Mac) shortcut to open a file.

3. Take some time to look at this project and its objects.

The project you just opened contains 20 slides, including those you worked with in the previous chapter. After reading the previous chapter, you have all the skills to complete everything in this sample file. We've added a few more slides into the project, applied Master Slides, and inserted standard objects, such as Text Captions, Images, and Smart Shapes.

Using the exercise files

In this chapter, you will use the sample files in the Chapter03 folder. In the Chapter03/final folder, you find the sample files as they should be at the end of this chapter if you follow all the step-by-step instructions. If you get confused by any of the step-by-step instructions, look at the final folder. Also, be aware that you'll have a fresh set of files to work with at the beginning of each chapter, so don't hesitate to experiment and mess around with the files while performing the exercises.

amazon.com

SGhSsKtNLc

Your order of May 2, 2023 (Order ID 112-6909237-4107420)

Qty.	Item	Item Price	Total
1	**Mastering Adobe Captivate 2019: Build cutting edge professional SCORM compliant and interactive eLearning content with A...** Jaisingh, Dr. Pooja --- Paperback **1789803055** 1789803055 9781789803051	$51.99	$51.99
1	**Adobe Creative Cloud All-in-One For Dummies (For Dummies (Computer/Tech))** Smith, Jennifer --- Paperback **1119724147** 1119724147 9781119724148	$38.36	$38.36

ˆment completes your order.			
	Subtotal		$90.35
	Order Total		$90.35
	Paid via credit/debit		$90.35

ˈace your item
ˈ/returns

RIC5-TWI/second-nominated-day/0/0504-02:00/0503-20:26   **A3-60**

Inserting external animations in the project

In this section, you will learn how to insert external animations in your Adobe Captivate project. These animations are called external, because they are created outside of Captivate in applications such as Adobe Animate CC or Adobe Photoshop CC.

Captivate lets you import three types of such animations:

- Animated GIF files
- Flash-based animations (with a .swf file extension)
- HTML5 animations

Since Adobe has announced the end of the Flash Player by 2020, this book only covers inserting GIF animations and HTML5 animations. In the final project, you will not need these animations. Therefore, the following two exercises are for demonstration purposes only. You will create a new slide in the takeTheTrain.cptx project to experiment with inserting external animations. At the end of this section, this slide will be deleted:

1. Make sure you are on slide 1 of the Chapter03/takeTheTrain.cptx project
2. Use the **Slides** icon of the toolbar to insert a new **Blank Slide** as the second slide of the project

You now have a blank slide in your project to experiment with, so it is time for hands-on action!

Inserting animated GIF files into the project

In this exercise, you will import an animated GIF file on the blank slide you have created in the previous section. You will then test your project to see the animation at work. Use the following steps to perform this exercise:

1. Make sure you are on slide 2 of the Chapter03/takeTheTrain.cptx project.
2. Use the **Media** | **Animation** icon on the Toolbar to insert a new animation on the current slide.

In the dialog that opens, you have to choose which animation file you want to import. By default, this dialog opens on the Captivate Gallery folder, which can be found at the following locations:

- Windows: `C:\Program Files\Adobe\Adobe Captivate 2019 x64\Gallery`
- macOS: `/Applications/Adobe Captivate 2019/Gallery`

The Gallery folder is further divided into several subfolders, with assets that you can use in your Captivate projects. However, in this exercise, you won't use the Gallery. Instead, you will use a custom `.gif` file.

3. Browse to the `Chapter03/DiDaXo-AnimatedGif.gif` file.
4. Import the selected file into the project.

As usual, Captivate inserts the object right in the middle of the current slide, which is fine for this exercise. You will now preview the project to test your animation.

5. Use the **Preview | Next 5 slides** icon of the toolbar to open the **Preview** pane and test your sequence.
6. When the image appears in the **Preview** pane, confirm that the animation plays as expected.
7. Close the **Preview** pane when done.

Inserting an animated GIF file in Captivate is easy and straightforward. Since we don't actually need this animation in the final project, you will now delete it before moving on to the next exercise.

8. Right-click the animation you just imported.
9. Choose **Delete** in the context menu that opens.
10. Confirm the deletion of the object.

If you have access to Adobe Photoshop CC, the source file that we used to create this `.gif` animation is available at `Chapter03/animation_source/DiDaXo-AnimatedGif.psd`. The process of creating and exporting `.gif` files into Adobe Photoshop CC is further explained at the following location: `https://helpx.adobe.com/be_en/photoshop/how-to/make-animated-gif.html`

Inserting Flash animations in the project

The same workflow that you used in this exercise can also be used to insert a Flash animation in the project. The only difference is that you will select a file with a .swf extension, instead of a .gif file. Be aware, that Flash-based animations are not supported in the HTML5 output. If you publish your project in HTML5, all the Flash-based animations contained in the project will be converted to static (non-animated) images upon publishing. In today's technological landscape, inserting Flash animations into your Captivate projects makes little sense. This is the reason why this feature is not covered in this book. The only reason why inserting Flash animations is still possible in Captivate 2019 is to guarantee backward compatibility with legacy projects.

Inserting HTML5 animations into the project

In this exercise, you will import an HTML5 animation created in Adobe Animate CC into the project. Since the final project does not require any HTML5 animation, the next exercise is for demonstration purposes only, and you will delete the animation at the end of the exercise.

If you have Adobe Animate CC installed on your computer, the source file of the animation you will use in this exercise is available at Chapter03/animation_source/SpeedLimit_120.fla in the exercise files. Feel free to take a look at that file to see how the animation was made.

Use the following steps to import an HTML5 animation in your course:

1. Click the **Media | HTML5 Animation** icon on the Toolbar to start the import.
2. Navigate to the Chapter03/SpeedLimit_120.oam file and import it into your slide.
3. When the animation has finished loading, hover over the newly imported object to preview it on the slide.

An .oam file is a special package created by Adobe Animate CC. It works just like a .zip file. That is, the .oam file is a wrapper that contains all the HTML, CSS, and JavaScript resources needed to make the animation run properly.

Inspecting the content of a .oam **file**

If you want to inspect the actual content of a .oam file, here is a simple trick: just change the .oam extension to .zip. Then, unzip the resulting file and inspect its content. Make sure you change the extension of the package back to .oam before continuing with this exercise.

You will now adjust the properties of the new HTML5 animation so it integrates nicely with the slide. The most obvious thing to do is to adjust the size of the object. When inserting these kinds of animation, Captivate creates a container of 400 pixels in width by 300 pixels in height, regardless of the actual size of the animation.

4. With the HTML5 animation still selected, look at the **Options** tab of the **Properties** inspector.
5. Deselect the **Constraint proportions** checkbox.
6. Change the width to 500 px and the height to 100 px. Use the *Enter* key to confirm the new values.
7. Return to the **Style** tab of the **Properties** inspector and look at the available options.
8. Deselect both the **Border** and the **Scrolling** checkboxes.

The size of the animation is now 500px by 100px.

If you have access to Adobe Animate CC, you can open the Chapter03/sources/SpeedLimit_120.fla file and confirm the size of this animation in the **Properties** panel of Adobe Animate CC.

You will now preview your new HTML5 animation using the **Preview** icon on the Toolbar.

9. Use the **Preview** | **Next 5 slides** icon on the Toolbar to open the **Preview** pane.

Well, it looks like you have a problem! Your HTML5 animation is not showing in the preview pane. Don't worry! There is nothing wrong with your project. The preview pane shows a temporary Flash file of whatever portion of the project you want to preview. But the HTML5 animation you just inserted is not supported in Flash and can't be previewed inside of Captivate. To test your HTML5 animation, you have to preview the HTML5 output in a web browser.

10. Close the preview pane and click the **Preview** icon on the Toolbar one more time.
11. Choose the **HTML5 in Browser** item in the list of options.

Because this project is not responsive, the **HTML5 In Browser** preview option only shows the entire project. When the preview reaches slide 2, make sure your HTML5 animation is displayed as expected.

 Responsive and VR projects can only be published in HTML 5, so all previewing options use the web browser. You will learn more about responsive projects in Chapter 10, *Creating a Responsive Project,* and about VR projects in Chapter 11, *Creating Virtual Reality Projects.*

 During the preview, keep in mind that the project is not finished. The arrangement of the objects on the slides, as well as the overall timing, is yet to be defined.

Since this project does not need any HTML5 animation, you will now delete slide 2 and return to the original project.

12. In the **Filmstrip**, right-click slide 2.
13. Click **Delete** and confirm the deletion in the dialog.

This concludes your overview of inserting external animations into Captivate. It is time to summarize what you have learned:

- Captivate lets you insert external .swf, .gif, and HTML5 animations in your projects.
- Creating .gif animations is done in an external application, such as Adobe Photoshop CC.
- .swf animations requires the Adobe Flash Player plugin. They are typically created in Adobe Animate CC and are not supported in HTML5.

- With Adobe Animate CC, you can create animations and compile them either as `.swf` or as HTML5 animations.
- Use Adobe Animate CC to package your HTML5 animations into `.zip` or `.oam` files before inserting them into Captivate.
- Captivate has the ability to import `.zip` and `.oam` packages directly into your project.
- Those HTML5 animations are not supported in Flash, and therefore do not appear in the Flash-based preview pane of Captivate. It is necessary to test the project in a web browser to see these animations.
- Flash animations are not supported in HTML5 and should be used in legacy projects only.

In the next section, you will continue learning about the multimedia capabilities of Captivate by inserting video files into your project.

Working with video

It's time for the next object in this chapter: the **video** file. Captivate allows you to insert various types of video files, including `.flv`, `.avi`, `.mov`, and `.mp4` files. However, Captivate always converts your videos to `.mp4` upon publishing.

 It is not Adobe Captivate that handles the conversion of your video files to the `.mp4` file format. Behind the scenes, this task is taken care of by the Adobe Media Encoder CC 2018. The Adobe Media Encoder CC 2018 is included in the Adobe Captivate 2019 installation package.

In this exercise, you will insert a new slide in the Take the Train project and add a video file to it:

1. Return to the `Chapter03/takeTheTrain.cptx` file.
2. Use the **Filmstrip** to go to slide 19.
3. Use the **Slide | Blank Slide** icon on the Toolbar to create a new blank slide.
4. If necessary, use the **Properties** inspector to apply the **contentBkg** Master Slide on the newly created slide.

The new slide is inserted as slide 20. Remember that new slides are always inserted *after* the active slide. You will now import a video file onto this new slide.

5. Go to the **Media | Video** icon on the Toolbar. Alternatively, you can also use the **Video | Insert Video** menu item.

The **Insert Video** dialog opens. At the top of the dialog, you have to choose either an **Event video** or a **Slide video**. The following table lists some of the differences between these two options:

	Event video	Slide video
Sync	Cannot be distributed over several slides.	Can be distributed over several slides or not.
Timeline	The Timeline of the video is independent from the Timeline of the project.	The video plays in sync with the slide or slides it appears on.
Playback controls	Event videos can have their own playback controls.	Has no specific playback controls associated because it uses the same playback controls as the project.
Number of videos	You can have several Event videos on the same slide.	You can have only one Slide video on any given slide.
Closed Captions	Cannot be closed-captioned	Can be closed-captioned.
Interactivity	Cannot be converted to interactive videos	Can be converted to interactive videos

In this case, you want the video to show on slide 20 only, something that both the **Event Video** and the **Slide Video** can achieve. But in Chapter 13, *Creating Accessible eLearning*, you will add Closed Captions to the video; something that only the **Slide Video** can do.

6. At the top of the dialog, choose the **Slide Video** option.
7. Make sure the **From Your Computer** option is selected. In this case, we don't want to import a YouTube video in the project.
8. Click the **Browse** button and navigate to the Chapter03/departure_sequence_EN.mp4 file of your exercises folder.

9. Click **Open** to insert the video onto the slide.

10. In the lower area of the **Insert Video** dialog, select the **Modify slide duration to accommodate video** option.

11. Make sure the **Insert Video** dialog looks like the following screenshot and click the **OK** button:

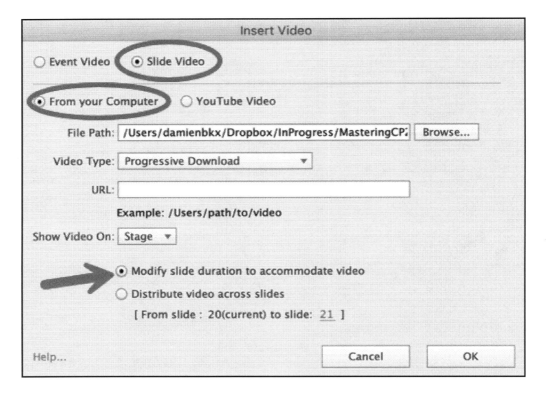

The video is inserted in the center of the slide. You will now take a quick look at the **Timeline** panel situated below the stage area.

12. Take a look at the **Timeline** panel (if the **Timeline** is not visible, double-click the **Timeline** button at the bottom of the screen or use the **Window | Timeline** menu item).

13. Notice that the duration of the slide matches the duration of the video file.

14. Save the file and use the **Preview | Next 5 slides** icon on the Toolbar.

15. When the preview is finished, close the **Preview** pane.

In this exercise, you have inserted an external video into your Captivate course. In `Chapter 5`, *Developing Interactivity*, you will go one step further and make the video interactive by adding Bookmarks and Overlays to your Slide Videos. But for now, it is time to summarize what you've learned about inserting videos in Captivate:

- There are two options available to insert videos in Captivate: **Event Video** and **Slide Video**.
- The key difference between an Event video and a Slide video is that Event videos have their own Timeline that is independent from the Timeline of the project. These can therefore have their own playback controls. Slide videos always play in sync with the project, so they don't need their own playback controls and can be Closed Captioned.
- Captivate allows you to insert various types of videos in your project, but will always convert your files to `.mp4` video upon publishing.
- The *Adobe Media Encoder* is an external application. It is part of Adobe Creative Cloud and part of the default Adobe Captivate package. The Adobe Media Encoder (AME) automatically converts any video file to `.mp4`, so it can be used in Captivate.

In the next section, you will start looking at audio support in Adobe Captivate.

Working with audio

In this section, you will discover how audio can be used in a Captivate project. In Captivate, you can add sound at three different levels:

- **Object level**: The audio associated with an object plays when the object appears on the screen. This is a great place to add small sound effects (whooshes, clings, bangs, tones, and so on) to the project.
- **Slide level**: The audio clip plays in sync with the slide. Most of the time, this option is used to add voiceover narration.
- **Project level**: Most of the time, project level audio is used to add background music to the entire course module.

You will now cover these three options in greater detail.

Adding audio to the objects

Sound can be added on each and every object in Captivate. The audio clip associated with an object plays when the object appears on the Stage.

While object level audio is the preferred place to add sound effects, nothing prevents you from adding narration or any other type of audio content at the object level. It may be used, for example, to read aloud descriptive text or to pronounce a difficult word. This book only shows the typical use case, but you should experiment and be creative in how you actually use this feature.

In the next exercise, you will associate a sound effect with one of the Character images present in the Take the Train project using the following steps:

1. Return to the `Chapter03/takeTheTrain.cptx` file and use the **Filmstrip** to select slide 2.
2. Select the Character image on the left side of the slide.
3. Refer to the **Properties** inspector and switch to the **Options** tab.
4. Click the **Add Audio** button.

You can also use the **Audio | Import To | Object** menu item, or right-click the object and choose the **Audio | Import to** contextual the menu. Whichever way you use, you will always end up with the following dialog:

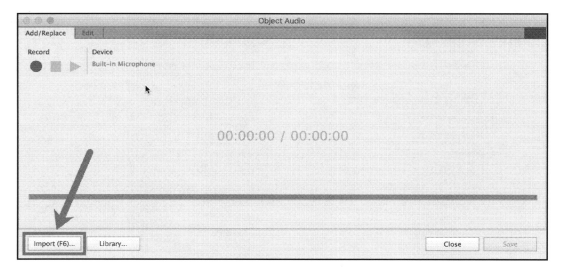

5. At the bottom of the **Object Audio** dialog, click the **Import** button (see the arrow in the preceding screenshot).

By default, the window that opens displays the content of the Sound directory of the Gallery. Remember that the Gallery is a collection of assets that ship with Captivate. If the **Import Audio** dialog does not show the content of the Sound directory, the Gallery is located in the C:\Program Files\Adobe\Adobe Captivate 2019\Gallery folder (Windows) or in the Applications/Adobe Captivate 2019/Gallery folder (Mac).

6. At the end of the list, choose the Whoosh 2.mp3 file and click **Open**.

The audio clip is imported into the project and the sound wave is loaded in the **Object Audio** dialog.

7. Click the **Play** button in the top-left corner of the **Object audio** dialog to control the imported sound.
8. Click the **Save** button at the bottom-right corner of the box.
9. Click the **Close** button to close the **Object Audio** box.

The audio clip is now associated with the selected Character image. If you open the **Timeline** panel, you will see a loudspeaker icon on the image layer, indicating that an audio clip is associated with that particular object (see the following screenshot):

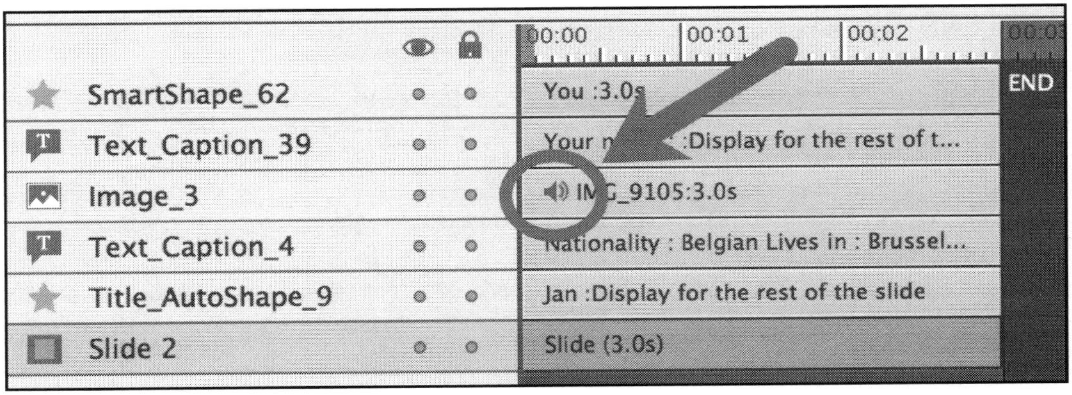

The sound effect plays in sync with the object. This means that you hear the sound effect whenever the Character image appears on the screen. You will now use the **Timing** panel to modify the timing of the selected image and give it a try.

10. Make sure the Character image you associated the audio clip with is still selected.
11. Open the **Timing** panel. Remember that the **Timing** panel is associated with the **Properties** inspector and appears on the right side of the screen.
12. At the top of the **Timing** panel, change the **Appear After** property to 5 seconds. Your object is now displayed for a **Specific Time** of 3 seconds and **Appears After five** seconds.

If the **Timeline** panel is open at the bottom of the screen, you see this change reflected in the **Timeline** panel. This is illustrated in the following screenshot (you can use the **Window | Timeline** menu item to open the **Timeline** panel if needed):

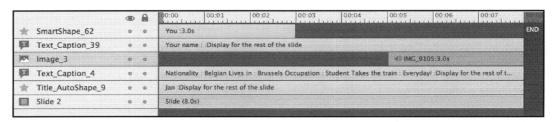

Even though we will discuss the **Timeline** in detail in Chapter 4, *Working with the Timeline and Other Useful Tools*, it is quite easy to see that the Character image is scheduled to appear 5 seconds into the slide and to be displayed for 3 seconds. It also means that your sound effect should play 5 seconds after the slide begins, in sync with the object. Let's check this out using the Preview feature of Captivate.

13. In the **Filmstrip**, select the first slide of the project.
14. Use the **Preview** icon on the Toolbar to preview the **Next 5 Slides** and test the sound effect.

15. When slide 2 displays in the **Preview** pane, make sure the sound effect is played in sync with the Character icon, 5 seconds after the beginning of the slide.

16. Close the **Preview** pane when done.

17. Don't forget to save the file when you are finished.

This concludes your overview of object level audio in Captivate. Let's summarize what you have learned:

- You can associate an audio clip with any object. The audio plays when the object appears on the Stage.
- Usually, object level audio is used to add sound effects to the course.
- Only sound clips in .wav or .mp3 format can be imported into Captivate.
- When a sound clip is added to an object, a loudspeaker icon appears in the corresponding layer of the **Timeline**.

Adding background music to the entire project

In this section, you will associate an audio clip with the entire project. Usually, project level audio is used to add background music, but nothing prevents you from adding other types of audio content at that level. To make sure that the music plays during the entire project, you will use a 15 to 30 second sound clip (called a sample) and make it loop for the duration of the course.

In the next exercise, you will add background music to the Take the Train project:

1. If needed, return to the Chapter03/takeTheTrain.cptx file.
2. Use the **Audio | Import To | Background** menu item.
3. Choose the Loop Acoustic.mp3 file from the /Sound directory of the Captivate Gallery and click **Open**.
4. The **Background Audio** dialog opens.

The **Background Audio** dialog informs you that the duration of the `loop Acoustic.mp3` sound clip is 16 seconds (see the arrow in the following screenshot):

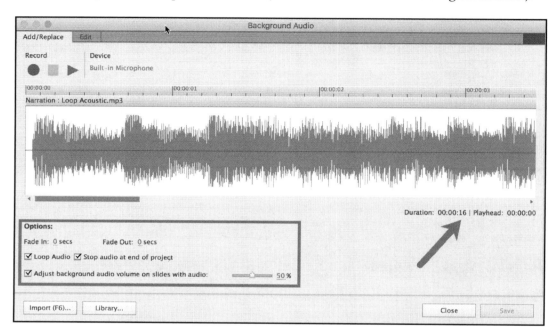

Some interesting options are located in the lower part of the **Background Audio** dialog (see the rectangle in the lower left area of the preceding screenshot):

- When the audio clip is finished, the **Loop Audio** option makes it start over, so the sound clip plays for the entire project.
- The **Stop audio at end of project** option should be selected at all times. If it is not selected, the background audio will keep playing even after the end of the course.
- The **Adjust background audio volume on slides with audio** option automatically lowers the volume of the background music on slides with associated slide-level audio. This option ensures that the slide audio is always louder than the background audio.

Most of the time, leaving these options at their default settings works just fine.

  5. Accept the defaults and click **Close** to close the **Background Audio** dialog.
  6. Use the **Preview** icon on the Toolbar to preview the entire **Project**.
  7. Close the **Preview** pane when you are done

If you need to modify the **Background Audio** or one of its associated options, use the **Audio | Edit | Background** menu item to reopen the **Background Audio** dialog. Use the **Add/Replace** tab of the **Background Audio** dialog to use another sound clip and the **Edit** tab to modify the current sound clip.

When to use background audio?

I have never used background audio in a Captivate project! I find it annoying and distracting. It drives the students away from what I want them to focus on. That being said, there are probably some use cases for which background audio would be useful. If you run into one of these use cases, don't hesitate to use the feature. There is only one thing to keep in mind: *you are teaching,* so the background music you use, as well as any other features of your Captivate project, *should serve the student's learning.*

You will now remove the background audio that you have added to the project.

  8. Use the **Audio | Remove | Background** to remove the background audio.
  9. Confirm you want to remove the audio clip.
  10. Save the file when you are done.

Before moving to the next section, this is a summary of what you have learned about background audio:

  • Audio can be added at the project level. Most of the time, this feature is used to add background music to the project.
  • Use the **Audio** menu to add, edit, and delete the background audio.

- To make sure the background music plays for the entire duration of the course, use a short sample of music and make it loop.
- Captivate has an option to lower the volume of the background audio when a slide with an associated sound clip plays.
- Use background audio with care! It should not distract your students.

Also, remember that background audio does not have to be music. It could, for instance, be the background sounds you may hear in a hospital setting when learning about hospital procedures. It can also be used in an introduction slide where students can check if they have audio or if it is a good volume. Again, this book shows the most typical use cases. It is your imagination and instructional design that will ultimately define how this feature is used.

Adding audio to the slides

Adding audio to the slides is by far the most interesting place to use audio in Captivate. Typically, slide level audio is where you add voiceover narration. Slide level audio is also the only audio where you can apply Closed Captions. You will learn more about closed captioning in `Chapter 13`, *Creating Accessible eLearning*.

There are three ways to add audio at slide level:

- The narration can be produced entirely within Captivate
- The narration can be produced in an external application and imported into Captivate
- Text-To-Speech can generate audio clips

In this section, you will experiment with these three options, one by one.

Recording narration with Captivate

The first way to insert audio at the slide level is to record your audio clips with the tools of Captivate. First, you have to make sure that your microphone or system audio communicates with Captivate.

The following exercise requires a microphone. If you do not have a microphone available, just read through the steps. You'll have a chance to catch up in a subsequent exercise.

Setting up the sound system

The exact setup procedure depends on your audio equipment and your operating system, but basically, setting up a sound system can be divided into three phases:

- **Phase 1**: Plug the microphone in the audio input port of your computer (usually it is the red plug of your sound card). If you have a USB microphone, plug it into any available USB port.
- **Phase 2**: Check out the audio options of your operating system (see the following screenshot):
  - **macOS**: In the **System Preferences**, use the **Input** tab of the **Sound** section
  - **Windows**: Use the **Manage Audio Devices** link in the **Hardware and Sound** section of the **Control Panel**
- **Phase 3**: Check out the audio options of Captivate:

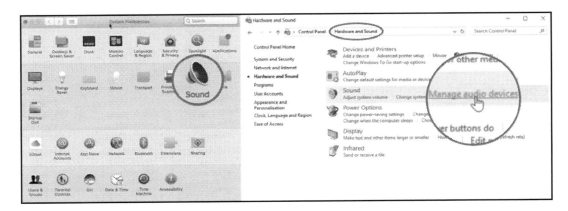

Once the audio options of the operating system are properly set up, you can adjust Captivate's audio settings:

1. Return to the `Chapter03/takeTheTrain.cptx` file.
2. Use the **Audio | Settings** menu item to open the **Audio Settings** dialog.
3. Open the **Audio input Devices** drop-down list and select your microphone or audio interface.

If your computer has multiple audio input devices (such as a microphone-in and a line-in), the **Audio Input Devices** drop-down list instructs Captivate on which device it has to use. This is the single most important part of the procedure. If the wrong device is selected, the audio data will never reach Captivate. In the following screenshot, I instruct Captivate to listen to the audio stream coming from the **Yeti Stereo Microphone**, which is an external microphone plugged in to my computer via a USB cable. The actual content of the drop-down menu depends on the audio equipment installed on your system:

For the **Bitrate** option, the default should be fine. If you later decide that the default audio quality is not good enough, you can test a new recording with a higher **Bitrate**. Be aware that the higher the **Bitrate**, the bigger the file. When choosing the **Bitrate**, you have to find the most appropriate balance between the quality of the sound and the size of the resulting file.

4. Leave the **Bitrate** option at its default and click the **Calibrate Input** button.

Calibrating the input is finding the right sensitivity for the microphone. If it is set too high, you'll have a saturated sound with lots of clipping, but if it is set too low, the recorded narration will be lost in the background noise. To help you out, Captivate provides an auto-calibrating feature. All you need to do is to say a few words into the microphone and let Captivate evaluate the input sensitivity to find the right value. Let's give it a try!

5. In the **Calibrate Audio Input** dialog, click the **Auto Calibrate** button.

6. Speak normally into your microphone until you have a message saying that the microphone has been calibrated (if you don't know what to say, just tell a joke! Don't worry, it's not recorded!).

7. Click the **OK** button to validate the sensitivity value and to close the **Calibrate Audio Input** dialog.

8. Close the **Audio Settings** dialog as well.

Recording the narration

Now that both your computer system and Captivate are properly set up, it is time to concentrate on the actual recording of the voiceover narration:

1. Still in the `Chapter03/takeTheTrain.cptx` file, use the **Filmstrip** to go to slide 2.

2. Use the **Audio | Record To | Slide** menu item, to open the **Slide audio** dialog.

This is one of the many ways to start a slide audio recording. Another option is to click the **Add Audio** button in the **Options** tab of the **Properties** inspector when a slide is selected.

 Make sure you use the **Audio | Record To | Slide** menu item with slide written with no **s**. If you click **Slides** (with an **s**), you'll end up in a very similar, but slightly different dialog.

The next step of the exercise is the actual recording of the sound clip. Before you press the record button, it is necessary to take some time to rehearse the narration. The following text is the script that you will record:

"Hi there! My name is Jan. I'm a student in Brussels, the capital city of Belgium. I'll be your guide during this short training on how to take the train in Belgium. Before we get started, I'd like to know a bit more about you. Please, type your name in the box below and click on the submit button."

Read those sentences aloud a few times. When you feel ready, you can move on to your first audio take!

3. Click the red **Record Audio** button at the top left of the **Slide Audio** dialog. After a short countdown, read the preceding sentences aloud at a normal speed and with a normal voice.

4. When the recording is complete, click the **Stop** button.

5. Listen to your recording by clicking the **Play** button. If you are not satisfied, start over with another take.

6. When you are satisfied, click the **Save** button and **Close** the **Slide Audio** dialog.

If the recorded sound clip is longer than the slide, you will be prompted to extend the duration of the slide to the length of the sound clip, as shown in the following screenshot. Click **Yes** to add the new sound clip into the slide:

7. Take a look at slide 2 in the **Filmstrip** panel and notice the small loudspeaker icon below the slide thumbnail.

8. Click the **Timeline** button at the bottom of the screen to open the **Timeline** panel.

In the **Timeline** panel, the new sound clip is displayed as an additional layer below the slide layer. If needed, you can move the sound clip in the **Timeline** to better synchronize it with the rest of the slide, but you cannot use the **Timeline** to change the duration of the sound clip. Now, don't worry about the proper syncing of the narration and the slide just yet. You will finalize this in Chapter 4, *Working with the Timeline and Other Useful Tools.*

Use the **Play** button at the bottom of the **Timeline** panel to test the slide. This plays only the current slide without opening the **Preview** pane. This does not let you test every single feature of the slide, but it is a quick and easy way to do basic testing and synchronization.

Recording narration is not an easy task, especially if you are not used to speaking into a microphone. Here are some tips and tricks to help you out:

- Write the script that needs to be recorded and rehearse it a few times before the recording.
- Keep in mind that you don't have to be perfect the first time. Try as many times as needed.

- Speak slowly, especially if you have an international audience where not all of the students speak the same language.
- Have a glass of water ready to avoid the dry mouth effect. Remember that lots of students will hear the narration through a headset.
- Position the microphone within four to six inches of your mouth and slightly to the side to avoid pops and hisses on the letters S and P.
- Standing up and gesturing while speaking can help you speak more clearly and confidently, and add more energy to your voice.
- Remove any objects that could get picked up in the audio, such as jewelry or a squeaky chair.
- A well-insulated room will give you better, warmer quality than a large cavernous room, which could add echo or distort your voice.

With these simple tips and tricks, a basic computer microphone, and a bit of practice, you should be able to record some pretty good audio clips in no time!

Whose voice should be recorded?

If you can afford it, hire a voiceover talent. You can also record your own voice or the voice of a colleague or a friend. When choosing the person who will read the lines, always have your students in mind. For my very first big Captivate project, I had to develop a course in English, but most of the students were not native English speakers. We met with the customer and agreed to record the voice of a non-native English speaker (it was an employee from the next-door office who was into theater). The recorded English was not perfect, the accent was a bit strange, but it was not important because it was adapted to the audience.

Editing a sound clip in Captivate

Even though Captivate is not a fully-fledged audio editing application, it does have basic audio editing capabilities. You will now explore these capabilities with the narration that you just recorded.

If you are not happy with the audio you recorded, you can use the `Chapter03/takeTheTrain_audio.cptx` file for the next exercise. It contains my own audio recording made with the techniques described in the previous section (please forgive my strange-sounding voice; I had a bad cold on that day).

Use the following steps to finalize the audio you have recorded in the previous section:

1. Return to the second slide of the `Chapter03/takeTheTrain.cptx` file.
2. Use the **Audio** | **Edit** | **Slide** menu item to edit slide level audio. You can also use the **Edit Audio** button in the **Options** tab of the **Properties** inspector when the slide is selected.

This action opens the **Slide Audio** dialog on the **Edit** tab (see the arrow in the next screenshot). It is the same dialog you used when recording the audio in the previous section. The only difference is that you used the **Add/Replace** tab when recording the audio:

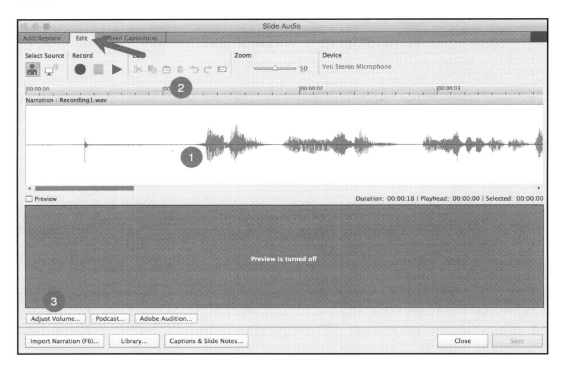

When recording the audio narration in the previous section, chances are you did not start speaking right after clicking the **Record** button. So, you probably have some silence between the beginning of the recording and the actual beginning of the narration. In the preceding screenshot, you can see that the actual audio waveform (the graphical representation of your audio file) is not at the very beginning of the audio clip (see **1** in the preceding screenshot). You will now select this silence and remove it.

3. Click the **Play** button to listen to the entire audio clip. Try to associate what you hear with the graphical representation of the waveform as displayed in the **Slide Audio** dialog.

4. Use your mouse to select from the beginning of the clip up to the actual beginning of the narration (from the beginning to **1** in the previous screenshot).

5. When done, hit the *Delete* key of your keyboard, or click the trash icon in the **Edit** section at the top of the **Slide Audio** dialog (see **2** in the preceding screenshot).

6. Repeat this operation with the silence at the end of the audio clip.

7. Click the **Play** button to test the new version of the clip.

Congratulations! You just took your first step into the fascinating world of audio editing! You will now use the **Adjust Volume** feature of Captivate to normalize the volume of your audio narration.

8. In the bottom-left corner of the **Slide Audio** dialog, click the **Adjust Volume** button (see **3** in the preceding screenshot).

9. Take some time to review the options of the **Adjust Volume** box, but do not change any of them at this time.

10. In the **Audio Processing** section of the **Adjust Volume** dialog, select the **Normalize** option and click the **OK** button.

Normalizing an audio clip means finding the best audio level for that particular sound clip.

Blog post

If you want to know more about the normalization process, I've written an entire blog post on this topic. It can be found at `http://en.didaxo.be/blog/producing-high-quality-audio-content-for-captivate-part-1-normalization/`.

11. Click the **Save** button at the bottom-right corner of the **Slide Audio** dialog.

12. Click the **Close** button to close the **Slide Audio** dialog.

In the next chapter, you will position this audio clip on the **Timeline** to sync it with the other slide event.

Round trip editing with Adobe Audition CC

Audition CC is the audio application from Adobe. It is available as part of a Creative Cloud subscription. Adobe Audition (formerly Cool Edit) is an awesome yet easy-to-use audio application. If Adobe Audition CC is available on your system, the **Adobe Audition** button of the **Slide Audio** dialog will be enabled. Clicking this button opens the audio clip in Audition, where you can use specialized and dedicated audio tools to edit your clip. When you're done editing, just save the file in Adobe Audition and return to Captivate to update it. Using Captivate with other applications is covered in more detail in Chapter 12, *Using Captivate with Other Applications.*

Importing an external sound clip

The second way to add audio at slide level is to import audio clips into the course. When taking this approach, the audio clips are recorded and produced in a dedicated audio application.

In this exercise, you will delete the audio narration recorded in the previous section and replace it with an imported audio file:

1. Return to the second slide of the Chapter03/takeTheTrain.cptx file.

2. Use the **Audio | Remove | Slide** to remove the audio clip associated with the selected slide.

   Note that this action removes the audio from the slide, but not from the **Library** of the project. You will learn more about the **Library** in Chapter 4, *Working with the Timeline and Other Useful Tools.*

3. In the **Options** tab of the **Properties** inspector, click the **Add Audio** button. The **Slide Audio** dialog opens.

4. Click the **Import Narration** button in the bottom-left corner of the dialog.

5. Browse the files on your computer and select the Chapter03/Slide02.wav file in the download associated with this book.

6. Click **Open**. The selected file is imported into the project.

7. Click the **Play** button to test the imported audio.

8. Save the changes by clicking the **Save** button in the bottom-right corner of the **Slide Audio** dialog.

9. It is possible that the duration of the slide has to be increased to match the duration of the new audio file. Click **Yes** if prompted to do so.

10. Close the **Slide Audio** dialog.

11. Save the file when done.

After these steps, the audio file appears in the **Timeline** panel as an extra layer at the very bottom of the stack.

Yes, it is that easy to import external sound clips into Captivate! In the next chapter, you will import the remaining audio clips and learn how to use the **Timeline** panel to synchronize the audio with the other slide elements.

Using Text-To-Speech to generate narration

The third way to insert audio at slide level is to use Text-To-Speech. The idea is to type the narration text into the **Slide Notes** panel and have Captivate convert it to a sound clip. To convert typed text to sound clips, Captivate uses preinstalled voices packages called speech agents.

Installing the Captivate speech agents

Due to their very large size, Adobe decided to make the installation of the Text-To-Speech agents optional. Adobe Captivate 2019 ships with one voice package that installs several speech agents for various languages. Note that Captivate is also able to pick up third-party speech agents installed on your system.

The speech agents of Captivate can be downloaded from the following locations:

- For Windows 64 bit:
  `http://www.adobe.com/go/Cp2019_win64_voices_installer`
- For Mac: `http://www.adobe.com/go/Cp2019_mac_voices_installer`

It is necessary to install the Text-To-Speech agents in order to go through the steps of the next exercise. The names of the speech agents provided by Captivate are Bridget, Chloe, James, Julie, Kate, Paul, and Yumi.

Working with the Slide Notes panel

The basic idea of Text-To-Speech is to transform a piece of typed text into a sound clip. In Captivate, you use the **Slide Notes** panel to type the text you want to convert to speech. The **Slide Notes** panel is not displayed by default, so your first task is to turn it on:

1. Go to slide 3 of the `Chapter03/takeTheTrain.cptx` file.
2. Use the **Window | Slide Notes** menu item to show the **Slide Notes** panel.

By default, the **Slide Notes** panel appears at the bottom of the screen next to the **Timeline** panel:

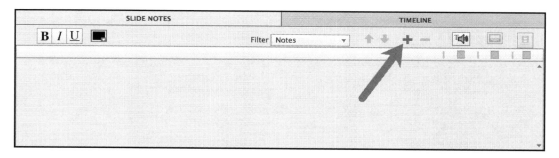

At the far-right side of the panel, the + icon is used to create a new note.

3. Click the + icon to add a new note.

4. Type `Thank you! It's great to know you!` in the new note.

5. Click the + icon to add a second note after the first one.

6. Type `Congratulations on your decision to come visit us in Belgium. It's a great country to visit, full of historical places, tourist attractions, awesome landscapes, and great food!` in the second note.

7. Add a third note to the **Slide Notes** panel and type `And to get around, the best way is the train! I take it every day, and I just love it!`

8. If needed, use the up and down arrows in the top-right corner of the **Slide Notes** panel to reorder the notes.

When typing the text into the **Slide Notes** panel, keep in mind that a program will convert it to an audio clip. This program will not work correctly if the spelling and punctuation aren't perfect, so double-check (and even triple-check) your typing. If it is wrong, you'll get unexpected (and sometimes hilarious!) results.

9. Use the **Filmstrip** to browse the remaining slides. Notice that the necessary Slide Notes have been added where appropriate.

Converting Slide Notes to speech is one of the many goodies of the **Slide Notes** panel. Before moving to the next section, take some time to experiment with the **Slide Notes** panel and notice the icons, boxes, and switches that surround it. In `Chapter 13`, *Creating Accessible eLearning*, you will return to this panel and use it to generate the Closed Captions.

Now that the Slide Notes have been correctly typed and carefully ordered, you can safely convert them to audio using Text-To-Speech.

Converting text to speech

Converting the text typed into the **Slide Notes** panel to speech is not difficult. All you need to do is choose the note(s) to be converted, assign a speech agent to each note, and generate the audio file:

1. Make sure you are on slide 3 in the `Chapter03/takeTheTrain.cptx` file.

2. At the top of the **Slide Notes** panel, click the **TTS** checkbox to select all three notes, as shown in the following screenshot:

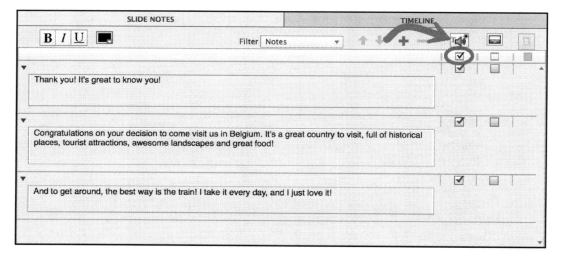

Most of the time, you'll want to convert all the notes to speech. But, if needed, you can deselect the notes that don't need to be converted to speech.

3. Click the **Text-To-Speech** button at the top of the **Slide Notes** panel (see the arrow in the preceding screenshot). The **Speech Management** window opens.

The **Speech Management** window is where you assign a speech agent to each of the note(s) you selected for Text-To-Speech conversion. The number of available speech agents depends on the voice packs installed on the system (see the *Installing the Captivate speech agents* section for more details).

For this exercise, you will use the speech agent named **Paul**. This speech agent is designed for US English text only, and is included in the voices installer of Captivate.

4. In the **Speech Management** window, use the drop-down menus in front of each note to assign the speech agent **Paul** to all three notes.

This action is illustrated in the following screenshot:

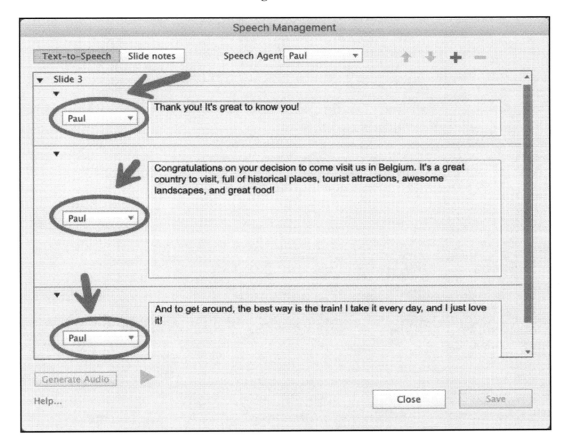

While assigning the speech agent to the Slide Notes, there are some interesting things to notice:

- You can assign a different speech agent to each Slide Note. This means that you can use different speech agents on the same slide. It is very handy to generate conversations, for example.
- Notice the **Speech Agent** drop-down menu at the very top of the **Speech Management** window. You can use it to assign the same speech agent to all the selected notes instead of going one note at a time.
- In the top-right corner of the **Speech Management** window, notice the same icons as those found in the **Slide Notes** panel. Use them to type new notes, delete existing notes, or reorder notes directly from the **Speech Management** window.

Now that you have assigned a speech agent to each note of the slide, it is time to generate the audio file.

5. Click the **Generate Audio** button at the bottom-left corner of the window. A progress bar appears on the screen as the audio is generated.
6. When the progress bar disappears, click the **Play** button located in the bottom-left corner of the dialog, next to the **Generate Audio** button. If you don't like the generated audio, feel free to restart the process using another text and/or another speech agent.
7. Click the **Close** button to close the **Speech Management** window.
8. At the bottom of the screen, switch to the **Timeline** panel.

Surprise! The **Timeline** panel now shows an audio layer beneath the slide layer.

9. Use the **Play** button of the **Timeline** panel to test the audio clip.

Great! The Slide Notes of slide 3 were successfully converted to speech using a speech agent named **Paul**. You will now repeat the same procedure on the other slides, but using a slightly different method.

10. Use the **Audio | Speech Management** menu item to reopen the **Speech Management** window.

Note that opening the **Speech Management** window this way displays the Slide Notes of the entire project rather than those of the selected slide.

11. In the top-left corner of the **Speech Management** window, switch to the **Slide notes** tab (see **1** in the following screenshot).

12. Use the **Speech Management** window to browse the Slide Notes in the project. As you do so, select them for Text To Speech (see **2** in the following screenshot) and assign the speech agent **Paul** to all of them (see **3** in the following screenshot):

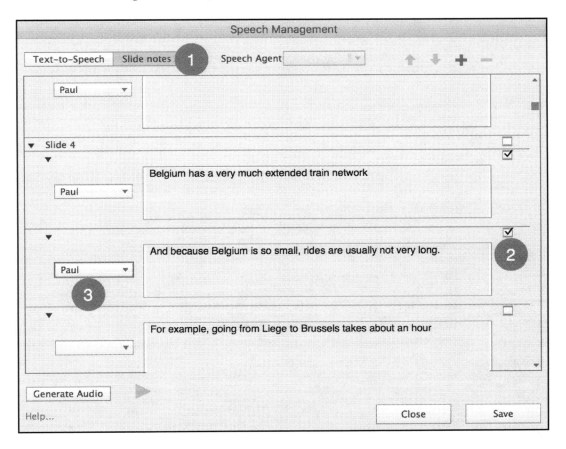

13. When this is completed for all the Slides Notes of the project, click the **Generate Audio** button.

14. When the audio generation is complete, click the **Play** icon just next to the **Generate Audio** button. This allows you to control the audio that was generated.

15. When you are ready, close the **Speech Management** dialog and switch to the **Timeline** panel.

With this technique, you can generate the audio of the entire project in a single operation! When Captivate has finished generating the audio files, examine the results and notice the following:

- Captivate has generated audio files for almost all the slides of the project. These can be identified easily thanks to the loudspeaker icon visible under each slide thumbnail in the **Filmstrip** panel.

- Text-To-Speech cannot reproduce every single word correctly. This is the case of the URL `www.sncb.be` on slide 15, for example.

- Text-To-Speech is very sensitive to any spelling or typing mistake (including punctuation and grammar!).

- You can always return to the **Slide Notes** panel of any slide, correct the typing, spelling, punctuation (or adjust the text in any way), and regenerate the audio files using the techniques covered earlier in this section.

- Captivate has matched the length of the slides with the length of the generated audio files as necessary.

Tweaking the speech agents

There are ways to have the speech agents correctly pronounce the words they initially mispronounce, such as technical terms. A thorough explanation is way out of the scope of this book. Kevin Siegel discusses it well in the following blog post: `http://iconlogic.blogs.com/weblog/2016/05/adobe-captivate-train-the-text-to-speech-agents.html`. You can also use the VTML language in your Slide Notes as described in the following documentation: `https://media.neospeech.com/document/vt_eng-Engine-VTML-v3.9.0-3.pdf`. Note that these techniques only apply to the speech agents included with Captivate. Third-party speech agents might have their own custom mechanisms.

You have now worked with all the options that can be used to insert audio at slide level. Here is a summary of the key points that have been covered:

- There are three ways to insert audio at slide level: recording audio with Captivate, importing an audio file produced in an external application, or generating the audio clips with Text-To-Speech.
- When recording audio with Captivate, ensure that the audio interface is correctly set up both in the operating system and in Captivate.
- The first time you record audio with Captivate, it is necessary to calibrate the sensitivity of your microphone. Captivate has an easy-to-use auto calibrating feature.
- Captivate provides some basic audio editing tools that allow you to perform simple operations, such as trimming the beginning and the end of your audio files or adjusting the volume of the audio.
- Audition CC is the dedicated audio application of Adobe Creative Cloud. If it is available on your system, use it to produce your audio clips.
- In Text-To-Speech, Captivate uses speech agents (computer voices) to convert text to audio clips.
- Captivate ships with a bunch of speech agents packed into an extra installer available for free on the Adobe website.
- Captivate also recognizes third-party speech agents installed on your system.
- Each speech agent is designed for a specific language.
- The **Slide Notes** panel is used to type the text to be converted to speech. You can choose to convert every Slide Note to speech or just some of them.
- A different speech agent can be assigned to the different notes of the same slide.
- The **Speech Management** window provides a quick and easy way to convert all the notes of the project to speech at once.

Most of the slides of your project now have an associated voiceover narration. Even though there is a lot of work left to be done, your course is definitely starting to provide a genuine multimedia experience.

Text-To-Speech versus manual voiceover recording

Is Text-To-Speech better than an actual recording? A real recording takes a lot of time and, consequently, costs a lot more money. But the result is perfect and can be tailored to fit the specific needs of a particular project. Text-To-Speech is fast, easy, and cheap, but the result may sound like an old Game Boy (for millennials, a Game Boy is a twentieth-century video game console), depending on the quality of the speech agents that you use.

Another thing to consider is how easy it is to update the project. Updating a Text-To-Speech audio file is easy. Just change the text in the **Slide Notes** panel and regenerate the audio to make your updates. Modifying a human recorded sound is much more difficult and costly. You may have to rent a sound studio, hire the voiceover talent a second time, and so on.

One possibility is to use Text-To-Speech during the development phase of the project, and once the narration is fully validated by the customer, you can hire the voice talent and the recording studio. No solution is perfect though. The choice is yours...

Using the Advanced Audio Management window

The Advanced Audio Management window provides a high-level overview of all the audio in your project. In the following exercise, you will open the Advanced Audio Management window and take a look at the tools it provides using the following steps:

1. Make sure you are still in the `Chapter03/takeTheTrain.cptx` file.
2. Use the **Audio | Audio Management** menu item to open the **Advanced Audio Management** window.

The **Advanced Audio Management** window contains a list of all the slides in the project along with their associated audio file(s), if any.

3. In the bottom-left corner of the **Audio Management** window, select the **Show object level audio** checkbox (see **1** in the following screenshot):

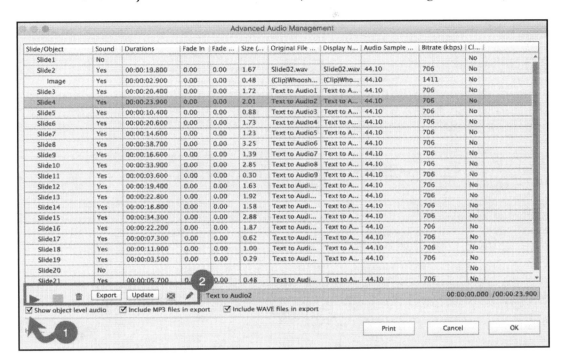

By selecting the **Show object level** audio checkbox, the list of audio files displayed in the **Advanced Audio Management** window includes the audio associated with the Character image on slide 2.

4. Select any of the audio files in the list.

When an audio file is selected in the **Advanced Audio Management** window, the buttons in the bottom part of the window are enabled (see **2** in the preceding screenshot). These buttons allow you to play the selected audio file, export it to a .wav and/or .mp3 file, edit the audio file, add Closed Captions, and more.

5. Inspect the other controls of the **Advanced Audio Management** window.
6. Close the **Advanced Audio Management** when you are done.
7. Save and close the takeTheTrain.cptx file.

There really is nothing more to say about the **Advanced Audio Management** window. It is just a nice and easy way to have a general overview of all the audio used in your course module.

Summary

In this chapter, your project took on a whole new dimension. With the addition of multimedia elements, your eLearning is much more fun and dynamic to look at, and your message is more powerful than ever.

You first learned how to import external animations into your project. These can be animated .gif files animations, or HTML5 animations packaged in .oam files. These animated items are created using external applications, such as Adobe Animate CC or Adobe Photoshop CC.

You also learned how to insert video files into your course module. You can insert them as Event Videos or as Slide Videos. Captivate lets you import various types of video files, but will always convert them to .mp4 videos upon publishing.

Finally, you studied the audio options in Captivate. You learned that sound can be added at the object level, slide level, or project level. To produce the audio files, Captivate offers the ability to record your own clips, but you can also import audio clips produced in an external application or convert text typed into the **Slide Notes** panel to speech using one of the speech agents provided by Captivate or already present on the system.

There is still a lot of work to do before your course module can be made available to the learners. One of the most important things to be done is the synchronization of the newly inserted audio files with the other elements of the slide. This process, along with many other tools, will be covered in the next chapter.

Meet the community

At the end of this chapter, we want to introduce you to Alice Acker. Alice has been part of the Captivate Community for many years. She holds the record for attending the most Adobe eLearning Summits, starting in 2011. She's used Captivate since version 2. Her attention to detail and sharp wit make her a valuable member of our community.

Damien

Alice served as a technical reviewer for *Mastering Adobe Captivate 2017*. She taught me that it's okay to say *"click"* instead of *"click on"* and made me implement this change throughout the entire book! Hopefully, she speaks a little bit of French, so I can take my revenge and teach her the subtleties of my native language.

Pooja

I've known Alice since my first Adobe Learning Summit in 2013. She's always been open about telling me what she likes about Captivate, and what can be improved. She's attended many of my webinars and is willing to chime in with her insights.

Alice Acker

Alice is the Principal at Aptus Learning Design. Alice specializes in project management and the development of electronic medical record eLearning.

After a successful career in healthcare administration, Alice decided to focus on elearning. She obtained a certificate in web management, where she gained proficiency in Adobe Creative Cloud. Her first forays into Captivate were reading Kevin Siegel's *Captivate 3* books and attending a seminar at Learning Solutions taught by Joe Ganci in 2011. (Alice is very thankful to both Kevin and Joe!) Her healthcare industry insight and hands-on development skills make her uniquely qualified. She now frequently writes blogs for the community and creates humorous 60-second videos for Mac Captivate Newbies.

Contact details

- Blog: http://elearning.adobe.com/
- Twitter: @Ackeral
- LinkedIn: https://www.linkedin.com/in/alice-acker-4781666/

4
Working with the Timeline and Other Useful Tools

You've already done a lot of work on the project you started two chapters ago. But you're not done yet! Now, we will focus on object alignment and positioning, as well as on audio synchronization with slide elements.

In this chapter, you will primarily focus on using the **Timeline** panel to synchronize elements of the slides with the audio. You will also learn about various tools and features used to manage and lay out the objects of the project.

In this chapter, you will learn about the following topics:

- Using the Library to manage the assets of the project
- Using Smart Guides to accurately arrange the objects
- Using the rulers and creating custom guides
- Learning how to group and ungroup objects
- Using the **Align** toolbar to perfectly arrange the objects on the slides
- Using the **Filmstrip** to manage the slides of the project
- Using the **Timeline** to synchronize the various elements of the slide
- Applying effects to the objects

At the end of this chapter, you will better understand how the features and objects discussed in the previous two chapters come together to build an eLearning course.

Preparing your work

To get the most out of this chapter, you should first reset your workspace. If you are using the default interface mode, restarting Captivate also resets your workspace to default. If you are using the advanced interface mode, use the **Window** | **Workspace** | **Reset 'Classic'** menu item to reset the classic workspace to default. In this chapter, you will use the exercise files in the Chapter04 folder. If you get confused by any of the step-by-step instructions, look at the Chapter04/final/takeTheTrain.cptx file, which is the project as it should look at the end of this chapter.

Working with the Library

The **Library** contains a list of the assets in your project. These assets include the background used on the Master Slides and all the external files imported into the project (images, video, sounds, and so on). Perform the following steps to open a project and explore its library:

1. Open or restart Captivate.
2. Open the Chapter04/takeTheTrain.cptx file.
3. When using default interface mode, a **Library** icon appears at the far right side of the toolbar, just next to the **Properties** icon. Click the big **Library** icon situated at the far right side of the toolbar. Alternatively, use the **Window** | **Library** menu item.

When the **Library** panel opens, it looks like the following screenshot:

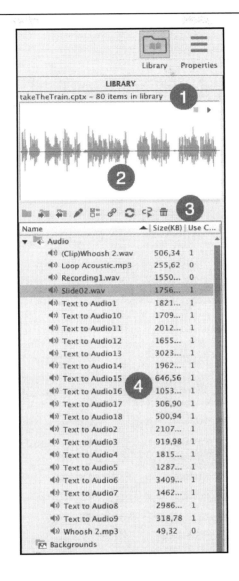

As shown in the preceding screenshot, the **Library** panel is composed of the following elements:

- At the top of the **Library** panel is the name of the file the **Library** belongs to (**1**). This means that the **Library** is associated with the currently active project only. When you switch to another project, you also switch to another **Library**.
- The preview area (2) gives a preview of the selected item. In the preceding screenshot, we have selected the **Slide02.wav** audio clip you imported in the previous chapter. Note that, by default, nothing is selected when you open the **Library** panel.
- Just below the preview area, the **Library** toolbar (3) displays useful icons. These are the tools used to manage the assets present in the **Library**.
- The main area of the **Library** panel (4) lists the assets of the project organized by type. You may not have files of each type in each project, but Captivate organizes the **Library** and creates these folders in case you add these types of files later.

You will now take some time to further explore the **Library** using the following steps:

4. Scroll down the **Library** panel and look at the available folders. The **Library** shows the assets that have been imported into this file. Look at the filenames. You should recognize many of these from the previous two chapters.
5. In the **Audio** section of the **Library**, select the Slide02.wav audio clip. It is the audio file you imported in the project during the previous chapter.
6. Click on the sixth icon on the **Library** toolbar (it looks like a chain link). This icon is called **Usage**.
7. A box pops up informing you that this particular audio clip is used as the background audio of slide 2.
8. Click **OK** to close the **Usage** dialog box.

The only purpose of the **Usage** window is to show you where the selected asset is being used in the project.

Using the Library to remove assets from the project

In the previous chapter, you used text-to-speech to generate slide audio. You'll now replace these files with real voiceover recordings made in an external audio application (in this case, the external application was Adobe Audition, but it could have been any external audio application).

Alternatives to Adobe Audition CC

If you don't have Adobe Audition CC on your computer, you can use any other audio application, such as Apple Logic, Steinberg Cubase, ProTools, and so on. If you don't want to spend any money on a dedicated audio application, Audacity (http://www.audacityteam.org/) is a great open source audio-editing application.

You will now use the **Library** to remove the text-to-speech generated audio clips using the following steps:

1. In the **Audio** section of the **Library**, select all the **Text to Audio...** files (select the first one, hold down the *Shift* key, and select the last one. This should select all the needed files).
2. Click the last icon on the **Library** toolbar (the trash can icon) to delete the selected files from the **Library**.
3. Confirm your intention by clicking **Yes** on the message that pops up.
4. A second message tells you that the selected file is currently used as the background audio of a slide. Click **Yes To All** to remove all the **Text to Audio** clips from the **Library**.

The selected audio files have been removed from the project. In the **Filmstrip**, notice that the loudspeaker icon that was associated with these slides has been removed, indicating that there is no more audio associated with these slides (except for slide 2, which uses the Slide02.wav file as background audio).

This is shown in the following screenshot:

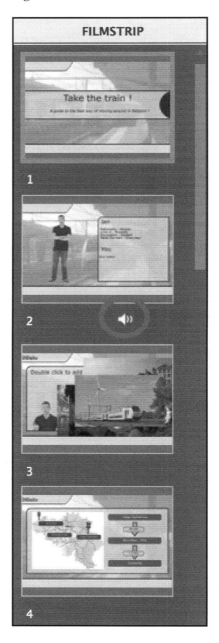

Thanks to the **Library**, you were able to remove multiple assets without having to go to individual slides. Using the **Library** is a big timesaver!

Importing external assets into the Library

Now, you will import the final audio files. You could select each slide of the project and import the new audio files one by one, but the **Library** gives you a better way. Using the following steps, you will import the audio files into the project and associate them with the corresponding slides:

1. In the chapter04/takeTheTrain.cptx file, make sure the **Library** panel is open.
2. Click the second icon on the **Library** toolbar. This icon is named **Import**.
3. Browse to the Chapter04/audio folder of the downloaded exercises and select all the .wav files it contains.
4. Click the **Open** button and let Captivate import the selected audio files into the **Library** panel.
5. When the import process is finished, you will see a message that **18 items has been successfully imported**. Click **OK** to acknowledge the message.

All of the required audio files have been imported into the project. Your next task is to associate each of the imported files with the correct slide:

6. Use the **Filmstrip** to go to slide 3 of the current project.
7. Drag the slide03.wav file from the **Audio** section of the **Library** and drop it on top of slide 4. Make sure you drop it on the slide itself, and not on one of the objects present on the slide.
8. If the **Audio Import Options** dialog pops up, choose to extend the duration of the slide to match the length of the audio file.

Yes, it is that easy to import external assets into the **Library**! On the **Filmstrip**, you'll notice a loudspeaker icon next to the slides you just added audio to. The only potential issue you have to be mindful of is to drop the audio clip on top of the slide, and not on top of one of the objects sitting on the slide.

Repeat the same process with the next audio clip (slide04.wav), except this time, drop the audio file on top of the scrap area (the dark grey area around the slide). Dropping the audio file on the scrap area is another way of associating the audio file with the slide. The benefit of this technique is that you limit the risk of dropping the audio file on top of an object rather than on top of the slide. Let's now explore yet another way to perform the same operation.

Repeat the same process once again with slide05.wav, but this time, drop the audio file on top of the slide 5 thumbnail in the **Filmstrip** panel. Dropping the audio file on the corresponding slide thumbnail in the **Filmstrip** panel is yet another way to ensure that the audio file is associated with the slide, and not with one of the objects present on the slide.

The rest of this exercise is quite simple! You'll use the exact same drag-and-drop technique to associate the remaining audio clips with their corresponding slides. Use the name of the sound clip to identify which slide to associate it with, the Slide10.wav audio clip goes on slide 10, and so on.

 Naming audio clips this way is a best practice and helps you to know which audio clip is associated with which slide.

At the end of this exercise, all of the audio files have been added to the project and associated with the correct slide. It is time to move to the next section and discover the other features of the **Library** panel.

Reusing Library items

One of the main benefits of the **Library** is that you can reuse assets. This means you don't have to reimport them every time. In this section, you will learn how to reuse the assets already imported in the project using the following steps:

1. In the Chapter04/takeTheTrain.cptx file, use the **Filmstrip** to navigate to slide 2.
2. Select the character image on the left side of the slide.
3. Right-click the image and click the **Find in the Library** menu item.

This action selects the IMG_9105.png image in the **Library**, as shown in the following screenshot:

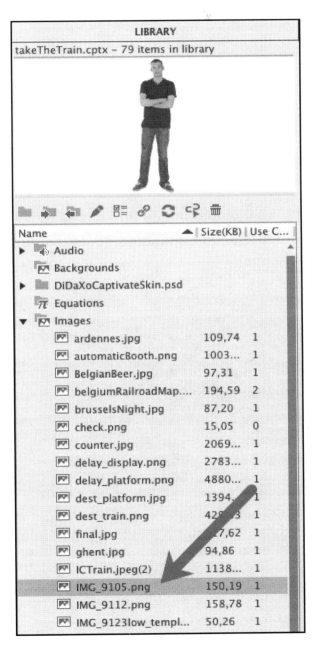

Renaming Library items

The default name of an item in the **Library** panel is the name of the file that was imported in the project. If you want, you can right-click a **Library** item to rename it and give it another, more meaningful name.

If you want to use the same image again, there is no need to import it a second time. It can be taken directly from the **Library** panel and reused as many times as needed throughout the entire project. Using multiple instances of the same file helps in keeping the file size as low as possible. You will now drag and drop another instance of the same image elsewhere in the project:

1. Use the **Filmstrip** to go to slide 8.
2. Drag the **IMG_9105.png** file from the **Images** section of the **Library** and drop it on the left of slide 8.
3. Move and resize the image so your slide looks like the following screenshot:

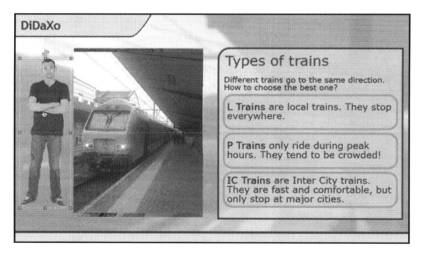

In this exercise, you have reused an image from the **Library**. If you look at the **IMG_9105.png** file in the **Images** folder of the **Library** panel, you'll see the **Use Count** is now **2**.

Importing objects from another Library

Another great feature is the ability to open the **Library** of another file. This makes it easy to share assets across different Captivate projects. In the next exercise, you will open the **Library** of another Captivate file and insert one of the assets it contains into the *Take the Train* project:

1. In the `Chapter04/takeTheTrain.cptx` file, use the **Filmstrip** to go to slide 7.
2. In the **Library** panel, click the **Open Library...** button. It's the first button on the toolbar.
3. Navigate to the `exercises` folder and open the `Chapter04/library.cptx` file. The **Library** panel of this file appears as an extra floating panel.

 Make sure the `Chapter04/library.cptx` file is closed when doing this operation, otherwise you'll have a file lock error.

4. If needed, enlarge the external **Library** panel. It contains a single image called `inAmsterdam.jpg`.
5. Drag the `inAmsterdam.jpg` image from the external library to the middle of slide 7.
6. Close the external library when done.

Oops, wrong image! Sorry folks, this is an image of me in Amsterdam a few hours before the AC/DC show during their 2009 *Black Ice* world tour! Well, even though this is not the intended picture, I've made my point: the **Library** can be used to share assets between Captivate files. Notice that the `inAmsterdam.jpg` image is now present in the **Images** folder of the **Library** of the current project.

7. Still on slide 7, select and delete the newly inserted image.

After you delete the image, look at the **Library** panel. The image remains in the **Library** even though it's not being used. The **Use Count** now displays a **0** confirming this.

Importing into the project Library from an external library
You can also drag assets from an external library and drop them directly in the **Library** of the current project (rather than on a specific slide). These assets are imported into the current **Library** with a **Use Count** of **0** and are ready to be used anywhere in the current project.

Deleting unused items from the Library

The unused items are the assets that are present in the project **Library**, but are no longer used in the project. To control the size of the .cptx file, it is a good idea to remove these items from the **Library**. In this exercise, you will use the **Library** panel to quickly identify and delete unused items:

1. In the **Library** panel, click the **Select Unused Items** icon. It is the second-to-last icon in the **Library** toolbar, as shown in the following screenshot:

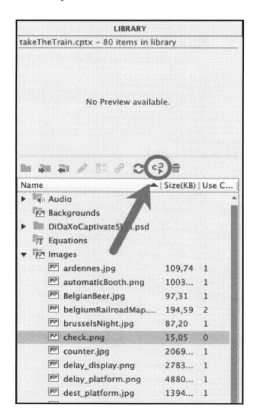

The unused items, including the `inAmsterdam.jpg` image, are now selected in the **Library**.

2. Click the last icon on the **Library** toolbar (the trash can icon) to delete the selected assets.
3. Click **Yes** to confirm the deletion.
4. Save the file when done.

That's it! Thanks to the **Library** panel, it has been quick and easy to identify and delete the unused assets. This will help you keep the size of your `.cptx` file as low as possible.

Be careful when deleting assets from the **Library**. Once an item has been removed from the **Library**, there is no way to get it back without reimporting it from outside of the project. Make sure you have a copy of the important files, should you ever need to import them again later.

You will discover a few more features of the **Library** panel later in the book, but for now, let's make a quick list of what you already know:

- The **Library** panel appears on the right side of the screen, next to the **Properties** inspector.
- The primary purpose of the **Library** is to maintain a list of all assets in the active project. These include the pictures, audio files, videos, animations, and so on, imported into the project.
- Each project has its own **Library**. If you open another project, you will get another **Library**.
- The **Library** panel provides the necessary tools to let you manage the assets used in the project.
- You can use the **Library** panel to insert multiple instances of the same asset in your project. This helps keep the project size as low as possible.
- You can share assets across projects by opening the **Library** of other `.cptx` files and importing the assets they contain in the current project.
- When you delete an asset from a slide, it is not deleted from the **Library**. As a result, you may end up with a **Library** containing many unused items. Captivate will alert you if you have too many unused **Library** items when you open a `.cptx` file.

- You can easily select and delete the unused items with the tools of the **Library** panel.
- Right-click any item in the **Library** panel to open a menu with additional functions, including the ability to rename the item you right-clicked.

Laying out the objects on the slides

In this section, you will examine a few practical tools to help you quickly and easily arrange the objects on your slides.

Using Smart Guides

The first of these tools are the **Smart Guides**. Smart Guides make it very simple to align various objects together. In this section, you will return to slide 8 of the takeTheTrain.cptx file and precisely align the Character image so it is located exactly in the vertical middle of the train image that sits on its right:

1. Return to the Chapter04/takeTheTrain.cptx project and use the **Filmstrip** to navigate to slide 8.
2. Open the **View** menu.
3. Make sure the **Show Drawing / Smart Guide** option of the **View** menu is enabled (a checkmark should be visible in front of the menu item). If not, enable it now.
4. Select the Character image you imported in the previous section and move it slowly toward the top of the slide. When the Character image is aligned with another object, you will see a horizontal and/or vertical green dotted line. The Character image will briefly snap to that line, allowing you to align the two objects together. This dotted green line is a Smart Guide. These Smart Guides appear automatically when some kind of alignment is possible, as shown in the following screenshot:

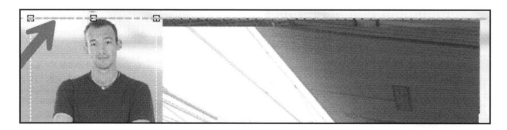

5. Release the mouse to place the Character image at the location defined by the Smart Guide.

6. Move the same Character image again. Move it slowly toward the bottom of the slide.

7. At some point, you will see a horizontal Smart Guide extending from the middle of the Character image to the middle of the train picture on the right.

8. Release your mouse when that Smart Guide is displayed to properly align these two images.

Using the Smart Guide, it is simple and fast to align an object with the other objects on the same slide. At the end of this exercise, slide 8 should look like the following screenshot:

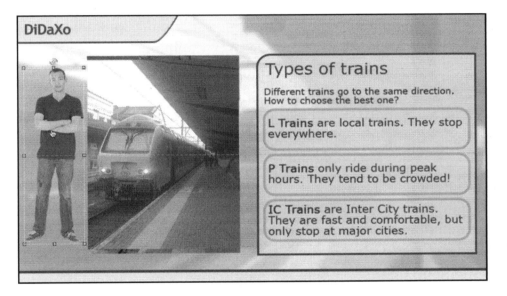

Using the rulers and the guides

Other features that will help you properly position objects on a slide are rulers and guides. The difference between the guides you will use in this section and the Smart Guides discussed in the previous section is that you will now draw the guides and decide where to position them. In the previous section, Smart Guides were temporary guides automatically generated by Captivate.

In the next exercise, you will properly position the images of slide 9 using the rulers and custom guides that you will place on the slide yourself. Your first task is to turn the ruler on and to draw the guides using the following steps:

1. In the `Chapter04/takeTheTrain.cptx` project, use the **Filmstrip** to navigate to slide 9.
2. Select the **Getting a ticket** title shape to see its boundaries and its resize handles.
3. Use the **View | Show Ruler** menu item to turn both the vertical and the horizontal rulers on.
4. Place your mouse on top of the vertical ruler, at the left edge of the stage area.
5. From there, drag a vertical guide. Place the guide so that it touches the left edge of the smart shape **Getting a ticket**.
6. Select the image of a train ticket on the right side of the slide to reveal its boundaries and its resize handles.
7. Place your mouse on top of the horizontal ruler at the top of the stage.
8. From there, drag a horizontal guide. Place the guide so that it touches the top edge of the selected image.

As shown in the following screenshot, you should now have two guides on your slide – one vertical guide and one horizontal guide:

 In the following screenshot, the guides have been made thicker to help you properly spot them. In real life, these guides are much thinner than on the image.

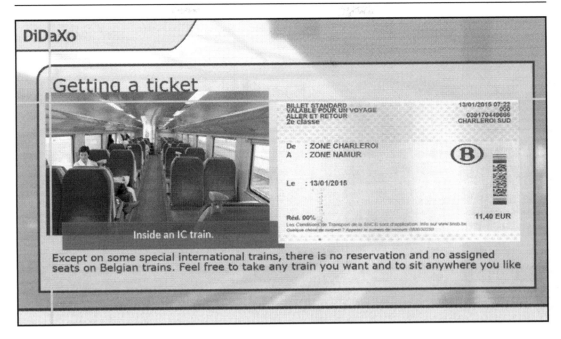

Before moving on with this exercise, it is important that you fully understand the operations that you can do with these guides:

- You can move the guides by placing your mouse on top of a guide until the mouse pointer turns into a double arrow. This allows you to fine-tune the position of an existing guide.
- To remove a guide, you can drag a horizontal guide back into the top ruler, or drag a vertical guide back to the vertical ruler at the left edge of the screen.
- Open the **View** menu to discover some more operations, such as hiding all the guides, clearing (removing) all the guides, locking the guides, and so on.

In this exercise, you want to move the train image (on the left-hand side of the slide) so that its top-left corner matches the intersection of the two guides. To help you out, you will activate the **Snap To Guide** feature before moving the image into position:

9. Use the **View | Snap to Guide** menu item to turn the **Snap to Guide** feature on.
10. Select the train image on the left side of the slide.

11. Slowly move the image so that its top-left corner matches the intersection of the guides. When the image touches the guides, these should turn purple.

Thanks to those custom guides, it was easy to properly position the image on the slide.

Extra credit – aligning the image legend

Now that the train image is in place, you can move the **Inside an IC train** Smart Shape into position. The bottom edge of the Smart Shape should touch the bottom edge of the train image. Move the Smart Shape around and use the Smart Guides to position it properly.

Alternate ways to create guides

In the previous exercise, you used your mouse to drag vertical and horizontal guides from the top and the rulers. This is just one of the available methods for creating guides. In this section, you will explore the other ways of creating guides:

1. Use the **Filmstrip** to return to slide 8. Note that the guides you created on slide 9 are also displayed on slide 8. Guides are not tied to a particular slide layout, but are added on top of the stage for the whole project.
2. Use the **View | Clear Guides** menu item to remove all the existing guides.
3. Use the **View | New Guide** menu item to open the **New Guide** dialog.
4. In the **New Guide** dialog, choose to generate a **Horizontal** guide located precisely at 89 pixels from the top of the slide. Click **OK** to validate and create the guide.

The **New Guide** dialog allows you to create new guides and to position them precisely on your slide:

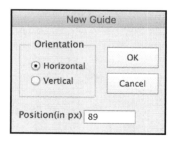

You will now explore yet another way of creating guides in Captivate.

Use the **View | Create Multiple Guides** menu item to open the **Create Multiple Guides** dialog. This box allows you to create multiple guides in a single operation. Designers use it to generate a grid of guides that they use to layout their slides in Captivate. These grids are very common among graphic designers because they simplify things and help in creating slick and flawless designs. You will now generate a grid of 12 columns by 3 rows using the following steps:

5. In the **Create Multiple Guides** dialog, select both the **Column** and the **Row** checkboxes.

6. In the **Columns** section of the box, you want 12 columns with a gutter of 20 px between each column (the gutter is the empty space between the columns).

7. In the **Rows** section, you want 3 rows.

8. Select the **Margins** checkbox and add margins of 50 px on all four sides.

9. Finally, select the **Clear Existing Guides** checkbox to remove the current guides and replace them by those you are generating.

Make sure the **Create Multiple Guides** dialog looks as follows before clicking the **OK** button:

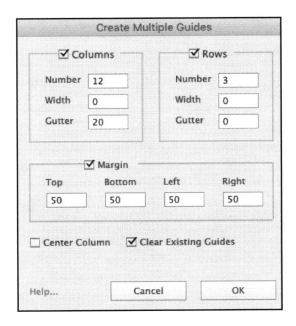

In the preceding screenshot, notice that the **Width** of both the columns and the rows is set at 0. It means that Captivate will calculate the width of those elements so that the slide is divided into 12 columns of equal width (with a space of 20 px between each columns) and in 3 rows of equal height.

 A grid of 12 columns is very popular among designers, because it allows for a lot of combinations. For example, if you want three elements side by side, you will give each of them a width of four grid columns (because *4 * 3 = 12*), but if you want two elements side by side, you will give each element a width of six grid columns (because *6 x 2 = 12*), and so on. Thanks to the 20 pixels gutter between each column, the elements you hang on the grid will be separated from each other by a space of 20 pixels.

You can now use this grid to organize the objects present on the slides of the project. However, you don't want to accidentally move these guides while placing the objects. Thankfully, Captivate has a feature that allows you to lock the guides in place:

10. Use the **View | Lock Guides** menu items to lock the guides in place.
11. With the **Lock Guides** feature active, try to grab and move one of the existing guides with your mouse.

Captivate should not let you move the guides around, thus preventing any accidental guide movement. The objects of the slide are not affected by this option and can to be moved with no restriction around the stage.

With all those guides on the screen, your work environment probably feels a bit cluttered. You can easily show and hide the guides using the following steps:

12. Use the **View | Hide Guides** menu item to temporarily hide the guides. While doing so, take good note of the keyboard shortcut associated with this feature (*Ctrl + ;* on Windows or *command + ;* on the Mac).
13. Use the keyboard shortcut (*Ctrl + ;* on Windows or *command + ;* on macOS) to turn the visibility of the guides back on.

Thanks to the **View | Hide Guides** menu item and its associated keyboard shortcut, it is very easy to temporarily hide the guides, thus reducing the clutter on the screen.

In the case of this particular project, we did not use this grid system to lay out the slides, so you will now delete the guides that you have created.

14. Use the **View | Clear Guides** menu item to delete the existing guides.

Using the Align toolbar

If you are looking for pixel-perfect alignment and positioning, the Align toolbar is the best tool. It contains the necessary icons to align, distribute, and resize the objects of your slides. By default, the Align toolbar is not displayed in the Captivate interface, so your first task is to turn it on:

1. Use the **Window** | **Align** menu item to turn the Align toolbar on. By default, it appears in the top-left area of the screen.

As shown in the following screenshot, the Align toolbar contains 14 icons. During the next exercise, you will use many of these. To make it clearer to know which icon to click, they are numbered in the screenshot:

 The Align toolbar actually contain 18 icons, but only the first 14 are used to align and resize items on the stage. The remaining four icons are used to arrange the stacking order of objects. Arranging the stacking order will be covered later in this chapter.

The icons become available to use when you've selected something. The selection you have determines which buttons are active:

2. Navigate to slide 4 of the `chapter04/takeTheTrain.cptx` file and select the **Liège Guillemeins** Smart Shape on the right side of the slide. With one object selected on the slide, only the **Center horizontally on the slide** (icon 7) and the **Center vertically on the slide** (icon 8) icons are available.

3. With the **Liège Guillemins** Smart Shape still selected, hold the *Shift* key down, while clicking the **Bruxelles -Midi** Smart Shape, to add it to the current selection. With two objects selected, most of the icons of the Align toolbar are available. Only the **Distribute Horizontally** (icon 9) and the **Distribute Vertically** (icon 10) icons are still disabled.

4. Hold the *Shift* key down while clicking the **Oostende** Smart Shape to add it to the current selection. With three (or more) objects selected, all the icons of the Align toolbar are available.

You can also access the tools of the Align toolbar by right-clicking an object and opening the **Align** menu item. The content of that menu depends on the current selection and will always match what is available on the Align toolbar.

Selecting multiple objects

Most of the tools of the Align toolbar require that at least two objects be selected. Selecting multiple objects is not difficult, and works the same way in Captivate as in most other applications. But Captivate has one behavior that is different from other applications. This is what you will explore in this section:

1. Still on slide 4 of the `Chapter04/takeTheTrain.cptx` file, click anywhere in the scrap area (the grey area around the slide) to deselect all the objects.
2. Click the map of Belgium to select it.
3. Hold the *Shift* key down while clicking the **Liège Guillemins** Smart Shape.

You now have two objects selected on your slide. The first object you selected (the map of Belgium) is surrounded by white selection handles while the **Liège Guillemins** Smart Shape is surrounded by black selection handles, as shown in the following screenshot:

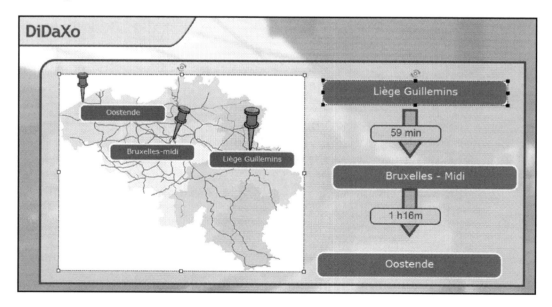

In Captivate, the first object selected is the **key object**. The Align toolbar aligns other objects to the key object. Key objects have white selection handles, all others have black selection handles.

4. Click the **Align top** (icon 4) button of the Align toolbar. This operation aligns the top edge of the **Liège Guillemins** Smart Shape to the top edge of the map of Belgium (because the map of Belgium is the key object).
5. Hold down the *Shift* key and click the **Liège Guillemins** Smart Shape again to remove it from the current selection.
6. Click the **Oostende** Smart Shape in the right side of the slide while holding down the *Shift* key to add it to the selection.

Once again, you have two objects in the selection. The key object (with the white handles) is still the map of Belgium. The second object is the **Oostende** Smart Shape.

7. Click the **Align bottom** (icon 6) button of the Align toolbar.

This operation aligns the bottom edge of the **Oostende** Smart Shape to the bottom edge of the map of Belgium, which is still the Key object. You will place the **Bruxelles-Midi** shape in the middle of the other two using the following steps:

8. Hold down the *Shift* key and click the map of Belgium to remove it from the current selection. Because the map of Belgium was the Key Object when you deselected it, Captivate automatically chose another object in the selection to be the Key Object. Since the **Oostende** Smart Shape was the only other object selected, it becomes the new Key Object and is surrounded by white selection handles.
9. While holding down the *Shift* key, click the **Bruxelles-Midi** Smart Shape and the **Liège Guillemins** Smart Shape to add them to the current selection. After this step, you should have three objects selected.
10. Click the **Align Left** icon (icon 1) of the Align toolbar to align the left edges of the three selected Smart Shapes to the left edge of the Key Object.
11. Click the **Distribute Vertically** (icon 10) icon of the Align toolbar to space the three selected objects equally.

With these operations completed, these three Smart Shapes are in their final position.

Extra credit – aligning the other objects of the slide

You now have all the skills you need to perfectly align the remaining Smart Shapes of this slide. Here is what you need to do:

- Select the objects you want to align, paying close attention to the first one you select. Remember that the tools on the Align toolbar are calibrated based on the first selected object.
- Use the tools on the Align toolbar to move the objects of the slide to their intended position.
- Save the file when finished.

At the end of this extra credit section, your slide should look like the following screenshot:

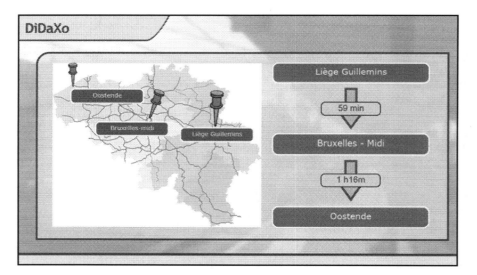

Grouping objects

The next tool discussed in this chapter is the ability to group objects together. When objects are grouped, you can manipulate them as a single entity. This means that you can, for example, move the entire group of objects without breaking their relative alignment.

You can also apply effects to a group (rather than applying effects to each object of the group) and control the visibility of an entire group of objects using actions and variables.

 Applying effects will be discussed later in this chapter. Variables and actions will be covered in Chapter 14, *Variables and Advanced Actions*.

In the following exercise, you will use the following steps to group the seven Smart Shapes you aligned in the previous section:

1. Make sure you are on slide 4 of the Chapter04/takeTheTrain.cptx file.
2. Click one of the seven Smart Shapes present on the right side of the slide.
3. Holding down the *Shift* key, click the other six Smart Shapes one by one to add them to the selection.
4. With all seven objects selected, use the **Edit** | **Group** menu item to group them together. Alternatively, you can use the *Ctrl + G* (Windows) or the *command + G* (Mac) keyboard shortcut.

The result of this last operation is shown in the following screenshot:

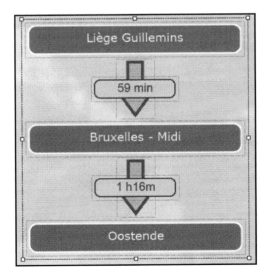

Now that these Smart Shapes have been grouped, they can be moved together without breaking their relative alignment:

5. Experiment with moving the group of seven Smart Shapes around the slide and confirm that these objects are moving together as a single entity.
6. When finished, use the green dotted Smart Guides to put the group of objects back into place.

Even though these objects have been grouped, you can still move and change the properties of individual group members:

7. Click an empty area of the slide to deselect any active object. The **Properties** inspector should display the properties of the slide.
8. Click the group once to select it. When a group is selected, the outline and the white handles surround the entire group. But, within the group, thin gray dashed lines identify the members of that group.
9. While the group is selected, click one of the objects within the group.

This action sub-selects the object you clicked within the group. Note that the white selection handles now surround the selected object, while the group it belongs to is identified by green handles, as shown in the following screenshot:

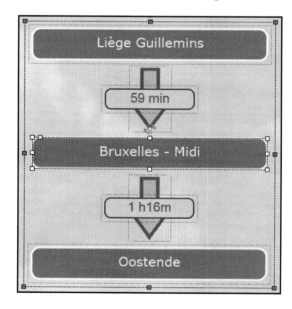

The **Properties** inspector shows you the properties of the currently selected object, in this case, the object you sub-selected within the group. If needed, you can use the controls and switches of the **Properties** inspector to modify the properties of the selected object without affecting the other objects of the group.

If you want to ungroup the grouped objects, all you need to do is select a group and use the **Edit | Ungroup** menu item. You can also use the *Ctrl + Shift + G* (Windows) or the *command + Shift + G* (Mac) keyboard shortcut to ungroup the selected group. Finally, you can also right-click a group and select **Ungroup** in the contextual menu.

In this section, you learned about four Captivate features you can use to easily position objects on your slides. These four features are the Smart Guides, the Rulers and Guides, the Align toolbar, and the ability to group objects. Before moving on to the next section, let's summarize what you learned in this section:

- Smart Guides are dotted green lines that automatically appear and disappear as you move objects around. These guides are used to help you align objects together. These are temporary guides that are automatically generated by Captivate.
- Smart Guides can be turned on and off using the **View | Show Drawing/Smart Guides** menu item.
- Use the **View | Rulers** menu item to turn both the horizontal and the vertical rulers on and off.
- When the rulers are on, you can drag custom horizontal and/or vertical guides from the rulers to the slide. These guides are meant to help you properly position the objects on the stage.
- These custom guides belong to the project, not to a specific slide. If you move to another slide of the project, your guides will still be there.
- Use the **View | Create Multiple Guides** menu item to create a grid of guides on your slides. Use this grid to layout the objects on your slides. Many designers use this grid technique.
- Use the **View | Clear Guides** menu item to remove all the guides.
- The Align toolbar is not part of the default interface. It is necessary to turn it on using the **Window | Align** menu item.
- There are 14 icons on the Align toolbar. The number of enabled icons depends on the number of objects selected.

- It is possible to select multiple objects in Captivate using the same techniques as in most other applications.
- The first selected object of a multiple selection is known as the key object of the selection. The tools on the Align toolbar are calibrated based on that key object.
- Captivate displays white selection handles around the key object, and black selection handles around the other objects of the selection.
- Different objects can be grouped into a single entity. When grouped, these objects can be moved together without breaking their relative alignment.

With a bit of practice, the Smart Guides, the Align toolbar, the Rulers and Guides, and the Group feature will soon count among your most commonly used tools in your Captivate toolbox!

Working with the Filmstrip

The **Filmstrip** is another interesting area of Captivate. By default, it's displayed on the left-hand side of the screen. The main purpose of the **Filmstrip** is to display the thumbnails of the slides in the project. There are a number of things you can do in the **Filmstrip** panel, such as changing the slide order, which you did earlier. In this section, we will discuss other **Filmstrip** operations.

Hiding and showing slides

You can use the **Filmstrip** to show and hide slides in your project using the following steps:

1. Make sure you are still in the `Chapter04/takeTheTrain.cptx` file.
2. In the **Filmstrip**, right-click slide 2 and select **Hide Slide** in the contextual menu. The context menu also shows you the keyboard shortcut for this operation (*command + Shift + H* on Mac or *Ctrl + Shift + H* on Windows).

Hidden slides are dimmed in the **Filmstrip**, and an eye icon appears just below the hidden slide, as shown in the following screenshot:

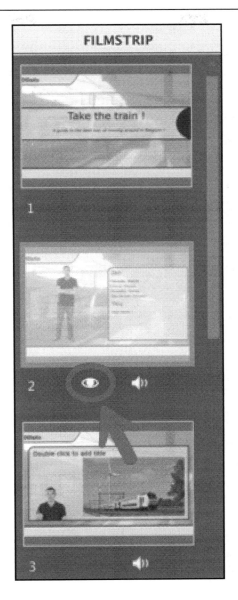

A hidden slide is still part of the project, but it is not displayed to the student taking the course.

3. Use the **Filmstrip** to return to slide 1 of the Chapter04/takeTheTrain.cptx file.

4. From there, use the **Preview | Next 5 slides** icon to preview your sequence in the **Preview** pane of Captivate.

5. Confirm that the second slide is no longer displayed in the **Preview** pane (that is, Captivate jumps from slide 1 directly to slide 3).

6. Close the **Preview** pane when done.

You will now unhide slide 2 using the following steps.

7. Right-click the slide 2 thumbnail in the **Filmstrip**.

8. Choose **Show Slide** in the contextual menu. Alternatively, you can also use the keyboard shortcut (*command + Shift + H* on the Mac or *Ctrl + Shift + H* on Windows), or simply click the eye icon below the slide thumbnail to unhide it.

Hiding slides is very useful in many situations. For example, you might want to keep an older version of a slide in the project for reference, but not show that slide to the students. Or you might have a slide at the beginning of the project with instructions for the Captivate developer on how to use a template. Such a slide is very useful, but must not be displayed to the student. You might also have several language versions of the same slide, but want to show only the version corresponding to a specific language.

Locking and unlocking slides

Another operation that the **Filmstrip** allows you to do is to lock and unlock slides. When a slide is locked, all the objects of the slide, as well as the slide itself, can no longer be edited. Use the following steps to experiment with locking and unlocking slides:

1. Still in the `Chapter04/takeTheTrain.cptx` file, right-click slide 2 in the **Filmstrip** and select **Lock Slide** in the contextual menu. Take good note of the associated keyboard shortcut (*command + K* on the Mac or *Ctrl + K* on Windows).

Notice that a blue lock icon appears in the top-right corner of the locked slide thumbnail in the **Filmstrip**:

Now that the slide is locked, you can no longer access the slide or the objects on it.

2. Use the **Filmstrip** to go to slide 2 of the project.
3. If necessary, open the **Properties** inspector.

Notice that the options and switches of the **Properties** inspector are all disabled. Because the slide is locked, you can no longer modify the properties of the slide.

    4. Try to select the objects present on slide 2.

Because the slide is locked, you can no longer select the objects present on the slide. This means that you can no longer modify the size, the position or the other properties of these objects.

    5. In the **Filmstrip**, right-click the slide 2 thumbnail and choose **Unlock Slide** in the contextual menu. Alternatively, you can also use the keyboard shortcut (*command + K* on the Mac or *Ctrl + K* on Windows), or simply click the lock icon in the upper-right corner of the slide thumbnail to unlock it.

    6. When the slide is unlocked, confirm that you can access its properties in the **Properties** panel, and that you can select the objects present on the slide.

Locking slides is very useful when you want to avoid any accidental modification of a finished slide.

Grouping and ungrouping slides

Another very useful operation is the ability to group and ungroup the slides of your project. This allows you to create sequences of slides and to reduce the clutter in the **Filmstrip**. Use the following steps to group and ungroup slides:

1. Return to slide 1 of the `Chapter04/takeTheTrain.cptx` project.
2. Hold the *Shift* key of your keyboard down as you click slide 3 of the **Filmstrip**. This operation selects the first three slides of the project.
3. Right-click any of the selected slides.
4. Choose **Group | Create** in the contextual menu.

This operation groups the selected slides in one sequence. On the **Filmstrip**, the first three slides of the project appear as a single entity called **Untitled Group.** This is shown in the following screenshot:

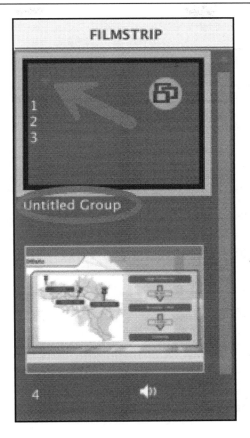

You will now rename the group using the following steps:

5. In the **Filmstrip**, make sure the group you just created is selected. When the group is selected, the **Properties** Inspector displays properties for the entire group.
6. Use the **Title** field at the very top of the **Properties** inspector to change the name of the group to **Introduction**. Note that the new name is displayed in the **Filmstrip** just below the group thumbnail.

Take some time to examine the other options available in the **Properties** inspector. You can change the color associated with the group. This color is used to identify the group in the **Filmstrip**. You can also apply one of the Master Slides of the theme to all the slides in the selected group.

You will now use the **Filmstrip** to expand and collapse the group of slides using the following steps:

7. In the **Filmstrip**, click the blue arrow located in the top-left corner of the group thumbnail (see the arrow in the preceding screenshot) to expand the group

8. Click the same arrow once again (this time, it is located in the top-left corner of the first slide of the group - slide 1 in this example) to collapse the group

9. Finally, right-click the group thumbnail in the **Filmstrip** and choose **Group | Ungroup** in the contextual menu to ungroup the slides

Another benefit of grouping slides and renaming the groups is that Captivate will use that information when generating the Table of Contents of the project. Creating the Table of Contents will be covered in Chapter 15, *Finishing Touches and Publishing*.

In this section, you have learned that the **Filmstrip** is much more than a simple listing of the slides in the project. There are a number of very useful operations that can be done on the slides of your project using the **Filmstrip**. Before moving on to the next section, let's make a quick summary of what you have learned in this one:

- The **Filmstrip** is displayed by default and appears on the left-hand side of the screen.
- The primary purpose of the **Filmstrip** is to show the sequence of slides that makes up the project.
- As covered in an earlier chapter, you can use the **Filmstrip** to reorder the slides of the project.
- You can use the **Filmstrip** to hide and unhide slides. A hidden slide is still part of the project, but is not displayed to the student taking the course.
- The **Filmstrip** allows you to lock and unlock slides. When a slide is locked, it can no longer be modified. All the controls of the **Properties** panel are disabled for locked slides.
- The objects present on locked slides can no longer be accessed and modified.
- You can use the **Filmstrip** to group and ungroup slides. The first benefit of grouping slides is to reduce the clutter on the **Filmstrip** in projects containing a large number of slides.
- When a group is selected, you can use the **Properties** inspector to rename the group and to change the color of the outline used to identify the group in the **Filmstrip**.

- You can use the **Properties** panel to quickly apply the same Master Slide to all the slides of a group.
- Captivate uses the groups and the name of the groups when generating the Table of Contents of the project.

Working with the Timeline

By default, the **Timeline** is closed at the bottom of the Captivate interface. To reveal it, click the **Timeline** bar at the bottom of the screen. The primary purpose of the Timeline is to organize the sequence of events on each slide, but the **Timeline** panel can be used for other things as well. This is what you will explore in this section.

Using the Timeline to select objects

Sometimes, objects are so close to each other that you might have a hard time selecting the correct one. Objects can also be stacked on top of one other so that selecting an object that is not on top of the stack can be tricky. Using the **Timeline** panel, you can make sure that the object you select is the one you want!

1. If necessary, return to the Chapter04/takeTheTrain.cptx file.
2. Click the **Timeline** bar at the very bottom of the screen to open the **Timeline** panel.
3. Use the **Filmstrip** to navigate to slide 3. This slide contains several images stacked on top of each other.
4. Look at the **Timeline** panel at the bottom of the screen.

In the **Timeline** panel, each line (layer) represents an object (with the exception of the bottommost line, which represents the audio clip associated with this slide).

You can make the **Timeline** taller by dragging the top edge of the **Timeline** panel toward the top of the screen.

The layer just above the audio clip represents the slide itself. Looking at that layer, you learn that duration of the slide is currently **21.7** sec, which matches the duration of the associated audio clip (see the ellipse in the following screenshot). The other lines represent the objects inserted on top of the slide. The brown line is the title placeholder Smart Shape that currently reads **Double click to add a title** (see the arrow in the following screenshot). The remaining lines represent the images that you see on the stage:

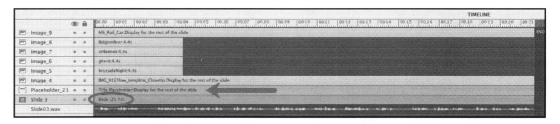

Counting the remaining lines, you learn that there are six images in this slide. One of them is the Character image in the bottom-left corner of the slide:

5. Click the Character image on the slide to select it.
6. In the **Timeline** panel, you'll see that the line corresponding to the Character image is also selected.
7. In the **Timeline** panel, click the topmost layer to select it. The corresponding image is also selected on the stage.

Selecting an object on the **Timeline** selects it on the stage and vice versa. This helps you to figure out which **Timeline** layer corresponds to which object. Using the **Timeline** to select an object is a great way to select objects that are difficult (or even impossible) to select with the mouse.

Labeling the objects

The **Timeline** panel shows the name of the objects. Use the text field at the top of the **Properties** inspector to label your objects. The name you type in the **Properties** inspector appears on the **Timeline** panel. Giving your objects a meaningful and custom name is considered best practice.

Using the Timeline to lock and unlock objects

Locking objects is another feature that helps you select the correct object. It also prevents you from accidentally modifying something you've completed. To illustrate this, you will now lock the group of objects you created in the previous section using the following steps:

1. Use the **Filmstrip** to return to slide 4 of the Chapter04/takeTheTrain.cptx file.

2. Click once on the group of Smart Shapes you created in the previous section.

3. Turn your attention to the **Timeline** panel and notice that the group has its own line and that this line is selected.

4. If needed, click the disclosure triangle located in front of the group label in the **Timeline** to expand the group and see its components (see 1 in the following screenshot).

5. Still in the **Timeline** panel, click the lock icon associated with the group layer (see 2 in the following screenshot):

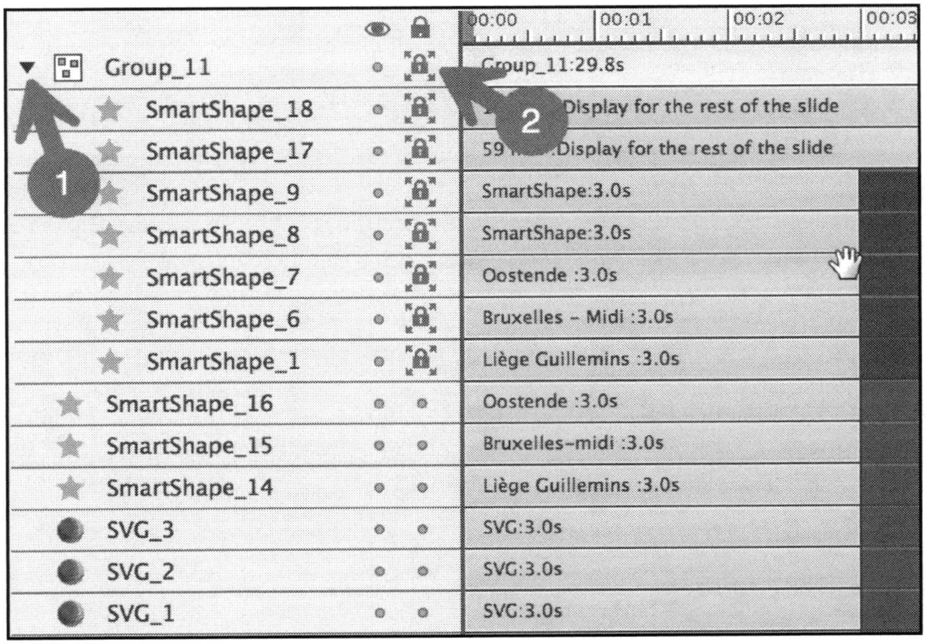

6. On the stage, click the group to select it. Note that Captivate allows you to select the group even though it is locked. In the **Properties** inspector, the properties of the group are displayed as usual.
7. Try to use the mouse to move the group around the slide. Captivate does not let you move the group.
8. With the group still selected, switch to the **Options** tab of the **Properties** inspector.

In the **Options** tab of the **Properties** inspector, note that the **Lock Size and Position** checkbox is selected. When a lock icon with arrows is displayed in the **Timeline** panel (as shown in the preceding screenshot), only the size and the position of the corresponding objects are locked. The objects can still be selected and their other properties (such as fill color, opacity, and so on) can still be accessed.

9. Click the lock icon associated with the group (marked as 2 in the preceding screenshot) again. Notice that another type of lock (without the arrows) now appears next to the group layer.
10. On the stage, try to click the group to select it. Because the group is locked, Captivate does not allow you to select the group. In the **Properties** inspector, the properties of the group are no longer accessible.
11. Click the same lock icon again to disable all the locks. There should be no lock icon on the group layer.

Clicking the lock icon several times circles you through three lock states:

- If no icon is present in the lock column of the **Timeline**, the corresponding object is completely unlocked and all its properties are accessible.
- If a lock icon with arrows is present, only the size and the position of the corresponding object are locked. The other properties (such as the fill and the stroke properties) are not locked and can be modified as usual.
- If a standard lock icon is displayed (without the arrows), then the object is completely locked and cannot even be selected.

The lock feature of Captivate prevents you from accidentally selecting or moving objects that have been already taken care of.

The lock icon at the very top of the **Timeline** panel allows you to lock and unlock all the objects of the slide in a single click! The lock command can also be accessed from the right-click menu, but for unlocking, you'll need to use the **Timeline**.

Using the Timeline to show and hide objects

In the **Timeline** panel, next to the lock/unlock icons, are the show/hide icons (the eye icons). These icons work the exact same way as the lock icons covered in the previous section. You can use them to hide objects from the slide. When the slide contains a large number of objects, the show/hide option can help you select and work with the correct objects, while keeping the others out of the way. Hiding an object with this tool hides it *from the Captivate interface only*, not from the final project as viewed by the students.

Using the Timeline to change the stacking order of the objects

The stacking order determines which objects go in front of or behind other objects. In the **Timeline** panel, the topmost object is in front of any other objects. It means that if objects overlap, the topmost object covers the one(s) below it. The slide is always at the bottom of the stack, since it serves as the background:

1. Use the **Filmstrip** to navigate to slide 3 of the Chapter04/takeTheTrain.cptx file.
2. In the **Timeline** panel, click the topmost layer to select the corresponding image on the stage. You have selected the image with the train and the wind turbines. It is the topmost image of the stack. On the stage, it covers the other images that are behind it.
3. In the **Timeline** panel, use your mouse to drag the top layer down. As you do so, look at the stage and notice that the train image now goes behind the other pictures.
4. Still in the **Timeline** panel, right-click the image you just moved down and use the **Arrange** | **Bring to Front** menu item. This takes the image back to the top of the stack, both on the stage and in the **Timeline** panel.
5. If needed, use the **Window** | **Align** menu item to turn the Align toolbar back on.

6. Notice that the last four icons of the Align toolbar also allow you to control the stacking order of the selected object.

The main takeaway of this section is that the layer stacking order in the **Timeline** matches the stacking order of the objects on stage. To change the stacking order, you have four options:

- You can drag the layers up and down in the **Timeline** panel.
- You can right-click an object and use the **Arrange** menu.
- You can use the last four icons of the Align toolbar.
- Finally, you can use the **Modify | Arrange** menu item.

Extra credit – aligning images

Before moving on to the next section, let's put your new skills to work by aligning the images on slide 3.

On the right side of the slide, there are five images of Belgium. These images are all the same size. Use the tools described in the preceding sections (Smart Guides, Rulers, the Align toolbar, and the **Timeline** panel) to position these five images precisely on top of one other and to place them on the right side of the slide, without changing their stacking order.

At the end of this assignment, your slide should look like the following screenshot:

Using the Timeline to set the timing of the objects

The primary purpose of the **Timeline** is to let you control the timing of the objects on the active slide. For each object, you can choose when it appears on the stage and how long it stays visible. By carefully and precisely arranging the objects on the Timeline, you'll be able to achieve great visual effects with minimal effort. This is what you will explore in this section, using the following steps:

1. Use the **Filmstrip** to navigate to slide 5 of the
   `Chapter04/takeTheTrain.cptx` project.
2. Look at the **Timeline** panel and notice how the six objects of the slide are organized.
3. Click an empty area of the slide or the scrap area around the slide to make it the active item. The **Properties** inspector updates and displays the properties of the slide. In the **Timeline** panel, slide 5 turns blue when it's active.
4. Switch to the **Timing** panel, which is located next to the **Properties** inspector.
5. At the top of the **Timing** panel, change the **Slide Duration** property to **16** seconds. This change is reflected in the **Timeline** panel.
6. In the **Timeline** panel, drag the right edge of the slide layer to the **14** second mark. This change is reflected in the **Slide Duration** property of the **Timing** panel. The changes made in the **Timeline** panel are reflected in the **Timing** panel and vice versa. This gives you two methods to organize the timing of your objects.

Adjusting the zoom level on the Timeline

At the very bottom of the Timeline panel, you find a horizontal slider that you can use to adjust the zoom level of the Timeline. Adjust the Zoom level of the Timeline until you get a view that works best for you:

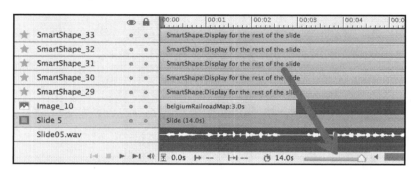

7. Click on the map of Belgium to make it the active object. The **Timing** panel updates and shows the timing properties of the selected image.

The **Timing** panel states that the image will **Appear After: 0 sec** and stays visible for a **Specific Time** of **3 sec**. The **Timeline** panel is a visual representation of this situation.

You will now adjust the timing of the audio file that was imported into this slide:

8. In the **Timeline** panel, place your mouse on top of the audio file layer until the mouse pointer turns to a grabbing hand.

9. Move the audio file to the right so it begins at the **0.5** second mark.

Sound can be very intrusive, so you must use it with care. One of the things I always do on slides with voiceover narration (such as the one you are working with) is to move the sound clip on the **Timeline** to the right, to make the audio narration begin half a second into the slide. This simple trick dramatically diminishes the intrusive and aggressive feeling that sound can induce without affecting the general rhythm of the project.

You will now adjust the timing of the map of Belgium so that it shows for the entire duration of the slide:

10. On the stage, select the map of Belgium.

11. In the **Timing** panel, open the **Display For** drop-down menu and change its value to **Rest of Slide**.

This operation is reflected in the **Timeline** panel. The layer representing the map of Belgium has been extended to the end of the slide. This image should now **Appear After: 0 sec** and will **Display For: Rest of Slide**.

Adjusting the default timing of the objects

When a new object is added to the stage, its timing is set to 3 seconds by default. This default timing can be adjusted for each type of object separately. Simply go to **Edit | Preferences | Defaults** (Windows) or **Adobe Captivate | Preferences | Defaults** (Mac), choose an object in the **Select** drop-down list, and adjust the default timing of the selected object type.

You will now arrange the timing of the five circle Smart Shapes using the following steps:

12. At the bottom of the **Timeline** panel, click the play icon to hear the audio narration.
13. Stop playing when the narration says "*Click on the map to see...*".
14. If necessary, use your mouse to move the red playhead approximately to the **8** second mark. This location corresponds to silence in the audio clip.
15. In the **Timeline** panel, place your mouse at the very beginning of the **SmartShape_29** object. This object is one of the five blue circles on top of the map. The mouse pointer will turn into a double arrow.
16. Use the mouse to drag the beginning of this object to the 8 seconds mark, where the red playhead is located.
17. Look at the **Timing** panel and confirm that the selected object is scheduled to **Appear After: 8 sec** and will **Display For: Rest ofSlide**.
18. Use the same technique to change the timing of the other blue circles. Make them begin half a second apart from each other.

When you are finished, the **Timeline** panel of slide 5 should look as follows:

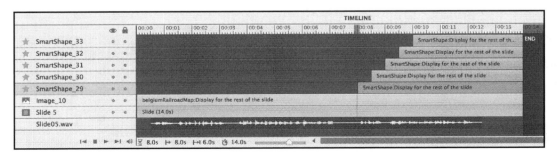

Finally, you will test your work using the Preview feature of Captivate. Use the **Preview | Next 5 slides** icon of the toolbar to test your sequence in the **Preview** pane.

Everything looks fine and syncs well. The **Timelime** shows exactly what you saw in the **Preview**. Before moving on to the next section, let's fine-tune one small detail:

19. On the stage, select the map of Belgium.
20. At the bottom of the **Timing** panel, open the **Transition** drop-down menu.
21. Change the **Transition** to **Fade In Only**.
22. Use the **Preview | Next 5 Slides** icon of the toolbar again to test your change. You should see that the map of Belgium appears on the stage with a nice fade in effect.

In Captivate, it is possible to apply a Fade In and/or a Fade Out effect on (almost) every object. By default, this **Transition** effect lasts half a second, but you can adjust its timing in the **Transition** section of the **Timing** panel.

Keep the **Transition** effect in mind when setting up the timing of your objects. Imagine a Text Caption that is set to be visible for 3 seconds with a default Fade In and Fade Out transition applied. The first half a second is used for the Fade In effect and the last half a second is used for the Fade Out effect. This effectively leaves only 2 seconds for the learner to read the text contained in the Text Caption!

Congratulations! You just synced your first slide in Captivate using the **Timeline** and **Timing** panels. This can take time, but it is straightforward. With practice, it will soon become second nature for you. Before moving on to the next section, let's summarize what you have learned so far:

- The primary purpose of the **Timeline** is to define the timing of the objects.
- The **Timeline** can also be used to select the objects, to lock them, to modify their visibility in the Captivate authoring environment, and to modify their stacking order.
- The **Timeline** panel is a visual representation of the properties found in the **Timing** panel. Changing the timing of the objects in the **Timeline** updates the **Timing** panel, and vice versa.
- It is possible to apply a Fade In and/or a Fade Out effect on an object using the **Transition** drop-down menu in the **Timing** panel. The default transition time is 0.5 sec, but this can easily be changed in the **Timing** panel.

Tips and tricks for great syncing

When it comes to syncing the objects of your project, the **Timeline** is your best friend. When you go the extra mile and combine different features in Captivate, you can achieve great syncing results. In this section, we would like to share with you some of the techniques we use when syncing the projects we work on.

Using the Sync with Playhead feature

The first trick is to use the Sync with Playhead feature. You will use it to sync slide 3 of the `Chapter04/takeTheTrain.cptx` file. The steps are as follows:

1. Return to or open the `Chapter04/takeTheTrain.cptx` file and use the **Filmstrip** to navigate to slide 3.
2. If needed, click the **Timeline** bar at the bottom of the screen to open the **Timeline** panel.

Remember that Slide 3 contains five images of Belgium that are the same size. Normally, these five images are positioned exactly on top of each other on the right side of the slide. The first step of the workflow is to define the beginning and the ending of the slide.

3. In the **Timeline** panel, move the audio clip to the right so it begins at the **0.5 sec** mark.
4. Go to the end of the **Timeline** and extend the duration of the slide to the **23 sec** mark. If you prefer, you can also modify the slide duration in the top section of the **Timing** panel.

The next step is to make each of the five images appear when the corresponding comment is spoken out in the narration.

5. In the **Timeline** panel, select the **brusselsNight** layer. This layer represents the image that is at the bottom of the stack.
6. Click the play icon in the bottom-right area of the **Timeline** panel.
7. Stop the playback when the narration says "*Congratulations on your decision...*" (around the **3.5 sec** mark).
8. With the red playhead in position, right-click the **brusselsNight** layer and choose **Sync with Playhead** in the contextual menu.

This action makes the selected object appear at the current position of the playhead. Since you'll be performing this kind of synchronization often, it's good to know the keyboard shortcut associated with the Sync with Playhead feature (*Ctrl + L* on Windows and *command + L* on the Mac).

9. At the bottom of the **Timeline** panel, click the play icon again to listen to the next part of the audio clip.
10. Stop the playhead when the narration says "*...full of historical places..*" (around the **9.5 sec** mark).
11. In the **Timeline** panel, select the **ghent** layer. This is the layer that is immediately above the one you just synced.
12. Use the *Ctrl + L* (Windows) or the *command + L* (Mac) shortcut to sync the selected image with the current position of the playhead.
13. Repeat the same sequence of actions for the remaining three pictures, using the following table as a reference:

Image	Narration	Approximate timing
Ardennes	*...awesome landscape...*	12.8 sec
BelgianBeer	*...and great food...*	14.7 sec
trainWindmills	*...the best way is the train...*	18.5 sec

By now, all the images should appear on the stage, in sync with the audio narration. Let's check it out using the Preview feature of Captivate:

14. Use the **Preview | Next 5 slides** icon on the toolbar to test your sequence. During the preview, pay close attention to how and when the images appear on the stage. You should see that the timing is correct, but a few remaining details need to be addressed. The most obvious issue is the duration of the first image, which is too short.
15. Close the **Preview** pane when you are finished.
16. Back in the **Timeline** panel, use your mouse to drag the right edge of the **brusselsNight** image to the **10.5 sec** mark. Alternately, you can achieve the same result by changing the value of the **Time** property at the top of the **Timing** panel with that image selected.
17. Finally, use the **Timeline** to select all five images, one by one. At the end of the **Timing** panel, make sure they all use the same **Fade In Only** transition.
18. Use the **Preview | Next 5 slides** icon of the toolbar to test your synchronization once again.

During the preview, make sure that the images are correctly synced with the audio. If necessary, return to the slide and adjust the timing of the images before testing again.

At the end of this exercise, the **Timeline** panel of slide 3 should look similar to the following screenshot:

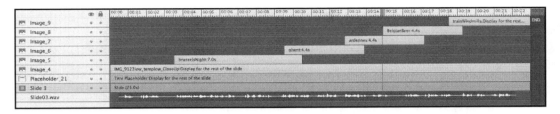

Because all the images are the same size and share the same position, you see a cross-fade effect between the images. Remember that the default Fade In and Fade Out transitions last 0.5 seconds. So, if you extend the duration of an image by at least 0.5 seconds (make that 1 second, just in case), you ensure that the images disappear from the stage when the next one is already visible on top of it. The **Fade In Only** transition brings the final touch to this effect.

To achieve the desired result, you applied several features together in this section:

- You used an image editing tool (such as Adobe Photoshop) to ensure that all the images have the exact same size (this had been done for you before the images were inserted into the slide).
- You used the Align toolbar to position all five images in the exact same place.
- You used the Smart Guides and/or the rulers and guide to align the image stack.
- You used the default 0.5 sec **Fade In Only** transition on your images.
- You used the **Timeline** panel and the **Sync with Playhead** feature to sync the images with the narration.
- You extended each image by at least 0.5 seconds to make sure an image disappears after the end of the Fade In transition of the next image to create a cross-fade effect.

This exercise demonstrates the power of these tools when they are used together.

Extra credit – adjusting the timing of the other slides

Now that you know the tools and techniques used to set the timing and the stacking order of objects, browse the other slides of the takeTheTrain.cptx project to adjust the timing of the objects on each slide. Refer to the Chapter04/final/takeTheTrain.cptx file of your exercise folder for examples and inspiration.

Here are some tips to keep in mind before you get started:

- Use the **Timeline** panel whenever possible. It is the most intuitive and visual way to adjust the timing of the objects.
- If you want precise timing, use the **Timing** panel.
- Remember the Sync with Playhead feature and its associated keyboard shortcut (*Ctrl* + *L* on Windows and *command* + *L* on the Mac).
- Use the tools of the Align toolbar to resize and relocate the objects on the slide. Proper size/location combined with precise timing can lead to strong, yet easy to achieve, visual effects.
- Finally, keep in mind that some objects (for example, buttons) are still missing and will be added in the next few chapters.

Not too fast and not too slow

When creating an online course with Captivate, you'll quickly discover that one of the most difficult aspects is to find the right pace for your instruction. When there is some audio narration, setting the pace is quite easy, because the narration dictates the overall rhythm of the project. When there is no narration, here is a simple trick. For text objects, use the stopwatch function of your cell phone and *slowly* read the content of the text aloud, then round up the timing to the upper half a second. For example, if it takes you 5.7 seconds to read the text aloud, make that object stay on the stage for a specific time of 6 seconds. If your audience is multilingual, add up to 1 second to that timing so that the students taking the course in a language other than their native language will be allowed extra time to read and understand. You can also use the **Calculate Caption Timing** preference of Captivate. When this preference is turned on, Captivate automatically calculates the length of the Text Captions based on their content. You can find this option under the **Defaults** category of the Captivate preferences.

Working with effects

Effects can be applied to any Captivate objects. In this section, you will discover that a wide range of animations can be created within Captivate. So, you may not need to import any external animations after all! You will now use these effects to animate some of the objects of the project.

Applying and removing effects

In this section, you will use the following steps to apply and remove effects:

1. Use the **Filmstrip** to navigate to slide 2 of the `Chapter04/takeTheTrain.cptx` file (use the `Chapter04/takeTheTrain_synced.cptx` file if you didn't sync during the last exercise).
2. Select the Character image on the left side of the slide.
3. If needed, open the **Properties** inspector, and then switch to the **Timing** panel.

The **Effects** section of the **Timing** panel is where you find the built-in effects of Captivate. The main area of this section (see 1 on the following screenshot) is comprised of the list of available effects:

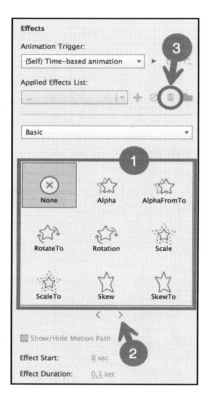

Take some time to inspect the **Timing** panel and get used to its icons before continuing with this exercise.

4. In the main area of the **Timing** panel (see 1 in the preceding screenshot), move your mouse to the top of the effects, and look at the selected Character image on the stage. You will see a preview of the effect you hover on.
5. Click the effect you like the most to apply it to the Character image.
6. If necessary, click the **Timeline** button at the bottom of the screen to reveal the **Timeline** panel.
7. Click the play icon in the bottom-left corner of the **Timeline** panel to preview your effect.

Now that you know how to apply an effect to an object, you will learn how to remove an effect. Then, you will explore additional effects available in Captivate:

8. With the Character image still selected, click the trash can icon on the **Timing** panel to remove the applied effect from the Character image (see 3 in the preceding screenshot).

9. In the **Effects** section of the **Timing** panel, open the **Basic** drop-down menu.

10. Take note of the five families of effects available in Captivate (**Basic**, **Emphasis**, **Entrance**, **Exit**, and **Motion Path**).

11. When ready, click the **Entrance** category. The list of **Entrance** effects appears in the main area of the **Timing** panel.

12. Click the arrow marked as 2 in the preceding screenshot to discover even more **Entrance** effects.

13. On the second page of the **Entrance** effects, click the **Fly In From Left** effect to apply it to the Character Smart Shape.

14. Use the **Preview | Next 5 Slides** icon on the toolbar to test your effect in the **Preview** pane. Close the **Preview** pane when done.

With this effect applied to the Character, you see a horizontal line starting with a green triangle and ending with a red square. This line is a Motion Path. It shows the movement of the character image on the slide. The beginning of the movement is the green triangle and the end of the movement is the red square. Note that you can move these two points with the mouse if you ever want to edit this path.

Place your mouse on top of the green triangle and move it to the right. This shortens the Motion Path. The Character will now make a shorter movement.

Moving the green triangle in a straight line
Hold down the *Shift* key while moving the green triangle, to move it in a straight line.

Make sure the effect is as shown in the following screenshot:

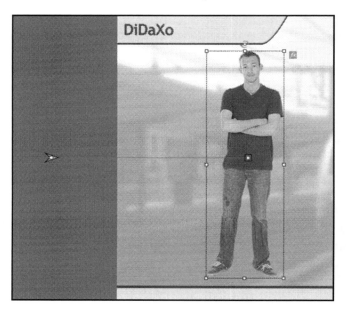

With this configuration, the Character image starts its motion off-stage, enters the stage in a sliding movement from left to right, and ends its motion at its current location. You will now modify the duration (and thus the speed) of the movement using the **Timeline** panel:

15. With the Character image still selected, look at the **Timeline** panel.
16. Click the small disclosure triangle in front of the selected layer of the **Timeline** (see 1 in the following screenshot). This reveals the timing of the effect applied to the Character image.
17. Reduce the duration of the effect to the first half a second of the duration of the object (see **2** in the following screenshot).

This action is shown in the following screenshot:

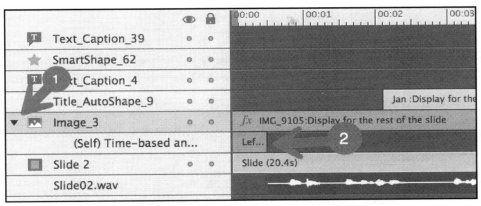

Congratulations! You just applied your first **Entrance** effect to one of the objects of your Captivate file! Use the **Preview | Next 5 Slides** icon on the toolbar to test your new effect in the **Preview** pane.

Applying other effects

Still on the same slide, you will now apply another effect to the Text Caption describing Jan, the Belgian student:

1. Still on slide 2 of the `Chapter04/takeTheTrain.cptx` file, select the Text Caption situated just under the title **Jan** on the right side of the slide.
2. In the **Character** section of the **Properties** inspector, increase the **Spacing** to `1.5`. This adds some space between the lines of text within the Text Caption.
3. With the Text Caption still selected, switch to the **Timing** panel.
4. Open the **Basic** drop-down menu and choose the **Entrance** family of effects.
5. Use the right arrow just below the list of available entrance effects to browse through the three pages of available effects.
6. On the third page, click the **StretchFromTop** effect to apply it to the selected Text Caption.
7. At the bottom of the **Effects** section of the **Timing** panel, change the **Effect Duration** to **0.5** sec.
8. Open the **Timeline** panel if necessary.

9. In the **Timeline** panel, open the little triangle at the beginning of the selected Text Caption layer (see the preceding screenshot for the exact location of that triangle). You should see your effect applied to the first half a second of the Text Caption.

Because the **Timeline** panel is a visual representation of the properties in the **Timing** panel, changing the effect duration can be done in either place.

10. Use the **Preview** | **Next 5 slides** icon on the toolbar to preview your effects in the **Preview** pane.

When watching the preview, notice how these two simple effects make the slide much more dynamic and visually appealing, but don't overshadow the content. This is the key to using effects. Effects have to enhance the content, to make it more appealing and meaningful. But if it ever takes precedence over the content of the slide, then you missed the point of adding effects. To help you use effects more effectively, here is a list of simple tips to keep in mind:

- Never forget that you are teaching. Just like any other feature you use in Captivate, effects must *serve the student's learning*.
- While there are a lot of built-in effects available, you will probably end up using the same two to five effects. That's perfectly fine!
- Don't add an effect to every object. Instead, carefully choose the objects you want to attract the student's attention to, and apply an effect only to those objects. Sometimes, you'll even have an entire slide without any effects applied. That's OK, too!
- Sometimes, a simple Fade In or Fade Out transition (found at the very end of the **Timing** panel) is just enough to make the slide stand out.

The key words when using effects are *simplicity*, *subtlety*, and *efficiency*!

Extra credit – adding effects to the remaining slides

Now that you have applied effects to the objects on slide 2, browse through the remaining slides. When you feel like an effect would be useful, use the **Timing** panel to apply the effect you feel is the most appropriate.

This is a good opportunity for you to familiarize yourself with the built-in effects of Captivate and to experiment with how they work. While doing this, you will certainly discover some features that were not covered in the previous section, such as the following:

- The ability to add multiple effects to the same object.
- The ability to combine effects to create new ones.
- The ability to fine-tune the parameters of the effects. The actual parameters you can edit depend on which effect you apply.
- The ability to trigger an effect with an action, rather than with the timeline (actions will be covered in `Chapter 14`, *Variables and Advanced Actions*).

Look at the `Chapter04/final/takeTheTrain.cptx` file to see how we have used effects in this project.

This *Extra credit* section concludes your overview of effects in Captivate. Feel free to experiment more by applying other effects to other objects and to your own projects. The possibilities are endless, and this book only shows a few examples of what is possible.

Before wrapping up this chapter, this is a list of what you have learned about effects:

- It is possible to add effects to any Captivate object.
- Use the **Timing** panel to apply and manage effects.
- The available effects are sorted into five categories: **Basic**, **Entrance**, **Emphasis**, **Exit**, and **Motion Path**. These categories are available in the **Timing** panel.
- A Motion Path describes a movement that is applied to an object. Captivate contains many predefined Motion Paths, but you can also define custom Motion Paths.
- You can see the effects applied to an object by opening the disclosure triangle on the **Timeline**.
- Effects can be combined to create sophisticated animations.
- Use effects wisely, keeping in mind that they should serve the content and facilitate the learning of the student.

Summary

At the end of this chapter, use the **Preview** | **Project** icon on the toolbar to take a look at the whole project and let yourself be amazed at the job you have already accomplished!

In this chapter, you learned how to use various tools to layout, animate, and synchronize the elements of your eLearning project. These tools include the **Library**, Smart Guides, the Align toolbar, Effects and, most importantly, **Timeline**.

Used individually, these tools are great, but it is when used in combination that they reveal all their power and flexibility.

By syncing the elements of the slides, you reached another milestone in the creation of your eLearning course. But the road is still long before the project can be considered finished.

One of the most impressive capabilities of Captivate is its ability to generate highly interactive animations. In the next chapter, you will learn how to add interactivity, taking your projects to an even higher level.

Meet the community

In this section, we would like to introduce you to Josh Cavalier. He had a secret identity in the Captivate community, which for years was a well-guarded secret. But now, we all know that *Captain Captivate*, the superhero of the Captivate community, was in fact Josh Cavalier! Even though he has announced his retirement as *Captain Captivate*, he will still be around and active in the community using his real name.

> *"I may have retired the cape, but Captain Captivate will always live on. I absolutely love where Adobe is taking Adobe Captivate, and I enjoy every opportunity to train eLearning developers on the tool."*

Josh Cavalier

Josh Cavalier, who founded Lodestone in 1999, is in charge of Lodestone's eLearning consulting services and leads the overall direction and operations of Lodestone's eLearning team. He brings 23 years of eLearning development experience, technology implementation, and vision to his clients. Prior to Lodestone, he was an art director for Handshaw, a leading eLearning services company. He was one of the key resources leading the effort for streamlining Handshaw's eLearning development process and transition from CD ROM delivery to the web. He holds a Bachelor's in Fine Arts from Rochester Institute of Technology.

Contact details

- Website: www.lodestone.com
- Twitter: @joshcav

Developing Interactivity

5

In this chapter, you will continue developing your Captivate project by adding interactivity. This will make it even more interesting, engaging, and fun to use for your students.

This interactivity is created by the interactive objects of Captivate. Three of those objects (Button, Click Box, and Text Entry Box) can stop the playhead and wait for the learner to do or type something. Captivate also provides other means of building interactivity. The **Drag and Drop Interaction** provides an easy way to build highly engaging interactions. The **Multi-States Objects** make it very easy to build sophisticated interactions without any programming, and, finally, the all-new interactive video feature takes your instructional videos to new levels of engagement and efficiency.

These features introduce a new level of complexity to your projects, as the students will receive feedback that is dependent on the action they perform. So, you will have to account for multiple possible answers from your students and act accordingly. This concept is known as **branching**.

Adding interactivity to your online courses will provide a compelling experience that drives student engagement and retention.

In this chapter, you will learn how to do the following:

- Insert different kinds of buttons to give students more control over the timing of the project
- Use Text Entry Boxes to capture the student's typed answers
- Use the Drag and Drop Interaction to add exciting interactivity to your content

- Use the Object State to build highly engaging interactions without any programming
- Make instructional video interactive
- Use the Learning interactions of Adobe Captivate

These will combine to create another chapter full of surprises and discoveries.

Preparing your work

To get the most out of this chapter, you should first reset your workspace. If you are using the default interface mode, restarting Captivate also resets your workspace to default. If you are using the advanced interface mode, use the **Window | Workspace | Reset 'Classic'** menu item to reset the classic workspace to default. In this chapter, you will use the exercise files in the Chapter05 folder. If you get confused by any of the step-by-step instructions, look at the Chapter05/final folder, which contains a copy of the exercises as they should look at the end of this chapter.

Working with Buttons

A Button can stop the playhead and wait for the student to click it. This triggers an action. Buttons are an essential part of every Captivate project and allow the student control the overall pace of the course.

You will now return to the takeTheTrain.cptx project and add a button to slide 3:

1. Open the Chapter05/takeTheTrain.cptx file.
2. Use the **Filmstrip** to navigate to slide 3.
3. In the Toolbar, use the **Interactions | Button** icon to insert a new button in the middle of the slide. Alternatively, you can also use the *Shift + Ctrl + B* (Windows) or the *shift + command + B* (Mac) keyboard shortcut.
4. With the new button selected, open the **Properties** inspector.

When a button is selected on the stage, the **Properties** inspector shows the properties that are relevant to a Button object. Notice that there are three tabs available (Style, Actions, and Options), as shown in the following screenshot:

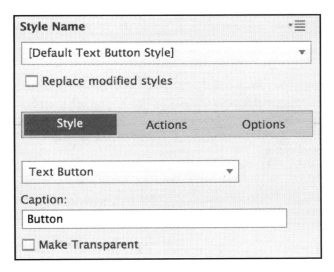

The **Actions** tab is displayed in addition to the usual **Style** and **Options** tabs. This tab only appears when an interactive object is selected.

5. In the **Style** tab of the **Properties** inspector, change the button **Caption** to Continue.
6. Inspect the other properties available in the **Style** tab of the **Properties** inspector, but do not change any of them at this time.
7. Switch to the **Actions** tab of the **Properties** inspector.
8. Open the **On Success** drop-down list and review the available options. When you have finished, make sure **Go to the next slide** is selected (this is the default option).
9. Use the resize handles to increase the size of the button so the new text fits in the object.

When increasing the size of the button, think about the learners who use mobile devices with touch screens. They will appreciate the bigger tap target of a bigger button.

10. Position the new button in the bottom-right corner of the slide below the images (don't forget that you can use the Smart Guides to align the button better).

11. If needed, click the **Timeline** label at the bottom of the screen to open the **Timeline** panel. You may need to use the zoom slider to make the button layer larger (see the following screenshot).

Now that the button is in place and performs the correct action, you need to arrange it on the **Timeline**. There are a few more options to take care of, since the button is an interactive object that stops the playhead. On the **Timeline** panel, the button object is separated into two areas. As shown in the following screenshot, the separator between the two areas is a *Pause* symbol. It represents the exact moment when the button will stop the playhead:

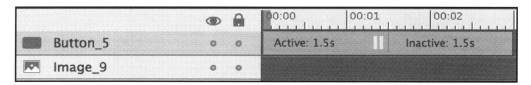

When the button is clicked, the action you selected in the **On Success** drop-down menu of the **Actions** tab in the **Properties** inspector is triggered. In this case, the action is **Go to Next Slide**. It means that when the learner clicks the button, the playhead jumps from the pause symbol to the first frame of the next slide. Consequently, your students will never see the frames of slide 3 situated in the **Inactive** area, after the pause symbol of the button.

12. Use the **Timeline** or the **Timing** panel to do the following:
    - Make the Button **Appear After** 20.5 **sec.**
    - Have the Button **Pause After** 1.5 **sec.**
    - Have the Button **Display For** the **Rest of** the **Slide.**

13. Use the **Preview** | **Next 5 Slides** icon on the Toolbar to test the new button.

The button appears just before the audio narration ends and pauses the playhead when the narration is over. When you click the button, the playhead jumps directly to the next slide and the project continues as usual.

Formatting the Buttons

In this section, you will use the **Properties** inspector to explore some of the properties available on the Button object using the following steps:

1. Still on slide 3 of the `Chapter05/takeTheTrain.cptx` file, make sure the new button is selected.
2. Return to the **Style** tab of the **Properties** inspector and open the **Text Button** drop-down menu.

This drop-down menu lists the three button types available in Captivate:

- **Text Button**: This is the default. It is a simple button whose text can be customized in the **Caption** field of the **Properties** inspector.
- **Transparent Button**: This is a sensitive area that serves as a button. The Transparent button may serve many purposes and has an Opacity slider to change the amount of transparency. It is typically added on top of a background picture.
- **Image Button**: This is an image (actually a set of three images) that acts as a button. Captivate provides predesigned image buttons. But you can also create your own buttons in an image-editing tool and import them in Captivate.

In this exercise, you will create a button from a set of images stored on your computer using the **Image Button** option:

3. Choose the **Image Button** option in the drop-down menu.
4. Inspect the list of predefined buttons provided by Captivate.
5. Next to the **Image Button** dropdown, click the folder icon.
6. Choose the `Chapter05/images/buttons/btn_continue_up.png` file of the exercises.

When browsing for the image file, note that the `Chapter05/images/buttons` folder contains three versions of the image:

- One version ends with _up. It is the normal state of the Button.
- Another version ends with _over. It is the Rollover State of the button. It is used to change the appearance of the button when the student rolls the mouse over the button.

- The third version ends with _down. It is the down state of the button, used when the student has the mouse over the button and presses the mouse button at the same time. The action occurs when the student releases the mouse button.

Captivate is able to import all three buttons and will apply them to the correct states if all three images are stored in the same location and share the same name with _up, _over, or _down added as a suffix:

7. Save the file and use the **Preview | Next 5 Slides** icon of the Toolbar to test the button.
8. When the button appears on the stage, the _up image is used by default.
9. Pass your mouse over the button without clicking to see the _over state of the button.
10. Click and hold on the mouse button to see the _down state.
11. When you release the mouse button, the action specified in the **On Success** menu of the **Actions** tab of the **Properties** inspector (in this case, **Go to the next slide**) is triggered.
12. Close the **Preview** window and save the file when you have finished.

Keep in mind that the button states will not behave the same way on a touch device (Tablet or Smartphone). On such devices, the RollOver state is not used. The Down state is briefly displayed whenever the student taps the button.

This exercise concludes your first overview of the Button object of Captivate. In the next section, you will discover yet another feature of the Smart Shape object.

Finding the Images Buttons

When choosing **Image Button** in the **Style** tab of the **Properties** inspector, Captivate proposes a list of predefined Image Buttons you can choose from. The image assets pertaining to these buttons are located at [Captivate install Path]/Gallery/buttons. This folder also includes a More subfolder, which contains a few extra **Image Buttons** that do not appear in the **Properties** inspector by default.

Using Smart Shapes as Buttons

Back in Chapter 2, *Working with Standard Objects*, you learned about Smart Shapes. If you are not yet convinced of the awesomeness of Smart Shapes, this section will win you over!

1. Return to slide 3 in the Chapter05/takeTheTrain.cptx file.
2. Select the image button you added in the previous section and delete it.
3. Use the **Shapes** icon on the Toolbar to open the Smart Shape menu.
4. Select the rounded rectangle shape and draw a rounded rectangle in the lower-left area of the slide.
5. Double-click the Smart Shape and write Continue in the rounded rectangle.
6. Use the **Style Name** dropdown of the **Properties** inspector to apply the **shape_As_Button** style to the rounded rectangle shape.

Remember that this style, along with all the other styles currently in use in the project, is defined in the Theme you applied in Chapter 2, *Working with Standard Objects*. When done, your slide should look like the following screenshot:

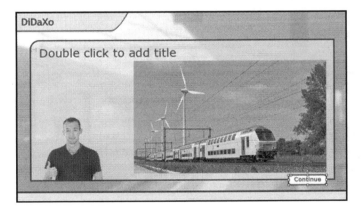

You will now turn your new Smart Shapes into a Button.

7. When the Smart Shape is selected, the **Properties** inspector contains the standard **Style** and **Options** tabs.
8. At the top of the **Properties** inspector, select the **Use as Button** checkbox. The **Actions** tab appears.
9. Switch to the **Actions** tab of the **Properties** inspector.
10. Make sure that the **On Success** action is set to **Go to the next slide**.

11. Look at the **Timeline** panel. If necessary, click the **Timeline** button at the bottom of the screen to open it.

In the **Timeline** panel, notice that the rounded rectangle Smart Shape now has a pause symbol, just like the Buttons you worked with earlier in this chapter.

12. Move the Smart Shape to the end of the **Timeline** so that the pause symbol corresponds to the end of the audio narration.

Make sure the end of the **Timeline** panel of slide 3 looks like the following screenshot. Then, use the **Preview | Next 5 slides** icon on the Toolbar to test your new button:

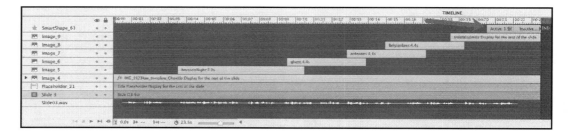

 In the preceding screenshot, note that the Button layer turns green when selected.

In this section, you have learned that any Smart Shape can be used as a button. This means that any shape can be turned into a clickable area you can attach an action to. This includes the custom shapes that you can draw using the polygon tool. So, are you still not convinced by the awesomeness and flexibility of Smart Shapes?

Extra credit – Creating the Continue button on Slide 4

Now that you have used a Smart Shape to create a Continue button on slide 3, you will repeat the very same steps to create the same Continue button on slide 4. Remember that the general steps go as follows:

- Go to slide 4 of the project.
- Draw a rounded rectangle Smart Shape in the bottom-right corner of the slide.
- Apply the **shape_As_Button** style.
- Turn the Smart Shape into a button using the **Use as Button** checkbox of the **Properties** Inspector.
- Make sure the **Action** of the new button is **Go to the next slide**.
- Place the new button on the **Timeline** so that the pause symbol roughly corresponds to the end of the narration.

This whole process will soon become second nature for you, as Buttons and Smart Shapes used as buttons are very common in most Captivate projects.

Branching with Buttons

Branching refers to providing a customized experience to the learners based on their actions in the project. In this exercise, you will create a sequence explaining the train ticket types to the student. You will let the student view the ticket types in any order, and as many times as needed. To do this, you will create a slide with three buttons, one for each ticket type. You will send the student back to this slide after viewing each ticket type.

Preparing the buttons

The first step is to prepare the necessary buttons. There are several ways to do it in Captivate. Here is one of them:

1. Use the **Filmstrip** to go to slide 11 of the `Chapter05/takeTheTrain.cptx` file.
2. Click the **Library** icon in the upper-right corner of the screen to open the Library.
3. In the **Images** section of the Library, locate the **Ticket.png** file.
4. Click the fifth icon of the Library toolbar to see the **Properties** of the selected image.

Notice the dimensions of the picture are 521 by 320 pixels:

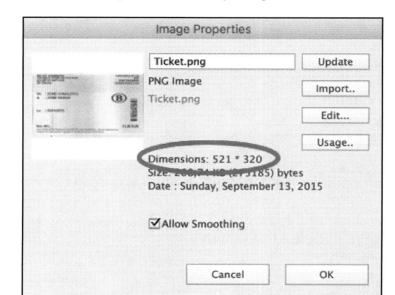

5. Click the **OK** button to close the **Image Properties** dialog.
6. Use the **Shapes** icon on the Toolbar to draw a rectangle on the slide. The size and the position of this rectangle do not matter at this time.
7. With the new rectangle selected, use the **Options** tab of the **Properties** panel to give the rectangle a Width of 521 pixels and a Height of 320 pixels (You may need to deselect the **Constraint Proportions** checkbox).

At this point of the process, you have a rectangle shape on the slide whose dimensions are exactly the same as the Ticket.png image. You will now use the **Image Fill** property of the rectangle shape and use the Ticket.png image as the fill of the rectangle.

8. With the rectangle shape still selected, return to the **Style** tab of the **Properties** inspector.
9. In the **Fill** section, use the first drop down to change the fill to **Image Fill**.
10. Click the second button to open the Image Fill properties.
11. Click the Folder icon next to the **Custom Image** field (see the arrow in the following screenshot).
12. In the **Select Image / Audio from Library** dialog, choose the Ticket.png image, which is already present in the project's Library.

13. As shown on the following screenshot, make sure the **Stretch** checkbox is selected and the **Tile** checkbox is deselected:

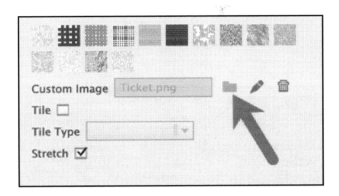

At this point, the slide contains a rectangle shape that uses the Ticket.png image as its Image Fill. You could have achieved the same visual result by simply adding an image onto the slide. The big advantage of the technique you are using in this exercise is that this object is *not* an image, but a Smart Shape. It means that you can write on top of the image and use this shape as a button.

14. Double-click the rectangle shape and write Using Standard Tickets.
15. Use the controls of the **Properties** inspector to format the text. In the Chapter05/final folder of the exercises, we have increased the font size to 48 points and we have used the **Highlight** color to make the text stand out on top of the picture.
16. Select the **Use as Button** checkbox in the **Properties** inspector to turn the Ticket.png rectangle into a clickable button.

Using this technique, any image can be a button! The only thing to be mindful of is to create a shape whose dimensions are exactly the same as the picture and then, use the picture as the Image Fill of the new shape. Also, if you ever need to resize this object, never forget to maintain the aspect ratio of the object to prevent the fill image from being distorted.

17. Resize the object using a corner handle while holding the Shift key down to maintain the aspect ratio.

18. Move and rotate the object until your slide looks like the following screenshot. Rotating the images can be done in the **Options** tab of the **Properties** inspector, or by using the rotate icon that appears on top of the selected object:

Creating the other buttons of the slide

Using images as buttons, as you did in the previous section, is a powerful, but somewhat advanced technique. That's why it is very important that you do it again on your own. In this section, you will use the same steps to create two more buttons on the slide. You will use the RailPass.png image and the Subscription.png image that are already present in the Library of the project.

Remember that you must draw a rectangle that is the exact same size of the picture. Also remember when resizing the object, it is critical that you maintain the aspect ratio.

As a reminder, these are the general steps of the process:

- Select the image in the **Library** and use the **Properties** icon of the Library toolbar to inspect the dimensions of the selected picture.
- Draw a rectangle shape of any size. Then use the **Options** tab of the **Properties** inspector to give your rectangle the same size as your image.

- Use the image as the Fill of the rectangle shape.
- Because the object is a rectangle Smart Shape and not an image, you can write on top of the image and turn the object into a button.
- You can now resize, rotate, and move the object in place. Remember to always maintain the aspect ratio when resizing the object; otherwise, the Image Fill will be distorted.

At the end of this section, your slide should look like the following screenshot:

In this section, you created the buttons you will use for your branching system. To do it, you have used Images, Smart Shapes, and Buttons, as well as a bunch of other tools of Captivate to place and size your objects correctly. This is another example of multiple tools working together to produce the desired effect.

To pause or not to pause?
In this particular situation, you have three buttons on your slide and, by default, each of them pauses the playhead. This is unnecessary, as you want only one of these buttons to pause the playhead at the end of the slide. You can remove the pause behavior from a button, by deselecting the **Pause After** checkbox in the upper portion of the **Timing** panel.

Creating the Branching scenario

In this section, you will use your new buttons to create the branching scenario. To do it, you will change the action associated with each button. To make it easier, you will also give names to some of your slides using the following steps:

1. Use the **Filmstrip** to select slide 11 of the Chapter05/takeTheTrain.cptx project.
2. At the very top of the **Properties** inspector, name the slide Ticket types navigation.
3. Hit the *Enter* key to confirm the name.

Naming slides this way is not required for branching to function properly. But it is a best practice and will make it much easier to work with these slides later in the process. It also has other benefits, such as increased accessibility (accessibility will be discussed in Chapter 13, *Creating Accessible eLearning*). You can name any object in Captivate, including groups of objects, using this technique:

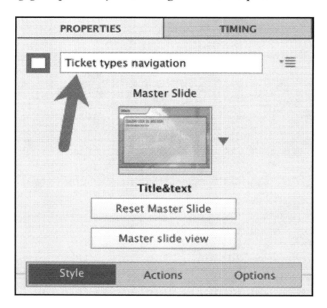

Before continuing with this exercise, look at slide 11 in the **Filmstrip**. Note that the name you gave to the slide appears below the slide thumbnail.

4. Repeat the same operation to give these names to the following slides:
   - Slide 12: `Using standard tickets`
   - Slide 13: `Using passes`
   - Slide 14: `Using subscriptions`
5. Use the **Filmstrip** to return to slide 11.
6. Select the **Using standard tickets** button.
7. In the **Actions** tab of the **Properties** inspector, change the action of the button to **Jump to slide**.
8. Choose slide **12 Using standard tickets** in the **Slide** drop-down menu. The name you gave to the slide makes it easy to select it in the dropdown.
9. Repeat the preceding operation to make the **Using passes** button jump to slide **13 Using passes,** and the **Using subscriptions** button jump to slide **14 Using subscriptions**.
10. Use the **Preview | Next 5 slides** icon on the Toolbar to test your buttons. Make sure they all jump to the correct slide before continuing with the exercise.

During the preview, you will certainly have noticed the rollover and down states of the three buttons that need to be fine-tuned. This will be done later in this chapter.

The first part of the branching is now in place: you can go from the *Navigation* slide (slide 11) to the other three slides of the sequence. Now, you will build the second part of the branching: going back to the *Navigation* slide from the other three slides of the sequence. To do it, you will change the action associated with the On Exit event of each slide.

11. Use the **Filmstrip** to select slide 12 of the current project.
12. With slide 12 selected, go to the **Actions** tab of the **Properties** inspector.
13. Open the **On Exit** drop-down menu and examine the available actions.
14. When ready, choose the **Jump to slide** option.
15. In the **Slide** dropdown, choose the **11 Tickets types navigation** item.
16. Repeat the same sequence of actions with slides 13 and 14.

This operation is illustrated in the following screenshot:

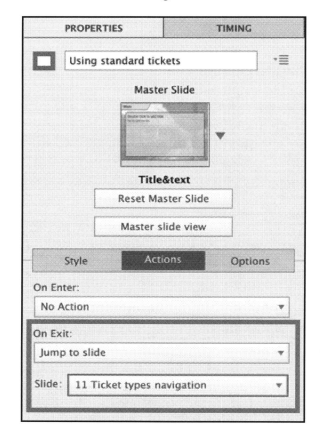

In `Chapter 14`, *Variables and Advanced Actions*, you will add a *Continue* button to the bottom of slide 11 to take the user to slide 15. You will also make sure that this button only appears when the student has seen all three slides (Standard tickets, Passes, and Subscriptions) at least once. But now let's make a quick summary of what has been covered in this section:

- The Button object is one of the interactive objects of Captivate.
- The Button object is able to pause the playhead and wait for the student to interact with the online course.
- When an interactive object is selected, the **Properties** inspector displays the **Actions** tab in addition to the usual **Style** and **Options** tabs.
- The **Actions** tab of the **Properties** inspector is used to define what happens when the Button is clicked.

- Captivate proposes three types of Buttons. These are the **Text Button**, the **Transparent Button,** and the **Image Button**.

- Image Buttons use three different images to create the _up, _over, and _down states of the Button.

- Because the Button stops the playhead, it displays a pause symbol on the **Timeline** panel. The pause symbol in the button represents the exact moment when the playhead is stopped.

- It is possible to convert a Smart Shape into a Button. The **Properties** inspector displays the **Actions** tab when the Smart Shape is selected. Use it to define the action that occurs when the Smart Shape is clicked. Because Smart Shapes are so powerful and flexible, this is the best way of creating buttons in modern versions of Adobe Captivate.

- When using an image as the Fill of a Shape, it is possible to write text on top of the image and to turn it into a button. This advanced technique can be used to turn any image into a button!

Before moving to the next section, take some time to add *Continue* buttons at the end of the slides of your projects, where you think it is appropriate to do so (you can copy/paste the Continue button of slide 3 to go faster). Don't forget to arrange the buttons on the **Timeline** of each slide to determine when the button appears and when it pauses the playhead. Look at the `Chapter05/final/takeTheTrain.cptx` file to see where we have added buttons in our version of the project.

The Button object and the pedagogy

Two of the most important things to keep in mind while teaching are the following: to keep the students focused and to adapt your teaching to each student (the latter is known as **differentiated instruction**). Basically, it means that it is the course that has to adapt to the student and not the other way around (see `http://en.wikipedia.org/wiki/Differentiated_instruction` for more).

The Button object helps you with both of these. While watching a longer sequence, your students' attention will inevitably drift away from the course. Each time you add a button, you make the students active, which helps refresh their attention. Another benefit of the button is that it lets each student manage the timing of the course. If you have a slide with a lot of text, it is important to pause the playhead with a button and let each student read the slide at their own pace.

Working with Text Entry Boxes

The second interactive object covered in this chapter is the **Text Entry Box**. Just like the Button, the Text Entry Box is able to stop the playhead and wait for the user to interact with it. The difference lies in the nature of the interaction. Using a Text Entry Box, the student is expected to *type*.

You will now insert a Text Entry Box on slide 2 to capture the name of the student. Use the following steps to create a Text Entry Box:

1. Use the **Filmstrip** to go to slide 2 of the `Chapter05/takeTheTrain.cptx` file.

2. Use the **Text | Text Entry Box** icon on the toolbar to create a new Text Entry Box. Alternatively, you can use the *command + shift + T* (Mac) or the *Ctrl + Shift + T* (Windows) shortcut to perform the same action.

The Text Entry Box system adds up to five objects to the slide (it is OK if only some of them are displayed on the slide):

- The Text Entry Box itself
- A Success caption
- A Failure caption
- A Hint caption
- A **Submit** button (the **Submit** button is sometimes hidden below the Success Caption)

You will now set up the Text Entry Box so it looks the way you want.

3. Move and resize the Text Entry Box to place it under the **Your name** title.

4. Move the **Submit** button and place it next to the Text Entry Box. Use the green dotted Smart Guides or the Align toolbar to align the objects correctly.

5. With the **Submit** button selected, use the **Style Name** drop-down menu of the **Properties** inspector to apply the **btn_quiz_submit** style to the button.

After this operation, your slide should look like the following screenshot:

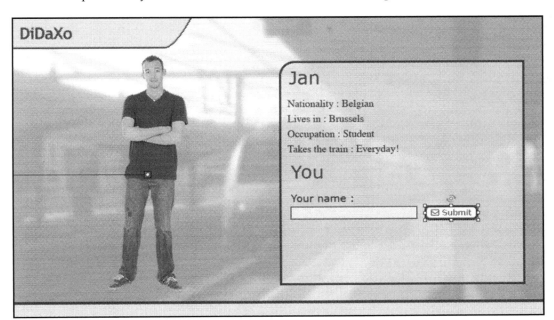

You will now look at the properties of the Text Entry Box object.

6. Select the Text Entry Box and look at the **Style** tab of the **Properties** inspector.
7. Inspect the available properties.
8. When you have finished, select the **Validate User Input** checkbox.

In Captivate, the Text Entry Box object serves two very different purposes. First, it can be used to gather data from the student. In such cases, there is no correct or incorrect answer. What is typed in the Text Entry Box does not need to be validated. But sometimes, you'll use the Text Entry Box to capture a specific answer to a question or to mimic a typing action that requires a precise answer. In these situations, there are correct and incorrect answers. In these instances, what is typed into the Text Entry Box needs to be validated.

When the **Validate User Input** checkbox is selected, the Correct Entries box is displayed. You use this box to specify the list of correct answers. Captivate will compare whatever the student types in the Text Entry Box with this list of answers. If it finds a match, the answer is considered correct; otherwise, the answer is false.

9. Still in the **Properties** inspector, click the **More Options** button. Inspect the additional validation options. Click **Cancel** when done.

10. Switch to the **Actions** tab of the **Properties** inspector and inspect the available options.

11. Select the **Success** and the **Failure** checkboxes.

When the **Validate User Input** checkbox is selected, (in other words, when there are right and wrong answers) it is important to give feedback to the learner. This is the purpose of the Failure and Success captions you just turned on. The Failure Caption is shown to the user after an incorrect answer has been submitted. The Success Caption is displayed after the student submits a correct answer.

In this example, however, the Text Entry Box is used to capture the name of the student, so there are no right or wrong answers. Therefore, you will now deselect the **Validate User Input** checkbox.

12. Return to the **Style** tab of the **Properties** inspector.

13. Deselect the **Validate User Input** checkbox. Note that the Correct Entries window, as well as the Failure and Success captions, disappear from the slide.

14. Return to the **Actions** tab of the **Properties** inspector.

15. Notice that the **Success** and **Failure** checkboxes are grayed out. These two options are only relevant when the **Validate User Input** checkbox is selected.

16. Change the **On Success** action to **Go to the next slide**.

In the **Actions** tab, another important option is the **Shortcut** option. This option lets you choose the keyboard key (or combination) the student can use to submit the Text Entry Box. This **Shortcut** option can be used as an alternative or as a replacement to the **Submit** button when it is removed from the slide. You will learn more about assigning shortcuts to interactive objects in Chapter 13, *Creating Accessible eLearning*.

The next step is to arrange the Text Entry Box on the timeline.

17. If necessary, click the **Timeline** button at the bottom of the screen to open the **Timeline** panel.

On the **Timeline**, the Text Entry Box is represented just like a button. It has a pause symbol that marks the exact moment when the playhead will be paused.

18. On the **Timeline**, move the Text Entry Box so that the pause symbol corresponds more or less to the end of the narration.

After this operation, the **Timeline** of slide 2 should look like the following screenshot:

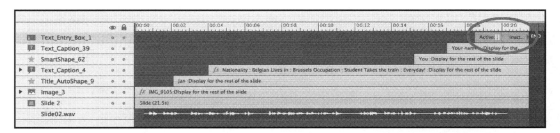

Use the **Preview | Next 5 slides** icon on the toolbar to test your slide. When the Text Entry Box appears, the playhead pauses to let you type your name. When you submit your name, the playhead jumps to the next slide and the course continues.

In Chapter 14, *Variables and Advanced Actions*, use the student name to create a custom welcome message. But for now, let's summarize what you have learned about the Text Entry Box:

- Just like a button, a Text Entry Box is able to stop the playhead and wait for the student to interact.
- When using Text Entry Boxes, you can decide whether the text entered by the student must be validated.
- If you decide to validate the text, you can define **Success** and/or **Failure** captions to give feedback to the student.
- If the **Validate User Input** checkbox is selected, you must also provide the correct answer(s) in the **Correct Entries** box.
- If the **Validate User Input** checkbox is not selected, the Text Entry Box is used to capture a piece of data. In that case, you want to store that data in a variable for later use.

Working with multi-state objects

In Adobe Captivate, objects can have multiple states. This feature allows you to define some sophisticated interactivity and interface effects without any programming. In this section, you will explore some of the possibilities offered by multi-state objects and discuss a few typical use cases.

Working with the built-in states of buttons

The multi-states feature allows you to define the rollover, down, and visited states of your buttons. This is what you will explore using the following steps:

1. Use the **Filmstrip** to go to slide 4 of the `Chapter05/takeTheTrain.cptx` file.
2. Select the **Continue** button in the lower-right corner of the slide. Remember that this button is a rounded rectangle Smart Shape used as a button.
3. At the top of the **Properties** inspector, click the **State View** button.

This action opens the State View of the selected button. All the objects of the slide are dimmed, except the selected **Continue** button you are viewing the states of.

Also notice that the Filmstrip panel is now the **Object State** panel. It displays the three built-in states of the selected button. This is shown in the following screenshot:

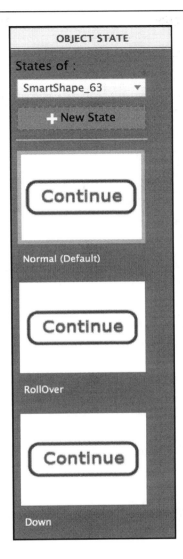

These three states are as follows:

- The **Normal** state is the initial Default state. (You can set any other custom state as default by right-clicking the state thumbnail). It defines the normal look of the Continue button when the student is not interacting with it.
- The **RollOver** state defines the look of the button when the student rolls the mouse over the button. When the student removes the mouse from the button, it reverts to the Normal state.

- The **Down** state defines the look of the button when the student has the mouse on top of the button and when the mouse button is held down. The button action occurs when the student releases the mouse button.

You will now slightly modify the **RollOver** and the **Down** states of the **Continue** button to create a nice effect.

4. In the **Object State** panel, click the **RollOver** state to select it.
5. Change the **Stroke** color to a lighter shade of blue.

When defining the RollOver state of a button, one subtle change such as the one you just applied is usually more than enough to produce the desired effect.

Now, you will define the Down state. But you would like to start from the current look of the RollOver state to define it. So, you will delete the current Down state and recreate it based on the current Rollover state using the following steps.

6. In the **Object State** panel, right-click the **Down** state of the button.
7. Click the **Delete State** menu item. Confirm your intention in the dialog that appears.
8. Next, right-click the **RollOver** state and choose **Duplicate State** in the contextual menu.
9. In the box that appears, choose **Inbuilt State** in the first drop-down list and **Down** in the second, as shown in the following screenshot.
10. Click the **OK** button to create the new Down state:

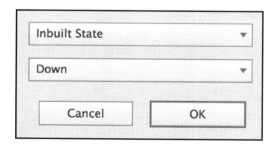

You will now slightly modify the Down state of the button to make it unique.

11. In the **Object State** panel, select the **Down** state.

12. Use the **Properties** inspector to change the font **Color** to the same shade of blue you used for the Stroke on the RollOver state (the recently used colors are available at the bottom of the color picker).

Now that you have defined the three states of the Continue button, you can exit the State View and test your work in the Preview pane using the following steps.

13. On the Toolbar, click the **Exit State** button (the last one with the large Red X) to return to the regular Captivate interface.

14. Use the **Preview | Next 5 slides** icon to preview your changes in the **Preview** pane.

When the **Continue** button appears, notice that the Normal state of the button is displayed by default. When you hover your mouse over the button, the RollOver state is displayed. And when you press and hold the mouse button, the Down state is displayed. The *Go to the next slide* action is triggered when you release your mouse button.

Keep in mind that you always test your projects on a computer (desktop or laptop). The button states will not behave the same way on a touch device (Table or Smartphone). On such devices, the RollOver state is not visible. The Down state is briefly displayed whenever the student taps the button.

15. Close the **Preview** pane when you have finished. Make sure the **Continue** button is still selected on the slide.

16. In the topmost section of the **Properties** inspector, open the **Normal (Default)** drop-down menu.

17. Choose the **RollOver** state in the list of available states.

This action displays the **RollOver** state on the slide. Use this drop-down menu to adjust the state using the tools of the **Properties** inspector without switching to the states view. Still in the **Properties** inspector, notice the **+** icon next to the state list. It allows you to create new states for the selected object. Also notice the trash icon, which allows you to delete the selected state.

18. In the topmost section of the **Properties** inspector, open the **RollOver** drop-down menu.

19. Choose **Normal (Default)** to return to the initial state of the button.

This exercise concludes your first approach to multi-state objects in Captivate.

Working with the Visited state

In this section, you will discover one additional built-in state available on buttons. This will help you apply the finishing touches to slide 11 using the following steps:

1. Use the **Filmstrip** to go to slide 11 of the `takeTheTrain.cptx` file. Remember that this is the slide you use as the navigation slide of the *Types of tickets* sequence.

 If you did not succeed in creating the button of slide 11 as described in the previous section, you will find a copy of the finished slide in the `Chapter05/slide11.cptx` file. Simply copy and paste that slide as slide 11 of your `takeTheTrain.cptx` project. When doing so, make sure to apply the correct Master Slide to the newly imported slide. Also make sure to correct the action to the three buttons. Refer to the *Branching with Buttons* section earlier in this chapter for precise instructions.

2. Select the **Using Standard Ticket** button (remember that if the object is a rectangle shape, the image is the fill of the rectangle).
3. At the top of the **Properties** inspector, click the **State View** button to switch to the state view.

Captivate has already created the default three states for this button. But, in this particular instance, the Rollover and Down states are not needed. You will need to delete these two states. Then, you will add the Visited state using the following steps.

4. In the **Object State** panel, right-click the **RollOver** state and delete it. Repeat this operation with the **Down** state.
5. At the top of the **Object State** panel, click the **New State** button. This is one of the many ways to create a new state.
6. In the box that appears, choose **Inbuilt State** in the first dropdown and **Visited** in the second.
7. Click **OK** to validate and create the **Visited** state.
8. With the new **Visited** state selected in the **Object State** panel, use the **Media | Image** icon of the Toolbar to insert a new image.
9. Browse to the `Chapter05/images/check.png` image to insert it in the **Visited** state of the transparent button.
10. Move, resize, and rotate the `check.png` image to place it in the top-right corner of the **Using Standard Ticket** button.

This exercise illustrates how you can add extra objects to the states of another one. In this case, the object you are changing the state of is the **Using Standard Tickets** button. The green checkmark is an additional object that will show only when the visited state of the button is displayed. Take some time to inspect the icons available on the main Toolbar. Notice that you can add most of the standard objects of Captivate. But you cannot add any of the interactive objects when in the states view.

Make sure the Visited state looks like the following screenshot before moving on with the exercise:

Before exiting the state view, notice the blue outline around the **Using Standards Tickets** button. This blue outline identifies the object you are viewing the states of. The green checkmark is surrounded by a red outline. This red outline identifies the extra object(s) added to the selected state.

You will now exit the State View and test your work in the Preview pane using the following steps.

11. Click the **Exit State** icon on the Toolbar to return to the default Captivate interface.
12. Use the **Preview** | **Next 5 slides** icon on the Toolbar to test your sequence.

In the **Preview** pane, click the **Using Standard Tickets** button. This takes you to slide 12. At the end of slide 12, you are brought back to slide 11, but the visited state of the button is not showing!

This is because Captivate forgets about the button states when going to another slide, unless you complete the following steps.

13. Close the **Preview** pane and return to slide 11.
14. Make sure the **Using Standard Tickets** button is selected.
15. In the topmost area of the **Properties** inspector, select the **Retain State on Slide Revisit** checkbox.
16. When you have finished, use the **Preview | Next 5 slides** icon on the Toolbar again to test your sequence. Confirm it works as expected before moving on.

The **Visited** state of the button now produces the desired effect. It adds a green check when a particular slide has been viewed. Your next task is to repeat the same sequence of actions on the remaining two buttons.

Creating the Visited state of the other buttons

In this section, you will repeat the actions of the previous exercise on the remaining two buttons. The general steps are as follows:

- First, you must select the button you want to modify the states of.
- Switch to the states view and delete the unnecessary states.
- Create the Visited state and import the green check image. (This image is now available in the Library. No need to import it a second time!)
- Return to the default Captivate interface, and don't forget to select the **Retain State on Slide Revisit** checkbox.
- When this is done for both buttons, save your file and give it a try in the **Preview** pane.

Working with custom states

In the previous two sections, you discovered the built-in states of the Button object. In this section, you will go one huge step further and add your own custom states to any object. This makes it incredibly easy to create complex interactions that are entirely compatible with any device, using either Flash or HTML 5.

In the next exercise, you will use custom states to create a complex interaction with the map of Belgium on slide 5 of your project. This slide contains five blue dots on top of the map of Belgium. When the student clicks a blue dot, more information about the selected train station should be displayed on the right side of the slide. To make it easier to know which blue dot to use, they will be numbered from **1** to **5**, as shown in the following screenshot:

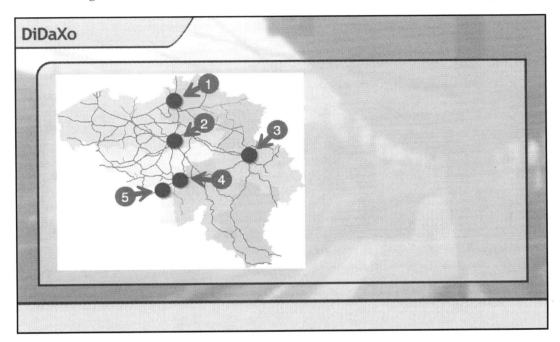

Creating the custom states

Use the following steps to create the necessary custom states:

1. Use the **Filmstrip** to go to slide 5 of the `Chapter05/takeTheTrain.cptx` project.
2. Select the map of Belgium image.
3. At the top of the **Properties** inspector, give the selected image the following name: `img_belgium`. Don't forget to hit the *Enter* key to confirm the new name.

Captivate allows you to name any object. Naming objects this way is not technically required, but it is a best practice and will make it much simpler later in the process.

4. With the map of Belgium image still selected, click the **State View** button in the upper section of the **Properties** inspector.

This action takes you to the State View of the selected image. Notice that Captivate has not created any default built-in states. Only some Interactive objects (such as Buttons) have built-in states. You will now add five custom states to your image, one for each blue dot, using the following steps.

5. In the **Object State** panel, click the **New State** button.
6. In the box that appears, give your new state the following name: Antwerpen.
7. Click **OK** to validate and create the new custom state.
8. With the new **Antwerpen** state selected in the **Object State** panel, use the **Text | Text Caption** icon to insert a new Text Caption in the selected state.
9. Type Antwerpen Centraal in the Text Caption.
10. Hit the *Esc* key to exit the text edit mode and select the Text Caption as an object.
11. In the **Properties** inspector, increase the font size to 24 and make the text bold.
12. Move and resize the Text Caption to place it in the upper area of the right-hand side of the slide.
13. Still in the **Antwerpen** state, add a second Text Caption below the first one.
14. Write the following text in the new Text Caption: This station has been nominated among the most beautiful train stations in the world.

The **Antwerpen** state of your image is now ready. The state should look like the following screenshot:

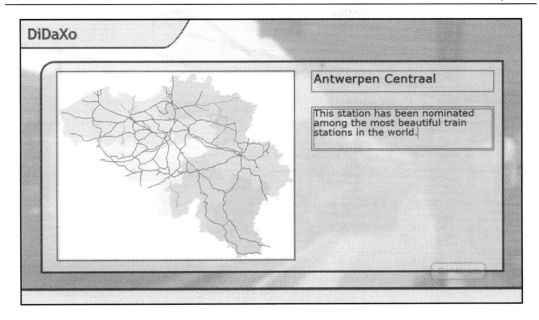

You will now use the same procedure to create the remaining four custom states. Use the following table to add content to the states:

Aligning content across states

To place the title and the description for the Text Captions at exactly the same location on every state, here is a very simple trick: Instead of creating new states, right-click an existing state and duplicate it. Then, simply update the title and the description text. This will not only speed up your work, but also ensure proper alignment across the custom states you create.

State name	Title	Description
Brussels	Brussels Centraal	This underground station was designed by world-famous architect Victor Horta.
Liege	Liege Guillemins	This brand-new station was designed by Spanish architect Santiago Calatrava. The grand opening took place on December 18, 2009.
Charleroi	Charleroi-sud	This 1847 building was entirely renovated in 2011. It now provides all the services of a modern station, while maintaining its historical character.
Thuin	Thuin	This rural station is unattended. Only local trains stop here. There is nothing special about it, except this is where I live!

After this process, you should have five custom states in addition to the **Normal (Default)** state on the map of Belgium image.

Using Buttons to change the state of an object

Now that the five custom states exist, you will use the five blue dots as buttons to change the state of the **img_belgium** image using the following steps:

1. If necessary, click the **Exit State** button on the Toolbar to return to the default interface.
2. Select the topmost blue dot (marked as **1** on the previous screenshot). Remember that this blue dot is a Smart Shape.
3. In the **Properties** inspector, notice that the **Use as Button** checkbox is selected and that an **Actions** tab is present.
4. Switch to the **Actions** tab of the **Properties** inspector.
5. Change the **On Success** action to **Change State Of**.
6. Select the **img_belgium** object in the next drop-down menu and the **Antwerpen** state in the last one.
7. If necessary, deselect the **Continue Playing the Project** checkbox.

This last step is very important. If you do not deselect the **Continue Playing the Project** checkbox, the button will release the playhead in addition to changing the state of the **img_belgium** object. In this example, you already have a **Continue** button at the bottom-right corner of the slide that is taking care of pausing and releasing the playhead, so the blue circle shapes should not interact with the playhead at all.

The **Actions** tab of the **Properties** inspector should look like the following screenshot:

Now, the rest of the process is very simple. Just repeat the preceding sequence of actions to link each blue dot to the corresponding state of the image:

- Blue dot **2** goes to the **Brussels** state.
- Blue dot **3** goes to the **Liege** state.
- Blue dot **4** goes to the **Charleroi** state.
- Blue dot **5** goes to the **Thuin** state.

When you have finished, use the **Preview** | **Next 5 slides** icon on the Toolbar to test your work. Make sure each button takes you to the correct state before moving to the next section.

Customizing the Normal (Default) state

By default, each object of Captivate has a single state called the *Normal (Default)* state. Using the State View of Captivate, this *Normal (Default)* state can be customized as well. In this extra credit section, you will add a Character image and a callout Smart Shape to the *Normal (Default)* state of the *map_belgium* image. The general steps are as follows:

- Return to the **State View** of the **map_belgium** image and select the **Normal (Default)** state.
- Add a Character image of your liking to the right-hand side of the slide.
- Also add a callout Smart Shape. Write `Click the blue dots to see more information on the corresponding station`. Arrange the callout so it points at the Character image.
- Exit the **State View** to return to the default Captivate interface.

Because you have added these two objects to the *Normal (Default)* state of your image, they will disappear and be replaced by the content of the other states whenever the student clicks a blue dot. The following screenshot shows what we have done with the Normal (Default) state of this image:

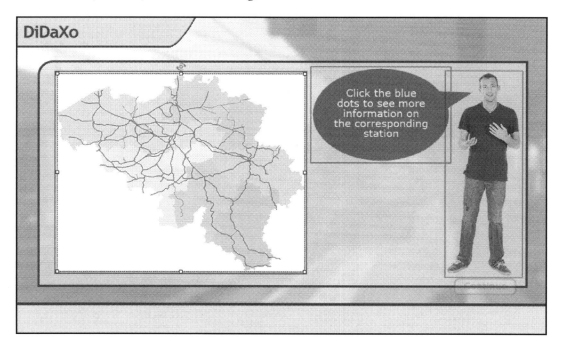

Working with the Go to Next State action

In this section, you will explore another use case for multi-state objects. The goal is to show you how diverse and flexible this feature is. To illustrate this use case, you will work on slide 7. You will add an image, define multiple custom states, and use the **Go to Next State** action to create another interesting interaction.

The steps are as follows:

1. Use the **Filmstrip** to go to slide 7 of the `Chapter05/takeTheTrain.cptx` file.

2. Use the **Media | Image** icon on the toolbar to insert the `Chapter05/images/scheduleDetail.png` image file.

3. Move and resize the image so it fits in the center of the slide. To speed up your work and make it easier, use the tools covered earlier (such as the Align toolbar, the Smart Guides, holding down the *Shift* key while resizing the images, and so on).

4. With the image selected, use the **Properties** inspector to give it the following name: `img_scheduleDetail`.

5. If there is no **Continue** button in the bottom-right corner of the slide, add one now (you can copy and paste the Continue button of another slide to go faster). Use the **Timeline** to make it pause the playhead when the narration finishes.

6. With the **Continue** button selected, use the *command + D* (Mac) / *Ctrl + D* (Windows) shortcut key to duplicate it.

7. Place the second **Continue** button to the left of the first one and change the label to *Next*.

8. On the **Timeline**, arrange the timing of the objects as you see fit. Just make sure that the `scheduleDetail.png` image stays visible for the entire duration of the slide, and that the buttons pause the playhead after the narration is finished.

Make sure the slide looks like the following screenshot before continuing with the exercise:

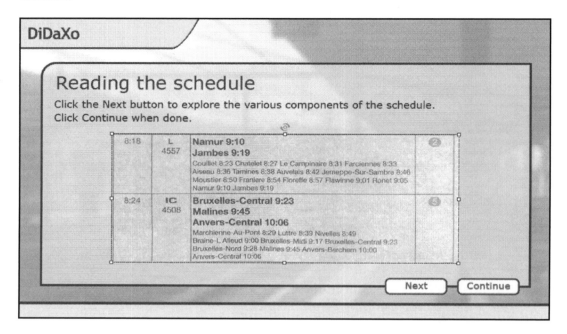

Now that the stage is set, you will define several custom states on the image and use the button to let the user circle through these states. Use the following steps to create the necessary states.

9. Select the **img_scheduleDetail** image. At the top of the **Properties** inspector, click the **State View** button to switch to the State view interface.

10. Right-click the **Normal (Default)** state and choose the **Add State** menu item. This is another way of creating a new state in the **State View** interface.

11. In the popup window, name the new state hour and click the **OK** button.

12. While in the hour state, use the **Shapes** icon of the toolbar to draw a rounded rectangle around the **8:18** text on top of the first column of the schedule image.

13. Use the **Style Name** drop-down menu to apply the **shape_As_HB** style to the rounded rectangle.

14. Use the **Shapes** icon of the toolbar again to draw a rounded rectangle callout shape on the image. Make it point to the rounded rectangle you drew in the previous step.

15. Apply the **alternate_Shape** style to that new shape.
16. Type `The departure time of the train` in the rounded rectangle callout.
17. Move and resize the shapes so the hour state looks like the following screenshot:

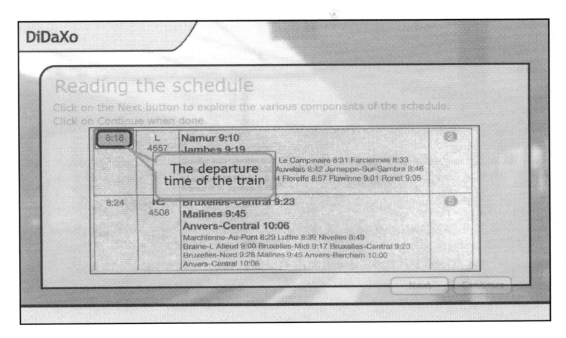

Repeat the preceding actions to create three additional states. Use the following table to add the proper content and shapes to the remaining states:

State name	Blue shape position	Callout text
typeNumber	Second column, on top of **L 4557**	The train type and number
destinations	Third column (on top of the list of destinations)	Destinations Main destinations in bold Other destinations in regular
platform	Last column (on top of the number 2)	Departure platform

After this process, you should have four custom states in addition to the **Normal (Default)** state. You will now return to the default interface of Captivate and apply the required action to the **Next** button.

18. Click the **Exit State** button on the Toolbar to return to the standard Captivate interface.

19. Select the **Next** button in the bottom-right corner of the slide.

20. In the **Actions** tab of the **Properties** inspector, change the **On Success** action to **Go to Next State**. Make sure the `img_scheduleDetails` image is selected in the drop-down menu that appears just below.

21. Deselect the **Continue Playing the Project** checkbox to prevent the **Next** button from releasing the playhead.

A new interaction is now in place. It is time to test your work using the **Preview | Next 5 slides** icon on the Toolbar.

Before moving to the next section, here is a quick summary of what you have learned about multi-state objects in this section:

- Captivate allows you to define multiple states on (almost) any object.
- Some objects, such as Buttons, Smart Shapes used as buttons, and so on, have predefined built-in states. These define RollOver effects, Down effects, and more.
- The Visited state allows you to define a state for the buttons that have been clicked.
- Select the **Retain State on Slide Revisit** checkbox to maintain the visited state even if you jump to other slides and come back.
- Click the **State View** button of the **Properties** inspector, or use the state drop-down list to see the states on the stage and edit them.
- When in State View, click the **Exit State** button on the toolbar to return to the default interface.
- You can define any number of custom states and make them look the way you want.
- You can add extra objects (such as Shapes, Text Captions, images, and so on) to the states of an object.
- You can use the **Change State of**, the **Go To Next State**, or the **Go To Previous State** actions with any button. This allows you to define interesting interactions without any programming.
- To make defining these interactions easier, don't forget to give names to your objects and slides. This is a good habit to get into and makes complex interactions easier to assemble.

Working with Drag and Drop interactions

In this section, you will explore some of the amazing possibilities of the **Drag and Drop** interaction. Drag and Drop requires at least two objects. One serves as the **Drag Source** and the second as the **Drop Target**:

- The Drag Source is the object that the student can drag
- The Drop Target is the object on which a Drag Source can be dropped

It does not matter what those objects are, as long as they are not interactive. In the following example, you will use images as both the Drag Source and the Drop Target, but you could as well use Text Captions, Highlight Boxes, Smart Shapes, and so on.

To make things more interesting, a single slide can contain multiple Drag Sources and multiple Drop Targets. Thanks to this capability, you are able to create complex and fun interactions. Best of all, Drag and Drop is supported in both Flash and HTML5.

Using the Drag and Drop Interaction wizard

For this first example, you will create a simple Drag and Drop. The goal is to ask your students which train car they can board with a second-class ticket. They have to drag the ticket on top of the car they can board. To create this, you will use the Drag and Drop interaction wizard using the following steps:

1. Use the **Filmstrip** to navigate to slide 19 of the Chapter05/takeTheTrain.cptx project.
2. Use the **Interactions | Drag and Drop** icon on the Toolbar to start defining your Drag and Drop.

The Drag and Drop Interaction wizard is a three-step process that helps you define a simple Drag and Drop. In the first step, you have to select the Drag Source(s). In this case, there is only one Drag Source, which is the image of the train ticket.

3. Click the image of the train ticket to select it as a drag source. This adds a green outline around the image to indicate that it is selected as a Drag Source. If you made a mistake and selected the wrong object, use the red *minus* sign in the top-right corner of the object to remove the object from the selection.
4. Click the **Next** button at the top of the screen to go to the second step of the wizard.

In the second step of the wizard, you have to select the Drop Target(s). In this example, the two train car images are the Drop Targets.

5. Click the two train car images to mark them as Drop Targets. A blue outline is used to identify the Drop Targets.
6. Click the **Next** Button at the top of the screen to go to the last step of the wizard.

The last step of the wizard is used to associate the Drag Source(s) with the matching Drop Target(s). In this example, you want to associate the train ticket with the train car on the right (because it is a second-class train car).

7. Select the image of the train ticket and notice the arrow icon in the middle of the image.
8. Click and drag an arrow from that icon to the image of the train car in the top-right corner of the slide.

You can use the lock feature of the **Timeline** panel to ensure that you don't accidentally move the images themselves.

Make sure your slide looks like the following screenshot before you click the **Finish** button at the top of the screen:

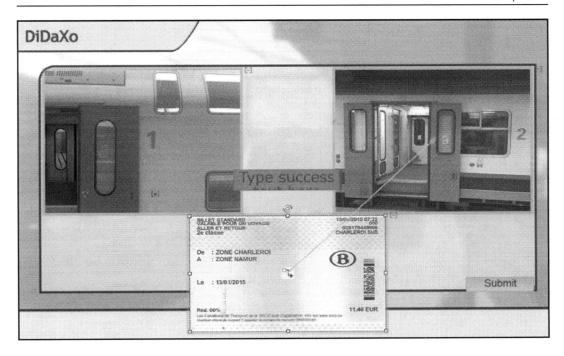

And now, the finishing touches are applied.

9. Move the green Success Caption that sits in the middle of the slide to reveal the red Failure Caption that is hidden underneath.

10. Type `Attention! You entered a first class coach with a second class ticket!!!` in the red Failure Caption. When you have finished, hit the *Esc* key to leave the text-editing mode and select the object.

11. Move and resize the Failure Caption so it sits in the middle of the slide.

12. Use the same process to write `Great! You are ready to discover Belgium by train.` in the green success caption.

13. Move and resize the success caption so it sits in the middle of the slide.

When moving and sizing the success and the failure captions, don't forget that these two messages will never be displayed together. The success caption is displayed when the student provides the correct answer and the failure caption, when the student provides the wrong answer. Therefore, it's perfectly fine if these two objects overlap on the slide.

14. Save the file and use the **Preview** | **Next 5 slides** icon to test your first Drag and Drop interaction.

In the **Preview** pane, drag the train ticket onto one of the two train cars. Hit the **Submit** button in the bottom-right corner of the slide and make sure the right feedback is displayed.

Congratulations! You have created your first Drag and Drop interaction with Captivate! It is not yet perfect, but your students will certainly enjoy this high level of interactivity.

Using the Drag and Drop panel

The power of the Drag and Drop interaction goes way beyond this first example. In the next exercise, you will explore the **Drag and Drop** inspector and use it to fine-tune the Drag and Drop you created in the previous section:

1. Make sure you are on slide 19 of the `Chapter05/taketheTrain.cptx` project.
2. Select the train ticket image.
3. Open the **Drag And Drop** inspector. It is located on the right edge of the screen, next to the **Properties** inspector and the **Timing** panel.

 If the **Drag and Drop** inspector is not visible, use the **Window** | **Drag and Drop** to display it.

The **Drag and Drop** inspector contains the options pertaining to the Drag and Drop interaction. The Drag and Drop Interaction wizard you used in the previous section only gives you access to a small subset of these options. The **Drag and Drop** inspector is divided into three tabs. At the very top of the **Drag and Drop** inspector, notice the trashcan icon that allows you to delete the Drag and Drop interaction if needed.

4. If you do not see the Drag and Drop interaction on the slide, click the eye icon at the top of the **Drag And Drop** inspector. This removes the red line and displays the Drag and Drop on the stage.
5. In the **Actions** tab of the **Drag and Drop** inspector, select the **Infinite Attempts** checkbox. This gives your students unlimited attempts to find the correct answer.

6. Select the **Reset All** radio button. This will move the Drag Sources back to their original locations when a wrong answer is submitted.

7. Also select the **Auto Submit Correct Answers** checkbox.

8. Select the second class coach image located in the upper-right corner of the slide.

9. Switch to the **Format** tab of the **Drag and Drop** inspector.

10. At the bottom of the **Format** tab of the **Drag and Drop** inspector, change the **Size** to 0% and the **Opacity** to 0%.

These two options change the size and the opacity of the drag source (in this case the ticket image) when it is dropped on the selected drop target. This will make the train ticket disappear into the coach image.

11. Select the first class coach image situated in the upper-left area of the slide.

12. In the **Format** tab of the **Drag and Drop** inspector, click the **Object Actions...** button.

13. In the **Accepted Drag Sources** dialog, deselect the **Image_65** entry.

14. Click the **OK** button to validate and close the dialog.

Image_65 is the image of the train ticket. Remember that this object is the only drag source of the current Drag and Drop interaction. In the previous step, you told the first class coach image (which is a drop target) that it should not accept the train ticket drag source. Consequently, the train ticket will only be accepted by the second class coach image (in the upper-right corner). Another consequence of the options you have set in this section is that the Submit button is no longer needed. Unfortunately, you cannot delete the Submit button, as it is a required part of any Drag and Drop interaction. But... there is a trick.

15. Select the **Submit** button at the bottom-right corner of the slide.

16. Move the submit button in the scrap area (the dark-grey area around the slide). This makes the button invisible to the student taking the course without needing to delete it.

17. Move the **Submit** button in place, to a location that you like at the bottom right of the slide.

18. Take some time to examine the other options of the **Drag and Drop** inspector before moving on.

19. Save the file and use the **Preview | Next 5 Slides** icon on the Toolbar to test your updated Drag and Drop.

When testing your interaction, try to drag the train ticket on top of the first class coach image. Captivate should not let you drop the train ticket at this location. Then, try to drop the ticket image on top of the second class coach image in the top-right area of the slide. You should see the ticket *disappearing* into the coach image before the green feedback message is displayed on the screen. With this setup, you will never see the red failure message.

Drag and Drop extravaganza

The exercise you just performed shows you the typical use case of a simple Drag and Drop interaction, but the true power of Drag and Drop goes way beyond this sole example. For a comprehensive overview of the Drag and Drop interaction feature of Captivate, don't hesitate to look at the following `lynda.com` course with Dr Pooja Jaisingh:

`https://www.lynda.com/Captivate-tutorials/Captivate-Project`
`s-Drag-Drop-Interactions/187496-2.html`.

Customizing the feedback messages

There are two feedback messages associated with the Drag and Drop interaction: The Success Caption and the Failure Caption (with the currently selected options, only the success caption will ever be displayed). These types of messages can also be associated with other interactive objects, such as Buttons, Click Boxes, Text Entry Boxes, and Quiz slides. Sometimes, a third feedback message (called the Hint caption) can be added, though this is not the case for the Drag and Drop interaction you are currently working with:

- The **Success Caption** shows only if the student submits the correct answer or performs the correct action.
- The **Failure Caption** shows only if the student submits the wrong answer or performs the wrong action.
- The **Hint Caption** shows when the student rolls the mouse over an interactive object (such as a Click Box, a Text Entry Box, or a Button).

In Captivate 2019, these feedback messages are based on the Smart Shape object. It means that they have the same formatting capabilities as a regular Smart Shape. You will now experiment with these feedback messages using the following steps:

1. Still on slide 19 of the `Chapter05/takeTheTrain.cptx` file, go to the **Actions** tab of the **Drag and Drop** inspector.
2. Deselect the **Failure Caption** checkbox to remove the red failure caption from the stage.
3. Select the green Success Caption.
4. Look at the **Properties** inspector and take good note of the available properties. These are the same as for a Smart Shape.
5. Right-click the green Success Caption and choose the **Replace Smart Shape** menu item.
6. In the list of available shapes, choose any shape of your liking.

By default, such a feedback message is based on the rounded rectangle Smart Shape. This exercise demonstrates the ability to use any of the available shapes of Adobe Captivate as a feedback message.

7. With the green feedback message still selected, click the **State View** button at the top of the **Properties** inspector.

This action takes you to the State View of the Success Caption. Notice that the usual **Normal (Default)** state is already available. But if you try to click the **New State** button at the top of the **Object State** panel, nothing happens! This is because you cannot add additional states to those feedback messages. But you can customize the **Normal (Default)** state!

8. Click the **Library** icon at the far right of the Toolbar to open the project library.
9. In the **Images** section of the **Library**, locate the **check.png** image.
10. Drag the **check.png** image from the **Library** panel to the **Normal (Default)** state of your Success Caption.
11. Move and resize the green checkmark as per your requirements.

At the end of this exercise, the normal (default) state of your success caption should look like the following screenshot:

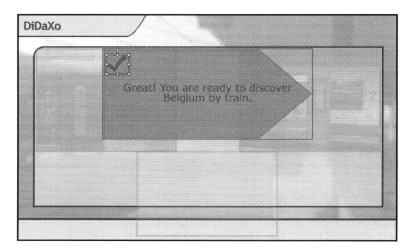

12. Click the **Exit State** button on the Toolbar to return to the default interface.
13. Use the **Preview | Next 5 slides** icon of the Toolbar to give your Drag and Drop interaction another try. Confirm that the green success caption displays as expected, before moving on to the next section.

In this section, you have customized the green Success Caption associated with the Drag and Drop defined in the previous section. Here is a summary of what you have learned:

- Captivate provides automatic feedback messages for a lot of interactive objects and features. This includes buttons, click boxes, text-entry boxes, drag and drops, and quiz slides.
- These feedback messages can be Success Captions, Failure Captions, Hint Captions, and so on. Note that the available messages depend on the interactive object being used and the settings of the drag and drop.
- By default, these feedback messages are based on the rounded Rectangle Smart Shape, but you can right-click a feedback message and choose the **Replace Smart Shape** menu item to choose which shape to use.
- Only the **Normal (Default)** state is available on those messages.
- You can use the **State View** button of the **Properties** inspector to access the **Normal (Default)** state and further customize the feedback messages.

Working with Interactive Video

Back in Chapter 03, *Working with Multimedia*, you inserted a video file on slide 20 of your takeTheTrain.cptx project. In this section, you will use some of the newest features of Adobe Captivate to turn this video file into an interactive experience. In Captivate 2019, there are two things you can do to make a video interactive:

- You can add bookmarks on the video. These bookmarks act as destination points for the playhead. You can, for example, use an action to jump the playhead to a certain bookmark. This allows you to play the video from a very precise point rather than from the beginning of the file.
- You can also add overlay slides on top of the video. This is typically used to pause the playback of the video at a certain point and overlay extra information, interactions, or a Question Slide right within the playback of the video file.

The Interactive Video feature is only supported in HTML5. It is very interesting to see that the newest features of Captivate are being developed in HTML5 only and do not work in the legacy Flash format. This tells a long story about where the product is heading to. It also reminds us that nowadays, only HTML5 publishing should be considered.

Inserting an interactive video

When you inserted the video, back in Chapter 3, *Working with Multimedia*, you learned that you can insert videos as either Event Videos or Slide Videos. The main difference between the two types of video is that the Slide Video is synchronized with the project. When it comes to making a video interactive, Captivate must be able to control the video. For example, Captivate must be able to jump to a certain place on the video, or to overlay a specific slide at a predefined timecode of the video. The only type of video that Captivate can control in such ways is the Slide Video, so only Slide Videos can be made interactive.

Let's now explore the different ways to insert such a video on a slide:

1. Still in the Chapter05/takeTheTrain.cptx project, use the **Filmstrip** to go to slide 20.
2. Use the **Video | Insert Video** menu item to insert a video file on the current slide.

3. At the top of the **Insert Video** dialog, choose to insert a **Slide Video**.

At this point, Captivate should warn you that a Slide Video is already present on slide 20 and that there can only be one Slide Video per slide. The action you are currently requesting is therefore not possible.

4. Click the **OK** button to acknowledge the message.
5. Click the **Cancel** button to close the **Insert Video** dialog.

In order to review the process of inserting a Slide Video in Captivate, you need to be on a slide that does not already contain a Slide Video.

6. Use the **Slide | Blank Slide** icon of the Toolbar to insert a new slide based on the Blank master slide of the theme. This new slide is inserted as slide 21 of the project.
7. Now, use the **Media | Video** icon on the Toolbar, or the **Video | Insert Video** menu item to reopen the **Insert Video** dialog.
8. At the top of the **Insert Video** dialog, choose to insert a **Slide Video**.

Take some time to reinspect the available options. Remember that the video can be a file stored on your computer or a YouTube video. Also remember that you can insert this type of video on the stage or in the table of content of the project. Finally, you have some options to control the duration of the slide on which you add the video. These options are shown in the following screenshot:

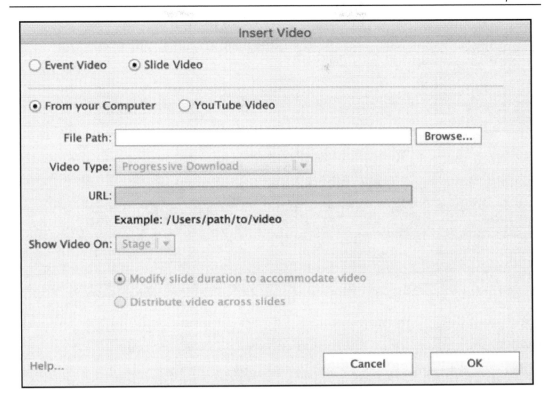

Adobe Captivate 2019 has a simplified workflow for inserting interactive video. Let's explore this new workflow using the following steps.

9. Click **Cancel** to close the **Insert Video** dialog.
10. Click the **Interactive Video** icon on the Toolbar.

The dialog that opens is a simplified version of the **Insert Video** dialog. It only gives you access to the options pertaining to inserting Interactive Videos. The other options are set automatically and are therefore not available in this version of the **Insert Video** dialog:

- Only Slide Videos can be made interactive, so the corresponding option is not present in this version of the **Insert Video** dialog.
- The video can only be inserted on the stage, so this option is also not present in this version of the **Insert Video** dialog.
- If the duration of the slide is shorter than the duration of the video, the duration of the slide will be increased in order to match the duration of the video.

The options available in this version of the Insert Video dialog are illustrated in the following screenshot. Notice that two additional options allow you to choose the **Start time** and the **End time** of the video:

In your project, you already inserted a Slide Video that can be made interactive on slide 20. Slide 21 is therefore not needed and can be safely removed.

11. Click **Cancel** to close the **Insert Video** dialog.
12. In the **Filmstrip**, right-click slide 21 and choose **Delete** in the contextual menu.
13. Confirm your intention to delete the slide.
14. Use the **Filmstrip** to return to slide 20.

In this section, you have learned how to insert a video on a slide so that it can be made interactive. In the next section, you will insert bookmarks on the Interactive Video.

Working with Bookmarks

Now that the video has been inserted in the project, you can start the process of adding interactive features to the video. In this section, you will start by adding bookmarks. In the next section, you will use these bookmarks to generate the needed interactions:

1. Make sure you are still on slide 20 of the Chapter05/takeTheTrain.cptx file.

2. If needed, open the **Timeline** panel at the bottom of the screen.

3. Use the play icon in the bottom-left corner of the **Timeline** panel to play the slide.

4. Pause the video just before you hear the train attendant whistling (around the 5.5 second mark on the **Timeline**).

The current location of the red Playhead is where you want to add the first bookmark. To do so, turn your attention to the Playhead in the **Timeline** panel. As shown on the following screenshot, two extra layers have been added to the **Timeline**: the **Bookmark** and the **Overlay** layers:

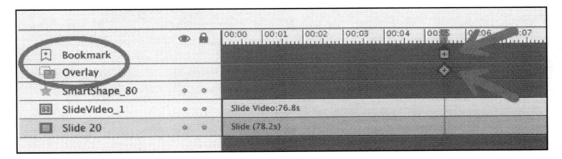

There are also two extra buttons on the playhead: a little square with a **+** sign to add a Bookmark at the playhead location, and a little diamond with a **+** sign to add an Overlay Slide at the playhead location (see the arrows in the preceding screenshot).

5. Click the square with a **+** sign to add a Bookmark at the current location of the playhead.

6. Name the bookmark `whistle` and press the `Enter` key to confirm the name.

You have created a first bookmark on your video file. This bookmark has a name (**whistle**) and a location (around the 5.5 second mark on the **Timeline**). You will now use the very same procedure to create three more bookmarks using the following table as a guide:

Timecode	Video narration	Bookmark name
44 sec	The train attendant now triggers the departure procedure...	trigger
56 sec	After a few seconds...	departure
1 min 09 sec	But if you made it on time	enjoy

You can also check the exact timecode of the red playhead at the bottom of the **Timeline**, next to the Zoom slider.

Now that you have added some bookmarks, you will test your video and see whether anything has changed when playing the project.

7. Still on slide 20 of the `Chapter05/takeTheTrain.cptx` project, use the **Preview** | **Next 5 slides** icon on the Toolbar to test your video file.

When viewing the project, you should not see any difference, despite the fact that you have added bookmarks on the video. Bookmarks are used as the destination of an action, but they don't do anything on their own. There is one more thing to do for the bookmarks to shine and make your video truly interactive. But, first, let's learn how you can modify and delete the existing bookmarks.

Modifying and deleting bookmarks

You should have four bookmarks added on your video. In this section, you will learn how to modify and delete a bookmark using the following steps:

1. On slide 20 of your project, return to the beginning of the **Timeline**
2. Click on the first bookmark located around the 5.5 second mark

When a bookmark is selected, you can use the text field to rename it. You can also click the trash icon to remove the bookmark. These operations are illustrated in the following screenshot:

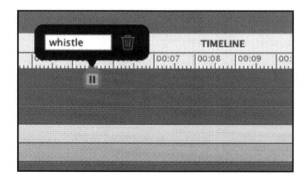

You can also drag the bookmark with your mouse to relocate it at another timecode on the **Timeline**.

Using the Jump to Bookmark action

Now that you have added bookmarks on the video, it is time to add the last piece of the puzzle and build some interactivity. In this section, you will create four buttons on your slide, one for each of the bookmarks you added in the previous section. These buttons will allow the students to jump back and forth between the bookmarks of the video. Use the following steps to add the first button:

1. Use the **Shapes** icon of the Toolbar to draw a rounded rectangle shape on the left side of the video.
2. Double-click the newly inserted shape and type `01 Whistle` inside of the rounded rectangle.
3. Hit the `Esc` key to leave the text editing mode and keep the new shape selected.
4. Use the **Style Name** drop-down menu located in the upper section of the **Properties** inspector to apply the **shape_As_Button** style to the new rounded rectangle.
5. Click the Align Left icon of the **Properties** inspector to align the text to the left side of the button.
6. Still in the **Properties** inspector, select the **Use as Button** checkbox.
7. Switch to the **Timing** inspector.
8. Deselect the **Pause After** checkbox (you already have a **Continue** button at the bottom-right corner of the slide that is taking care of pausing the playback of the project).
9. In the **Timing** inspector, make sure your new button is **Displayed for** the **Rest of** the **Slide** and **Appears After 0 sec**.

After this process, slide 20 of your project should look like the following screenshot:

You will now assign the **Jump to Bookmark** action to your new button using the following steps.

10. Make sure the **01 Whistle** button is still selected.
11. In the **Actions** tab of the **Properties** inspector, open the **On Success** drop-down list.
12. Choose the **Jump to Bookmark** action. Then, choose the **whistle** bookmark in the Bookmark drop-down menu.

You will now test this first button in the web browser. Remember that the Interactive Video feature is only supported in HTML5. Consequently, it will not work in the Preview pane of Captivate, which is still using the Flash technology behind the scenes. That is why you must test this feature using the HTML 5 in Browser, using the following steps.

13. Use the **Preview | HTML 5 in Browser** icon on the Toolbar to test your project in a web browser.
14. When the preview reaches slide 20, click the **01 Whistle** button and confirm that it takes you to the Whistle bookmark that you placed on the video.

Creating the remaining buttons

Now that your **01 Whistle** button is working, you can safely generate the three remaining buttons. Use the following general steps to do so:

- Use the *Ctrl + D* (Windows) / *command + D* (Mac) shortcut to duplicate the **01 Whistle** button.
- Change the text of the duplicated button so it matches the name of the corresponding bookmark.
- Change the action of the button, so it jumps to the right bookmark.
- When all four buttons are present on the slide, use the tools of the **Align** toolbar to properly align and distribute them.

At the end of this process, your slide should look like the following screenshot:

Of course, don't hesitate to use the **Preview | HTML 5 in Browser** icon on the Toolbar to give your new buttons a try. You should be able to jump back and forth between the four bookmarks you added on top of the video.

Working with Overlay Slides on the video

Another aspect of Interactive Videos in Adobe Captivate 2019 is Overlay Slides. The idea is to pause the video at a predefined moment and display a slide on top of the video. The student then interacts with the slide and the video resumes when done.

In this section, you will add an extra slide in the project and use it as an Overlay Slide on the video of slide 20.

Preparing the Overlay Slide

The first step of the process is to create an extra slide in the project and get it ready to be used as an Overlay Slide. Use the following step to insert the Overlay Slide in the project:

1. Open the `Chapter 05/overlay.cptx` file.
2. In the **Filmstrip**, right-click the first (and only) slide of the `overlay.cptx` project.
3. Select **Copy** in the contextual menu.
4. Return to the `Chapter05/takeTheTrain.cptx` project and use the **Filmstrip** to navigate to slide 20.
5. Paste the slide you copied from the `overlay.cptx` file.
6. Use the **Properties** inspector to apply the **ContentBkg** Master Slide of the theme to the new slide.

The new slide has been inserted as slide 21 of the project. This is not a requirement. Technically, you can insert the slides you want to use as Overlay Slides anywhere in the project, but for the sake of clarity, let's keep all the slides involved in this exercise together in the **Filmstrip**. Also, as soon as you mark a slide as an Overlay, it is automatically moved in the Filmstrip and positioned after the Video slide. And if there are multiple overlays on the same video, they are placed in the exact order of their appearance.

The slide you just inserted is a very simple slide containing a text caption and a **Continue** button. The **Continue** button stops the playhead to let the user interact with the slide at their own pace.

7. Select the **Continue** button.

8. In the **Actions** tab of the **Properties** inspector, change the **onSuccess** action to **Continue**.

The **Continue** action simply releases the playhead. Keep in mind that this slide will be used as an Overlay Slide on top of an Interactive Video. It means that the playback of the video will be paused and the slide will be shown to the student on top of the paused video. The **Continue** action will simply unpause the playhead and continue playing the video.

Adding the Overlay Slide on the Interactive Video

Now that you have a slide that can be used as an Overlay Slide, let's return to the Interactive Video to choose the exact moment when the video should be paused and the slide shown to the learner:

1. Use the **Filmstrip** to return to slide 20 of the `Chapter05/takeTheTrain.cptx` project.

2. If necessary, open the **Timeline** panel.

3. Use the play icon at the bottom-left corner of the **Timeline** to play the video in Captivate.

4. Stop the playhead around the **5:00** second mark (after the narration says "*...using a very precise procedure,*" but before the *Whistle* bookmark).

5. Click the diamond icon located on the red playhead. This opens the **Overlay** dialog.

This action is illustrated on the following screenshot:

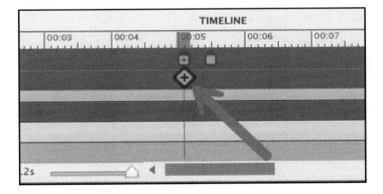

The diamond icon is used to insert an Overlay Slide at the current location of the playhead. This diamond marks the precise moment when the video will be paused and when the Overlay Slide will be displayed.

6. Click the Info icon in the top right corner of the **Overlay** dialog. Take some time to read the message about the type of slides you can use as Overlay Slides.
7. Click the **OK** icon to dismiss the message.
8. Select **slide 21** in the **Overlay** dialog.
9. Close the **Overlay** dialog by clicking the **Insert** button.

Slide 21 is now marked as the Overlay Slide that should be displayed at the 5:00 second timecode of slide 20. Notice that on the **Filmstrip**, the thumbnail of slide 21 is a little smaller than the other thumbnails. You can consider slide 21 as being kind of a *sub-slide* of slide 20. This is shown on the following screenshot:

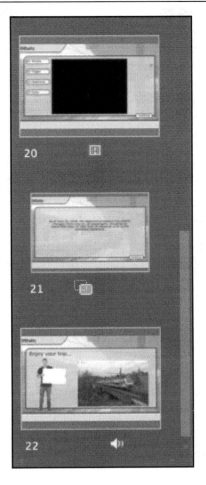

It is now time to test the new Overlay Slide in the HTML 5 browser using the following step.

10. Use the **Preview | HTML 5 in Browser** icon on the Toolbar to test the project in the HTML 5 browser.

When the preview reaches slide 20, the video should start playing automatically. After 5 seconds, the video pauses and the Overlay Slide is displayed. When you click the **Continue** button, the Overlay slide is dismissed and the video resumes.

Modifying the Overlay Slide

In this section, you will quickly review the workflows allowing you to modify and unlink the Overlay Slide using the following steps:

1. Return to slide 20 of the `Chapter05/takeTheTrain.cptx` file and open the **Timeline** panel if necessary.
2. In the **Timeline** panel, hover the mouse over the Overlay Slide diamond around the 5:00 second mark.

As shown in the following screenshot, this action reveals a popup with the image of the overlay slide:

Notice the two icons in the bottom-right corner of this pop-up window.

3. Click the first icon (the two rectangles with a + sign).

This action reopens the **Overlay** dialog allowing you to change the slide used as the Overlay Slide.

4. Click the **Cancel** button to close the **Overlay** dialog.

5. Back in the dark pop-up window, click the second icon (the icon of a broken link).

This action removes the Overlay slide and the yellow diamond from the **Timeline**. On the **Filmstrip**, slide 21 is no longer a *sub-slide* of slide 20.

6. Use the **Edit | Undo Delete Item** or the *Ctrl + Z* (Windows) / *command + Z* (Mac) shortcut to undo the last action.
7. In the **Timeline** panel, click the Overlay Slide diamond around the 5:00 second mark to select it.
8. In the **Properties** Inspector, click the **21. Slide 21** thumbnail.

This action reopens the **Overlay** dialog. This is another way of changing the slide used as the Overlay Slide.

9. Click the **Cancel** button to close the **Overlay** dialog.
10. In the **Properties** inspector, notice the Unlink icon next to the Slide 21 button. If needed, you can use this icon to unlink the Overlay Slide.
11. Also notice the Background Opacity drop-down menu. This lets you choose how much of the video slide is visible through the Overlay Slide.

This exercise concludes your first overview of the new Interactive Video feature of Adobe Captivate 2019. In Chapter 07, *Working with Quizzes*, you will return to this slide and discover some additional Interactive Video features. But, for now, let's make a quick summary of what you have learned in this section:

- Adobe Captivate 2019 introduces new features allowing you to make your videos interactive.
- There are two things you can do to make a video interactive. You can add bookmarks and Overlay Slides to the video.
- Because they can be controlled by the Captivate project, only Slide Videos can be made interactive. Event videos have their own playback controls and are therefore not eligible as interactive videos (In Chapter 09, *Producing a Video Demo*, you will learn that Video Demo slides can also be used as Interactive Videos).
- For a Slide Video to be made interactive, it needs to be inserted on the stage, not in the table of contents of the project.
- The video can be stored on your computer, or can be a YouTube video.

- You can use the **Media** | **Video** icon on the Toolbar or the **Video** | **Insert video** menu item to insert the video file in Captivate. But Adobe Captivate 2019 also proposes a simplified workflow to insert the interactive video. When using the **Interactive Video** icon on the Toolbar, only the options pertaining to inserting an interactive video are available.
- To add a bookmark, move the red playhead at the timecode where you want the bookmark to be added. Then, click the square icon with a + sign and give your bookmark a name.
- You can use the **Timeline** panel to select the existing bookmarks. When a bookmark is selected, you can rename it, delete it, or move it to another timecode.
- Bookmarks do not do anything on their own. You have to use an interactive object with a **Jump To Bookmark** action to appreciate the benefit and the real power of the bookmarks.
- To add an Overlay Slide, move the red playhead at the timecode you want the Overlay Slide to. Then, click the diamond icon with a + sign and choose the slide you want to use as an Overlay.
- When a slide is used as an Overlay Slide, the size of its thumbnail is reduced in the **Filmstrip**.
- You can use the **Timeline** to select the existing Overlay Slide markers to unlink the Overlay Slide, change the slide used as the Overlay slide, or move the diamond marker to another timecode.
- Only content slide and knowledge check questions can be used as Overlay slides. The other types of question slides as well as the slide containing videos cannot be used as Overlay slides as of this writing.

Working with Learning Interactions

Learning Interactions are complex interactive objects with built-in logic and behavior. As such, they represent the easiest way to add interactivity to your courses. Captivate contains a selection of Learning Interactions by default. You will explore them in this section. When inserted on a slide, Learning Interactions can be used as is, or customized in various ways. The best part is that Learning Interactions are entirely compatible with both Flash and HTML5.

Working with the Accordion interaction

One of the available Learning Interactions is the Accordion Widget. In this exercise, you will add one more slide to the *takeTheTrain* project and insert the **Accordion** Learning Interaction using the following steps:

1. If necessary, return to the `Chapter05/takeTheTrain.cptx` file.
2. Use the **Filmstrip** panel to go to the first slide of the project.
3. Use the **Slides | Blank Slide** icon on the Toolbar to insert a new slide based on the **Blank** Master Slide of the Theme. The new slide is inserted as slide 2.
4. Use the **Filmstrip** to go to slide 4 of the project.
5. Select the **Continue** button in the bottom-right corner of the slide.
6. Use the *Crtl + C* (Windows) or the *command + C* (Mac) shortcut to copy the selected button.
7. Use the **Filmstrip** to return to slide 2.
8. Use the *Crtl + V* (Windows) or the *command + V* (Mac) shortcut to paste the **Continue** button in the bottom-right corner of slide 2.

The stage is set! You now have a new slide with a **Continue** button whose job is to stop the playhead in order to let the student interact with the Accordion Widget. It is now time to insert the Learning Interaction, using the following steps.

9. Use the **Interactions | Learning Interaction** icon on the Toolbar to open the **Select Interaction** dialog.
10. Review the available interactions. When you have finished, select the **Accordion** interaction (the first one on the list).

11. Click the **Insert** button to insert it on to slide 2. This is shown in the following screenshot:

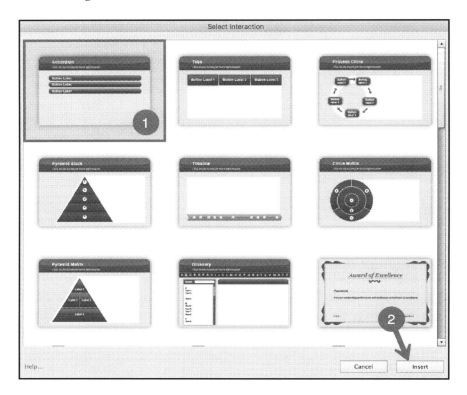

This inserts the Accordion interaction into slide 2 and opens the **Widget Properties** dialog box. You will use it to customize the content and the look and feel of the Accordion.

12. Use the column on the left of the **Widget Properties** dialog to choose a Theme that you like (in the example of the Chapter05/final folder, we chose Theme 4).

13. Double-click the interaction title in the header area and type Objectives of this course module as the title of the Accordion interaction.

14. Repeat the same operation to customize the subtitle of the interaction.

You will now customize the content of the panels of the Accordion widget.

15. In the main area of the **Widget Properties** dialog, double-click the first button of the Accordion. Change its title to Moving around in Belgium.

16. Triple-click the content area of the first Accordion to select all the text. Then, type a short text such as `Belgium is a small country with a lot of people, so roads and highways tend to be over crowded. However, Belgium has an extensive train network that makes it easy and cheap to travel the country.`

17. Change the **Button Label 2** title to `Finding your way in a Belgian train station` and the **Button Label 3** title to `Travel cheap and relaxed.`

18. Double-click the **Button Label 4** title. Click the *Minus* button that appears on the left side of the label to delete it from the Accordion.

You should now have three panels left in the Accordion Interaction, as shown in the following screenshot:

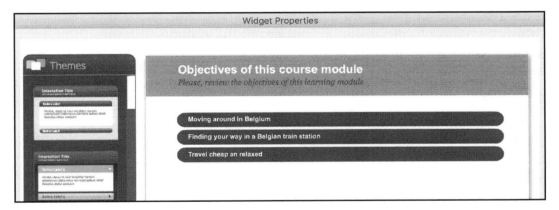

19. Add a descriptive text in each of the three panels.

20. Explore the other options available to further customize your Accordion interaction. When you are done, click the **OK** button.

21. Move and resize the Accordion so it integrates nicely into the slide.

22. Use the **Preview** | **Next 5 slides** icon on the Toolbar to test your interaction.

Your exploration of the Accordion interaction is now finished. If you want to customize your interaction further, double-click it to reopen the **Widget Properties** dialog.

The Accordion Widget is just one of the available interactions. Take some time to review the other available interactions. You will find great ideas to pump up your next Captivate project. The basic principle is always the same, and it goes as follows:

- A Learning Interaction is a self-contained interactive item that contains built-in actions.
- Inserting a Learning Interaction into the slide does not stop the playhead. Make sure you also add a button that stops the playhead to give the student a chance to interact with the widget.
- Learning Interactions can be customized in many ways, but the extent of this customization is up to each interaction. This is both the strength and the weakness of these objects. They are simple to use and customize, but only go so far in what they allow you to do.
- To modify an interaction, double-click it on the slide to reopen the **Widget Properties** dialog.
- Learning Interactions are supported in both Flash and HTML 5.

Using the Rollover objects

There are three more interactive object that have not yet been covered in this chapter. These objects are known as the **Rollover Objects**. They are originally hidden and show only when the user *rolls over* a specific area of the slide with their mouse. This behavior makes the Rollover Objects impossible to use on touch devices such as tablets and smartphones. This is the reason Rollover Objects are not supported in HTML5 and will not be used in the project you are working on. These objects are as follows:

- The Rollover Caption (and the Rollover Smart Shape)
- The Rollover Image
- The Rollover Slidelet

Because these objects are not supported in HTML5, they will not be further discussed in this book. Remember that Adobe will stop supporting the Flash Player as of 2020, so you should not use these objects in any new eLearning modules. The only reason why these objects are still present in Captivate 2019 is to ensure compatibility with legacy projects.

If you want more information on these objects, our dear friend Paul Wilson has published a great video on this topic on his YouTube channel; you can watch this video at the following URL: `https://www.youtube.com/watch?time_continue=1v=ipJaoPl5klA`

Summary

At the end of this chapter, your project is quite different than what it was at the beginning. By adding interactive elements to your slides, you have come a long way in making your online course engaging and fun to use. From a pedagogical standpoint, this interactivity is paramount in maintaining the students' attention and in improving their retention.

In this chapter, you studied the Button and the Text Entry Box objects. These objects have the ability to stop the playhead and wait for the learner to interact with the course. You used the Button object to provide content that is driven by your student's input in your course, a concept known as Branching.

You discovered the awesome power of Multi-State objects, which allow you to define sophisticated interactions without the need of any programming skills. You have worked with the Drag and Drop interaction and with the associated feedback messages. You have transformed a video file into a fully interactive digital experience. Finally, you have discovered how Learning Interactions work.

In the next chapter, you will focus on the aesthetics of your project. You will learn how to create and apply a consistent look and feel that will further help your learners get the most out of your teaching.

Meet the community

In this section, we want to introduce you to Joe Ganci. He is a veteran eLearning developer and instructional designer. Joe is almost always presenting at all the major eLearning events around the world. Chances are that you will meet him sooner rather than later!

Damien

Joe has reviewed two of my previous Captivate books. The first time I contacted him via email, he was kind enough to include a small quote in French (my native language) in his reply. We finally met in October 2014 during the Adobe Learning Summit in Las Vegas. In 2018, I was fortunate enough to spend a few days with him and his family in his house in the Washington DC area. Thanks, Joe, for all the good moments and discussions we have had together.

Pooja

I first met Joe at the Training 2012 conference in Atlanta, and since then we've been close friends. I always look forward to seeing him at conferences, breaking bread, co-presenting sessions, and spending time with him. He has a great sense of humor and is always keen to learn new things and share what he knows with others.

Joe Ganci

Joe Ganci is an eLearning consultant with a long track record. His design approaches and his innovative use of tools, such as Adobe Captivate and many others, has caused many to improve how they design and develop their eLearning and to implement new and better methods. His personal and hands-on style of consulting keeps his services constantly in demand, and he is privileged to have visited many clients from all over the world.

He has been involved in every aspect of learning development since 1983. He holds a degree in Computer Science and is a published author, having written several books, research papers, and many articles about eLearning. He is widely considered a guru for his expertise in eLearning development and conducts classes and seminars at commercial companies, government facilities, leading universities, and at many industry conferences, where he often serves as the keynote speaker. Most recently, he has been honored to present and speak in Moscow, Shanghai, Warsaw, Dubai, and many other locations. He is on a mission to improve the quality of eLearning with practical approaches that work. Call on Joe for your training needs and to have Joe help with your eLearning projects.

Joe makes his home in Northern Virginia outside Washington, DC. He is certain that he is privileged to call both Damien Bruyndonckx and Dr. Pooja Jaisingh his friends!

Contact details

- Website: http://elearningjoe.com/
- Twitter: @elearningjoe
- Email: joe@elearningjoe.com
- Joe's Tool Reviews: http://bit.ly/GanciReviews

6
Crafting the Graphical Experience with Styles and Themes

In this chapter, we will focus on the aesthetic aspect of the project by using Styles, Master Slides, Themes, and Templates. Your primary goal is to reach a high level of consistency in the look and feel of your eLearning content.

When developing eLearning, always keep in mind that your students will most likely experience your content while alone in front of their computer or mobile device with no one around to guide them. In this chapter, you will discover that a consistent look and feel is an efficient way to get your students on task. The idea is to free them from learning how eLearning works and looks so that they can be fully available for the actual teaching.

Captivate offers a few features to help you achieve this high level of consistency. The first feature that will be discussed in this chapter is **Styles.** You will also learn about **Master Slides**, **Themes**, and **Templates**.

In addition to serving your pedagogical efficiency, the proper use of Master Slides, Templates, Styles, and Themes will dramatically speed up the development of your eLearning content.

In this chapter, you will do the following:

- Import the color scheme of the project
- Experiment with Styles and the Object Styles Manager
- Learn about different fonts that are available in Captivate

- Experiment with predefined Themes
- Create a Theme containing Styles and Master Slides
- Create and use a Template

There's a lot to cover, so let's dive into the first discussion of this chapter.

Preparing your work

To get the most out of this chapter, it is important to reset your workspace. If you are using the default interface mode, restart Captivate to reset your workspace to its default state. If you are using the advanced interface mode, use the **Window | Workspace | Reset 'Classic'** menu item.

In this chapter, you will use the exercise files in the Chapter06 folder. If you get confused by any of the step-by-step instructions, take a look at the Chapter06/final folder, which contains a copy of the exercises as they should look by the end of this chapter.

Importing the colors

When working on an eLearning project, it is very important to precisely format the objects that are present in your course. Never forget that you are teaching! In such situations, most students will try to make sense out of every single formatting anomaly. Inconsistent formatting can mislead and confuse your learners.

Consistent formatting in eLearning

In my first eLearning project with Captivate, I used blue Text Captions to *explain* things to the learners and black Text Captions when I wanted them to *do* something. After a short while, the learners knew that, when seeing a blue Text Caption, they just had to read through the text, and when seeing a black Text Caption, they made themselves ready to do something. Learners have reported that this formatting consistency helped them structure their learning.

When it comes to color, it is important to define a good-looking color scheme at the beginning of the project and stick to it throughout the development. Sometimes, this color scheme is enforced by company regulations. At other times, you must respect a strict color scheme that's been defined by a graphic designer. In some situations, you are the only person involved and you can define your own color scheme.

One of the techniques that's used to import the needed colors in Captivate is to import an image containing the needed color swatches in the scrap area of the project. You will now use the following steps to create a new project and import the needed colors on the scrap area:

1. Open Captivate.
2. Use the **File** | **New Project** | **Blank Project** menu item to create a new Captivate project.
3. Choose **1024 x 627** as the new project size.
4. Save the new project as Chapter06/styles.cptx.
5. Use the **Media** | **Image** icon on the Toolbar to insert a new image. Navigate to the Chapter06/images/DiDaXo_colors.png file and import it into the project.

Just like any other new object, the image is imported in the center of the currently selected slide. You will now move the new image to the scrap area so that it is present in the project without being displayed to the learner (the Scrap Area is the dark grey background around the slide).

6. Move the image to the dark grey area on the left-hand side of the slide.
7. At the top of the **Timing** panel, use the **Display For** drop-down menu to display the selected image for the **Rest of** the **Project**.

Using this simple technique, it is very easy to import the needed color swatches into the project without displaying them to the learners. Your slide should now look like what's shown in the following screenshot:

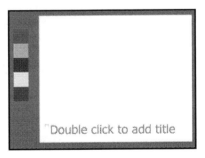

This example also emphasizes the usefulness of the Scrap Area. You can use this area to import utility objects that are needed when developing the project, but which should not be displayed to the user. In this example, you imported a picture with the needed color swatches. You could also leave notes or instructions for your fellow developers in the Scrap Area using Text Captions or leave sample objects that you want the developers to use and reuse throughout their projects. This makes the Scrap area one of the most useful areas of Captivate!

 For this exercise, we've used an online service named **Adobe Color CC** to create the color scheme. Then, we used the CC libraries to sync our color scheme with Photoshop and created the image of the five colored squares. Finally, we exported the image as a .png file from Photoshop. You can find out more about Adobe Color CC at https://color.adobe.com/.

Using the imported colors

Now that the corporate colors of DiDaXo have been imported into the project, you will use them to format the standard objects of Captivate:

1. Still in the Chapter06/styles.cptx project, select the title placeholder at the bottom of the slide.
2. Open the **Properties** inspector if necessary.
3. In the **Character** section, open the **Color** picker by clicking the downward arrow in the color swatch.
4. At the top of the color picker, click the eyedropper icon.
5. With the eyedropper tool activated, click the topmost color swatch of the picture you imported in the Scrap Area.

The result of your last action is that the characters of the title placeholder take the same purplish color as the first swatch of the image.

Using the Eyedropper tool

If you are not familiar with the eyedropper tool, take some time to learn how to use it. This tool is available in many (if not all) design-centric applications. It allows you to sample the color of the pixel you click when the tool is activated. You can, for example, activate the eyedropper tool and click the picture of a logo to sample the exact color that's used on the logo image. In this chapter, you will use the eyedropper tool to sample the five color swatches of the image you placed in the scrap area.

What's true for the font color is true for any other color properties. In other words, each time you have a color picker, you have access to the eyedropper tool. Let's experiment with this.

6. With the title placeholder still selected, open the color picker associated with the **Fill** color property in the **Properties** inspector.

7. At the top of the color picker, activate the eyedropper tool.

8. With the eyedropper tool activated, click the second swatch of the picture you imported at the beginning of this section (light blue). This color is now used as the fill color of the title.

9. Change the opacity of the selected object to 30% for better viewing.

10. Use the same process to change the **Stroke** color to the third available swatch (dark blue).

11. Finally, increase the stroke **Width** to 4 pixels. (Notice that *pixels* is the default unit, so 4 means 4 px.)

After this process, the slide should look as follows:

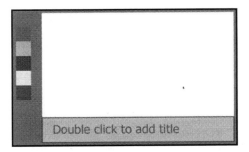

Thanks to the picture you inserted in the Scrap Area and to the eyedropper tool, you've been able to import the custom colors of the DiDaXo brand into the project and use them to format the Title Placeholder of the first slide. Using the same techniques, you can use the same set of five colors throughout the entire project. This is your first step toward consistent formatting. Your learner will appreciate this high level of professionalism when taking the course.

Working with styles

In Captivate, the formatting properties of an object can be saved in a style. This allows you to reapply the same properties on other objects of the same type. Captivate comes with predefined styles, but you can modify these default styles and even create your own custom styles.

Managing styles with the Properties inspector

In this section, you will explore how the **Properties** inspector can be used to apply and create styles:

1. Still in the `Chapter06/styles.cptx` file you created in the previous section, select the title placeholder on the first slide of the new project.
2. If needed, click the **Properties** icon on the Toolbar to open the **Properties** inspector.

The **Style Name** drop-down list (shown as **1** in the following screenshot) tells you that the style that's currently applied to the selected object is the **+[Default Title Smart Shape Style]** style. The **+** sign in front of the style name means that the formatting has been manually changed on top of the original style. Technically, this is called a *style override*. There's no way of knowing which formatting changes have been made on top of the original style:

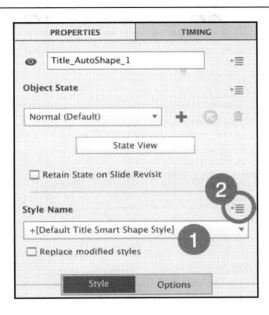

Just above the **Style Name** drop-down menu of the **Properties** inspector is another icon (marked as **2** in the preceding screenshot). This icon gives you access to additional options pertaining to the selected object. In this chapter, we will refer to this icon as the *Style Options* icon.

3. Click the Style Options icon and inspect the available items.

The menu items that are available in the Style Options icon are used to manage the styles in different ways. In the upcoming sections, you will explore these options one by one.

Resetting a style

Resetting a style is one of the operations that's available in the Style Options icon:

1. With the formatted placeholder still selected, open the Style Options icon.
2. Click the **Reset Style** menu item.

The original **[Default Title Smart Shape Style]** style is reapplied to the selected object and the **+** sign disappears from the **Style Name** in the drop-down list.

3. Use the **Edit** | **Undo** menu item or the *Ctrl + Z* (Windows) or *command + Z* (Mac) shortcut to undo the last action.

Resetting a style is very practical when you want to reset the format of the selected object back to its default state.

Creating new styles

Creating new styles is another operation that can be done with the Style Options icon. In this section, you will save the current formatting of the placeholder object as a new style using the following steps:

1. Make sure the formatted title placeholder is selected.
2. Look at the **Style Name** drop-down list of the **Properties** inspector. Confirm that the applied style is the **+[Default Title Smart Shape Style]** style.
3. Open the Style Options icon and click the **Create New Style** item.
4. In the **Save New Object Style** dialog box, name the new style `DiDaXo-MainTitle` and click **OK**.

Take another look at the **Style Name** drop-down menu on the **Properties** inspector. It tells you that the new **DiDaXo-MainTitle** style is applied to the selected object. This style can now be applied to any other Smart Shape in the project.

Applying styles

Applying styles to existing objects is yet another operation that can be done from the **Properties** inspector. In the next exercise, you will apply your new **DiDaXo-MainTitle** style to another Smart Shape of the project:

1. Use the **Slide | Content Slide** icon on the Toolbar to add a second slide to the `Chapter06/styles.cptx` file.
2. Use the topmost section of the **Properties** inspector to apply the **Content 03** Master Slide to the new slide.
3. Select the title placeholder in the topmost area of the slide.
4. At the top of the **Properties** inspector, open the **Style Name** drop-down menu.
5. Select the **DiDaXo-MainTitle** style.

Two title placeholders on two different slides now share the same look and feel thanks to your own custom style! You will now try to apply this same style to yet another object.

6. Select one of the Text Caption placeholders of slide 2.
7. At the top of the **Properties** inspector, open the **Style Name** drop-down menu.

Notice that your custom **DiDaXo-MainTitle** style is *not* available in the drop-down menu. This is because the selected object is not a Smart Shape, but a Text Caption.

In Captivate, each object type has its own set of styles. So, a style defined for a Smart Shape can only be applied to Smart Shapes, and a style defined for a Text Caption can only be applied to Text Captions. In this case, your custom **DiDaXo-MainTitle** style can only be applied to Smart Shapes. This can be tricky as, in some cases, a Smart Shape containing text and a Text Caption can be formatted to look the very same way. But since they are not of the same object type, they'll never share the same style.

Modifying a style

Modifying a style is the next action that you will perform. In this exercise, you will modify the formatting of one of the Smart Shapes that has the **DiDaXo-MainTitle** style applied. You will then update your custom style to the new formatting and see how the other object reacts:

1. Make sure that the title placeholder in the topmost area of slide 2 is selected.
2. Look at the top of the **Properties** inspector. Confirm that the **DiDaXo-MainTitle** style is currently applied to the selected object.
3. In the **Style** tab of the **Properties** inspector, change the font size to 48.

Because you have made a formatting change, the + sign appears in the **Style Name** drop-down menu. The style that's currently applied to the selected Text Caption is **+ DiDaXo-MainTitle**.

4. Open the Style Options icon and click the **Save changes to Existing Style** item.
5. This action updates the **DiDaXo-MainTitle** style after the current look of the selected object. The **+** sign disappears from the **Style Name** drop-down list.
6. Use the **Filmstrip** to return to the first slide of the project.
7. Select the main title placeholder. In the **Characters** section of the **Style** tab of the **Properties** inspector, confirm that the new font size is also applied to the selected title placeholder.

By updating the **DiDaXo-MainTitle** style, you have updated the formatting of every object this style is applied to throughout the entire project.

Applying styles automatically

Imagine the style that's currently applied to the title placeholders of slide 1 and slide 2 is the one you want to apply to *every* slide title throughout the project. You could browse each slide one by one and manually apply the new style to each and every title. But there's another, more automated, way:

1. Make sure you are on slide 2 of the `Chapter06/styles.cptx` file.
2. Use the **Slide | Content Slide** icon on the Toolbar to add a third slide to the project.
3. Repeat the preceding operation three more times.

You should now have six slides in your project. The first slide uses the *Title* Master Slide. The remaining five are using the *Content 03* Master Slide. Your goal is to apply the **DiDaXo-MainTitle** style to every slide title throughout the project. However, so far, only the first two slides are correctly using this style.

4. Use the **Filmstrip** to navigate to slide 3 and select the title slide placeholder.
5. Look at the **Style Name** drop-down menu on the **Properties** inspector. Take good note of the style that is currently applied to the selected object. (On my computer, it is the **[Default Title Smart Shape Style]**).
6. Use the **Properties** inspector to change one of the formatting properties of the selected object. For example, change the font size to 36. After this operation, a + symbol appears in front of the style name. (On my computer, the style that's applied is now **+[Default Title Smart Shape Style]**).

Now, you can apply your custom **DiDaXo-MainTitle** style to all of the slide titles of the project.

7. Use the **Filmstrip** to return to slide 2. Select the slide title placeholder.
8. Open the Style Options icon and click the **Apply this style to...** item.
9. In the **Apply Object Style** box, select the style that's currently applied to the objects of the other slides (on my computer, I chose the **[Default Title Smart Shape Style]** style in the drop-down list) and click **OK**. This operation is illustrated in the following screenshot.

By doing this, you apply the **DiDaXo-MainTitle** style to every title placeholder of the project currently using the **[Default Title Smart Shape Style]** style:

10. Use the **Filmstrip** to browse slides 4 and 5 of the project. Confirm that your custom **DiDaXo-MainTitle** style is correctly applied to the title placeholder of each slide.

11. Use the **Filmstrip** to navigate to slide 3 of the project. You should see that the current look of the slide title does not reflect the properties of your style.

12. Select the title placeholder of slide 3 and look at the **Properties** inspector.

The **DiDaXo-MainTitle** style has been properly applied to the title placeholder, but the manual style override is still active. So, the actual style is **+DiDaXo-MainTitle**.

13. Open the Style Options icon and click the **Reset Style** item.

This action removes the style overrides, which properly applies the genuine **DiDaXo-MainTitle** style.

Automatically replacing the overrides

Before moving on to the next section, take note of the **Replace modified styles** checkbox. When this checkbox is selected, the style overrides are automatically cleared when a new style is applied to the selected object. This may sound very tempting, but it may lead to unwanted changes throughout the project, so use it with great care.

This concludes your first exploration of styles in Captivate. Using styles, it has been easy and quick to format every Title Placeholder of the project. This helps you achieve the high degree of formatting consistency that assists your students in the learning process and creates a professional-looking project.

Before moving on to the next topic, let's summarize what you have learned:

- Styles help create and maintain consistent formatting throughout the entire project.
- In the topmost section of the **Properties** inspector, use the **Style Name** dropdown to apply a style to the selected object.
- When additional formatting is applied, a + sign appears in front of the style name. This indicates that the style has been overridden by some manual adjustments.
- Use the **Reset Style** feature to clear the overrides and reapply the original style.
- When you modify a style, you change the formatting of all of the objects using that particular style, throughout the entire project.
- The Style Options icon in the top-right corner of the **Properties** inspector contains the necessary options to create, update, reset, and apply styles.

Working with the Object Style manager

So far, you have used the Style Options icon of the **Properties** inspector to apply and manage styles. This icon provides quick and easy access to the main styling features. However, behind the scenes, the **Object Style Manager**, a much more sophisticated engine, is at work! The items of the Styles Options icon are just shortcuts to the actual Object Style Manager. Everything these icons made possible is also possible through the Object Style Manager. However, the Object Style Manager has much more to offer.

Renaming styles

One of the extra features offered by the Object Style Manager is the ability to rename an existing style. In this section, you will experiment with this ability hands-on, using the following steps:

1. Make sure you are in the Chapter06/styles.cptx project.

2. Use the **Edit | Object Style Manager** menu item to open the Object Style Manager. You can also use the *Shift + F7* (Windows) or the *shift + fn + F7* (Mac) shortcut to do the same thing.

The Object Style Manager will open, as shown in the following screenshot:

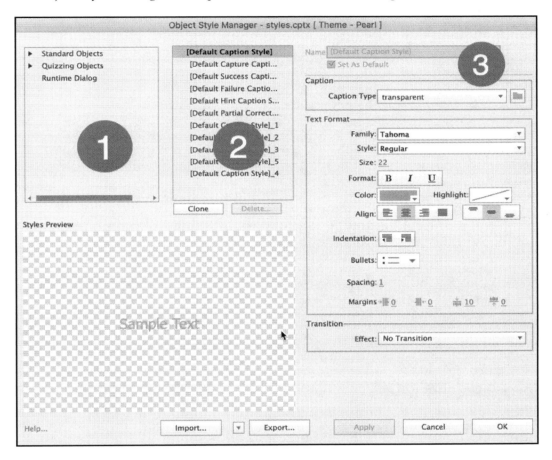

The left-hand side of the Object Style Manager (shown as (**1**) in the preceding screenshot) lists the object types of Captivate.

3. In the left column of the Object Style Manager, expand the **Standard Objects** section.

4. In the **Standard Objects** section, expand the **Smart Shape** subsection and select the **Title** object.

The middle column (shown as (**2**) in the preceding screenshot) shows a list of styles that can be applied to the object type that's selected in the first column. In this case, the styles listed in the middle column can be applied to the Smart Shape object. Among them is your custom **DiDaXo-MainTitle** style. You will now use the Object Style Manager to rename it.

5. In the middle column, select the **DiDaXo-MainTitle** style.

When a style is selected in the second column of the Object Style Manager, its properties are displayed in the third column. One of these properties is the name of the style that appears at the very top of the third column (see **3** in the preceding screenshot).

6. Change the name of the selected style to **DiDaXo-SlideTitle.**

7. Click the **OK** button in the bottom-right corner of the Object Styles Manager to confirm this change and close the dialog.

8. Select the title placeholder of the slide you are on.

9. Look at the **Style Name** drop-down menu of the **Properties** inspector and confirm that the selected object now uses the **DiDaXo-SlideTitle** style.

Renaming existing styles is one of the many capabilities of the Object Style Manager. In the next two sections, you will experiment with exporting and importing styles.

Exporting a style

Exporting styles is another feature offered by the Object Style Manager. Let's experiment with this capability using the following steps:

1. Still in the `Chapter06/styles.cptx` file, use the **Edit** | **Object Style Manager** or the *Shift + F7* (Windows) or *shift + F7* (Mac) shortcut to reopen the Object Style Manager.

2. In the left column, select the **Standard Objects** | **Smart Shape** | **Title** object.

3. In the middle column, select the **DiDaXo-SlideTitle** style.

4. At the bottom of the **Object Style Manager**, click the **Export** button.

5. Save the style as `Chapter06/DiDaXo-SlideTitle.cps`.
6. Click the **OK** button to acknowledge the successful export.
7. Click **OK** to close the **Object Style Manager**.
8. Save the `Chapter06/styles.cptx` file.

Exporting a style creates a `.cps` file. This file will be used to import the style in another project.

Exporting multiple styles
Clicking on the drop-down arrow next to the **Export** button in the Object Style Manager gives you the ability to export all of the Styles of a specific object type or all of the Styles of all of the objects.

Importing a style

To use your custom **DiDaXo-SlideTitle** style in another project, you will now use the Object Style Manager to import the `.cps` file, which we created in the previous section, in the `takeTheTrain.cptx` project. We will do this by using the following steps:

1. Open the `Chapter06/takeTheTrain.cptx` file.
2. Use the **Edit | Object Style Manager** menu item to open the Object Style Manager.
3. In the **Object Style Manager**, expand the **Standard Objects** section and then the **Smart Shape** subsection.
4. Select the **Title** object.

Notice that your **DiDaXo-SlideTitle** style is *not* listed in the middle column. This is because the styles listed in the Object Style Manager are specific to the active file only. In Captivate, each project has its own list of styles.

5. At the bottom of the **Object Style Manager** dialog, click the **Import** button.
6. Browse to the `Chapter06/DiDaXo-SlideTitle.cps` file and click **Open**.
7. Read the message and click **Yes** to discard it.
8. Close the **Object Style Manager** dialog by clicking the **OK** button.

After this operation, the **DiDaXo-SlideTitle** style will be transferred to the `takeTheTrain.cptx` project. You are now able to apply it to the Smart Shapes of this project as well.

9. In the **Filmstrip**, select slide 1.
10. Select the main title of the project that reads **Take the train!.**
11. Use the **Style Name** dropdown in the topmost area of the **Properties** inspector to apply the **DiDaXo-SlideTitle** style to the selected Smart Shape.

This confirms that your custom style has been correctly transferred from one project to the other and that it is now available in both projects.

12. Use the **Edit | Undo** menu item or the *command + Z (Mac)/Ctrl + Z* (Windows) shortcut to undo your last action.
13. Save and close the `Chapter06/takeTheTrain.cptx` file when done.

Thanks to the Object Style Manager, you've been able to transfer a style from one project to another. This workflow helps you achieve formatting consistency—not only within each project, but also across different projects.

Adding styles globally

If you want to add styles to the Object Style Manager and make them available to every (future) project of your Captivate installation, close all open files and go to the **Edit | Object Style Manager** menu item of Captivate when no file is open. This allows you to open the Object Style Manager of your Captivate installation rather than the Object Style Manager of a specific project.

Creating a style in the Object Style Manager

To create the **DiDaXo-SlideTitle** style, you used the **Create New Style** item of the Style Options icon in the **Properties** inspector. You will now create another style using the Object Style Manager:

1. Return to the `Chapter06/styles.cptx` file.
2. Use the **Edit | Object Style Manager** menu item or the *Shift + F7* (Win)/*shift + F7* shortcut (Mac) to reopen the Object Style Manager.
3. In the leftmost column, select the **Standard Objects | Smart Shapes** category.
4. In the middle column, select the **DiDaXo-SlideTitle** style.

5. Just below the middle column, click the **Clone** button. Captivate duplicates the **DiDaXo-SlideTitle** style and saves the clone as **DiDaXo-SlideTitle1**.

6. In the rightmost column of the **Object Style Manager** dialog, rename the new style `DiDaXo-ProjectTitle`.

7. In the **Text Format** section, change the font from **Family** to **Verdana** and the font **Size** to `56`.

8. In the **Fill & Stroke** section, change the fill **Opacity** to `0%` and the stroke **Width** to `0` to make the Smart Shape transparent.

Make sure that the Object Style Manager looks similar to what's shown in the following screenshot:

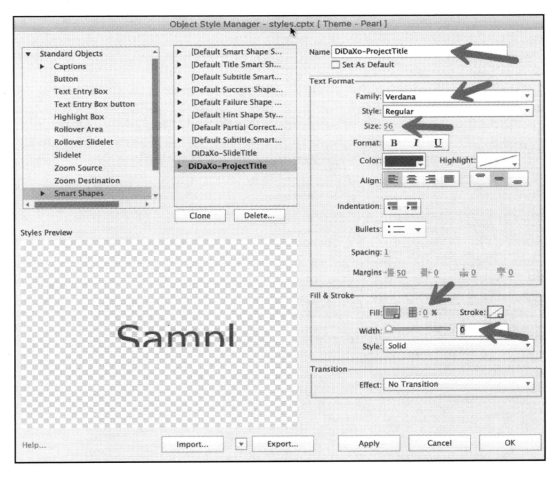

9. Leave the other options at their current settings and click **OK** to close the Object Style Manager.
10. Use the **Filmstrip** to go to slide 1.
11. Select the Title Placeholder.
12. Use the **Style** drop-down list of the **Properties** inspector to apply the new **DiDaXo-ProjectTitle** style to the selected object.
13. Save the `Chapter06/styles.cptx` file when done.

This exercise concludes your overview of the Object Style Manager. Before moving on, let's summarize what you've learned:

- The items in the Style Options icon of the **Properties** inspector act as shortcuts to the Object Style Manager
- The Object Style Manager provides extra tools compared to the Object Options icon
- The leftmost column of the Object Style Manager lists all of the object types of Captivate
- Using the Object Style Manager, styles can be exported from a project and imported into another
- The Object Style Manager also provides the ability to rename existing custom styles
- It is possible to create entire styles in the Object Style Manager

Working with fonts

In this section, you will learn how to properly use fonts in Adobe Captivate. This may sound a bit surprising. After all, when an object is selected, there is a **Font** property in the **Properties** inspector that works the same way in most applications you commonly use. Just open the **Fonts** dropdown and pick the font you want to use—this is very simple. However, there is one thing you should keep in mind.

When working with Adobe Captivate, the last step of the process is to publish your work in Flash or HTML5. When publishing in HTML5, your course is exported as a self-contained mini website that's viewed in a web browser by the learner. Well, here's the thing: on the internet, a website uses the fonts that are installed on the client machine to render text. This means that if you use a font in Captivate when designing your course, that very same font must be installed on the computer of all your learners for the text to render correctly on their side.

This problem is not limited to producing courses with Captivate. This is something the whole web design industry has struggled with for years! But the industry has come up with various solutions that you can use in Captivate.

Using web safe fonts

The first solution is to use fonts that are known to be available on most, if not all, computers around the world, regardless of the system (Windows, Mac, or Linux) or version used by the learner. Using one of these fonts is therefore considered safe, hence the name *Web Safe Fonts*. Let's discover the list of Web Safe fonts available in Captivate using the following steps:

1. Make sure you are in the `Chapter06/styles.cptx` file.
2. Use the **Filmstrip** to go to slide 2 of the project.
3. Select one of the Text Caption placeholders.
4. Open the Fonts drop-down menu situated in the **Character** section on the **Style** tab of the **Properties** inspector.

Notice that the list of available fonts is divided into categories. One of these categories is **Web Safe Fonts** and another one is **System Fonts**, as shown in the following screenshot:

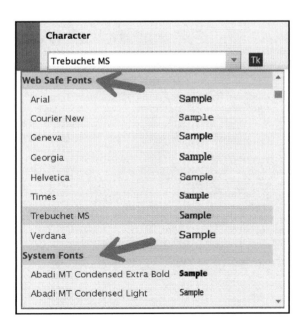

If you use one of the fonts listed under the **Web Safe Fonts** category, you are certain that the font used to render text on the learner's computer is the exact same font you used when you designed the course on your computer. This is because the Web Safe fonts are known to be available on every computer in the world. The trade-off is that the list of available fonts is quite limited and very widely used.

Working with System Fonts

The second category of fonts available in the **Properties** inspector is **System Fonts**. The System Fonts category is a list of all of the fonts that are installed on your computer not in the Web Safe fonts category. Using these fonts when developing a website (and remember that your Captivate courses are exported as mini-websites) is risky, because there is no guarantee that the fonts that are available on your computer are also available on the computer that's used to view your content.

When using a System Font, Captivate exports the Text Captions and Smart Shapes with text as images. This is the only way to make sure your text content is rendered exactly as you designed it.

When creating a Responsive Project, text is never exported as images because it is difficult to make an image truly responsive. This stresses the danger of System Fonts even more. When developing eLearning content, you definitely don't want to use System Fonts. You will learn more about Responsive Projects in Chapter 10, *Creating a Responsive Project*.

Using images for text is really not an optimal solution:

- First, image file sizes are larger than text, so the use of System Fonts dramatically increases the size of your published content.
- Another problem is the accessibility of the content. Text written on images is not visible to the assistive technologies being used by students with disabilities (you will learn more about accessibility in Chapter 13, *Creating Accessible eLearning*).
- Finally, an image has a fixed size, which makes it very difficult to use in a responsive situation. For example, reflowing the text based on the available screen dimension is barely possible when using an image (you will learn more about responsive projects in Chapter 10, *Creating a Responsive Project*).

For all of these reasons (plus the ones not listed here), you will want to avoid using System Fonts in your projects.

Working with web fonts

A third solution is to use web fonts. This idea is very simple to understand. Instead of relying on fonts that are installed on your student's computer, you can use fonts hosted on the internet. The chosen font is downloaded before it is used to render text, which makes it available to all of your students. Sure enough, this impairs performance, as an extra file (the font) must be downloaded from the server before the content is made available to the viewer. Also, some students working on restricted networks or being behind a proxy server might not be able to download the font from the public internet. However, on the other hand, you have a much wider range of fonts to choose from. (Not mentioning that the caching technologies used by web browsers makes the performance issue a very minor annoyance.)

Adobe has developed an online font library called Adobe Fonts. Adobe Captivate 2019 is fully integrated with the Adobe Fonts online Library. Let's explore this feature using the following steps:

 Adobe Fonts was previously known as Adobe Typekit. Adobe decided to rebrand the service on October 15, 2018. Since Captivate 2019 was released in August 2018, a few months prior to Typekit being renamed Adobe Fonts, Captivate still refers to this service as Typekit. This is likely to change in the next Adobe Captivate update, so by the time you read this book, Captivate may have been updated to use the new Adobe Fonts brand. Consider the terms Adobe Typekit and Adobe Fonts to be interchangeable in the few upcoming pages. More information about this rebranding can be found at `https://blog.typekit.com/2018/10/15/time-for-a-change-typekit-has-become-adobe-fonts/`.

1. If needed, return to `Chapter06/takeTheTrain.cptx` and use the **Filmstrip** to navigate to slide 8.
2. Select the slide title Smart Shape that reads **Reading the schedule**.
3. In the **Properties** inspector, notice that this text uses the **Verdana** font family.

Verdana is a Web Safe font because it is available on every single system. This is the main reason why it is used in this project. Using a Web Safe font ensures that the text is rendered correctly on every system without adding any extra file size to the project, without impairing accessibility, and with the ability to resize and reflow the text on smaller screens if necessary.

The trade-off is that Verdana is so widely used that it does not convey any graphical uniqueness anymore. To make this project stand out, you will need to replace the Verdana font with another one from the Typekit online font library.

Adobe Fonts and the Adobe ID

Adobe Fonts is a commercial online service from Adobe. Access to the Adobe Fonts library requires a free Adobe ID. Syncing the fonts with your computer also requires the installation of the Creative Cloud desktop app, which is available at

`http://www.adobe.com/creativecloud/desktop-app.html`.

4. With the slide title still selected, click the **Tk** icon just next to the Font drop-down menu in the **Properties** inspector. This action takes you to the Adobe Fonts website (keep in mind that this icon may be updated to reflect the new Adobe Fonts branding).
5. If needed, log in with your Adobe ID using the **Sign In** button in the top-right corner of the Adobe Fonts website.

The Adobe Fonts website allows you to browse the entire online font library. The column on the left-hand side of the screen provides an easy-to-use search interface. Feel free to explore the capabilities of the site at your own pace before resuming this exercise:

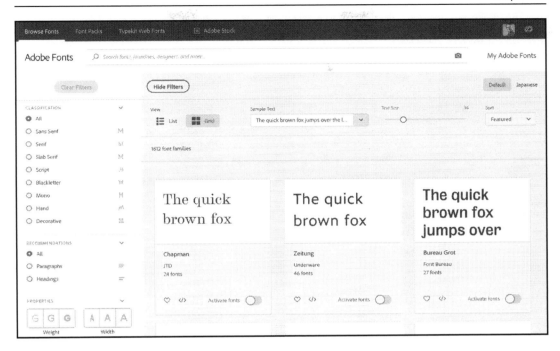

Before choosing the font you want to use, there are a few things you need to be aware of:

- Adobe Fonts is a commercial online service from Adobe that requires an Adobe ID and an extra subscription that is *not* included in the Captivate license. You can find more information on the available plans at `https://fonts.adobe.com/plans`.

- A small subset of the Adobe Fonts library is available for free.

- This exercise uses fonts that are available for free at the time of writing. If the font is no longer available for free by the time you read this book, don't hesitate to choose another free font of your liking from the library.

- More information on the integration of Adobe Fonts in Captivate can be found at `https://helpx.adobe.com/captivate/using/typekit-plan-captivate.html`.

You will now select a font from the Adobe fonts library, sync it with your computer, and use it in your Captivate project.

6. Use the search field in the upper area of the Adobe Fonts website to search for the *Cooper Black* font.

7. Click the font name to reach the font page on the site (available at `https://fonts.adobe.com/fonts/cooper-black`).

8. Click the **Activate All Fonts** button associated with the **Cooper Black Std** font.

9. After a few moments, you will receive a notification from the Adobe Creative Cloud Desktop app that the font has been successfully activated.

10. Return to slide 8 of the `Chapter06/takeTheTrain.cptx` file. Make sure that the slide title is still selected.

11. In the **Style** tab of the **Properties** inspector, open the font list.

At the top of the list, you should see a third category called **Typekit Fonts**. This category lists the online fonts that you have activated on your computer. Among them, you will find the **Cooper Std** font, which is now available on your system:

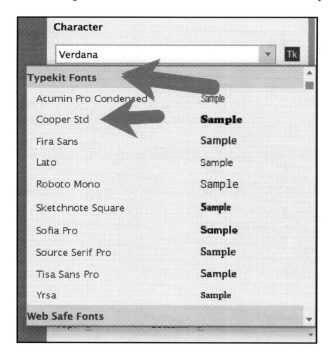

You can now use this new font in the same way as any other font that's installed on your system.

12. Select the new **Cooper Std** font to apply it to the selected slide title. Notice that the style applied to this object is now **+SlideTitle**.

13. Click the Style Options icon and choose the **Save Changes to Existing Style** item.

14. Browse the other slides of your project and confirm that every slide title now uses the new Typekit font.

15. If necessary, resize, move, and reset the styles so that the font applies to all slide titles throughout the project.

This concludes your first exploration of the Adobe Fonts Library. Adobe Fonts and the Web Fonts technology give you access to a tremendous amount of creative flexibility and opportunities. Thanks to this technology, your online course will shine like never before, providing an even better training experience to your learners.

Syncing a second Adobe Fonts web font

Now that you've used Adobe Fonts for the slide titles, why not sync a second web font that you can use for regular text? In this section, you will return to the Adobe Fonts site, find a great font for the body text, activate it, and use it in your project. The general steps go as follows:

1. Go to the Adobe Fonts website and search for a suitable font (in the project in the `Chapter06/final` folder, we have used the *Lato* font: `https://fonts.adobe.com/fonts/lato`).

2. Activate the chosen font with your computer using the Adobe Fonts website and the Creative Cloud desktop application.

3. Use the newly activated font in Captivate for Text Captions and Smart Shapes containing body text.

4. Don't forget to save your changes in existing styles to quickly update the font used by the objects throughout the project.

5. Save and close the `Chapter06/takeTheTrain.cptx` file when done.

At the end of this extra credit section, your project should convey a completely updated look and feel, thanks to the use of two Typekit web fonts.

Before moving on the next section, let's quickly summarize what you've learned about fonts in this section:

- When published in HTML5, your Captivate course is exported as a self-contained mini-website. As such, the technical possibilities and limitations of your published course are similar to those of a regular website.
- On the internet, web browsers use the fonts that are installed on the computer of the learner to render text. To see the course as you designed it, each learner must have the same fonts as the ones you used when creating the course.
- The *Web Safe Fonts* is a short list of fonts known to be installed on most (if not all) computers and devices in the world, regardless of the system or version. Using these fonts on the internet is therefore considered safe.
- System Fonts are the fonts that are available on your local computer that are not in the Web Safe fonts list. Using these fonts for designing sites is dangerous, as they might not be available on the learner's computer.
- When using System Fonts in non-responsive projects, Captivate exports the text as images. This is the only way to ensure that the text looks as intended. But it comes with many undesirable side effects, such as increased file size, limited accessibility, and limited responsiveness.
- When creating a Responsive Project, the text is never exported as images.
- Web Fonts are fonts that are hosted on the internet. They can be downloaded to the viewer's computer when visiting a site/course.
- Adobe Fonts is a Web Fonts library maintained by Adobe. Adobe Fonts is available in Captivate 2019, so you can use the Adobe Fonts library to design your courses. This ensures that the font you used to design a course is also available to your learners.
- Access to the Adobe Fonts library requires an Adobe ID, the Creative Cloud desktop application, and a subscription that is not included in the Captivate license. However, a small subset of the Adobe Fonts library can be used for free, without any extra subscription.
- Adobe fonts was previously known as Adobe Typekit. Depending on the version of Captivate that you are using, Captivate may still refer to this service as Adobe Typekit.

Working with Themes

A **Theme** is a file that collects all the formatting properties of a project, including (but not limited to) Object Styles. Captivate comes installed with a handful of ready-to-use themes. To have a better idea of what a Theme is, we will start with some simple experiments using the predefined Themes of Captivate:

1. Save and close every open file.
2. Use the **File | New Project | Blank Project** menu item to create a new blank project.
3. In the **New Blank Project** dialog, use the **Select** drop-down menu to choose a size of **1024 x 627**. When you are done, click the **OK** button.

Captivate creates a new blank project of the chosen size. When a new project is created this way, a single slide is automatically added to the **Filmstrip**. This new slide is already formatted.

Creating a Blank project from the Welcome screen
To create a new blank project, you can also use the **New** tab of the Welcome screen. In such cases, you must choose the size of the new project in the bottom left corner of the Welcome screen. If you do this, the **New Blank Project** dialog does not open.

Applying a theme to an existing project

When you install Captivate, predefined themes are installed along with the application. You will now apply one of these themes to your new project and explore what a Theme is made of:

1. Still in your new blank project, click the **Themes** icon on the Toolbar.

As shown in the following screenshot, the **Themes** icon lists the available themes. Looking at this list, you also learn that the theme that's currently applied is the **Pearl** theme, as indicated by the frame around its thumbnail (see the arrow in the following screenshot):

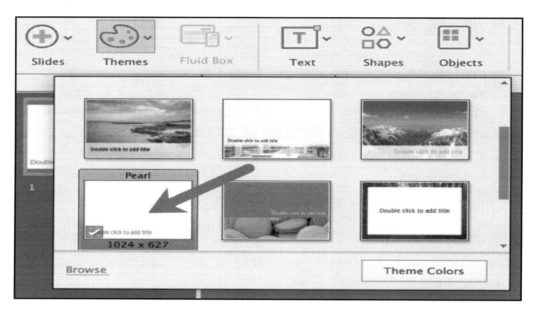

Choosing the default theme

In the preceding screenshot, also notice the checkmark in the bottom-left corner of the **Pearl** theme. This checkmark indicates that the **Pearl** theme is the default theme that's applied to every new project. To choose another theme as the default, right-click a Theme and choose the **Set as Default Theme** menu item.

2. Click any thumbnail to apply the corresponding theme to the current project.
3. Read the warning message about the style overrides. Click **Yes** to acknowledge and clear the message.

The new theme is now applied to the project. Take some time to look at what has changed. You should notice that not only has the background of the slide changed, but also the formatting of the title placeholder.

Before moving on to the next section, you will reapply the original *Pearl* theme to the project.

4. Click the **Themes** icon on the Toolbar to reopen the list of available themes.
5. Click the **Pearl** theme thumbnail to reapply it to the current project.
6. Click **Yes** to acknowledge and clear the warning message.

Now that you know how to apply themes, you will further explore this feature and discover what Themes are made of.

The elements of a Theme

A Captivate Theme is a collection of graphical elements and assets. In the next few pages, you will discover what Themes are made of by manipulating different Themes and exploring how they affect the slides and objects of the project.

The Master Slides

The first element that makes up a Captivate Theme is a set of **Master Slides**. To better understand what they are, your first stop is the **Master Slide** panel:

1. Make sure that your new project is still open. If you closed it, just recreate a new one.
2. Use the **Window | Master Slide** menu item to switch to the **Master Slide** view.

The **Master Slide** panel now replaces the **Filmstrip** panel on the Captivate interface. In this view, the **Filmstrip** is not visible.

3. Enlarge the **Master Slide** panel by dragging the vertical separator between the **Master Slide** panel and the stage to the right.

The Pearl theme that is currently applied to the project contains an entire set of predefined Master Slides. Each of these Master Slides defines a layout that you can apply as-is to any slide of the project.

To ensure visual consistency across the Master Slides of a theme, the first Master Slide visible in the **Master Slide** panel is known as the **Main Master Slide** (shown as **1** in the following screenshot).The Main Master Slide contains the visual elements that are common to most (if not all) slides of the project:

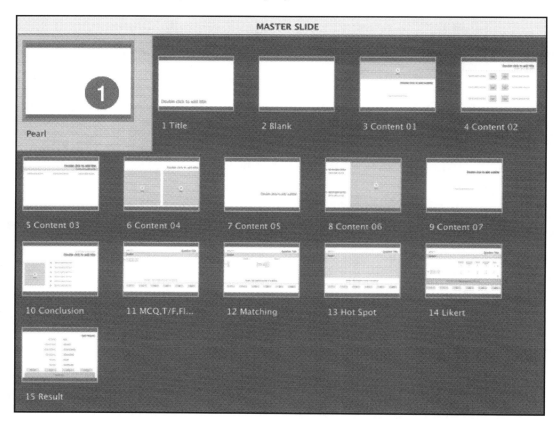

Creating slides based on Master Slides

Master Slides are used as templates for the individual slides of a Captivate project. In this section, you will create slides in your new project and explore how to apply Master Slides using the following steps:

1. Use the **Exit Master** icon on the Toolbar to switch back to the **Filmstrip** view. You can also use the **Window** menu and deselect the **Master Slide** item.
2. If needed, reduce the width of the **Filmstrip** by dragging the vertical separator between the **Filmstrip** and the stage to the left.
3. Use the **Insert** | **New Slide From** | **Content 02** menu item to insert a new slide based on the Content 02 Master Slide of the Theme.

The new slide already contains objects. To be exact, the elements contained on the slides are not actual objects yet. These elements are objects **Placeholders**. They are used to predefine the location, size, and other formatting options of a future object.

4. Double-click the **Double click to add title** Placeholder.
5. Type some text into the object and hit the *Esc* key.

Now that some text has been typed into the object, it is no longer a placeholder. It is an actual Smart Shape with text. The size, position, font family, font size, color, and so on of this object are inherited from the placeholder, while the content has just been typed in.

Changing the Master Slide of an existing slide

Sometimes, you want to change the Master Slide that's applied to an existing slide. This is what you will learn about in this section. Follow these steps to get started:

1. Use the **Slide** | **Content Slide** icon on the Toolbar to insert a third slide in the project.
2. With the new slide selected, look at the **Properties** inspector.

Remember that new slides are always inserted after the selected slide. When it comes to the Master Slide, Captivate uses whatever Master Slide is applied to the selected slide when inserting a new one.

3. In the topmost section of the **Properties** inspector, open the **Master Slide** drop-down menu and apply the **Content 01** Master Slide of the theme to the selected slide. This operation is illustrated in the following screenshot:

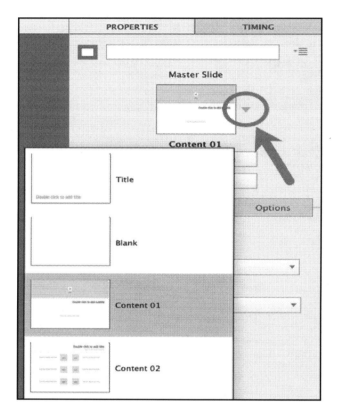

In this section, you learned how to change the Master Slide and applied the selected slide using the **Properties** inspector.

Inserting a blank slide in a themed project

In this section, you will insert a new blank slide into your project and see which Master Slide is applied by default:

1. Use the **Filmstrip** to select the third slide of the current project.
2. Use the **Slide | Blank Slide** icon on the toolbar to insert a new blank slide.
3. With the new slide selected, look at to the topmost section of the **Properties** inspector.

Notice that the **Blank** Master Slide has been automatically applied to this new slide.

4. Open the **Background** menu situated in the **Style** tab of the **Properties** inspector.
5. Select the **Custom** option. Extra icons appear in the **Properties** inspector.

Inspect the available options. Take note of how you can change the background color, create a gradient, or use a picture as the slide's background.

This exercise concludes your first exploration of Master Slides in Captivate. Now, you will explore the second element of a Theme.

The Styles

The second element of a Theme is a set of object Styles. You will now experiment with Styles in Themes by using the following steps:

1. Use the **Filmstrip** panel to return to the second slide of the project.
2. Select the title (a Smart Shape with text) that you created in the previous section.
3. Inspect the **Properties** inspector of the selected object. Note the **Font, Color, Font Size**, and other formatting properties that are currently in use.

You will now apply another Theme to the project and see how this change affects the slides and the objects.

4. Open the **Themes** icon on the Toolbar.
5. Click the **Abstract** theme to apply it to the project.
6. Read the warning message and click **Yes** to continue.

The new Theme is applied to the project.

7. Use the **Filmstrip** panel to go through the slides of the project one by one.

Note how the new Theme affects the look and feel of the project. The most obvious change is the new background picture, but a Theme is far more than that.

8. When on the second slide, select the Title Smart Shape.
9. In the **Properties** inspector, note how the formatting properties of the selected object have changed.

This illustrates that, in addition to Master Slides, a Theme also contains Object Styles. So, by applying another theme to a project, you update the Master Slides *and* the styles that are applied to the objects.

The third element of a Theme

In addition to Master Slides and Object Styles, a Theme affects a third element, called the **Skin**. The Skin of the project is covered in Chapter 15, *Finishing Touches and Publishing*.

You now have a much better understanding of what a Theme is. In the next section, you will take a look at how we created the takeTheTrain_Theme.cptm theme you applied to the TakeTheTrain.cptx file back in Chapter 2, *Working with Standard Objects*. But for now, let's summarize what you already know about themes:

- A Theme is a collection of graphical assets and Styles. It is used to quickly define the look and feel of an entire project.
- Captivate contains predefined Themes. These are available in the **Themes** icon on the Toolbar.
- A Theme is composed of three basic elements: a collection of Master Slides, the Styles applied to the objects of the project, and the Skin of the project.
- When inserting a new slide, Captivate tries to determine the best Master Slide to apply.
- The **Properties** inspector makes it easy to change the Master Slide that's applied to any slide at any time.

Creating a custom Theme

In this section, you will recreate (part of) the theme you applied to the takeTheTrain.cptx file at the beginning of this book. While doing so, keep in mind that creating a theme should come much earlier in the production process of your Captivate courses. As a matter of fact, it should probably be one of the first things you do when starting a new project. In this book, it comes after you have sufficient knowledge of the basic objects and concepts of Captivate for pedagogical purposes only.

To create a custom theme, you must first apply one of the predefined Themes of Captivate to a new project. You must then modify the Master Slides and the Styles of this theme to slowly build your own theme:

1. Close every open file in Captivate.
2. Use the **File** | **New Project** | **Blank Project** menu item to create a new blank project.
3. In the **New Blank Project** dialog, use the **Select** drop-down menu to choose a size of **1024 x 627** for the project. When you are done, click the **OK** button.
4. Save the new project as `Chapter06/themeMaker.cptx`.
5. Use the **Themes** icon on the Toolbar to apply the **Blank** theme to the project.
6. Click **Yes** to acknowledge and clear the warning message.

The Missing Blank theme

If the Blank theme is not available in the **Themes** icon of the Toolbar, click the small **Browse** link in the bottom left corner of the Themes window and look for the `~Documents/My Adobe Captivate Projects /Layouts/11_0/en_US/Blank.cptm` file (Mac) or the `C:\Program Files\Adobe\Adobe Captivate 2019\Gallery\Layouts11_0\en_US\Blank.cptm` file (Windows).

By applying the **Blank** theme to the project, you modify the overall look and feel as well as the styles that are already present in the project. The **Blank** theme is an excellent starting point for creating your own themes.

7. Use the **Themes** | **Save Theme As** menu item to create a new Theme.
8. Save the new Theme as `Chapter06/DiDaXo-Theme.cptm`.
9. Acknowledge the successful creation of the new Theme by clicking the **OK** button.

With your new Theme saved, you can move to the next step, in which you will customize the Master Slides of the Theme.

Making the Blank theme the Default theme

Lots of Captivate developers decide to use the Blank theme as the default theme that's applied to new projects. This saves a step in the preceding procedure. To do so, open the **Themes** icon on the toolbar, right-click the **Blank** theme, and choose **Set as Default Theme**.

Customizing the Master Slides of the Theme

You create Master Slides with visual elements (backgrounds, logos, headers, and so on) so that you can apply them to the standard slides of your project that need to share the same basic layout. If you are a PowerPoint or Keynote user, this process probably sounds very familiar:

1. Still in the `Chapter06/themeMaker.cptx` file, use the **Window** | **Master Slide** menu item to switch to the Master Slide view.

As shown in the following screenshot, the **Blank** theme that you applied to the project contains seven Master Slides (shown as **1** in the following screenshot), in addition to the Main Master Slide (shown as **2** in the following screenshot). Note that the **Master Slide** panel has been enlarged to capture the screenshot. Also notice that the name of the applied theme (here, **DiDaXo-Theme**) appears below the Main Master Slide thumbnail:

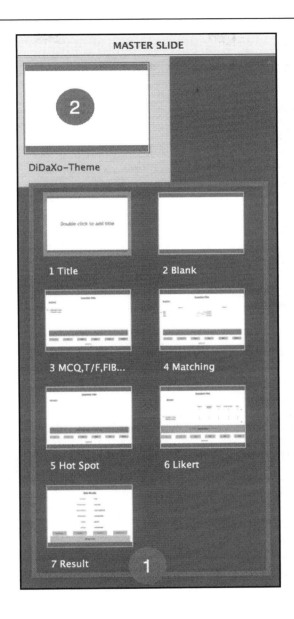

Now, try to delete one of these Master Slides and see what happens using the following steps.

2. Right-click any of the Master Slides (just make sure you don't right-click the Main Master Slide at the very top of the **Master Slides** panel).

3. Click the **Delete** menu item and confirm your intention to delete the selected Master Slide.

A second message appears, indicating that the selected Master Slide cannot be deleted. This is because at least one Master Slide for each type of slide must be present in the Theme. In other words, the seven Master Slides of the current theme represent the minimal set of Master Slides each Theme must contain.

Customizing the Main Master Slide

The Main Master Slide is the first one in the **Master Slide** panel. You use it to insert the main graphical elements shared by most (if not all) of the other Master Slides of the project:

1. In the **Master Slide** panel, click the Main Master Slide to select it.

2. If needed, open the **Properties** inspector. Make sure it shows the properties of the Main Master Slide.

3. Use the **Media | Image** icon on the Toolbar to insert the `Chapter06/images/mainBackground.png` image on the main Master Slide.

4. With the image selected, look at the **Options** tab of the **Properties** inspector.

5. Make sure that both the **X** and the **Y** properties are set to 0 so that the image is positioned exactly in the top-left corner of the slide.

6. Open the **Timeline** panel and completely lock the image using the corresponding lock icon.

With the addition of this single image, your project already looks far different than it did a few minutes ago, as shown on the following screenshot:

If you take a look at the **Master Slide** panel, you will notice that all of the Master Slides of the Theme (except the Blank one) are now using the background image we defined on the Main Master Slide.

The Main Master slide is also the perfect place to add legal mentions such as a copyright notice.

7. Still on the Main Master Slide, use the **Text** | **Text Caption** icon on the Toolbar to create a new Text Caption.
8. Double-click the new Text Caption to enter the text edit mode.
9. Delete the default text.

10. In the **Character** section of the **Style** tab of the **Properties** inspector, click the **Insert Symbol** icon. This operation is illustrated in the following screenshot:

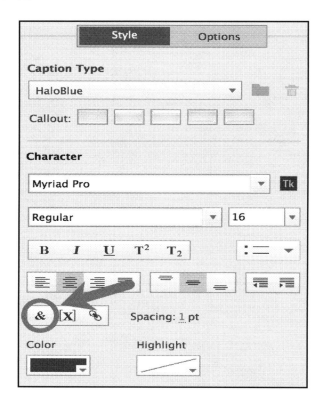

11. Double-click the copyright symbol to insert it into the Text Caption.
12. Type copyright - DiDaXo - 2019 after the copyright symbol.
13. When you are done, hit the *Esc* key to leave the text edit mode and select the Text Caption.
14. In the **Style** tab of the **Properties** inspector, change the font to **Lato** (or whatever other Typekit font you chose to use earlier in this chapter) and the font size to 8 points (it is possible to type it if it is not in the list).
15. Change the **Caption Type** to **Transparent** if needed.
16. Switch to the **Options** tab of the **Properties** inspector and set the **Angle** to 270°.
17. Move and resize the Text Caption so it fits along the left edge of the slide, just above the footer area.

18. In the **Timing** panel, make sure the **Transition** is set to **No Transition**.

19. Switch back to the **Properties** inspector and use the Style Options icon to create a new style after the current formatting of the copyright notice. Give that new style the name of `DiDaXo-Copyright`.

20. Finally, use the lock icon on the **Timeline** panel to completely lock this object.

21. Save the file when you are done. Browse the other Master Slides of the project and note that the copyright notice appears on (almost) every one of them. The fact that the Main Master Slide controls the general look and feel of the entire project also makes it the perfect place to add the color scheme of the project in the Scrap area:

22. Still on the Main Master Slide of the `Chapter06/themeMaker.cptx` project, use the **Media | Image** icon to add an image to the Main Master Slide.

23. Browse to the `Chapter06/images/DiDaXo_colors.png` file and import it into your project.

24. Move the newly imported image to the scrap area of the Main Master Slide.

At the beginning of this chapter, you added the same image in the scrap area of the first slide of the project and used the display for the Rest of Project option of the Timing panel. Using the scrap area of the Main Master Slide is another technique you can use to make this image available to (almost) all of the slides of your project.

Changing the background of a Master Slide

You will now customize the **Title** Master Slide of the theme. This Master Slide should use a different background than the one that's inherited from the Main Master Slide. You also want to remove the copyright notice so that it does not appear on Title slides. Use the following steps to apply a different background image to the title Master Slide:

1. Still in the Master Slide view of the `Chapter06/themeMaker.cptx` file, use the **Master Slide** panel to select the **Title** Master Slide.

2. In the **Properties** inspector, deselect the **Show Main Master Slide Objects** checkbox.

This action removes the objects that are inherited from the Main Master Slide. This leaves you with a blank slide containing one placeholder.

3. Use the **Media | Image** icon on the Toolbar to insert the `Chapter06/images/titleBackground.png` image on the slide.

4. Use the **Timeline** panel to lock the image so it cannot be accidentally modified.

In this section, you've used the **Show Main Master Slide Objects** checkbox of the **Properties** inspector to import a slightly different background image on the Title Master Slide. Note that this checkbox hides all of the objects defined on the Main Master Slide. This explains why the copyright notice as well as the color scheme do not show on the Title Master Slide.

5. Use the **Media | Image** icon on the Toolbar to insert the `Chapter06/images/DiDaXo_colors.png` image on the slide.

6. Move the color scheme image to the scrap area of the Title Master Slide.

7. In the **Master Slide** panel, select the **Blank** Master Slide.

8. Look at the **Properties** inspector and notice that the **Show Main Master Slide Objects** checkbox is already deselected for this particular Master Slide.

Now, you know why the Blank Master slide is ... blank!

Adding a Master Slide to the Theme

You will now add a new Master Slide to the theme. You will name it `Content` and insert another image onto it:

1. Still in the Master Slide view of the `Chapter06/themeMaker.cptx` file, use the **Master Slide** panel to select the **Title** Master Slide.

2. Use the **Insert | Content Master Slide** menu item to insert a new Master Slide in the project.

The new Master Slide is inserted as Master Slide number 2. Note that this new slide inherits the elements of the Main Master Slide by default. You will now give a name to this Master Slide and import another image.

3. Select the newly inserted Master Slide in the **Master Slide** panel and look at the **Properties** inspector.

4. At the very top of the **Properties** inspector, enter `Content` in the **Name** field and hit the *Enter* key to validate this.

Note that the new name also appears below the Master Slide thumbnail in the **Master Slide** panel.

5. Use the **Media | Image** icon on the Toolbar to insert the `images/chapter06/contentBkg.png` image.

6. Use the Lock icon on the **Timeline** panel to completely lock the new image, preventing any accidental edits.

The project contains eight Master Slides in addition to the Main Master Slide, as illustrated in the following screenshot (the **Master Slide** panel has been enlarged to capture the screenshot):

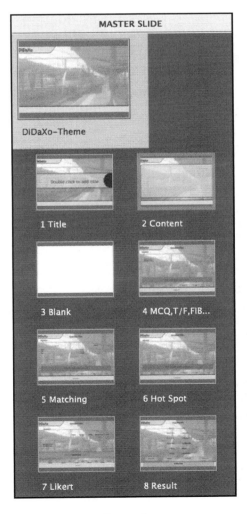

Adding more Master Slides to the theme

In this section, you will add three more Master Slides to the theme using the same procedure as the one you used in the previous section. The general steps are as follows:

1. Use the **Insert | Content Master Slide** menu item to insert new Master Slides in the Theme.
2. Use the **Properties** inspector to change the name of the **Master Slides**.
3. Insert the required images onto each new Master Slide.
4. Lock the imported images using the lock icon of the **Timeline** panel.

Use the following table to name the new master slides and add the correct image:

Master Slide name	Image to import
Content 2 Cols	Chapter06/images/2colsBkg.png
Content Left Col	Chapter06/images/leftColBkg.png
Content Right Col	Chapter06/images/rightColBkg.png

At the end of this extra credit section, you should have eleven Master Slides in your Theme.

This concludes your first exploration of the Master Slides in a Theme. Of course, you can add more Master Slides, import additional background images and objects, and so on. Feel free to further experiment with these concepts before moving on to the next section. But before that, let's quickly summarize the key concepts you've learned in this section:

- To create a new Theme, apply one of the predefined Themes to your project and use the **Themes | Save Theme As** menu item
- A Theme is saved as a .cptm file, and it will appear in the list of themes in the **Theme** icon on the toolbar
- The first element contained in a Theme is a set of Master Slides
- The Main Master slide is used to quickly define the general look and feel of the whole project
- By default, all of the Master Slides of the project inherit the elements that are defined on the Main Master Slide
- Deselect the **Show Main Master Slide objects** checkbox to prevent the elements of the Main Master Slide from showing on another Master Slide
- Use the **Insert | Content Master Slide** menu item to insert new Master Slides into the project

In the next section, you will define new Styles and save them in your custom Theme.

Adding Styles to the Theme

To create new styles, you will return to the Styles Options icon of the **Properties** inspector. You will save these new styles in the Theme at the end of this exercise.

Let's start by giving the proper look and feel to the standard objects of the project.

Styling the titles

In this section, you will return to the Title Master Slide of the Theme and modify the formatting of the Title Smart Shape using the following steps:

1. Still in the Master Slide view of the `Chapter06/themeMaker.cptx` file, use the **Master Slide** panel to select the **Title** Master Slide.
2. Select the **Double click to add title** placeholder.

A placeholder object, such as the one you just selected, is a special object used to predefine the size, location, and styling properties of a future Captivate object. You will now use this placeholder to predefine the look and feel of the future titles of the future Captivate projects that will use this particular theme.

The **Properties** inspector of the selected Title Placeholder shows the same properties as a Smart Shape. This is because the Title Placeholder is based on a Smart Shape object. This means that all of the features and flexibility offered by Smart Shapes are available to the Title Placeholder.

3. Move and resize the selected placeholder to the top of the central area of the **Title** Master Slide.
4. In the **Character** section of the **Style** tab of the **Properties** inspector, increase the font size to `60` points.
5. Change the Font to **Cooper Std** (or whatever Typekit Web Font you chose to use earlier in this chapter).
6. Change the color of the text as well. Use the eyedropper tool to select the topmost swatch (purple) of the `DiDaXo_colors.png` file that you imported in the Scrap Area earlier in this section.
7. Use the Style Options icon to save the current formatting of the selected placeholder in a new style named `DiDaXo-ProjectTitle`.

After the preceding actions, the title placeholder on the Title Master Slide has the proper look and feel, as shown in the following screenshot:

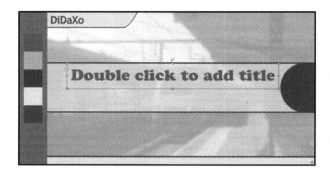

In the next section, you will learn how to add extra placeholders to your Master Slides.

Adding placeholders to the Master Slides

The power of Master Slides goes way beyond defining common backgrounds and objects. By adding Placeholder objects, you can predefine the location and styling of future objects (such as Images, Text Captions, Smart Shapes, and so on). In this exercise, you will add a slide title placeholder to the Content Master Slide we created in the previous section:

1. In the **Master Slide** panel, select the **Content** Master Slide.
2. Use the **Insert | Placeholder Object | Title** menu item to add a Title Placeholder on the Master Slide.
3. Move and resize the Placeholder object so that it fits in the top left corner of the content background image.
4. With the Title Placeholder selected, look at the **Style** tab of the **Properties** inspector.
5. In the **Style** tab of the **Properties** inspector, change the font to **Cooper Std** (or any other Typekit font).
6. Change the alignment to **Align Left**.
7. Change the color of the text as well. Use the topmost swatch (purple) of the image you imported in the Scrap Area.
8. Switch to the **Timing** panel and apply a **Fade In Only** transition to the Title Placeholder.

9. Switch back to the **Properties** inspector and use the Style Options icon to create a new style after the current formatting of the placeholder. Give this new style the name `DiDaXo-SlideTitle`.

When developing a project that uses this theme, the eLearning developer simply double-clicks the placeholder and types the title of the slide. The size, location, and formatting properties of this title are inherited from the placeholder. This ensures visual consistency and considerably speeds up the development process. The Content Master Slide should look as follows:

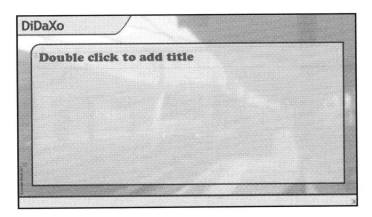

Note that Placeholder objects can only be inserted into Master Slides. In other words, it is not possible to insert a Placeholder object into regular slides.

Adding Title Placeholders to the other Master Slides

In this section, you will repeat the preceding sequence of actions to add a Title Placeholder into the **Content 2 Cols**, **Left Content**, and **Right Content** Master Slides. The general steps are as follows:

1. Select the desired Master Slide in the **Master Slide** panel and use the **Insert | Placeholder Object | Title** menu item to insert a new Title Placeholder on the selected Master Slide.
2. Apply the **DiDaXo-SlideTitle** style to the newly inserted placeholder object.
3. Resize the placeholder so that it fits in the upper area of the slide.

At the end of this section, you should have added one Title placeholder to each new Master Slide.

Don't forget that you can use the Align toolbar, the **Options** tab of the **Properties** inspector, and the Guides to make sure that the objects are placed the same way on each Master Slide.

Saving the Styles in the Theme

You've now been exposed to (pretty much) all of the tools, techniques, and features we used to create the `takeTheTrain_Theme.cptm` theme that you applied to your project at the beginning of the second chapter of this book. Of course, we could have defined additional Master Slides, inserted more placeholder objects of different types, and defined additional styles. For the sake of time, we will not go any further into defining the theme.

Feel free to open to the `final/chapter06/takeTheTrain.cptx` file and use the **Window | Master Slide** menu item to examine the Master Slides, Placeholders, and Styles that we've defined in the theme.

However, there's one additional step that we want to emphasize before moving on to the next topic. To save the newly created styles and Master Slides into the theme, you need to save the theme file itself. By saving the Theme, you update the `DiDaXo-Theme.cptm` file so that you can apply this theme to other projects. You can do this by using the **Themes | Save Theme** menu item to update the current Theme with the new styles and Master Slides.

In the next section, you will discover the Captivate templates, but first, let's summarize what you've learned about Themes in this section:

- It is possible to create a custom theme in Captivate. Just use the **Themes | Save Theme As...** menu item to create a `.cptm` file on your computer.
- Always start by applying one of the predefined themes of Captivate that you can customize to create your own theme.
- The **Blank** theme is one of the predefined themes. It is an excellent starting point when creating your custom themes from scratch.
- Use the **Window | Master Slide** menu item to switch to the Master Slide view. Alternatively, there's a **Master slide view** button at the top of the **Properties** inspector when a slide is selected.

- When in the Master Slide view, there are several ways to return to the regular Filmstrip view. You can use the **Filmstrip view** button on the **Properties** inspector (when a Master slide is selected), the **Exit Master** icon on the Toolbar, or deselect the **Window** | **Master Slide** menu item to return to the regular Filmstrip view.

- The Main Master Slide is used to define the general look and feel of all of the Master Slides of the theme. It is also a great place to add utility objects (such as the color scheme of the project) to the scrap area.

- A theme must contain at least seven Master Slides, in addition to the Main Master Slide. This is to ensure that every possible type of slide is covered by at least one Master Slide.

- It is possible to add additional Master Slides to a theme by using the **Insert** | **Content Master Slide** menu item.

- When a Master Slide is selected, deselect the **Show Main Master Slide Objects** on the **Properties** inspector to define a custom background for that Master Slide.

- You can add different types of Placeholders into Master Slides. A Placeholder is a template object that's used to define the size, location, and formatting properties of a future object.

- The styles you create and modify are saved in the Theme, along with the Master Slides.

- Don't forget to use the **Themes** | **Save Theme** menu item to update the `.cptm` file. You will see your theme in the Themes icon on the toolbar so that you can apply it to other projects.

Working with Templates

The basic idea of a Template is to create a project that can be used as a blueprint for future projects. When creating a project from a Template, a duplicate of the Template is created, which serves as the starting point of a new project. In the new project, the teacher can edit, remove, and add objects, with no restrictions.

A Template can contain the same slides and objects as a regular project. The preferences that are applied to the Template become the default preferences of future projects based on that Template. The Theme applied to a Template becomes the default Theme of future projects based on that Template.

In the next exercise, you will create a Template that will be used for all of the Captivate files of the `Take the train` project. To do so, let's pretend that the instructional and graphic designers at DiDaXo decided upon the following:

- All files should have a resolution of 1,024 x 627 pixels (so they fit on an iPad screen in landscape mode).
- All files should use your custom `DiDaXo-Theme.cptm` theme.
- All files should begin with a title slide. The title should be written in a Smart Shape using the **DiDaXo-ProjectTitle** style.
- The second slide of each project should state the objectives of the project.
- The actual course begins on the third slide.
- When the main course is finished, a summary slide should emphasize the key points of what has been covered in the project.
- The project should end with a quiz.
- The final slide should be similar to the first one, but with closing text.

Creating a Template

To help the company enforce these rules, you will create a Template that the eLearning developers will use to create future courses. This Template will help in producing consistent content and design across projects. It will also speed up the development of the eLearning courses by reusing common designs, properties, and content:

1. Save and close every open project.
2. Use the **File | New Project | Project Template** menu item to start the creation of a new template. (Make sure to use the **Project Template** item, not the **Project From Template** item.) Alternatively, you can use the *command + T* (Mac)/*Ctrl + T* (Windows) menu item.
3. In the **New Project Template** box, select the **1024 x 627** resolution, and click **OK**.

The first rule is already enforced! All of the files that will be based on this Template will be of the same **1024 x 627** size by default.

4. Open the **Themes** icon on the Toolbar.
5. Click the **Browse** link in the bottom-left corner of the **Themes** panel.
6. Navigate to the `Chapter06/DiDaXo-Theme.cptm` file you created earlier in this chapter to apply that theme to the new Template.

 If you didn't succeed in creating the theme file by following the instructions in the previous sections, you can use the `Chapter06/final/DiDaXo-Theme.cptm` file.

Second rule enforced! All future projects based on this Template will use your custom `DiDaXo-Theme.cptm` theme.

7. Make sure that the **Properties** inspector shows the properties of the first slide of the project.
8. At the top of the **Properties** inspector, use the **Master Slide** drop-down menu to apply the **Title** Master Slide of the Theme to the selected slide if necessary.
9. At the top of the **Properties** inspector, change the slide name to `Intro Slide` and press *Enter* to confirm.

Third rule enforced! The first slide of the Template is based on the Title Master Slide of the Theme and contains a Title Smart Shape placeholder with the **DiDaXo-ProjectTitle** style already applied.

10. Use the **Slide | Content Slide** icon on the Toolbar to insert a new slide into the template.
11. Use the **Properties** inspector to change the name of this slide to `Objectives`.
12. Also, make sure that the **Title&Content** Master Slide of the Theme is applied to the new slide.
13. Double-click the slide title placeholder and write `Objectives of this module` in the placeholder.
14. Hit the *Esc* key to exit Text Edit mode and select your slide title as an object.

The second slide of your template should now look as follows:

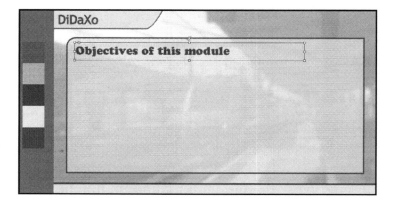

Fourth rule enforced! The second slide of the Template is ready to receive the objectives of the project. The layout and styling of that content is already predefined in the Theme and Master Slides.

15. Use the **Slide | Content** icon on the Toolbar to insert a third slide based on the **Content** Master Slide of your Theme.
16. Use the **Text | Text Caption** icon on the Toolbar to add a Text Caption in the center of this new slide.
17. Type `Your project begins here` in the Text Caption and hit the *Esc* key.

Fifth rule enforced! The third slide of the Template is where the course module actually begins. When using the template, eLearning developers will be able to add extra slides, change the Master Slides, add more objects, and so on.

18. Use the **Slide | Content Slide** icon of the Toolbar to insert a new slide into the project.
19. Use the **Properties** inspector to change the name of this slide to `Summary`.
20. Still in the **Properties** inspector, make sure that the **Content** Master Slide of the Theme has been applied to the new slide.
21. Double-click the slide title placeholder and write `Summary of this course module` in the placeholder.
22. Hit the *Esc* key to exit Text Edit mode and select your slide title as an object.

Sixth rule enforced! After the main course, a summary slide should list the key takeaways of this course module.

Adding Placeholder Slides

The next slide of the Template is where the question slides of the project should be placed. When developing the template, you do not know what question types will be used and what the actual questions will be. You only know that the quiz begins on that slide. To enforce this rule, you will add **Placeholder Slides** to the Template.

There are two types of Placeholder Slide available:

- A **Recording Slide Placeholder** is meant to be replaced by a screenshot-based recording using the techniques you will learn about in Chapter 8, *Capturing Onscreen Action*.
- A **Question Slide Placeholder** is meant to be replaced by a Question Slide. Quizzes and Question Slides will be covered in Chapter 7, *Working with Quizzes*.

In this case, you need a Question Slide Placeholder. Use the following steps to insert it into the Template:

1. If needed, use the **Filmstrip** panel to go to the last slide (slide 4) of the Template.
2. Use the **Insert** | **Placeholder Slides** | **Question Slide Placeholder** menu item to add a Question Slide Placeholder at the end of the Template.

Seventh rule enforced! A Question Slide Placeholder has been added at the end of the Template.

Just like Placeholder objects can only be added to Master Slides, Placeholder slides can only be added to Captivate templates. Also note that the options of the **Properties** inspector, as well as most icons on the Toolbar, are grayed out when a placeholder slide is selected. This is because this Placeholder is not an actual slide. Therefore, there are no properties to show in the **Properties** inspector and no objects can be added onto it.

Adding the last slide

You will now create the last slide of the Template. Because it is very similar to the first slide, you will duplicate the first slide, move the duplicated slide to the end of the Template, and change the text content of the title Smart Shape using the following steps:

1. In the **Filmstrip** panel, select the first slide of the Template.

2. Use the *Ctrl + D* (Windows)/*command + D* (Mac) shortcut to duplicate the selected slide.

3. In the **Filmstrip** panel, drag the duplicated **Intro Slide** to the very end of the project. After this action, the duplicated slide is the sixth and last slide of the Template.

4. Use the **Properties** inspector to change the name of that last slide to *Ending slide*.

5. Double-click the Title placeholder and type `Thank you for taking this online course with us.`

6. Resize the title Smart shape so that the text fits on the slide.

Eighth rule enforced! The last slide of the Template is very similar to the first one, with a nice closing comment.

Saving the Template

For the sake of time, let's consider that this Template is complete. Keep in mind, though, that you could go much further in the development of a Captivate Template. For example, you could use the **Preferences** dialog to define project properties directly in the Template. These would become the default preferences that are used by future projects based on that Template:

1. Save the Template as `Chapter06/DiDaXo-Train.cptl`.

Note that the file extension that's used for a Captivate Template is `.cptl` and not `.cptx` as for a regular project. Next, you'll create a new project from this template.

Creating a new Captivate project from a Template

In this section, you will play the role of an eLearning developer who has to use your new Template to develop a new course module for the DiDaXo Company:

1. Close every open file so that you can see the Captivate Welcome screen.

2. Use the **File** | **New Project** | **Project From Template** menu item to start creating a new Captivate project based on an existing template.

3. Navigate to the `Chapter06/DiDaXo-Train.cptl` Template file you created in the previous section to choose it as the base of a new project.

The new project that opens in Captivate is a copy of the Template you created in the previous section. Note that the new project uses the standard `.cptx` file extension. Before moving on, you will quickly preview the project.

    4. Use the **Preview** | **Project** icon on the Toolbar to preview the entire project.

When the project appears in the **Preview** pane, note that the Smart Shape Placeholder of the first slide does not appear in the final output. Also, note that the Question Slide Placeholder is not part of the final output. Actually, the slide count (shown at the top-left corner of the **Preview** pane) is **5** and not 6. As long as *actual* objects and slides haven't replaced the Placeholder objects and slides, they do not appear in the published version of the project.

    5. Close the **Preview** pane to return to Captivate.
    6. Use the **Filmstrip** panel to go to the first slide of the project.
    7. Double-click the Title Placeholder and type `Take the train in Belgium`. Hit *Esc* when done to quit Text Edit mode and leave the shape selected.

This action turns the Title Placeholder into an actual Smart Shape object. Note how quick it was to insert the project tile on the first slide. Rapid development is one of the key advantages of using Themes, Templates, Styles, and Placeholders.

    8. With the title selected, look at the **Style** tab of the **Properties** inspector.
    9. Try to change the font to another one of your choice.

No warning messages appear to tell you that this property is locked by the Template and cannot be changed. In other words, the developer has the freedom to override the choices that were made on the Template. Remember that the Template sets the *default* properties of slides and objects, but it does not force the teacher/developer to use them in the final version of the project.

    10. Use the **Filmstrip** panel to go to slide 5 of the project.

Slide 5 is the **Question Slide Placeholder**. Remember that it did not show up in the **Preview** pane when we tested the project earlier in this section.

    11. Double-click the **Question Slide Placeholder** slide.
    12. In the box that appears, select the **Multiple choice** checkbox and click the **OK** button

Captivate replaces the Question Slide Placeholder with a Multiple Choice question slide. You will learn more about Quizzes and Question Slides in the next chapter, `Chapter 7`, *Working with Quizzes*.

13. Keep experimenting with this file. Try to add more slides, change the applied Master Slides, modify the content of Placeholders, and so on. Notice that you have full freedom to do so.

14. When you are done, close the project without saving it.

This exercise concludes your overview of Templates. Before moving on to the next chapter, let's quickly summarize what has been covered in this section:

- A Captivate Template is a blueprint that's used as a starting point for standard Captivate projects.
- A Template contains the same objects and slides as a standard project.
- The Theme that's applied to a Template serves as the default Theme for all future projects based on that Template.
- Placeholder Slides are used to mark the location of a screen recording or the location of Question Slides in the Template.
- A Template sets the default properties and objects, but it does not strictly enforce them. In other words, a teacher/developer can override the choices made on a Template when designing the project.
- A Template file has a `.cptl` file extension. When you create a course using a template, remember to save it as a `.cptx` file.

Summary

In this chapter, you concentrated on the graphic design aspect of the project. You discovered that it is important to create a consistent learning environment in which your learners feel comfortable enough to concentrate on learning the content and not on how the online course works.

In the first part of this chapter, you learned about the Styles and the Object Style Manager. You focused on the different fonts that you can use and discovered the Adobe Fonts (formerly Typekit) collection of Web Fonts that's available in Captivate 2019. You then used the predefined Themes to better understand what Themes are and how they work. Next, you moved on to creating your own Theme, and finally, you created a Template and used that Template to create a new project.

By using Styles, Master Slides, Themes, and Templates, you created a consistent and professional look and feel that can be used across multiple projects. You've also made the life of your eLearning developers much easier by giving them a tremendous amount of assets they can use and reuse in their future projects. This will dramatically speed up their work.

With the completion of this chapter, an important part of this book comes to an end. The project you've been working on is pretty much ready to be published.

In the next few chapters, you will learn about the more advanced features of Captivate, such as Quizzes, Capturing on-screen actions, and Advanced Actions. If all you need is to create simple projects such as the one you just completed, feel free to jump directly to `Chapter 15`, *Finishing Touches and Publishing*, to learn about the publishing phase, which is the last of the Captivate Production processes.

In the next chapter, you will jump into Quizzes, one of the most powerful and popular features of Captivate.

Meet the community

In this section, we want to introduce you to James Kingsley. James is a usual speaker at eLearning conferences and summits. If you ever participate in one of these events, make sure you attend James' session. You'll certainly find insights on innovative ways to use Captivate and learn an advanced trick or two!

James Kingsley

James Kingsley has worked in the eLearning industry since 2001. James enjoys making tools, desktop, and web applications do things they were not meant to do. He keeps an eye on the latest web and mobile technologies and looks for ways to combine them with eLearning to create new solutions. James is a regular speaker at conferences and has won several awards for combining technologies to produce better eLearning.

During his time in the military, James was the Course Supervisor for Instructor Training and Curriculum Design. When he joined the civilian workforce, he combined his love for programming and software development with his military experience.

As an entrepreneur, James has founded several software, web, and mobile development companies, primarily in the eLearning arena, including *ReviewMyElearning.com*, which is the first feature-packed solution to collect feedback from SMEs, team members, clients, and so on, when reviewing online courses with almost any authoring tool. It is also the only course review tool that works with Adobe Captivate.

James is also the founder of *CoursePortfolios.com* – the best solution for sales teams and developers to host and share demos of eLearning courses, videos, and image galleries with clients and potential customers. This solution creates portfolios that you can customize for each client and industry with your own logos, colors, contact information, and more. In addition, it is a great place to browse demos and get inspiration for your next project!

Currently, James is available to help you solve your eLearning puzzles. James regularly blogs for eLearning Brothers, and hosts webinars to showcase how to think outside of the box when working with Captivate, JavaScript, and xAPI.

Contact details

- LinkedIn: https://www.linkedin.com/in/jameskingsley/
- Twitter: @onEnterFrame
- Blog: http://elearningbrothers.com/author/jkingsley/
- Site: http://jameskingsley.com

Working with Quizzes 7

Assessing students' knowledge has always been a primary concern for anyone involved in teaching activities. When it comes to eLearning, assessment is both a pedagogical and a technical issue.

On the pedagogical side, one of the factors that characterizes the eLearning experience is that learners sit alone in front of computers or mobile devices. As teachers, we have to leave lanterns along the learner's path to make sure that the lonely learner does not get lost and confused. Constant assessment helps in keeping the learners on track. By giving them many opportunities to test and validate their knowledge, the learners can build new knowledge on solid grounds.

On the technical side, Captivate contains a powerful quizzing engine that lets you insert different kinds of **Question Slides** in your projects. At the end of the Quiz, Captivate is able to send a detailed report to a **Learning Management System** (**LMS**). An LMS is a server that is used to host eLearning content and track the learner's progression withg your online courses.

In this chapter, you will perform the following:

- Inserting various kinds of Question Slides in your Captivate projects, using several different techniques
- Exploring how some of the objects of Captivate can be added to the Quiz
- Creating Knowledge Check questions throughout the course
- Using Knowledge Check Questions as overlay slides of Interactive Videos
- Creating a Question Pool and inserting random Question Slides in the project
- Exploring and setting Quiz Preferences

- Providing feedback to the students by using the branching capabilities of the Question Slides and the Quiz
- Setting up the reporting to an LMS
- Discussing the SCORM, AICC, and xAPI standards used to communicate the quiz results to the LMS

Preparing your work

To get the most out of this chapter, reset the Captivate interface to default. If you are using the default interface mode, just close and restart Captivate. If you use the advanced interface mode, use the **Window | Workspace | Reset 'Classic'** menu item to reset Captivate to default. In this chapter, you will use the exercises stored in the Chapter07 folder. If you get confused by any of the step-by-step instructions, take a look at the Chapter07/final folder, which contains a copy of the files, as they will be at the end of this chapter.

Introducing the Quiz

During the first part of this chapter, you will insert a Quiz at the end of the takeTheTrain.cptx project. For pedagogical reasons, it is important to introduce the Quiz to the students. You should explicitly state what is going to happen and how the student will be graded. You will now insert one more slide in the project, using the following steps:

1. Open Captivate.
2. Open the Chapter07/takeTheTrain.cptx.
3. Use the **Filmstrip** to go to slide 21.
4. Use the **Slides | Content Slide** icon on the Toolbar to insert a new slide in the project. Confirm that the new slide is slide 23 of the project.

Remember that Captivate inserts new slides *after* the selected one. But this case is a bit special. Because slide 22 is used as an Overlay Slide for the Interactive Video of slide 21, these two slides form a single *system*. Therefore, the new slide has been inserted after that *system*. In other words, the new slide is slide 23, regardless of slide 21 or 22 being the selected one at the time of the insertion of the new slide.

5. In the **Properties** inspector, apply the **Title&Text** Master Slide to the new slide.
6. Double-click the Title placeholder and type Time for the Quiz.
7. Double-click the Caption placeholder and type the following text: Answer the following questions the best you can.[Enter] Your answers will be reported to the LMS. [Enter] You must score 50 % or higher to pass.
8. Draw a Rounded Rectangle Smart Shape in the bottom area of the slide.
9. With the rounded rectangle selected, look at the **Properties** inspector.
10. Select the **Use as Button** checkbox and apply the **shape_As_Button** style.
11. Change the text of the button to Start the Quiz.
12. Adjust the size and the position of the button to your taste.
13. Don't hesitate to add additional decorative elements (such as a Character image). Also, feel free to modify the properties of the existing objects further.
14. Arrange the **Timeline** of the new slide, making sure that the **Start the Quiz** button stops the playhead at the end of the slide and jumps to the next slide when being clicked.

See how easy and fast it is to insert new slides when a Theme is applied to the project. Because the visual aspect is, for the most part, taken care of by the Master Slides and the Object Styles, you can concentrate on the content to deliver.

Your new slide should look similar to the following screenshot:

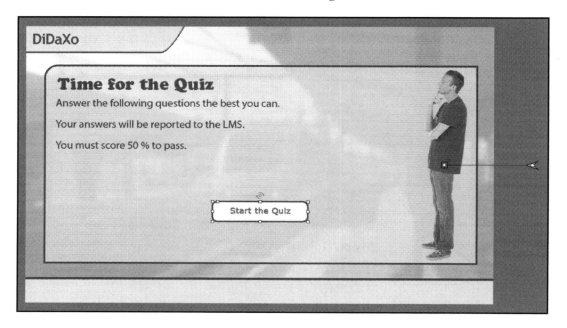

Creating Question Slides

In Captivate, a Question Slide is a very special type of slide. When inserting the first Question Slide in a project, you automatically create a Quiz. There are many options that you can set either for each individual Question Slide or for the entire Quiz.

Although very powerful, the Quiz engine of Captivate has some limitations. While it is possible to insert regular slides in between the Question Slides, all the Question Slides of a project (excluding the Knowledge Check questions) belong to the same Quiz. In other words, each project can only contain a single Quiz.

Captivate supports eight types of Question Slides. In the upcoming sections, you will explore each of these question types, one by one.

Inserting the first Question Slide

To get started, you will now insert the first Question Slide in your project by performing the following steps:

1. Return to the `Chapter07/takeTheTrain.cptx` project.
2. Use the **Filmstrip** panel to go to slide 23. Notice that the project currently contains 24 slides.
3. Click the **Slides | Question Slide** icon on the Toolbar. You can also use the **Quiz | Question Slide** menu item to perform the same action. The **Insert Questions** dialog opens.

The **Insert Questions** dialog lists the types of Question Slides available in Captivate. For this first example, you will add a single **Multiple Choice** question to the project.

4. In the **Insert Questions** dialog, select the **Multiple Choice** checkbox.
5. Open the **Graded** drop-down list associated with the **Multiple Choice** question.

The dropdown provides three options: **Graded**, **Survey**, and **Pretest**:

- **Graded**: This type of question has correct and incorrect answers. For example, *Does Belgium have an extensive train network? (True/False)* is a question that has a correct and an incorrect answer, so it is a graded question (by the way, the answer is *True*!).
- **Survey**: This type of question is used to gather the learner's opinion. As such, it has no correct or incorrect answer. For example, *Would you recommend this eLearning course to your friends? (Yes/No)* is a survey question.
- **Pretest**: This type of question is graded, but is not a part of the Quiz. In other words, the answer to a Pretest question is not considered when calculating the score of a Quiz. Also, these answers are never reported to the server. A pretest is used to assess the student's knowledge before taking the course. It is possible to add branching based on the outcome of the pretest. For example, the students passing the pretest can skip the course if they want to. But the students failing the pretest have to take the course to gain the required knowledge.

There is a fourth type of Question Slide available in Captivate called Knowledge Check Slides. These will be covered at the end of this chapter.

In this example, you will add a single *Graded* Multiple Choice question.

    6. Select **Graded** in the drop-down list.

Make sure the **Insert Questions** dialog looks like the following screenshot:

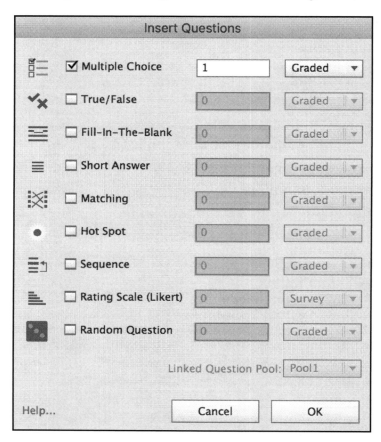

    7. Click the **OK** button to generate the Question Slide and to close the **Insert Questions** dialog.

Take a look at the **Filmstrip**. It now contains *26* slides. This means that the operation you just completed has added *two* slides to the project:

- As expected, the Multiple Choice question has been inserted after the active slide. In this case, the Multiple Choice question is slide 24.
- Because the new slide is the first Question Slide of the project, Captivate has also generated the **Quiz Results** slide as slide 25.

The **Quiz Results** slide contains a lot of automatically generated elements.

8. Use the **Filmstrip** to go to slide 24.
9. Inspect the various elements that have been automatically added to the Multiple Choice question slide.

The only element that may require an explanation is the **Review Area**. This area is used to display feedback messages to the student at the end of the Quiz. The content of these messages depend on how the students answered this particular question.

10. Use the **Filmstrip** to go to slide 25.
11. Inspect the elements of the **Quiz Result** slide.

The **Quiz Results** slide is generated by default when a new Quiz is created (or, in other words, when the first Question Slide is added to the project). It is possible to turn this slide off if you want to.

12. Use the **Quiz | Quiz Preferences** menu item to open the Quiz Preferences dialog.
13. On the left side of the **Preferences** dialog, click the **Settings** category of the **Quiz** section.

Watch out! There is another **Settings** category in the **Recording** section. Make sure you use the one in the **Quiz** section, as shown in the following screenshot:

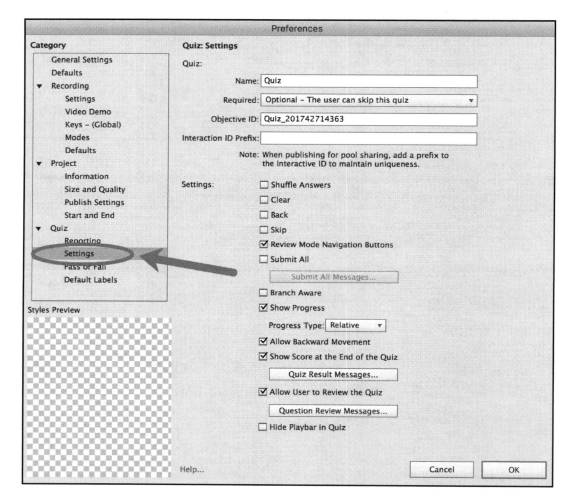

14. Deselect the **Show Score at the End of the Quiz** checkbox.
15. Click the **OK** button to apply the changes and close the **Preferences** dialog.

When this operation is complete, look at the **Filmstrip**. Note that slide 25 is grayed out and that an eye icon appears under its thumbnail. This means that the slide is hidden. In other words, it is still in the project, but it won't be displayed to the students.

16. On the **Filmstrip**, click the eye icon below slide 25.

This action turns the visibility of slide 25 back on. It is equivalent to returning to the **Preferences** dialog to select the **Show Score at the End of Quiz** checkbox again.

Turning the visibility of slides on and off

Turning the visibility of slides on and off is not limited to the **Quiz Results** slide. You can use this handy feature on any slide of the project. Simply right-click a slide in the **Filmstrip** and choose **Hide Slide** in the contextual menu. This might be useful when a slide has been updated, but you want to retain a record of the original slide. It can also be used on multilingual projects to hide or show the slides pertaining to a particular language version.

Completely removing the Quiz Results slide is only possible when there are no more Question Slides in the project. But if you have a Quiz in the project (in other words, if you have at least one Question Slide), the Quiz Results slide is mandatory. This is because, behind the scenes, most of the variables and internal logic associated with a Quiz refer to this particular slide.

Using the Multiple Choice question

The basic principle of a Multiple Choice question is to provide multiple answers to a given question. The student has to choose the correct answer from a predefined list.

In the following exercise, you will configure the Multiple Choice question you added in the previous section by performing the following steps.

1. Return to the Chapter07/takeTheTrain.cptx project.
2. Use the **Filmstrip** to go to slide 24.

Slide 24 is the first Question Slide of the project. Lots of objects have been automatically generated on this slide.

Watch out! It is possible that some objects sit on top of other objects. For example, move the yellowish *Incomplete Caption* to reveal the *Incorrect Caption* and the *Correct Caption*!

The purpose of most of the generated objects should be obvious, but some of them require more explanation:

- The **Review Area** is related to the **Review Quiz** button on the **Quiz Results** slide (currently, slide 25). If the learner clicks that button at the end of the Quiz, the learner will be allowed to review the Quiz. In such a case, the **Review Area** is used to display an appropriate feedback message to the student.
- The student uses the buttons at the bottom of the slide to interact with the Quiz. It is possible to control the visibility of most of those buttons either for the entire Quiz or for each individual Question Slide.
- The **Progress Indicator** in the top right corner of the slide can also be customized in the **Preferences** dialog.
- During the Quiz, the feedback messages in the middle of the slide are hidden by default. They are automatically revealed depending on the student's answer to the question. It is therefore not a problem if they overlap.

Every element of the Question Slide can be customized. If needed, you can even insert extra objects (such as Images, Animations, or additional Text Captions), using the same techniques as those used for a standard slide. Note that extra buttons and other interactive objects cannot be added to a Question Slide.

To add extra interactive objects to a question slide, add a Smart Shape and select the **Use As Button** checkbox.

Understanding the basic question properties

Text Captions and Smart Shapes are used to display the question and the list of possible answers. Your next task is to customize these objects by performing the following steps.

1. Triple-click the placeholder that reads **Type the question here** to select it in text edit mode and to select its content.

2. Type `What type of ticket would you choose if you use the train every day to go to work or school?` and hit the *Esc* key.

3. Click the thin blue line that wraps the answers. This selects the Answer Area on the slide.

4. Use the *Shift* + down arrow shortcut several times to move the Answer Area down 10 pixels at a time.

Remember that when using the arrow keys, you move the selected objects *one pixel* at a time. But when combining the arrow keys with the *Shift* key, you move the objects *10 pixels* at a time. This is one of the shortcuts we use the most in Adobe applications, because, yes.... it also works in other applications such as Photoshop, Illustrator, InDesign, and more!

5. Now, you can increase the height of the Question Smart Shape, so the text fits in the object.

6. Triple-click the first possible answer to select it in the edit mode and select its content. Type `A standard one-way ticket.` as the first answer.

7. Don't hesitate to move the feedback messages out of the way before continuing with this procedure.

8. Use the same technique to write `A standard round trip ticket.` as the second answer.

To make this question more interesting, you need to add more possible answers to the list.

9. Open the **Quiz** inspector next to the **Properties** inspector in the panel group on the right edge of the screen. You may need to click the **Properties** icon of the Toolbar to open the panel group.

10. In the topmost section of the **Quiz** inspector, change the number of **Answers** to 4. Captivate generates two more answers on the Question Slide.

11. Type `A 10 trips pass in first class.` and `A renewable three months subscription.` in the newly generated answers.

12. Click the radio button associated with the last answer (**A renewable three month subscription.**) to mark it as the correct answer.

Your multiple choice Question Slide should now look as follows (note that the success, failure, and incomplete feedback messages have been moved to the scrap area before taking the screenshot):

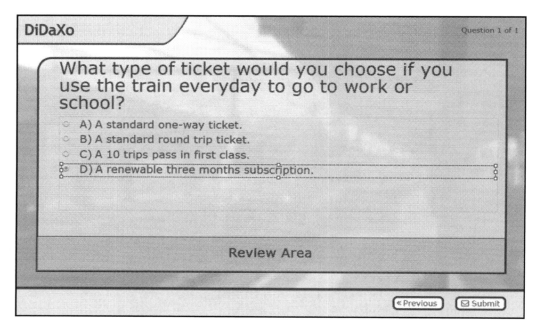

Working with Partial Scoring

In this particular example, the first question is complete. But, sometimes, you'll need a more sophisticated Multiple Choice with multiple correct answers. Fortunately, Captivate has an option that allows the Multiple Choice question to accept multiple correct answers. You will now experiment with this feature by performing the following steps:

1. Return to the `Chapter07/takeTheTrain.cptx` project.
2. Use the **Filmstrip** to go to slide 24.
3. Select the **Multiple Answers** checkbox in the topmost section of the **Quiz** inspector.

On the Question Slide, this action changes the radio buttons associated with each possible answer to checkboxes. You can now tell Captivate what the right answers are.

4. On the Question Slide, select any three answers out of the four available. (Remember that in this example, what you need is a single correct answer, so this exercise is made for demonstration purposes only. The actual answers you select are therefore not important).

At this moment, the question is either entirely correct (if the user selects all three correct answers) or entirely wrong (in every other case). **Partial Scoring** allows you to make this question partially correct if the student selects some of the right answers but not all. This advanced option is currently available on Multiple Choice questions only. You will now turn Partial Scoring on using the following steps.

5. Select the **Partial Score** checkbox in the topmost section of the **Quiz** inspector.

Note that by selecting the **Partial Score** checkbox, the **Points** and **Penalty** options of the **Quiz** inspector are disabled. When Partial Scoring is turned on, each possible answer of the Multiple Choice question is assigned a specific score.

6. Select the first answer you marked as correct.
7. Switch to the **Properties** inspector and go to the **Options** tab. Change the **Points** of this answer to 5.
8. Repeat the same procedure with the other two answers you marked as correct.
9. Finally, select the only answer not marked as correct and make sure the **Points** property is set at 0 (note that you can also assign a negative score to the incorrect answer).

In this configuration, the student can be awarded, 0, 5, 10 or 15 points for this question, depending on the answers provided. You will now return to the initial situation by performing the following steps.

10. Return to the **Quiz** inspector and deselect the **Multiple Answers** checkbox. On the Question Slide, the checkboxes associated with each answer revert to radio buttons.
11. Also deselect the **Partial Score** checkbox. This action reactivates the **Points** and the **Penalty** properties.
12. Make sure the **Points** property has a value of 10 and the **Penalty** property has a value of 0.

13. On the slide itself, make sure to mark the last answer (**A renewable three months subscription**) as the only correct answer.

Even though you don't need the *Multiple Answers* and *Partial Scoring* options in this example, you now have the required knowledge about these features if you ever need to use them.

Branching with Question Slides

The last thing to do with this Question Slide is to decide how Captivate should react when the learner submits an answer. Remember that Captivate can react differently when the correct or the incorrect answer is submitted. This concept is known as **Branching**. Perform the following steps to implement branching on this Question Slide:

1. Make sure you are still on slide 24 of the Chapter07/takeTheTrain.cptx file.
2. Scroll down the **Quiz** inspector until you see the **Actions** section.
3. Make sure the **On Success** action is set to **Continue.**
4. Also confirm that the **No. of Attempts** option is set to **1.**
5. Open the **Last Attempt** dropdown and inspect the available options.
6. Select the **Jump to slide** action and choose **11 Slide 11** in the **Slide** dropdown that appears just below.

Slide 11 explains the main types of train tickets available in Belgium. If the students does not answer the Multiple Choice question correctly, you want to redirect them to that slide to re-explain this particular topic.

7. Use the **Filmstrip** to return to slide 11 of the project.
8. Select the **Continue** button in the bottom center of the slide.
9. In the **Action** tab of the **Properties** inspector, change the **On Success** action to **Return To Quiz**.

If a Quiz is in progress, this action redirects the student to the current Question Slide in the Quiz. If no quiz is in progress, this action has no special effect and the **Continue** action is assumed.

10. When you have finished, use the **Filmstrip** to return to slide 24 of the project.

Discovering the other options of the Quiz inspector

In this section, you will explore the other options of the **Quiz** inspector. While doing so, keep in mind that the features and properties that you are about to discover are available regardless of the question type (Multiple Choice, True/False, Matching, and so on). Perform the following steps to experiment with the options of the **Quiz** inspector:

1. In the **Quiz** inspector, locate the **Buttons** section.
2. Select the **Clear**, **Back**, and **Skip** checkboxes.

This adds the corresponding buttons to the question slide (note that the **Clear** button appears just above the **Previous** button; therefore, you might want to move the **Clear** button a little bit to reveal the **Previous** button that is underneath).

 These buttons have been customized using the Theme that is applied to the project.

3. Return to the previous situation by deselecting the **Clear**, **Back**, and **Skip** checkboxes.
4. Still in the **Quiz** inspector, locate the **Actions** section.
5. Change the number of attempts to 2.
6. Select the **Retry Message** checkbox to see the corresponding **Try Again** Smart Shape appearing on the stage.

You can, of course, customize the content and the styling of this feedback message. But for this example, you will disable it.

7. Deselect the **Retry Message** checkbox to discard the **Try Again** message.
8. Open the **Failure Messages** dropdown. Notice that it allows you to choose between **None**, **1**, or **2**.
9. Close the **Failure Messages** dropdown and change the number of **Attempts** to 3.
10. Reopen the **Failure Messages** dropdown. Notice that this time it allows you to choose between **None**, **1**, **2**, or **3**.

The options visible in the **Failure Messages** dropdown depend on the **No. of Attempts** property. The highest number available in the **Failure Message** dropdown always matches the defined number of attempts.

11. Change the **Failure Messages** to **3**.

This inserts three failure messages (in red) on the stage. Be aware that some of them might overlap, so it is possible that you don't see three distinct failure messages until you move them around. You can now customize the failure message displayed to the user for each failed attempt.

 There is no visible difference in the failure messages. All three of them look identical. To identify them, you can hover over the caption, and it will show the incorrect shape number.

12. Still in the **Quiz** inspector, open the **Failure Messages** dropdown and choose **None**.

In this configuration, there is no failure message displayed to the student when a wrong answer is submitted.

13. Change the **No. of Attempts** back to 1 (notice that this, logically, disables the **Retry Message** checkbox).
14. Open the **Failure Messages** drop-down menu and choose **1**. This generates a single red failure caption at the bottom of the slide, which is the default configuration.
15. In the **Captions** section, deselect the **Incomplete** checkbox to discard the corresponding caption on the stage.
16. Take some time to inspect the remaining options available in the **Quiz** inspector, but do not change any of them at this time.

Pay particular attention to the following:

- You can still change the question **Type** (**Graded** or **Survey**).
- You can set a **Time Limit** and a corresponding **Timeout Caption** to answer this particular question.

Customizing the feedback messages

Providing quality feedback to the students is paramount in any pedagogical situation, eLearning, or classroom. In this section, you will look into the basic ways of creating feedback messages on Question Slides. Keep in mind, though, that more sophisticated feedback strategies can also be implemented.

For example, you can use the Branching capabilities of the Question Slides to redirect the student to a specific slide or sequence of slides. But, for now, let's start with the basics by performing the following steps:

1. On slide 24 of the `Chapter07/takeTheTrain.cptx` project, select the red failure caption.
2. Double click the object and change the text of the red failure message to `Sorry, this is not the correct answer – Click anywhere or press 'y' to continue..`
3. Change the text of the green feedback message to `Great answer! – Click anywhere or press 'y' to continue..`
4. Hit the *Esc* key to leave the text edit mode and select the green success message as an object.
5. Turn your attention to the **Properties** inspector.

Notice that the properties available in the **Properties** inspector are the same as those available when a Smart Shape is selected. This is because the feedback messages of a Question Slide are Smart Shapes with text. Therefore, all the capabilities of standard Smart Shapes are available, including the ability to change the shape of the messages.

6. Select the red rectangular failure message.
7. If needed, move and resize it so the text fits in the shape.
8. Right-click the rectangular failure message and choose the **Replace Smart Shape** menu item.
9. In the list of available shapes, select the rounded rectangle. This changes the shape of the underlying object to a rounded rectangle.

Keep this capability in mind when working with feedback messages as the shape used to provide the feedback message might reinforce the message itself.

Now, remember that in Chapter 2, *Working with Standard Objects*, you have used another object to display text to the learner. This object is the Text Caption. If you prefer to use Text Captions instead of Smart Shapes for your feedback messages, you can do so by performing the following steps.

10. Right-click the red failure caption and choose the **Revert to Text Caption** menu item.
11. With the red Text Caption selected, turn your attention to the **Properties** inspector.

Notice that the available properties are those of a Text Caption. Most Captivate developers tend to prefer using Smart Shapes over Text Captions, as Smart Shapes provide much more creative and pedagogical capabilities. This includes a wealth of shapes to choose from, the ability to control opacity, or to use image backgrounds. Therefore, you will now revert to using a Smart Shape for your red failure message before finalizing your first question slide.

12. Right-click the red failure caption and choose the **Convert To Smart-shape** menu item.
13. Choose the Rounded Rectangle in the Smart Shape gallery.
14. Move and resize the red Failure Caption and the green Success Caption to your taste.

While resizing and moving your feedback messages, don't hesitate to use the Align toolbar (remember to use the **Window | Align** menu item to display it) and the Smart Guides to align and size the objects easily. When you have finished, your Question Slide should look as follows:

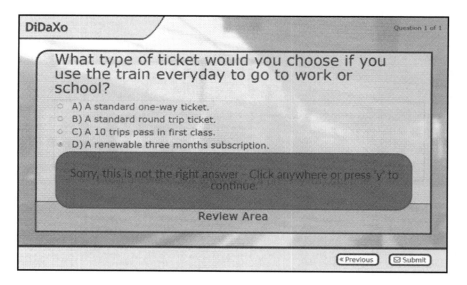

Notice that we've used the Align toolbar to give both feedback messages the same size and the same position, so they overlap on the screenshot. This is not a problem, since Captivate only displays one message *or* the other depending on the submitted answer.

This concludes your exploration of the Multiple Choice question. As you can see, there are a multitude of options available to help you fine-tune your assessments.

Importing Question Slides from a GIFT file

GIFT stands for **General Import Format Technology**. A GIFT file is a text file, which allows you to use a simple text editor to write various types of questions. Such a text file can then be imported into any GIFT-compliant eLearning application and system, making it easy to share question banks across these systems.

Captivate offers the ability to import GIFT files into your projects. Thanks to this feature, you can import into Captivate questions that were originally created in another GIFT-compliant application. Note that Captivate can only import GIFT files created in other systems, but it cannot export the Question Slides of a Quiz into a GIFT file.

 The GIFT format was invented by Moodle, a popular open source LMS. To learn more about the GIFT format, see the following page on the official Moodle website: `https://docs.moodle.org/en/GIFT_format`.

In the following exercise, you will take a look at a GIFT file and import it into the `takeTheTrain.cptx` project by performing the following steps:

1. Open the `Chapter07/takeTheTrain_GIFT.txt` file in a text editor such as Text Edit (Mac) or Notepad (Windows).
2. Read through this text file, making sure you don't change any of its content.

A GIFT file is a specially formatted text file, with a `.txt` file extension. Even without knowing anything about the GIFT format, reading it is easy. This particular file contains three questions. The first one is a **Matching** question, the second a **Short Answer** question, and the last one is a **True/False** question. Notice that the feedback messages for those questions are also included in the GIFT file.

3. Return to the `Chapter07/takeTheTrain.cptx` project and use the **Filmstrip** to return to slide 24.
4. Use the **Quiz | Import GIFT Format File** menu item.
5. Navigate to the `Chapter07/takeTheTrain_GIFT.txt` file and click **Open** to begin importing the file.
6. Read the message stating that the feedback captions will, unfortunately, not be imported. Click the **OK** button to continue.

Captivate parses the GIFT file and creates three additional Question Slides in the project. These new slides are added after the selected one as slides 25, 26, and 27.

The GIFT file you just imported is a Moodle question bank that has been exported with the built-in export feature of Moodle. To learn more about creating question banks with Moodle, see `https://docs.moodle.org/en/Question_bank`. To learn more about exporting Moodle questions to a GIFT file, see `https://docs.moodle.org/en/Export_questions`.

After this simple process, you should have four Question Slides and a total of 29 slides in your project.

Our good friend Paul Wilson published a video tutorial on this feature. Don't hesitate to take a look at it (and the other videos on his YouTube channel) to have yet another perspective on creating GIFT files and inserting them in Captivate: `https://www.youtube.com/watch?v=tkXM2d8lcag`

Importing Question Slides from a CSV file

In the previous section, you have learned how to import questions from a GIFT file. This workflow makes it easy to import Question Slides in Captivate. That being said, importing from a GIFT file has its own shortcomings:

- The biggest problem is to create the GIFT file. You need a GIFT compliant application or platform. And even when using such an application, you sometimes need to tweak the generated GIFT file before it can be inserted in Captivate with no errors.
- While there are lots of GIFT compliant applications, there are many Captivate users who do not have access to such a system.

Thankfully, Captivate 2019 provides a brand-new workflow for importing Question Slides to your projects. The idea is very similar, but instead of importing a GIFT file, you will now import a CSV file.

CSV stands for **Comma-Separated Value**. Just like a GIFT file, a CSV file is a special type of text file that can be opened and edited by any basic text editor (such as Notepad on Windows or Text Edit on the Mac). But CSV files have a lot of advantages over GIFT files.

The biggest advantage is that CSV files can be created and edited by most spreadsheet applications, such as Microsoft Excel, Open Office Calc or Apple Numbers. This means that anyone that has access to such spreadsheet applications (which means virtually anyone!) can create questions for your Captivate projects.

In this section, you will first delete the three Question Slides that you imported using the GIFT workflow. Then, you will review the CSV file that you will import in Captivate before discussing ways to create such a CSV file.

Deleting the Question Slides

The first step of this process is to delete the Question Slides that have been imported using the GIFT workflow earlier in this chapter. Use the following steps to do so:

1. Return to the `Chapter07/takeTheTrain.cptx` project and use the **Filmstrip** to return to slide 25.
2. Hold the `Shift` key down and click on slide 27 in the **Filmstrip**. This action should select from slide 25 to slide 27. In other words, the three Question Slides imported earlier should be selected.
3. In the **Filmstrip**, right-click any one of the selected slides.
4. Choose the **Delete** menu item in the contextual menu and confirm your intention.

After this operation, your project contains a single Multiple Choice Question Slide for a total of 26 slides in the project.

Inspecting the CSV file

You will now inspect the CSV file that you will import in Captivate using the following steps:

1. Open the `Chapter07/takeTheTrain_CSV.csv` file in any basic text editor (Use Notepad if you are on Windows and Text Edit if you are on a Mac).

When the file opens, you should see the same three questions as those imported with the GIFT file, but written in another format. In the `takeTheTrain_CSV.csv` file, notice the following:

- The first line represents the title of the columns. For example, the name of the first column is **//Question Type**, the name of the section column is **//Points**, and so on.
- The other three lines represent the three questions contained in this CSV file.

- The pieces of data in this file are separated by the comma , symbol. In other words, each time Captivate encounters a comma in the file, it switches to the next column. For example, **MAT** is the //**Question Type** of the first question (**MAT** stands for **MAT**ching Question), **SA** is the //**Question Type** of the second question (**SA** stands for **S**hort **A**nswer Question), and so on.
- When a column contains no data, you simply see the comma symbol in the CSV file. This explains why some lines of data end with lots of commas with no data between them.

The following screenshot shows the CSV file as seen on a Mac in Text Edit:

```
takeTheTrain_CSV.csv — Edited

//Question Type,//Points,//Question Stem,//Answer Option 1,//Answer
Option 2,//Answer Option 3,//Answer Option 4,//Answer Option 5,//Answer
Option 6,//Answer Option 7,//Answer Option 8,//Answer Option 9,//Answer
Option 10,//Answer Option 11,//Answer Option 12,//Answer Option 13,//
Answer Option 14,//Answer Option 15
MAT,10,Match the type of train with the corresponding description,L
Trains|Local trains are the only way to reach rural areas.,IC Trains|
Inter City trains run only between major cities.,P Trains|Peak trains
only run during peak hours,,,,,,,,,,,,
SA,10,"What type of train only runs during peak hours? (choose between
L , IC or P)",P,,,,,,,,,,,,,
TF,10,It is necessary to make a reservation when traveling on Belgian
trains.,TRUE,*FALSE,,,,,,,,,,,,
```

Lines in a CSV file

What we consider a *line* in the CSV file you are working with is everything that stands between two carriage returns (the carriage return being an invisible character). With this definition of *line* in mind, it is quite possible that a *line* of data in the CSV file spans multiple lines on your screen. This is because the *lines* in the CSV file are usually much wider than your screen so the text editor is displaying a single *line* of data over several lines on the screen.

One of the advantages of a CSV file is that it can be opened in most spreadsheet applications. You will now close your basic text editor and open the same CSV file in a spreadsheet application (such as Microsoft Excel, Open Office Calc, or Apple Numbers) to have yet another perspective on the data you will soon import in to Captivate.

2. Close your basic text editor (Notepad or Text Edit) without saving any changes to the CSV file.

3. Reopen the same CSV file using any spreadsheet application available on your system.

> If you do not have access to any spreadsheet application on your system, you can download the free and open source Open Office from the following URL `https://www.openoffice.org/`. Open Office contains a spreadsheet application called Calc that can be used for this exercise.

When the CSV file opens in the spreadsheet application, you should have a much clearer view of what exactly is going on:

- You should see four lines on your spreadsheet, the first line being the name of each column and the three remaining lines being the three questions defined in the CSV file.

- When opening the file, the spreadsheet application uses the comma character present in the CSV to delimit each cell of the table. The carriage return character of the CSV file is used to delimit each line of the table (note that the carriage return character is invisible in the CSV file).

- Some cells of the table are empty, which correspond to the suites of commas you have seen in the CSV.

The following screenshot represents the same CSV file as seen in Microsoft Excel for Mac. Note that the zoom level as well as the column width has been increased to make the screenshot:

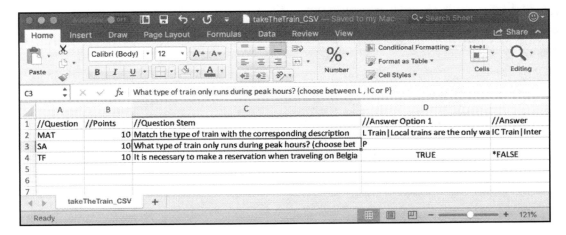

The ability to open and edit CSV files in any spreadsheet application makes CSV much easier to create and edit than GIFT files. It also enables other members of your teams, who do not know anything about Adobe Captivate, to participate in the production of your eLearning projects by writing questions in those CSV files using Microsoft Excel or a similar application.

4. Close your spreadsheet application without saving any changes made to the CSV.

Importing the CSV file in Adobe Captivate

Now that you have a precise idea of the CSV file you are working with, let's import it in Captivate using the following steps:

1. Return to the `Chapter07/takeTheTrain.cptx` project and use the **Filmstrip** to return to slide 24.
2. Use the **Quiz | Import CSV Format File** menu item.
3. Navigate to the `Chapter07/takeTheTrain_CSV.csv` file and click **Open** to begin importing the file.
4. Make sure you save the file before continuing with this exercise.

After this operation, three additional Question Slides are added as slides 25, 26, and 27 of the project.

Creating CSV files for importing in to Captivate

Now that the Question Slides defined in the CSV file have been imported in Captivate, let's discuss the creation of CSV files. The biggest advantage of CSVs over GIFT files is that you can use any spreadsheet application to generate and edit CSV files. To help you generate compliant CSV that can be imported flawlessly into Captivate 2019, the Captivate team provides two templates to help you out. This is what you will review in this section, using the following steps:

1. [Windows] Use Windows Explorer to navigate to `C:\Program Files\Adobe\Adobe Captivate 2019 x64\Gallery\Quiz`
2. [MAC] Use the Finder to navigate to *`/Applications/Adobe Captivate 2019/Gallery/Quiz`*

The following screenshot shows the content of this folder as seen on a Mac:

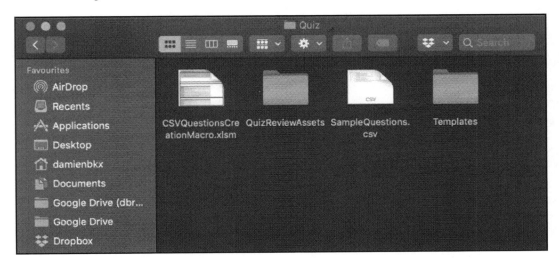

There are two important template files that you can use to create CSV files that can be imported in Adobe Captivate 2019:

- SampleQuestions.csv is a CSV file containing one example of each of the supported question type. Use this file as a template to create your own CSV files using any text editor or spreadsheet application.
- CSVQuestionsCreationMacro.xlsm is a Microsoft Excel file containing macros. If you have Microsoft Excel on your system, you can use this file to generate the CSV files using an automated process that uses Excel macros. If you have Microsoft Excel available on your system, don't hesitate to open this file and see the instructions it contains.

You will find more information on using the CSVQuestionsCreationMacro.xlsm file in the following blog article by Dr Pooja Jaisingh: https://elearning.adobe.com/2018/08/adobe-captivate-2019-release-and-csv-question-import-template/.

Working with Matching questions

The first question that has been imported from the CSV file is a **Matching Question**. The Matching Question provides two columns of elements. The student has to match an element of the first column with one or more element(s) of the second column. In this exercise, you will take a look at the imported Matching question and modify some of its properties by performing the following steps:

1. In the `Chapter07/takeTheTrain.cptx` project, use the **Filmstrip** to go to slide 25.
2. Move the feedback messages out of the way if necessary.
3. Take some time to inspect this slide and to compare it with the content of the CSV file.
4. When ready, select the **Column 1** and the **Column 2** captions (remember to hold the *Shift* key while selecting the second object to add it to the selection).
5. Move the two captions down using the *Shift* + down arrow key on the keyboard.
6. When you have done this, you should have enough room to increase the size of the Question Smart Shape to see the whole text.
7. Double-click in the **Column 1** text area and change the text to `Type of train`.
8. Use the same process to change the text of the **Column 2** object to `Description`.

To make the question more interesting (and the answer more difficult to find), you will provide a different number of items in both columns.

9. In the topmost area of the **Quiz** inspector, increase the number of items of **Column 2** to `4`.
10. Select the **Shuffle Column 1** checkbox.

The **Shuffle Column 1** checkbox instructs Captivate to display the options of the first column in a random order each time a student takes the Quiz.

You will now change the text of the new item you just added to the **Description** column.

11. Type `T trains are for tourists only` in the extra item of the **Description** column.

12. Move and resize the four items of the **Description** column so the text fits in each one of them. You can use the tools of the Align toolbar to make it easier.

13. Select the **L Train** item in the first column of the Matching question.

14. Open the dropdown that appears in front of the **L Train** item.

This dropdown is used to tell Captivate the right answer. In this case, this operation is useless, as the right answer is part of the information that has been imported from the CSV file. Note that many items of the first column can match a single item of the second column. This can be used to create very interesting and complex Matching questions.

15. Click an empty area of the slide to deselect the currently selected object and close the associated dropdown.

16. In the **Captions** section of the **Quiz** inspector, deselect the **Incomplete** Caption to remove the yellow feedback message.

17. In the **Buttons** section, make sure that only the **Clear** button is selected.

18. Leave all the other options of the **Quiz** inspector at their current values.

19. Customize the green correct message and the red failure message to taste.

Before moving on to the next question type, feel free to move and resize the objects of this slide so they look good to you. Remember that when it comes to aligning and resizing objects, great tools are available on the Align toolbar. Your slide should look similar to the following screenshot when complete.

Connecting the lines

In the following screenshot, notice how the lines are connected to the elements of the **Type of train** column. To achieve this result, we have manually reduced the width of each elements of the first column to better fit the actual length of the text:

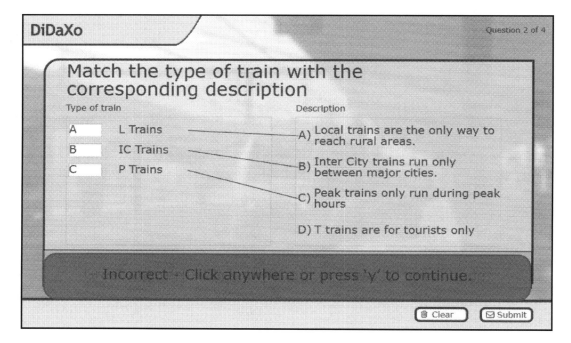

Working with Short Answer questions

The second question inserted from the CSV file is a Short Answer question. In a Short Answer question, the student must type in a few words or a short sentence as the answer. Captivate then matches the supplied answer against a predefined list of correct answers. Let's take a look at the Short Answer question by performing the following steps:

1. In the `Chapter07/takeTheTrain.cptx`, use the **Filmstrip** to go to slide 26.
2. Inspect this slide and compare it with the content of the CSV file.
3. Move the feedback messages out of the way.

4. Move the answer area down using the *Shift* + down arrow shortcut and increase the height of the question text object.

5. Select the big Answer Area in the middle of the slide. When selected, the **Correct Entries** box is displayed.

6. Compare the content of the **Correct Entries** box to the content of the CSV file.

The **Correct Entries** box contains the list of entries that the answer provided by the student will be matched against. You can add more correct answers by clicking the + icon in the top right corner of the **Correct Entries** box. You can also make the correct entries case sensitive if needed.

Coming up with the right question

As a teacher, coming up with the right question is always a challenge. This is especially true with the Short Answer question type. You need to find a question whose answer is obvious enough for a computer to correct, complicated enough to have some pedagogical value, and flexible enough to allow the students to type the same answer in different versions. All in all, I must admit that I don't use the Short Answer type very often for graded questions. That being said, it is a great survey question. Something like *"Do you have any comment to make regarding this online course?"* is easily done using a Short Answer survey question.

The main properties of this question are now in place. It's time for some fine-tuning.

7. In the topmost section of the **Quiz** inspector, change the **Points** value to 5 and the **Penalty** value to 1.

The **Penalty** value removes one point from the student's score if an incorrect answer is submitted.

8. In the **Captions** section of the **Quiz** inspector, deselect the **Incomplete** Caption. This removes the yellow feedback message.

9. In the **Buttons** section of the **Quiz** inspector, make sure **Clear** is the only selected checkbox.

10. Leave the other options of the **Quiz** inspector at their current settings.

11. Don't hesitate to rearrange the elements of the slide, keeping in mind that the success and failure captions will never be displayed at the same time. Therefore, it is not a problem if they overlap.

That's it for the Short Answer question. Make sure your slide looks similar to the following screenshot and save the file before moving on:

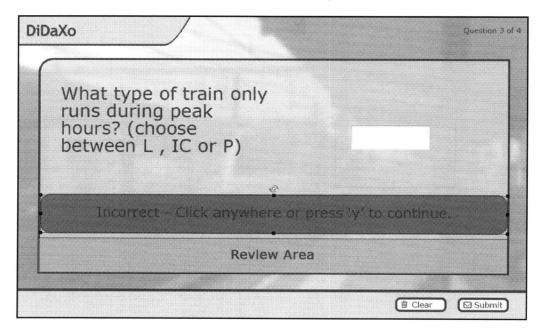

Working with True/False questions

The third question imported from the CSV file is a **True/False** question. A True/False question is a Multiple Choice question with only two possible answers. By default, these two answers are *True* and *False*, but you can change these defaults to anything you like (such as Yes/No, Man/Woman, and so on) as long as there are no more than two different answers. Perform the following steps to explore and modify the imported True/False question:

1. In the `takeTheTrain.cptx` file, use the **Filmstrip** to go to slide 27.
2. Move the feedback messages out of the way if needed.
3. Move the Answer Area a few pixels down to allow for a higher question text.
4. Double-click the **True** answer and try to change the text.

You should be able to change the text without any problems. This illustrates that the possible answers of a True/False question can actually be something other than *True* or *False*. The important point here is to ask a question that has no more than two possible answers, whatever these answers are. Make sure to undo your changes so the text actually reads **True** before continuing with this exercise.

5. Make sure that **False** is marked as the correct answer. (This should have been imported from the CSV file, but a double-check is always a good thing!)

As usual, you will now fine-tune the other properties of this question slide.

6. In the **Quiz** inspector, deselect the **Incomplete** Caption to remove the yellow feedback message.
7. Make sure the **Clear** button is the only one selected in the **Buttons** section.
8. Leave all the other options of the **Quiz** inspector at their current value.
9. Rearrange the elements of the slide however you want, and customize the success and failure feedback messages too.

When you have finished, your slide should look like the following screenshot:

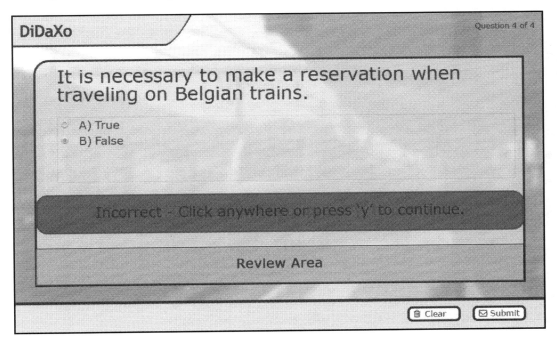

Adding the remaining Question Slides

To speed you up and let you focus on the Question Slides, specifics, the remaining Question Slides of this project have already been created for you. They are stored in the `Chapter07/additionalQuestions.cptx` file. In this section, you will copy and paste the questions of the `additionalQuestions.cptx` file into the `takeTheTrain.cptx` file:

1. Open the `Chapter07/additionalQuestions.cptx` project.
2. Use the **Filmstrip** of the `additionalQuestions.cptx` file to select the first slide.
3. Hold the *Shift* key down and select slide 3 in the **Filmstrip** panel.

This action selects from slide 1 to slide 3. In other words, you have selected all but the last slide of the `additionalQuestions.cptx` file. The last slide of this project is the automatic **Quiz Result** slide of the Quiz, which cannot be copied and pasted to another project.

4. Use the *Ctrl + C* (Windows) or the *Cmd + C* (Mac) shortcut to copy the selected slides to the clipboard.
5. Return to slide 27 of the `takeTheTrain.cptx` file.
6. Use the *Ctrl + V* (Windows) or the *Cmd + V* (Mac) shortcut to paste the slides.

Three Question Slides are added to the project after slide 27. At the end of this section, there should be 32 slides in the `takeTheTrain.cptx` file.

7. Save the `TakeTheTrain.cptx` file.
8. Close the `additionalQuestions.cptx` file.

The stage is set for you to explore the remaining Question Types available in Captivate.

Working with the Fill-in-The-Blank question

The next question type is the **Fill-in-The-Blank** question. The idea is to take one or more words out of a given sentence. The student has to *fill in the blank(s)* either by typing the missing words or by choosing them from a drop-down list. Perform the following steps to explore the Fill-in-The-Blank question:

1. Use the **Filmstrip** panel to go to slide 28 of the `Chapter07/takeTheTrain.cptx` project.
2. Click an empty area of the slide.
3. In the **Properties** inspector, click the **Reset Master Slide** button.

This action reapplies the Master Slide to the imported Question Slide. This ensures that the styles defined in the theme and the elements defined in the Master Slide are properly applied.

4. As usual, move the feedback messages out of the way, move the answer area, and increase the height of the question text.
5. Inside the answer area, select the sentence that begins with **Belgium is so small...**
6. Increase the height of the selected element to reveal the whole sentence.

This sentence is the one from which some words will be taken out. In this case, you will delete three words and replace them by three drop-down lists of possible answers.

7. Select the word **Small**.
8. At the top of the **Quiz** inspector, click the **Mark Blank** button.

Note that a dashed line now underlines the selected word. This is how Captivate marks the words that are taken out of the original sentence. You will now tell Captivate that you want to replace this word with a drop-down list.

9. Click the underlined word until the **Correct Entries** box appears on the screen.
10. In the bottom left corner of the box, change **User Input** to **Dropdown List** (see **1** in the following screenshot).
11. Click the **+** icon (see **2** in the following screenshot) three times to add three additional entries in the list. There are now four possible answers in the list.
12. Type `big`, `wide`, and `strange` as possible entries.
13. Show Captivate the right answer by selecting the checkbox associated with the **small** option (note that you can mark multiple entries as correct).
14. Select the **Shuffle Answers** checkbox.

The **Shuffle Answers** checkbox instructs Captivate to display the options of the drop-down list in a random order each time a student takes the Quiz. Make sure your list looks like the following screenshot before moving on:

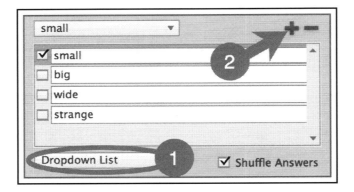

15. Repeat the same procedure to mark the **..not very long..** part of the sentence and the **...two hours.** part at the end of the sentence as blanks.

16. Replace those two additional blanks with drop-down lists of answers. Don't forget to select the correct answer in order to let Captivate know how to grade this question.

17. In the **Quiz** inspector, deselect the **Incomplete** Caption and make sure the **Clear** button is the only one selected.

18. Customize the feedback messages and arrange them on the slide as you see fit.

The other properties of this Question Slide have already been taken care of for you. Feel free to arrange the object contained on the slide to your taste.

Spacing the answer

Make sure you place the longest answer at the top of the list, since Captivate uses the width of the first item of the drop-down menu to determine the width of the blank and of the dropdown. You can also add extra spaces at the end of the first answer of the drop-down list to make it the widest one.

When it comes to grading a sentence with multiple blanks, Captivate awards points only if the whole sentence is correct. This question type does not support partial scoring and is, therefore, completely correct or completely incorrect!

That's it for the Fill-in-The-Blank question. Make sure it looks like the following screenshot before moving on to the next question:

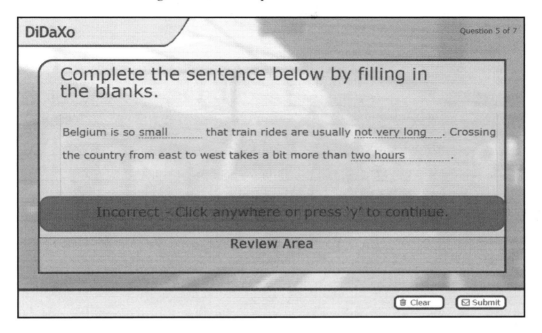

Working with Hotspot questions

The idea of the **Hotspot** question is to display an image on the slide and let the student choose the right spot(s) on this image. In this example, you will display an extract of the train schedule and ask the student to click the departure platform information of a specific train:

1. Return to the takeTheTrain.cptx file and use the **Filmstrip** to go to slide 29.
2. Click the **Reset Master Slide** button in the topmost section of the **Properties** inspector to reapply the Master Slide.
3. Move the feedback messages out of the way and increase the height of the question text.

Slide 29 has been imported from the `additionalQuestions.cptx` file. A picture of an extract of the train schedule is visible in the middle of the slide. There is also a single rectangular Hotspot on top of the image. The students will be asked to click the image. The goal is to click inside the area defined by the hotspot.

4. In the topmost section of the **Quiz** inspector, notice the **Answers** property.

This property allows you to create additional hotspots that you can place on top of the image. This allows you to define multiple areas of the picture as the correct answer. Note that this question type does not support partial scoring, so if you have multiple hotspots on your image, the students have to mark all the hotspots for the answer to be considered correct.

5. Select the only hotspot of the slide in the bottom right corner of the image.
6. In the **Style** tab of the **Properties** inspector, change the stroke **Width** to 0 and set the **Opacity** to 0%. This makes the hotspot completely transparent.
7. At the top of the **Properties** inspector, click the Style Options icon and choose the **Create New Style** item in the list.
8. Save the current formatting of the selected hotspot as a new style called `transparentHotspot`.

The next time you need the same type of hotspot, you'll be able to reapply this style, which will save you some steps.

9. In the **Quiz** inspector, deselect the **Incomplete** Caption and make sure the **Clear** button is the only one selected.
10. Customize the feedback messages and arrange them on the slide as you see fit.

At the end of this section, the Hotspot Question Slide should look similar to the following screenshot:

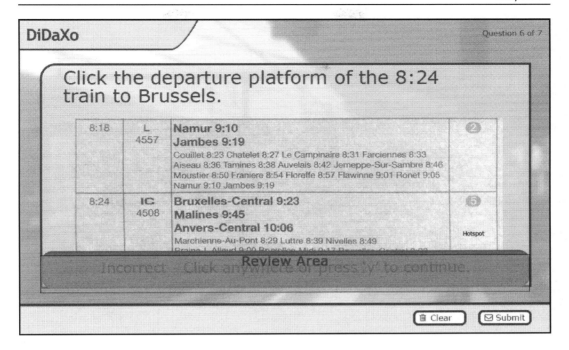

That's it for the Hotspot question! This question type is particularly well suited when assessing computer-related skills. You can, for example, display the screenshot of a toolbar and ask the student to click the correct icon. As you can see, there is nothing really difficult about this question type; it's just another great assessment tool in your teacher's toolset.

Working with Sequence questions

The idea of the **Sequence** question is to provide the student with a set of steps that have to be arranged in the correct order. Perform the following steps to use the Sequence question:

1. In the `Chapter07/takeTheTrain.cptx` project, use the **Filmstrip** to go to slide 30.
2. In the upper section of the **Properties** inspector, click the **Reset Master Slide** button to reapply the Master Slide to the currently selected question.

Resetting the Master Slide resets the formatting of the slide to default. It is very practical when you want to apply another Master Slide to an existing slide, when you copy and paste a slide from another project or when you need to restart formatting a slide from scratch.

3. Move the feedback messages out of the way and increase the height of the question text.
4. In the top section of the **Quiz** inspector, notice the **Answers** property.

This property controls the number of steps that students will have to put in order. In this case, it has been set to **5,** and the five steps have already been filled in for you.

With the Sequence question, there is no need to show Captivate the correct answer. Captivate displays these steps in a random order each time a student takes the Quiz. The correct answer is the order in which you typed the sentences on the slide.

5. In the **Quiz** inspector, make sure the **Points** option is set to **10**. Also, add a **Penalty** value of **2** points.

These options instruct Captivate to add *10* points to the student's score in case the answer is correct and to subtract two points from the score when the answer is wrong. Note that the answer is considered correct only when all the steps are in order. This type of question does not support partial scoring.

6. In the **Quiz** inspector, make sure the **Clear** button is the only one selected.

Notice that the **Incomplete** option is grayed out. This makes sense since the answer will always include the five displayed steps. Technically, this question type can therefore never be incomplete.

7. To get rid of the yellowish incomplete caption, just select and delete it as if it was a regular object.
8. Customize the feedback messages and arrange them on the slide however you want.
9. As usual, feel free to arrange the objects of this Question Slide further so it looks good to you.

This concludes your overview of the Sequence question. Make sure it looks like the following screenshot before continuing:

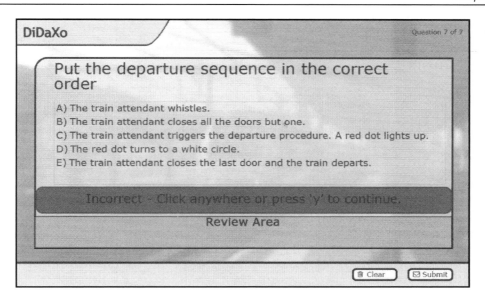

There is one last question type to go through before you can give your quiz a first test run in the **Preview** pane.

Creating surveys with Likert questions

This one is a bit special. It is the only question type that cannot be graded. The **Rating Scale (Likert)** question is used to gather feedback and opinions, so there is no right or wrong answer for this type of question. The idea is to display statements on the screen and have students express their level of agreement with these statements using a rating scale.

Reporting Likert questions to an LMS

It is the LMS that determines the amount of information that may be extracted from the course. Some LMSes support a very detailed set of information, while other LMSes only support basic information about the course and the quiz. Although Captivate sends a comprehensive report to the LMS, all the items of the Likert question might not be available for data analysis on your server. Check the documentation of your LMS to find out what exactly is supported. There will be more on LMS and reporting in the *Reporting scores to an LMS* section later in this chapter.

In the following exercise, you will configure a Likert question by performing the following steps:

1. Go to slide 30 of the `Chapter07/takeTheTrain.cptx` project.
2. Use the **Slides | Question Slide** icon on the Toolbar to open the **Insert Questions** dialog.
3. Choose to insert a single **Rating Scale (Likert)** question.

The **Insert Questions** dialog should now look like the following screenshot. Note that the **Survey** dropdown associated with this type of question is grayed out, which means that it cannot be used as a graded question:

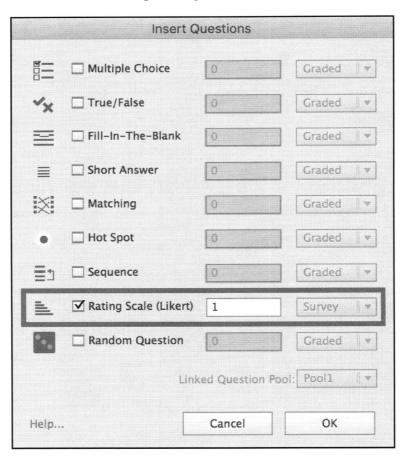

4. Click the **OK** button to proceed with the insertion of the new Question Slide.

5. Move the Incomplete Caption out of the way. Notice that, since the question cannot be graded, there are no success or failure captions on survey questions.

6. Double-click the question text placeholder and type `Please, fill this quick survey.`

7. In the **Quiz** inspector, change the number of **Answers** to 3. Notice that Captivate generates two additional items in the answer area.

8. Open the **Rating Scale** drop-down list to reduce the scale to 3 items. This property controls the number of radio buttons associated with each statement.

9. Expand the box on the stage that holds the ratings. Notice that this puts an equal amount of space between them.

10. Before leaving the **Quiz** inspector, make sure the **Clear** button is the only one selected.

11. Change the text of the three statements to `I learned interesting things in this online course.`, `eLearning is a great learning solution.`, and `I would recommend this course to a friend.`.

12. Change the label of the three columns to `Disagree`, `Neutral`, and `Agree`.

13. Customize the Incomplete message and move it back to the stage where you see fit.

14. Feel free to move and resize the other objects of this slide as per your taste.

15. It is a good idea to save the file when you have finished.

At the end of this section, your survey question should look as follows:

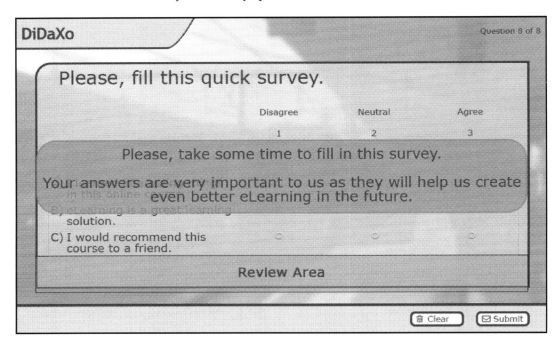

In this exercise, you created a **Rating Scale (Likert)** question. Remember that this question can only be used as a survey question. However, keep in mind that you can use any type of question as survey questions. You could, for example, decide to use Multiple Choice, True/False, or Short Answer questions as additional survey questions as well.

You have now inserted one question of each type in your Captivate Quiz. Before moving on to the next section, let's summarize what you have learned in this one:

- There are eight types of Question Slides available in Captivate.
- Each question can either be a Graded, a Survey, or a Pretest question. The only exception to this is the Rating Scale (Likert) question that can only be a Survey question.
- When inserting the first Question Slide, Captivate automatically generates the **Quiz Results** slide. This slide can be hidden in the Quiz Preferences or in the **Filmstrip**, but it cannot be deleted from the project.
- Use the **Slides | Question Slide** icon on the Toolbar to insert Question Slides into the project.

- A Graded question has correct and incorrect answers. A Survey question is used to gather feedback and opinions from the students. It does not have correct or incorrect answers. A Pretest question is not part of the Quiz and is used to assess the student's knowledge before taking the online course or as a method of keeping the student engaged.
- The GIFT file format can be used to import questions created in third-party systems. Captivate is not able to export the questions of a Quiz in a GIFT file. It can only import a GIFT file created externally.
- In Captivate 2019, the CSV file format can also be used to import questions in the project. The main advantage of CSV over GIFT is that CSV files can be created and modified using any spreadsheet application, such as Microsoft Excel, Open Office Calc, or Apple Numbers.
- Excel and CSV templates can be found in the [Captivate 2019 installation folder]/Gallery/Quiz folder. Use these templates to create CSV files that can be imported flawlessly in Adobe Captivate 2019.
- The **Quiz** inspector is used to control the options specific to each type of Question Slide.
- Each Graded question can be weighted by using varying **Points** when the student answers the question correctly. If the answer is incorrect, it is possible to remove points from the student's score by applying a **Penalty**.
- Partial Scoring is available for Multiple Choice questions only.
- By default, the feedback messages contained on a Question Slide are based on a customizable Smart Shape object.

Previewing the Quiz

Now that you have one example of each possible question type in the project, it is time to experience the quiz hands-on! Since you have not changed any of the Quiz preferences yet, you will go through the default Quiz experience. Perform the following steps to preview the Quiz:

1. Use the **Filmstrip** to return to slide 23 of the Chapter07/takeTheTrain.cptx file.
2. Use the **Preview | From this slide** icon on the Toolbar to preview the project from slide 23 to the end. You may see a popup telling you some of the objects are not supported in SWF format. Click **OK** to discard the message if needed.

3. Go through the entire Quiz as a learner would.

4. When you reach the **Quiz Results** slide, click the **Review** button.

The **Review Quiz** button takes you back to the first slide of the Quiz. Use the **Previous** and the **Next** buttons to go through each Question Slide. Note how Captivate shows the correct, incorrect, incomplete, and expected answers.

When you get back to the **Quiz Results** slide, inspect the information it contains. Pay particular attention to the message at the end of the slide (**Sorry you failed** or **Congratulations, you passed**). It is a general feedback message that depends on the outcome of the whole Quiz. Obviously, you have to set a passing score to let Captivate know when to display one or the other message.

5. Click the **Continue** button to move on to the last slide of the project.

6. When you are done, close the **Preview** pane to return to Captivate and save the file.

Remember that you have not changed any of the Quiz preferences yet. In *The Quiz Preferences* section later in this chapter, you will review the options that allow you to customize the Quiz. But before that, you will take a deeper look at the Quiz modes.

Understanding the Quiz modes

When previewing the Quiz in the previous section, you noticed that, by default, you are presented with a button allowing you to review the Quiz. This button is, logically, located on the Quiz Result slide. To make it work, Captivate defines two different viewing modes for the Quiz:

- The **Quiz Mode** is the initial viewing mode. It is used when you take the quiz, which means when all the questions of the Quiz have not yet been answered. The Quiz Mode begins when the playhead enters the first question slide of the Quiz and ends at the Quiz Result slide.
- The **Quiz Review Mode** is used when all the questions of the Quiz have been answered and the student has clicked the **Review Quiz** button on the Quiz Result slide.

Captivate allows you to define navigation buttons that are specific to each of these viewing modes. In other words, some buttons are displayed in the regular Quiz Mode, while other buttons only appear in Quiz Review Mode. Let's experiment with this feature by performing the following steps:

1. In the `Chapter07/takeTheTrain.cptx` file, use the **Filmstrip** to return to slide 24, which is the first Question Slide of the Quiz.
2. In the **Quiz** inspector, select the **Back** and the **Skip** buttons.

This adds two more buttons at the bottom of the Question Slide. You should now have four buttons labeled **Previous**, **Next**, **Clear,** and **Submit** displayed at the bottom of the slide.

3. Select the **Clear** button and move it toward the top of the slide to reveal the **Previous** button that was hidden underneath.
4. Do the same with the **Submit** button to reveal a **Next** button that was hidden underneath the **Submit** button.

You now have six buttons on your question slide. Two of these are labeled **Next**, two others are labeled **Previous,** and the remaining two are labeled **Clear** and **Submit**. This is illustrated in the following screenshot:

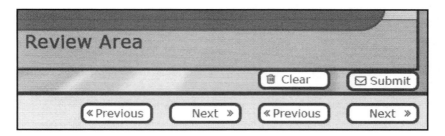

The **Clear** and the **Submit** buttons are only displayed when in the regular Quiz Mode (that is, when taking the Quiz). When in the Quiz Review mode, these buttons are hidden, which explains why they can be placed on top of other buttons that only appear in the Quiz Review Mode.

Regarding the **Previous** and **Next** buttons, two of these are displayed in the regular Quiz Mode, and the other two only appear when in the Quiz Review mode. Perform the following steps to determine which one is which.

5. Select the leftmost **Previous** button (based on the preceding screenshot).
6. At the very top of the **Properties** inspector (see the following screenshot), notice that this object is called **Back Button**. It means that it is the back button of the normal Quiz Mode.
7. Now, select the leftmost **Next** button (based on the preceding screenshot). At the very top of the **Properties** inspector, this button is the **Next Button**. It means that it is the Next button of the normal Quiz Mode.

8. Select the rightmost **Previous** button (the one that was hidden beneath the **Clear** button).

9. At the top of the **Properties** inspector, this object is called the **Review Mode Back Button**. This is the Back button that only shows when in the Quiz Review Mode.

10. Finally, select the rightmost **Next** button (that used to be hidden beneath the **Submit** button). At the top of the **Properties** inspector, this button is called the **Review Mode Next Button**. This is the Next button of the Quiz Review Mode.

Having all these buttons at your disposal allows you to very precisely define the user experience when taking and when reviewing the Quiz. Just remember to take a look at the top of the **Properties** inspector to make sure you are working with the right button:

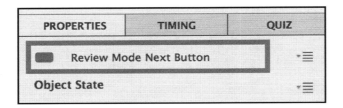

You will now revert to the initial project using the following steps.

11. In the **Quiz** inspector, deselect the **Back** and **Skip** buttons. This turns off the **Previous** and the **Next** buttons of the normal Quiz Mode.

12. If needed, use the **Window | Align** menu item to display the Align toolbar.

13. Select the remaining **Previous** button (which is the Previous button of the Quiz Review Mode).

14. Hold down the *Shift* key while selecting the **Clear** button. This adds the **Clear** button to the current selection.

Note that white selection handles surround the **Previous** button, while the **Clear** button is surrounded by black selection handles. As you remember from Chapter 4, *Working with the Timeline and Other Useful Tools*, it means that the tools of the Align toolbar are currently calibrated based on the **Previous** button.

15. Click the last available icon of the Align toolbar. This action places both buttons exactly on top of one another. (Use the **Window | Align** menu item to display the Align toolbar if needed).

16. Repeat the same sequence of actions to place the **Submit** button exactly on top of the **Next** button.

In this section, you have seen the normal Quiz Mode and the Quiz Review Mode. You have discovered that each mode has an associated set of navigation buttons, which gives you a high level of control over the user experience of your Quiz. Let's make a quick summary of your new findings before moving on to the next section:

- When the playhead enters the first Question Slide of the project for the first time, Captivate switches to Quiz Mode behind the scenes. The Clear, Submit, Back, and Skip buttons are specific to this mode.
- By default, the students are allowed to review the Quiz, which gives them access to some more extensive feedback. The **Review Quiz** button is located on the Quiz Results slide.
- When the student is reviewing the Quiz, Captivate switches to Quiz Review Mode behind the scenes. Special Previous and Next buttons are available to enable navigation when reviewing the Quiz.

Understanding Pretests

So far, you have created Graded and Survey questions. But the **Insert Questions** dialog allows a third type of question slide. Pretest questions are exactly the same as the Survey or Graded questions. What makes them special is the following:

- First, the Pretest questions are not part of the Quiz. Their result is not considered when generating the **Quiz Results** slide.
- Second, the Pretest questions are not part of the interaction report that is sent to your LMS (there is more on reporting to an LMS in the *Reporting scores to an LMS* section later in this chapter).

The idea of a pretest is to assess the student's knowledge prior to taking the course. The decision to take the course module or to skip it can be made based on the outcome of the pretest. However, in practice, we usually use the LMS to do this. For example, you can develop a dedicated course module (a regular Captivate Quiz for instance) as a pretest and use the branching capabilities of your LMS to display or not display the next module depending on the outcome of that pretest. Check with your LMS administrator to see what are the branching capabilities of your particular LMS.

Because Pretest is a feature of Captivate that not many people use, it has not been inserted into the sample files associated with this book and will not be further explored in this chapter. If you want more information about this feature, please refer to the following page of the Adobe Captivate help site: `https://helpx.adobe.com/captivate/using/insert-pretests.html`, and to the following YouTube video: `https://www.youtube.com/watch?v=alSvWTMTyBIt=9s`.

Exploring the Quiz Preferences

Now that you have a better idea of how a Quiz works by default, you will return to the **Preferences** dialog to take a deeper look at the available Quiz options by performing the following steps:

1. Return to the `Chapter07/takeTheTrain.cptx` file.
2. Make sure you are on one of the Question Slides you inserted in the previous section.
3. Use the **Quiz | Quiz Preferences** menu item to open the **Preferences** dialog.

By default, the **Preferences** dialog opens on the **Reporting** section. This section will be discussed later in this chapter.

4. On the left side of the **Preferences** dialog, click the **Settings** category of the **Quiz** section, as shown in the following screenshot:

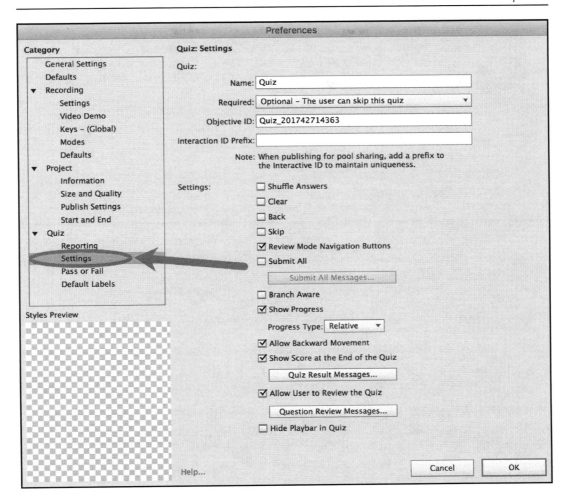

Take some time to review the options of this page.

>   5.   Deselect the **Show Progress** checkbox. This removes the progress indicator in the top-right corner of the Question Slides.

The progress indicator is used to provide the students with an indication of their progress in the Quiz. The default progress indicator of Captivate can show the relative progress (**Question 1 of 3**) or the absolute progress (**Question 1**) to the student.

A customized progress indicator

Lieve Weymeis, also known as *Lilybiri*, is the queen of Advanced Actions. She has found a way to create a customized progress indicator using Advanced Actions and Variables. See her blog post at http://blog.lilybiri.com/customized-progress-indicator. Advanced Actions and Variables will be covered in Chapter 14, *Variables and Advanced Actions.*

6. Select the **Skip** checkbox and read the message that appears.
7. Click **Yes**.
8. Click **OK** to apply the changes.

Use the **Filmstrip** to browse through the Question Slides of the Quiz and confirm that a **Next** button is now displayed at the bottom of each Question Slide. Also notice that the progress indicator that used to be displayed in the top right corner of each Question Slide is now gone.

9. Return to the Quiz Preferences by using the **Quiz | Quiz Preferences** menu item and return to the **Settings** category.
10. Deselect the **Skip** checkbox and click **Yes** to remove all the **Next** buttons from the Question Slides of the Quiz.
11. Select the **Clear** checkbox, and then click **Yes** to display a **Clear** button on each Question Slide.

This should not change much in your project, as you should have enabled the **Clear** button on each Question Slide individually during the previous section. This tells you a bit more about the options of the Quiz Preferences dialog. They represent the *default* settings of new Question Slides, but you can always override those preferences in the **Quiz** inspector of each individual Question Slide.

If you deselect the **Allow Backward Movement** checkbox, Captivate removes all the **Previous** buttons (of the Normal Quiz Mode) present on the question slides. It also grays out the **Back** checkbox. Make sure that you leave this option selected in this example.

12. Make sure the **Show Score at the End of Quiz** checkbox is selected.
13. Click the **Quiz Results Messages...** button. The **Quiz Results Messages** dialog opens.

The **Quiz Results Messages** dialog is where you can customize the information that appears on the **Quiz Results** slide.

14. Deselect the **Correct Questions, Total Questions**, and **Quiz Attempts** checkboxes.

This removes the corresponding messages from the **Quiz Results** slide.

15. If needed, customize the **Pass Message** and **Fail Message**.

These are the messages displayed in the **Review Area** of the **Quiz Results** slide at the end of the Quiz.

16. Click the **OK** button to confirm your changes and close the box.
17. Deselect the **Allow User to Review the Quiz** checkbox.

This action removes the **Review Quiz** button from the **Quiz Results** slide and the **Review Area** from each Question Slide. It also grays out the **Review Mode Navigation Buttons** option. This option lets you choose whether or not to display the special Previous and Next navigation buttons of the Quiz Review Mode. But since you just turned off the ability for the students to review the Quiz, this option doesn't make sense anymore.

18. Reselect the **Allow User to Review the Quiz** checkbox.
19. Select the **Hide Playbar in Quiz** checkbox.

This option hides the Playback Controls during the Quiz. This is made to ensure students cannot use the Playback Controls to go back and forth in the Quiz or to skip the Quiz.

Note the **Submit All** checkbox. When selected, the answers to the questions are all submitted together at the end of the Quiz. This allows the students to travel back and forth into the Quiz and change their answers before submitting them all at once at the end.

20. Click the **OK** button to validate the changes and close the **Preferences** dialog.
21. Use the **Filmstrip** to go to slide 32.

Slide 32 is the **Quiz Results** slide. Note that it contains less information than before and that the **Review Quiz** button has been removed. This matches the checkboxes configuration you created in the **Preferences** dialog.

22. Feel free to move some of the content of the Quiz Results slide to remove the large space in the center of the stage. Remember that you can use the Smart Guides and the Align toolbar to lay out your slides easily.

Setting the passing score of a Quiz

When the student reaches the **Quiz Results** slide, Captivate displays a Pass/Fail message that depends on the Quiz score. To display this message, Captivate must be informed of what the passing score of the Quiz is. If the student reaches that passing score, Captivate displays the **Pass Message**; otherwise, the **Fail Message** is displayed.

In this section, you will set the passing score of the Quiz and add some branching. First, you will import an additional slide in the project and place it after the Quiz. This slide should be displayed only to the students that passed the Quiz. Perform the following steps to import the new slide:

1. Open the `Chapter07/quizFeedback.cptx` file.
2. In the **Filmstrip**, select the one and only slide of that project.
3. Use the *Ctrl+C* (Windows) or the *Cmd+C* (Mac) shortcut to copy the selected slide.
4. Return to slide 32 of the `takeTheTrain.cptx` file and paste the slide using the *Ctrl+V* (Windows) or the *Cmd+V* (Mac) shortcut.
5. Use the **Filmstrip** to go to slide 33 and take some time to review the objects of that slide. Feel free to rearrange them however you like.
6. Use the **Properties** inspector of slide 33 to apply the **contentBkg** Master Slide of the theme to slide 33.

After this procedure, the `takeTheTrain.cptx` file should contain 34 slides.

The stage is set! You will now return to the **Preferences** dialog to set the passing score of the Quiz and arrange the branching.

7. Use the **Quiz | Quiz Preferences** menu item to return to the **Preferences** dialog.
8. Click the **Pass or Fail** category in the **Quiz** section of the **Preferences** dialog.

The main **Pass or Fail** option is at the top of the dialog box. Note that there are two ways to set the passing score for a Quiz: as a *percentage* or a certain amount of *points*. The total number of points is the sum of the points set for all the Question Slides of the quiz (excluding the points of the Pretest slides, if any).

9. In the **Pass/Fail Options** section, set the passing score to 50 percent (make sure the % radio button is selected).

10. In the **If Passing Grade** section, set the **Action** dropdown to **Jump to slide**. Then, select the **33 Quiz Passed** slide from the **Slide** drop-down list.

11. In the **If Failing Grade** section, allow the user one attempt and set the **Action** dropdown to **Jump to slide**. Then, select the last slide (labeled **34 slide34**) from the **Slide** drop-down list.

Setting the Pass and Fail options and adding some branching to the Quiz is that easy! Before moving on to the next step, take a quick look at the **Default Labels** preferences pane.

12. Click the **Default Labels** category situated on the left side of the **Preferences** dialog.

The **Default Labels** preferences are used to change the default text and the default styles applied to the various elements of a Question Slide. It is best to define these options as part of your preparatory work or in a Template. In this case, it is too late!

13. Click the **OK** button to confirm the changes and close the **Preferences** dialog.

14. Use the **Preview | Project** icon on the Toolbar to test the entire project. When you have finished, close the **Preview** pane and save the file.

Your Quiz is now up and running. In the next section, you will add some spice to the mix by creating a Question Pool. Before that, let's summarize what you have just learned:

- By default, Captivate generates a **Quiz Results** slide and displays it at the end of the Quiz.
- By default, the **Quiz Results** slide contains the **Review Quiz** button that allows the student to return to each Question Slide and get feedback on the submitted answer.
- The **Clear, Back,** and **Skip** options of the Quiz Preferences are used to define which buttons should be displayed by default on the Question Slides. It is possible to override these defaults using the **Quiz** inspector of each individual Question Slide.
- You can allow students to go backward in the Quiz, but once a question has been submitted, the student cannot change the answer.
- The **Submit All** checkbox allows the students to change their answers until they click the **Submit All** button at the end of the Quiz.

- The **Preferences** dialog contains many options to let you fine-tune the student experience. Some of these options are used to turn the objects of all the Question Slides of the Quiz on or off.
- You can use the **Preferences** dialog to set the passing score of the quiz and to add branching that is dependent on the quiz score.

Working with Question Pools

A **Question Pool** is a repository of Question Slides. The idea is to let Captivate randomly choose questions from the pool to create a unique Quiz for each student. You can have as many Question Pools as needed, and each pool can contain an unlimited number of Question Slides.

Perform the following steps to create a Question Pool:

1. Make sure you are in the `Chapter07/takeTheTrain.cptx` project.
2. Use the **Quiz | Question Pool Manager** menu item to open the **Question Pool Manager** dialog.

As described in the following screenshot, **The Question Pool Manager** dialog is divided into two main areas:

- On the upper-left side of the box is a list of all the Question Pools of the current project. Just above the list of pools, the **+** and **-** icons (see **1** in the following screenshot) are used to add or remove Question Pools.
- The right side of the box shows the list of the Question Slides associated with the pool selected on the right side. The **+** and **-** icons (see **2** in the following screenshot) are used to add Questions into the selected pool or to remove existing Questions from the selected Pool.

Also, notice the ability to import GIFT and CSV files directly into the selected
Question Pool:

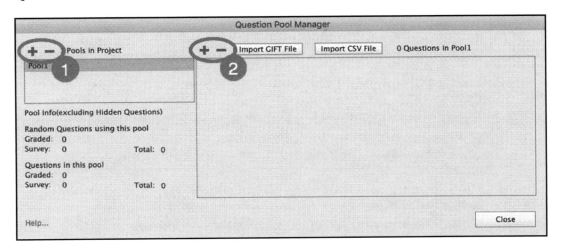

A first Question Pool named **Pool1** has been automatically created by Captivate when
you opened the **Question Pool Manager**. You will now rename this Question Pool by
performing the following steps.

3. On the left side of the **Question Pool Manager** dialog, double-click the
   Pool1 entry of the list of pools.
4. Name the pool takeTheTrain_Questions and press the *Enter* key. This
   confirms the new name and closes the Question Pool Manager.

Now that you have a Question Pool available, you will add questions to it.

The name of a Question Pool cannot exceed 100 characters and
cannot contain any spaces or special characters.

Inserting questions in a Question Pool

You could have used the **Question Pool Manager** dialog to create new Question Slides directly into the Pool. But you will use another technique. Instead of creating new Question Slides to fill the Question Pool, you will move the existing Question Slides of the Quiz into the new Pool by performing the following steps:

1. Use the **Filmstrip** to select slide 30 of the project. It is the Sequence Question Slide that you have created earlier in this chapter.
2. Right-click this Question Slide in the **Filmstrip** and delete it (we have another plan in mind for this question later in the chapter).
3. Use the **Filmstrip** to go to slide 24 (which is the first Question Slide of the Quiz).
4. Hold down the *Shift* key and click slide 29. This operation selects six slides from slide 24 to slide 29.
5. In the **Filmstrip** panel, right-click one of the selected slides.
6. In the contextual menu, click the **Move Questions to | takeTheTrain_Questions** item.

This operation removes the selected slides from the **Filmstrip** and moves them into the Question Pool. The **Filmstrip** now contains 27 slides.

7. Open the **Question Pool** panel that appears next to the **Timeline** panel at the bottom of the screen (if the **Question Pool** panel is not visible, use the **Window | Question Pool** menu item to turn it on).

Six Question Slides are displayed in the **Question Pool** panel indicating that they have been moved into the **takeTheTrain_Questions** Question Pool correctly. Another way of accessing the same information is using the **Question Pool Manager** dialog.

8. Use the **Quiz | Question Pool Manager** to open the **Question Pool Manager** dialog.
9. Make sure that the **takeTheTrain_Questions** Question Pool is selected on the left side of the dialog and look at the right side.

When the **takeTheTrain_Questions** is selected, the right side of the **Question Pool Manager** lists the Question Slides included in the pool.

10. Click the **Close** button to close the **Question Pool Manager** dialog.

The Question Pool is now ready for action! The next step is to pick questions from the pool randomly and add them to the Quiz.

Sharing Question Pools with other projects
You may have noticed the **Quiz | Import Question Pools** menu item. Using this feature, you can import a Question Pool from another project into this project. This makes it easy to share Question Pools across projects.

Inserting Random Question Slides in the project

Remember that the idea of a Question Pool is to have a repository of questions available to generate random quizzes. In this section, you will randomly pick three questions from the **takeTheTrain_Questions** Question Pool and insert them into the quiz by performing the following steps:

1. Use the **Filmstrip** to go to slide 23 of the `takeTheTrain.cptx` file. Slide 23 is the introduction slide of the Quiz that you created at the beginning of this chapter.
2. Use the **Quiz | Random Question Slide** menu item to insert the first random question into the main project.

Another way of inserting Random Question Slides in the project is to use the **Insert Questions** dialog.

3. Use the **Slides | Question Slides** icon on the Toolbar to open the **Insert Questions** dialog.
4. At the bottom of the dialog, select the **Random Question** checkbox.
5. Set the number of questions to insert to 2.

The **Insert Questions** dialog should now look like the following screenshot. Notice the **Linked Question Pool** dropdown that you can use to choose the Question Pool to pick questions from:

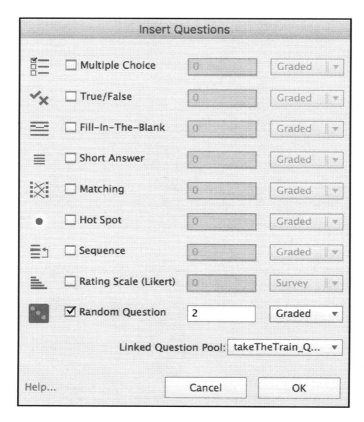

6. Click **OK** to confirm and insert two additional Random Question Slides in the project.

The Quiz currently contains three Random Question Slides, as well as the Survey slide (slide 27), which is the same for every student. This illustrates the capability to mix standard Question Slides and Random Question Slides in the same Captivate Quiz.

7. Use the **Filmstrip** to go to slide 24, which is the first Random Question Slide of the Quiz.
8. Take a look at the **Quiz** inspector.

The **Quiz** inspector of a **Random Question** Slide only contains a fraction of the options available in the **Quiz** inspector of a regular Question Slide. Two of the available options are the **Points** and **Penalty** properties.

9. If needed, open the **Question Pool** panel next to the **Timeline** panel at the bottom of the screen.
10. Select any Question Slide in the **takeTheTrain_Questions** Question Pool.
11. When the selected question appears in the main area of the Captivate interface, take a look at the **Quiz** inspector.

Notice that, here again, the **Quiz** inspector contains fewer options than the **Quiz** inspector of a regular Question Slide. Two of the missing options are the **Points** and **Penalty** properties.

When combining the options of the **Quiz** inspector of the Random Question Slide in the main project with the options of the **Quiz** inspector of a Question Slide within a Question Pool, you more or less obtain the **Quiz** inspector of a regular Question Slide.

12. Return to slide 24 of the main **Filmstrip**. In the topmost section of the **Quiz** inspector, make sure the **Points** property is set to 10 and the **Penalty** property is set to 1.
13. Set the same **Points** and **Penalty** values for the other two Random Question Slides.

Now that you have Random Questions in the Quiz, you can give your random Quiz a try.

14. Use the **Preview** | **Project** icon on the Toolbar to test the project in the **Preview** pane.

When you reach the Quiz, pay close attention to the questions asked. Try to provide the correct answers so that the **Quiz Passed** slide is displayed when the Quiz is finished.

15. When you are done, close the **Preview** pane.
16. Use the **Preview** | **Project** icon to test the entire project a second time.

When you reach the Quiz for the second time, the questions should not be the same as compared to your first attempt (if they are, close this book and get a Lottery ticket right away! This is your lucky day!).

17. Provide wrong answers so that you fail the Quiz.
18. Make sure the **Quiz Passed** slide is *not* displayed at the end of the Quiz.

Your random quiz is now up and running. It is time to summarize what you have just learned:

- A Question Pool is a repository of Question Slides from which Captivate randomly picks questions at runtime.
- A Captivate project can include as many Question Pools as needed. A Question Pool can contain as many Question Slides as needed. It's a good idea to use the **Question Pool Manager**, which gives your Question Pools unique names so you know where to pull the questions from.
- The **Quiz | Import Question Pool** menu item can be used to import a Question Pool of another project into the current project.
- Use the **Quiz | Question Pool Manager** menu item to create new Question Pools and to add Question Slides to the available pools.
- GIFT and CSV files can be imported directly into a Question Pool.
- If the project already contains Question Slides, they can be moved to a Question Pool at any time. Questions in a Question Pool can also be moved back to the main project using the same technique.
- A Quiz can be made up of a mix of standard Questions Slides and random questions from different question pools.
- The **Quiz** inspector of a Random Question Slide contains only a fraction of the options available for a regular Question Slide. The remaining options are associated with each Question Slide in the **Question Pool**.

Great! You now have a pretty good idea of what a Captivate Quiz is and of the myriad options available to them.

Styling the elements of the Question Slides

In this section, you will return to the Master Slide view and take a quick look at the Master Slides that define the look and feel of the Quiz by performing the following steps:

1. Make sure you are in the `Chapter07/takeTheTrain.cptx` file.
2. Use the **Window | Master Slide** menu item to return to the Master Slide view.

Some of the Master Slides listed on the left side of the screen control the look and feel of the Question Slides and of the **Quiz Results** slide.

3. In the **Master Slide** panel, right-click the **MCQ, T/F, FIB, Sequence** Master Slide (slide 10) and try to delete it.

Captivate informs you that at least one Quiz Master Slide of each type must be present in the project. The selected Master Slide can therefore not be deleted. This particular Master Slide is used to control the look and feel of the Multiple Choice, True/False, Fill-in-The-Blank, and Sequence Question Slides.

4. Take a quick look at the other Master Slides present in the **Master Slides** panel.

The **Matching** Master Slide is used by the Matching questions, the **Hot Spot** Master Slide is used by the Hot Spot questions, and the **Likert** Master Slide is used by the Likert questions. Finally, the **Result** Master Slide controls the look and feel of the Quiz Results slide.

5. While in the Master Slide view, open the **Insert | Quiz Master Slide** menu item.

From this menu item, you can insert additional Question Master Slides and define alternative layouts for the various question types.

6. Use the **Window | Question Pool** menu item to return to the Question Pool panel.
7. Within the **Question Pool** panel, select the Multiple Choice question.
8. With the Multiple Choice question selected, look at the **Properties** inspector.

As shown in the following screenshot, Captivate has automatically applied the **MCQ, T/F, FIB, Sequence** Master Slide to the Multiple Choice question. When inserting a Question Slide into the project, Captivate automatically applies the proper Master Slide to the new question depending on the type of question:

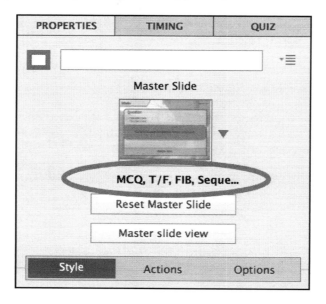

You will now try to apply a different Master Slide to this question slide.

9. In the **Properties** inspector, click the arrow next to the **Master Slide** thumbnail.

Even though there are multiple Master Slides in the Theme, only that one Master Slide can be applied to the selected question. If you insert additional Master Slides for that particular question type, the **Properties** inspector will filter the list of available Master Slides to those that can be applied to the selected question.

Before moving on to the next section, let's quickly summarize what has been covered in this section:

- When a Question Slide is added to the project, Captivate automatically applies the proper Master Slide based on the type of question being inserted.
- In the Theme, there are five Master Slides that are used to control the look and feel of the Question Slides and of the Quiz Results slide.

- You can insert additional Question Master Slides in the Theme using the **Insert | Question Master Slide** menu item when in the Master Slide view.
- There must be at least one Master Slide for each question type in the theme.
- The position and formatting of the object as defined on these Master Slides are inherited by the Question Slides of the main project.

Reporting scores to an LMS

LMS stands for **Learning Management System**. The help files of Captivate give the following definition for an LMS:

> *"You can use a learning management system (LMS) to distribute a computer-based tutorial created using Adobe Captivate over the Internet. A learning management system is used to provide, track, and manage web-based training."*

An LMS offers many services to both teachers and students involved in eLearning activities. The following list states some of them:

- An LMS is a website that is able to host your eLearning courses.
- An LMS maintains a list of teachers and students. Thanks to this listing, an LMS can be used to enroll students in online courses and to define one or more teachers for each course.
- An LMS is able to enforce the pedagogical decisions of the teacher. For example, the LMS can be programmed to give access to the next activity of the course only if the current activity has been completed. Some LMSes can also enforce branching by automatically providing an additional activity for students who have failed a quiz, and so on.
- An LMS is able to communicate with your Captivate content (and vice versa). This gives you access to many pieces of information, such as the number of students that have taken the course, the time it took to complete an activity, the results of the quizzes, and even a detailed report of every interaction performed by each student while taking the course.
- There are many other services that an LMS has to offer.

There are many LMSes available, and there are a myriad of companies, schools, and universities that have deployed some kind of LMS to deliver, track, and manage their web-based trainings. Some LMSes are commercially licensed and can be quite expensive, but there are also several open source LMS platforms that are free to use and easy to deploy on a web server.

Moodle

Moodle is one of the most popular and powerful open source LMS solution. Personally, I have used Moodle for many eLearning projects, and it has never let me down. However, Moodle has a fairly steep learning curve. Packt Publishing has published an impressive array of titles on Moodle, providing the necessary documentation to get you started. More information on Moodle is available at `http://www.moodle.org`. More information about Packt books on Moodle is available at `https://www.packtpub.com/all/?search=moodle`.

Captivate Prime

Captivate Prime is the LMS solution developed by the Captivate team itself! It is a paid solution available in **SAAS (Software as a Service)** mode. The course modules that you create with Adobe Captivate can be published and uploaded to your Adobe Captivate Prime account right from within Captivate. More information about Captivate Prime can be found at `http://www.adobe.com/products/captivateprime.html`. The co-author of this book, Dr. Pooja Jaisingh, also has a dedicated course on this topic on LinkedIn Learning. It can be found at `https://www.linkedin.com/learning/adobe-captivate-prime-essential-training`.

For a list of the most popular LMSes, see the following web page on Wikipedia: `http://en.wikipedia.org/wiki/List_of_learning_management_systems`
.

Understanding SCORM, AICC, and xAPI

Each LMS has its pros and cons, and each contains a unique set of features. However, every LMS must be able to host eLearning content created by a myriad of different authoring tools (Adobe Captivate being one of the many eLearning authoring tools available).

To make web-based learning possible, it is important to ensure that the course modules can communicate with the underlying LMS platform. This communication should be possible regardless of the Authoring tool/LMS combination. This is where SCORM, AICC, and xAPI come into play.

These are three internationally accepted standards used to make the communication between your eLearning content and your LMS possible. When choosing an LMS for your organization, make sure that the chosen solution is either SCORM, AICC, or xAPI compliant. Captivate is SCORM, AICC, and xAPI compliant. So Captivate courses can be integrated in virtually every LMS available on the market. Let's now discuss these three standards in more detail:

- **SCORM** stands for **Sharable Content Object Reference Model**. SCORM is maintained by the **Advanced Distributed Learning** (ADL) (http://www.adlnet.org/) project of the US Department of Defense. SCORM is a **reference model**. It means that it aggregates standards created by other organizations. The goal is to build a single standard based on the work done by other organizations that are active in the eLearning field. See the Wikipedia page on SCORM at http://en.wikipedia.org/wiki/SCORM.

- **xAPI** is the newest standard, launched in April 2013. During its development phase, this standard was known as the **Tin Can API**, and many people still refer to it as *Tin Can*, even though its official name is now the **Experience API** (xAPI). This new specification allows eLearning content and Learning Management Systems to speak to each other in a manner that records and tracks all types of learning experiences. Learning experiences are recorded in a **Learning Record Store** (**LRS**). LRSes can exist within traditional LMSes or on their own. You can find out more about the xAPI at http://experienceapi.com/.

- **AICC** stands for **Aviation Industry Computer-based Training Committee**. The initial idea was to provide a unique training and testing environment for the aviation industry to ensure the same training and testing standard for all airline companies throughout the world. For more information, see the AICC page on Wikipedia at http://en.wikipedia.org/wiki/Aviation_Industry_Computer-Based_Training_Committee. On December 11, 2014, the AICC committee announced that AICC would be dissolved and the AICC standard would no longer be maintained. All the work of AICC has been transferred to ADL, which oversees both the SCORM and the xAPI standards. Captivate still maintains an AICC option for backward compatibility with older LMSes.

Now that you have a better idea of what an LMS is, and of the standards used, you will enable reporting in your Captivate project.

Enabling reporting in Captivate

To have Captivate publish an LMS-ready package, you have to set options at different locations throughout the project.

In the next exercise, you will make your Quiz ready to be integrated in a SCORM-compliant LMS. You will first inspect the options available at the interaction level before moving on to project level reporting options.

Reporting options at the Question Slide level

Each of the scorable objects of Captivate are automatically assigned with a unique **Interaction ID**. This Interaction ID is what makes data tracking by the LMS possible. Perform the following steps to view and change the Interaction IDs:

1. Use the **Filmstrip** to go to slide 24 of the `Chapter07/takeTheTrain.cptx` file.
2. At the bottom of the **Quiz** inspector, notice the **Report Answers** checkbox.

This checkbox allows you to choose which interactions are reported to the LMS. For Question Slides, this checkbox is checked by default, because it is assumed that you want to report these interactions to the LMS. It means you must explicitly deselect this option if you don't want to report a particular question of the Quiz.

3. If needed, use the **Window | Question Pool** menu item to open the Question Pool panel.
4. Select any Question Slide within the Question Pool.
5. At the end of the **Quiz** inspector, notice the **Interaction ID** in the **Reporting** section.

Captivate automatically assigns a random **Interaction ID** to each Question Slide. Most of the time, this default random **Interaction ID** is fine. But you can assign a unique **Interaction ID** on your own if you want to. Note that there can be no spaces or special characters in the **Interaction ID**. If you type your own **Interaction ID** with a prohibited character, Captivate turns the spaces and special characters into underscores. You may also have to check with your LMS vendor for specific naming conventions that will work smoothly.

Finally, when working with regular Question Slides (versus Question Slides within a Question Pool), these two options are grouped in a single **Reporting** section at the end of the **Quiz** inspector, as shown in the following screenshot:

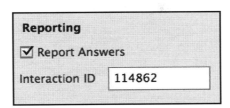

Reporting other types of interactions

The Question Slides that make up a Quiz are not the only interactions that can be reported to an LMS. Other objects also have this capability.

For example, the Drag and Drop interaction has built-in reporting capabilities that are very similar to those of a regular Question Slide, as you will see by following these simple steps:

1. Use the **Filmstrip** to return to slide 20 of the `Chapter07/takeTheTrain.cptx` file. This is the slide where you defined a Drag and Drop interaction earlier in this book.
2. Select one of the objects of the Drag and Drop (for example, select one of the two images).
3. Look at the **Drag And Drop** panel on the right side of the screen. It may be necessary to use the **Window | Drag And Drop** menu item to make this panel visible.
4. Open the **Actions** tab of the **Drag And Drop** panel and notice the **Reporting** section at the very end of the panel.
5. Select the **Include In Quiz** checkbox.

This last action reveals more options. These are very similar to the **Reporting** options found in the **Quiz** inspector when a standard Question Slide is selected. It is therefore very easy to include Drag and Drop interactions into the Quiz, and to report the results to the LMS. Note, however, that those interactions are not included in the Quiz by default. You must explicitly include them by selecting the **Include In Quiz** checkbox. This is very different than the behavior of a regular Question Slide, which is reported by default.

6. If needed, also select the **Report Answer** checkbox to have this interaction reported to the LMS.

7. In this example, however, you don't need to include this Drag and Drop interaction in the Quiz, so you can safely deselect the **Include In Quiz** checkbox.

8. Save the file when you have finished.

If you ever need to grade a Drag and Drop interaction and to report it to the LMS, you now have the required knowledge to do so.

When selecting the **Include In Quiz** checkbox, and not the **Report Answer** checkbox, you include an interactive object in the Quiz without reporting the interaction to the LMS. Captivate then uses these objects to calculate the score displayed on the **Quiz Results** slide, but does not report these interactions to the LMS. This allows you to use the interaction as an informal Knowledge Check question or in a practice exam.

In addition to regular Question Slides and the Drag and Drop interaction, other Captivate objects can also be scored and tracked by an LMS. These are the three interactive objects that have the ability to stop the playhead. These objects have been covered in Chapter 5, *Developing Interactivity*. They are the Click Boxes, the Buttons, and Text Entry Boxes. Let's take another look at these objects by performing the following steps.

9. Use the **Filmstrip** to return to slide 3 of the Chapter07/takeTheTrain.cptx file.

10. Select the Text Entry Box object and look at the **Properties** inspector.

11. At the end of the **Actions** tab, notice the **Include in Quiz** checkbox in the **Reporting** section.

In this case, the **Include in Quiz** checkbox is grayed out. This is because you have deselected the **Validate User Input** option on the **Style** tab of the **Properties** inspector when creating this object back in Chapter 5, *Developing Interactivity*. If you decide to validate the user input, it is easy to add this Text Entry Box interaction to the Quiz and to report the answer to the LMS.

12. Use the **Filmstrip** to go to slide 4 of the Chapter07/takeTheTrain.cptx file.

13. Select the **Continue** button in the bottom right corner of the slide and look at the **Properties** inspector.

14. At the end of the **Actions** tab, select the **Include in Quiz** checkbox.

As for the Drag and Drop interaction, this action reveals the options used to assign points when clicking that button and to report this interaction to the LMS. In this case, however, reporting a **Continue** button makes little sense. You will now deselect this checkbox before wrapping up this section.

15. At the end of the **Actions** tab, deselect the **Include in Quiz** checkbox of the selected button.

In this section, you have explored the scorable objects of Captivate and learned that the reporting capabilities are not limited to Question Slides.

The Advanced Interaction dialog
Use the **Project | Advanced Interaction** menu item or the *F9* shortcut key to open the **Advanced Interaction** dialog. This floating panel provides a list of all the scorable objects of the project in addition to a summary view of their current settings.

In the next section, you will explore project-level reporting options.

Setting up the project-level reporting options

Now that you have decided which interactions will be included in the Quiz and reported to the LMS, it's time to focus on project level reporting options. This is where you configure the global settings used to report the data to the LMS.

Before putting in all this effort, it is important to check with your LMS vendor what level of information your LMS can receive and what is the standard (SCORM, AICC, or xAPI) that your LMS supports. In this exercise, you will report the data to a Moodle LMS. A quick look at the Moodle documentation (`https://docs.moodle.org/en/SCORM_FAQ#Supported_Versions`) tells you that Moodle is SCORM 1.2 compliant.

Perform the following steps to create a SCORM 1.2 package that can be integrated into Moodle:

1. If needed, return to the `Chapter07/takeTheTrain.cptx` file.
2. Use the **Quiz | Quiz Preferences** menu item to open the **Preferences** dialog.
3. In the left side of the **Preferences** dialog, make sure you are on the **Reporting** category.

4. At the top of the page, select the **Enable reporting for this project** checkbox.

When I teach a Captivate class, I often refer to this checkbox as being the *main circuit breaker* of the reporting system.

5. Open the **LMS** drop-down menu.

The LMS dropdown lists some of the most popular LMSes and lets you quickly apply specific settings that are optimized for each LMS.

6. Choose **Moodle** as the LMS.

This action automatically adjusts most of the options of **Reporting Preferences** to the values that a Moodle LMS expects. If your LMS is not listed, you would use the **Other Standard LMSs** item and complete the form manually. Check with your LMS vendor which settings are expected by your LMS.

7. Open the **Standard** drop-down list.

The **Standard** drop-down menu probably is the single most important option of this **Preferences** page. It allows you to choose the reporting standard used to communicate with the LMS. By choosing **Moodle** as the LMS in the previous step, this option has been automatically set to **SCORM 1.2**.

8. Make sure you choose the **SCORM 1.2** option in the drop-down list.

You will now decide how Captivate should report the status of the course. If there is a Quiz in the project, you probably want the status to be either *Pass* or *Fail*. If the project does not contain a Quiz and you just want to track the completion status of the project, choose *Complete/Incomplete*. Knowing your LMS and how it receives and deals with the information is important for making these decisions. In this case, Moodle can accept both representations of the status, but it might not be true for every LMS.

9. In the **Status Representation** section, select the **Incomplete --> Passed/Failed** option.

You will now instruct Captivate that you want to consider this eLearning module complete when the student has passed the Quiz.

10. In the **Success/Completion Criteria** section, choose the **Slide views and/or quiz** option.
11. If needed, deselect the **Slide Views** checkbox, but leave the **Quiz is Passed** checkbox selected.

Finally, you need to decide what data you want to report to the LMS. You can choose to report only the final score of the student or to report the final score plus some details about each interaction. In this case, you want to report the score of the student as a percentage as well as the interaction data.

12. In the **Data To Report** section, choose to report **Quiz Score** as a **Percentage**.
13. Make sure the **Interaction Data** checkbox is selected.

At the end of these steps, make sure your **Preferences** dialog looks like the following screenshot:

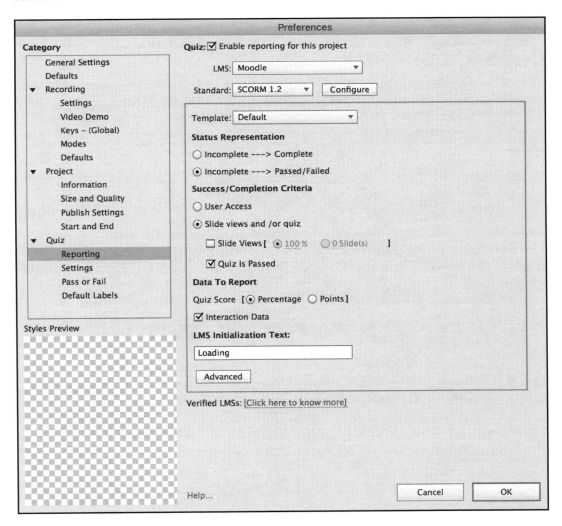

Because you are using the SCORM standard, there is one extra step to go through. This extra step is the creation of the SCORM manifest file. Note that a manifest is also required when using the xAPI standard. When using AICC, a Manifest file is not required.

Enabling reporting in a project with no Quiz

These reporting options are not limited to projects containing a Quiz. Reporting can be used to track only the completion status of a project. Some LMSes are able to reveal the next activity of a course when and only when they receive the *complete* status report from the current activity.

Creating a SCORM manifest file

A SCORM manifest is a `.xml` file named `imsmanifest.xml`. This manifest file is an essential component of any SCORM package. It is used to describe the course to the SCORM-compliant LMS. Without this file, the LMS is unable to integrate SCORM enabled content in a course or to gather the tracking data sent by the course module.

If this sounds too technical, don't worry! Captivate has you covered and can generate that manifest file for you by using the very simple procedure described here:

1. Still in the **Reporting** category of the **Preferences** dialog, click the **Configure** button next to the **SCORM 1.2** standard at the top of the box.

The first section of the **Manifest** dialog is the **Course** section. The **Course** section is used to enter the metadata of the project. This metadata is used by the LMS to display the course information to the student and to enhance the integration of the project into the LMS.

2. In the **Course** section of the **Manifest** dialog, enter the following information:
   - **Identifier**: `takeTheTrain101`
   - **Title**: `Take the train in Belgium`
   - **Description**: Enter any meaningful description here

The second part of the **Manifest** dialog is named **SCO**.

SCO stands for **Shareable Content Object**. This concept is at the heart of the SCORM standard. In the SCORM specification, a course can be composed of many activities. Each of these activities must have a unique SCO identifier. Using a SCORM Packager application (such as the *Multi SCO Packager* or *Reload*), it is possible to integrate a Captivate project in a larger SCORM-compliant course containing lots of other content made by lots of other SCORM-compliant authoring tools. This is why it is important to specify the SCO identity of your Captivate project.

3. Enter `takeTheTrain101` in the SCO **Identifier** field (no spaces allowed).
4. Enter `Take the train in Belgium` in the SCO **Title** field.

The **Manifest** dialog should now look like the following screenshot:

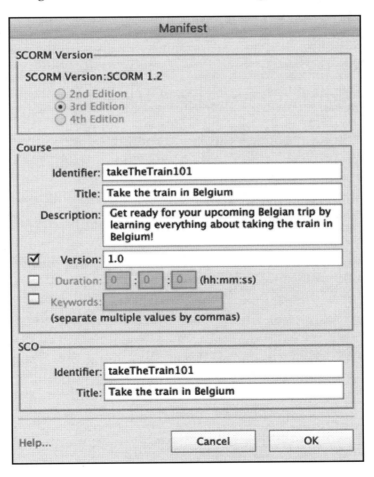

5. Click **OK** to validate the changes and close the dialog box.
6. Also click the **OK** button of the **Preferences** dialog.
7. Make sure you save the file when you are done.

The project is now ready to be published as a SCORM package. This step will be covered in `Chapter 15`, *Finishing Touches and Publishing*.

Testing your SCORM enabled projects with SCORM Cloud

Now that you have enabled the reporting capabilities of your course module, you can take advantage of another Captivate feature that helps you test the communication between your course module and the LMS. To do so, Adobe has teamed up with SCORM Cloud. SCORM Cloud is an eLearning hosting service developed by a company called Rustici Software.

Rustici Software is a well-known company in the eLearning industry. It helped develop both the SCORM and the xAPI standards. SCORM Cloud is just one of the services it provides. You can find more info about Rustici Software at `https://rusticisoftware.com/` and more info about SCORM Cloud at `https://scorm.com/cloud`.

You will now upload your course module to SCORM Cloud and test the communication between your Captivate module and the LMS by performing the following steps:

Even though SCORM Cloud is a commercial service from Rustici Software, testing your eLearning content with SCORM Cloud is included in your Captivate license. You don't need to sign up for a SCORM Cloud account or subscribe to an extra service:

1. In the `Chapter07/takeTheTrain.cptx` file, use **the Preview | Preview in SCORM Cloud** icon on the Toolbar.
2. Click the **OK** button to clear the message telling you that negative scoring is not supported in SCORM 1.2 and that your content will be tested using the SCORM 2004 standard. This issue will be addressed later in the book.
3. Captivate generates a temporary preview of the entire project. When this operation is finished, Captivate displays a message on the screen. Read the message and click the **Accept** button.

4. Captivate uploads the generated preview to SCORM Cloud.
5. When the upload is complete, the preview appears in a special Preview pane. At the bottom of the Preview pane, you will find a log of all communications between the course content and the LMS.

This is shown in the following screenshot:

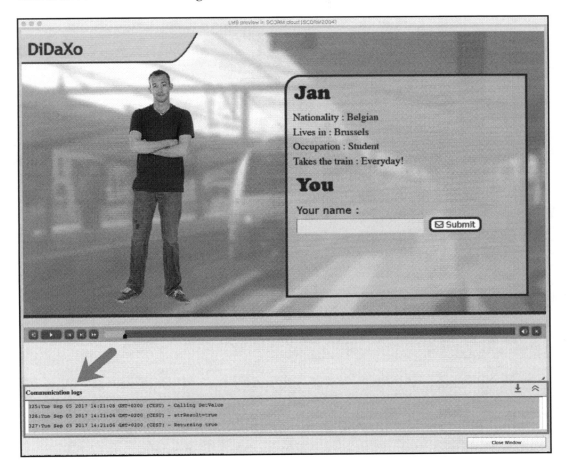

Thanks to this special preview option, you can test the communication between your course module and the LMS. If an error occurs, an error message will appear in the **Communication Log** window. This allows you to diagnose and fix the errors before releasing your course module to the students.

6. When you are done, click the **Close Window** button in the bottom right corner of the Preview pane.
7. Click the **Get Results** button in the message that appears.

This action opens your web browser with a page showing a digest of the data available to the LMS. This gives you a pretty good idea of what SCORM is capable of. Note that the actual data gathered by your LMS and the way it is presented to you depends on the LMS you use. Check with your LMS vendor for more details.

8. Return to Captivate.
9. Click the **Close** button in the **Relaunch the Preview** message.

Captivate deletes the course you uploaded to SCORM Cloud and closes the **Relaunch the Preview** message.

Thanks to this handy feature, you have been able to test the SCORM communication between your course content and the LMS. Note that, despite the name, SCORM Cloud is also able to test your xAPI and AICC content.

Working with Knowledge Check Slides

The typical use case of a Quiz is to assess the student's knowledge either at the end of a learning process or at the very beginning.

But you can use Question Slides for other purposes as well. Sometimes, all you need to do is to check and reinforce what the student has just learned right in the middle of a learning module. In such cases, you don't need to grade the questions or to track these interactions using your LMS. All you need is an informal question that challenges the learners and helps them identify the topics needing more attention. This is precisely what Knowledge Check Slides are for.

Knowledge Check Slides work exactly like regular Question Slides. The differences are as follows:

- Knowledge Check Slides are never graded, though they do have correct and incorrect answers.

- Knowledge Check Slides are never reported to the LMS. Therefore, they cannot be tracked or otherwise used in any kind of formal assessment activity.

In this section, you will experiment with Knowledge Check Slides by performing the following steps:

1. Use the **Filmstrip** to go to slide 8 of the `takeTheTrain.cptx` file.
2. Use the **Slides | Knowledge Check Slide** icon on the Toolbar to open the **Insert Questions** dialog.
3. Choose to insert a single **Hotspot** question. Notice that the **Graded** drop-down menu is completely disabled when inserting a Knowledge Check Slide.

Make sure the **Insert Questions** dialog looks like the following screenshot before clicking the **OK** button:

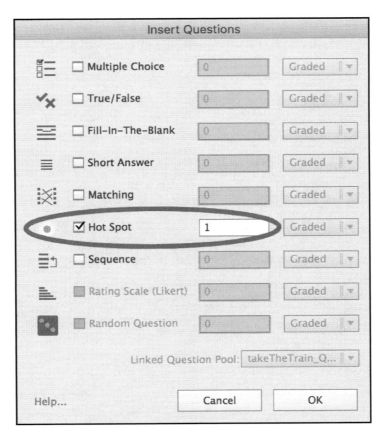

Your new Knowledge Check Slide is inserted as slide 9 of your project. It should look exactly like a standard Hotspot Question, with a few differences in the **Quiz** inspector.

4. Turn your attention to the **Quiz** inspector of your newly inserted Knowledge Check Slide.

Notice that, even though you can turn the **Correct** and the **Failure** captions on (indicating that correct and incorrect answers are indeed supported), there are no properties to set a number of *Points* or a *Penalty* value. Also, there is no *Reporting* section at the end of the **Quiz** inspector.

5. Write `Click the yellow poster to use when traveling by train on a Saturday.` in the Question Text placeholder.
6. Increase the height of the Question Text so the question is entirely visible on the slide.
7. In the **Quiz** inspector, deselect the **Incomplete** and the **Infinite Attempts** checkboxes. The corresponding captions disappear from the stage.
8. Use the **Media | Image** icon on the Toolbar to add the `Chapter07/images/ScheduleWeek.png` file.
9. Place the image on the left side of the slide.
10. Use the **Media | Image** icon on the Toolbar a second time to add the `Chapter07/images/ScheduleWeekEnds.png` file.
11. Place this image on the right side of the slide.
12. Don't hesitate to use the tools of the Align toolbar and other tools (such as the Smart Guides, the ability to group objects, and so on) to properly place and align those two pictures on the slide.
13. At the top of the **Quiz** inspector, set the number of **Answers** to 2. This adds a second hotspot on the slide.
14. Move and resize the Hotspots to place one Hotspot on top of each image.
15. At the top of the **Quiz** inspector, select the **Allow Clicks Only on Hotspots** checkbox.

With this checkbox selected, the students will only be able to click on the Hotspots when answering the question. Obviously, you should now tell Captivate which one of the two Hotspots is the correct answer.

16. Select the Hotspot on top of the `ScheduleWeek.png` image (the one on the left side, with a blue strip at the top).

17. In the **Style** tab of the **Properties** inspector, deselect the **Correct Answer** checkbox.

In this configuration, the students can only click the Hotspots when answering the question. Captivate knows that the Hotspot on the right is the correct answer. Notice that the Hotspot representing the correct answer has a blue checkmark, as shown in the following screenshot:

The main properties of this Knowledge Check Question are now in place. You should now provide some meaningful and engaging feedback to the students. This is what you will do in the next section.

Using the object states to customize the feedback messages

In this section, you will create the feedback messages of your Knowledge Check Slide. You need to create a correct caption and a failure caption. You could use the exact same techniques as those already discussed earlier in this chapter. However, this time, you want to go a little further, using the Object States feature of Captivate.

Perform the following steps to create a meaningful failure message:

1. Still on slide 9 of the `Chapter07/takeTheTrain.cptx` file, look at the **Quiz** inspector.

2. Open the **Failure Messages** drop-down menu and choose 1 in the list of options. A single red failure message appears on the stage.

3. Write `Nope! Click anywhere or press 'y' to continue.` into the failure message.

4. Right-click the failure message and choose the **Replace Smart Shape** menu item.

5. In the list of available shapes, choose the **Oval Callout** (or any other callout of your liking).

6. Move and resize the callout Smart Shape so the text fits in the object.

You will now add a character image to your failure callout. Inserting a character image is very easy and has been covered in `Chapter 2`, *Working with Standard Objects*. But in this case, the red failure callout and the character image you are about to insert are both part of the failure feedback. In other words, both those objects are initially hidden from the slide and should appear together only if and when the student provides an incorrect answer. Creating a multi-object feedback message is possible using the Object States, as shown in the following steps.

7. Make sure the red failure message is selected and click the **State View** button at the top of the **Properties** inspector.

8. Once in the State View, use the **Media | Characters** icon on the Toolbar to open the **My Assets** dialog.

9. In the top left corner of the dialog, open the **Category** drop-down menu and select the **Casual** option.

10. In the left column, select the last character of the **Casual** category.

11. In the central section of the dialog, choose the most appropriate image.

12. In the rightmost column, choose the most appropriate shot (**CloseUp**, **Half**, or **Full**).

13. Arrange the objects so they look good to you.

14. Click the **Exit State** icon on the Toolbar to return to the normal view.

Your Knowledge Check Slide should now look similar to the following screenshot:

Because you have inserted the Character image to the Normal state of the failure message, both the message and the associated image are part of the failure feedback. This is how you can use the Object States (covered in more detail in `Chapter 5, Developing Interactivity`) to create sophisticated, fun, and engaging feedback messages for your students.

 Even though you can add objects to the Normal state of such feedback messages, you cannot add extra custom states to these objects.

Creating the Correct feedback message

In this section, you will create the correct feedback message and associate a character image, using the same procedure.

As a reminder, the general steps are as follows:

- Select the **Correct** caption checkbox in the **Quiz** inspector to generate the green Correct caption on the stage.
- Customize the message and replace the Smart Shape with a callout of your liking.
- Switch to the **State View** of the green Correct caption and add the most appropriate character image.

Using Knowledge Check Slides with Interactive Video

Back in Chapter 05, *Working with interactive objects*, you worked with the new Interactive Video feature of Adobe Captivate 2019. You learned that any Slide Video inserted in Adobe Captivate can be made interactive through the use of Bookmarks and Overlay Slides. In this section, you will return to the Interactive Video you worked with in Chapter 5, *Developing Interactivity*, and explore how Knowledge Check Slides can be used as Overlay Slides for an Interactive Video using the following steps:

1. In the Chapter07/takeTheTrain.cptx project, use the **Filmstrip** to return to slide 22.
2. If needed, open the **Timeline** panel situated at the bottom of the screen.

Take some time to look at the Timeline of slide 22. Remember the bookmarks and the overlay slide that you have added on this Slide Video back in Chapter 5? You will now add yet another Overlay Slide using the following steps.

3. With slide 22 still selected in the **Filmstrip**, use the **Slide | Knowledge Check slide** icon on the Toolbar to reopen the **Insert Question** dialog.
4. Insert a single **Sequence** question. (Remember that because you are inserting a Knowledge Check slide, the **Graded** drop-down is not available).
5. Click the **OK** button to insert the new question and close the **Insert Question** dialog. The new slide is inserted as slide 24 of the project.
6. At the top of the **Quiz** inspector, change the number of **Answers** to 5. Captivate generates three more answers on the slide.

7. In the **Quiz** inspector, deselect the **Infinite Attempts** checkbox.

8. Change the question stem to `Put the departure sequence in the correct order.`

9. Rearrange the objects of the slide so that the question stem is not truncated.

10. Change the text of the five answers to the following:

    - A) `The train attendant whistles.`
    - B) `The train attendant closes all the doors but one.`
    - C) `The train attendant triggers the departure procedure. A red dot lights up.`
    - D) `The red dot turns to a white circle.`
    - E) `The train attendant closes the last door and the train departs.`

11. Add a Correct and an Incorrect caption using the tools and techniques you have learned earlier in this chapter.

You will now add some branching to this Question slide. What you want to achieve is the following:

- If the learner answers the question correctly, you simply want to close the Overlay Slide and continue with the video.
- If the learner provides the wrong answer, you want to play the video again. To do that, you will use the **Jump To Bookmark** action to redirect the user to the **whistle** bookmark you created in Chapter 05.

Use the following steps to setup the branching for this Knowledge Check Question Slide.

12. On slide 24 of the `Chapter07/takeTheTrain.cptx` project, turn your attention to the **Quiz** Inspector.

13. In the **Actions** section of the **Quiz** inspector, make sure the **On Success** action is set to **Continue**.

14. Open the **Last Attempt** drop down menu and change the action to **Jump To Bookmark**.

15. Make sure the **whistle** bookmark is selected in the **Bookmark** dropdown.

The **Actions** section of the **Quiz** inspector should now look like the following screenshot:

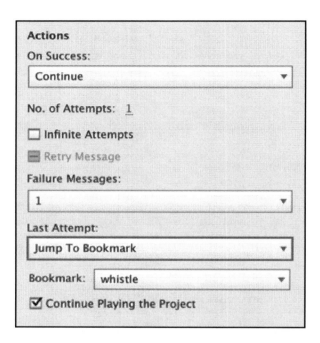

The last step of the process is to define your new Knowledge Check question as an Overlay Slide of the Interactive Video of slide 22. You will do that using the following steps.

16. Use the **Filmstrip** to return to slide 22 and open the **Timeline** panel if necessary.
17. In the **Timeline** of slide 22, place the red playhead just after the **1:08** sec mark (just before the *enjoy* bookmark). This is the timecode at which you want to display the Knowledge Check question as an Qverlay Slide of the Interactive Video.
18. Click the yellow diamond with a + sign, located on the red playhead.
19. Select **Slide 24** in the **Overlay** dialog and click the **Insert** button.

These actions are depicted in the following screenshot:

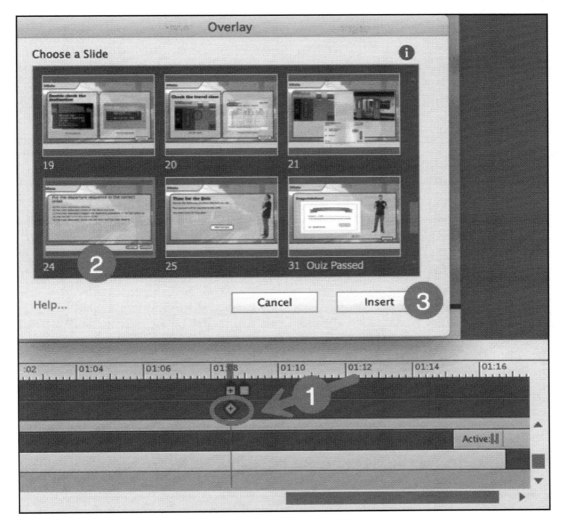

You have now used a Knowledge Check question as an Overlay Slide of an Interactive Video.

 At the time of this writing, only Knowledge Check slides can be used as Overlay Slides of an Interactive Video. Regular (graded) Question Slides are not (yet) supported.

Remember that the Interactive Video feature is only supported in the HTML 5 output. In other words, you cannot test your new Overlay Slide in the standard **Preview** pane of Captivate (which uses Flash behind the scenes).

20. Use the **Preview | HTML 5 in Browser** icon on the Toolbar to test your new Overlay Slide. Make sure both scenarios (when you answer incorrectly and when you answer correctly) work as expected before returning to Captivate.

In this section, you have added Knowledge Check Slides to your project. You have also used the Object States to provide much more sophisticated and engaging feedback messages to your students. It is time to summarize what has been covered in this section:

- Knowledge Check slides work just like regular Question Slides, apart from two important exceptions: They cannot be graded, and they cannot be reported to your LMS.
- Because of these two exceptions, Knowledge Check slides are not included in the Quiz that is in the project.
- Knowledge Check Slides are an invaluable pedagogical tool allowing you to help students reinforce their knowledge and identify areas needing attention. This is done without interfering with the formal assessment (and thus with the scores) of the students.
- These slides are used as informal challenges to check and reinforce the knowledge of the student throughout the learning module.
- You can use the Object State view of the feedback messages to further customize those messages and create even more engaging eLearning modules.
- Knowledge Check slides can be used as Overlay Slides of an Interactive Video.

Allowing the students to fail

Failure is a normal step of any learning process, and every teacher should allow students to fail while learning something new. By using the Knowledge Check Slides, you allow students to test themselves, and potentially to fail, but without any consequences on the final outcome (in other words, on their score) for the course. This makes the Knowledge Check Slides an invaluable pedagogical tool. Don't hesitate to use them in your own teaching.

Summary

With the addition of Question Slides and Quizzes, your project has reached an important milestone. It is now a highly interactive eLearning package that is able to integrate nicely in virtually every LMS on the market. On the pedagogical side, you have discovered the eLearning answer to the assessment challenge, which is one of the primary concerns of any teacher. On the technical side, you have discovered the SCORM, AICC, and xAPI standards that make communication between the eLearning content and the LMS possible.

In this chapter, you have learned about each of the eight question types of Captivate. You created a Question Pool before exploring the **Quiz Preferences** and the myriad options available. In the second part of this chapter, you learned how the Quiz results and other interactions can be reported to an LMS, before discovering the pedagogical power of the Knowledge Check Slides.

In the next chapter, you will learn how to capture onscreen action using Captivate. Be ready to discover a completely different and exciting type of project.

Meet the community

In this section, we will introduce you to two individuals from the same family. Together with two other members of the family, they own and manage Infosemantics, an Australian-based company specialized in eLearning development and Captivate widgets.

Rod Ward

The director of Infosemantics, Rod is a technical author, information designer, and eLearning developer with over a decade of industry experience. Based in Perth since 1986, he has worked for companies large and small across Australia. Rod's specialties are the design and development of eLearning courses using sound instructional design principles and Adobe's suite of eLearning software tools. Rod is also the author of four eBooks about Adobe Captivate, three about troubleshooting issues in various versions of Captivate, and one about using Advanced Actions and Variables to create custom interactivity.

Tristan Ward

Tristan is an expert in Adobe Captivate and Adobe Animate, as well as an accomplished HTML5 programmer. He builds many animations and interactivity add-ons included in Infosemantics' eLearning courses. He is the creator of the CpExtra HTML5 widget that has quickly become the most popular widget for creating powerful HTML5 and Responsive Design content in Adobe Captivate. CpExtra is now widely regarded as an essential part of any serious Captivate developer's toolkit.

Contact details

- Website: http://www.infosemantics.com.au/
- Twitter: @Infosemantics
- CpExtra: http://www.infosemantics.com.au/adobe-captivate-widgets/cpextra

Capturing Onscreen Action 8

So far, you have learned how to create an eLearning course with text, shapes, audio, video, interactions, and quiz questions. Now, it's time to explore how Captivate 2019 creates simulations.

Software simulation modules enable you to teach skills, such as performing specific steps in an application, or demonstrating how a website works.

Recording software simulations can be compared to filming a movie. When filming a movie, the director wants to capture all the images, sequences, and shots he or she needs. In the movie industry, this raw footage is called the **rushes**. After filming, the director begins post-production. This is the stage where the raw material from filming is shaped into the final movie. Only the best rushes make their way to the movie theater while the others are discarded. The post-production phase is only successful when the filming provides enough good-quality material to create a great movie.

This same idea applies to Captivate. When you're recording screens, you need to have enough quality slides to give you the flexibility to shape the final product during post-production.

At the end of this chapter, you will have recorded and edited your first simulation project.

In this chapter, you will cover the following topics:

- Choosing the right size/resolution for the project
- Touring the recording preferences and the recording modes
- Recording demonstrations and simulations
- Recording System Audio
- Discussing and using the Full Motion Recording
- Using Manual Panning
- Recording a responsive simulation
- Resizing a project
- Modifying the object properties

If you are ready, it's almost time to turn the camera on and start the real action!

Choosing the right resolution for the project

Choosing the right resolution is the first critical decision you have to make. This is important because the size of the captured slides plays a critical role in the quality of the final movie.

Describing the problem

A typical Captivate project, such as the Encoder demonstration you experienced in `Chapter 1`, *Getting Started with Adobe Captivate 2019*, involves taking screenshots of an actual piece of software. At the end of the process, the project will be published in HTML5 or SWF format and placed on a web page. Most of the time, that web page displays many other page elements (such as logos, headers, footers, navigation bars, and so on) in addition to incorporating your Captivate movie. While the application may look fine when recording, you need to be aware of how it will look in the final product. In the following screenshot, you can see the crowded display space the recording needs to fit into:

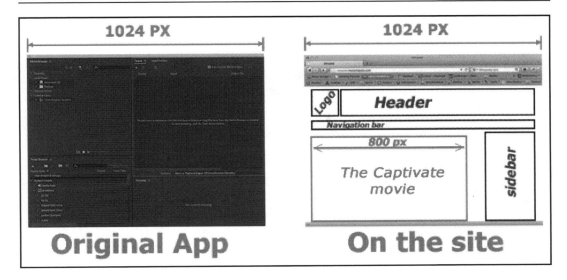

Let's pretend this application requires a minimal width of 1024 pixels to be displayed without horizontal scrollbars. On the right-hand screenshot is the wireframe of the web page you must embed the finished recording on. The page has been designed to fit a 1024 pixel-wide screen and has to display lots of elements in addition to the Captivate content. To cope with the design requirement of the web page, your project should not be wider than 800 pixels.

So, here is your problem: you have to find a way to fit 1024 pixels in 800 pixels! Several approaches are available to address this situation. Each of these has its pros and cons, and we will go through a brief review of each.

Resizing the project after the initial shooting

The first approach is a two-step process. The initial step is recording the project with a width of 1024 pixels. The second step is to use the Rescale Project feature to downsize the project to 800 pixels.

By recording with a screen width of 1024 pixels, the application is captured in its intended size, matching the student's experience of the application.

The main disadvantage of this approach is that it requires resizing the project. In Captivate, the resize operation is an irreversible operation! It always has a cost in terms of image quality. Surprisingly, the resize operation can result in a larger file size, even if the new resolution is smaller than the original one. Also, in case the new resolution is smaller, the screenshots will be smaller and the information they contain might become difficult to read.

Here are a few things you need to keep in mind when resizing a project:

- It is always better to downsize a project than to make it bigger.
- Always keep a backup copy of the project in its original resolution! Remember that the resize operation is an irreversible operation. Your backup copy is the only way to roll back the resize operation, in case something goes wrong!

Downsizing the application during shooting

The second approach is to change the size of the application during recording to match the size of the final product. In this example, it means that the application would be 800 pixels wide instead of 1024 pixels during the capture.

This is the easiest solution, as no irreversible or complex resize operation is needed. But when capturing the application, the screen is very crowded. Remember that the application you capture requires a minimal width of 1024 pixels. So, by downsizing it to a width of 800 pixels, it does not have enough room to display all its components and creates horizontal scrollbars. The scrollbars and any scrolling actions will be recorded and appear in the final Captivate project. Scrollbars sometimes hide important information from the screen, and therefore, from your students.

Using the Panning feature of Captivate

In the movie industry, panning refers to moving the camera while filming. In Captivate, it means that you can move the recording area while capturing the slides.

This approach is a way to try and meet both the requirements of the application to record, and the requirements of the movie to be produced.

The idea is to leave the application at its intended width of 1024 pixels, and at the same time define a capture area that is 800 pixels wide. During the recording, the smaller capture area can be overlaid on the bigger application, as shown in the following screenshot:

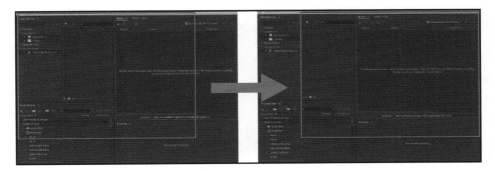

In the preceding screenshot, the capture area is the red rectangle. Captivate only captures what is inside the red rectangle. As you can see, the capture area does not always cover the same part of the application during the recording.

This approach is a good compromise, but it has two major disadvantages. Moving the recording area while filming increases the file size of your final movie. But more importantly, using this approach, your learner never sees the application entirely, which could compromise the quality of the learning process.

Using the Scalable HTML Content feature

The Scalable HTML Content feature makes the published movie scalable, so it fits the screen it is viewed on (even as the screen is resized!).

For example, say you shoot and publish your movie at a size of 1024 pixels, but the movie is viewed on a website where the maximal resolution can only be 800 pixels. In such a case, the Scalable HTML Content feature scales the movie down to 800 pixels so that it fits in the available space.

This approach is quick and easy to implement, but it has a major flaw: you lose control over how your content will actually be experienced. Only the learners who have exactly the same size screen as yours will see the course as you designed it. The other learners will see the course either bigger (which means possibly pixelated) or smaller (which probably means too small to be comfortable).

This option will be covered in Chapter 15, *Finishing Touches and Publishing*.

Using a Responsive Project

Creating a responsive simulation also helps you solve this problem. By using a Responsive Project, you can rearrange the layout and the course content to make it fit various screen sizes.

The main advantage of this approach is that you can control almost every aspect of your project on virtually any screen size. On the other hand, the projects built using this solution can only be published in HTML5, so only objects supported in HTML5 can be used in such projects. Creating a Responsive Project takes more time and requires using special tools and features of Captivate, like the Fluid Boxes.

Building a Responsive Project will be covered in `Chapter 10`, *Creating a Responsive Project*.

Conclusion

None of these approaches are perfect, but you'll have to choose one anyway. The best approach depends on the project, on your learners, and on your personal taste. Here are some general guidelines to help you make the best choice:

- The size of the capture area should match the size of the application to capture whenever possible.
- If you need to resize the project, take a bigger project and make it smaller to help maintain the best possible image quality. Also, make sure you keep a backup copy of the project at its original size.
- Use panning only if you really need it.
- When panning, move the camera (the red capture area) only when necessary, and move it slowly enough to help the students build a mental picture of the entire application.
- If you use the Scalable HTML Content feature, make sure you test your work on an array of different screens and devices to ensure the best possible learning experience in the majority of the scenarios.
- Responsive Projects can only be published in HTML5. They also require some more work and the use of special tools.

Finally, never forget that you are teaching. Your learners don't care about your sizing concerns; they just want to learn something. If the chosen approach compromises the quality of the learning process, then it is not the correct approach!

About screen sizes
For more information about the screen sizes in use, visit
`http://www.websitedimensions.com/.`

Recording the first project

It is time to have our first hands-on experience of an actual recording session.
Recording a Captivate project is a five-step process:

1. Preparing the application to record
2. Rehearsing the scenario
3. Resetting the application
4. Recording the project
5. Previewing the rushes

Let's review these five steps one by one.

Preparing the application to record

For this exercise, the application you will record is Adobe Media Encoder CC 2018.
This application is used to convert video and audio files into a wide range of formats.
Adobe Media Encoder (AME) is included in the standard Captivate package; if you
have Captivate (even the trial version) installed on your machine, you also have
AME.

First, you will open AME by performing the following steps:

1. Open Captivate. If Captivate is already open, close all the open files.
2. Open AME. On Mac, it is in the `/Applications/Adobe Media Encoder`
   `CC 2018` folder. On Windows, a shortcut to AME should be available in the
   Start menu.

When AME opens, make sure it looks like what's shown in the following screenshot:

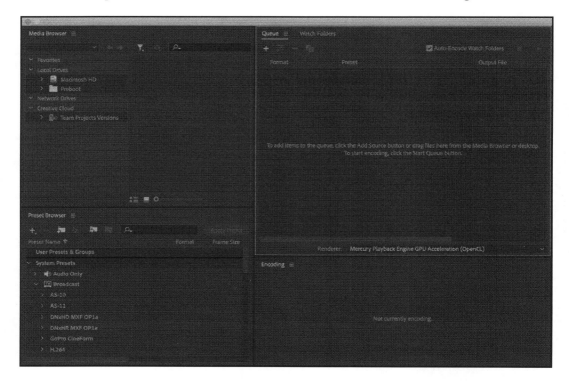

This exercise and the screenshots are based on Adobe Media Encoder CC 2018, which is the version that was installed with Adobe Captivate 2019, but it also works with Adobe Media Encoder CC 2019, which is a part of Creative Cloud.

Rehearsing the scenario

The goal of this Captivate project is to teach students how to use AME to convert a QuickTime movie (with a .mov extension) to a 400x300 pixels dimension video (with a .mp4 extension). This scenario follows the exact same steps as those used in the demonstration and simulation in the first chapter. Make sure that the audio system of your computer is turned on before rehearsing the following scenario. Here are the steps:

1. Go to the Adobe Media Encoder application.
2. Under the **Queue** panel, click the + icon on the top left corner.

3. Browse to the `Chapter08\video\MOV` folder of the exercise files.

4. Select the `demo_en.mov` QuickTime movie and click **Open**.

5. Open the **Format** drop-down list and be sure the **H.264** format is selected.

6. Open the **Preset** drop-down list and apply the **YouTube 480p SD** preset.

7. Click the hyperlink of the preset name to open the **Export Settings** dialog.

8. Go to the **Video** tab in the lower right area of the **Export Settings** dialog.

9. Make sure the Maintain Aspect Ratio icon (the chain icon) is active, and change the width of the video to `400` pixels. The new height of the video will be automatically set to `300` pixels.

10. Click the **OK** button to validate the new export settings.

11. Click the Start Queue button (the green play icon) on the top right corner to start the actual encoding.

The encoding process begins. In the **Encoding** panel at the bottom of the screen, you will see a progress bar for this operation. When the operation is complete, the system plays a brief chime sound effect and the Start Queue button is greyed out.

 If you don't hear the chimes sound effect at the end of the encoding process, go to AME **Preferences** and select **Play chime when finished encoding**.

If you need more practice, feel free to rehearse this scenario a few more times before the recording. After all, on a real movie set, even the most famous actors rehearse their scenes many times before the director finally decides to turn the camera on. Make sure you master these steps, and make sure AME behaves as expected before continuing.

Resetting the application

When you are ready to record the sequence, don't forget to reset AME to its original state. The best way to do this is to perform the following steps:

1. Close and restart AME

2. When the application reopens, make sure it looks like the previous screenshot again

Also, delete the `.mp4` file(s) generated during the rehearsal(s) by performing the following steps:

3. Open the **Finder** (Mac) or the **Windows Explorer** (Windows) and browse to the `Chapter08\video\MOV` folder of the exercises
4. Delete every `.mp4` file present in this folder

On a real movie set, this is the job of the script supervisor!

Recording the movie

The scenario and Adobe Media Encoder are ready to be captured. Let's head back to Captivate and start the actual recording process.

Enabling access to assistive devices (Mac users only)

If you work on Mac, there is one system option to change before Captivate can record the project. Use the following steps to make your Mac ready to record:

1. The first time you create a new software simulation with Captivate, a warning message appears to turn on Adobe Captivate in **System Preferences** to allow Captivate to control your computer
2. Click **OK** to dismiss the message, and then click **Cancel**
3. Open the **System Preferences** application
4. In the **System Preferences** dialog, click **Security & Privacy**
5. Go to the **Privacy** tab
6. If needed, click the lock icon at the bottom left corner of the **System Preference** application and authenticate as an administrator
7. Select the **Captivate** option to grant Captivate access to the assistive devices

Without this step, macOS does not broadcast the events that Captivate uses to capture user interactivity (clicking a button, typing into a text entry, and so on).

Preparing Captivate to record the sequence

For this first practice recording, you will use the default options of Captivate to record the sequence using the following steps. Make sure that Adobe Media Encoder has been reset and is open at this time.

1. Close every open file so that the Captivate Welcome screen is displayed.
2. On the **New** tab of the Welcome screen, double-click the Software Simulation thumbnail. You can also use the **File | Record a New Software Simulation** menu item to achieve the same result.

The Captivate interface disappears and you should see a red rectangle on the screen. This red rectangle is the recording area.

3. In the recording window, choose **Application** to record an application.
4. In the **Select the window to record** drop-down list, choose to record the **Adobe Media Encoder CC 2018** application.

The Adobe Media Encoder application opens and the red recording area snaps to the application window.

5. In the **Snap to** section of the box, choose to record at **Custom Size**.
6. Choose the **1024 x 768** size from the drop-down list. The red recording area and AME are both resized to the chosen size.

If you are using scaled display settings for your computer, the Adobe Media Encoder application might not resize to exactly **1024 x 768** pixels. In such a case, use the smallest display resolution allowed for the Adobe Media Encoder application as the size for your Captivate project.

7. Leave the remaining options at their default settings.

8. The recording window should look like what's shown in the following screenshot:

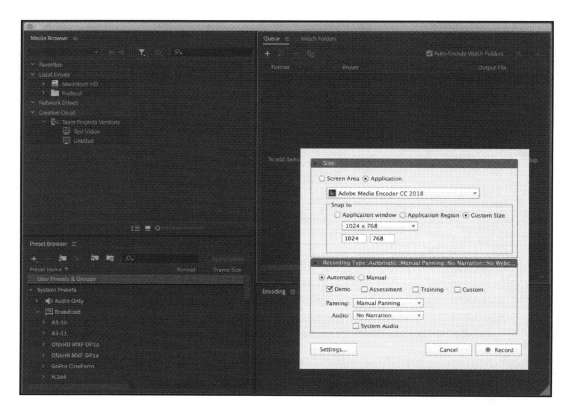

In the preceding screenshot, notice the **Demo** checkbox in the lower part of the window. Make sure that this checkbox is the only one that's selected.

 For Mac users, the **System Audio** checkbox might be unavailable on your system. This problem will be addressed later in this chapter.

The stage is set and the actors are in place. Everyone is waiting for the director's signal to get started!

And action!

The signal is the red **Record** button at the bottom of the recording window. Once you click it, all your actions are recorded by Captivate until you stop the capture:

 If you have a problem while doing this exercise, refer to the `Chapter08/final/encoderDemo_1_1024.cptx` file of your exercises folder.

1. Click the red **Record** button at the bottom of the recording window. After a short countdown, you'll be in the recording mode.
2. In the Adobe Media Encoder window, perform the actions as written in the scenario you rehearsed earlier in this chapter.

During the recording, pay close attention to the following things:

- Each time you click, you should hear a camera shutter sound
- When you type in the **Width** field, you should hear keystrokes
- After clicking the Start Queue button, AME displays a progress bar in the bottom right panel
- When the encoding process is finished, the application plays a brief chimes sound effect and the Start Queue button is greyed out

Also, make sure you perform the actions slowly to allow Captivate enough time to capture all the needed images and actions. Don't worry about being too slow. The captured slides will still be three seconds long.

3. After completing all the steps, hit the *End* key (Windows) or use the *command + enter* shortcut (Mac) to stop the recording and generate the slides in Captivate.

 Shortcuts on Mac
On some Mac models, it is necessary to add the *fn* key into the mix. In this instance, some Mac models require the *command + fn + enter* shortcut to stop the recording. You can also click the Captivate icon in the notification area to stop the recording.

4. When the project has finished loading in Captivate, save it as `Chapter08/encoderDemo_1_1024.cptx`.
5. Close the Adobe Media Encoder application.

The recording phase of the project is now over. If you don't get it right the first time, don't worry – you can simply discard your sequence and start over. On a real movie set, even the most famous actors are granted many chances to do it right.

Previewing the rushes

The project should be open in Captivate. To launch the preview, you will use the same icon as in `Chapter 1`, *Getting Started with Adobe Captivate 2019*, as explained in the following steps:

1. Click the Preview icon on the Toolbar. From the drop-down list, choose **Project** to preview the entire project (you can also use the *F4* shortcut key to do the same thing).
2. Captivate generates the slides in a temporary Flash file and opens the **Preview** pane.
3. Click the Play button at the center of the Preview dialog.
4. Close the Preview pane when done.

Captivate has already generated lots of objects on the slides. Remember that in the recording window, the **Demo** mode was selected by default. The **Demo** mode automatically adds Text Captions, Highlight Boxes, and Mouse movements to the slides.

Of course, some of the content of the Text Captions must be corrected; the size and position of the Highlight Boxes and Text Captions must be fine-tuned; and the overall rhythm of the project is probably too fast, but this is an acceptable start point.

The main problem with these rushes is how the movie ends. While previewing the project, you probably noticed that the progress bar has not been captured by Captivate.

To understand why Captivate did not capture this progress bar, it is necessary to further dive into the inner workings of the Captivate capture engine.

The inner workings of the Captivate capture engine

For you techies, the Captivate capture engine is based on static screenshots. Going back to the Adobe Media Encoder project, let's review what exactly happened when you clicked the mouse during screen capture using the following steps:

1. Return to the `Chapter08/encoderDemo_1_1024.cptx` file
2. Make sure the first slide is selected in the **Filmstrip** panel

The first slide shows the mouse clicking the Add Source icon of AME. When you clicked this icon, Captivate launched a sequence of actions behind the scenes:

- Captivate recorded the position of the mouse at the time of the click (using x and y coordinates).
- Adobe Media Encoder executed the action.
- When Adobe Media Encoder completed its action, Captivate took a second static screenshot to capture the new state of the application. This second screenshot is used as the background image of slide 2.

You then used your mouse a second time to select the `demo_en.mov` file. When this second click occurred, Captivate launched the same sequence of actions and took a third static screenshot to use as the background image of slide 3.

When the movie plays, the static screenshot of the first slide (a `.bmp` image) is displayed. When the mouse has to move, Captivate recreates a movement from the top left corner of the slide to the position of the click, as recorded during filming. Just after the click, Captivate displays the static (`.bmp`) screenshot of the second slide.

When it is time to move the mouse over the second slide, Captivate recreates a movement from where the click occurred on the first slide to the location of the click on the second slide, as recorded during filming. Right after the second click, Captivate displays the third static screenshot. This process repeats itself until the end of the movie.

It may sound very simple and logical, but the way this process works has lots of implications, as mentioned in the following list:

- Only the start and the end points of the mouse movements are recorded by Captivate. During the playback, a movement is recreated between these points.
- The actual mouse movements made during the recording between two clicks are therefore not recorded.
- The animations displayed by the Captured application (in this case, the progress bar) are not captured.
- The Timeline of the generated movie is independent of the time that has passed during filming.

This system creates a very lightweight animation: a bunch of images and a few coordinates are enough to reproduce an entire movie.

However, this system is limited. Some mouse actions, such as drag and drop and scrolling actions, cannot be reproduced that way. These actions require an actual frame-by-frame video recording to be played back correctly. In Captivate, such a frame-by-frame sequence is known as **Full Motion Recording** (**FMR**).

Understanding the FMR mode

To make sure you understand this concept, let's take a look at some of the preferences of Captivate:

1. In Captivate, use the **Edit** | **Preferences** (Windows) or **Adobe Captivate** | **Preferences** (Mac) menu item to open the **Preferences** dialog.

Once the **Preferences** dialog opens, click **Settings** under the **Recording** section, as shown in the following screenshot:

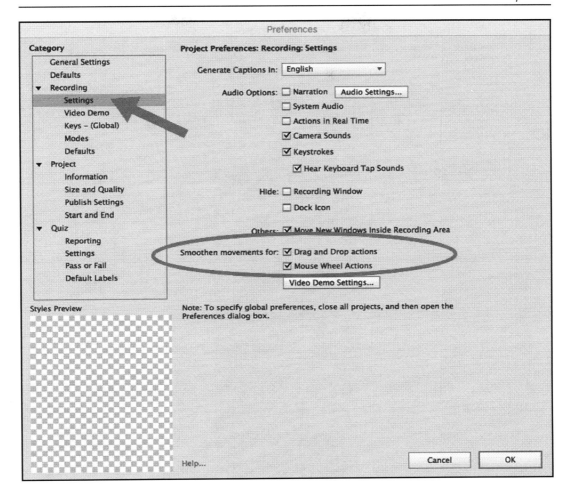

At the end of the **Preferences** dialog, there are two options that help you control the FMR behavior of Captivate: **Smoothen movements for Drag and Drop actions** and **Smoothen movements for Mouse Wheel Actions**. These two options should be selected by default.

2. Make sure these two options are selected and close the **Preferences** dialog.
3. In the **Filmstrip** panel, take a close look at the icons beneath each of the slide's thumbnails.

While most of the slides display the icon of a mouse, one slide should display the icon of a video camera. This is shown in the following screenshot:

As shown in the preceding screenshot, slide 8 is where the scrolling movement in the preset list of AME occurs.

 The actual slide number may vary depending on how your particular recording session went.

Because the **Smoothen movements for Drag and Drop actions** and **Smoothen movements for: Mouse Wheel Actions** options were turned on, Captivate has detected this scrolling movement and has automatically switched to the FMR mode when capturing that particular slide.

One of the limitations of FMR is that it does not allow any kind of interaction. During the playback, the learners cannot perform such scrolling movement themselves. Another limitation of FMR is that it increases the file size of the simulation.

The FMR mode will also help you capture the progress bar at the end of the project. The only problem is that the progress bar is not linked to any scrolling or drag-and-drop action. Fortunately, there is another way to control FMR mode.

Controlling Captivate during the recording session

Controlling Captivate during the recording session is quite a challenge for your operating system (Mac or Windows). Even though both Windows and Mac OS are multitasking operating systems (it means they can handle multiple applications running at the same time), there can only be one active application at any given time. The active application is the one you currently interact with and therefore is the one that currently listens to the keyboard, the mouse, and other input devices.

When recording with Captivate, there are two active applications: the application you capture and Captivate itself. You should be able to interact with both of these applications, so they both share the same mouse and the same keyboard at the same time. This is a very unusual situation to deal with for an operating system.

By default, the mouse and the keyboard send their data to the application you record, except for a few keys and shortcuts that are wired to Captivate. Let's take a deeper look at this system using the following steps:

1. Use the **Adobe Captivate | Preferences** (Mac) or **Edit | Preferences** (Windows) menu item to open the **Preferences** dialog of Captivate.
2. In the left column of the **Preferences** dialog, open the **Keys - (Global)** category.

This part of the **Preferences** dialog lists all the keys and shortcuts that allow you to interact with Captivate during the recording, as shown in the following screenshot:

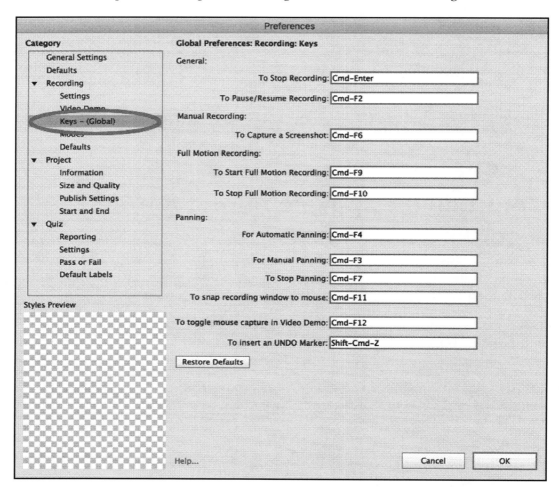

 The preceding screenshot has been taken on a Mac. If you work on Windows, the dialog will be exactly the same with the exception of the shortcuts, which are a bit different on Windows.

Remember that all the other keys as well as the mouse are wired to the application you capture.

3. Take some time to review the available keys and shortcuts.

Of special interest are the keyboard shortcuts you can use to manually start and stop a FMR. Also, notice that you can use a keyboard shortcut (*Print Screen* on Windows or *command + F6* on Mac) to manually take extra screenshots if needed. Finally, the *End* (Windows) or *command + enter* (Mac) shortcut is used to stop the recording.

In some situations, you may need to change these recording keys. For example, if the software you are recording uses the same shortcut keys that are defined for Captivate recording functions, you will need to change the key combinations.

Here are the steps you can follow to modify the shortcut keys assigned for each task:

4. Click the field where the key used to stop recording is defined (*End* on Windows or *command + enter* on Mac).
5. Type the *Ctrl + E* shortcut on your keyboard. The *Ctrl + E* shortcut is now assigned to the stop recording action.
6. At the bottom of the window, click the **Restore Defaults** button to return to the default settings.
7. Leave the **Preferences** dialog open.

Now, take some time to inspect the remaining preferences of Captivate.

Exploring the Preferences

In this section, you will explore the remaining recording preferences of Captivate. You will start by exploring the automatic recording modes.

Exploring the automatic recording modes

In the previous section, your first recording experience was based on the default preferences of Captivate. To take full control of the situation, you will explore and fine-tune the automatic recording modes before having a second try. Perform the following steps to explore the automatic recording modes:

1. In the left panel in the **Preferences** dialog, select the **Modes** category under the **Recording** section.

2. At the top of the **Preferences** dialog, make sure the **Mode:** drop-down list is set to **Demonstration**, as shown in the following screenshot:

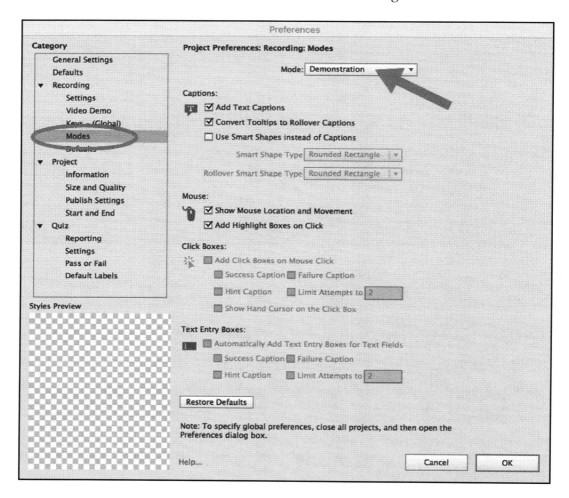

The **Preferences** dialog currently displays the settings of the **Demonstration** recording mode you used during your first capture session. As expected, this recording mode adds Text Captions to the slides.

If you wish to use Smart Shapes instead of Text Captions to have more flexibility to style the text, select **Use Smart Shapes instead of Captions**.

It also shows the mouse and adds a Highlight Box each time the mouse is clicked during the capture.

3. These settings reflect what you have seen when previewing the rushes of the first movie. At the top of the **Preferences** dialog, open the **Mode:** drop-down list.
4. Choose the **Assessment Simulation** option.

The **Assessment Simulation** mode is the second automatic recording mode of Captivate. As discussed earlier, a simulation is a project in which the user is active, so the **Show Mouse Location and Movement** option is, logically, not selected. Instead, each time a mouse click occurs during the filming, a **Click Box** is automatically added to the slide.

The Click Box is one of the interactive objects of Captivate. It can pause the module and wait for the learner to click the same location where you clicked during the capture. Because the **Failure Caption** option is selected, a failure notice will be displayed if the learner does not click the right spot.

If you use the keyboard during the recording process, Captivate generates a Text Entry Box. The Text Entry Box is another interactive object of Captivate that stops the playhead and waits for the learner to interact with the course.

5. Open the **Mode:** drop-down list again.
6. In the list, choose the **Training Simulation** mode.

The **Training Simulation** mode is very similar to the **Assessment Simulation** mode. The only difference is the **Hint Caption** option that is selected for both the Click Box object and the Text Entry Box object. A Hint Caption is a Text Caption or a Smart Shape that is displayed when the student hovers the mouse over the hit area of the Click Box / Text Entry Box.

7. Open the **Mode:** drop-down list one last time.
8. In the drop-down list, choose the **Custom** mode.

Surprise! When choosing the **Custom** mode, no option is selected by default. In fact, the Custom mode is yours to create, so let's go!

9. In the **Caption:** section, select the **Add Text Captions** box.

10. In the **Click Boxes:** section, select the **Add Click Boxes on Mouse Click** option. Also, select the **Failure Caption** and **Hint Caption** boxes.

11. Finally, in the **Text Entry Boxes:** section, select the **Automatically Add Text Entry Boxes for Text Fields** option with a **Failure Caption** and a **Hint Caption**.

Depending on the recording mode, Text Captions, Failure Captions, and/or Hint Captions will be added to the slides.

Exploring the recording settings

Now let's focus on the **Recording: Settings** category of the **Preferences** dialog:

1. Open the **Recording: Settings** category by clicking **Settings** under the **Recording** category in the left pane of the **Preferences** dialog

The first available option at the top of the recording settings preference pane is the **Generate Captions In:** drop-down list. Use it to choose the language used by Captivate to generate the various types of captions:

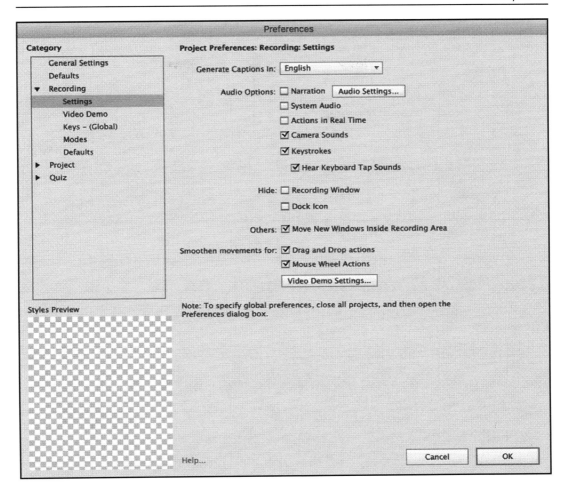

Other options available on this pane include the following:

- When the **Actions in Real Time** checkbox is selected, the recording is played back at the same speed as the actions performed during the recording.
- The **Camera Sounds** check box is used to turn the camera shutter sound on or off during the recording. Make sure this option is selected.
- The **Keystrokes** and **Hear Keyboard Tap Sounds** options are responsible for recording the keystrokes and for the keystroke's sound during filming. It is best to leave these options selected.

- The **Move New Windows Inside Recording Area** option is used during the capture when the application you record opens a new window or a dialog. It prevents the new window from opening outside or partially outside of the recording area. This option should be selected at all times.
- The **Hide Recording Window** option turns off the display of red border around the recording area.
- (For Windows only) The **Hide System Tray Icon** and **Hide Task Icon** checkboxes are great when you record fullscreen. When turned on, they hide the Captivate button from the Windows taskbar and the Captivate icon from the notification area.
- (For Mac only) The **Hide Dock Icon** checkbox is used to remove the Captivate icon from Dock during the filming. This option is very useful when recording fullscreen.

The Video Demo preferences pane

To finish off with the **Recording** preferences, you will now explore one last **Preferences** pane:

1. Click the **Video Demo** category to open the **Video Demo** preferences pane.

The **Video Demo** preferences pane shows options to control and optimize the conversion of an FMR into HTML5 or SWF video. Normally, the default options should work fine in almost every situation, so there is no need to change anything on this page right now.

2. Click **OK** to close the **Preferences** dialog and save the changes.

Now that you have a better idea of the available preferences, it is time to have a second try at recording your project.

Recording the other versions of the project

It is now time to start another recording session. For this second experience, you will pursue the following objectives:

- You will generate four different versions of the project in a single recording session

- At the end of the project, you will use an FMR to capture the progress bar of the encoding process

Before turning on the camera for the second time, here are some additional tips and tricks for successful capture:

- Use the automatic recording modes whenever possible.
- If you have to record fullscreen, reset your desktop to its default appearance, that is, remove your custom wallpaper, and turn off any custom color scheme, or mouse pointer sets, and preferably set it to a solid color like dark blue or gray. Your computer should look like any computer.
- Turn off your screensaver.
- Turn off the instant messaging apps or make yourself unavailable.
- Turn off the notifications.
- Turn on the sound so that you can hear the camera shutter and the keystrokes. This will help you have better control over the recording process.
- If you are not sure whether or not Captivate took a given screenshot, don't hesitate to take one manually using the *Print Screen* key (Windows) or the *command + F6* shortcut (Mac). During the editing phase that follows, it is much easier to delete an extra slide than to generate a missing slide.
- Perform the actions slowly, especially the text typing actions and the actions that require an FMR. You'll be able to set up the timing of each slide with great precision during the editing phase.
- Rehearse your scripts before recording.

With these tips and tricks in mind, let's concentrate on the actual recording. Your first concern is to reset the stage by performing the following steps:

1. Reopen AME. When the application appears, make sure it looks like the screenshot in the *Preparing the application to record* section earlier in this chapter.
2. Delete all the `.mp4` files in the `videos/MOV` folder of the exercise files.
3. Return to Captivate and close every open file, if needed.
4. Use the **File | Record a New Software Simulation** menu item or the Software Simulation thumbnail on the **New** tab of the welcome screen to create a new project. The main Captivate interface disappears and the red recording area is displayed.

5. In the recording window, choose **Application** to record **Adobe Media Encoder CC 2018**. The red recording area snaps to the **Adobe Media Encoder** window.

6. Use a **Custom Size** of **1024 x 768** pixels to record your application.

7. In the recording modes section of the recording window, select all four automatic recording modes (**Demo**, **Assessment**, **Training**, and **Custom**).

8. Leave the other options at their current value.

9. Make sure your recording window looks like the following screenshot:

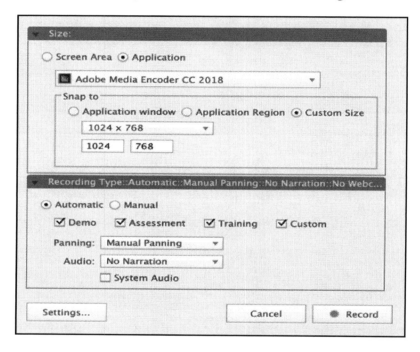

10. When you are ready, click the red **Record** button. After a short countdown, you'll be back in recording mode.

11. In Adobe Media Encoder, perform the actions as rehearsed earlier in this chapter. Behind the scenes, Captivate is recording!

You should hear a camera shutter sound each time you click and a keystroke sound each time you use the keyboard. Notice that, even though two applications are currently active, the mouse and the keyboard are interacting with AME, not with Captivate.

12. Just before clicking the Start Queue button (the Play icon), press the *Print Screen* (Windows) or *command + F6* (Mac) keys to take an extra screenshot manually.

This extra screenshot is necessary to correctly capture the progress bar with an FMR. A camera shutter sound lets you know that an extra screenshot has indeed been captured.

 Mac users, if you don't hear the camera shutter sound, remember that some Mac models require that you add the *fn* key to the mix. The shortcut to take an extra screenshot might therefore be *command + fn + F6*.

You will now turn FMR on and click the Start Queue button.

13. Use either the *F9* (Windows) or *command + F9* (Mac) shortcut to turn FMR on.
14. Click the Start Queue button of AME to start the actual encoding of the video.
15. When the encoding is finished, use either the *F10* (Windows) or *command + F10* (Mac) shortcut to stop FMR.
16. Finally, use the *End* key (Windows) or the *command + enter* shortcut (Mac) to stop the recording.

Captivate generates the slides. When that process is over, Captivate has a nice surprise for you!

 An alternate way to stop a Captivate recording
In addition to the keyboard shortcuts we discussed previously, you can also use your mouse to stop a Captivate recording. On Windows systems, click the Captivate taskbar icon at the bottom of the screen. On Mac, the same icon is in the notification area at the top right corner of the screen.

Previewing the second rushes

The nice surprise is that Captivate has generated four versions of the same project. This is due to the four checkboxes that you selected at the bottom of the recording window just before pressing the **Record** button:

- The `untitled_demo1.cptx` file was generated based on the **Demo** mode. Save it in your exercises folder as `Chapter08/encoderDemo_1024.cptx`.
- The `untitled_assessment1.cptx` file was generated based on the **Assessment Simulation** mode. Save it in your exercises folder as `Chapter08/encoderAssessment_1024.cptx`.
- The `untitled_training1.cptx` file was generated based on the **Training Simulation** mode. Save it in your exercises folder as `Chapter08/encoderTraining_1024.cptx`.
- The `untitled_custom.cptx` file was generated with the settings of your very own **Custom** mode. Save it in your exercises folder as `Chapter08/encoderCustom_1024.cptx`.

Now that these files have been saved, you will preview them one by one:

1. Select the `Chapter08/encoderDemo_1024.cptx` file.
2. Use the **Preview | Project** icon on the Toolbar to preview the entire project.

Captivate generates the slides and opens the **Preview** pane.

 If you did not succeed in producing great recordings, you can use the files in the `Chapter08/final` folder of the exercises.

The **Demo** version of the project is quite similar to the one you shot earlier in this chapter. The only major difference is the progress bar that has been correctly captured by FMR.

3. When the preview is finished, close the **Preview** pane.
4. Select the `Chapter08/encoderAssessment_1024.cptx` file.
5. Use the **Preview | Project** icon to preview the entire project.

As described in the **Assessment Simulation** recording mode, the mouse pointer and the Text Captions have not been added to this version of the project. After a short while, the project pauses. If you don't do anything, nothing happens as Captivate is waiting for you to click the right spot.

If you click the right icon, the project moves on to the next slide and pauses again, waiting for your second action. If you do not perform the right action, a Failure Caption is displayed.

6. When you complete the entire project, close the **Preview** pane.
7. Return to the `Chapter08/encoderTraining_1024.cptx` file.
8. Once again, use the **Preview** | **Project** icon on the Toolbar to preview the entire project.

As expected, this version of the project is similar to the previous one. The only difference is the Hint Caption that is displayed when the mouse is over the hit area of the Click Boxes or Text Entry Boxes. This Hint Caption can provide some useful information on the action to be performed by the learner.

9. When you are through the entire project, close the **Preview** pane.
10. Go to the `Chapter08/encoderCustom_1024.cptx` file.
11. Use the Preview icon one more time to preview the entire project.

Your **Custom** recording mode has added Text Captions, Click Boxes, and Text Entry Boxes to the slides, effectively providing an entirely new customized experience.

Of course, none of these four versions of the project are final in any way. There is a lot of work to be done before these projects can be published. That being said, the automatic recording modes of Captivate have successfully provided enough raw material of a good quality to get you started. Remember, this is exactly what you should expect from the capture step of the process.

Recording with System Audio

System Audio is the audio that is generated from the application you capture or from your operating system. In the AME example, it is the chimes sound effect that is played when the encoding is finished. In this exercise, you will once again capture the sequence of actions described in the scenario. This time, Captivate will record the System Audio in addition to screenshots and mouse movements.

First, you should reset your applications to their original state:

1. Close AME if it is still open.
2. Reopen AME and change the presets to their default values.
3. Delete every `.mp4` file that is in the `video/MOV` folder of the exercise.

The second step is to get Captivate ready for the capture session.

4. Return to Captivate and use the **File | Close All** menu item to close all open files (if any).

5. Use the **File | Record a New Software Simulation** menu item or the Software Simulation thumbnail under the **New** tab of the Welcome screen to create a new project.

6. In the recording window, choose **Application** to record the Adobe Media Encoder application. The red recording area snaps to the AME window.

7. Use a **Custom Size** of **1024 x 768** pixels to shoot your application.

8. In the recording modes section of the recording window, make sure the **Demo** mode is the only one selected.

9. Also, select the **System Audio** checkbox.

System Audio on Mac

If you are on a Mac, the **System Audio** checkbox is not available. You will need to install the Soundflower system extension and configure your audio system accordingly before being able to use the System Audio feature of Captivate. This procedure is explained in the knowledge base article at
`http://helpx.adobe.com/captivate/kb/system-audio-disabled.html`.

On Windows, System Audio should work right out of the box!

Once **System Audio** has been correctly set up, the recording window should look like the following screenshot:

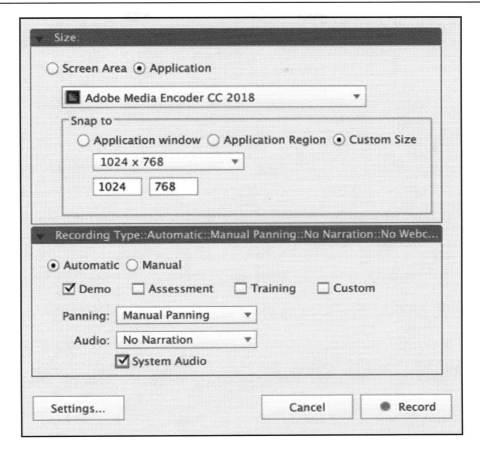

10. When you are ready, click the red **Record** button. After a short countdown, you'll be back in the recording mode.

11. In Adobe Media Encoder, perform the actions as rehearsed earlier in this chapter. Behind the scenes, Captivate is recording!

Notice that you do not hear the camera shutter sounds and the keystrokes sounds anymore. When System Audio is activated, these sounds are automatically disabled, because obviously they don't need to be recorded.

12. Just before clicking the Start Queue button (the Play icon), press the *Print Screen* (Windows) or *command + F6* (Mac) shortcut to take an extra screenshot manually.

13. Use the *F9* (Windows) or *command + F9* (Mac) shortcut to turn FMR on.

14. Click the **Start Queue** button in AME to start the actual encoding of the video.

15. When the encoding is finished, use the *F10* (Windows) or *command + F10* (Mac) shortcut to stop FMR.

16. Finally, use the *End* key (Windows) or the *command + Enter* shortcut (Mac) to stop the recording.

17. When Captivate has finished generating all the slides, save this file in the exercises folder as `Chapter08/encoderDemo_sysAudio_1024.cptx`.

As usual, let's preview the rushes of this new recording session.

18. Use the **Preview** | **Project** icon on the Toolbar to preview the entire project.

This version of the project is, again, similar to the demonstrations you saw earlier. However, you should notice one significant difference. At the end of the project, when the encoding process is completely finished, you should hear the chimes sound of AME that has been captured, thanks to the System Audio feature of Captivate!

Automatic and Manual Panning

In the movie industry, panning refers to moving the camera during filming. In Captivate, the camera is the red recording area. When panning is turned on in Captivate, it simply means that the red recording area can be moved during the recording. This enables you to capture a bigger application with a smaller recording area.

Earlier in this chapter, we had a discussion about how to solve the project-sizing problem. Panning was one of the possible approaches. Let's take a closer look at it:

 If you have a problem while doing this exercise, refer to the `Chapter08/final/encoderDemo_panning.cptx` file of your exercises folder.

1. Restart AME to reset the user interface.
2. Delete all the `.mp4` files present in the `videos/MOV` folder of the exercise.
3. Return to Captivate and use the **File | Record a New Software Simulation** menu item or the corresponding thumbnail of the **New** tab of the Welcome screen to start a new project.

The Captivate interface disappears, and the red recording area shows up.

4. In the recording window, choose to record a **Screen Area** (and not an **Application** as before). Give the area a **Custom Size** of **800 x 600** pixels.

Normally, the size of the Adobe Media Encoder application should still be **1024 x 768** pixels from the previous filming sessions.

5. Move the red recording area so that its top right corner corresponds to the top right corner of the **Adobe Media Encoder** application window.

In this configuration, the size of AME does not match the size of the red recording area. The recording area should be smaller than AME.

6. In the bottom part of the recording window, make sure that the **Demo** mode is the only one selected.
7. In the **Panning:** drop-down list, choose **Manual Panning**.
8. If necessary, set the **Audio:** dropdown to **No Narration** and deselect the **System Audio** checkbox.

Your computer screen should look like the following screenshot:

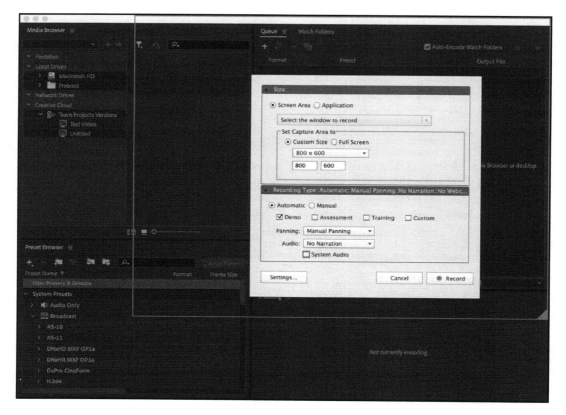

9. When ready, click the red **Record** button to switch to the recording mode.

10. After the countdown, perform the first few steps of the scenario in the Adobe Media Encoder application.

11. When the **Export Settings** window opens, place your mouse above the red line of the recording area until the mouse turns into a grabbing hand. Then, slowly move the red recording area until it covers more or less the lower right section of the **Export Settings** window.

12. In AME, modify the size of the video, as defined in the scenario.

13. When the **Export Settings** dialog closes after you clicked the **OK** button, move the red recording area back to its original position.

14. Just before clicking the **Start Queue** button (the Play icon), press the Print Screen (Windows) or *command* + F6 (Mac) shortcut to take an extra screenshot manually.

15. Use the *F9* (Windows) or *command + F9* (Mac) shortcut to turn FMR on.

16. Click the **Start Queue** button in AME to start the actual encoding of the video.

17. When the encoding is finished, use the *F10* (Windows) or *command + F10* (Mac) shortcut to stop the FMR.

18. Finally, use the *End* key (Windows) or the *command + Enter* shortcut (Mac) to stop the recording.

19. Use the **Preview | Project** icon on the Toolbar to preview the entire project.

20. When the movie is finished, close the **Preview** pane, and save the file as `Chapter08/encoderDemo_panning.cptx`.

Back in Captivate, take a look at the **Filmstrip** panel. Beneath some of the slide thumbnails, you should see the camera icon, indicating that there are some FMR slides in the project. FMR is used to reproduce the panning movements made during the capture.

In this example, you have used Manual Panning. When using Automatic Panning, Captivate places the mouse at the center of the red recording area. During filming, the red recording area automatically follows any mouse movement. Automatic Panning produces a lot of unnecessary movements, and, consequently, a lot of extra FMR slides.

Responsive capture

Responsive Projects were first introduced in Adobe Captivate 8. They allow you to adapt the content and the layout of your Captivate project for different device sizes.

When it comes to screen capture, the Responsive Projects allow you to capture static screenshots and to pan to the relevant area which contains the Highlight Box or Click Box. The exact procedure is as follows:

1. Restart AME to reset the user interface.

2. Delete all the `.mp4` files present in the `videos/MOV` folder of the exercise.

3. Return to Captivate and close any open files so that you see the Welcome screen.

4. Double-click the Responsive Project thumbnail on the **New** tab of the Welcome screen. You can also use the **File | New Project | Responsive Project** menu item.

This action creates a new Responsive Project. For this first experiment with the Responsive Projects, you will use the default settings of Captivate. At the top of the stage, you should see the **Layout Preview** bar, which gives a quick preview of how the content will be displayed on different device sizes.

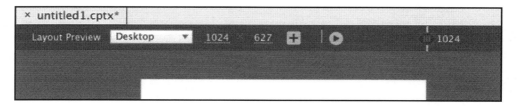

Notice that the desktop size is set to **1024 x 627**. To record the AME window correctly, we will need to increase the height of the desktop view to 768 pixels.

5. To do so, click **Modify | Rescale Project.**
6. Change the height to 768 pixels and click **Finish.**
7. Click **OK** to close the alert box.
8. You will now see that a **Custom** preset has been added to the **Layout Preview** dropdown, with the dimensions set to **1024** x **768**, which will allow us to capture the screen perfectly.
9. Optionally, click the **+** sign to add this custom size to the **Preview in** drop-down list.

Now, it's time to start recording the responsive simulation. You can use the following steps to add slides into this Responsive Project using the capture engine of Captivate.

10. Click the **Slides** icon, which is the first icon on the Toolbar.
11. Choose the **Software Simulation** option from the drop-down list:

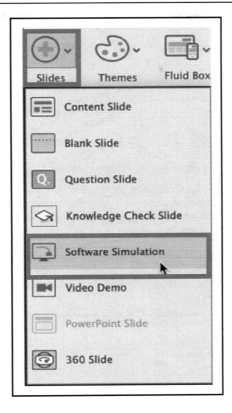

12. Click **OK** at the bottom right corner of the **Record Additional Slides** dialog to insert the new slides after the first (and only) slide of the project.

The Captivate interface disappears and the red recording area shows up.

13. In the drop-down list at the top of the recording window, choose to record the **Adobe Media Encoder CC 2018** application.

14. Make sure that the **Snap to window** checkbox is selected to have the red recording area snap to the AME window.

15. Make sure that the **Demo** mode is selected from the **Mode** drop-down list.

16. If needed, reset the **Panning** dropdown to **No Panning** and the **Audio** dropdown to **No Narration**.

Unlike your previous recording experiences, you cannot choose the recording size. This is because the project already exists and already has a size of 1024 x 768 pixels. Therefore, the red recording area already has the same size as the project. Your screen should now look like the following screenshot:

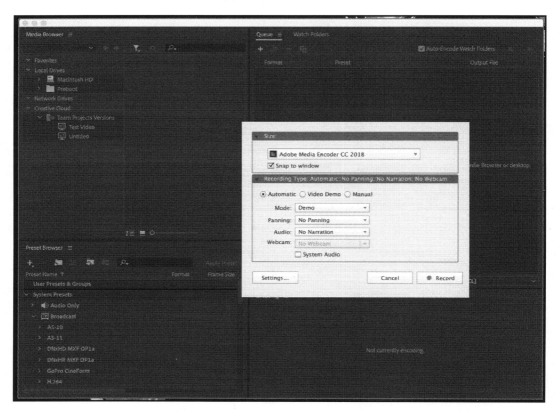

You are now ready for your first responsive capture!

17. Click the red **Record** button. After a short countdown, you'll be back in the recording mode.
18. In Adobe Media Encoder, perform the actions as rehearsed earlier in this chapter. Behind the scenes, Captivate is recording!
19. Finally, use the *End* key (Windows) or the *command + enter* shortcut (Mac) to stop the recording.
20. When Captivate has finished generating all the slides, save this file in the exercises folder as `Chapter08/encoderDemo_responsive.cptx`.

So far, so good! The story is almost exactly the same as before. However, this project is a bit special.

21. To see what's special, use the **Filmstrip** panel to select the second slide of the project.

22. Notice that there's a blue rectangle on the slide. This blue rectangle is the focus area of your simulation, and the screen area inside the blue rectangle will always appear on your slide. The size of this blue rectangle is the minimum supported device size for Captivate Responsive Projects.

23. You can reposition this blue rectangle to any other location. But while doing so, make sure you don't move the rectangle away from the click area/Highlight Box and the Text Captions.

24. To preview the simulation in different device sizes, select different device options from the **Preview-in** drop-down list. Notice that the blue rectangle defines the area that is always visible, regardless of the device.

25. Use the **Preview | Project** icon on the Toolbar to preview the entire project. Because you are in a Responsive Project, this option opens the demonstration in the default web browser.

26. When in the browser, feel free to use the slider at the top of the preview to test the responsiveness of the project.

27. When done, close the browser and return to Captivate.

 When you publish these simulations and view them on devices, you will be able to pan to the areas that are not shown in the simulation. And because of this special Panning functionality for simulations, the default Swipe Right, Left, Up, or Down gestures are disabled for the responsive simulation.

While there is a lot more to learn about the new Responsive Projects of Captivate, you will now move on to the next section of this book. You will cover this topic in much more detail in Chapter 10, *Creating a Responsive Project*.

Rescaling a project

This chapter opened with a discussion on choosing the right size for the project. This discussion led to four possible approaches to manage the size difference between the application to capture and the course to produce.

The first approach was to shoot big and then downsize. In the initial step, you used a resolution of 1024 x 768 pixels to record your first sequence. You will now perform the second step: resizing the movie to 800 x 600 pixels.

Remember that resizing a project is a one-way operation that always results in data and quality loss. If another solution that does not require resizing the project is available, go for it! If a resize operation cannot be avoided, always keep a backup copy of your project at its original size.

1. In Captivate, open the `chapter08/encoderDemo_1024.cptx` file.

If you did not successfully save this file earlier in this chapter, you can use the one saved in the `chapter08/final` folder.

Or, if you have a problem while doing this exercise, refer to the `Chapter08/final/encoderDemo_800.cptx` file of your exercises folder.

2. Use the **File | Save As** menu item to save the file as `Chapter08/encoderDemo_800.cptx`.
3. When the project is saved, use the **Modify | Rescale Project** menu item to open the **Rescale Project** dialog.

This window is divided into three parts. The top part allows you to define the new size of the project. It is the only part that's available at the moment:

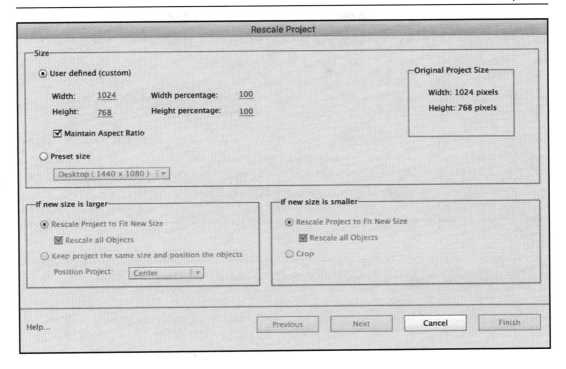

4. Make sure the **Maintain Aspect Ratio** box is selected.

5. Reduce the **Width** of the project from **1024** to **800** pixels. The new **Height** of **600** pixels should be calculated automatically.

Since the new size is smaller than the original size, the lower right part of the box becomes available. It is titled: **If new size is smaller**. The lower left part of the box is still inactive. It would activate if the new size of the project were larger than the original size.

6. Take some time to review the available options, but leave the default unchanged. When ready, click **Finish**.

7. A dialog box informs you that resizing a project cannot be undone. Click **OK** to confirm you want to resize the project anyway.

8. Captivate resizes each slide, one by one.

9. Save the file when the resize process is complete.

Although Captivate does a great job of resizing all the objects on the slides, you should always review each slide and object to verify that the conversion was successful.

Modifying the object properties

Now that you have finished recording a demonstration, assessment, simulation, and a custom project, let's talk about the objects that are automatically generated with these screen recordings. You will also learn how to modify the properties and styles of these objects to suit your project requirements and match your project style-guide.

The objects that are generated with screen recording projects are Text Captions, Text Entry Boxes, Mouse, Highlight Boxes, and Click Boxes. In Chapter 2, *Working with Standard Objects*, you learned how to modify the properties of Text Captions, and in Chapter 5, *Developing Interactivity*, you learned how to use Text Entry Boxes. In this chapter, let's learn how to work with Highlight Boxes, Click Boxes, and Mouse in screen capture projects.

The Highlight Box object

Let's start by talking about the **Highlight Box**. As its name implies, a Highlight Box is used to highlight a specific area of the screen. A Highlight Box is a rectangle that appears and disappears from the screen according to its position on the **Timeline** panel.

When using the Demo recording mode during the capture, Captivate adds a Highlight Box for each mouse click:

1. In Captivate, open the chapter08/encoderDemo_800.cptx file.
2. Use the **Filmstrip** panel to go to the first slide.

On Slide 1, you will see three objects: a Text Captions, a Mouse, and a small Highlight Box below the mouse pointer:

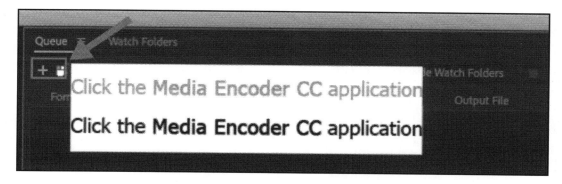

This Highlight Box was automatically added by Captivate during filming.

3. Click the Highlight Box to make it the active object.

Selecting the Highlight Box
Because the Highlight Box is so close to the Mouse object, you may end up selecting the Mouse instead of the Highlight Box. You can use the **Timeline** panel to select the desired object.

Selecting the Highlight Box updates the **Properties** inspector. At the top of the **Style** tab, notice the **Fill** and the **Stroke** sections that provide the formatting options of the selected Highlight Box:

- **Fill** indicates the color *inside* of the object.
- When the **Opacity** parameter is set to **0%**, the object is completely transparent. When the **Opacity** is set to **100%**, the object is completely opaque.
- The **Stroke** is the border *around* the object. You can change both the stroke **Style** and the stroke color.
- The last option is **Width**. This option lets you choose the width of the stroke. Set this option at **0** to remove the stroke from the object.

Now that you have a better idea of the available options, you will change the formatting of the selected Highlight Box.

4. Choose a dark orange as the **Fill** color.
5. Leave the **Opacity** value at 20%.
6. Click **Stroke**. In the color picker, choose the same orange color as the one you chose for the fill. Notice that the recently selected colors are available at the bottom of the color swatches.
7. Set the stroke **Width** to 2 pixels.

Make sure your **Fill** and **Stroke** sections look like the following screenshot:

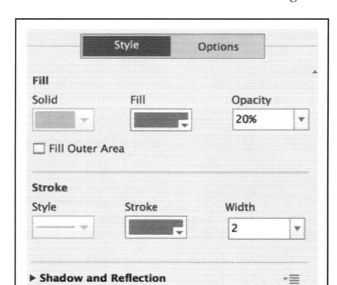

Finally, you will use the **Options** tab of the **Properties** inspector to modify the size and the position of the Highlight Box.

8. Still on Slide 1 of the `encoderDemo_800.cptx` file, make sure that the Highlight Box is the selected object.
9. Switch to the **Options** tab of the **Properties** inspector.
10. For the size, change the **Width** to 24 pixels and **Height** to 19 pixels (to be able to modify the **Height** independently from the **Width**, make sure the **Constrain proportions** checkbox is deselected).
11. For the position, give the Highlight Box an **X** coordinate of 357 pixels and a **Y** coordinate of 38 pixels.

The Highlight Box should precisely cover the **Add Files (+)** icon.

12. Use the **Preview** | **Next 5 Slides** icon on the Toolbar to test your sequence.

Captivate generates the slides and opens the **Preview** pane. Take a close look at the Highlight box of slide 1.

When the preview is finished, close the **Preview** pane. There is one last option to experiment with.

13. Return to Slide 1 of the `encoderDemo_800.cptx` file and select the orange Highlight Box.
14. In the **Style** tab of the **Properties** inspector, change the **Opacity** value to `70%`.
15. Select the **Fill Outer Area** checkbox just below the **Fill** color section.

With this option selected, the fill color of the Highlight Box will be applied to the area outside the object. The only part of the slide that will not be covered by the fill color will be the inside the Highlight Box. It is necessary to see the project in preview mode to see the **Fill Outer Area** option in action!

16. Still on slide 1 of the `encoderDemo_800.cptx` file, use the **Preview** | **Next 5 Slides** icon on the Toolbar.

When the project starts playing in the **Preview** pane, pay close attention to the way the Highlight Box behaves:

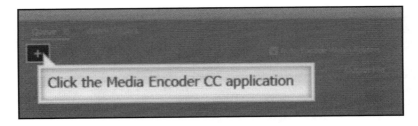

17. Return to slide 1 of the `encoderDemo_800.cptx` file and select the orange Highlight Box one last time.
18. In this particular case, you want the Highlight Box to behave normally. So, in the **Style** tab of the **Properties** inspector, deselect the **Fill Outer Area** checkbox and reduce the **Opacity** value back to `20%`.
19. Save the file when done.

Here is a summary of what you learned about in this section:

- A Highlight Box is a rectangle that's used to highlight a particular spot on the slide.
- **Fill** is the inside of the Highlight Box object. The **Style** tab of the **Properties** inspector lets you choose the color and the opacity of the fill.

- **Stroke** is the border around the Highlight Box object. You can choose the style, the color, and the width of the stroke in the **Properties** inspector.
- Select the **Fill Outer Area** option to apply the fill color to the outside of the Highlight Box rather than to the inside.

Working with the Mouse

The second object to study is the **Mouse**. Remember that during filming, only the coordinates of the mouse clicks were recorded and that the mouse movements are recreated during the playback.

Understanding mouse movements

You will start your study of the Mouse object by discovering how Captivate manages the mouse movements:

1. If needed, use the **Filmstrip** panel to return to Slide 1 of the `encoderDemo_800.cptx` file.

You should see four red dots in the top left corner of the slide. These four dots mark the starting point of the mouse.

2. Use your mouse to move the four red dots anywhere on the slide.

By moving the four red dots, you change the starting point of the mouse on slide 1, as illustrated in the following screenshot:

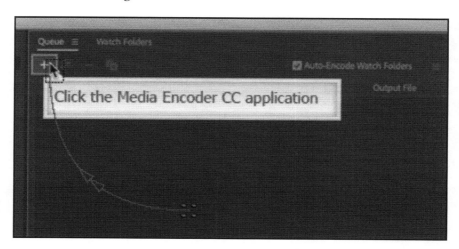

From the chosen spot, Captivate generates a curved blue line that represents the mouse movement. This curved line ends with the mouse pointer.

3. Click the mouse pointer at the end of the curved blue line to select the Mouse object. The **Properties** inspector updates.

When a Mouse object is selected, the **Properties** inspector does not contain any tabs.

4. Select the **Straight Pointer Path** checkbox.

By selecting this checkbox, Captivate generates a straight line between the start and the end points of the mouse movement.

5. Deselect the **Straight Pointer Path** checkbox.
6. Use the **Filmstrip** panel to select slide 2.

On the second slide, the four red dots that are visible on slide 1 are not visible. You can only change the starting point of the mouse on the first slide with a mouse path. Every slide after will use the ending point of the previous mouse path to determine the starting point of the new mouse path.

7. Use the **Filmstrip** panel to browse the remaining slides of the project.
8. When done, return to slide 1.
9. Take the mouse pointer and move it to a random location.
10. Use the **Filmstrip** panel to select slide 2.

On slide 2, the starting point of the curved blue line has changed and corresponds to the location you chose on slide 1.

11. On the **Filmstrip** panel, click slide 1 to make it the active slide.
12. Move the mouse pointer back to its original location.
13. Use the **Filmstrip** panel to go to the last slide of the project.

On the last slide, the mouse makes a long movement. This mouse movement is not necessary. Let's remove the Mouse object from the slide.

14. On the last slide, right-click the mouse pointer at the end of the blue line.
15. In the contextual menu, deselect the **Show Mouse** item. You can also use the **Modify** | **Mouse** | **Show Mouse** menu item to achieve the same result.

Note that the coordinates of the Mouse object as recorded during the filming are saved with the slide, if you change your mind about the Mouse being hidden on the last slide, you can add it back.

16. Use the **Filmstrip** panel to go to slide 14 of the `encoderDemo_800.cptx` file.

This is the slide where you typed `400` in the **Width** field of AME. The next slide (slide 15) is where the Mouse moves to click the **OK** button of the **Export Settings** dialog. For this particular sequence, you want to have a single action per slide. So, slide 14 should only show the typing in the **Width** field with no mouse movement. Slide 15 should show the entire Mouse movement.

17. Still on slide 14, right-click the mouse pointer to select the Mouse object.
18. In the contextual menu, select **Align to Previous Slide**.

By selecting the **Align to Previous Slide** option, the mouse pointer on slide 14 is aligned to the mouse pointer on slide 13. The start and end points of the Mouse object on slide 12 have the same coordinates and the mouse no longer moves on slide 12. The starting point of the mouse on slide 13 has changed to match the location of the mouse on slide 12, effectively moving the mouse movement to slide 13.

19. Go to the **Preview** icon on the Toolbar to preview the entire project.
20. In the Preview pane, pay close attention to the mouse movements. Make sure each click occurs at the right place.
21. When the preview is complete, close the **Preview** pane.
22. If needed, adjust the position of the Mouse on the slides where the click area is not well-positioned.
23. Save the file when done.

Formatting the Mouse object

During the preview, you will see a small blue circle and hear a click sound on most mouse clicks. These mouse options can be managed in the **Properties** inspector. The steps are as follows:

1. Use the **Filmstrip** panel to return to slide 1.
2. Once on slide 1, select the mouse pointer to make it the active object.
3. Take some time to inspect the properties that are available in the **Properties** inspector, as shown in the following screenshot:

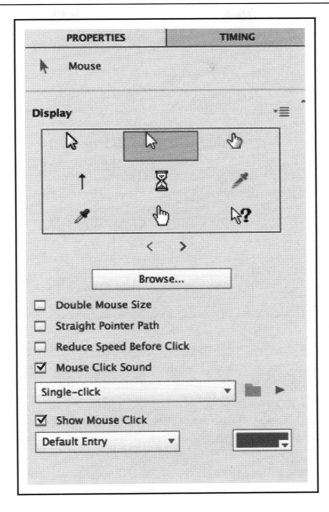

Notice the two drop-down lists that let you choose the click sound to use (single-click or double-click) and the shape of the visual click. You can also change the color of the visual click, if necessary.

The top of the **Properties** inspector lets you choose the mouse pointer. In this example, the default pointer is perfect, so you will not change it.

Choosing the right mouse pointer

My very first big eLearning project was to build an online course on SAP for a big multinational company. SAP uses custom mouse pointers that I wanted to reproduce in Captivate. A mouse pointer is a .cur file, so I clicked the **Browse** button right below the collection of mouse pointers in the **Properties** inspector and searched for the appropriate .cur file in the C:\Program files folder of Windows. I eventually found the .cur file I was looking for, and I could import it in Captivate. If you work on a Mac, you can inspect the content of an .app file by right-clicking on the file and choosing **Show package content**. You might find the .cur file you are looking for in the package. The bottom line is, your Captivate project should reproduce the behavior of the actual application as close as possible.

Let's quickly summarize what you learned in this section:

- During the capture, only the position of the mouse at each click is recorded. A mouse movement is recreated between these positions at runtime.
- By default, the mouse movement uses a curved line, but you can change it to a straight line in the **Properties** inspector.
- The first slide of the project is the only slide where you can move both the start and the end points of the mouse movement.
- To prevent the mouse from moving on a given slide, right-click the mouse pointer and choose **Align to Previous Slide** in the contextual menu.
- Removing the Mouse from a slide does not remove its coordinates. This makes it easy to turn the Mouse back on the slide, if you change your mind.
- Moving the mouse pointer on a slide moves the origin of the mouse movement on the next slide.
- You can add or remove a visual click and a click sound in the **Properties** inspector.

Working with Click Boxes

There is one more interactive object that has the ability to stop the playhead and wait for the student to interact. This object is the **Click Box**. A Click Box is used to define an invisible clickable area on the screen. If the learner clicks inside the Click Box, the correct action is performed. If the student clicks outside the box, the wrong action is performed and the appropriate feedback should be displayed.

The Click Box object is similar to the transparent button object that you used in Chapter 5, *Developing Interactivity*, with a few key differences:

- Click Boxes are invisible. There are no Fill, Opacity, or Stroke properties.
- Because a Click Box is always invisible, it does not have states.

When using the Training recording mode during the capture, Captivate adds a Click Box for each mouse click:

1. In Captivate, open the chapter08/encoderTraining_1024.cptx file.
2. Use the **Filmstrip** panel to go to the first slide.

On Slide 1, you will see three objects: A Click Box, a Failure Caption, and a Hint Caption:

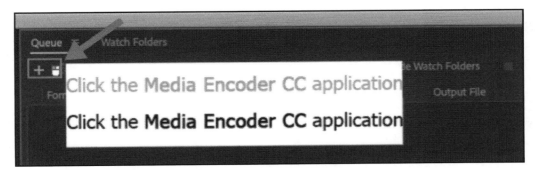

This Click Box was automatically added by Captivate during filming.

3. Select the Click Box to make it the active object.

Selecting the Click Box updates the **Properties** inspector. There is no Style tab for the Click Box because it is an invisible object.

4. Under the **Actions** tab, you can change the action settings. These settings are the same as Buttons and Shape Buttons.
5. You can modify the size and position of these Click Boxes by using either the resize handles of the Click Box or by changing the properties under the **Others** tab in **Properties** inspector.

The Text Caption object

As you learned in `Chapter 2`, *Working with Standard Objects*, the **Text Caption** is the most basic object in Captivate. It is typically used to display text to learners.

During the screen recording, Text Captions automatically generate instructions to perform the steps, success captions, failure captions, and hint captions. Some of these might be just right, but most of them--if not all of them--need some extra work.

Modifying the content of a Text Caption

You already learned in `Chapter 2`, *Working with Standard Objects*, how to modify Text Captions to change the formatting and timing of the Text Caption, and change the text in these captions.

Now, you can modify the Text Caption properties and replace the text in the captions with meaningful instructions for the learners. When you are ready, save the file in the `chapter08` folder and name it as `encoderDemo_800_final.cptx`.

Summary

In this chapter, you have explored different options to capture screens and edit object properties. Your main concern was to adjust the content during or after the recording process to produce the required final recording dimensions.

While experiencing each of these approaches, you uncovered three important features of Captivate: Full Motion Recording (FMR), Panning, and responsive capture.

You also discovered that Captivate has four automatic recording modes, that is, **Demonstration**, **Assessment Simulation**, **Training Simulation**, and a **Custom** mode that is yours to create. Each of these automatic recording modes adds Text Captions and other objects to the slides.

The System Audio feature allowed you to capture application and system sound effects. You also learned how to edit the styles and properties of objects.

In the next chapter, you will learn how to record a Video Demo and generate an `.mp4` video file that can be uploaded to YouTube.

Meet the community

In this section, it is our pleasure to introduce you to Akshay Bharadwaj. Akshay leads the Adobe team that builds Adobe Captivate. (He is the one we try to steal information from during conferences, but it never works!) He is also active in the community portal, writing blog posts, helping Captivate users, and commenting on Captivate news.

Damien

When I asked Akshay to author the foreword of my fourth Captivate book, he was very enthusiastic and he wrote a great foreword. Whenever I have a chance to meet with him, I'm always impressed by his simplicity and his great sense of humour.

Pooja

I've worked with Akshay since 2011, and there's never been a conversation where I've not learned anything new from him. He has missed no chance to impress me with data and current trends about eLearning and his fantastic ideas to take Captivate to the next level. I feel privileged to have him as a colleague and friend!

Akshay Bharadwaj

Akshay Bharadwaj is the Principal Product Manager for Adobe Captivate. Akshay has helped build products across eLearning and internet domains. In his ten years at Adobe, Akshay has seen Captivate evolve from primarily being a simulation tool to comprehensive responsive authoring. Apart from authoring tools, Akshay is also interested in building learning communities, as well as the psychology of learning and building next-generation learning experiences. Some of our experiments in this space can be seen in Adobe Knowhow, now rebranded to Adobe Captivate Prime – Content Catalog. Akshay also loves interacting with customers and eLearning folks. You can reach him on any of his social media accounts.

Contact details

- Blog: `https://elearning.adobe.com/`
- Twitter: `https://twitter.com/akshay_bh`
- Facebook: `http://www.facebook.com/adobecaptivate`
- LinkedIn: `https://www.linkedin.com/in/akshaybharadwaj/`
- YouTube: `http://www.youtube.com/adobeelearning/`
- Email: `akshay@adobe.com`

Producing a Video Demo

9

Sometimes, all you need is a good old video file that you can embed into your website or upload to YouTube. In such cases, you need a Video Demo project. Video demos are used to create .mp4 video files that the learner experiences from the beginning to the end in a linear fashion. Therefore, the interactivity features of Captivate are not supported in Video Demos.

In this chapter, you will experience the entire Captivate production process using a Video Demo file as an example. First, you will record a Video Demo. Second, you will turn it into a professional screencast using the features in Captivate. Finally, you will publish it as a .mp4 video file. If you happen to have a YouTube account, you will even upload the video file to YouTube from within Captivate.

In this chapter, you will do the following:

- Discuss and experience the Video Demo recording mode
- Remove and replace the background for a webcam video feed
- Tour the Video Demo interface
- Resize and reposition the webcam feed
- Mask the Video and Webcam layers in the Timeline
- Trim unwanted portions of the Video Demo
- Add objects in a Video Demo project
- Remove unwanted popups
- Add Transitions and Pan & Zoom effects
- Publish the Video Demo as a .mp4 file
- Publish the Video Demo to YouTube

Preparing your work

To get the most out of this chapter, it is a good idea to reset the Captivate interface to default. If you are using the default interface mode, just close and restart Captivate to reset it. If you are using the Advanced Interface mode, use the **Window** | **Workspace** | **Reset 'Classic'** menu item to reset Captivate to default. In this chapter, you will use the exercises stored in the Chapter09 folder of the download associated with this book. If you get confused by any of the step-by-step instructions, take a look at the Chapter09/final folder, which contains a copy of the files as they will be at the end of this chapter.

The Video Demo recording mode

The Video Demo recording mode allows you to create a video file by capturing the onscreen actions. A Video Demo recording project actually is a big Full Motion Recording. In the 2019 release of Adobe Captivate, you also get the ability to record your webcam feed alongside the screen capture.

A Video Demo project is quite different from the other projects you have worked on so far. Because a Video Demo project can only be published as an .mp4 video file, no interactive objects can be included in such projects. In other words, it can only be a demonstration. Because a Video Demo project is based on a single big video file, there is no slide or **Filmstrip** panel in a Video Demo project. This makes Video Demo projects particularly suitable for upload to an online video hosting service, such as YouTube, Vimeo, or Dailymotion.

Selecting the Video Demo recording settings

In this exercise, you will create a Video Demo version of the Encoder Demonstration that you recorded in Chapter 8, *Capturing Onscreen Action*.

The first step is to reset your system:

1. Restart the Adobe Media Encoder application.
2. Delete all the .mp4 files present in the videos/MOV folder of the exercise files.

Now that your system is ready, let's create a Video Demo project.

 If you have a problem while doing this exercise, refer to the `Chapter09/final/encoderVideo.cpvc` file of your exercises folder.

3. Use the **File** | **Record a New** | **Video Demo** menu item to start a new Video Demo project.

This option is also available on the **New** tab of the Welcome screen of Captivate when no file is open.

The recording dialog appears. You can see the recording settings on the left and your Webcam feed on the right side of the dialog:

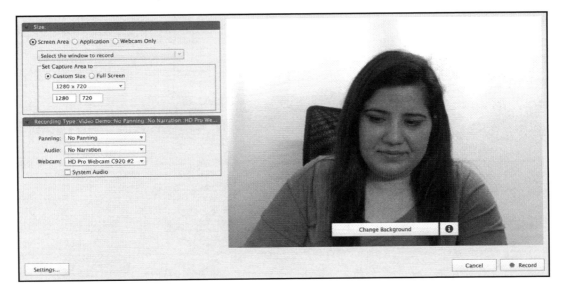

4. At the top of the recording dialog, select **Application**.
5. In the drop-down list below **Application**, select **Adobe Media Encoder CC 2018**.
6. In the **Snap to** section, choose to record at **Custom Size** of **1280 x 720** pixels.

Most of the time, a narration is added to such projects. If you have a microphone available, you'll record your voice in addition to the onscreen action. If you don't have a microphone available, just read through these steps. Audio can also be added later in the process, if needed.

7. If a microphone is available, open the **Audio** drop-down list and choose your microphone (or the audio interface the microphone is plugged into) in the list of entries.

Adobe Captivate 2019 supports webcam capture. You can decide to record the webcam feed or disable it.

8. If you don't wish to record the webcam feed, select **No Webcam** from the drop-down list. If you want to record the **Webcam** feed, select the required webcam from the drop-down list.

The recording window should now look like the following screenshot:

Changing the background of the webcam feed

If you have chosen to record the webcam feed, you can also remove the background and replace it with another background of your choice. This is called the Chroma Key effect, or the green screen effect, because it usually uses a green screen to detect the background.

You don't need a green screen to accomplish this. Use any wall that is handy, as long as the wall is a solid color. You will want to choose wall colors that are different from the color of your skin or clothing. Decorative wallpaper or ornate backgrounds are not usually good candidates for replacement.

Let's take a look at the steps to do this:

1. With a webcam selected in the **Settings** section, you can see your webcam feed on the right side of the Recording dialog. To begin the Chroma Key process, click the **Change Background** button at the bottom of the video preview.

2. Then, click the **Take my snapshot** button to let Captivate start filtering your image from the background:

3. In the next step, you will see the cursor turn into a green plus symbol. Click and drag the mouse to draw a vertical line from your forehead to the bottom of the screen:

4. Then, draw a horizontal line across your shoulders. This will isolate you from the background:

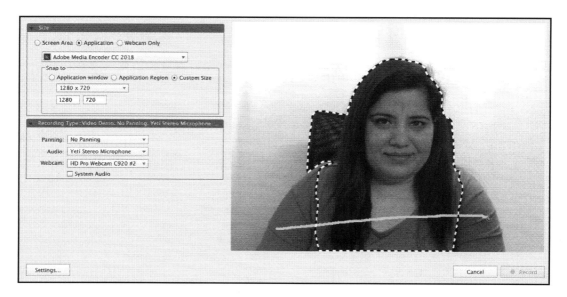

5. If you miss any portion, you can always go back and draw over the missing elements.

6. If you accidentally select a portion of the background, press and hold the *option* (for Mac) or *Alt* (for Windows) key. This will turn the green plus symbol into a red minus symbol.

7. Draw a line carefully on the area that you need to deselect.

8. Once you have completed the selection, click **I am fully selected** to move on to the next step.

Captivate displays a preview of your video, this time with the background clipped away and a new background substituted. Check your image to verify that it is doing a good job of clipping out the background and replacing it will a new background:

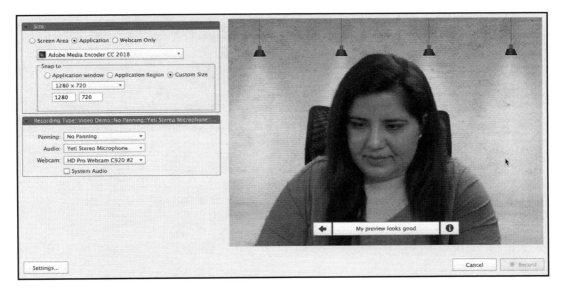

9. Once you are satisfied, click the **My preview looks good** button to explore additional backgrounds.

10. You can now change the background by clicking the background itself.

11. After a few background images, you will come to one that is a checkerboard pattern. The checkerboard represents transparency. When you use this background, your image will be placed directly over the screen capture, making the background the screen capture itself:

12. You are all set! Click the red **Record** button to start the recording.

If it is the first time you are recording sound with your Captivate installation, you'll have to calibrate the sensitivity of your microphone.

In the **Calibrate Audio Input** dialog, click the **Auto Calibrate** button. Speak normally into the microphone until the **Input level OK** message appears on the screen. Click **OK** to validate the sensitivity settings and to discard the dialog.

13. After a short countdown, the recording begins.
14. In Adobe Media Encoder, perform the actions rehearsed in `Chapter 8`, *Capturing Onscreen Action*.
15. Make sure to leave some silence before or after the recording, or make a mistake or two and then correct it. You will be able to trim the unwanted portions of the recording later in the process.
16. If you have a microphone, speak as you go through the steps of the scenario.
17. When done, press the *End* key (Windows) or the *command* + *Enter* shortcut (Mac).

Captivate finalizes the video capture. When the finalization process is finished, your entire video is played back. It includes both the screen you captured and the webcam video with a transparent background. Enjoy the show!

18. When the video has finished playing, click the **Edit** button in the bottom-right corner of the screen.

By clicking on the **Edit** button, you leave the preview mode of the Video Demo project and enter the editing mode. Note how the interface of a Video Demo project is different from the interface of a standard Captivate project.

19. Save your file as `Chapter09/encoderVideo.cpvc`.

Notice that a Video Demo project does not use the standard `.cptx` file extension, but uses the `.cpvc` file extension instead.

The Video Demo interface

Now, it's time to take a look at the Video Demo file that you recorded:

1. With the `encoderVideo.cpvc` file still open, use the **Preview | Project** icon on the Toolbar and take the necessary time to view the entire project.

As you click the **Preview** icon, note that most of the previewing options are grayed out. The only thing that you can actually do is preview the entire project. Remember that a Video Demo project is aimed at producing a `.mp4` video file. Such content plays in one big chunk from the beginning to the end with no interactivity whatsoever. Technically, it is said that a video file offers a *linear* experience, versus the nonlinear interactive experience of a regular project. It is therefore not based on slides, so the previewing options involving slides (**Preview From this Slide**, **Preview Next 5 slides**, and so on) are, logically, unavailable.

2. At the end of the preview, click the **Edit** button in the bottom-right corner of the screen to return to Edit mode.
3. Take some time to inspect the interface of Captivate.

When working on a Video Demo project (with a `.cpvc` file extension), the Captivate interface is a bit different than what you've been used to when working on a regular project (with a `.cptx` file extension). All these interface changes come down to the simple fact that the published version of the project can only be a `.mp4` video file.

First, note that there is no **Filmstrip** panel on the left side of the screen. Since the project is not based on slides, this makes perfect sense. Also, note that the **Interactions** icon on the **Toolbar** is grayed out. Since video files do not support any kind of interaction, this again makes perfect sense.

4. Browse the other icons on the **Toolbar** and take good note of the objects that are available in a Video Demo project.
5. Click the **Properties** icon at the right end of the **Toolbar**.

As expected, this action opens the **Properties** inspector. Just next to the **Properties** inspector is the **Video Effects** panel.

6. Switch to the **Video Effects** panel and take some time to examine the available properties.

The **Video Effects** panel contains options and tools that are specific to Video Demo projects.

7. Take some time to further explore the interface. Try to spot other differences between the standard Captivate interface and the one used for Video Demo projects.

This concludes your first overview of Video Demo projects and the associated Captivate interface. Before moving on, let's see a quick summary of what you have learned so far:

- Video Demos are used to generate linear video files in .mp4 format.
- Video Demos use their own .cpvc file extension that is different from the .cptx extension used by the standard projects of Captivate.
- When working on a .cpvc project, the Captivate interface is slightly different from the standard interface of .cptx projects. Some panels, such as the **Filmstrip** panel, are not relevant to video files and are therefore not present in the interface. Other panels, such as the **Video Effects** panel, are specific to Video Demo projects, and are not available in standard Captivate projects.

The post-production phase of a Video Demo

Remember that the Captivate production process is made up of three phases. When it comes to this particular project, the first phase (the Capture phase) is now complete. You will now dig into the second phase of the process.

Resizing and repositioning the webcam feed

The webcam feed in a Video Demo project is recorded and added to the project as a separate layer. This gives you the power to resize and reposition it the way you like:

1. With the `encoderVideo.cpvc` file still open, click the **View** | **Magnification** | **Best Fit** menu item.

 If you had a problem recording the Video Demo, use the `Chapter09/encoderVideo_Start.cpvc` file from your exercises folder.

Notice that the webcam recording is placed at the bottom-right corner of the screen. This is the default placement of the webcam recording.

2. Click the webcam recording and drag it to the bottom-left corner of the stage.

Most of the action takes place in the right side of the screen in this Video Demo, so the left side is the best place for the webcam feed for this screen recording.

3. You can also increase or decrease the size of the webcam recording to your liking. Click and drag the top-right handle of the webcam recording to increase or decrease the size.

Notice that it maintains the aspect ratio of the video even when you are not pressing and holding the *Shift* key on your keyboard.

4. Undo the resize changes by pressing the *Ctrl + Z* (Windows) or *command + Z* (Mac) key combination on your keyboard to bring it back to the original size.

Changing the webcam background image

At the time of recording the Video Demo, you selected the transparent background image. If you wish to replace it with any other image, you can do so by following these steps:

1. With the webcam feed still selected, go to the **Properties** inspector.
2. Click the **Change Background** button.
3. For Windows, use Windows Explorer to navigate to `C:\Program Files\Adobe\Adobe Captivate 2019 x64\Gallery\Webcam Background`.
4. For Mac, use the Finder to navigate to `/Applications/Adobe Captivate 2019/Gallery/Webcam Background`.
5. Select any image from this folder and click **Open**. The new background is now applied to the webcam feed.
6. Now, let's get back to the transparent background. For that, click the **Change Background** button again.
7. Select the `Screen.png` image and click **Open**.

This feature allows you to create amazing video effects without a green screen or other sophisticated studio gear. Remember that the only thing you need is a solid color background and some decent lighting. The rest is up to the Adobe Captivate magic!

Masking the Video and Webcam layers in the Timeline

In the Video Demo project, both the screen recording and the webcam recordings are visible all the time. If you wish to hide one of the feeds during the playback of the Video Demo, you can use the Mask feature to hide a video feed for a defined amount of time.

For example, when you are introducing the topic, concluding it, or explaining a concept, you can hide the screen capture recording and just show the webcam feed. Similarly, if you want the students to concentrate on the step you are showing instead of looking at the webcam feed, you can mask the webcam feed.

Let's take a look at the steps to do that:

1. In the `encoderVideo.cpvc` file, open the **Timeline**.
2. Move the Playhead to the beginning of the video.
3. Then, select the **Video/Audio** layer in the **Timeline**.
4. Click the **Mask Video** button:

5. You can see two black handles, used to make a selection on the Timeline to mask the video. Move the handles to the desired position. Feel free to click the **Play/Pause** icon on the **Timeline** to play the video in order to determine the correct position.
6. Click the **Mask Video** button again.

This masks the video. On the **Video/Audio** layer, you see that the masked portion of the layer is now dark blue and has an eye icon on top of it, indicating that this layer portion is masked:

7. Click the **Play** icon on the **Timeline** to preview the Video Demo.

Notice that the webcam recording appears full screen with a white background applied to it. Once the mask duration is over, you see both feeds (Video and Webcam) on the screen.

Similarly, you can mask the screen recording by selecting the Webcam layer and then masking the portion of the layer that you want to hide. During the masked section, only the screen recording is visible.

8. To delete the mask, click the masked area on the Timeline layer, and it will be removed.
9. Undo the deletion step by pressing the *Ctrl + Z* (Windows) or *command + Z* (Mac) key combination on your keyboard.

You can follow the same steps to mask these layers at multiple positions on the **Timeline** to highlight the desired layer in the Video Demo.

Deleting unwanted portions of the Video Demo

When you are recording videos, it's very difficult to get everything right in one take. Adobe Captivate understands that, and allows you to trim out the unwanted portions from your Video Demo. Let's trim these unwanted portions from the video using the following steps:

1. With the `encoderVideo.cpvc` file still open, go to the **Timeline** panel.
2. Move the Playhead to the position where you left some silence or made a mistake.

 If you made a perfect recording with no mistakes, feel free to open the `Chapter09/encoderVideo_Start.cpvc` file from your exercises folder, where I've made quite a few mistakes to help you practice the trim functionality.

3. Click the **Play** button at the bottom of the **Timeline** to play the video and confirm the duration of the silence/mistake.
4. You need to trim that portion now. To do so, bring the red playhead back to the start of the silence/mistake.
5. Then, click the **Trim** button at the bottom of the **Timeline**.
6. You will get Trim *Start* and *End* markers around the playhead. Either move the Trim Start marker so that it begins at the playhead position, or click the **Snap trim start marker to playhead** button at the bottom of the **Timeline**.
7. Listen to the audio and place the Trim End marker at the end of the silence/mistake. You can also position the playhead at the end position, and then click the **Snap trim end marker to playhead** button.

8. If required, listen to the audio multiple times and make sure the marking is correct. Once you follow the next step, you will not be able to recover the deleted video portion.

As a best practice, save a copy of the Video Demo before making any further changes so that if something goes wrong, you have a master recording to fall back on.

9. Now, click the **Trim** button again to remove the unwanted portion of the video:

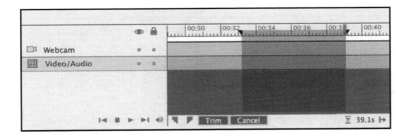

The unwanted portion of the Video Demo is now removed. Play the video to confirm that it looks and sounds good.

Now, check the rest of the video and follow the same steps to remove all the areas of silence or mistakes.

Adding objects to a Video Demo

Next, you will take a closer look at the objects that can be added in a Video Demo project and explore how they can be used in the context of a linear video file.

Inserting images in a Video Demo project

You will create the beginning and the ending of the video using an image that you will overlay on top of the video track. Use the following steps to insert an image into the Video Demo:

1. Go to the **Timeline** panel. If it is not open, click the **Timeline** button at the bottom of the screen.

2. In the **Timeline** panel, make sure that the playhead (the vertical red line) is at the very beginning of the project. If it is not at the beginning, click the **Move the playhead to the beginning** icon, as shown in the following screenshot:

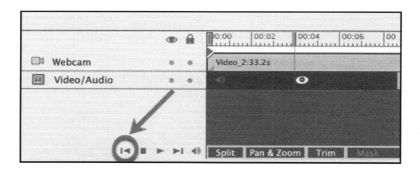

3. Play the video and then pause before you introduce the topic. If you are using the Chapter09/encoderVideo_Start.cpvc file, pause at 2.5 seconds on the **Timeline**.

4. Use the **Media | Image** icon on the Toolbar to insert Chapter09/images/mftc-titleBkg_VideoDemo.png at the playhead position.

The imported Image appears in the **Timeline** panel, at the position of the playhead, as an extra layer on top of the Webcam layer.

5. Use the **Timeline** or the **Timing** panel to extend the duration of the Image until the end if the topic introduction. If you are using the encoderVideo_Start.cpvc file, extend the duration of the Image to 5 seconds.

The **Properties** and **Timing** panels of the Image are exactly the same as in a regular project. Inserting images in a Video Demo is also quite similar to inserting images in a standard Captivate project.

Extra Credit – inserting the end image of the Video Demo

In this Extra Credit section, you will insert the very same image at the end of the Video Demo. Because the image has already been inserted in the project, it is available in the project Library and does not need to be imported a second time. The general steps go as follows:

1. Move the Playhead to the position where you are about to make the concluding statement.
2. Drag the `mftc-titleBkg_VideoDemo.png` file from the **Library** panel and drop it on top of the video.
3. Place the image in the top-left corner of the video (**X** = 0 and **Y** = 0).
4. Extend the duration of the image to the end of the Video Demo.

After this Extra Credit section, `mftc-titleBkg_VideoDemo.png` should be displayed at the beginning and at the end of the project.

Inserting objects in a Video Demo project

A small subset of the Captivate objects is supported in a Video Demo project. Supported objects include Smart Shapes, Highlight Boxes, and Text Captions, among others. Inserting and formatting these objects in a Video Demo happens the exact same way as in a standard Captivate project. That's why this section of the book will not contain any step-by-step instructions, as it usually would. Instead, you will apply the skills you learned in the previous chapters to insert objects in the Video Demo project.

Your assignment goes as follows:

1. Insert a rectangle Smart Shape at the beginning of the project, on top of the image you inserted in the previous section. Write a nice title for the Video Demo and format it to your liking.
2. Repeat the preceding operation to add a closing comment at the end of the project.
3. When you feel like an area of the screen should be further highlighted, insert a Smart Shape and format it as a Highlight Box. Don't forget to use the **Timeline** panel to sync these Highlight Boxes with the rest of the video file.
4. Feel free to add other objects or Text Labels as you see fit.

After this section, your project Video Demo should contain Images, Highlight Boxes, and other objects used to further enhance the screencast. As far as these objects are concerned, there is nothing new to learn in this section. Just take this as an opportunity to practice your new skills in a new situation. If you get confused by this assignment, don't hesitate to take a look at the Chapter09/final/encoderDemo.cpvc file for clarification and inspiration.

Themes in a Video Demo

You probably noticed that the **Themes** icon on the Toolbar is disabled in a Video project. This is because Themes are, unfortunately, not supported in a Video Demo project. Styles, however, are fully supported, including importing and exporting slides to and from other Captivate projects regardless of these projects being Video Demos or regular Captivate files.

Removing unwanted popups

In your Video Demo projects, you have the ability to remove unwanted popups and tooltips that were captured during the recording.

In the Chapter09/encoderVideo_Start.cpvc project, there is such a tooltip between the **00:49** and the **00:51** mark in the **Timeline** panel. You will now remove this unwanted tooltip using the following steps:

1. Use the **Timeline** panel to place the red playhead around the **00:49** mark.
2. Use the **Play/Pause** icon at the bottom-left corner of the **Timeline** panel to spot the exact timing where the unwanted tooltip appears and disappears.
3. When done, place the playhead at the point on the **Timeline** that the tooltip appears on the screen.
4. Turn your attention to the **Video Effects** panel.

Remember that the **Video Effects** panel is tied to the **Properties** inspector. It may therefore be necessary to open the **Properties** inspector to access the **Video Effects** panel. Also remember that the **Video Effects** panel contains options that are specific to Video Demo projects.

5. Switch to the **Popup** tab of the **Video Effects** panel.
6. Click the **Replace** button and draw a rectangle on top of the unwanted yellow tooltip.

7. In the **Timeline** panel, extend the duration of the **Popup_Freeze_Item** so it matches the duration of the unwanted tooltip of the video track.

At the end of this process, this portion of the Timeline should look like the following screenshot:

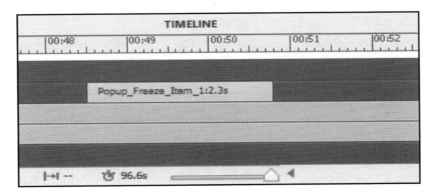

Thanks to this awesome and yet easy-to-use feature of Captivate, you are now able to clear your video captures of unwanted popups and tooltips!

Adding Pan & Zoom

Another very nice and easy-to-use feature of Video Demos is the **Pan & Zoom** animation. It allows you to zoom in on a specific area of the video and to move the camera during the movie. In the next exercise, you will add **Pan & Zoom** animations into this particular project by performing the following steps:

1. In the **Timeline** panel, click the Play icon to start playing the video, and pause right after the **Export Settings** dialog appears. If you are using the `Chapter09/encoderVideo_Start.cpvc` project, pause at the **00:55** mark in the **Timeline** panel.
2. Turn your attention to the **Pan & Zoom** tab of the **Video Effects** panel.
3. In the **Pan & Zoom** panel, click the **Add Pan & Zoom** button.

The **Pan & Zoom** panel updates and shows the available pan and zoom controls, along with a thumbnail image of the current frame of the video. A blue bounding box with eight handles surrounds this thumbnail image.

4. Resize and move the blue bounding box so it covers the bottom-right corner of the thumbnail (see **1** in the following screenshot).

5. Increase the **Speed** value of the **Pan & Zoom** animation to 1.0 second (2), as shown in the following screenshot:

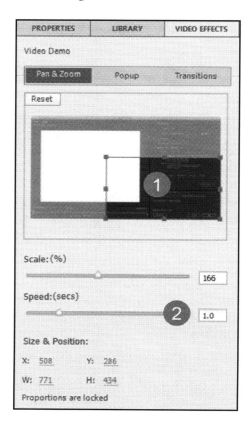

After this procedure, a **Pan & Zoom** icon appears in the **Timeline** panel. If you want to modify or delete the **Pan & Zoom** animation, just click this icon to load the properties of this **Pan & Zoom** animation in the **Pan & Zoom** panel.

6. Earlier in this chapter, you trimmed an unwanted portion of the video. As a result of this trim, the video is split in two parts. Go ahead and add one more **Pan & Zoom** effect at the start of the second video portion. Make sure the size and position of the effect is the same as the previous **Pan & Zoom** effect.

7. Also, decrease the **Speed** value of this Animation to 0.0 second.

8. Because of the **Pan & Zoom** effect, it may be necessary to move and resize some of the objects you added on top of the video in the previous section.

You will now move the playhead ahead on the **Timeline** panel and add the corresponding *Zoom Out* animation.

9. In the **Timeline** panel, place the red vertical playhead at the time when you click the **OK** button to close the **Export Settings** dialog.
10. Return to the **Pan & Zoom** tab of the **Video Effects** panel and click the **Zoom Out** button to restore the view.
11. Increase the **Speed** value of the animation to 1.0 second.
12. Adjust any Highlight Boxes or other objects to fit in the zoom area, if needed.

These actions add another **Pan & Zoom** animation in the project, as indicated by the second **Pan & Zoom** icon in the **Timeline** panel shown in the following screenshot:

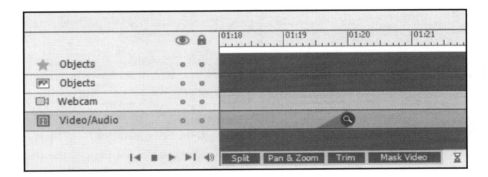

Adding Transitions

Another way of adding a kind of animation to a Video Demo project is to add **Transitions**. A Transition defines how the project moves from one video clip to the next.

Because you trimmed the original video, you have two or more video clips in your project. The only places you can add Transitions to are between different video clips (which includes the trimmed videos), as well as at the very beginning and at the very end of the project. To add Transitions in any other portion of the video clip, you first have to *split* the video into smaller sequences. You will then be able to add Transitions between these sequences.

Let's check it out by performing the following steps:

1. In the **Timeline** panel, move the playhead to where the front title of the video finishes (see **1** in the following screenshot).

2. At the bottom of the **Timeline** panel, click the **Split** button, shown as (**2**) in the following screenshot:

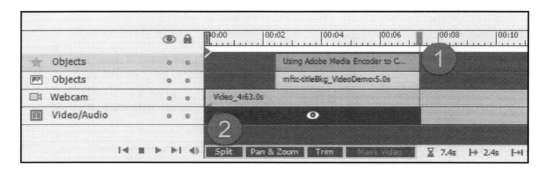

This effectively splits the video file into two separate sequences, as indicated by the small diamond that appears in the **Timeline** panel at the exact location of the split. Because you have now split the video, it is possible to add a Transition between these two sequences.

3. Turn your attention to the **Transitions** tab of the **Video Effects** panel.

4. In the **Timeline** panel, click the diamond between the two sequences that you have split.

5. In the **Transitions** panel, choose a Transition of your liking. Note that as soon as you apply a transition effect, the color of the diamond on the Timeline changes.

6. At the top of the **Transitions** tab, adjust the **Speed** of the Transition to your liking (Fast, Medium, or Slow).

7. Repeat the same sequence of actions at the end of the project, before the end title appears.

8. When done, use the **Preview** | **Project** icon on the Toolbar to take a look at the entire Video Demo.

During the preview, pay particular attention to the newly added **Pan & Zoom** and **Transitions**.

9. When the preview is finished, click the **Edit** button at the bottom-right corner of the screen to return to edit mode.
10. Save the file when done.

This exercise concludes the post-production step of the process. Your Video Demo is now ready for publication, but before that, let's make a quick summary of what has been covered in this section:

- You can resize and reposition the webcam feed anywhere on the screen.
- If you selected the **Change Background** option before recording, you can replace the background image of the webcam feed after the recording process.
- You can mask the Video or Webcam feed at any position on the **Timeline** to show just one of the feeds and hide the other.
- Unwanted portions of the video can be deleted using the **Trim** functionality in the Video Demo.
- Objects can be added on top of a Video Demo using the very same procedures and options as in a standard Captivate project.
- The only difference is that Video Demos only support a small subset of the objects available in Captivate. Interactive objects, such as Buttons and Text Entry Boxes, are not supported.
- Video Demos do not support Themes, but they fully support Styles, including importing and exporting styles to and from other projects.
- The **Video Effects** panel contains options that are exclusive to Video Demos.
- You can remove the unwanted popups and tooltips from the video.
- **Pan & Zoom** animations can be used to zoom in on a specific part of the screen and move the camera while playing the movie.
- **Transitions** can be added between two video clips. If your project is composed of a single big video track, you can split it into smaller sequences and add Transitions between these sequences.

Publishing a Video Demo

Due to its very nature, a Video Demo project can only be published as an `.mp4` video file. In the following exercise, you will explore the available publishing options and publish the `Chapter09/ecoderVideo.cpvc` project using the following steps:

1. Open or return to the `Chapter09/encoderVideo.cpvc` file.
2. Make sure the file opens in edit mode.
3. If you are not in edit mode, click the **Edit** button at the lower-right corner of the screen (if the **Edit** button is not displayed on the screen, it simply means that you are already in edit mode).
4. Click the **Publish** | **Publish to Computer** icon or use the **File** | **Publish** menu item. In both cases, the **Publish Video Demo** dialog opens.
5. In the **Publish Video Demo** dialog, make sure the **Name** of the project is `encoderVideo`.
6. Click the **...** button and choose the `Chapter09` folder of your exercises as the destination of the published video file.
7. Open the **Preset** dropdown. Take some time to inspect the available presets. When done, choose the **Video** | **Apple iPad** preset.
8. Make sure the **Publish Video Demo** dialog looks similar to that shown in the following screenshot and click the **Publish** button:

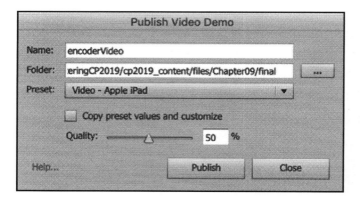

Publishing a Video Demo project can be quite a lengthy process, so be patient. When the process is complete, a message asks you what to do next. Note that one of the options enables you to upload your newly created video to YouTube directly.

9. Click the **Close** button to discard the message.
10. Use Windows Explorer (Windows) or the Finder (Mac) to go to the Chapter09 folder of your exercises.
11. Double-click the encoderDemo.mp4 file to open the video in the default video player of your system.

While enjoying the final product of your hard work, remember that a Video Demo project can only be published as a video file. Also, remember that the published .mp4 video file can only be experienced in a linear fashion, and does not support any kind of interactivity.

Publishing to YouTube

Captivate includes a workflow that allows you to upload the published video file to your YouTube account without even leaving Captivate. In the next exercise, you will experiment with this workflow using the following steps:

 This exercise requires a working YouTube account. If you do not have a YouTube account, you can create one for free on the YouTube website (see https://support.google.com/youtube/answer/161805?hl=en for details) or just read through the steps of the exercise.

1. Still in the Chapter09/encoderVideo.cpvc file, use the **File | Publish to YouTube** menu item to start the procedure.

Captivate directly converts your Video Demo into an .mp4 video file without asking you to choose a preset. Since Captivate already knows that this video will be uploaded to YouTube, an appropriate preset is applied automatically.

2. When the publishing process is complete, click **Log in** in the **Publish To YouTube** window.
3. Sign in using your YouTube credentials.
4. You will get an alert that Adobe Captivate would like to manage your YouTube account and YouTube videos. Click **Allow** to confirm.

5. Once logged in, enter the relevant project information:

- Enter the title of the movie in the **Title** field.
- Enter a description in the **Description** field.
- Choose the level of **Privacy** (**Public**, **Private**, or **Unlisted**).
- Click the terms and conditions link, read it, and then click the **Back** button.
- Select the **I have read the terms & conditions** checkbox and click the **Upload** button.

Captivate then uploads the video to YouTube. When the process is complete, you can see a preview of the video in the same dialog. To go to the YouTube page and view the video, click the **YouTube** button in the bottom-right corner of the video.

6. Now, return to Captivate and click the **Close Window** button to close the **Publish to YouTube** window.

As you can see, Captivate makes it incredibly easy to publish a Video Demo to YouTube!

For more information on YouTube's privacy settings and the difference between a public and private video, visit
`https://support.google.com/youtube/answer/157177?hl=en`.

Inserting a Video Demo project in a regular project

When in a regular Captivate project based on slides (using the `.cptx` file extension), use the **Insert | CPVC Slide** menu item to create a new slide based on a Video Demo project. This is a great feature if you want to have your Video Demo file in the middle of a regular interactive project, or if you want to add quiz slides after your Video Demo.

To further edit the embedded Video Demo project, go to the Properties inspector and click **Edit Video Demo**. This will open the Video Demo project for you. Here, you can make the changes and then click the **Exit** button on the top-left corner to save the changes and return to the main project.

Summary

In this chapter, you have gone through the entire recording and production process of a Video Demo project.

During the capture phase, you decided to record both the onscreen actions and your webcam feed. You also learned how to remove and replace the background image of the webcam feed.

During the post-production phase, you resized and repositioned the webcam feed, changed the background of the webcam feed, and learned how to mask one of the video layers. Then you trimmed out the unwanted portions from your Video Demo and applied video effects that are specific to Video Demo projects. You have also learned how to place Captivate objects on top of the video file in order to enhance the screencast and provide the best possible experience to your learners.

Finally, you performed the third and last step of the production process by publishing your project as an `.mp4` video file. You even uploaded that video directly to your YouTube channel without even leaving Captivate.

In the next chapter, you will explore responsive projects. These projects are yet another special type of project, using a slightly customized interface. They allow you to optimize your eLearning course for multiscreen delivery, placing Captivate at the cutting edge of the multiscreen content production workflow.

Meet the community

In this section, we want to introduce you to Paul Wilson from Canada. Besides being a talented eLearning designer and Adobe Captivate developer, Paul is a YouTuber. He publishes YouTube video tutorials on his own YouTube channel dedicated to Adobe eLearning. You definitely want to bookmark his awesome YouTube channel, which contains over 300 free video tutorials at the time of writing this book.

Damien

I first met with Paul in Washington DC in April 2016, during the first annual Adobe eLearning conference – East Coast. If you've ever been to Washington, DC, you know that the international airport is very far away from the city. On our way back home, Paul and I shared the same taxi ride to get to the airport, which gave us 50 minutes of quality time chatting together.

Pooja

Paul is truly a hero in the Captivate community. The number of videos he has produced to teach eLearning professionals how to use Captivate is mind-blowing. I got to meet Paul in person during the last two Adobe conferences, and really enjoyed talking to him.

Paul Wilson

Paul has been designing and developing with Adobe Captivate for over 13 years. Getting into the training field by accident, Paul has worked as a senior instructional designer for companies such as Bell Canada and the Greater Toronto Airports Authority. When he decided to start his own eLearning development company, he began creating video tutorials on YouTube to share his knowledge of Adobe Captivate. As of the summer of 2017, his videos have been seen all over the world by hundreds of thousands of viewers and his channel has over 9,000 regular subscribers. He works with companies all over the globe, consulting, designing, and teaching eLearning for a variety of organizations.

Contact details

- Blog: `https://CaptivateTeacher.com/`
- Twitter: `@CaptivateTeachr`
- LinkedIn: `https://www.linkedin.com/in/paul-wilson-ctdp-b096559/`
- YouTube: `http://www.youtube.com/PaulWilsonLearning`

10
Creating a Responsive Project

In today's ultra-connected world, the majority of your students probably own multiple devices. And, of course, they want to be able to take your eLearning course on all of their devices. They might want to start the course on their desktop computer at work, continue it on their phone while commuting home, and finish it at night on their tablet. In other situations, students might only have a mobile phone available to take the course, and sometimes the topic being taught only makes sense on a mobile device. To address these needs, you want to deliver your course on multiple screens, which is possible by creating a Responsive Project in Captivate.

A Responsive Project is a project that you can optimize for different device sizes. It is like providing several different versions of the course in a single project.

In this chapter, you will be introduced to the key concepts and techniques required to create a Responsive Project in Adobe Captivate 2019. Keep in mind that everything you have learned so far can be applied to a Responsive Project.

In this chapter, you will do the following:

- Create a new Responsive Project in Captivate 2019
- Explore the interface differences in Responsive Projects
- Use Fluid Boxes to create screen layouts
- Add objects to Fluid Boxes and modify their properties
- Use Optional and Static Fluid Boxes
- Modify text properties in Responsive Projects
- Distribute objects equally in a Fluid Box
- Convert a non-responsive project to be responsive
- Switch to the Breakpoint Mode

At the end of this chapter, your first Responsive Project will be ready for publishing and you will be at the cutting edge of the mobile learning revolution.

Preparing your work

To get the most out of this chapter, it is a good idea to reset the Captivate interface to the default. If you are using the default interface mode, just close and restart Captivate to reset it. If you are using the Advanced Interface mode, use the **Window | Workspace | Reset 'Classic'** menu item to reset Captivate to the default. In this chapter, you will use the exercises stored in the Chapter10 folder. If you get confused by any of the step-by-step instructions, take a look at the Chapter10/final folder, which contains a copy of the files as they will be at the end of this chapter.

Responsive Projects

A Responsive Project is meant to be used on multiple devices, including tablets and smartphones that do not support Flash technology. Therefore, it can only be published in HTML5 format. This means that all the restrictions of a traditional HTML5 project also apply to a Responsive Project. For example, you will not be able to add Text Animations or Rollover Objects in a Responsive Project because these features are not supported in HTML5 content.

Creating a Responsive Project

It is now time to open Captivate and create your first Responsive Project, using the following steps:

1. Open Captivate or close every open file.
2. On the Welcome screen, under the **New** tab, double-click **Responsive Project**. Alternatively, you can also use the **File | New Project | Responsive Project** menu item.

This action creates a new Responsive Project. The choice to create a Responsive Project or a regular Captivate project must be done upfront when creating the project. You can also convert an existing regular project created using Captivate 9, 2017, or 2019 to a Responsive Project. You will learn about this workflow later in the chapter.

The responsive workspace of Captivate is similar to what you are used to, with the exception of the **Layout Preview** bar across the top of the stage. The **Layout Preview** bar will help you view how the content will be displayed on different device sizes, right inside the Captivate edit area:

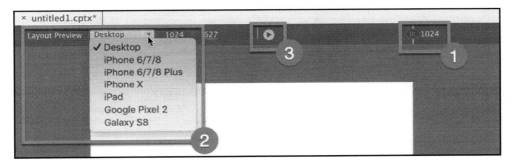

3. Move the **Preview Slider** (1) on the top-right corner of the stage area to preview how the content will display on different devices.

4. You can also open the **Layout Preview** (2) drop-down list to view the slide content in specific device sizes.

5. If you wish to add more devices to the **Layout Preview** device list, first drag the **Preview Slider** to the position where it reflects the width of the new device. Alternately, you can enter the value in the width and height fields.

6. Then, click the **+** symbol, enter the new device name in the dialog, and click **OK**.

7. To delete these additional devices from the list, select the device name from the list, click the **-** symbol, and click **Yes** to confirm.

8. You can click the **Layout Preview** (3) button to automatically preview the slide and see your content automatically wrap, scale, and align across device sizes.

9. You can also use the same option from the **Properties** inspector, next to the **Wrap Options**:

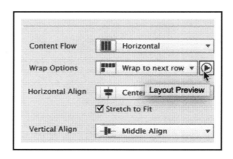

Resizing the Responsive Project

The default maximum width and height of Responsive Projects in Captivate 2019 is set to 1024 x 627. You can increase or decrease this by re-scaling the project. Let's take a look at the steps required:

1. Make sure you have **Desktop** selected in the **Preview in** drop-down list. If not, open the dropdown and select **Desktop**. Notice that the width and height of the project are set to 1024 x 627.

2. To increase the width and/or height of the project, use the **Modify | Rescale Project** menu item.

3. In the **Rescale Project** dialog, deselect **Maintain Aspect Ratio** if needed.

4. Enter the new width and height in pixels or as a percentage. Let's set the new width and height to 1280 x 768, which is a 16:10 ratio.

5. Click **Finish**:

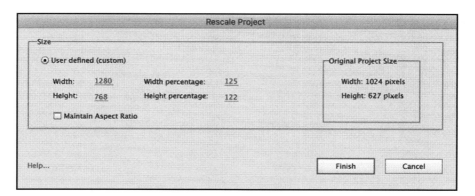

6. You will see an alert that the resize project operation cannot be undone. Click **OK** to confirm.

7. The maximum width and height of the project will now be changed to `1280 x 768`. The new project height will automatically be reflected on the slide. You can move the Preview Slider to the right to view the slide contents at the maximum width.

Fluid Boxes

Now that you have learned how to create a Responsive Project and resize the maximum width and height, it's time to design responsive slides. The first step of designing responsive slides in Captivate 2019 is to add Fluid Boxes.

Fluid Boxes are containers that display and move your content based on the settings you choose.

Adding Fluid Boxes

Let's take a deep dive into learning how to add Fluid Boxes, change their properties, and add content to these Fluid Boxes:

1. If you still have the project open from the last exercise, close it. Then, open the `Chapter10/FluidBoxes.cptx` file.

2. Go to slide 3. You can start adding Fluid Boxes to this blank slide.

3. On the Toolbar, click **Fluid Box**. It gives you the option of selecting either a **Horizontal** or **Vertical** flow based on your screen layout requirements. Let's select **Vertical** in this example.

4. Add 3 vertical Fluid Boxes in this example:

 Note that you can add up to 10 Fluid Boxes in each direction.

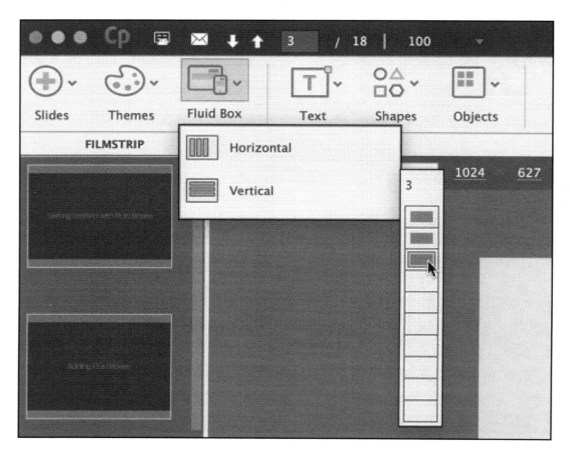

This creates one main Fluid Box on the screen, with three child Fluid Boxes. You can see the hierarchy of the Fluid Boxes anytime in the **Select Fluid Box** section in the **Properties** inspector. Please note that the Fluid Box number you see on your computer might be different from the number you see here in the screenshot:

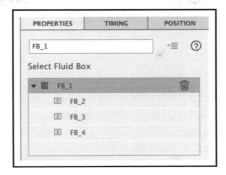

5. You can then resize the child Fluid Boxes by selecting the main Fluid Box and clicking and dragging the resize handles on the slide:

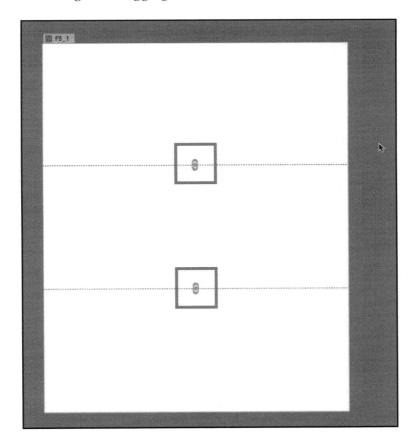

6. Alternately, you can select the Fluid Box for which you wish to change the size. Select the first Fluid Box on this slide.

7. Then, go to the **Properties** inspector, and switch to the **Position** inspector.

8. Open the dropdown and select %, and then enter 10 in the field. This will change the Fluid Box size on the stage:

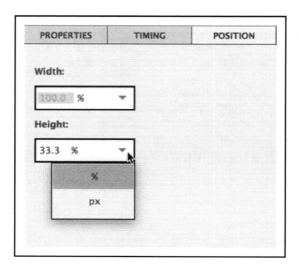

9. Similarly, select the last Fluid Box and change the height to 10 from the Position Inspector.

10. You can further add child Fluid Boxes to these Fluid Boxes. To do that, select the Fluid Box on the slide to which you wish to add child Fluid Boxes. Let's select the second Fluid Box here.

11. On the Toolbar, click **Fluid Box | Horizontal** or **Vertical** based on your preferences and then select the number.

12. Resize the Fluid Boxes using the resize handles, if required.

13. Continue adding Fluid Boxes until you get the desired layout for the screen. Notice that the **Select Fluid Box** section in the **Properties** inspector starts showing all the Fluid Boxes in a nested view:

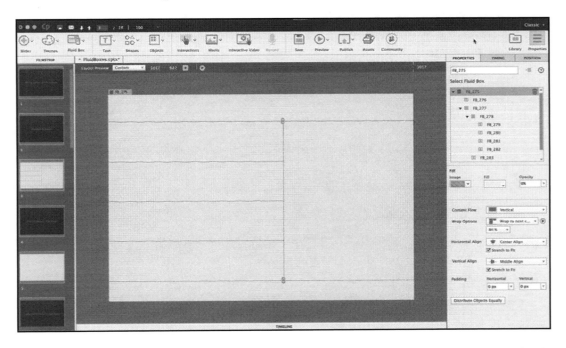

14. From the **Select Fluid Box** section, you can easily switch to any other Fluid Box and modify their properties, or you can directly select the Fluid Box on the slide by clicking anywhere on the Fluid Box.

15. The selected Fluid Box appears with a blue outline and a label with the Fluid Box name in the top-left corner. This is also reflected in the **Select Fluid Box** section.

16. Alternately, you can make a selection in the **Select Fluid Box** section, and it will be reflected on the slide as well.

17. When you hover over another Fluid Box, you will see a green highlight, outline, and label. This can be seen in the **Select Fluid Box** section too:

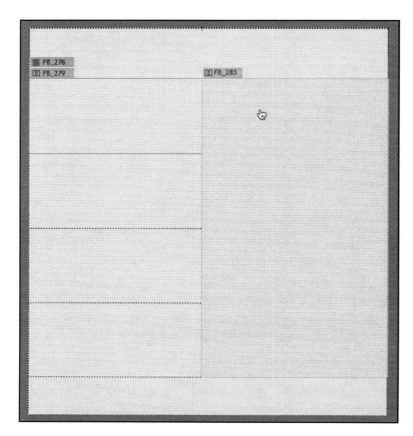

18. The selected Fluid Box also shows the parent Fluid Box label in orange above the child Fluid Box label. To select the parent Fluid Box, you can click the orange label:

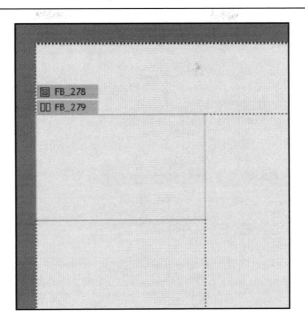

19. Similarly, if an object is selected, the parent Fluid Box's name appears in the orange label. You can click the orange label to select the Fluid Box. You will learn how to add objects to a Fluid Box in the next section.

20. You can also rename each of these Fluid Boxes by selecting the Fluid Box and changing the name in the **Properties** inspector from FB_<number> to something more meaningful.

You have now successfully created a slide layout using Fluid Boxes. In the next section, you will learn how to add objects to Fluid Boxes. But before that, let's summarize the key points we've covered up to this point:

- A Responsive Project works well on any device size
- Responsive Projects can be published only in HTML5 format
- You can preview how the content will be displayed on different device sizes in the Captivate edit area, using the **Layout Preview** drop-down list
- The default maximum dimensions of Responsive Projects are 1024 x 627, and you can increase or decrease dimensions by rescaling the project
- Fluid Boxes are the containers that lay out your content intelligently as per the defined settings

- The objects placed inside Fluid Boxes can flow either vertically or horizontally
- You can add up to 10 Fluid Boxes in each direction on the slide
- The Fluid Boxes can be resized on the slide using the resize handles or from the **Position** inspector
- You can add child Fluid Boxes to each Fluid Box on the slide

Adding objects to Fluid Boxes

Now, let's learn how to add objects to a Fluid Box:

1. In the `FluidBoxes.cptx` file, go to `Slide 5`. Fluid Boxes are already added to this slide.
2. Select one of the Fluid Boxes and then go to the Toolbar, click **Media | Image,** and open the `Chapter10/Images/Image1.png` file.

The image has now been added to the selected Fluid Box.

If you don't have a Fluid Box selected when adding objects to the slide, the object will be added to the center of the slide and not linked to any of the Fluid Boxes. You can then drag and move the object to the desired Fluid Box.

3. To move the image to another Fluid Box, click and drag the image to another Fluid Box. When you see a green highlight in the desired Fluid Box, drop the image. The image will now move to the new Fluid Box.

The size of the image changes when it is moved to a smaller or bigger Fluid Box, but the aspect ratio for the image is maintained. This happens because the **Maintain Aspect Ratio** option for images is selected by default:

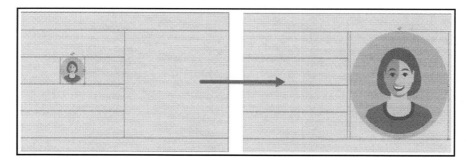

4. With the image still selected, go to the **Properties** inspector and you will notice that the **Maintain Aspect Ratio** option is selected. Deselect the option and the image will be resized to fill the entire Fluid Box.

5. Selecting the **Maintain Aspect Ratio** option again will bring it back to normal.

For objects such as Images, Shapes, Buttons, and so on, the **Maintain Aspect Ratio** option is selected by default. For Text Captions, it is disabled by default, so that the text is able to fill the entire Fluid Box and flows based on the device's width and height.

6. Now, select an empty Fluid Box.

7. Go to the Toolbar and click **Text | Text Caption**.

8. Notice that the Text Caption takes up the entire Fluid Box space end to end.

9. Now, select the Fluid Box to which you added the `Image1.png` image. Then, go to the Toolbar, click **Media | Image,** and open the `Chapter10/Images/Image2.png` file.

Notice that the `Image1.png` image resizes to make space for `Image2.png`.

10. Similarly, add `Image3.png` and `Image4.png` in the same Fluid Box. The images will further resize to make space for new objects:

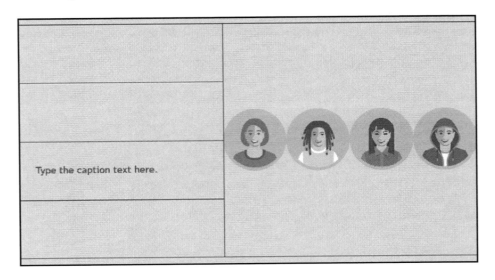

11. You can also change the order of these objects by dragging and dropping the object at the desired location in the Fluid Box.
12. Drag the **Preview Slider** on the top-right corner of the slide to see how these objects will realign on the slide, based on the dimension of the device.

Another requirement when adding objects can be that you want to add the object, but don't want to associate it with any Fluid Box. You want this object to be present on the screen at the same position, regardless of the device size.

13. In such cases, you can select the object and select **Unlock from Fluid Box** in the **Properties** inspector.
14. Unlike the other objects, moving the unlocked object will not prompt you to add it to any of the Fluid Boxes. To add it back to one of the Fluid Boxes, uncheck **Unlock from Fluid Box** and move it to the desired Fluid Box.

This will give you an idea of how well the objects are sized and positioned automatically on the slide. If you don't like the way the objects are flowing, don't worry, you will learn how to change the properties of Fluid Boxes and objects so that you can make them look the way you like!

Using the Fill option for Fluid Boxes

The Fill option for Fluid Boxes is the best way to add a background color, gradient, or images to the slide or objects. The Fill option for Fluid Boxes works in exactly the same way as the Fill option for Smart Shapes, which was covered in Chapter 2, *Working with Standard Objects*.

1. In the FluidBoxes.cptx file, go to Slide 7. Fluid Boxes are already added to this slide.
2. Select the main Fluid Box. Remember that you can use the **Select Fluid Box** section in the **Properties** inspector to easily select the main Fluid Box, which is the outermost Fluid Box that covers the entire slide.
3. In the **Properties** inspector, you'll find the **Fill** properties under the **Select Fluid Box** section. You can fill the Fluid Boxes with a solid color, gradient, or an image. Let's fill the main Fluid Box with an image.

4. Select the **Image Fill** option from the first dropdown under the **Fill** section:

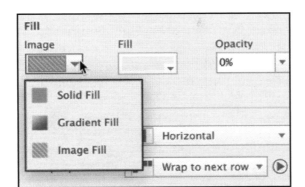

5. Then, open the second dropdown and click the **Browse** icon (the icon of a folder).
6. In the **Select Image/Audio from Library** dialog, click **Import**.
7. Open the Chapter10/Images/Background.jpeg file.
8. Similarly, if you wish to apply background fill to any other Fluid Box on the slide, you can select that Fluid Box and apply the Fill property.

Modifying the properties of Fluid Boxes

You've got a good headstart with creating responsive courses in Captivate 2019 using Fluid Boxes. You have learned how to add Fluid Boxes, resize the boxes on the slide, add objects to Fluid Boxes, and fill them with background color or images.

Captivate assigns some default properties to the Fluid Boxes, which automatically flow, align, and wrap the objects on smaller device sizes. Now, let's learn how to modify these default settings to get your desired result:

1. In the FluidBoxes.cptx file, go to Slide 9. Fluid Boxes and some images are already added to this slide.
2. Select the main Fluid Box and go to the **Properties** inspector.
3. Here you will find the **Content Flow**, **Wrap Options**, **Horizontal** and **Vertical Align,** and **Padding** properties for the Fluid Box.

Let's talk about these properties before making any modifications.

- **Flow**: The **Content Flow** property denotes the direction in which the objects will be laid out. When this Fluid Box was added to the slide, the direction specified was **Vertical**. The same is shown in the Flow dropdown. If, after adding the Fluid Box, you wish to change the direction, you can change it from the **Properties** inspector by changing the **Vertical** flow to **Horizontal**, or the **Horizontal** flow to **Vertical**.

- **Wrap**: With the **Wrap Options** property, you can control when and how the objects wrap to the next row on the smaller device sizes. There are four different wrapping options available for the horizontal flow:

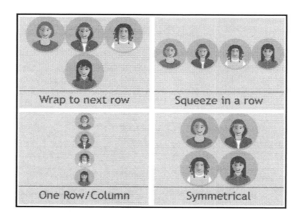

- **Wrap to next row**: This is the default wrap property for Fluid Boxes. When the wrap point reaches its threshold and can no longer hold all of the objects in the same row, the last object in the Fluid Box is moved to the next row, and then when it hits the threshold again, the second to last object is moved to the next row. This happens in a sequence and the objects are moved to the next row one at a time.

- **Squeeze in a row**: If you don't want the images to wrap to the next row and want them all to appear in the same row, you can select the **Squeeze in a row** option. With this property, instead of the images moving to a new row, the image size will shrink to allow them all to fit when the screen size gets smaller.

- **One Row/Column**: This property will squeeze the objects in a single row or a single column. When the wrap point reaches the threshold, the objects move from being horizontally aligned to vertically aligned.

- **Symmetrical**: The last wrap property is symmetrical, which moves the objects to the next row in groups, instead of moving one object at a time. For example, if you have four objects in a Fluid Box, it will move two objects together to the next row on smaller device sizes so that the first and the second rows have an equal number of objects.

Similar to these options, there are four wrapping options available for the vertical flow: **Wrap to next column**, **Squeeze in a column**, **One Row/Column**, and **Symmetrical**.

Now let's modify these properties to see how the objects behave:

4. We are still on `Slide 9` in the `FluidBoxes.cptx` file. Select the Fluid Box on the right side of the screen, which has four images added to it. Notice that the **Content Flow** for the Fluid Box is set to **Horizontal**.

5. Notice that the **Wrap Options** is set to **Wrap to next row**. Click the **Layout Preview** icon next to **Wrap Options** to see the wrapping behavior of the objects.

6. Then, change the **Wrap Options** property to **Squeeze in a row** and click the **Layout Preview** icon next to **Wrap Options** to see how the images wrap differently on smaller device sizes:

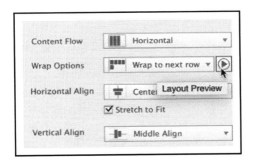

7. Similarly, switch to the other two **Wrap Options** properties and preview how the images wrap on smaller device sizes for those wrap properties.

8. Now, change the **Content Flow** for the Fluid Box to **Vertical**, change the **Wrap Options** property, and preview how the images wrap on smaller devices.

Align: As the name indicates, this option will allow you to decide how to align the objects in the Fluid Boxes.

- **Left align**: Use this option to left-align the objects. The first object will be placed at the left-hand side of the Fluid box and the others will follow.
- **Center align**: The objects will be center-aligned in the Fluid Box.
- **Right align:** The objects will be right-aligned in the Fluid Box. The last object will be placed at the right of the Fluid Box and the others will be placed after it in a right-to-left direction.
- **Top align**: The objects will be top-aligned in the Fluid Box.
- **Middle align**: The objects will be middle-aligned in the Fluid Box.
- **Bottom align**: The objects will be bottom-aligned in the Fluid Box.
- **Space in Between**: The objects will be evenly distributed in the Fluid Box. The first object will be placed on the left and the last object on the right side of the Fluid Box.
- **Space Around**: The objects will be evenly distributed in the Fluid Box with equal space around the objects.

Now, let's apply these alignment options one by one to the Fluid Box with images to see how it appears.

9. But before that, deselect the **Stretch to Fit** option for both the **Horizontal** and **Vertical Align** properties:

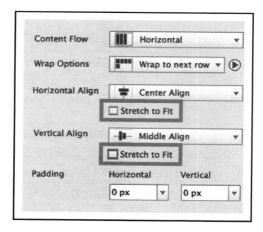

10. Now, select each option from the **Horizontal** and **Vertical** alignment drop-down list and see how the alignment changes based on your selection.

Padding: If you need some space around the objects in the Fluid Boxes, you can add padding from 0 to 100 pixels in both the horizontal and vertical directions. This option is especially useful for text inside the Fluid Boxes.

You have now covered all the basics for adding objects to Fluid Boxes and modifying the properties of the Fluid Boxes. Let's summarize what you have learned so far:

- You can add an object to a Fluid Box by selecting it and then adding the object. Alternately, you can first add the object to the slide and then move it to the required Fluid Box.
- Objects can be easily moved from one Fluid Box to another Fluid Box by dragging and dropping the objects on the stage.
- Use the **Maintain Aspect Ratio** option to avoid distorting the shape of the object added.
- You can add multiple objects to a single Fluid Box. The size and position of the existing objects are adjusted to accommodate the new objects added to the Fluid Box.
- The order of objects in the Fluid Box can be changed by dragging and dropping the object at the desired position.
- You can position the object outside the Fluid Box by selecting the **Unlock from Fluid Box** option.
- You can fill the Fluid Boxes with a background color, gradient, or image. The Fluid Box Fill option is similar to the Smart Shape Fill option.
- You can change the flow of the objects in Fluid Boxes from horizontal to vertical, and vice versa.
- By default, the objects will be wrapped to the next row/column when they reach the threshold, but you can change the wrapping behavior to squeeze in a row/column, one row/column, or symmetrical.
- You can also align the objects in the Fluid Boxes. The options available are **Left align**, **Center align**, **Right align**, **Top align**, **Middle align**, **Bottom align**, **Space in Between**, and **Space Around**.

Marking Fluid Boxes/objects as Optional

In eLearning courses, some objects are critical for learning, while others are less important, and may simply be decorative. Less important objects can take up a lot of space on smaller devices and distract from the critical objects. Also, objects can be less useful for learners if they become too small. For example, a map of a company property is helpful when it's large, but it's unreadable when viewed on smaller devices. If this happens, you can mark less important content as Optional. This will show all the objects on larger screens, but as the screen sizes get smaller, the optional objects will disappear to make more space for the critical objects.

Let's first look at the workflow for marking objects in a Fluid Box as Optional:

1. In the `FluidBoxes.cptx` file, go to `Slide 11`. A Fluid Box and some images are already added to this slide.
2. Select one of the images on the slide.
3. Go to the **Properties** inspector and select **Optional:**

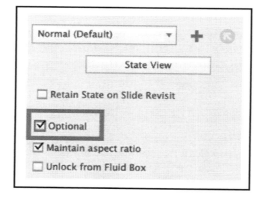

4. Then, select the Fluid Box and change the **Wrap Options** property to **Squeeze in a row**.

This step is very important, as the **Optional** property works only with the **Squeeze in a row** wrap setting.

5. The **Wrap** threshold is set to 80%. You can increase or decrease it, if needed:

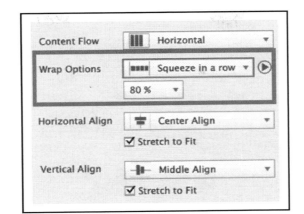

 By default, the Wrap threshold property is available only for the main Fluid Box on the slide. If you need to set different threshold properties for the child Fluid Boxes as well, open the **Preferences** dialog and switch to the **Defaults** category. In the **General** section, select **Enable WrapPoint** and click **OK**. This will enable the Wrap threshold for all Fluid Boxes.

6. Click the **Layout Preview** icon. For smaller device sizes, the image marked as Optional disappears from the screen and the others automatically adjust their size and position to cover the entire space.

Similarly, you can mark the entire Fluid Box as Optional. Here are the steps required:

7. In the `FluidBoxes.cptx` file, go to `Slide 12`. On this slide, the images are placed in separate Fluid Boxes.
8. Select one of the Fluid Boxes with images.
9. Go to the **Properties** inspector and select **Optional**.
10. Then, select the main Fluid Box and change the **Wrap** property to **Squeeze in a row**.
11. Click the **Layout Preview** icon. You will notice that for smaller device sizes, the Fluid Box marked as optional disappears from the screen and the other Fluid Boxes automatically adjust their size and position to cover the entire space.

Modifying the text properties

When you add text to Fluid Boxes in Captivate 2019, the text automatically scales down on the smaller device sizes, corresponding to the font size selected for the Text Caption. You also have the ability to define a Minimum Font Size so that the text is readable on smaller devices:

1. In the `FluidBoxes.cptx` file, go to `Slide 14`. Notice that this slide has a lot of text.
2. Let's preview this slide to see how the text scales on smaller devices. For previewing text, you should not use the **Layout Preview** options in the edit area, as they will not show you the true text scaling. Go to the Toolbar and click **Preview | Next 5 Slides** to preview the slide.
3. In the browser, click the **Play** icon on the slide.
4. Then, click the **Pause** button on the Course Playbar.
5. Adjust the slider to show how the content will appear on smaller devices. As you move to the smaller device sizes, the text scales to fit the width and height of the viewing area:

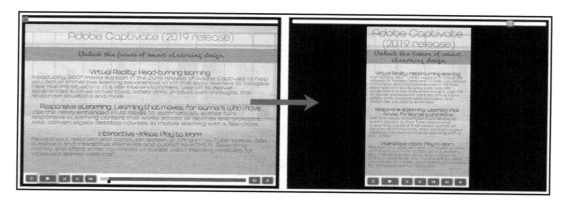

6. When the text is no longer able to fit on the slide, a **Read More** button appears. You can click the button to read the whole text; after reading, click or tap anywhere on the screen to dismiss it:

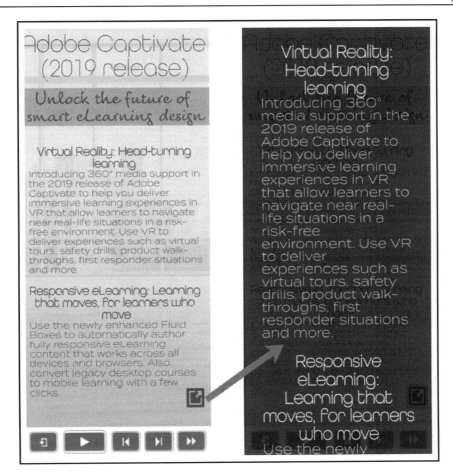

7. Close the browser and get back to the Captivate project.

8. In the **Properties** inspector for the slide, under the **Style** tab, you can change the **Minimum Font Size**. The default size is set to 14 pixels. You can increase or decrease the minimum size based on your requirements.

Enabling Uniform Text Scaling

If you have text with different lengths in different Fluid Boxes, you will need to make sure that all the captions scale at the same time:

1. In the `FluidBoxes.cptx` file, go to `Slide 15`. On this slide, unlike the previous slide, text is added to multiple Fluid Boxes.
2. Let's preview it to see how the text scales on smaller device sizes. Go to the Toolbar and click **Preview | Next 5 Slides** to preview the slide.
3. In the browser, click the **Play** icon on the slide.
4. Then, click the **Pause** button on the Course Playbar.
5. Adjust the slider to show how the content will appear on smaller devices.

You will notice that as you move to the smaller device sizes, the text scaling is not consistent, which makes the font size for some of the text larger than the others. Let's see how we can fix this.

6. In the `FluidBoxes.cptx` file, go back to `Slide 15`.
7. In the slide **Properties** inspector, select the **Enable Uniform Text Scaling** option:

8. Go to the Toolbar and click **Preview | Next 5 Slides** to preview the slide.
9. In the browser, click the **Play** icon on the slide.
10. Then, click the **Pause** button on the Course Playbar.
11. Move the slider above the slide. You will see that now all the Text Captions on the slide scale at the same time and look consistent.

Distributing objects equally

Let's take a look at a new option added in Captivate 2019, which is to distribute objects equally.

If you have objects in the Fluid Box that are not equally sized, you can use the **Distribute Objects Equally** option to ensure that all objects in a Fluid Box are equally spaced and are of the same size:

1. In the `FluidBoxes.cptx` file, go to `Slide 17`. Notice that in the bottom Fluid Box, the Back, Menu, and Next shapes are of different sizes.
2. Select the bottom Fluid Box, which is the last Fluid Box listed in the **Select Fluid Box** section.
3. In the **Properties** inspector, click the **Distribute Objects Equally** button. This will equally resize and distribute the objects in the Fluid Box.

As a best practice, you should use this option for objects that do not have the **Maintain Aspect Ratio** option selected. If you use this option for objects that have aspect ratio maintained, it might result in distortion in the size of the objects.

Also, you can use this option for Fluid Boxes in which the objects look of the same size in the desktop mode, but when you view the slide on smaller device sizes, they don't look equal. Selecting this option will make them look equal on all device sizes.

Marking Fluid Boxes as Static

In eLearning courses, we often have content that is overlaid on top of each other or is positioned relative to each other, for example, a Highlight Box on top of a screenshot, an arrow around the Button indicating that it needs to be clicked, a Caption close to the Character image, a description on top of the image, and so on. In such situations, the regular Fluid Boxes will not work, as they will line up the objects next to each other and will not allow you to overlay them and change the position of the object to be absolute.

If you have to use a multi-state object on the slide and need to add additional objects to the states, it will not be supported by normal Fluid Boxes. In such cases, you will need to convert the normal Fluid Boxes to static Fluid Boxes.

Here are the steps required:

1. In the `FluidBoxes.cptx` file, go to `Slide 19`.
2. There is a caption shape in the scrap area. We need to place this caption next to the image in the right Fluid Box. To do so, drag the caption to the Fluid Box. The caption takes its own area in the Fluid Box and cannot be overlaid on the image as the objects in the Fluid Boxes are placed side by side. To make it overlay, we will need to make the Fluid Box static.

3. Undo the previous step so that the caption is back to the scrap area.
4. Then select the Fluid Box with the image.
5. Go to the **Properties** inspector and select the **Static** option. This will give you control to add overlaid objects and manually change the placement of objects inside the Fluid Box:

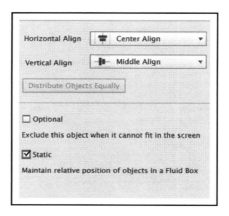

6. Now, you have the control to move and resize the image inside the Fluid Box. Move the image to the bottom-left corner of the Fluid Box, and make it a little smaller so that you have some space for the Text Caption.
7. Drag the caption from the scrap area to the static Fluid Box and position it on the top-right corner of the Fluid Box, with the caption overlapping the image a bit:

8. Move the **Preview Slider** to see that even when the Fluid Boxes are realigned, the relative position of the image and caption remain the same.

In Adobe Captivate 2019, you can also define the alignment properties for the static Fluid Boxes by selecting the horizontal and vertical alignment properties. When the learner views the course on smaller device sizes, the content will follow the alignment properties defined by you, instead of using the default center and middle align properties.

Using Fluid Boxes with Master Slides

Fluid Boxes on Master Slides work in the same way as they work on normal slides, apart from a few differences, as follows:

- Fluid Boxes on Master Slides cannot be named
- When a slide is associated with a Master Slide, the Fluid Boxes from the Master Slide are inherited by the slide
- Inherited Fluid Boxes cannot be deleted, but they can be resized
- New Fluid Boxes can be added or deleted

Question slides in Captivate projects also inherit the Fluid Boxes from the associated Master Slide. The same differences apply to the Fluid Boxes inherited from the Master Slides on the question slides.

Exploring the possibilities

Now that you have covered all the basics of using Fluid Boxes in Captivate, you are ready to create responsive courses using Fluid Boxes. Like any new workflow, you might need to tweak your course design a bit in order that it lends itself well to the responsive layout. Don't shy away from reimagining how you would be presenting the content to your students.

To get some ideas on how to create responsive courses using Fluid Boxes, explore the example course included with Captivate 2019:

1. Start Captivate 2019. If you already have the Captivate application open, close all the open projects so that you have the Welcome screen visible.
2. On the Welcome screen, go to the **Resources** tab.
3. Select the **Responsive Learning Sample** thumbnail and click **Open:**

4. This opens the responsive sample course for you. Explore how the content is laid out on the slides and how different Fluid Box and object properties have been used to bring it all together.

Converting a non-responsive project to responsive

If you have an existing non-responsive course created using Captivate 9, 2017, or 2019, you can convert it to a responsive course with Adobe Captivate 2019. This will allow you to repurpose the static courses into responsive ones, and this will save you from spending hours converting the course to responsive from scratch.

 Please note that you can convert a non-responsive project to responsive but not the other way round.

Let's look at an example of converting a non-responsive course to a responsive one:

1. Open the `Chapter10/Non-responsive.cptx` file. This course was created using Captivate 9 and has a fixed dimension of `1024` by `627` pixels.
2. To convert this course to responsive, click **File | Save as Responsive**.
3. You will get an alert that some of the items in non-responsive projects may not be supported after upgrading. Do you wish to proceed? Click **Show Unsupported Items** to see the unsupported slides or objects in the HTML5 output, or click **Save** to proceed.
4. Rename the project as `Responsive.cptx` and save it in the `Chapter10` folder.
5. Click **Save**. The project has now been converted to a Responsive Project, but the Fluid Boxes are not yet added to the project.

There are two options for adding Fluid Boxes to each slide. The first option is to manually add Fluid Boxes by using the options from the Toolbar, and then to drag the objects inside the Fluid Boxes. Alternately, you can click the **Suggest Fluid Boxes** button in the **Properties** inspector, and Captivate will automatically add Fluid Boxes and add all the slide objects to them.

6. Let's add Fluid Boxes to one of the slides in this project. Select the second slide.

7. Go to the **Properties** inspector and click **Suggest Fluid Boxes:**

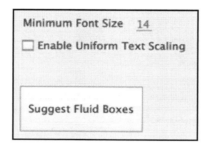

8. The Fluid Boxes are automatically added to the slide and the objects are placed inside the Fluid Boxes. Click **Preview | Next 5 slides**.

By following these few simple steps, you can convert existing non-responsive courses to responsive. If you don't like the way content is flowing on your slide, change the properties of the Fluid Boxes to your liking, and you'll have a perfectly responsive course ready to be served to students!

Although the steps to convert a static project to responsive are pretty simple, you need to follow some guidelines before and after you consider conversion:

Guidelines Part 1: https://elearning.adobe.com/2017/06/guidelines-for-considerations-before-and-after-upgrading-a-blank-project-to-a-responsive-project-part-1/

Guidelines Part 2: https://elearning.adobe.com/2017/06/guidelines-for-considerations-before-and-after-upgrading-a-blank-project-to-a-responsive-project-part-2/

Switching to Breakpoint Mode

The responsive eLearning workflow was added to Captivate back in version 8, and the Fluid Boxes workflow was added in version 2017. In Captivate 8 and 9, you could create responsive eLearning courses using the Breakpoint Mode. This approach, based on breakpoints, is still available in the Captivate 2017 and 2019 release:

- **Breakpoints** are the different layouts that are designed based on the viewport size of the devices your students use.
- **Viewport size** is the visible area (excluding the area covered by the address bar and other menu options) in the device browser.

You can use the Breakpoints approach if you have an older Responsive Project to maintain, or if you feel more at ease with the Breakpoint approach rather than with the Fluid Boxes approach.

Follow these steps to switch to the Breakpoint Mode in Captivate 2019:

1. Create a new Responsive Project in Captivate 2019.
2. Click **File | Save**, navigate to the `Chapter 10` folder, and save the file as `Breakpoints.cptx`.
3. Click the **Project** menu and select **Switch to Breakpoint Mode:**

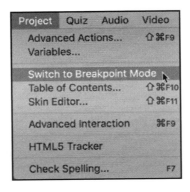

4. You will get an alert that all your Fluid Box layouts will be lost. Click **Yes** to confirm.
5. This will give you another opportunity to save the file with a new name so that you don't lose your work. We have created a brand new project, so let's click **Save** to continue using the same name.

6. Click **Yes** to replace the existing project.

7. This creates the project in Breakpoint Mode and you can continue from here to create Responsive Projects in a similar fashion as in Captivate 9.

Responsive eLearning with Breakpoints:
Here are a few handy resources for learning how to create Responsive Projects in the Breakpoint Mode:

How do I create my first responsive project?: `http://bit.ly/Cp9FirstResponsive`

Tips and Tricks for Creating Responsive Courses: `http://poojajaisingh.com/pooja/cp9/responsive.pdf`

Summary

After reading this chapter, you have been exposed to the tools and techniques used to create a responsive eLearning project.

Remember that Responsive Projects let you optimize the way your content looks on mobile devices. To do this, Captivate uses Fluid Boxes to automatically lay out the content on the screen so that it looks good on all device sizes. The default properties of Fluid Boxes give you a nice result, but you can modify these defaults to make the content look better for smaller devices.

If you are more comfortable creating your responsive eLearning courses using the legacy Breakpoint Mode, or if you have to maintain Responsive Projects created with Captivate 8 or 9, you can still switch to the legacy Breakpoint Mode.

You also have the ability to save a regular (non-responsive) Captivate project as a Responsive Project. However, as a Responsive Project can only be published in HTML5, keep in mind that some objects cannot be carried over in a Responsive Project, and you might need to adjust a few things manually before or after the conversion.

With a bit of practice and a lot of testing throughout your development, you'll soon be an expert at creating responsive eLearning content that your students will be able to use across all their devices.

In the next chapter, you will learn how to create Virtual Reality courses and add 360° slides to normal courses in Adobe Captivate 2019.

Meet the community

At the end of this chapter, we want to introduce you to Richard Vass. Richard is one of the co-founders of the custom division at eLearning Brothers. He was designing and developing in Captivate before it was even called Captivate (back in the RoboDemo days).

Richard Vass

Richard is a dynamic, experienced consultant and professional facilitator with over 20 years of experience in the field of human performance and development. He is a co-founder and Director of Custom Solutions Strategies at eLearning Brothers Custom and has forged a number of deep relationships with leaders in the field of professional learning services, where he has been fortunate enough to provide significant contributions to an impressive list of clients. As a Certified Professional in Learning and Performance (CPLP), Richard has designed and developed Captivate solutions ranging from mobile responsive to complex branching, and has been a key resource on learning showcase projects for Adobe's Captivate releases since 2012.

Contact details

- LinkedIn: https://www.linkedin.com/in/richvass/
- Twitter: https://twitter.com/rvass2
- Blog: https://elearningbrothers.com/elearning-blog/

11
Creating Virtual Reality Projects

In addition to being trendy, **Virtual Reality (VR)** is a very effective way to approach eLearning in a growing number of situations. With Adobe Captivate 2019, you can now add 360° media assets (images and videos) to your Captivate projects and create courses that can be consumed on Virtual Reality devices. This new mode of content delivery will allow you to engage your learners in near-real-life scenarios.

Typical topics for such VR courses include virtual tours, safety drills, first responder situations, crisis management, and so on, but of course the sky's the limit, and it is your imagination that will ultimately define what VR will be used for.

Traditionally, these courses have been created in a 2D environment. VR allows learners to explore an immersive environment, where they take center stage and look around to get a clear and complete picture of the environment.

In this chapter, you will do the following:

- Create a Virtual Reality project
- Insert 360° images and videos
- Add Labels, Hotspots, and quiz questions to 360 slides
- Use Guided and Exploratory options
- Add 360° slides to static and responsive projects

Preparing your work

In this chapter, you will use the exercises stored in the Chapter11 folder. If you get confused by any of the step-by-step instructions, take a look at the Chapter11/final folder, which contains a copy of the file as it will be at the end of this chapter.

Creating a Virtual Reality project

In Chapter 01, *Getting Started with Adobe Captivate 2019*, you experienced a completed VR project. In this chapter, you will learn how to create this project yourself. The first step is to create a new VR project in Adobe Captivate 2019:

1. Open Adobe Captivate 2019, or close any open file, so you see the Welcome screen.
2. On the Welcome Screen, under **New** tab, double-click **Virtual Reality Project**. You can also use the **File | New Project | Virtual Reality Project** menu item to perform the same action.

This creates a new VR project for you. After a few seconds, you will see the familiar Captivate interface, but on the stage, you will find a 360° placeholder image. Before learning about 360 images and videos, let's make a quick tour of the Captivate interface when a VR project is open.

3. Take a look at the **Toolbar** at the top of the screen and try to spot the differences between the Toolbar of a VR project and the regular Toolbar of Adobe Captivate.

You should see the following differences:

- First, you see a new icon called **Hotspots**. *Hotspots* are special objects that are only relevant in a VR project. This explains why this icon was not available when you were working on other types of projects. You will learn more about Hotspots later in this chapter.
- Lots of icons on the Toolbar (such as the **Themes** icon, the **Objects** icon, the **Interactions** icon, and so on) are disabled. This is because the objects that these icons allow you to insert in Captivate are not supported by the VR project type.

Finally, be aware that a VR project can only be published in HTML5 format, so all the restrictions and unsupported objects of a regular HTML5 project also apply to VR projects. You will now save your new VR project using the following steps.

4. Use the **File | Save** menu item, the **Save** icon on the **Toolbar,** or the *Ctrl +S* (Windows)/*command + S* (Mac) shortcut to save the new VR project.
5. Navigate to the Chapter 11 folder and save the file as VR_Project.cptx.

Now that the project exists and is saved to disk, you can add 360 assets to the project.

Adding 360 images and videos

A 360° image is a photographic/graphic image that is designed to be rendered by the computer as a 360° sphere, with your learner looking out from the absolute center of the sphere. If you take a look at a 360° image outside Captivate, it appears distorted, with curved edges at the top and bottom. Let's take a look at one such image:

1. Use Windows Explorer (Windows) or Finder (Mac) to navigate to the `Chapter11/images` folder for the exercises.
2. Double-click the `Living Room.jpeg` image to open it in the default image viewer of your system.

The following screenshot represents the `Living Room.jpeg` image as seen on a Mac using the Preview application:

This is the same image that was used in the example project you previewed in `Chapter 01`, *Getting Started with Adobe Captivate 2019*. Notice how the image is distorted and has curved edges when viewed outside Captivate.

3. Close the image and return to the Captivate project.
4. In the `VR_Project.cptx` project, click the **Add 360 Image / Video** button located at the center of the first slide.

5. Navigate to the `Chapter11/images` folder of the exercise, and select the `Living Room.jpeg` image. Click **Open** to insert the selected picture into Captivate.

The image is added as the background of slide 1. The first thing you should notice is that the distortions and curved edges that were visible when viewing the image from outside of Captivate are gone! This is because each slide of a VR project is its own 360° virtual world! Let's experiment with this hands-on approach, using the following steps.

6. Click and drag the mouse on the image to rotate the view and see different parts of the image. Notice how the image you have seen outside Captivate is used as the background image of an entire 360° experience! Now, let's add one more 360° slide to this project.

7. Go to the Toolbar, and click **Slides | 360 Slide**. Notice that the **Slides** icon on the Toolbar only lets you add 360 slides when in a VR project. In other words, regular slides are not supported in a VR project. That being said, it is possible to add 360 slides in a regular Captivate project (with a few restrictions though). But, you will learn about that workflow later in the chapter. First, let's add another 360 background image to slide 2.

8. On slide 2, click the **Add 360 Image / Video** button located at the center of the slide. The **Select 360 degree Image/Video** dialog opens.

9. Click the **Import** button.

10. Navigate to the Captivate Gallery (remember, the Gallery is located at `C:\Program Files\AdobeAdobe Captivate 2019 x64\Gallery\` if you are on Windows and `/Applications/Adobe Captivate 2019/Gallery/360BGAssets` if you are on a Mac).

11. Go to the `360BGAssets` subfolder of the gallery. In the `360BGAssets` folder, you can find seven different `.jpg` images. You can use these images as background images for your 360° slides in Captivate projects.

12. Select any of these images and click **Open**. The selected image is now used as the background of slide 2. These 360° background images can be easily replaced with other images. Use the following steps to replace the 360 background image of slide 2.

13. Go to the **Properties** inspector.

14. Under the **Style** tab, click the button with the image name.
15. In the **Select 360 degree Image/Video** dialog, click **Import**.
16. In the `360BGAssets` folder, select any other image and click **Open**.

The selected image now replaces the previous background on slide 2. If you ever want to delete this 360° image from the slide background, go to the **Properties** inspector and click the **Clear** icon next to the background image's name. These operations are illustrated in the following screenshot:

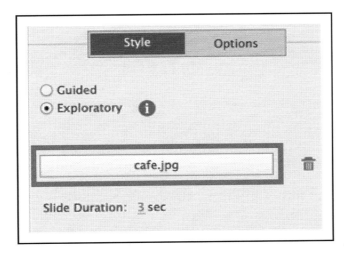

Similar to 360° images, you can also add 360° videos to the slides in a VR project. You can follow the same steps to add, replace, or delete a 360° video for the slide.

You can use a 360 camera to record 360° pictures and videos. These cameras typically take two 180° pictures and then stitch them together to provide you a complete 360° view.

Some phone apps also allow you to click 360° pictures by taking and stitching together multiple pictures as a single 360-degree image.

Alternately, you can search for 360° images or videos in a Stock photo library such as Adobe Stock: `https://stock.adobe.com/`

Adding Text Labels

After adding 360° images or videos as slide backgrounds for 360 slides, you can add several objects on top of those special slides. In this section, let's add Text Labels to the 360 slides:

1. Go back to Slide 1. You have already added a 360° image to this slide.
2. Click and drag the mouse on the image to rotate the view and stop when you have the main view visible (refer to the next screenshot).
3. Use the **Text | Label** icon on the **Toolbar**. This adds a text label at the center of the slide. Use the **Properties** inspector to modify the content and the formatting of the Text Label.
4. With the new Text Label selected, turn your attention to the **Properties** inspector.
5. In the **Label** field, delete the placeholder text and enter Wei's Apartment.
6. Change the font style to **Verdana** and increase the font size to **72** points.
7. Change the **Highlight** color to white. The Highlight Color is the background of the Text Label.
8. Change the **Color** of the text to any contrasting color.
9. Feel free to further adjust the formatting properties.

After these steps, slide 1 should look similar to the following screenshot:

You will now take some time to move the label to get a sense of how this label integrates into the virtual 3D environment of the slide.

10. Grab the label with your mouse and move it around the slide. See how the label integrates into the 3D space.

11. Also, grab the background image and move it around to see how the label moves with the background image. Now, the only thing missing on this slide is the narration. Let's add it and finalize slide 1.

12. Go to the **Toolbar**, and use the **Media | Audio** icon.

13. Navigate to the `Chapter11/audio/Introduction.wav` file and click **Open**.

14. In the **Audio Import Options** dialog, select the **Show the slide for the same amount of time as the length of the audio file** option and click **OK**.

This adds the narration file as the Slide Audio of Slide 1.

15. Click the **Timeline** bar at the bottom of the screen. Notice that the slide duration is 15.7 seconds, but the Label display duration is just 3 seconds.

16. To increase the duration of Label to match the slide duration, right-click the **Label** object in the **Timeline** panel and select **Show for the rest of the slide**. You can also use the *Ctrl + E* (Windows)/*command + E* (Mac) shortcut to perform the same operation.

Slide 1 is now ready and gives a good introduction to the topic. It's now time to add the Hotspots!

Adding Hotspots

Hotspots are special objects that can be added to 360 slides only. They are used to add interactivity to 360 slides. You can use them to display text, play some audio, or display an image. You can also use them to navigate to other slides inside your project. You will now add Hotspots to the second slide of your project, using the following steps:

1. Go to slide 2 and turn your attention to the **Properties** inspector.

2. Under the **Style** tab, click the trash can icon to remove the current 360 image from the slide background.

3. Click the **Add 360 Image / Video** button located at the center of the slide.

4. In the **Select 360 degree Image/Video** dialog, select the `Living Room.jpeg` image and click **OK**. Since this image is already present in the **Library** (it is used as the background image of slide 1), there is no need to import it again.

5. Click and drag the mouse on the image to move the sofa to the center of the slide.

You will now add a first interactive Hotspot to your VR project, using the following steps.

6. Click the **Hotspots** icon on the **Toolbar**. As shown in the following screenshot, this opens a list of pre-made hotspots. You can either use these or add your own by clicking the **Image** button:

In this example though, you will use one of the predefined Hotspots provided by Captivate.

7. Select any of the Hotspot icons from the Hotspots drop-down menu to insert a new interactive hotspot into your project. A Hotspot appears at the center of the slide.

8. Click anywhere on the slide to deselect the hotspot. You should see that the size of the Hotspot decreases when it is not selected.

9. Click the Hotspot to select it. Now, the size of the Hotspot increases to let you know it is selected.

10. With the Hotspot still selected, turn your attention to the **Properties** inspector.

11. Open the **On Click** dropdown.

Take some time to inspect the list of available actions, as depicted in the following screenshot:

You may select any one of these actions to be performed when the learner clicks the Hotspot during the VR experience. The default action is **Go to the next slide**. This will cause the project to move to the next available slide, and the learner would leave the 360 VR space currently displayed.

12. Select the **Display Text** action from the drop-down list, and then enter a short sentence or paragraph into the available field. Now, it's time to preview this slide and see the Hotspot in action.

13. Go to the **Toolbar** and click **Preview | From this Slide**. Remember that a VR project can only be published in HTML5, so after a few seconds, the preview opens in your default web browser and not in the **Preview** pane of Captivate.

14. Click the **Play** button to begin previewing the project.

15. Once your project is loaded, click and hold the left mouse button down, while dragging the mouse to the left and right, and up and down, to move in the 3D space.

16. When you have seen the space, navigate back to the Hotspot and click it.

The text you entered in the **Properties** inspector appears as an overlay and automatically disappear after a few seconds. You then see a green check mark in the top-right corner of the Hotspot, which indicates that the Hotspot has been visited. Don't hesitate to click it again if you wish to see the text overlay again. Congratulations! You have successfully added your first interactive hotspot to a 360 slide. You have used it to trigger an action that displays some text when clicking the Hotspot. Now, let's return to Captivate in order to take a look at the other options available for Hotspots.

17. Close the preview and go back to Captivate.

18. Make sure the Hotspot is selected and turn your attention to the **Properties** inspector.

Using the **Properties** inspector, you can adjust the amount of time that the text overlay appears using the **Display Duration** property below the text entry field. If you want to force the learner to click a given Hotspot before moving on to the next slide, check the **Must view once** option. You will now remove this Hotspot before moving on to the next section.

19. Select the Hotspot on the slide and press the *Delete* key on your keyboard.
20. Click **OK** to confirm the deletion.

Now that you have a better idea of what Hotspots are and the available options, you will add the required Hotspots to your project in the next section.

Adding Hotspots to display text

In the next few sections, you will be adding some custom Hotspot images and assigning different actions to them. Let's start with the **Display Text** action:

1. Return to slide 2 of the VR_project.cptx file.
2. To add a custom image as a Hotspot, go to the **Toolbar** and click **Hotspots | Image**.
3. Navigate to the Chapter11/hotspots folder.
4. In the **Enable** dropdown, select **Png Files(*.png)**.
5. Select Angle.png and click **Open**.
6. Click and drag the Angle Hotspot right above the sofa.
7. With the Hotspot still selected, turn your attention to the **Properties** inspector.
8. Open the **On Click** dropdown and select **Display Text**.
9. Go to the Chapter 11 folder and open the Text.txt file in any text editor.
10. Copy the paragraph below [text display - over sofa].
11. Go back to Captivate and paste this text into the **Text** field of the **Properties** inspector.
12. Change the display duration to 9 seconds.

After these steps, the **Properties** inspector of your first Hotspot should look like the following screenshot:

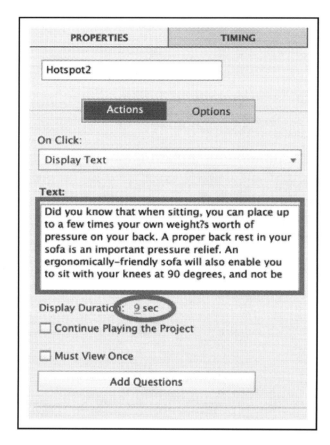

Don't hesitate to use the **Preview** icon to test this new Hotspot before moving on to the next section.

Extra credit – Adding another display text Hotspot

In this extra credit section, you will repeat the sequence of actions of the previous section to add a second text Hotspot to your 360 slide. Click and drag the 360 background image to the right to bring the right side of the balcony into focus. You need to add the Seasons hotspot to the top-right corner of the balcony and display a text caption upon clicking that Hotspot.

These are the general steps to follow:

1. Add a custom hotspot, using `Seasons.png` image.
2. Apply the **Display Text** action.
3. Copy and paste the text from the `Text.txt` file to the **Text** field in Captivate.
4. Change the **Display Duration** to `12` seconds.

Don't hesitate to use the **Preview** icon to test the new Hotspot before moving on to the next section.

Adding Hotspots to display images

Now, it's time to add the third Hotspot to the slide, but this time you want to display an image when the learner clicks the Hotspot:

1. Click and drag the 360 background image to the right to bring the balcony door into focus.
2. Go to the **Toolbar** and click **Hotspots | Image**.
3. Navigate to the `Chapter11/hotspots` folder.
4. In the **Enable** dropdown, select **Png Files(*.png)**.
5. Select `Garden.png` and click **Open**.
6. Click and drag the Garden hotspot to place it on the balcony door.
7. With the Hotspot still selected, turn your attention to the **Properties** inspector.
8. Open the **On Click** dropdown and select **Display Image**.
9. Click the **Browse** icon (the yellow folder icon) below the dropdown and navigate to the `Chapter11/images` folder.
10. Select the `360GardenImage.jpg` file and click **Open**.

After these steps, the **Properties** inspector of the new Hotspot should look like the following screenshot:

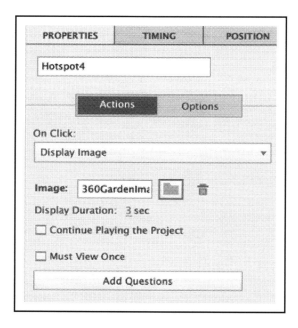

Feel free to modify the other properties of the Hotspot (such as the **Display Duration** property) and to test your new Hotspot using the **Preview** icon on the **Toolbar** before continuing to the next section.

Adding Hotspots to play audio

For the next Hotspot, you want to experiment with the **Play Audio** action. Use the following steps to add the next Hotspot to your 360 slide:

1. Click and drag the 360 background image to the right to bring the bedroom door into focus.
2. Go to the **Toolbar** and click **Hotspots | Image**.
3. Navigate to Chapter11/hotspots folder.
4. In the **Enable** dropdown, select **Png Files(*.png)**.
5. Select Sleep.png and click **Open**.

6. Click and drag the Sleep hotspot to place it correctly on the bedroom door.
7. With the Hotspot still selected, turn your attention to the **Properties** inspector.
8. Open the **On Click** dropdown and select the **Play Audio** action.
9. Click the **Browse** icon next to **Audio**.
10. In the **Select Audio from the Library** dialog, click the **Import** button.
11. Navigate to the `Chapter11/audio` folder.
12. Select the `Sleep.wav` file from the folder and click **Open**.

Take some time to examine the other options available in the **Properties** inspector when the **Play Audio** action is selected. Also, don't hesitate to test the new Hotspot using the **Preview** icon on the **Toolbar** before moving on to the next section.

Adding quiz questions

Now that you have a good idea of how to add Hotspots and associate actions with them, let's take a step forward. In this section, you will use Hotspots to display quiz questions in the 3D environment of your VR project. This allows you to create highly engaging and immersive eLearning content. Use the following steps to add an extra Hotspot and associate a Question slide to it:

1. Click and drag the 360 background image to the right to bring the kitchen area into focus.
2. Go to the **Toolbar** and click **Hotspots**.
3. Select the question mark hotspot from the second row (Note that you can associate Question slides with any Hotspot; just pick the one that is best suited for the situation).
4. Click and drag the Question Hotspot to place it below the kitchen chimney.
5. With the Hotspot still selected, click the **Add Questions** button in the **Properties** inspector.

This opens the **Insert Questions** dialog. Notice that, at the time of writing, only **Multiple Choice** and **True / False** questions are supported in VR projects. These questions can be either Graded or Knowledge Check questions. Survey and Pretest questions are not supported in VR projects.

In this dialog, you can select one or more questions to be presented to the learners when the Hotspot is clicked. For this exercise, let's just select one True/False question.

6. Select the checkbox for **True/False**. Let the count be at 1 and the question type as **Graded**, then click **OK**.

Captivate adds three additional slides after slide 2. In the upcoming sections, you will review these three slides one by one.

Working with slide 3 – the Question Slide

The first slide that has been added by Captivate when generating the True / False question in the previous section is the Question Slide itself. Observe the differences and similarities between this slide and the other slides in your Captivate project:

- This is a True/False question slide.
- Notice that the background image from the previous slide is already applied to this slide.
- Take a look at the **Filmstrip** and notice that this slide is set as an Overlay slide, similar to the Overlay slides for Interactive Videos.
- The appearance of this question slide is different than the regular questions and looks more like an overlay.
- The **Quiz** inspector has the same options as the regular quiz questions.
- To populate the question, you need to double-click the text for question stem, options, and feedback captions.
- To select the correct response, you need to click the radio button for the correct option, just like you do for regular questions.
- The Quiz Reporting for these questions is enabled by default in the **Quiz** inspector.

Now, let's start populating this question slide:

1. Copy and paste the question stem from the `Chapter 11/Text.txt` file to the Question slide.
2. Select the question stem text on the slide, go to the **Properties** inspector, and change the font size to 20 points so that it fits correctly on the slide.
3. Let the correct answer selection remain **True**.
4. Copy and paste the correct and incorrect feedback captions from the `Chapter 11/Text.docx` file to the Question slide.

Don't worry about the feedback text not fitting in the area, as only one of the feedback will be displayed in the top-right corner of the question overlay when the learner answers the course.

The question slide should now look like the following screenshot:

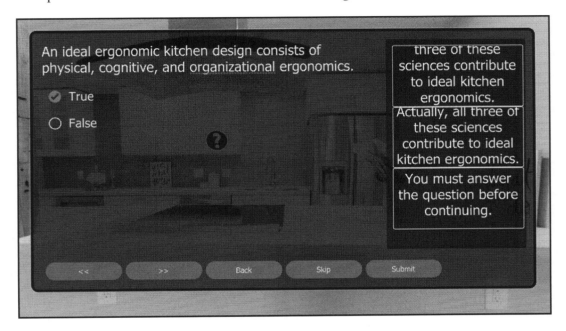

Now that the Question slide is in place, let's take a look at the other two slides that were generated by Captivate when adding the True/False question to the project.

Working with the Quiz Results Slide

The other two slides added by Captivate when creating the True/False question allow you to display the Quiz Result slide. Slide 4 is the background slide for the Quiz Results overlay, which is slide 5:

1. Use the **Filmstrip** to go to slide 4.
2. Click the **Add 360 Image / Video** button located at the center of the slide.

3. In the **Select 360 degree Image/Video** dialog, select the `Living Room.jpeg` image, and click **OK**. The image used as the background of slide 1 and 2 is now added to slide 4.

4. Use the **Filmstrip** to switch to slide 5. Notice that the background image from slide 4 is applied to this slide.

The functionality of the Quiz Results slide is exactly the same as for a Quiz Results slide in any other Captivate project.

5. Use the **Filmstrip** to go back to slide 2. Here, you need to add an Exit hotspot, which will take the learner to the Quiz Results slide.

6. Click and drag the 360 background image to the right to bring the dining area into focus.

7. Go to the **Toolbar** and click **Hotspots**.

8. Select the **Exit** hotspot from the second row.

9. Position the Exit hotspot somewhere near the floor.

10. With the Hotspot still selected, go to the **Properties** inspector and make sure the **On Click** action is set to **Go to the next slide**.

Remember that in this case, the next slide is slide 4, as slide 3 is the Question Slide used as an overlay of slide 2.

11. Now, click and drag the background image so that the sofa is the main focus.

This last step is extremely important to test your new Hotspot. When viewing the project, Captivate always loads the 360 image from the view you leave the slide at in the authoring environment. Don't hesitate to give it a try using the **Preview** icon on the Toolbar.

You have almost finished creating the VR project. In the next section, there are a few more options and settings to explore.

Guided and Exploratory options

Now, let's talk about the **Guided** and **Exploratory** options available for VR projects in Captivate. You will find these options in the Slide **Properties** inspector. As shown in the following screenshot, the default value for this option is **Exploratory**:

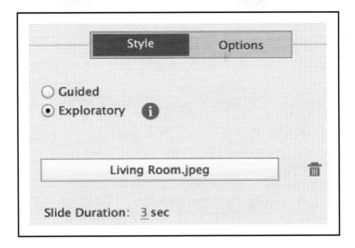

In an **Exploratory** VR slide, learners experience the content with no guidance about which Hotspot should be clicked. They are free to choose which Hotspots they click and in what order you they click them, while exploring the 360 space. Let's preview the project to better understand the **Exploratory** option:

1. In the `Chapter11/VR_project.cptx` file, go to the Toolbar and click **Preview | Project**. After a few seconds, your VR project opens in the default web browser of your system.

2. Click the **Play** icon in the browser window.

3. Click the **Forward** button on the Playbar to go to slide 2.

4. On this slide, click the Hotspots in any order you like. Just save the Exit hotspot for the end, as that will take you to the next slide.

5. After previewing the project, close the browser and go back to the Captivate project.

6. Make sure slide 2 is still selected in the **Filmstrip**.

7. Go to the **Properties** inspector, and select **Guided**.

In a **Guided** experience, learners will be "led" to the next sequential Hotspot, after each Hotspot is triggered. Captivate uses the sequence in the **Timeline** to determine the order of the Hotspots. When viewing the project, Captivate animates the camera to go to the next Hotspot in the sequence automatically. You can easily change the sequence of Hotspots by moving the Hotspots up and down in the **Timeline** panel. Now that slide 2 is set to be a Guided slide, let's preview the project again.

8. Go to the Toolbar and click **Preview** | **Project**.
9. Click the **Play** icon in the browser window.
10. Click the **Forward** button on the Playbar to go to slide 2. This time, you will be guided to the first Hotspot. When you click the first Hotspot, content related to it is displayed. When the content display duration is over, you are automatically redirected to the next Hotspot.
11. After previewing the project, close the browser and go back to the Captivate project.
12. Click the **File** | **Save** menu item to save the changes you made to the project.

You have now explored all the options available in Captivate 2019 when creating a VR project. Let's quickly summarize them all before moving on to the next section:

- VR projects are a new feature of Captivate 2019. They allow you to recreate a complete 360 environment to provide an immersive and efficient eLearning experience to your learners.
- A VR project can only be published in HTML5. Consequently, all the restrictions that apply to a regular HTML5 project also apply to a VR project. Another consequence is that a VR project is always previewed in the default web browser of the system, and not in the **Preview** pane of Captivate.
- In a VR project, each slide is a complete 360 environment. Also, remember that you cannot add regular Captivate slides to a VR project. Only 360 slides can be added in such a project.
- You must add a 360 image or a 360 video as the backgrounds of those 360 slides to generate the 360 environment. Captivate provides a bunch of 360 images in the Gallery to get you started. You can find additional 360 images in Adobe Stock. You can also use your own 360 camera to create your own custom 360 images.
- You can add Text Labels on the 360 slides. Use these labels to add some static text to your 360 environment.

- Hotspots are special Captivate objects that can be added on top of a 360 slide. They are used to add interactivity in the 360 environment.
- Use these Hotspots to perform various actions such as displaying text and images, or playing an audio file right in the 360 environment.
- Hotspots can also be used to display Multiple Choice and True/False Question Slides in the 360 space.
- Each 360 slide can provide either an Exploratory or a Guided experience. In an Exploratory slide, the learner explores the 360 space with no guidance. In a Guided experience, the learner is automatically taken to the next Hotspot in the sequence.
- The Hotspot sequence of a Guided slide depends on the ways the Hotspots are arranged in the **Timeline** panel.

Previewing and publishing VR courses

VR projects in Captivate have the same previewing options as those available for responsive projects. This is because VR projects and Responsive projects have in common the fact that they can only be published (and thus previewed) in HTML5.

One of the new preview options added for both Responsive and VR projects in Adobe Captivate 2019 is the Live Device Preview option. Let's check it out!

Live Device Preview

When developing responsive or VR courses, it is important to experience your eLearning content directly on a mobile device. This allows you to test the touch interactions of a responsive project or to preview a VR project using a real VR device. You can use the live preview feature in Adobe Captivate to generate a QR code that you can scan using a mobile device and mirror the project in real-time on your device browser.

Once the initial connection is done, you can keep previewing all your work across projects as long as the Adobe Captivate session is active. Use the following steps to preview your VR project on your mobile device:

1. Make sure you are still in the `Chapter11/VR_project.cptx` file.
2. On the **Toolbar**, click **Preview | Live Preview on Devices**.

3. This generates a QR Code for you in a browser.
4. Scan the code on your device to see the preview. Make sure your computer and the mobile device are on the same Wi-Fi network.

Some phones, such as iPhone (with OS 11), can scan QR codes with the camera. You can also find free apps that do this.

You can also share the QR code with others who are on the same network, and they will also be able to preview the course.

5. The course preview is now available directly on you mobile device. Tap the **Play** icon to begin.
6. If you have a VR device, tap the **VR** icon on the course playbar.
7. Then, place your phone in the VR device and preview to get a complete 360 experience of your Captivate project.

You can use any VR device to view the VR courses created using Captivate 2019. Here's a list of VR devices by the Captivate engineering team:

- Cardboard: `https://vr.google.com/cardboard/get-cardboard/`
- Google Daydream: `https://vr.google.com/daydream/`
- Galaxy Gear VR: `https://www.samsung.com/global/galaxy/gear-vr/`
- Oculus Go: `https://www.oculus.com/go/`

In the VR space, you can simply move your head to navigate. Because you now have limited ways to interact with the 360 environment, Adobe Captivate 2019 adds a method of triggering events called **Gaze**. Captivate monitors what the learner is looking at, and if an interactive element is the focus of your gaze for more than a few seconds, it clicks or triggers that interaction:

Look for the green animated timer to learn how active gaze will assist learners in clicking by simply looking at an object.

Captivate also adds arrows to guide the learner, rather than automatically shifting the focus to the next Hotspot, when a Guided experience is enabled for the project:

Finally, Captivate provides additional guidance in the form of a navigation menu. If the learner looks downward, they will be given a blue navigation button. This set of four squares launches the control menu, and learners may navigate using this menu:

The VR course is now ready to be published. You can publish and host the VR course on an LMS or a web server. You will learn about the steps to publish a VR course in Chapter 15, *Finishing Touches and Publishing*.

Adding 360 slides to normal projects

Similar to VR projects, you can add 360° slides to normal and responsive projects, and they will work seamlessly alongside the video slides, simulations, quizzes, and so on. When reaching a 360 slide, the learners will be able to navigate the 360° world, using their mouse. But these slides cannot be viewed in VR devices, as the rest of the project uses a 2D environment. Let's experiment with this capability, using the following steps:

1. Use the **File** | **New Project** | **Blank Project** menu item to create a new blank or responsive project in Captivate.
2. Accept the default dimensions for the new project.

3. On the **Toolbar**, click **Slides | 360 Slide**. This adds a 360 slide to your project.

4. Click the **Add 360 Image / Video** button located at the center of the slide.

5. Select the `Chapter11/images/Living Room.jpeg` image and click **Open**.

Now, just like the 360 slide in the VR project, you can add Hotspots and associate different actions to the Hotspots. The only option missing in the 360 slides added to normal projects is that you can't associate question slides with the Hotspots. You can add normal quiz slides for that purpose and use the slide navigation actions.

Also, if you add a 360 slide to your project, you will need to publish the course in HTML5 format, as this workflow is not supported in the Flash (SWF) output.

Summary

In this chapter, you explored the workflow of creating VR courses using Captivate 2019. You learned how to create a VR project in Captivate, add a 360 slide to the project, and add 360° media as a background for the 360 slide.

You then learned how to make the 360 slides interactive by adding Labels, Hotspots, and questions. You also explored the differences between the Guided and Exploratory modes for the slides, and learned about best practices along the way.

Finally, you looked at the workflow to add 360 slides and Hotspots to static and responsive projects, in order to give a 360° experience to your learners in the middle of a regular 2D project.

In the next chapter, you will learn how Captivate integrates with other applications such as Microsoft PowerPoint, Microsoft Word, Adobe Audition, and Adobe Photoshop.

Meet the community

In this section, we would like to introduce you to Debbie Richards. If you wish to know about the latest tech trends and cool gadgets, Debbie is your go-to-person. Her drive to learn about new things and train people on them is truly infectious. She is well-known in the eLearning and Captivate world, and frequently speaks at conferences about the latest innovations and trends in eLearning!

Debbie Richards

Debbie Richards, president of Creative Interactive Ideas, was named one of the most influential people in corporate eLearning in 2018. She works with organizations to design, develop, and deliver technology-based adult learning programs with measurable impact. Debbie loves working with Adobe eLearning programs. She was an early adopter of Adobe Captivate and Dreamweaver. Active in emerging technologies, her latest publication is the ATD at Work issue "Seeing the Possibilities With Augmented Reality."

Passionate about working with and mentoring other learning professionals, she is the president-elect of the Association for Talent Development Houston Chapter and a past ATD national adviser for chapters. She is the 2019 ATD Technology Conference Advisory Council chairperson.

Contact details

- Twitter: @cre8iveii
- LinkedIn: https://www.linkedin.com/in/cre8iveii/

Using Captivate with Other Applications

12

In this chapter, you will explore how Captivate can be used with other applications. These external applications include Adobe products such as Audition, Illustrator, and Photoshop. However, Captivate can also integrate with third-party applications such as Microsoft Word and Microsoft PowerPoint.

There are many benefits to using Captivate with external applications. If you already have a significant amount of training material made with PowerPoint, you'll be able to build on what already exists. If you are localizing your content, you can export Text Captions and Slide Notes to Microsoft Word. This makes it easy for translators to help you localize your eLearning content.

In this chapter, we will do the following:

- Create a new Captivate project from a PowerPoint presentation
- Add a PowerPoint slide in the middle of an existing Captivate project
- Explore the round trip editing workflow between Captivate and PowerPoint
- Localize a Captivate project by exporting Text Captions and Slide Notes to Microsoft Word, and reimporting them back into Captivate once they've been translated
- Import a Photoshop file into Captivate
- Explore round tripping operations with Adobe Audition
- Edit SVGs in Captivate projects with Adobe Illustrator
- Export the project as an XML file

Preparing your work

Before you start this chapter, it is a good idea to take some time and reset the Captivate interface to its default state. If you are using the default interface mode, just close and restart Captivate and you're good to go. If you are using the advanced interface mode, use the **Window | Workspace | Reset 'Classic'** menu item to reset Captivate to its default state. In this chapter, you will use the exercises that are stored in the Chapter12 folder. If you get confused by any of the step-by-step instructions, take a look at the Chapter12/final folder, which contains a copy of the files as they will be at the end of this chapter.

Integrating Captivate with PowerPoint

In this section, you will discover the integration that unites Microsoft **PowerPoint** and Adobe Captivate. This includes features such as creating a new Captivate project from a Microsoft PowerPoint presentation and including slides from a presentation in an existing Captivate project.

Captivate shares these features with another software product from Adobe, called **Adobe Presenter 11**. Adobe Presenter 11 is a Microsoft PowerPoint plugin. In PowerPoint 2007 and later versions, Presenter installs an extra ribbon at the top of the PowerPoint interface. Presenter can be used to publish a PowerPoint presentation to HTML5 and/or SWF using a technique that is similar to what is used in Captivate. Presenter also includes the ability to add narration and subtitles to PowerPoint presentations. It includes pretty much the same quiz engine as the one in Captivate. One of the best features of Presenter is Adobe Presenter Video Express, which allows you to create stunning professional screencasts. The Adobe Presenter PowerPoint plugin is only available on Windows. Adobe Presenter Video Express is available on both Mac and Windows. More information can be found at
http://www.adobe.com/products/presenter.html.

Converting an existing presentation into a Captivate project

In the first exercise of this chapter, you will convert an existing PowerPoint presentation into a new Captivate project. You will use a simple workflow that allows you to open a PowerPoint file from the **Welcome Screen** of Captivate. But first, let's take a look at the original PowerPoint presentation.

Viewing the presentation in PowerPoint

If PowerPoint is available on your system, take a look at the presentation before converting it into a Captivate project. Perform the following steps to view the presentation in PowerPoint:

1. Open Microsoft PowerPoint.
2. When in PowerPoint, open the `Chapter12/Presentation.pptx` presentation in the exercises files.
3. Use the **Slide Show** | **From Beginning** menu item or hit the *F5* shortcut key to start the slideshow.

While viewing the presentation, focus your attention on the following:

- The presentation has 11 slides.
- There is a transition between all of the slides in the presentation.
- The presentation is mainly composed of text and images. Most of it is animated.
- The presentation also contains smart art, shapes, and a table.
- Some of the effects used to animate objects in PowerPoint have an equivalent in Captivate, but some do not.
- Sometimes, a mouse click is needed to go to the next step of the presentation, but sometimes it isn't.
- Slide 2 of the presentation includes Slide Notes.
- The last slide of the presentation has a hyperlink to a blog article that's on the Adobe eLearning Community page.

Grammatical errors and typos have been intentionally left in the presentation. Don't correct them; they will be used to demonstrate the round tripping workflow between Captivate and PowerPoint.

4. Close PowerPoint without saving any changes made to the presentation.

You will now convert this presentation into a Captivate Project and see how the PowerPoint features listed previously are carried over (or not) into Captivate.

Creating a Captivate project from a PowerPoint presentation

In this section, you will convert the file you viewed in PowerPoint into a Captivate project.

Should you use .ppt or .pptx?
Captivate can import both .ppt and .pptx files. However, when importing a .pptx file, it must first be converted into .ppt before being imported into Captivate. Conversion from .pptx to .ppt requires opening the file in PowerPoint. Consequently, PowerPoint must be installed on your computer when importing a .pptx file into Captivate. When importing a .ppt file, conversion is not needed, and therefore PowerPoint is not mandatory.

Before starting this exercise, make sure you have closed the file in PowerPoint. Perform the following steps to convert the PowerPoint presentation into a Captivate project:

1. Return to Captivate and close any open files. The exercise begins on the **Welcome Screen** of Captivate.
2. Switch to the **New** tab of the **Welcome Screen**, if needed.
3. Double-click the **From PowerPoint** Thumbnail, as shown in the following screenshot (alternatively, you can use the **File | New Project | Project From MS PowerPoint** menu item to perform the same operation):

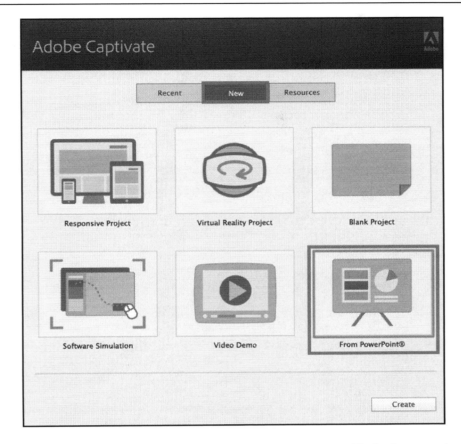

4. Navigate to the `Chapter12/Presentation.pptx` file in the exercises folder and click **Open**. If you don't have PowerPoint installed on your system, open the `Chapter12/Presentation.ppt` file.

Captivate converts PowerPoint slides into Captivate slides. Depending on the presentation to convert, and on the capabilities of your computer, this operation can be quite lengthy, so be patient. When the conversion is finished, Captivate opens the **Convert Microsoft® PowerPoint Presentations** dialog.

5. There are two sections in this dialog, **Project Properties** and **Slide Preview**. In the **Project Properties** section, change the **Name** of the project to `Introduction to Fluid Boxes`.

6. Notice that the **Width** and **Height** of the project is set to `1280` and `720` pixels, respectively. This is a direct conversion of the dimension of the PowerPoint presentation from inches to pixels.

7. Open the **Preset Sizes** dropdown and review the available preview sizes. You can pick one of the presets or you can input the custom values in the **Width** and **Height** fields.

8. If you have made any changes to the values for **Width** and **Height**, change them back to 1280 and 720.

9. In the Slide Preview section, there are thumbnails for all of the slides in the PPT with a small checkbox, allowing you to include or exclude the slide from the Captivate project.

10. You can also use the **Clear All** and **Select All** buttons to quickly select or deselect the entire set of slides. In this case, you want to import the entire PowerPoint presentation into Captivate, so make sure all the PowerPoint slides are selected before moving on.

11. At the end of the dialog, set the **Advance Slide** option to **On mouse click**.

12. Make sure the **Linked** checkbox is selected.

It is very important to get these last two options right! The **Advance Slide** option lets you decide how Captivate advances from one slide to the next:

- By choosing **On mouse click**, Captivate will generate a Click Box on top of every imported slide. This Click Box stops the Playhead and waits for the student to click anywhere on the slide to continue to the next step of the project.

- The **Automatically** option moves to the next slide automatically after the defined duration. You can also select **Automatically** if you wish to use your own navigation buttons in the Captivate project.

The **Linked** checkbox is even more important. Captivate proposes two ways to insert a PowerPoint presentation in a project. They are as follows:

- When **Linked** is not selected, you create an **Embedded** presentation. This means that a copy of the original PowerPoint presentation is entirely integrated into the .cptx file. This copy is completely independent from the original .pptx (or .ppt) file.

- When the **Linked** checkbox is selected, the PowerPoint presentation is also embedded in Captivate, but Captivate maintains a link between the copy of the PowerPoint file that is embedded in the .cptx file and the original PowerPoint file. This link can be used to update the Captivate file when a change is made to the PowerPoint presentation.

13. If you are on the Windows platform, make sure you select the **High Fidelity** option. This will ensure that all the PowerPoint objects, such as animations, Smart Art, effects, tables, triggers, and so on are imported into your Captivate project correctly. This option is not available on Mac.

Make sure the **Convert Microsoft® PowerPoint Presentations** dialog box looks like what's shown in the following screenshot before moving on. It might look different when you see it on Mac. Also, if you are importing a .ppt file instead of .pptx, you will not see the **High Fidelity** option on either the Windows or Mac platforms:

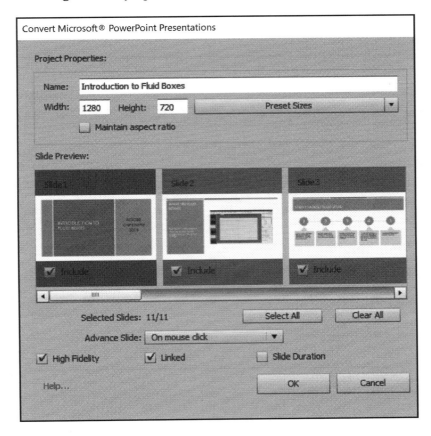

14. Click the **OK** button.

Captivate creates a new project from the original PowerPoint presentation. Depending on the presentation to convert and on the capabilities of your computer, this process can be quite lengthy, so be patient. When the import process has finished, an 11 slides project is loaded into Captivate. In the **Filmstrip** panel, notice that each slide has a name that is derived from the slide title, as it was entered in PowerPoint.

You will now test the entire project to see how well (or how badly) Captivate handles the conversion from PowerPoint.

15. Save the file as `Chapter12/Introduction to Fluid Boxes.cptx`.

16. Use the **Preview** | **Project** icon on the Toolbar to test the entire project in the Preview pane.

Now, test the entire project. You will notice the following:

- Captivate does a pretty good job of converting a PowerPoint presentation into a Captivate project.
- Most animations are carried over from PowerPoint, even if a corresponding effect does not exist in Captivate.
- Slide transitions are NOT carried over from the PowerPoint presentation. If you need to apply slide transitions, you will have to apply them again inside Captivate using the **Timing** inspector. However, if you plan to publish the course in HTML5 format, Transitions applied to Captivate slides will not work, as they are not supported in HTML5 format.
- On slide 11, the link is NOT functional. You will make it functional in the following exercise.

The conversion of the PowerPoint presentation into a Captivate project is now complete.

17. Close the **Preview** pane when done.

What you just experienced in the **Preview** pane is close to how students will experience the project. You will now take a closer look at the Captivate editing environment to discover other properties from the original presentation that are carried over in Captivate.

18. Now, let's make the link work on slide 11. Use the **Filmstrip** to return to the last slide of the project.

19. Select the Click Box covering the slide and press the *Delete* key on the keyboard. This big Click Box, which was added as a consequence of selecting the **Advance Slide on mouse click** option in the Import dialog, was hindering the functionality of the hyperlink on the slide. Removing it will make the hyperlink functional.

20. Use the **Preview | From this slide** icon on the Toolbar to test the slide in the Preview pane.

21. Click the hyperlink text at the bottom-left corner of the slide. It will open the **Adobe Captivate (2019 release) and Fluid boxes 2.0** article on the Adobe eLearning Community site.

22. Go back to Captivate and close the **Preview** pane.

23. Use the **Filmstrip** to go to slide 2 of the project.

24. Use the **Window | Slide Notes** menu item to open the **Slide Notes** panel. Remember that, by default, this panel appears at the bottom of the screen, next to the **Timeline**.

The Slide Notes typed in Microsoft PowerPoint have been imported into the **Slide Notes** panel of Captivate. Remember that these Slide Notes can be converted into Speech and Closed Captions. The fact that Captivate imports this data from PowerPoint is a great productivity feature and a huge time-saver.

 Warning:
The Slide Notes that are added to the original PowerPoint file after it has been converted into a Captivate project will not be synced with the Captivate file.

25. Use the **Filmstrip** to go to slide 3.

26. At the bottom of the screen, open the **Timeline** panel.

In PowerPoint, this slide is made up of quite a few pieces of text and objects. You would expect the Captivate version of that slide to contain a lot of objects. Unfortunately, the PowerPoint-to-Captivate conversion does not go that far. In Captivate, each PowerPoint slide is considered a single animated object. The individual components of this animation do not show up in the **Timeline** panel.

Consequently, modifying the content or the layout of the project must be done in PowerPoint, not in Captivate. In the next section, you will learn how you can modify the project in PowerPoint and import the edits in Captivate through a process called Round Tripping.

Round Tripping between Captivate and PowerPoint

Round Tripping is the process by which you can invoke PowerPoint from within Captivate, edit the presentation in PowerPoint, and import the modifications back into Captivate. If you are working on Windows, PowerPoint can even be displayed within the Captivate interface, so you won't even have to leave the Captivate environment. If you are working on a Mac, you'll be redirected to the actual PowerPoint application.

The following exercise requires both PowerPoint and Captivate to be installed on your computer. On Windows, Office 2003 (SP3) or higher is required. On Mac, Office 2004 or higher will do.

In the next exercise, you will modify a slide in PowerPoint and return to Captivate using the following steps:

1. Still in the `Chapter12/Introduction to Fluid Boxes.cptx` file, use the **Filmstrip** to go to slide 3.
2. Right-click anywhere on the slide and choose **Edit With Microsoft PowerPoint | Edit Presentation**, as shown in the following screenshot. Please note that this screenshot is from a Windows machine. You might not see some of the menu items on Mac:

If you get a message saying that Captivate is unable to open the PowerPoint presentation because of a permission problem, return to PowerPoint to make sure that the presentation is closed before starting this procedure in Captivate.

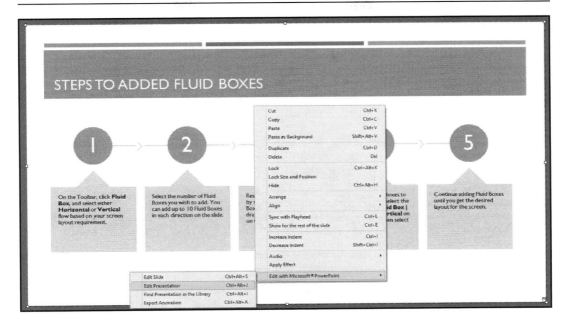

What follows depends on the operating system you are working on. On **Windows**, PowerPoint opens within the Captivate Interface, allowing you to edit the presentation using all the tools and features of PowerPoint without even leaving Captivate. On **Mac**, PowerPoint automatically opens in its own separate window and loads the presentation you want to edit.

Pay close attention to the remaining steps of this exercise. The round tripping experience on Windows is very different from the one on Mac.

3. [**Mac Only**]: When PowerPoint is open, go to slide 3 of the PowerPoint presentation.
4. [**Everyone**]: On slide 3, change **ADDED** to ADD in the title.
5. [**Mac Only**]: Use the **File | Save** menu item of PowerPoint to save the presentation.
6. [**Mac Only**]: Return to Captivate. A message asks if you want to import the updated presentation. Click **Yes** and let Captivate make the necessary changes in the project.
7. [**Mac Only**]: Close the PowerPoint application manually.

8. **[Windows Only]**: Click the **Save** button in the upper-left corner of the interface. PowerPoint closes and the Captivate project is automatically updated.
9. **[Everyone]**: Save the Captivate file when done.
10. **[Everyone]**: Use the **Preview | Project** icon on the Toolbar to preview the entire project in the preview pane.

When the preview reaches slide 3, pay close attention to the text in the title. The modification that's been made in PowerPoint should be reflected in the Captivate project.

Updating a linked PowerPoint presentation

In the next exercise, you will open PowerPoint and modify the presentation in the PowerPoint application. This is very different from what you did in the previous exercise, where the workflow was triggered from Captivate. You will then return to Captivate and update the project accordingly. The steps are as follows:

1. Return to PowerPoint and open the `Chapter12/Presentation.pptx` file.
2. Go to slide 6 of the presentation and change **WRAPP** to `WRAP` in the title.
3. **Save** the presentation and close PowerPoint.
4. Return to Captivate.

Because you selected the **Linked** checkbox when converting the PowerPoint presentation, Captivate is able to pick up on the changes made in the PowerPoint file and should display the same message, asking if you want to import the updated presentation. If the message is not displayed automatically, the **Library** panel offers a way to manually update the Captivate Project so that it reflects the changes made in the PowerPoint presentation.

5. If the message is displayed on your screen, click **No** to close the message without updating the Captivate project.
6. Open the **Library** panel next to the **Properties** inspector on the right-hand side of the screen.
7. In the **Presentations** section of the **Library**, locate the **Presentation** object.

Notice the red dot in the **Status** column, as shown in the following screenshot. It indicates that the linked PowerPoint presentation and the Captivate project are out of sync:

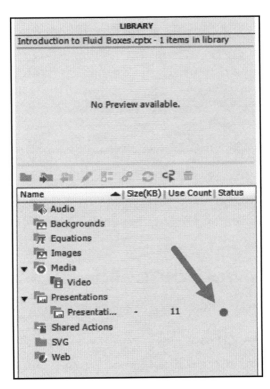

8. In the **Library** panel, click the red dot associated with the presentation.

This refreshes the linked presentation and puts the Captivate project and the PowerPoint presentation back in sync. At the end of the process, the **Status** color should turn back to green.

Using the **Library** panel, there are a few more operations that can be performed on a PowerPoint presentation.

9. In the **Library** panel of Captivate, right-click the **Presentation** object.
10. In the contextual menu, click the **Change To "Embedded"** menu item.
11. Click **OK** to clear the acknowledgment message.

After this operation, the link between the copy of the PowerPoint file that is embedded in Captivate and the external PowerPoint presentation is broken. The changes that were made to the external PowerPoint file will no longer be picked up by Captivate.

12. Still in the **Presentations** folder of the **Library**, right-click the **Presentation** object again.
13. In the contextual menu, click the **Change To "Linked"** menu item.
14. Browse to the `/Chapter12` folder of the exercises files and save the PowerPoint file as `Chapter12/Presentation_linked.ppt`.
15. Again, click the **OK** button to clear the message.
16. Save the Captivate project when done.

This operation saves a new copy of the embedded PowerPoint presentation as a new PowerPoint file and creates a link between this new file and the Captivate Project. It is not possible to actually recreate the link to the original PowerPoint file. Instead, you create a new PowerPoint file, and link that new file to the Captivate project.

Inserting a PowerPoint slide into a Captivate Project

In the previous two sections, you learned how to convert an entire PowerPoint presentation into a new Captivate project. But sometimes, only a few PowerPoint slides must be inserted in the middle of an existing Captivate project.

In the next exercise, you will insert a single PowerPoint slide in the middle of the *Introduction to the Fluid Boxes* project you created in the previous exercise, using the following steps:

1. Open the `Chapter12/Additional PPT Slides.cptx` file in the exercises folder.
2. In the **Filmstrip**, make sure Slide 1 is selected. You need to add a new slide with course objectives after this slide.
3. Click the **Slides | PowerPoint Slide** icon on the Toolbar.

4. In the dialog box, make sure that **Slide 1** is selected, as shown in the following screenshot:

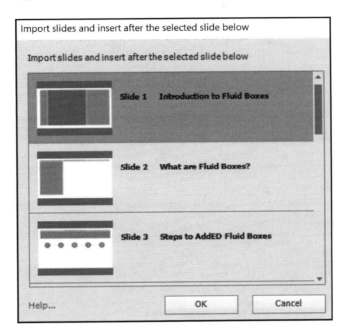

The imported PowerPoint slide(s) will be inserted after the slide that was selected in this dialog.

5. Click the **OK** button and browse to the Chapter12/Objectives.pptx PowerPoint file in the exercises folder. Click the **Open** button.

6. In the **Convert PowerPoint Presentations** dialog, open the **Advance Slide** dropdown and select the **Automatically** option.

This time, you do not want Captivate to generate an extra Click Box on top of the slide, as you did when converting a PowerPoint file earlier in this chapter.

7. Select the **High Fidelity** option if you are on Windows and have imported a .pptx file.

8. Leave the other options at their current value and click the **OK** button.

The PowerPoint slide is inserted as slide 2 of the *Additional PPT Slides* project.

You will now insert a native Captivate object on top of the imported PowerPoint slide. Note that adding a PowerPoint slide to a Captivate project can be done with any Captivate project, including projects that do not originate from a converted PowerPoint presentation.

9. With the new Objectives slide selected, use the **Shapes** icon on the Toolbar to draw a rounded rectangle on the bottom-right corner of the slide.
10. Double-click in the rounded rectangle and write Continue into the shape.
11. In the **Properties** inspector, select the **Use as Button** checkbox.
12. In the **Actions** tab of the **Properties** inspector, make sure that the **On Success** action of the new button is set to **Go to the next slide**.
13. Move and resize the button so that it integrates nicely with the rest of the slide.
14. Save the file when done.
15. Use the **Preview | Project** icon on the Toolbar to test the entire project.

In this exercise, you have inserted a PowerPoint slide in the middle of an existing Captivate Project. This presentation is available in the **Library** of the project and can be edited using the same round tripping workflow that we discussed earlier in this chapter.

This exercise also demonstrates the ability to add standard Captivate objects on top of the imported PowerPoint slides.

Controlling the user experience

Importing the PowerPoint slides with the **Advance Automatically** feature and adding your own buttons on top of the imported slides allows you to have better control of the user experience of imported projects. Lots of Captivate developers adopt the workflow described in this exercise rather than letting Captivate create a Click Box on top of every single PowerPoint slide, as you did in the first exercise of this chapter when choosing **Advance On a Mouse Click**.

This concludes our overview of the integration between Microsoft PowerPoint and Adobe Captivate. Before moving on, it is time to emphasize the key points of what has been covered. They are as follows:

- It is possible to convert an entire PowerPoint presentation into a Captivate project.
- Captivate can import both `.ppt` and `.pptx` files. A `.ppt` file can be imported in Captivate, even if PowerPoint is not installed on the computer. When importing a `.pptx` file, however, PowerPoint must be installed on the system, along with Captivate.
- When converting PowerPoint to Captivate, most animations, effects, and triggers are carried over, even if they are not natively supported by Captivate.
- Each PowerPoint slide is imported as a single animation. It is not possible to access each individual object of the original PowerPoint slide in Captivate.
- An imported presentation cannot be updated in Captivate. To update a presentation, it is necessary to use PowerPoint.
- An imported PowerPoint presentation is either an Embedded presentation or a Linked presentation. An Embedded presentation is entirely integrated into the Captivate project. A Linked presentation is also integrated into the Captivate project, but maintains a link with the original PowerPoint presentation. This link can be used to keep the PowerPoint presentation and the Captivate project in sync.
- **Round Tripping** is a concept that enables you to invoke PowerPoint from within Captivate, update the presentation in PowerPoint, and import the changes back into Captivate.
- The actual Round Tripping experience depends on the operating system in use (Mac or Windows).
- It is also possible to insert only a few PowerPoint slides in the middle of an existing Captivate project.
- All of the objects of Captivate can be inserted on top of the imported PowerPoint slide(s).

In the next section, you will use a workflow that involves Captivate and Microsoft Word to localize a Captivate project.

Importing PowerPoint versus animating native Captivate objects
In early versions of Captivate, the **Effects** panel did not exist. As it was impossible to animate objects directly in Captivate, it was very common to create slides in PowerPoint and insert them in Captivate. Since the introduction of the **Effects** panel in Captivate 5, any native Captivate object can be animated in ways that are very similar to what is found in PowerPoint. In our opinion, PowerPoint integration is a great tool to recycle existing content that's made in PowerPoint, or to involve non-Captivate developers in the production process. That being said, we think that new content should be developed entirely in Captivate whenever possible because it offers far more flexibility and does not require constant back and forth between two heavy applications.

Localizing a Captivate project using Microsoft Word

In this section, you will create the French version of the `takeTheTrain` course (but don't worry if you don't know French!). To produce the French version of the project, there are two basic things to do. They are as follows:

- Translate the Text Captions and the Slide Notes
- Localize the other assets (such as the video file, narration, or additional imported images)

In the following exercise, you will concentrate on the first step of this process and see how Microsoft Word can help you translate the Text Captions and the Slide Notes of your Captivate project using the following steps:

1. Open the `Chapter12/takeTheTrain_English.cptx` file.
2. You need to make a copy of this project for the French version. To do so, use the **File | Save As** option.
3. Navigate to the `Chapter12` folder, change the name of the CPTX file to `takeTheTrain_French.cptx`, and click **Save**.

The file is now ready for the translation of the Text Captions and the Slide Notes in Microsoft Word.

 The following exercise requires Microsoft Word to be installed on your computer, along with Captivate.

4. Make sure you are still in the `Chapter12/takeTheTrain_French.cptx` file.
5. Use the **File** | **Export** | **Project Captions and Closed Captions** menu item to export the Text Captions and the Slide Notes to a Word document.

The export process might take some time. Do not switch between Word and Captivate while the file is generating. Let it run untouched until it's finished.

6. Save the file as `Chapter12/takeTheTrain_French Captions.doc`. Notice that Captivate exports the Word file to `.doc` format and not `.docx` format.

 After exporting and before importing the captions, do not change the name of the Captivate or Word file. Also, do not make any text changes to the Captivate file. It might result in either the import not working, or the incorrect placement of translated captions.

When the export is complete, Captivate displays a message, asking if you want to see the generated Word document.

7. Click **Yes** to open Microsoft Word and view the generated document.

The generated Word document should look like what's shown in the following screenshot:

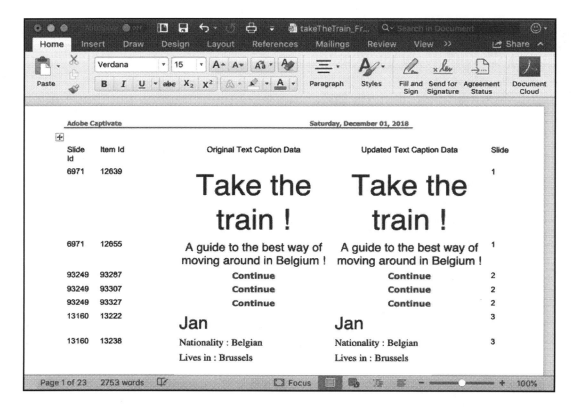

The generated Word document is a five-column table. The first two columns contain the **Slide ID** and **Item ID**. **Do not change anything in the first two columns**. When the translated text is imported back into the project, these two pieces of information will be used by Captivate to uniquely identify the object into which the text needs to be imported.

The third column is the original text as written in the source language. The fourth column is where the translator will work. **The translated text should be entered in the fourth column of the table**.

The last column is the slide number on which the object is found.

If you used white font for the Text Captions in your Captivate project, you might not be able to see them in the Word document, as the background of the Word file is also white. To see the text clearly, change the page background color of the Word file to a shade of grey, so that both black and white text is visible in the document.

8. Change the text in the fourth column of the Word document.

If you don't know French, don't worry. For the sake of this exercise, you can translate the first few captions into any language you want (or just update the text in any way!). After completing this task, save and close the Word document.

You will now import the updated Text Captions and Slide Notes back into the Captivate project.

9. Return to Captivate in the `takeTheTrain_French.cptx` file.
10. Use the **File | Import | Project Captions and Closed Captions...** menu item.
11. Import the updated `Chapter11/takeTheTrain_French Captions.doc` file.

Captivate imports the Word document, reads the data it contains, and updates the Text Captions, the Slide Notes, and the Closed Captions of the project. This process can be quite lengthy, so be patient. When the import process is complete, use the **Filmstrip** to browse through the slides of the project, and view the updated Text Captions and Slide Notes.

If you are on a Windows platform, and don't see the updated captions after importing the Word file, try running Adobe Captivate as an Administrator and then import the captions again. To run Captivate as an administrator, right-click the **AdobeCaptivate 2019** icon on your toolbar or in the installation folder and select **Run as administrator**.

12. Don't forget to save the `takeTheTrain_French.cptx` file when done.

This simple workflow is only one step toward translating an eLearning project into a foreign language. At this point in the exercise, the Text Captions, the Smart Shapes with text, the Slide Notes, and the Closed Captions have been updated. However, the localization work is not over. The videos, images, text used in Learning interactions, and so on are not affected by this workflow. Also, the narration needs to be re-recorded in the new language and imported into Captivate.

These remaining actions are beyond the scope of this book, but all the techniques that are needed to complete them have been discussed in previous chapters.

Importing a Photoshop file into Captivate

Photoshop is one of the most famous and widely used Adobe applications. It is an amazing image editing tool aimed at professional designers. Many design companies around the world use Photoshop as one of their primary tools to develop the look and feel of the projects they work on.

Therefore, it is common to have a designer make use of Photoshop to create the look and feel of a Captivate project. This is why the Captivate engineering team came up with a specific feature to import Photoshop files into Captivate.

In Photoshop, each piece of an image is stored on a separate **layer**. Layers are arranged in a way that is similar to what is found in the **Timeline** of Captivate.

The **Import from Photoshop** feature is able to retain the layers and layer comps of the original Photoshop file during the import process, thus creating separate images for each of the layers contained in the Photoshop document. You will see the benefit of this approach in the next exercise.

Examining the file in Photoshop

If Photoshop is available on your system, don't hesitate to open the `Chapter12/DiDaXoTitlePage.psd` file in Photoshop and further examine its content. Just make sure you don't make any changes to the file.

The following screenshot is the Photoshop file, as seen in Adobe Photoshop CC 2019:

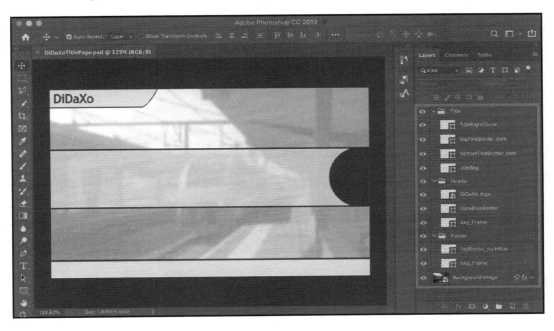

Notice that this image has one layer and three layer groups. They are as follows:

- At the bottom of the stack, the Background Image layer is the image of the train with some effects applied to it
- Above it is the Footer layer group, which includes the footer background frame and the Dark Blue color border
- Above the Footer layer group is the Header layer group, which is composed of the background frame, the Dark Blue color border, and the logo, which is visible in the top-left corner of the image
- At the top of the stack is the Title layer group, which includes the background frame, Dark Blue borders for the top and bottom of the title bar, and the blue semi-circle on the right-hand side of the slide

You will now import this Photoshop document into a blank Captivate project to create a title slide.

Close every open project before starting the following exercise:

1. On the **Welcome** screen, select the **Blank Project** thumbnail.
2. Select the **1024 x 627** canvas size and click **Create**.

3. When the project is open, use the **Window | Master Slide** menu item to switch to Master Slide view.

4. Use the **Master Slide** panel on the left-hand side of the screen to select the **Title** Master Slide.

5. Delete the Placeholder Title Text from the slide.

The Title Master Slide should now be completely blank. Next, you will insert the Photoshop file that we described on the previous page into this Master slide.

6. Still on the Title Master Slide, use the **File | Import | Photoshop File** menu item to start the procedure.

7. Import the `Chapter12/DiDaXoTitlePage.psd` Photoshop file of the exercises folder (notice that the file extension of a Photoshop file is `.psd`, which stands for PhotoShop Document).

Captivate opens the **Import "DiDaXoTitlePage.psd"** dialog, like so:

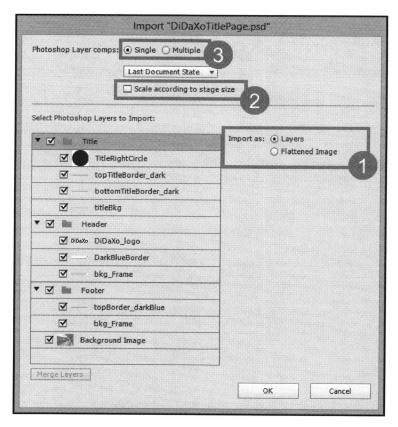

First of all, notice that you can import all the **Layers** of the original Photoshop file or import a **Flattened Image** (1). A **Flattened Image** is an image where all the layers have been combined into one single image.

Also, notice the **Scale according to stage size** checkbox (2). If selected, the Photoshop image will be automatically enlarged or reduced to fit the size of the Captivate project.

Photoshop users should notice the **Photoshop Layer comps** option at the top of the dialog (3).

8. Make sure that **Import as Layers** (1) is selected.
9. Make sure all the layer groups and layers are selected in the left-hand panel.
10. Click the **OK** button to import all the Photoshop layers into Captivate.
11. When the import is complete, click the **Timeline** button at the bottom of the screen to open the **Timeline** panel.

This is where the import from Photoshop feature shows its awesomeness. 10 images have been imported on the new Master Slide. This means that **a separate image has been created for each of the imported layers**.

12. Select the DiDaXo logo on the Master Slide.
13. Go to the **Timing** inspector and apply a **Fade In Only** transition to the logo.

This illustrates that, in Captivate, these images can be treated as entirely separate objects. Transitions, Effects, and other treatments can be applied to each image separately. You can even arrange each component of the imported Photoshop file on the Timeline.

14. While on the **Title** Master Slide, use the **Insert** | **Placeholder Objects** | **Title** menu item to insert a Title Smart Shape placeholder on the Master Slide.
15. Use the **Properties** inspector to change the font style and properties.
16. Arrange the objects of the Master Slide as you see fit. The goal is to come up with the greatest title slide ever created in the entire universe!

Inserting a Photoshop file in Captivate is just that easy. The last step of the process is to use this new Master Slide in the Project.

17. Use the **Window | Filmstrip** menu item to return to the main project.
18. You will see that the Title Master Slide has been applied to the slide. Now, you can change the title of the slide, as required.
19. Use the **File | Save** option to save this project as a `Chapter12/DiDaXoTitlePage.cptx` file.

In the next section, you will examine the round tripping workflow between Captivate and Photoshop.

Round Tripping between Captivate and Photoshop

Now that the Photoshop file has been imported into the Captivate project, let's pretend you want to modify the Photoshop file a little bit. The Round Trip editing workflow that exists between Captivate and Photoshop allows you to do it without re-importing the whole Photoshop document again. Let's examine this workflow hands-on, using the following steps:

 The following exercise requires Photoshop to be installed on your system, along with Captivate. If Photoshop is not available on your computer, just read through the steps to get an idea of the workflow. You can also download a trial version of Adobe Photoshop, which is a part of Adobe Creative Cloud, at the following URL: `http://www.adobe.com/products/photoshop.html`.

1. Still in the `Chapter12/DiDaXoTitlePage.cptx` file, click the **Library** icon on the Toolbar to open the **Library** panel.
2. In the **Library** panel, you will see the **DiDaXoTitlePage.psd** folder.
3. Use the disclose triangle to toggle the folder open, if necessary.

In the **Library** panel, the imported Photoshop file is viewed as a folder, and each of the imported layers are viewed as images within that folder. This is shown in the following screenshot:

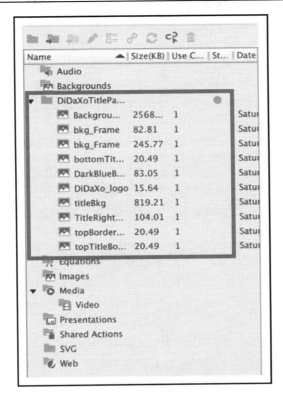

4. Right-click the **DiDaXoTitlePage.psd** folder or on any of the images it contains and choose the **Edit PSD Source File** item of the contextual menu.

This action opens the .psd file in Photoshop. Note that all the layers of the .psd document are available in Photoshop, not just the one you right-clicked on in Captivate. From here, you can use all the tools in Photoshop to modify your image.

5. Feel free to modify the image using the tools of Photoshop.
6. When done, save and close the Photoshop file.
7. Captivate automatically updates the components of the .psd document.

This simple procedure illustrates the tight integration that exists between Captivate and Photoshop. If you have Photoshop available on your system, this Round Trip editing workflow will greatly enhance your authoring experience.

In the next section, you will explore the integration between Captivate and Adobe Audition, but before that, let's quickly summarize what has been covered in this section:

- Photoshop is a professional image editing application developed by Adobe.
- Photoshop uses a layer-based system to create complex compositions.
- Captivate contains a specific tool to import Photoshop files into a project.
- You can import a flattened image into Captivate or maintain the layers found in the Photoshop file during the import process.
- If Photoshop layers are maintained, each layer is imported as a separate image in Captivate. This allows you to arrange these images on the **Timeline** and apply different effects to the different parts of the imported image.
- You can edit the original .psd file using the round trip editing workflow between Captivate and Photoshop.
- In the **Library** panel, the Photoshop document is a folder.

Editing audio with Adobe Audition

Adobe Audition (formerly Cool Edit) is the audio editing and mixing application of Creative Cloud. It allows you to manipulate your audio clips in ways that are impossible in Captivate. Thanks to Audition, you can apply effects and filters to your audio clips and create sophisticated multi-track sessions. Audition is also particularly good at sound restoration, so if you have background noise, a pop or a hiss to remove, Audition is the way to go!

The following exercise requires that Adobe Audition CC is installed on your computer, alongside Captivate. If you don't have access to Audition, which is a part of Adobe Creative Cloud, you will not be able to complete this exercise. In that case, just read through the steps to get an idea of the workflow. You can also download a trial version of Adobe Audition, which is a part of Adobe Creative Cloud, at the following URL:
http://www.adobe.com/products/audition.html.

If Audition is installed on your computer alongside Captivate, you can take advantage of some special workflows that unite these two applications. You will now discover these workflows hands-on using the following steps:

1. Return to the `Chapter12/takeTheTrain_English.cptx` file.
2. Use the **Filmstrip** to go to slide 3 of the project.
3. Open the **Timeline** panel and notice that there is an audio track attached to the slide.
4. Double-click on the audio track in the **Timeline**. This will open the Slide Audio dialog for you, with the contents for the **Edit** tab visible.

The **Slide Audio** dialog was covered in `Chapter 3`, *Working with Multimedia*. It allows you to change and modify the audio clip using the tools of Captivate. However, sometimes, the audio editing tools of Captivate are not enough. If Adobe Audition is installed on the same computer as Captivate, an Adobe Audition button will become available at the bottom of the **Slide Audio** dialog.

5. Click the **Adobe Audition** button in the bottom area of the **Slide Audio** dialog:

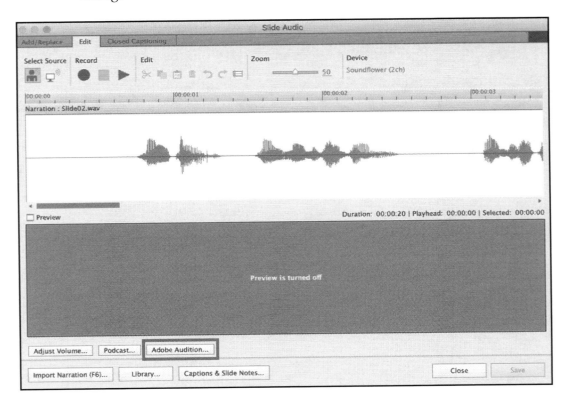

A dialog appears in Captivate, stating **Edit and Save Audio in Adobe Audition. Click OK in this dialog to import changes**. Don't click any buttons in this dialog yet. You will need to take action once you finish the edits in Adobe Audition.

Along with this dialog, an Adobe Audition window opens and loads the audio clip from slide 3. The following screenshot shows the audio clip as seen in Adobe Audition CC 2019:

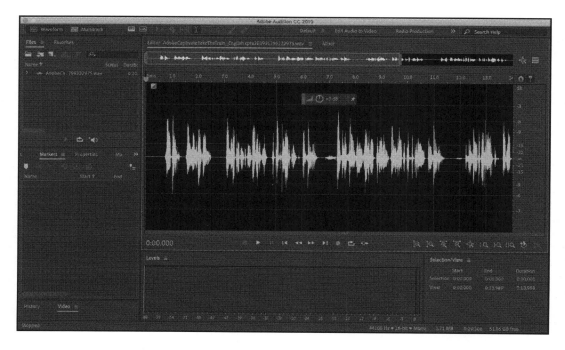

6. Edit the audio clip in Adobe Audition using all the tools, filters, and presets that you want to. When done, save and close the file in Audition and return to Captivate.
7. Click **OK** in the dialog.

Captivate will now pick up all the changes and update the audio clip.

8. Click the **Save** button on the bottom-right corner of the **Slide Audio** dialog and close the dialog.

Thanks to this simple workflow, Adobe Audition is only one click away when working in Captivate. Your students will certainly enjoy the crystal clear noise-free audio clips that you will produce for them. Note that this workflow also works with audio clips associated with objects, or with the background audio associated with the entire project.

You will now return to the **Library** panel of Captivate and explore yet another way to use Audition from within Captivate.

9. Make sure that the `Chapter12/takeTheTrain_English.cptx` file is still open.
10. Use the **Filmstrip** to go to slide 4 of the project.
11. Open the **Timeline** panel, if needed.
12. While in the **Timeline** panel, right-click the sound clip associated with the slide.
13. Choose the **Find in Library** menu item.

This action opens the **Library** panel and automatically selects the audio clip you right-clicked on (in this case, the **slide03.wav** audio clip, which is being used for Slide 4 in this project).

14. Right-click the **Slide03.wav** item in the **Library**.
15. Choose **Edit With...** in the contextual menu.
16. Browse to the Adobe Audition executable file. On Mac, look for the `/Applications/Adobe Audition CC 2019/Adobe Audition CC 2019.app` file. On Windows, look for the `C:\Program Files\Adobe\Adobe Audition CC 2019\Adobe Audition CC.exe` file.
17. The selected audio clip opens in Adobe Audition. You can now use the tools, filters, and presets of Audition to edit this audio clip in many ways that are not available in Captivate. When done, save and close the audio file.
18. Captivate should automatically pick up the changes and load a new version of the audio clip in the Library.

This simple exercise concludes the overview of the integration between Adobe Captivate and Adobe Audition. Along with Adobe Audition, you can also use this procedure with any other audio editing tool installed on your computer to tweak an audio file.

Let's quickly summarize what has been covered in this section:

- Adobe Audition is the professional audio editing application of Adobe Creative Cloud.
- If Captivate and Audition are both installed on the same computer, the **Adobe Audition** button of the Audio Edit dialog will be active.
- The **Adobe Audition** button allows you to open Audition from within Captivate. You can then use the advanced tools of Audition to manipulate your audio file in many ways that are not possible in Captivate.
- When you save the file in Audition, Captivate automatically picks up on any changes and adapts your eLearning project accordingly.
- You can right-click an element of the **Library** and choose the **Edit With...** menu item to open it in an external application.

You can also use Audacity for recording and editing narration for your eLearning courses. Audacity is a free and open source audio recording and editing software. You can download Audacity from the following URL: https://www.audacityteam.org/.

Editing SVGs with Adobe Illustrator

Adobe Illustrator is a vector graphic design application that allows you to create icons, logos, typography, and complex illustrations. It also allows you to create Scalable Vector Graphics, also known as SVGs. Adding SVGs in Captivate projects was covered in Chapter 2, *Working with Standard Objects*.

Adobe Captivate allows you to insert SVGs into your courses, which is especially beneficial for responsive courses, as SVGs scale beautifully in projects, without any loss of quality. The SVG images that you insert in Captivate can be edited by Adobe Illustrator using the same kind of round tripping workflow that you used with Audition and Photoshop in the previous sections.

The following exercise requires that Adobe Illustrator CC is installed on your computer, alongside Captivate. If you don't have access to Illustrator, which is a part of Adobe Creative Cloud, you will not be able to complete this exercise. In that case, just read through the steps to get an idea of the workflow. You can also download the trial version of Adobe Illustrator at the following URL: http://www.adobe.com/products/illustrator.html.

Now, you will learn how to edit the already added SVG in Captivate using the round tripping feature with Adobe Illustrator:

1. Return to the `Chapter12/takeTheTrain_English.cptx` file.

2. Use the **Filmstrip** to go to slide 5 of the project.

3. Select one of the pins on the map, which is an SVG.

4. In the **Properties** inspector, notice the name of the pin mentioned as `mapSymbolPin.svg`.

5. Select the other two pins and notice that they are also linked to the same SVG. You will modify this SVG in Adobe Illustrator, which will apply the changes to all three pins on this slide.

6. To make edits to the SVG file in Adobe Illustrator, select **Edit with Adobe Illustrator** and then click **Edit SVG** in the **Properties** inspector:

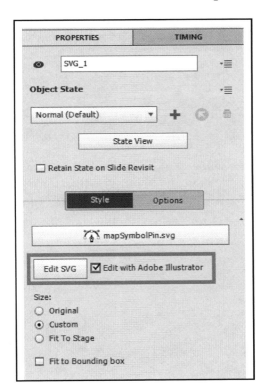

7. This opens the SVG file in Adobe Illustrator CC 2019, as shown in the following screenshot:

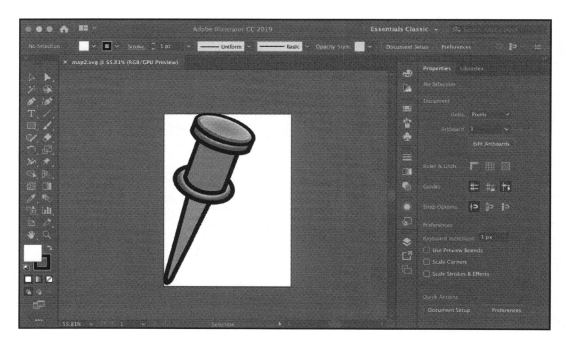

8. Make the required changes to the SVG file. For this pin, let's change the color red to green. Select the pin in the **Illustrator** window.
9. Use the **Edit** menu and select **Edit Colors | Recolor Artwork**.
10. In the **Recolor Artwork** dialog, double-click the color red below the **New** section:

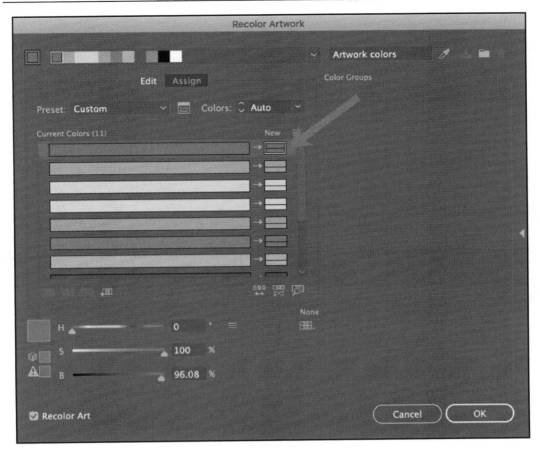

11. In the **Color Picker** dialog, select the dark green color and click **OK**.

12. Click **OK** to close the **Recolor Artwork** dialog.

13. You will see the new color applied to the pin. Now, save the changes to the Illustrator document and close it.

14. These changes will be immediately reflected in your Adobe Captivate project on all three pins:

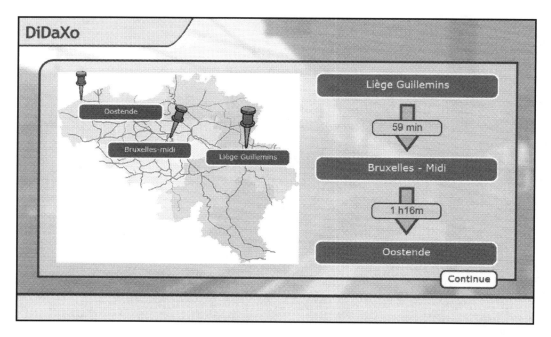

15. This brings us to the end of the round tripping workflow between Captivate and Illustrator to edit the SVG files that were added to the Captivate projects.

Exporting the project to XML

In this section, you will export the project as an XML file. Exporting the Captivate project to .xml gives you access to a much wider range of properties and content than the Export to Microsoft Word feature you used earlier in this chapter. According to the official Adobe Captivate blog, an exported XML file contains the following:

> "Text Captions, Text Animations, Rollover Captions, Default text and correct entries in Text Entry Box, Success/Failure/Hint Captions and button text for all interactive objects, Text Buttons, Slide Notes, Text and Rollover Captions in Rollover Slidelets, Quiz Buttons and Feedback captions, Project Info, Project Start and End options, text messages for password and Expiry Messages."

See the original post at `https://elearning.adobe.com/2009/05/quick_editing_of_text_using_xm_1/`.

Here are the steps to export your project as an XML file:

1. If needed, return to the `chapter12/takeTheTrain_English.cptx` file.
2. You need to make a copy of this project for the French version. To do so, use the **File | Save As** option.
3. Navigate to the `Chapter12` folder, change the name of the CPTX file to `takeTheTrain_French_xml.cptx`, and click **Save**.
4. Use the **File | Export | To XML** menu option.
5. Export the project as `chapter12/takeTheTrain_French_xml.xml` in the exercises folder.

When the export is finished, Captivate asks if you want to open the resulting XML file.

6. Click **No** to close the message box and return to Captivate.

The resulting XML can be opened and updated with any XML editor. When the editing is done, the **File | Import | From XML...** menu item can be used to import the updated data back into Captivate.

 To edit XML documents, you can use Brackets, which is a modern, open source text editor. You can download Brackets at the following URL: `http://brackets.io/`.

Summary

In this chapter, you have learned some of the workflows that integrate Captivate with other applications. Some of these applications, such as Photoshop, Illustrator, and Audition, are a part of the Adobe product line, and others, such as Microsoft Word and Microsoft PowerPoint, are third-party applications.

By using PowerPoint workflows, you are able to reuse existing content made in PowerPoint. When it comes to localization, you can export Text Captions and Slide Notes to a Microsoft Word document, send it to a translation service, and import it back into Captivate. There is no need for the translators to know anything about Captivate to make this workflow work. When importing a Photoshop file into Captivate, you can decide to maintain the layers of the original Photoshop file, which gives you a great deal of flexibility to further customize the imported images using the tools and effects of Captivate. Exporting to Audition allows you to tweak your audio files in many ways, and the round tripping workflow between Captivate and Illustrator will help you edit the SVG files that you add to your Captivate projects.

When used correctly, these workflows are huge time-savers that help you streamline the production process of your eLearning content.

In the next chapter, you will learn how to make your eLearning courses accessible for people with special needs.

Meet the community

In this section, we want to introduce you to Phil Cowcill. Phil is known as a dynamic instructor and has delivered numerous workshops at a wide variety of conferences. One of the most memorable things that he does when he teaches or demonstrates Captivate is showing "Creativity in Restriction." While Captivate is a powerful tool, it is restricted in all it can do. Phil likes to show unique ways of getting past restrictions within Captivate by incorporating JavaScript scripts or Animate projects.

Damien

Phil is one of those individuals I always look forward to meeting whenever I travel to a conference. In addition to being exceptionally knowledgeable and an awesome instructor, he is simply a great guy! I have attended several of his sessions on using Adobe Captivate with Adobe Animate CC and on using JavaScript in Adobe Captivate. The next step for us would be to teach a class together. Are you up to the challenge, Phil?

Pooja

Phil is a great friend and an awesome instructor! He always has a trick or two to get past product limitations. He adds a Phil touch to the workflow to make it look magical. Phil is always a delight to talk to and I feel honored to be a part of his friend circle.

Phil Cowcill

Phil Cowcill started his career in education when he was hired by Canadore College as an Educational Technologist in 1983. In 1984, he joined a unique team that developed Canada's first Interactive Videodisc (IVD). On this project, Phil wore many hats. He created some of the 3,000 graphics, shot and edited video, applied instructional design as he wrote some of the detailed storyboards, and programmed the IVD using a C-style language called MicroNATAL.

Phil worked in a variety of roles at the college. In 1995, he took on a full-time teaching position, becoming the coordinator of the post-graduate Interactive Multimedia program. Here, he worked with non-programming students and taught them how to develop websites and interactive CD-ROM productions. It was during this time that he led his students in building one of the first news websites that had streaming video (1996). In 2011, Phil developed the curriculum and taught Canada's first dedicated mobile application development program. He recorded over 700 instructional videos on all the topics in the mobile program so that his students had access to all the lessons at their convenience. In 2015, he left the college and started working as a contractor with Canada's Department of National Defence as a Senior eLearning Specialist.

Over the years, Phil has written numerous articles and tutorials on a variety of subjects. In 2001, Thompson Publishing released his first textbook on building database-driven websites using Dreamweaver. He was also a contributing author to Dr. Michael Allen's 2011 eLearning Annual book.

Phil continues to speak at conferences around the world and develop mobile applications for Android and iOS devices. If the opportunity arises, join in on one of his sessions at a conference and listen to a skilled eLearning professional share his vast experience.

Contact details

- Email: phil@pjrules.com
- Website: www.pjrules.com
- LinkedIn: www.linkedin.com/in/philcowcill

13
Creating Accessible eLearning

When delivering eLearning courses to large groups of people, it's important to be mindful of how people with different abilities experience your course. Learning is the right of every individual. You need to design your content in a way that benefits everybody and provides the best possible experience to all the eager learners.

An accessible project can be accessed by people with disabilities. These learners use some specific input and output devices (such as Braille readers, text-to-speech utilities, screen readers such as JAWS, and so on). To improve the experience for those learners, it's important that you take the time to enter some extra metadata in your projects.

Many countries around the world have adopted some kind of accessibility standards, rules, or laws. Most of the time, these standards are based on the **Web Accessibility Initiative (WAI)**; see `https://www.w3.org/WAI/`, a document developed by the **World Wide Web Consortium (W3C)**. In the US, these standards are an amendment of the US Rehabilitation Act of 1973. It's more commonly known as Section 508. When a project is 508 compliant, it means that it complies with the accessibility requirements of this legal document.

 To learn about the accessibility laws followed in different parts of the world, visit this web page created by **WebAIM**: `http://webaim.org/articles/laws/world/`.

Thankfully, Captivate allows you to create accessible eLearning courses by adding Accessibility text, language options, Closed Captions, keyboard shortcuts, and tabbing order to your course module. These features help you make your content accessible for people with special needs.

In this chapter, you will do the following:

- Enable accessibility for Captivate projects
- Select the language option for a project and objects
- Add project information for the course
- Add accessibility text for slides and objects
- Assign keyboard shortcuts to interactive objects
- Set the tab order for interactive objects on the screen
- Add Closed Captions for Slide Audio and Slide Video
- Add a CC button to the playbar

Preparing your work
At the beginning of this chapter, it is a good idea to take some time and reset the Captivate interface to default. If you are using the default interface mode, just close and restart Captivate. If you are using the advanced interface mode, use the **Window | Workspace | Reset 'Classic'** menu item to reset Captivate to default. In this chapter, you will use the exercises stored in the Chapter13 folder. If you are not able to follow the step-by-step instructions, take a look at the Chapter13/final folder, which contains a copy of the files as they will be at the end of this chapter.

Enabling accessibility in Captivate projects

In this section, you will learn how to enable accessibility for Captivate courses, at the project level, by following these steps:

1. Open the Chapter13/takeTheTrain.cptx file.
2. Open the **Preferences** dialog by using the **Edit | Preferences** (Windows) menu item or the **Adobe Captivate | Preferences** (Mac) menu item.
3. In the **Preferences** dialog, navigate to the **Publish Settings** category under the **Project** section.
4. In this section, make sure the **Enable Accessibility** option is selected.

This will ensure that the screen readers are able to read the slides and the objects in your course. If this option is not selected, the accessibility options that you set throughout the project will be useless.

5. Below the **Enable Accessibility** option is the **Restrict keyboard tabbing to slide items only** option. Select this option as well.

The keyboard tabbing option restricts the tabbing order to the slide, disabling tabbing for the Table of Contents and Playbar. The Playbar is automatically added by Captivate. In Chapter 15, *Finishing Touches and Publishing,* you will review the Playbar options and create a Table of Contents for your project:

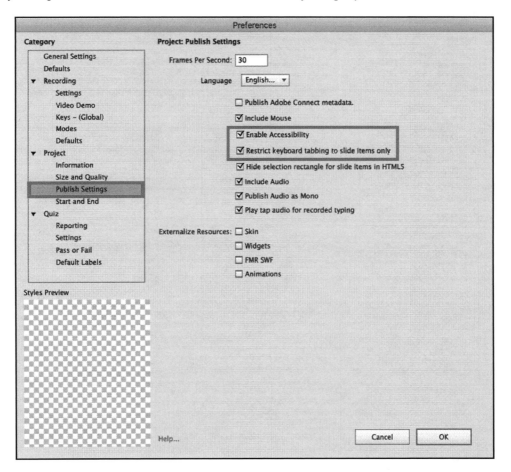

You can also define the language option for your Captivate project and objects. This option is used by screen readers for enhanced accessibility.

The **Language** option defines the HTML `lang` attribute, which identifies the language of textual content on the web. This attribute is used by screen readers to switch language profiles and provide the right accent and pronunciation.

6. To define the language attribute, open the **Language** dropdown and select the required language for your Captivate project:

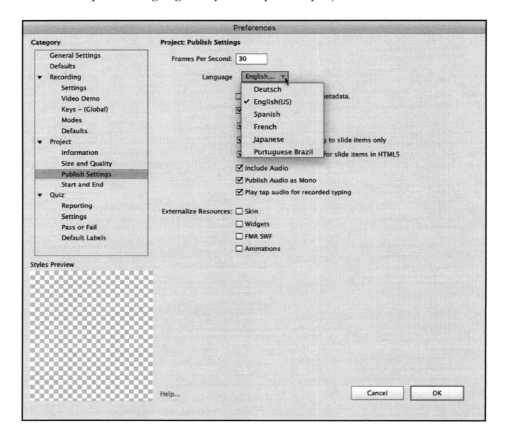

You can also define the language attribute at an object level for your multi-language project. You will learn these steps in a later section of this chapter.

7. Now, switch to the **Information** category under the **Project** section.

In this section, you will need to fill out the project information. The screen readers will be able to fetch this information and read it out for the learners. It also helps in indexing the content in search engines.

8. Type DiDaXo in the **Company** field.

9. Type 2019-DiDaXo in the **Copyright** field.

10. Enter Take the Train in the **Project Name** field.

11. Type This is a short training on how to take the train in Belgium. in the **Description** field.

12. Fill the remaining fields (**Author, Email**, and **Website**) with your own name, email address, and website URL. Note that none of these fields are mandatory. If you do not have a website, just leave the field blank.

Your screen should now look similar to the following screenshot:

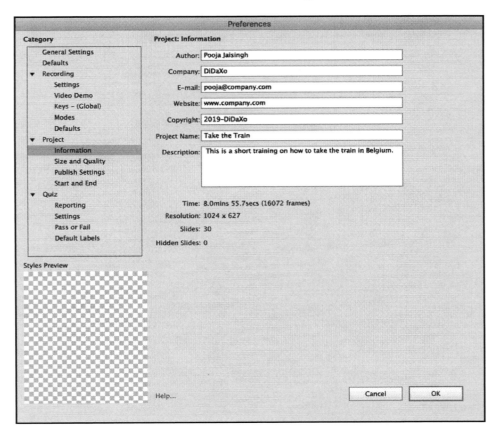

13. Click the **OK** button when you're done.

By entering the project information and enabling accessibility, you have taken an important step toward making the project 508 compliant. This is a good start, but there is more that can be done to further enhance the accessibility of the project.

Adding accessibility text for slides

The next step is to add accessibility text to the slides and objects. Remember that this accessibility text will be read aloud by the screen readers for visually impaired learners. Let's look at the workflow to add slide-level accessibility text first:

1. If needed, return to the Chapter13/takeTheTrain.cptx file.
2. Use the **Filmstrip** panel to go to slide 3.
3. Click the **Properties** icon on the Toolbar to open the **Properties** inspector.
4. Click the button on the right side of the Name field and select **Accessibility:**

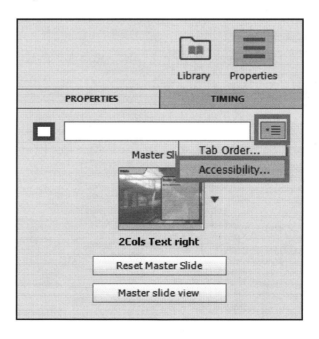

5. This will open the **Slide Accessibility** dialog. You can enter the text in the field, or if you have slide notes added for the slide, you can click the **Import Slide Notes** button.

This will add the slide notes to the field, and you can use them as Accessibility text. You can also edit this text, if required:

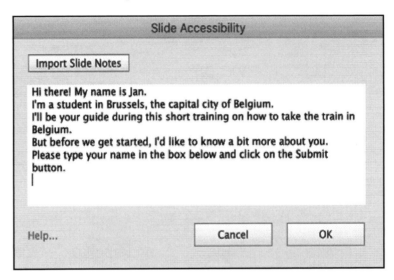

6. Click **OK** to confirm the addition of notes and close the dialog.

You can follow the same steps to add accessibility text to each of the slides in the project.

Adding accessibility text for objects

After you have finished adding accessibility text to the slides, you can add accessibility text to the objects on the slide.

Let's begin adding accessibility text to the objects on slide 3:

1. Select Jan's picture on the slide.
2. In the **Properties** inspector, click the button on the right side of the Name field and select **Accessibility**.

This will open the **Item Accessibility** dialog. Notice that the **Auto Label** option that is selected by default and the **Accessibility Name** and **Accessibility Description** sections are grayed out. The **Auto Label** option will automatically label the objects based on their name in the Name field:

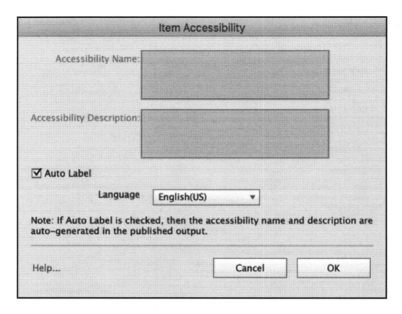

3. Deselect the **Auto Label** option to add meaningful information regarding this image.

4. This will allow you to add details in the **Accessibility Name** and **Accessibility Description** fields. Enter the name for the object and add the description. For this image, type Jan in the **Accessibility Name** field and Picture of Jan. in the **Accessibility Description** field.

Notice that in the **Language** dropdown, the language option you selected in the **Preferences** dialog is pre-selected here. If you have multiple languages supported in your project, you can change the language preference for each object here.

5. To change the language attribute for Jan's image, open the **Language** dropdown and select any other language.

6. Then, change the **Language** option back to **English(US)**, as the text you have added is in the English language.

7. Click **OK** to confirm the addition of the details and close the dialog:

And that's how you add accessibility text to the objects in Captivate projects. Select the other objects on the screen and add the accessibility text to them.

Make sure you follow these best practices while adding accessibility text for the objects on the screen:

- Keep the accessibility information about the objects to the point. Do not add extra or duplicate information.
- All objects that provide textual or non-textual information should have accessibility text assigned to them.
- As far as possible, avoid using the Auto Label option for graphical elements and provide a meaningful description for them.
- If you have any decorative objects on the slide that do not contribute to the information being provided on the screen, uncheck the Auto Label option and then leave the description blank so that the screen reader excludes it from the slide.
- If you have several objects on the screen that are placed together to create a single visual on the screen, add accessibility text to only one of the objects of the group, which provides the main idea of the content for the entire group of objects. This will help you avoid repetition of information.

For more accessibility best practices, visit the official Captivate documentation page for creating accessible courses in Adobe Captivate at `https://helpx.adobe.com/captivate/using/creating-accessible -projects.html`.

Adding accessibility text can be a tedious process, but you are sure to create a meaningful learning experience for all your learners and bring smiles to their faces!

Assigning keyboard shortcuts

When you are designing interactions for your courses, which need to be accessible, avoid using hover- and drag-based interaction. The only types of interactions that support accessibility are click-based interactions. Similarly, when adding quiz questions, you can choose from Multiple Choice, True/False, and Rating Scale questions, as they support accessibility.

Now, let's talk about making interactive objects accessible. Apart from adding accessibility text, you need to follow a few more steps to make the interactive objects fully accessible. The next important step is to assign keyboard shortcuts, so that your learners are able to complete the course without using a mouse.

Here are the steps to assign keyboard shortcuts to buttons in Captivate projects:

1. If needed, return to the `Chapter13/takeTheTrain.cptx` file.
2. Use the **Filmstrip** panel to go to slide 2.
3. Select the **Continue** button on the bottom-right corner of the slide.
4. Click the **Properties** icon on the Toolbar to open the **Properties** inspector.
5. In the **Properties** inspector, open the **Actions** tab.

Notice the **Shortcut** option under the **Actions** tab. This option lets you choose the keyboard key (or shortcut) the learners can use to execute the action attached to the button.

6. The **Shortcut** option for the interactive objects is disabled by default. Select the radio button under the Shortcut section to enable it.

7. Use your keyboard to press a key or key combination, to assign that shortcut to the button:

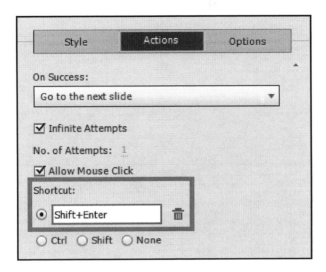

8. After assigning a shortcut to the button, make sure you add the information about the shortcut key to the accessibility text for the button.

The shortcut key will now be assigned to the button. If you add the shortcut key by mistake, you can click the **Delete** icon for the shortcut.

Setting the tab order

When your learners are using screen readers to access your course, they can use the *Tab* key to navigate through interactive objects. If you have multiple interactive objects on your screen, you might want to check the tab order for these objects and place the interactive objects in the desired order.

Here are the steps for setting the tab order of the interactive objects on the slide:

1. Make sure you are still on slide 2 of the takeTheTrain.cptx file.
2. If you have any object selected on the slide, click the slide 2 thumbnail on the **Filmstrip** or click anywhere on the scrap area around the stage to make the slide the active object.

3. Open the **Properties** inspector.

4. In the **Properties** inspector, click the button on the right side of the Name field and select **Tab Order:**

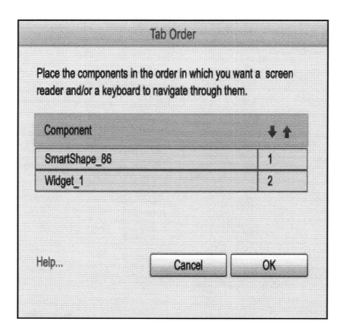

You will see the Interaction widget and the button listed in the **Tab Order** dialog. The button is placed above the widget in the tab order.

Notice how the **Continue** button is named **SmartShape_86** in the Tab Order dialog, which doesn't indicate at all that it's the **Continue** button. So, make sure when you add objects to slides to name them appropriately for easy identification.

5. To change the order, so that the widget interaction is active before the **Continue** button, select the **SmartShape_86** item. Notice that when you select it, the **Continue** button is selected on the slide as well.

6. Then, click the **Move Selected Row Down** arrow. This changes the order for the interactive objects on the slide.

7. Click **OK** to confirm the changes and close the dialog.

You can follow the same steps on other slides with more than one interactive object to change the tab order.

Here's a quick summary of what you have learned so far:

- Captivate helps you create accessible courses for learners with special needs.
- You can make the courses accessible by adding accessibility text, language attributes, Closed Captions, keyboard shortcuts, tabbing order, and so on.
- You need to enable accessibility for the project to ensure that the screen readers are able to read the slides and the objects in your course.
- You can add accessibility text to slides as well as objects. The accessibility text added throughout the project is read aloud by the screen readers of visually impaired students, which will dramatically enhance their experience of the course content.
- Avoid using hover- and drag-based interaction for courses that need to be accessible.
- You can choose from Multiple Choice, True/False, and Rating Scale questions for a quiz.
- For interactive objects, you need to add keyboard shortcuts as well as set the tab order.

Adding Closed Captions for slide narration

You have done a good job so far to make your course accessible. Give yourself a pat on the back!

The last thing you need to do is to add Closed Captions on the slides with navigation. Closed Captions make your eLearning content more accessible and more interesting for the learners. There are many situations where Closed Captions are useful:

- They make your Captivate projects accessible for hearing-impaired students
- They make the project easier to understand for foreign students
- They are useful for learners who have to take the online course in an office and don't want to bother their colleagues with the voiceover narrations

For these reasons (plus ones not listed here), it is a good idea to use Closed Captions each time you add voiceover narration to a slide.

In Captivate, Closed Captions are always associated with a Slide Audio or a Slide Video. They are not supported for object audio, system audio, triggered audio, and event videos.

In the next exercise, you will add Closed Captions to the Take the Train course by performing the following steps:

1. Return to the `Chapter13/takeTheTrain.cptx` file.
2. Use the **Filmstrip** panel to go to slide 3.
3. If needed, use the **Window | Slide Notes** menu item to reopen the **Slide Notes** panel.

Slide 3 is the first slide of the course to which you added narration. There are five notes in the **Slide Notes** panel. They exactly reflect what is said in the audio file associated with the slide.

4. At the top-right corner of the **Slide Notes** panel, click the **Audio CC** checkbox next to the Text-to-Speech checkbox. This operation is shown in the following screenshot:

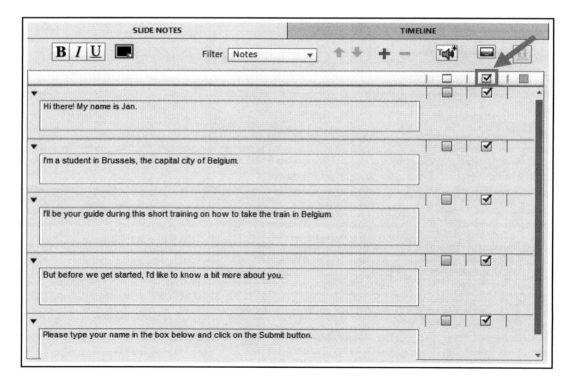

This action selects all the slide notes for closed captioning.

 Note that the **Audio CC** checkbox is available only if an audio file is associated with the slide.

5. In the top-right corner of the **Slide Notes** panel, click the **Closed Captioning** button.

The **Slide Audio** dialog opens, with the **Closed Captioning** tab (**1**) active:

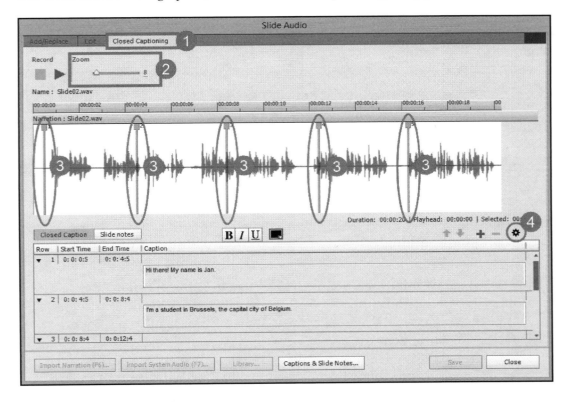

6. Use the Zoom slider (**2**) to reduce the zoom level so you can see the entire sound clip.

Each of the vertical bars (**3**) represents one of the **Slide Notes** you marked for Closed Captioning.

7. Click the **Play** button. Notice that the yellow bars mark when the slide notes are supposed to be displayed.

8. Adjust the position of the notes so they match the audio. Test again and make adjustments until all the Closed Captions are synced with the audio.

9. Now, it's time to make some formatting changes to the Closed Captions. Click the **CC Settings** button (4) at the center right of the dialog.

The **CC Settings** dialog appears, which lets you define the formatting of the Closed Captions. If required, you can also have a different look and feel and placement for Closed Captions on each slide.

In the top section of the **CC Settings** dialog, you will see a live preview of how the Closed Captions will appear on the screen. In the bottom section, you will find all the alignment and formatting options.

10. You will make some formatting changes to the Closed Captions area. To apply these changes to the entire project, open the dropdown that has **Slide 3** selected, and change it to **Project**.

11. Notice that the Closed Captions are currently set to appear at the bottom center of the screen. Open the drop-down list for the Align option and switch to the bottom left. This moves the captions to start from the bottom-left corner.

12. Open the drop-down list again and select **Custom**.

This option will help you decide the starting point of the closed caption by modifying the **X** and **Y** coordinates, and the size of the Closed Captions area by modifying the Width and Height properties.

13. Set the Width of the Closed Captions area to 100%, so that it covers the slide end-to-end.

14. Then, reduce the height to 9%, so that the Closed Captions appear exactly inside the bottom bar area.

15. Then, set the **X** and **Y** properties to 0% and 91%, respectively, so that it covers the entire bottom area. You can also drag and drop the Closed Caption area in the slide preview area to change the **X** and **Y** coordinates. Unfortunately, it does not work with size.

16. Change the font and background properties, if required.

17. If you want to show the Closed Captions as soon as this slide loads, select **Show Closed Captions**. For this exercise, let's leave it unchecked, so that you can see another workflow to turn on the Closed Captions in the course:

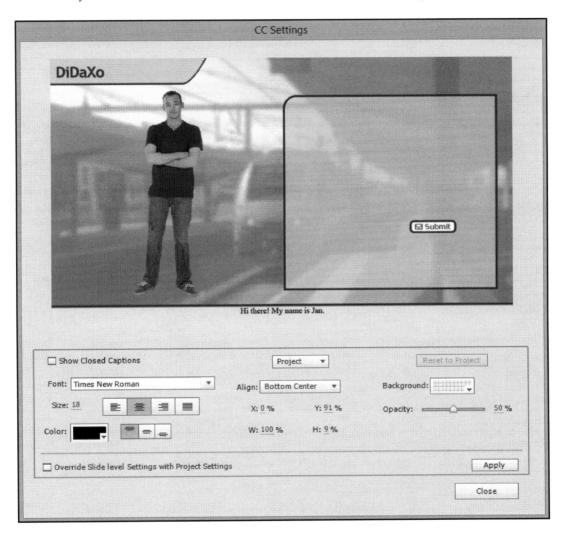

18. When you are satisfied with the result, click the **Apply** button on the bottom-right corner and then click the **Close** button.
19. Click the **Save** button at the bottom-right corner of the **Slide Audio** dialog.
20. Close the **Slide Audio** dialog.

Don't forget to save the file when you are done!

Viewing the Closed Captions

Now that Closed Captions have been added to slide 3 of the project, you will test it in the preview pane and control the newly inserted Closed Captions:

1. Still in the `takeTheTrain.cptx` file, use the **Filmstrip** to return to slide 1.
2. Use the **Preview** icon on the Toolbar to test the **Next 5 Slides**.
3. When the preview reaches the third slide (the first one with audio and Closed Captions), notice that the Closed Captions do not appear.

By default, the Closed Captions do not appear in the resulting Captivate output. It is up to the student to turn them on or leave them off while watching the project.

To let the student turn them on, you need to add a closed captioning button on the playback controls bar that appears at the bottom of the project. To add this button, you need to use the **Skin Editor**.

 In `Chapter 14`, *Variables and Advanced Actions*, you will use an advanced action to create a custom toggle button for Closed Captions.

This chapter only shows how to use the Skin Editor to add a Closed Captions toggle button to the playback controls bar. You will study the other features of the Skin Editor in `Chapter 15`, *Finishing Touches and Publishing*.

4. Close the **Preview** pane.
5. Use the **Project | Skin Editor** menu to open the floating **Skin Editor** panel.
6. On the left side of the **Skin Editor**, select the **Closed Captioning** checkbox to add a CC button on the playback controls bar.
7. Click the **Skin Editor** panel.

8. You can also click the **Settings** button below the Closed Captions checkbox to access the Closed Captions settings and make any modifications. This is the same dialog that you accessed while formatting the Closed Captions in the previous section.

Everything is now ready to test the Closed Captions you have added to the project.

9. Make sure you are still on slide 1 of the project and use the **Preview | Next 5 Slides** icon on the Toolbar to test the new CC button in the preview pane.

10. When the project opens in the preview pane, click the **CC** button on the right of the playback controls bar to turn the Closed Captions on.

11. When the preview reaches slide 3, you should see the associated Closed Captions displayed in sync with the audio.

You have successfully added Closed Captions to help make the project more accessible!

Closed captioning a video file

The last thing that you will do in this chapter is to add Closed Captions to the video file you imported on slide 22 of the `takeTheTrain.cptx` project:

 Note that you can add Closed Captions to a video file only if it has been imported as a **Slide Video**.

1. Still in the `Chapter13/takeTheTrain.cptx` project, use the **Filmstrip** to return to slide 22. It is the slide where you imported the video file in `Chapter 3`, *Working with Multimedia.*

2. Go to the **Slide Notes** panel. If it is not open, use the **Window | Slide Notes** option to open it.

3. Click the **+** sign to add a new note.

4. Type `Now, it is time for the departure using a very precise procedure.`

5. Click the + sign one more time and type `First the train attendant whistles and closes all the doors but one.`

6. Click the + sign for the third and last time and type `If you are late, this is your very last chance to board the train.`

This video is a lot longer and requires more Closed Captions. For this exercise, we will add captions for a small portion of the video. You can follow the same steps to add captions to the rest of the video.

7. Select the **Video CC** checkbox on the top-right corner of the **Slide Notes** panel.

8. Then, click the **Video CC** button located above the checkbox. The **Edit Video Timing** dialog opens.

The **Edit Video Timing** dialog can be used to edit the imported video file. In this exercise, that's not what you want to do. You only want to add Closed Captions to the video.

9. Click the **Closed Captioning** tab at the top-left corner of the **Edit Video Timing** dialog.

Notice that the three yellow vertical bars appear in the upper area of the **Edit Video Timing** dialog.

Watch out! It is possible that these three bars sit on top of each other at the same location, giving the false impression that there is only one vertical bar.

10. Move these vertical bars to synchronize the Closed Captions with the video file. This is the exact same procedure as for the Closed Captions associated with the slide audio.

11. Click the **Play** button in the top-left corner of the **Edit Video Timing** dialog to test the synchronization between the video and the Closed Captions. It will probably be necessary to adjust the position of the vertical bars and to retest the video a few times before the yellow bars are properly positioned.

At the end of this exercise, the **Edit Video Timing** dialog should look like the following screenshot:

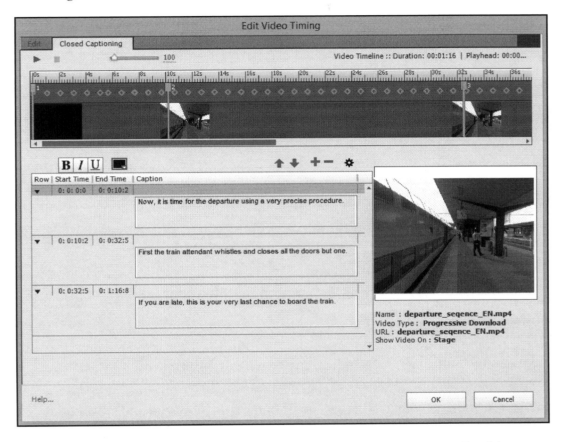

12. When done, click **OK** to validate the changes and close the **Edit Video Timing** dialog.
13. Use the **Preview | Next 5 Slides** icon on the Toolbar to test your new Closed Captions.
14. When the **Preview** pane appears, click the **CC** icon of the playback controls bar to turn the Closed Captions on. Confirm that the Closed Captions have been successfully added to the video file of slide 22.
15. Save the file when finished.

This exercise concludes your overview of the Closed Captioning system of Captivate. Here is a quick summary of what has been covered:

- Closed Captions are associated either with Slide Audio or Slide Video.
- The text for the Closed Captions can be added to the **Slide Notes** panel.
- The **Slide Notes** panel is not displayed by default. Use the **Window | Slide Notes** menu item to turn it on and off.
- Use the **Skin Editor** to add the **CC** button to the playback controls bar. The **CC** button is used by the learners to turn the Closed Captions ON or OFF.

Summary

In this chapter, you learned how to add accessibility text to slides and slide objects. Remember that this text is read aloud by screen readers for students with disabilities. Then, you learned how to make the interactive objects of Captivate accessible by assigning a shortcut key and by fine-tuning the tab order.

These options can be a little tedious to set, but taking the time to do it dramatically enhances the experience of students who need it. Learning is a right everyone has, so it is part of our duty, as teachers, to ensure that all students can access our course content.

In some countries, making course content accessible is a legal requirement. Accessibility guidelines and standards are commonly known as Section 508 in reference to an amendment of the US Rehabilitation Act of 1973.

In the next chapter, you will discover some of the most powerful and advanced features of Captivate. With variables and advanced actions, you will be able to add an even higher degree of interactivity and customization to your projects.

Meet the community

In this section, we want to introduce you to Kevin Siegel. Kevin is an awesome technical writer. He has written several Adobe Captivate books and developed several courses. Kevin regularly speaks at Adobe and eLearning-related events throughout the United States. Look for one of his sessions during your next conference!

Damien

As an Adobe Captivate Certified Instructor, I teach a lot of Captivate classes. Before I had my own book, I used Kevin's courseware for my teaching, so I can tell you with no hesitation that these are great resources if you want to learn Captivate.

Pooja

I have known Kevin for several years but got to spend quality time with him a few years back during my first trip to Washington DC. He, along with his wife, took me and my colleague for a tour of Washington DC monuments. It was a day full of history, humor, and excitement.

Kevin Siegel

Kevin Siegel is the founder and president of IconLogic, Inc. He has written hundreds of step-by-step computer training books on applications such as Adobe Captivate, Articulate Storyline, Adobe RoboHelp, Adobe Presenter, Adobe Technical Communication Suite, Adobe Dreamweaver, Adobe InDesign, Microsoft Word, Microsoft PowerPoint, QuarkXPress, and TechSmith Camtasia.

Kevin spent five years in the US Coast Guard as an award-winning photojournalist and has more than 30 years of experience as a print publisher, technical writer, instructional designer, trainer, and eLearning developer. He is a certified technical trainer, a veteran classroom instructor, certified master online trainer, and a frequent speaker at trade shows and conventions.

Kevin holds multiple certifications from companies such as Adobe, CompTIA, and the International Council for Certified Online Trainers (www.iccotp.com).

IconLogic offers online classes on Captivate that are attended by students worldwide. The company also offers full development and one-on-one mentoring on Captivate and other eLearning development tools.

Contact details

- Kevin's email: ksiegel@iconlogic.com
- IconLogic's website: www.iconlogic.com
- IconLogic's blog: https://blog.iconlogic.com

14
Variables and Advanced Actions

In this chapter, you will take advantage of the scripting capabilities of HTML5 and Flash. The HTML5 technology includes a programming language named JavaScript. When publishing a Captivate project in HTML5, a lot of JavaScript code is generated behind the scenes. It is the web browser that executes this JavaScript when the project is played back by the learner. If you decide to publish your projects in Flash, Captivate generates a lot of ActionScript code instead. It is the Flash Player that executes this ActionScript code at runtime.

Captivate exposes part of this scripting technology to the eLearning developer. Now let's be honest – most eLearning developers won't actually be writing real JavaScript or ActionScript in Captivate (being an ActionScript or JavaScript developer requires proper training and solid programming skills), but you will be able to create some simple scripts using buttons, drop-down lists, and dialog boxes. In Captivate, these small scripts are called **Advanced Actions**. That being said, more advanced users do have the ability to write actual JavaScript in Captivate!

Thanks to Advanced Actions, you will be able to dramatically enhance the eLearning experience of your students. For example, you can do the following:

- Dynamically generate text in Text Captions based on student input
- Show and hide objects in response to system or user events
- Trigger a sequence of actions instead of a single action when a Click Box or a Button is clicked to make one interaction accomplish more than one thing
- Evaluate if a condition is true or false before executing an action etc

Most of the time, Advanced Actions need to store and read data in the memory of the computer, so you need a robust system to manage these pieces of data. This task is handled by **Variables**. Basically, a variable is a named space in the memory of the computer in which you can store pieces of data. When referencing the name of a variable, you can access the data it contains and manipulate this data with Advanced Actions.

In this chapter, you will do the following:

- Learn about and use System Variables
- Store student input in a User Variable
- Use Variables to generate text dynamically
- Create Standard and Conditional Advanced Actions
- Create and use Shared Actions
- Create and use a Geolocation Variable
- Generate random feedback messages using JavaScript

Preparing your work

Before you start this chapter, take some time and reset the Captivate interface to its default state. If you are using the default interface mode, just close and restart Captivate. If you use the advanced interface mode, use the **Window | Workspace | Reset 'Classic'** menu item to reset Captivate to its default. In this chapter, you will use the exercises stored in the Chapter14 folder. If you get confused by any of the step-by-step instructions, take a look at the Chapter14/final folder, which contains a copy of the files as they will be at the end of this chapter.

Working with Variables

Every single programming language in the world makes use of **variables** to store and retrieve data to and from the memory of the computer. JavaScript and ActionScript are no exception! In Captivate, it is enough to know that a variable is a named space in the memory of the computer in which data can be read or written.

To cut a long story short, a variable is made up of two things:

- **A name**: This name must comply with strict naming rules and conventions. In ActionScript, for instance, the name of a variable cannot contain any spaces or special characters (such as @, é, è, ç, à, #, ?, /, and so on). When writing a script, the programmer uses the name of the variable to access the data it contains.
- **A value**: The value is the piece of data that the variable contains. This value can change (vary) during the execution of the script or each time the script is executed, hence the name *variable*.

For example, `v_firstName = "Damien"` defines a variable:

- `v_firstName`: This is the name of the variable
- `Damien`: This is the value of the variable

Next time the script is executed, you might have `v_firstName = "Phil"` or `v_firstName = "Pooja"`, depending on the first name of the student taking the course.

System and User-defined Variables

In Captivate, there are two types of variable:

- **System Variables**: These Variables are automatically created by Captivate. You can use them in your scripts to retrieve information about the project, about the system, or to control various aspects of the project.
- **User Variables**: These Variables are your own custom Variables that you create for your own specific use.

Exploring System Variables

Enough talking for now! Let's go back to Captivate to start our hands-on exploration of Variables by performing the following steps:

1. Open the `Chapter14/takeTheTrain.cptx` file.
2. Use the **Project | Variables** menu item to open the **Variables** dialog.

3. Open the **Type** dropdown, and choose **System** (see **1** in the following screenshot):

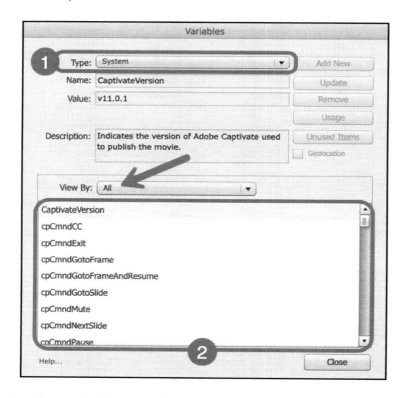

When selecting **System** in the **Type** dropdown, the list of available System Variables appears in the main area of the **Variables** dialog (marked as **2** in the preceding screenshot). Notice the **View By** dropdown (see the arrow in the preceding screenshot), which filters the Variables by their category.

4. Open the **View By** dropdown, and take some time to examine the available items. When you are done, select the **Movie Information** category.

Only Variables pertaining to the **Movie Information** category are now displayed in the **Variables** dialog.

5. Select the **CaptivateVersion** variable.

The upper area of the **Variables** dialog now displays the information for the **CaptivateVersion** variable. The **CaptivateVersion** variable gives you access to the version number of your Captivate installation.

6. Take some time to review the other **System Variables** available.
7. When you are done, click **Close** to close the **Variables** dialog.

Now that you have a better idea of the available System Variables, you will use one of them to dynamically generate the content of a Text Caption.

 You can find more information about the Variables that are available in Captivate at the following URL:
`https://helpx.adobe.com/captivate/using/captivate-variables`
`-list.html`.

Generating text dynamically

In Captivate, you can include Variables pretty much anywhere text is supported, typically within Text Captions and Smart Shapes. To be more exact, you will use the names of a Variable to specify the piece of data you want to show on the screen. At runtime, the web browser (if the project is published in HTML5) or the Flash Player (if the project is published in Flash) will replace the name of the Variable with the current value of that Variable.

In the next exercise, you will use the following steps to create a small note on the last slide containing the version of Captivate that was used to create the project:

1. Still in the `Chapter14/takeTheTrain.cptx` file, use the **Filmstrip** to go to the last slide of the project (slide 32).
2. Insert a new Text Caption on the last slide. Type `This project is powered by Captivate` in the Text Caption.
3. In the **Timing** or **Timeline** panel, make the Text Caption **Appear After 0 sec** and **Display for** the **Rest of** the **Slide**.
4. Still in the **Timing** inspector, make sure that the **Transition** is set to No Transition.
5. Feel free to further customize the formatting of this object.

6. Move and resize the Text Caption so that it fits on top of the white placard held by the Character. Remember that you can rotate an object using the icon just above the Text Caption, or the **Options** tab of the **Properties** inspector.

So far, so good! This is just about inserting a new Text Caption. Now, what you want is to automatically insert the version number of Captivate at the end of the Text Caption.

7. Double-click the new Text Caption and place your cursor at the end of the text, after the word **Captivate**.
8. Add a space in the Text Caption after the word **Captivate**.
9. On the **Style** tab of the **Properties** inspector, go to the **Character** section and click the **Insert Variable** icon, as shown in the following screenshot:

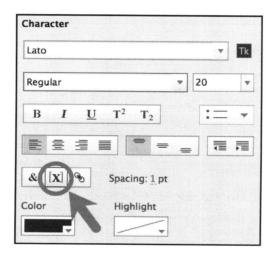

This action opens the **Insert Variable** dialog. You can use this dialog to choose the Variables whose value is to be inserted in the Text Caption.

10. In the **Insert Variable** dialog, change **Variable Type** from **User** to **System** if necessary.
11. In the **View By** dropdown, choose the **Movie Information** category.

12. Open the **Variables** dropdown and choose the **CaptivateVersion** Variables in the list of available variables.
13. Click **OK** to append the Variable to the Text Caption.
14. Use the **Timeline** or the **Timing** panel to have the Text Caption **Display For** the **Rest of** the **Slide**.

Thanks to this sequence of actions, you have added the **CaptivateVersion** system variable to the end of the new Text Caption. Actually, it is the name of the Variables that has been added to the Text Caption. The Text Caption now reads **This project is powered by Captivate $$CaptivateVersion$$**. At runtime, the **$$CaptivateVersion$$** part of the sentence will be automatically replaced by the value of the CaptivateVersion variable.

It is now time to test the new Text Caption in the **Preview** pane.

15. Use the **Filmstrip** to return to slide 31.
16. Use the **Preview | From This Slide** icon on the Toolbar to preview your sequence in the **Preview** pane (click **OK** to discard the warning about interactive videos not being supported in the **Preview** pane).
17. When the last slide appears in the **Preview** pane, pay close attention to the newly added Text Caption.
18. Close the **Preview** pane when you are done and save the file.

Normally, the Text Caption should read something like **This project is powered by Captivate 11.0.0!**

This first experience with Variables teaches you what **Dynamic Text** is. It is a piece of text that is generated dynamically at runtime.

Using User-defined Variables

What is true for System Variables is also true for User Variables. In this section, you will create a User Variable to store the first name of the student taking the course. To capture the value of that variable, you will use the Text Entry Box that you added at the beginning of the project in Chapter 5, *Developing Interactivity*.

Creating a User Variable

First, you will create your own User Variable using the following steps:

1. Return to the `Chapter14/takeTheTrain.cptx` file.
2. Use the **Project** | **Variables** menu item to open the **Variables** dialog.
3. Make sure that **User** is selected in the **Type** dropdown.

Note that Captivate has already generated a few User Variables for you. Two of these variables expose the name and the ID of the student when the course is hosted on an LMS (this data is transmitted from the LMS to your course module using the SCORM, AICC, or xAPI standard).

4. Click the **Add New** button to create a new variable.
5. Type `v_name` in the **Name** field.

This is the name of your new Variable. Remember that the name of a variable must comply with a strict set of rules and conventions, which are as follows:

- A variable name cannot contain any spaces
- A variable name cannot contain any special characters

In addition to these rules, some names are reserved by ActionScript/JavaScript and cannot be used as the names of your user-defined variables.

See the Captivate Help at
`https://helpx.adobe.com/captivate/using/create-user-defined`
`-variable.html` for a complete list of ActionScript reserved names.

6. Leave the **Value** field empty.
7. Optionally, add a meaningful **Description** to the new variable.
8. Click **Save** to create the variable and **Close** the **Variables** dialog.

Now that the Variable exists, you will use the Text Entry Box you added on slide 3 earlier in this book to capture the value to be stored in it.

Capturing values with Text Entry Boxes

Back in `Chapter 5`, *Developing Interactivity*, you added a Text Entry Box on slide 3 of this project. In this section, you will assign your new User Variable to this object. Whatever the student types in the Text Entry Box becomes the value of your `v_name` custom variable. Follow these steps to get started:

1. Use the **Filmstrip** to go to slide 3 of the `takeTheTrain.cptx` project.
2. Select the Text Entry Box on the right-hand side of the slide.
3. If needed, click the **Properties** icon on the Toolbar to open the **Properties** inspector.
4. In the **Style** tab of the **Properties** inspector, make sure that the **Validate User Input** checkbox is *not* selected.

Remember that a Text Entry Box can be used for two very different purposes. You can use it in a Quiz and ask your students to type something specific. In this case, you have correct and incorrect answers, and the value typed into the Text Entry Box must be validated.

However, in this example, you want to use a Text Entry Box to grab a piece of data (the name of the learner). There are, therefore, no correct or incorrect answers, so there is no need to validate what the user types into the Text Entry Box. Instead, you will associate this Text Entry Box with the custom `v_name` variable you created in the previous section.

5. Still in the **Style** tab of the **Properties** inspector, open the **Variable** dropdown.
6. Select the `v_name` variable from the list of available variables.

Your Text Entry Box is now associated with the `v_name` variable. This means that whatever the student types into the Text Entry Box at runtime becomes the value of the `v_name` variable.

Using the right variables

When creating the Text Entry Box, Captivate automatically creates the `Text_Entry_Box_1` User Variable. We suggest that you don't use these automatically created variables. Instead, take the necessary time to create your own Variables and give them meaningful names. This is critical for developing and maintaining your projects over time, especially when working in a team. Note that you can create your custom Variable directly from the **Properties** inspector by clicking the **[x]** icon next to the **Variables** dropdown in the **Style** tab. You can also safely delete the `Text_Entry_Box_1` user variable using the **Project | Variables** menu item.

The Text Entry Box is now ready to capture the student's first name and store that value in the `v_name` variable.

Using User-defined Variables to dynamically generate text

The last step of this sequence is to use the `v_name` Variable and its associated value to dynamically generate the title of slide 4. You can do this by using the following steps:

1. Use the **Filmstrip** to go to slide 4 of the `takeTheTrain.cptx` project.
2. Double-click the title placeholder and type `Welcome` followed by a space.
3. In the **Character** section of the **Style** tab of the **Properties** inspector, click the **Insert Variable** icon.
4. In the **Insert Variable** dialog, choose the `v_name` **User** variable.
5. When the **Insert Variable** dialog looks similar to the following screenshot, click the **OK** button:

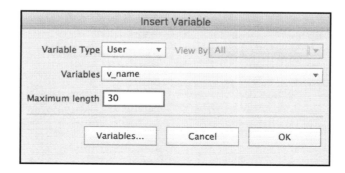

This action inserts the `v_name` variable in the title of slide 4 and encloses it in double **$** signs. The full text of the Caption is now **Welcome $$v_name$$**. Remember that, at runtime, the **$$v_name$$** part of the sentence is automatically replaced by the first name of the student, as typed in the Text Entry Box of the previous slide.

6. When you are done, save the file and return to the first slide of the project.
7. Use the **Preview | Next 5 Slides** icon on the Toolbar to preview the first few slides.

On the third slide, type your first name in the Text Entry Box, and click the **Submit** button. On slide 4, your name should be displayed in the title (if your name was longer than the 30 characters maximum length you defined, it will be truncated. You can always increase that value).

8. Close the **Preview** pane and save the file when you are done.

This exercise concludes your first exploration of System and User Variables. Before moving on to create more variables and use them in Advanced Actions, let's quickly summarize what you have learned so far:

- A variable is a named space in the memory of the computer. When referencing the *name* of a variable, you can access the *data* that the variable contains.
- There are two types of Variable in Captivate. System Variables are automatically created by Captivate. User Variables are yours to create.
- It is possible to insert Variables in Text Captions and in Smart Shapes to add dynamic text into the project.
- Dynamic text is a piece of text that is generated at runtime. The Flash Player or the browser's JavaScript engine retrieves the current value of a given Variable to generate the content of a Text Caption/Smart Shape.
- A Text Entry box can be associated with a User Variable. Whatever value is typed by the student into the Text Entry Box becomes the value of the associated Variable. Once captured and stored in a Variable, that piece of data can be used later in the project for various purposes, including generating dynamic text.

Working with Advanced Actions

An Advanced Action is a small program that is executed at runtime by the JavaScript engine of the web browser or the Flash Player. These Advanced Actions can be used to manipulate the data that's contained in Variables, Capitative objects, or even the project itself. In Captivate, there are three types of Advanced Action:

- **Standard Actions**: These actions are simple procedures that are always executed the same way in a linear fashion.
- **Conditional Actions**: These actions are a bit more complex. They can evaluate if a given condition is true or false and act accordingly. Consequently, they do not always perform the same set of actions each time they are executed.
- **Shared Actions**: These actions can be reused throughout a given project or even shared across projects.

In the next exercise, you will create a couple of Standard Actions to get a sense of what they can achieve.

Using Standard Actions

A Standard Action is the simplest form of Advanced Action that can be created in Captivate. A Standard Action is simply a list of instructions that the JavaScript engine of the browser or the Flash Player executes one by one and in order in response to an event. This is the main difference between a Simple Action (an action that you can perform from the **Properties** Inspector) and a Standard Advanced Action. When using the Simple Actions of the **Properties** Inspector, you can only select one action, but using a Standard Advanced Action, you can perform a series of Actions in response to a single event.

Using a Button to mute and unmute audio

In this section, you will use an Advanced Action to mute and unmute the audio of the project. Your goal is to provide the student with a Button in the top-left corner of the slide to toggle audio on and off. To do so, you first need to prepare and identify all of the ingredients that will make up this action.

Step 1 – Creating the Mute button

The first ingredient is the Mute button itself, which you will create using the
following steps:

1. Still in the `Chapter14/takeTheTrain.cptx` file, use the **Filmstrip** to
   return to the first slide of the project.
2. Use the **Shapes** icon on the Toolbar to create a new oval anywhere on the
   slide.
3. With the new shape selected, look at the **Properties** inspector.
4. In the **Options** tab, deselect the **Constrain proportions** checkbox and give
   your oval a Width and Height of 35 px. This is the best way to ensure that
   the oval is actually a circle.
5. In the **Style** tab, change the **Fill** type to **Image Fill**.
6. Click the **Fill** button (1) and choose to use a custom image (2). This
   operation is illustrated in the following screenshot:

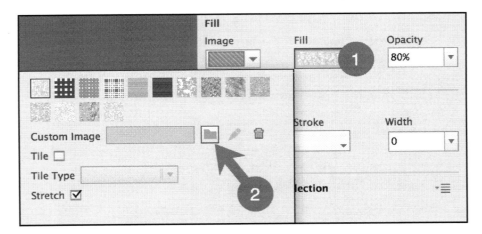

7. In the **Select Image/Audio from Library** dialog, click the **Import** button.
8. Navigate to the `Chapter14/images/Mute_Button_up.png` image file
   and use it as the image fill for the circle shape.
9. At the top of the **Properties** inspector, select the **Use as Button** checkbox.
10. Click the **State View** button to switch to the State view.

Notice that three built-in states are automatically generated by Captivate when
selecting the **Use as Button** checkbox. You will now customize these states and add
an additional custom state.

11. In the **Object State** panel, on the left-hand side of the screen, select the **RollOver** state.

12. In the **Style** tab, change the **Fill** type to **Image Fill**.

13. Click the **Fill** button and choose to use a custom image. Navigate to the `Chapter14/images/Mute_Button_over.png` image file and use it as the image fill for the circle shape in the **RollOver** state.

14. Repeat the same operations to change the image used in the **Down** state. Use the `Chapter14/images/Mute_Button_down.png` image file.

15. In the **Object State** panel, right-click the **Down** state and choose the **Duplicate State** menu item.

16. Duplicate the **Down** state as a **Custom** state named `Active`.

You should now have four different states for your Mute button. The **Normal, Rollover,** and **Down** states are three built-in states that are created automatically by Captivate. You simply customized them by changing the background image of the button in each state. On top of that, you have created an additional custom state called **Active**. This last state is simply a copy of the built-in **Down** state.

17. Use the **Exit State** icon on the Toolbar to return to the standard Captivate interface.

18. Move the Button in the header area of the slide next to the **DiDaXo** logo.

19. At the top of the **Properties** inspector, give your Button a meaningful name such as `btn_mute`. Don't forget to confirm the button name with the *Enter* or *Tab* key.

20. Switch to the **Timing** inspector.

21. Make sure your button appears **After 0 sec**.

22. Deselect the **Pause After** checkbox.

23. In the **Display For** drop-down menu, select the **Rest of Project** option. This ensures that the button will be displayed at this exact same location throughout the whole project.

24. Select the **Place Object on Top** checkbox. Since this button is displayed during the whole project, you want to make sure that it is always on top of whatever object you may add on the other slides of the project.

The first piece of your action is now in place. It should look like what's shown in the following screenshot:

Step 2 – Finding out which action to create

The second ingredient that you need is the name of the System Variable that you want to manipulate. Let's find it using the following steps:

1. Use the **Project | Variables** menu item to open the **Variables** dialog
2. In the **Type** drop-down menu, choose the **System** variables
3. In the **View By** drop-down menu, choose the **Movie Control** category
4. Select the **cpCmndMute** variable

This is the System Variable that you need to use to mute and unmute the audio. Take some time to read its description. Note that this variable accepts only two values. If it is set to 1, the audio is muted and if it is set to 0, the audio is un-muted. For you techies, this is an example of a Boolean variable in Adobe Captivate.

Step 3 – Creating the Action

The third ingredient is the Action itself. It should mute the audio and change the state of the Button. Use the following steps to create this standard Advanced Action:

1. Still in the `Chapter14/takeTheTrain.cptx` file, use the **Project | Advanced Actions** menu item to open the **Advanced Actions** dialog.

2. In the top left corner of the dialog, type `muteAudio` into the **Action Name** field.

Note that the name of the action must comply with the same strict rules as the name of the Variables (no spaces, no special characters, no reserved names).

3. In the **Actions** area of the dialog, double-click the first line of the table.

This adds a first step to the Advanced Action. In the first column, a yellow warning sign indicates that the action is invalid in its current state. In the second column, you will find a dropdown menu containing a list of possible actions.

4. Open the **Select an Action...** dropdown and take some time to inspect the list of possible actions.
5. When done, choose the **Assign** action in the list (unfortunately, these actions are not alphabetized).
6. Open the **Select Variable** dropdown and take some time to inspect the available Variables.

The **Select Variable** dropdown proposes a list of Variables whose values can be changed. (For instance, the `CaptivateVersion` Variable you used earlier is not listed, because you cannot change the value of this Variable. It is a read-only Variable.)

7. Select the `cpCmndMute` Variable.
8. Open the second **Variable** dropdown and choose **Literal**.
9. Type `1` in the field that appears, and press *Enter*.

The whole sentence becomes `Assign cpCmndMute with 1`. In plain English, it translates to *Turn off the audio*. Notice that the yellow warning sign in front of the action changed into a green checkmark. This is an indication that Captivate understands the first instruction of your Advanced Action, which is very good news!

10. Double-click the second line of the table to add a second step to the action.
11. In the **Select an action...** dropdown, choose the **Change State Of** action.
12. In the next dropdown, choose the object you want to change the state of. In this example, choose your **btn_mute** Button.
13. In the third and final dropdown, choose the custom state of the selected object you want to go to. In this case, you need the **Active** state.

Notice that only the **Normal** state and whatever custom states you created for the selected object are displayed in the list. The other built-in states (in this case, the *RollOver* and the *Down* states) are not listed. This is the reason why you had to duplicate the Down state as a custom state (you decided to name it *Active*) earlier in this procedure.

The reason why built-in states are never displayed when creating an Advanced Action is because these states are triggered automatically by internal Captivate actions. In this example, the *RollOver* and *Down* states of the Button were not available in the Advanced Actions dialog. You will see the same behavior while working with any other object that has built-in states.

Make sure that the **Advanced Actions** dialog looks like what's shown in the following screenshot before continuing with this exercise:

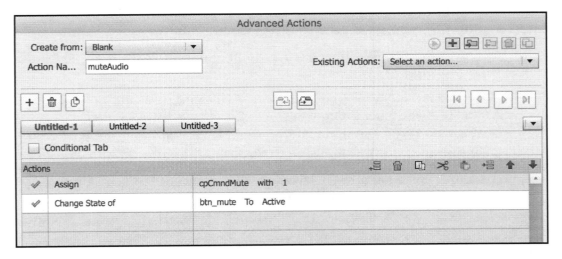

14. Click the **Save As Action** button at the bottom of the dialog to save the Advanced Action.
15. Acknowledge the successful saving of the Advanced Action and **Close** the **Advanced Action** dialog.

Your Advanced Action is now ready, but one last piece of the puzzle is still missing. You need to tell Captivate *when* you want your action to be executed. In other words, you need to attach the action to the **event** that will trigger it.

Step 4 – Assigning the Action to an event

In Captivate, there are lots of events you can attach Actions to. Some of them are **system events** (for example, the start of a course, the beginning of a slide, and so on), and some of them are **student-driven events** (typically, clicking a button). In this case, you will ask Captivate to execute the action when the student clicks the Mute button you created earlier in this chapter. Follow these steps to get started:

1. Still on slide 1 of the `Chapter14/takeTheTrain.cptx` project, and make sure that the **Properties** inspector displays the properties of the mute button.
2. In the **Actions** tab of the **Properties** inspector, change the **On Success** action to **Execute Advanced Actions**.
3. In the **Script** dropdown that appears just below, make sure that the **muteAudio** action is selected.
4. Save the file and use the **Preview | Project** icon on the Toolbar to test the project.

When the **Preview** pane opens, there are a few things to test to make sure that the action works properly:

- First, make sure your Mute button appears on the first slide and stays visible on the other slides of the project.
- When the audio narration starts (on slide 3), click the Mute button. Confirm that the audio stops and that the button switches to the Active state.

This first example illustrates how an Advanced Action can be used to manipulate a System Variable and how to attach an action to an event. By providing a way to mute the audio, you enhance the overall experience of your students.

Note that your Advanced Action is actually performing two things: it mutes the audio *and* it changes the state of your Mute button. In other words, clicking the Mute button does not trigger only one action, but a whole bunch of actions, as defined in the *muteAudio* Advanced Action. The ability to perform multiple actions as a response to a single event (in this case, clicking the Mute button) is the real power of those Advanced Actions.

Now there is one more problem to solve. When you click the Mute button, you turn the audio off, but there is currently no way of turning the audio back on (in other words, to unmute the audio). In the next section, you will use a Conditional Advanced Action to turn your Mute button into a toggle button that has the ability to turn the audio on, if it is currently off, and to turn the audio off, if it is currently on.

Using Conditional Actions

A Conditional Action is a bit more complex than a Standard Action as it is able to evaluate whether a condition is true or false and act accordingly. To illustrate this capability, you will now turn the Mute button you created in the previous section into a toggle button. This means that you want your button to be able to do two entirely different things:

- First, it needs to be able to *mute* the audio and change the state of the Mute button to *Active*
- Second, it needs to be able to *unmute* the audio and change the state of the Mute button back to *Normal*

To choose which set of actions to perform, your button needs to evaluate whether a condition is true or false. In this example, you first need to verify whether the audio is currently on or off. This is what will decide which set of actions to perform.

You will now update the Standard Advanced Action you created in the previous section and make it a Conditional Action using the following steps:

1. Still in the `Chapter14/takeTheTrain.cptx` project, use the **Project |
   Advanced Actions** tab to reopen the **Advanced Actions** dialog.
2. In the upper right corner of the dialog, open the **Existing Actions** drop-
   down menu and choose the **muteAudio** action. This is how you can update
   an existing action instead of creating a new one.
3. Just above the main area of the dialog box, select the **Conditional Tab**
   checkbox (see **1** in the following screenshot).

This turns your action into a Conditional Action. The **Advanced Actions** dialog updates and shows the interface that you will use to create the Conditional Advanced Action. Notice that you now have two main sections in the **Advanced Actions** dialog:

- At the top of the dialog, you have the **If** section (see **2** in the following screenshot). This is where you define the condition(s) to check before performing an action.
- The bottom half of the dialog (see **3** in the following screenshot) is used to define the actions to perform if the condition(s) defined above is (are) true. Note that the set of actions you defined earlier in this chapter has been moved to that section.

At the very bottom of the box, notice the optional **Else** section (see 4 in the following screenshot), which allows you to optionally provide an alternative set of actions to perform if the condition(s) evaluates to *false*:

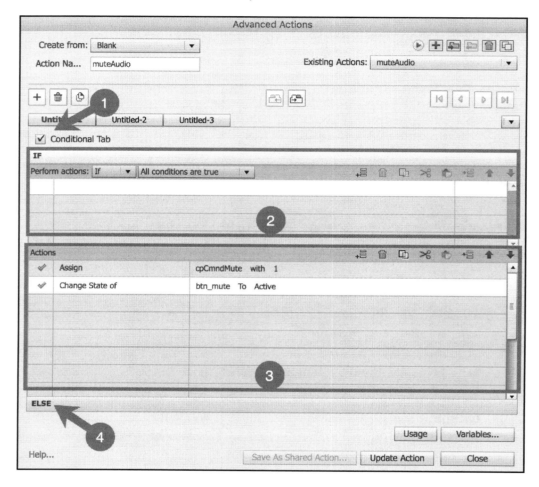

In this example, you want to execute the actions defined in the Actions section (**3** in the preceding screenshot), but only if the audio is turned *on* when the student clicks the Mute button.

4. In the **If** part of the box, double-click the first line of the table to add the first condition.

5. Open the **Variable** dropdown and select the **Variable** option from the list. Then, open the list again to select the cpCmndMute System Variable.

6. Open the **Select comparison operator** dropdown and choose the **is equal to** option from the list of available operators.

7. Open the last dropdown and choose **Literal** from the list. Then, type 0 in the field that appears.

The whole expression now reads `cpCmndMute is equal to 0` and a green checkmark appears in the first column of the table. In plain English, this translates to *If the audio is currently not muted*.

Notice the **AND** word at the end of the condition. It tells you that you can add more conditions and that these can be united by an `AND` operator. In other words, every individual condition should be true for the entire condition to be true.

8. Open the **All conditions are true** dropdown and choose the **Any of the conditions true** option from the list.

Note that the **AND** keyword switches to **OR**. In this case, the entire condition would be true if any one of the individual conditions evaluates to true.

9. Open the **Any of the conditions true** dropdown and choose the **Custom** option from the list.

In this situation, it is up to the developer to choose between **AND** and **OR** at the end of every condition. This allows you to create very complex conditions. In this exercise, you only have a single condition, so the choice between **AND** and **OR** is not relevant.

Another interesting functionality of the **Conditional Tab** is the *While* loop. The While loop is not used in this example, but you can find out more about it on the following blog article by our friend James Kingsley at `https://elearning.adobe.com/2017/06/making-the-most-of-adobe-captivate-2017s-while-loop/`.

10. Open the **Custom** dropdown one last time and revert to the **All conditions are true** option to return to the initial situation.

11. Click the **Else** button (marked as 4 in the preceding screenshot) to open the list of actions to perform if the condition evaluates to *false*.

12. Double-click the first row of the **Else** action pane.

13. Open the **Select Action...** dropdown and choose the **Assign** action in the list.

14. Open the next dropdown and select the `cpCmndMute` variable.

15. Open the second **Variable** drop-down list and choose **Literal**.

16. Type 0 in the field that appears and press *Enter*. This is the action that turns the audio back on if it is already muted when the student clicks the button.
17. Double-click the second line of the table to add a second step into the action.
18. In the **Select Action...** dropdown, choose the **Change State Of** action.
19. In the next dropdown menu, choose your **bnt_mute** button.
20. In the third and final dropdown list, choose the **Normal** state.

The **ELSE** part of your Advanced Action should look like what's shown in the following screenshot:

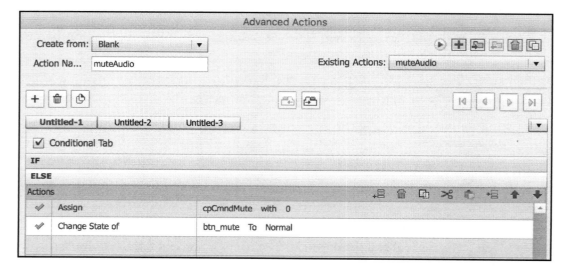

You will now update the name of your advanced action to better reflect what it actually does, and save it using the following steps.

21. In the **Action Name** field, in the top left corner of the dialog, change the name of the action to toggleAudio.
22. At the very bottom of the dialog, click the **Update Action** button.
23. Acknowledge the successful update and close the **Advanced Actions** dialog.

Your Advanced Action has been updated and is now much more sophisticated than before. It is now a conditional action that is able to execute different sets of actions based on whether a condition is *true* or *false*. Let's test it out.

24. Save the file and use the **Preview** | **Project** icon on the Toolbar to test the project.

When the **Preview** pane opens, test the following things:

- When the audio narration starts (on slide 3), click the Mute button. Confirm that the audio stops and that the button switches to the Active state.
- Click the same button again and confirm that the audio switches back on and that the button reverts to the Normal state.

Congratulations! You now have a toggle button in your project that your student can use to mute and unmute the audio.

Extra Credit – Creating a Closed Captions toggle button

In this Extra Credit section, you will create an additional button next to the **Mute** button you created in the previous sections and develop a Conditional Advanced Action to turn the Closed Captions on and off. The main difference between this button and the Mute button is the System Variable you need to manipulate. In this example, use the cpCmndCC variable to turn Closed Captions on and off. The general steps for this procedure go as follows:

- Create a Closed Captions button using the images stored in the Chapter14/images folder. Make sure you create a custom **Active** state for the button and place it next to the **Mute** button. Don't forget to give this new button a name in the topmost section of the **Properties** inspector.
- Use the **Timing** panel to make the button visible for the whole project on top of any other elements.
- Use the **Project** | **Variables** dialog to read the description of the cpCmndCC system variable.
- Create a conditional advanced action to determine the current value of the cpCmndCC Variable and act accordingly.
- Assign your Advanced Action to the click event of your new button.
- Test your button in Captivate's Preview.

This concludes your first exploration of Conditional Advanced Actions in Captivate. In the next section, you will discover Shared Actions.

Using Shared Actions

A Shared Action is an Advanced Action (standard or conditional) that can be reused multiple times in a single project or shared across multiple projects.

Shared Actions make sharing actions across projects easy. But there are other ways to share actions across projects. Dr. Pooja Jaisingh has written a great blog post about this that you can find at: `https://elearning.adobe.com/2013/12/the-most-awaited-enhancements-in-advanced-actions-and-variables-are-here/`.

Programming a conditional Button

In `Chapter 5`, *Developing Interactivity*, you created a sequence of slides to teach students about the different types of train ticket available in Belgium:

- On slide 13 of your `takeTheTrain.cptx` project, you have three Buttons, one for each ticket type. Each of these Buttons takes you to the corresponding slide in the sequence.
- Slides 14, 15, and 16 are the three destination slides of the Buttons defined on slide 13. Remember that, at the end of each of these three slides, the playhead jumps back to slide 13.
- Also remember that you used the Visited state of the Buttons to add a checkmark next to the ticket type that has already been viewed by the student.

In this section, you will make sure that the student goes through the three ticket types before clicking the **Continue** button that you added in the bottom right corner of slide 13.

To do so, you will first hide the **Continue** button. Then, you will create three User Variables to track which ticket type has been viewed by the student. When the student has viewed each ticket type at least once, you will reveal the **Continue** button on slide 13, allowing the student to jump to the next sequence and continue with the rest of the course.

Step 1 – Creating the necessary variables

The first step toward creating this advanced interactive sequence is to create the Variables that you will need to track the ticket types that are visited by the students:

1. Still in the `Chapter14/takeTheTrain.cptx` file, use the **Project |
   Variables** menu item to open the **Variables** dialog.
2. At the top of the **Variables** dialog, click the **Add New** button.
3. Type `v_standardTicket_visited` as the Variable name.
4. Type `0` as the initial value of the Variable.
5. Optionally, type a meaningful description into the **Description** field.
6. Click the **Save** button to save the new Variable.
7. Repeat the preceding process to create the `v_pass_visited`
   and `v_subscription_visited` Variables. Be sure to give the new
   Variables a value of `0`.

Make sure that the **Variables** dialog looks like the following screenshot before moving on:

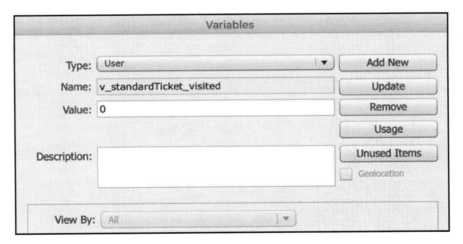

Each of these three Variables has an initial value of `0`, indicating that the corresponding slides have not yet been viewed by the student. You will use an action to turn the value of these variables to `1` when the student clicks the buttons on slide 13.

About naming variables

You already know that the name of a variable must comply with strict naming rules (no spaces, no special characters, and so on). That being said, any name that complies with these rules is not necessarily right.

When naming variables, it is important to stick to **conventions** in addition to complying with the rules, especially when working in a team. If no naming convention exists among the developers of a team, everyone ends up with his/her own naming rules and habits. In such a case, it is nearly impossible to keep track of variables and to maintain the projects over time. In this chapter, you will use the v_ prefix to mark your custom variables. It also helps you find your custom variables among the alphabetically ordered list of variables in Captivate. This is one of many possible naming conventions, but any other convention will do! The bottom line is: complying with the technical rules is not enough!

Step 2 – Creating the Shared Action

You will now create the actions that will update the value of the Variables that you created in the preceding section to 1 and jump the playhead to a different slide when the student clicks the buttons on slide 13.

If you think about it, you have three Buttons on slide 13 to which you want to apply a similar behavior (changing the value of a Variable to 1 and jumping to a slide). The only differences between the actions you'll create are the specific Variable to update and the specific slide to jump to. Thanks to Shared Actions, you will create a single Advanced Action that you will reuse multiple times, only changing some parameters each time you use the action.

In this exercise, you will use the following steps to create an Advanced Action that updates the value of the v_standardTicket_visited variable to 1 and jumps the user to slide 14:

1. Still in the Chapter14/takeTheTrain.cptx file, use the **Project | Advanced Actions** menu item to open the **Advanced Actions** dialog.
2. Type viewTicketType into the **Action Name** field.
3. Double-click the first line of the **Actions** list.
4. Choose **Assign** in the list of available actions (tip: you can type a when the menu is open to go to **Assign**).
5. Open the **Variables** dropdown and click the **Variables** item.

6. Choose the `v_standartTicket_visited` Variable in the list.

7. Open the second **Variable** dropdown and choose the **literal** item.

8. Type *1* in the field that appears and confirm this with the *Enter* key.

9. Double-click the second row of the **Actions** list to add a second action.

10. Choose **Jump to Slide** in the list of available actions.

11. In the next dropdown menu, choose the **14 Using standard tickets** slide.

Your Advanced Action is now complete. The two actions should read: *Assign the v_standardTicket_visited variable with 1*, and *Jump to slide 14*. This is illustrated in the following screenshot:

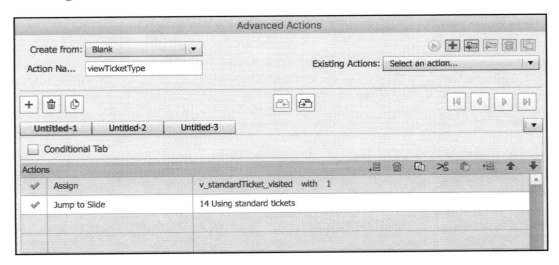

So far, creating a Shared Action is no different than creating a regular action. You will now save your new Advanced Action as a Shared Action.

12. Click the **Save As Shared Action** button at the bottom of the dialog.

This action opens the **Save As Shared Action** box. In this box, you need to define the parameters of the Shared Action. Remember that a Shared Action is meant to be reused multiple times in the project (or even across projects). The parameters of the Shared Action are the elements that differ each time the action is executed. In this case, you need two parameters: the Variable to update and the Slide to jump to.

Note that Captivate has automatically identified the potential parameters. It has already selected one of those parameters automatically, and there is no way to deselect the checkbox that Captivate has selected for you. The Variables and their values are not mandatory to parameterize in Shared Actions, as opposed to the objects and their states. This explains why, in this example, the *Slide to Jump to* parameter is mandatory, while the other two are optional.

You will now create those two parameters using the following steps:

13. Select the checkbox associated with the **v_standardTicket_visited** parameter.
14. Type `Variable to update` in the associated **Parameter Description** field.
15. Type `Slide to jump to` in the **Parameter Description** field associated with the **14 Using Standard Ticket** slide.
16. Take the time to type a meaningful **Description** as it will help you use this same action in other situations later.

Make sure that the **Save As Shared Action** dialog box looks like what's shown in the following screenshot before continuing:

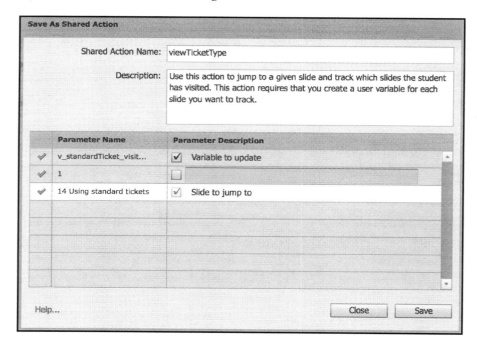

17. When you are done, click the **Save** button in the **Save As Shared Action** dialog.

18. Clear the information message and **Close** the **Advanced Actions** dialog.

The Shared Action is now complete and saved in the project. The next step is to attach this action to an event. In this case, the event is a click on the buttons associated with each ticket type.

Step 3 – Using and reusing the Shared Action

The last step of this process is to use and reuse your Shared Action. As with any other action, you have to attach your Shared Action to an event – only this time, you will attach the same Shared Action to many different events and set different action parameters each time. You will test it on the *Using Standard Ticket* button using the following steps:

1. Still in the takeTheTrain.cptx file, use the **Filmstrip** panel to go to slide 13.
2. Select the **Using standard tickets** button.
3. In the **Actions** tab of the **Properties** inspector, open the **On Success** dropdown list.
4. Choose the **Execute Shared Action** item.
5. Make sure that the **viewTicketType** action is selected in the dropdown that appears just below.
6. Click the little {P} icon next to the name of the action. This opens the **Shared Action Parameters** dialog.
7. Choose **v_standardTicket_visited** as the value of the **Variable to update** parameter.
8. Choose **14 Using standard tickets** as the value of the **Slide to jump to** parameter.

These actions are illustrated in the following screenshot:

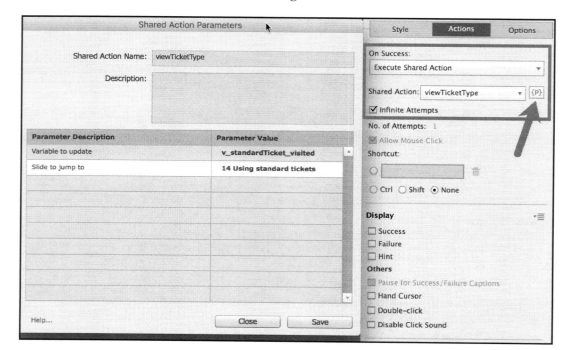

9. Click the **Save** button in the **Shared Action Parameters** dialog to finalize the process.

Reusing the Shared Action

All you need to do now is attach the same Shared Action to the **On Success** event of the other Buttons on slide 13. For each Button, the same Shared Action will be executed but using different parameters. These are the general steps to follow:

- Select the Button associated with one of the remaining ticket types.
- In the **Actions** tab of the **Properties** inspector, attach the viewTicketType Shared Action to the **On Success** event of the selected Button.
- Click the {P} icon and choose the parameters pertaining to the selected Button.
- When you are done, use the **Project | Next 5 slides** icon on the Toolbar to test your sequence and make sure you jump to the correct slide when clicking the Buttons.

Refer to the following table to choose the right parameters for the Shared Action:

Button	Variable to update	Slide to jump to
Using passes	v_pass_visited	15 Using passes
Using Subscriptions	v_subscription_visited	16 Using subscriptions

Reusing Shared Actions across projects

In the previous section, you created a Shared Action and used it three times in the same project. It is also possible to share actions across projects using two different techniques:

- With regard to the first technique, take a look at the **Library** panel and notice the **Shared Actions** section toward the bottom of the panel. In Chapter 4, *Working with the Timeline and Other Useful Tools*, you learned how to open the **Library** of another project in the current project to share assets (including Shared Actions) across projects.
- The second technique is to use the icons located in the top right corner of the Advanced Actions dialog. Using these icons, you can Import Shared Actions in the project or Export Shared Actions from the project. Captivate uses a file with the .cpaa extension to save a shared action externally:

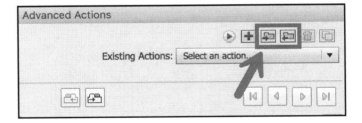

Shared Advanced Actions is a very powerful and advanced feature of Captivate. If you want to know more about it, consult the official Captivate help page on Shared Actions at
http://helpx.adobe.com/captivate/using/shared-actions.html.

Hiding and showing objects using Advanced Actions

The reason why you created the Shared Action in the previous section is to be able to track which ticket type students have visited. In this section, you will use that information to show the **Continue** button on slide 13, but only when all three ticket types have been visited at least once. The first step is to hide the **Continue** button and give it a name:

1. Use the **Filmstrip** to go to slide 13 of the Chapter14/takeTheTrain.cptx file.
2. Select the **Continue** button in the bottom right corner of the slide.
3. At the top of the **Properties** inspector, give this Button a meaningful name (for example, btn_continue) and press *Enter* to confirm.
4. Use the **Timeline** panel or the **Timing** inspector to make sure the **Continue** button **Appears After** 0 sec and stays visible for the **Rest of the Slide**.
5. Click the eye icon in the topmost section of the **Properties** inspector to hide this object from the student in the published project.

Make sure the topmost section of the **Properties** inspector looks like the following screenshot:

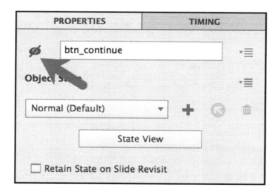

Visibility versus visibility

Notice that the **Continue** button is still visible on the stage, even though you have clicked the eye icon at the top of the **Properties** inspector. This is because the eye icon you clicked controls the visibility of the object *in the published project only*, but not in the authoring environment of Captivate. Use the **Preview | Next 5 slides** icon of the Toolbar to confirm that the **Continue** button is *not* displayed to the student. Remember that you have another eye icon located in the **Timeline** panel that controls the visibility of the object in the Captivate authoring environment only.

Now that the **Continue** button is hidden, you will create a Conditional Advanced action that will check whether the three slides associated with each ticket type have been visited. If all three slides have been visited, the action should turn the visibility of the **Continue** button back on.

6. Use the **Project | Advanced Actions** menu item to open the **Advanced Actions** dialog.

7. Type `showContinueButton` into the **Action Name** field.

8. Select the **Conditional Tab** checkbox.

9. In the **If** area of the **Advanced Actions** dialog, check whether the `v_standardTicket_visited` variable **is equal to 1**.

10. Add two more conditions in the **If** section to check whether the `v_pass_visited` variable **is equal to 1** and whether the `v_subscription_visited` variable **is equal to 1**. All three variables must be equal to 1 for the whole condition to be true.

11. In the **Actions** section of the **Advanced Action** dialog, add the **Show btn_continue** action.

In this case, there is no need to specify an action in the **ELSE** section. Make sure your **Advanced Actions** dialog looks like the following screenshot before moving on:

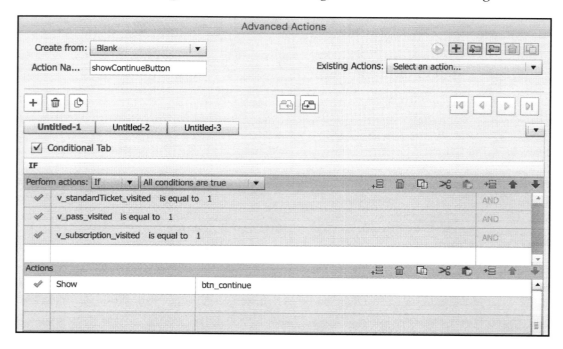

12. Save this as an Action and close the **Advanced Actions** dialog.

The last step of this process is to attach this action to the **On Enter** event of slide 13. Since the student goes back to slide 13 multiple times, your action will be executed multiple times as well. But it is only when all three variables are equal to 1 (in other words, when the student has visited all three ticket types) that the **Continue** button will appear on the slide.

13. Still on slide 13 of the `Chapter14/takeTheTrain.cptx` file, click once in the gray area around the slide to select the slide itself. After this operation, the **Properties** inspector displays the properties of the slide.
14. Switch to the **Actions** tab of the **Properties** inspector.
15. Open the **On Enter** dropdown and choose the **Execute Advanced Action** item.
16. Choose the **showContinueButton** action in the **Script** dropdown menu.

17. Use the **Preview | Next 5 slides** icon on the Toolbar to test your new action. Make sure that the **Continue** button displays only when you have visited the three ticket types.

In this section, you have used Advanced Actions to show an object when certain conditions are met. Using Advanced Actions to show and hide objects is another very common use case found in many Captivate projects.

While there is still so much more to say about Advanced Actions (they probably deserve their own book), let's consider your first exploration of the Advanced Actions of Captivate complete. It is time to quickly summarize what has been covered before moving on to the next section:

- There are three kinds of Advanced Action in Captivate: Standard Actions, Conditional Actions, and Shared Actions.
- A Standard Action is a simple list of instructions executed one by one and in order at runtime.
- A Conditional Action checks if a condition is met before executing an action.
- A Shared Action is an Advanced Action that can be reused multiple times in a project or even across multiple projects.
- Use the **Conditional Tab** checkbox of the **Advanced Actions** dialog to decide whether your action is a Standard Action or a Conditional Action.
- Advanced Actions can be used to manipulate Variables (System or User-defined), to manipulate objects in the project, or to manipulate the project itself.
- It is possible to give a name to any Captivate objects. This makes it easier to manipulate these objects with Advanced Actions or to use them as parameters of Shared Actions.
- Make sure you create and name all the Variables you need before creating your Advanced Actions.
- It is necessary to attach an Action to an event to instruct Captivate about when an Action should be executed.
- There are two types of event in Captivate: system events and student-driven events.
- System events are triggered automatically by the project. Examples of system events include the beginning or the end of a slide, the start of the project, and so on.

- Student-driven events are triggered by an action that's performed by the student. The typical student-driven event is clicking a Button, but it can also be clicking a Click Box, answering a Question Slide, and so on.

Variables and Advanced Actions are among the most advanced topics found in Captivate. You've only scratched the surface of this powerful feature in this book. With time and experience, you'll be able to take full advantage of this powerful tool.

 For more on Advanced Actions, make sure you subscribe to the blog of Lieve Weymeis, also known as Lilybiri, at `http://blog.lilybiri.com/`. She is a world-class specialist in Advanced Actions, and her blog is second to none when it comes to Variables, Advanced Actions, and other advanced tips and tricks for Captivate.

Geolocation in Adobe Captivate

What makes mobile learning so exciting and promising is the unique capabilities of the mobile devices used by the students when taking their online courses. One such capability is called **Geolocation**. It is the ability to detect where the learner is located while using his/her mobile device. Many apps take advantage of this ability to provide different content based on the user's location. For example, you can ask your mobile device to look for a restaurant within a 5-mile radius of your current location.

Captivate allows you to leverage this power in your eLearning course modules. You can access the location of the learner and provide content based on where the learner is located.

For the `takeTheTrain.cptx` file, the target audience is foreigners who want to visit Belgium. In other words, this project is not aimed at Belgian residents. In the next exercise, you will use the Geolocation capabilities of Captivate to detect the location of the learner taking the course. If you detect that the learner is in Belgium, you should display a warning message and give the learner the opportunity to skip the course. In every other situation, the course will run normally.

Inserting an extra slide

First, you need to insert a new slide into the project. To speed you up, this slide has already been created for you. All you need to do is copy-paste it using the following steps:

1. Still in the `chapter14/takeTheTrain.cptx` project, use the **Filmstrip** to return to the first slide of the project.
2. Open the `Chapter14/geolocation.cptx` file.
3. In the **Filmstrip**, select and copy the first and only slide of the project.
4. Return to the `takeTheTrain.cptx.cptx` file and paste the slide just after the first slide of the project. The new slide is inserted as slide 2.
5. Select the **No I will Skip It** button.
6. In the **Actions** tab of the **Properties** inspector, change the action of the button to **Jump To Slide**.
7. Select the last slide of the project (**Slide 33**) in the **Slide** dropdown that appears just below it.
8. Make sure that the **Action** of the other button is set to **Go to the next slide**.

This new slide should be displayed to Belgian learners only. In the next section, you will learn how you can access the location of the learner taking the course.

Detecting the location of the learner

One System Variables in Adobe Captivate returns the position (the latitude and the longitude) of the learner taking the course. Use the following steps to inspect this Variable and understand how it works:

1. Still in the `takeTheTrain.cptx` project, use the **Project | Variables** menu item to open the **Variables** dialog.
2. At the top of the **Variables** dialog, change the **Type** to **System**.
3. Open the **View By** dropdown.
4. Scroll to the end of the list and choose the **Mobile** item.
5. Select the **cpInfoGeolocation** variable.

As explained in the **Description** field, the cpInfoGeoLocation variable returns the geographic coordinates of the learner taking the course. It actually returns the Latitude and the Longitude coordinates of the learner (as well as the Accuracy, which is the range of the detected location). This ability is based on the Geolocation capabilities of the device that's used when taking the course.

Note that desktop and laptop computers can also be geolocalized based on the network they are connected to and on their IP address. This means that Geolocation is not specific to mobile devices. That being said, the accuracy of the Geolocation data largely depends on the device and the data connectivity being used.

Geolocation and privacy

Many users (including us!) decide to disable the geolocation capabilities of their devices for privacy reasons. This means that you may not have access to this data even if the learner uses a geolocation-aware device. You must respect this decision of the learner and always provide a default scenario that does not depend on the learner's location. In this example, the default scenario when geolocation information is not available is to skip the slide and continue the course normally, as if the student is not in Belgium.

Creating a custom Geolocation variable

Now that you have a way to detect the user's location, you will create a new User Variable in which you will store the geolocation coordinates of Belgium. At runtime, you will compare the cpInfoGeolocation System Variable, to your custom Belgium variable. If you detect that the learner is in Belgium, you should display the slide that you inserted in the project earlier in this section. Use the following steps to create a custom Belgium variable:

1. Still in the **Variables** dialog of the takeTheTrain.cptx file, use the **Type** dropdown to return to the **User** Variables.
2. Click the **Add New** button to create a new **User Variable**.
3. Type v_locationBelgium in the **Name** field.
4. Select the **Geolocation** checkbox below the **Unused Items** button.

By selecting this checkbox, you are telling Captivate that you want to create a custom Geolocation variable. The difference between a Geolocation variable and a standard variable lies in the way you express the value of the variable. When defining a standard variable, you simply type its initial value into the **Value** field of the **Variable** dialog. When defining a Geolocation variable, you must supply the **Latitude**, the **Longitude,** and the **Accuracy,** as shown in the following screenshot:

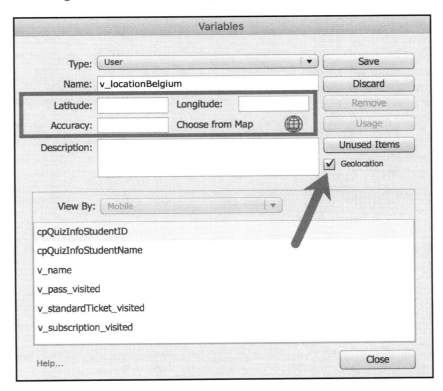

The **Latitude** and the **Longitude** are used to define a precise spot on Earth. The **Accuracy** is measured in meters. It defines the radius of a circle whose center is the precise spot defined by the **Latitude** and **Longitude** coordinates. If the location of the learner, as returned by the cpInfoGeolocation system variable is within that circle, the learner is considered to be at the custom location.

5. Click the **Choose From Map** icon to find out the **Latitude**, **Longitude**, and **Accuracy** values that you need.

The dialog that opens is based on Google Maps, which explains why you must be connected to the internet to make it work. Note that a circle and two points are present on top of the Google Map.

6. Type `Belgium` in the search field in the top area of the window.
7. Then, adjust the position of the two points so that the circle more or less covers Belgium on the map.
8. When you are done, click the **Submit** button just below the Search field.

Note that the **Latitude, Longitude,** and **Accuracy** values of the Geolocation variable have been automatically filled in. The center of the circle is used to define the **Latitude** and the **Longitude** values; the radius of the circle is used for the **Accuracy** value of the variable.

9. Click the **Save** button to save the new variable and close the **Variables** dialog.

In the next section, you will use this new Variable to check whether the learner is in Belgium or not and act accordingly.

Altering content based on the learner's location

The `cpInfoGeolocation` variable gives you access to the location of the learner, and your custom `v_locationBelgium` variable defines what area of the world you consider as *Belgium*. In this section, you will create a conditional Advanced Action that will compare these two Variables and decide whether slide 2 must be displayed to the learner or skipped. We will do this by using the following steps:

1. Use the **Project | Advanced Actions** tab to open the **Advanced Actions** dialog.
2. Type in `checkBeLocation` as the name of the action.
3. Select the **Conditional Tab** checkbox.
4. In the **If** part of the action, check whether the `cpInfoGeolocation` variable **is equal to** the `v_locationBelgium` variable.
5. In the **Action** section of the dialog box, double-click the first line and choose the **Continue** action.
6. Click the **Else** button at the bottom of the dialog box.

7. Double-click the first line of the **ELSE** panel and choose the **Go to Next Slide** action.

8. Click the **Save As Action** button at the end of the dialog box.

9. Acknowledge the successful creation of the script and **Close** the **Advanced Actions** dialog.

The last piece of the puzzle is to decide *when* the action needs to be performed. In this case, you want to attach this action to a system event.

10. Use the **Filmstrip** to go to slide 2 if necessary. Make sure that the **Properties** inspector displays the properties of the slide.

11. In the **Actions** tab of the **Properties** inspector, open the **On Enter** dropdown.

12. Choose the **Execute Advanced Actions** item in the list.

13. Select the **checkBeLocation** action in the **Script** dropdown menu.

The Advanced Action is executed when the playhead enters slide 2. If the geolocation of the learner is within the circle defined by the `v_locationBelgium` variable, the playhead continues normally. In the other situation, the playhead directly jumps to the next slide and skips slide 2.

To make this work, there is one last thing that we must check.

Enabling Geolocation capabilities

Before testing this new action, you need to make sure that Geolocation capabilities are enabled for this project. You can do this by using the following steps:

1. Still in the `Chapter14/takeTheTrain.cptx` file, use the **Window | Mobile** palette menu item to open the **Mobile Palette** dialog.

2. Make sure that the **Geolocation** checkbox is selected in the bottom section of the **Mobile Palette** dialog.

This action is illustrated in the following screenshot:

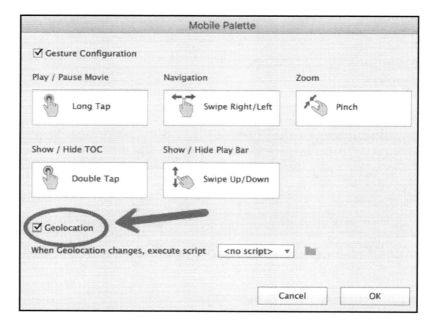

If this checkbox is not selected, Captivate will not be able to access the geolocation data. In other words, the **cpInfoGeolocation** system variable will always have a value of *undefined*.

Before closing the **Mobile Palette** dialog, take some time to inspect the other options that are available. For example, take good note of the ability to automatically run a script (in other words, an Advanced Action) each time a location change is detected.

3. Click the **OK** button to save these changes and close the **Mobile Palette** dialog.

Now that Geolocation has been enabled for this project, you can safely test your project.

4. Return to the first slide of the project and use the **Preview | HTML5 In Browser** icon to test your project.

When the project appears in the browser, notice the **Emulate Geolocation** dropdown menu. Use it to test your project, as if you were in Belgium, and confirm that slide 2 is displayed. Use the first icon of the playbar to rewind your project and test the Advanced Action. Test your project a second time, leaving the **Emulate Geolocation** option at its default value of **<nowhere>**, and confirm that slide 2 is skipped:

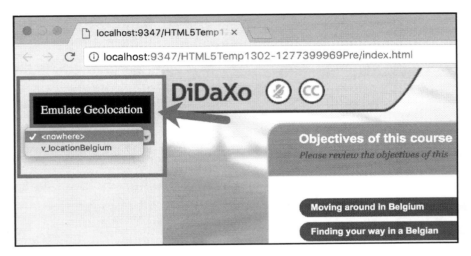

This exercise illustrates how you can use the Geolocation capabilities of Captivate to modify the content that is supplied to the learner based on their location.

Blog Post

Dr. Allen Partridge, Group Technology Evangelist for Adobe, has written an excellent blog post that illustrates another use case for these Geolocation capabilities. Even though this blog post was written with Captivate 8, it is still very relevant to Captivate 2019. See this blog post and download the sample files at `https://elearning.adobe.com/2014/06/location-aware-learning-example-with-complete-source-files-for-the-australia-zoo-app/`.

This concludes your exploration of the geolocation capabilities of Captivate. Let's list the main takeaways:

- Adobe Captivate leverages the geolocation capabilities of the devices used by the learner to take the course and gives you access to that information using a System Variable.

- The `cpInfoGeolocation` System Variable exposes the learner's location when taking the course. This ability depends on the device being used by the learner and on his/her privacy settings.
- Select the **Geolocation** checkbox in the **Variables** dialog to create custom User Variables that define a location. These variables define a circle on the globe. If the user is in the circle, Captivate considers that the user is at the custom-defined location.
- The center of this circle is a point defined by Latitude and Longitude coordinates. The radius of the circle is defined by the Accuracy parameter, expressed in meters.
- You can use Geolocation variables (System or User-defined) in any Advanced Actions, the same way you use standard variables.
- It is necessary to activate the Geolocation capabilities of Captivate in the **Mobile Palette** dialog to be able to detect the learner's location.

Working with JavaScript in Adobe Captivate

JavaScript is the programming language of web browsers. In the introduction to this chapter, you learned that Captivate generates a lot of JavaScript code during the publication process. In this section, we will take this concept one step further by providing Captivate with your own custom JavaScript.

This approach has a lot of benefits, as well as some drawbacks. First, let's look at some of the benefits:

- The ability to leverage the full power of the JavaScript technology gives you access to a tremendous amount of power. Remember that Captivate only exposes a small subset of this technology through Advanced Actions and Variables.
- The ability to leverage all the native capabilities of the web browser (such as local storage, cookies, fetch mechanism, and so on).
- The ability to define powerful custom interactions that are not natively available in Captivate.

Now, let's go over the drawbacks:

- JavaScript is a very broad and technical topic that requires proper training
- Lots of Captivate JavaScript features are undocumented

- Captivate does not (yet?) have a real JavaScript editor
- It is nearly impossible to test and debug JavaScript without publishing the Captivate project or previewing it in a web browser

This section will give you a glimpse of what can be done in Captivate with some simple JavaScript. But learning JavaScript is way beyond the scope of this book! While reading this section, keep in mind that this example is only the tip of a giant iceberg.

Generating random feedback messages with JavaScript

During the course of this book, you have discovered a lot of objects and interactions that make use of automatic feedback messages. For example, the Question Slides of the Quiz can display a red Failure Caption or a green Success Caption that depends on the answer supplied by the learner.

Using JavaScript, you will randomize these messages. The idea is to provide Captivate with a list of possible Failure and Success messages. When Captivate needs to display a feedback message, it will randomly pick one in the list of available messages and display it to the learner.

Let's start this process by creating two additional user variables in the takeTheTrain.cptx project.

 This exercise was inspired by our good friend Phil Cowcill during his session on JavaScript and Captivate at DevLearn 2018. DevLearn is the biggest eLearning conference in North America. If you ever travel to DevLearn, we might have a chance to meet in person! More information can be found at https://www.elearningguild.com/content/24/about-our-conferences/.

Creating Captivate Variables

First, you must create two additional User Variables in the takeTheTrain.cptx project by using the following steps:

1. Return to the Chapter14/takeTheTrain.cptx file.
2. Use the **Project | Variables** menu item to open the **Variables** dialog.
3. Click the **Add New** button to create a new User Variable.

4. Name the variable v_randomSuccess and leave the value field empty.
5. Click the **Save** button to save the new variable.
6. Repeat the same procedure to create the v_randomFailure variable.
7. Close the **Variable** dialog when done.

You now have two additional variables in your project. These two variables will be used to store the random success and failure messages that will be generated by the JavaScript function. The next step of this process is to create the necessary pools of messages using JavaScript arrays.

JavaScript is case-sensitive
When performing this exercise, be aware that JavaScript is case-sensitive. Make sure that you create variables that have the exact same name as what's given in this book. Any typo or case error will result in the code not functioning properly.

Creating pools of messages

To create pools of messages, we will use two JavaScript arrays. To make a long story short, a JavaScript array is a variable that has the ability to contain multiple pieces of data. Each piece of data in a JavaScript array is stored at a specific and unique index within the array.

Use the following steps to create the necessary arrays:

1. Return to the Chapter14/takeTheTrain.cptx file.
2. Use the **Filmstrip** to go to the first slide of the project.
3. Make sure that the slide is selected and open the **Properties** inspector.
4. In the **Actions** tab of the **Properties** inspector, open the **On Enter** drop-down menu.
5. Select **Execute JavaScript** in the list of actions.
6. Click the **Script Window** button.

This action opens an empty **JavaScript** window. It is in this window that you can write the JavaScript code that you want Captivate to execute when entering the first slide of the project. In this example, the JavaScript code has already been written for you, so you will simply copy/paste it in this window.

7. Navigate to the `Chapter14/js` folder in the exercise files.
8. Open the `01-createArrays.js` file in any text editor (you can use Notepad if you are on Windows and Text Edit if you are on Mac).
9. Use the *Ctrl + A* (Windows) or the *command + A* (Mac) shortcut to select all the content of this file.
10. Use the *Ctrl + C* (Windows) or the *command +C* (Mac) shortcut to copy the content to the clipboard.
11. Return to Captivate and paste the code (*Ctrl + V* on Windows/*command + V* on the Mac) in the empty **JavaScript** window.

When done, the **JavaScript** window associated with the **On Enter** event of slide 1 should look like what's shown in the following screenshot:

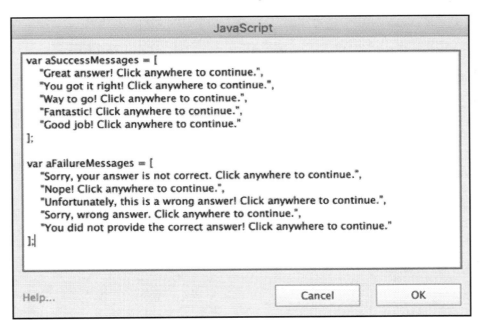

If you do not know JavaScript, don't worry! This code simply creates two JavaScript variables:

- The `aSuccessMessages` variable is a JavaScript array containing five possible success messages
- The `aFailureMessages` variable is a JavaScript array containing five possible failure messages

Take some time to read and understand this simple code and leave the **JavaScript** window open for the next section.

Creating the pickMessages() function

In this section, you will create a JavaScript function that will randomly pick one message in each array and save it as a Captivate variable. Use the following steps to copy/paste the code into the JavaScript window that is currently open in Adobe Captivate:

1. Navigate to the `Chapter14/js` folder of the exercise files.
2. Open the `02-pickMessages.js` file in any text editor available on your system.
3. Use the *Ctrl + A* (Windows) or the *command + A* (Mac) shortcut to select all the content of this file.
4. Use the *Ctrl + C* (Windows) or the *command +C* (Mac) shortcut to copy the content to the clipboard.
5. Return to Captivate and paste the code (*Ctrl + V* on Windows/*command + V* on the Mac) in the empty **JavaScript** window after the code already present in the window.

The **JavaScript** window associated with the **On Enter** event of slide 1 should now look like what's shown in the following screenshot:

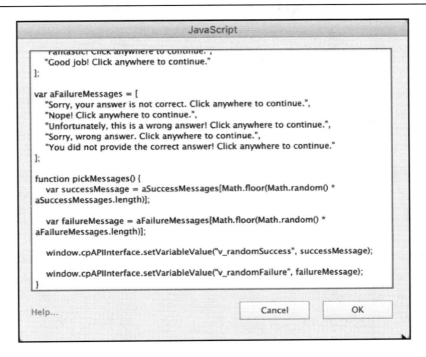

```
                            JavaScript
  Fantastic! Click anywhere to continue.",
    "Good job! Click anywhere to continue."
];

var aFailureMessages = [
    "Sorry, your answer is not correct. Click anywhere to continue.",
    "Nope! Click anywhere to continue.",
    "Unfortunately, this is a wrong answer! Click anywhere to continue.",
    "Sorry, wrong answer. Click anywhere to continue.",
    "You did not provide the correct answer! Click anywhere to continue."
];

function pickMessages() {
    var successMessage = aSuccessMessages[Math.floor(Math.random() *
aSuccessMessages.length)];

    var failureMessage = aFailureMessages[Math.floor(Math.random() *
aFailureMessages.length)];

    window.cpAPIInterface.setVariableValue("v_randomSuccess", successMessage);

    window.cpAPIInterface.setVariableValue("v_randomFailure", failureMessage);
}

  Help...                        Cancel              OK
```

The code you just added to the window defines a JavaScript function called `pickMessage()`. Each time the function runs, it will do the following:

- The first line of the function picks a random success message in the `aSuccessMessages` array
- The second line of the function picks a random failure message in the `aFailureMessages` array
- The third line of the function sets the value of the **v_randomSuccess** Captivate variable you created earlier to the randomly chosen success message
- The fourth line of the function sets the value of the **v_randomFailure** Captivate variable to the randomly chosen failure message

The magic takes place in the third and fourth lines of the function. This is when we make the connection between our JavaScript code and the Captivate project. To do that, we use something called the **Common JavaScript Interface for Adobe Captivate**.

Understanding the Common JavaScript Interface for Adobe Captivate

The Common JavaScript Interface for Adobe Captivate is a JavaScript object that is automatically provided by Captivate when viewing a project in a web browser. It is used as an interface between your Captivate content and the web browser used by the student to view the course. In this example, we need one function (called a *method* in geeky JavaScript jargon) from the Common JavaScript Interface for Adobe Captivate.

We will use the `setVariableValue()` method to give a value to the `v_randomSuccess` and `v_randomFailure` Captivate variables using JavaScript. To use this method, you must provide two parameters. The first one is the variable you want to assign a value to, and the second one is the value itself. Thus, the basic syntax of this method is as follows:

```
window.cpAPIInterface.setVariableValue("name_of_Captivate_variable",
"value_of_the_variable");
```

This corresponds to what you see on the third and fourth lines of the `pickMessages()` function.

Discussing the Common JavaScript interface for Adobe Captivate is more detail is way beyond the scope of this book. Just remember that it is a JavaScript object provided by Captivate and that it is used to link your JavaScript application with the Captivate project.

Learning about the Common JavaScript interface for Adobe Captivate

If you are into JavaScript, the Common JavaScript interface for Adobe Captivate is documented at the following URL: `https://helpx.adobe.com/captivate/using/common-js-interface.html`. Don't hesitate to consult that page whenever you need to use JavaScript in a Captivate project.

Before moving on to the next step of this process, you will need to close the **JavaScript** window:

1. Take some time to read the code you have pasted into the JavaScript window associated with the **On Enter** event of slide 1.
2. When ready, click the **OK** button to close the **JavaScript** window.
3. Save the file when done.

Next, you will use the `v_randomSuccess` and `v_randomFailure` variables to display random feedback messages to the learner.

Displaying random feedback messages

Now that the JavaScript code is in place, we can safely use the new *random feedback messages* capability of the project. You can do this by following these steps:

1. Still in the `Chapter14/takeTheTrain.cptx` file, use the **Filmstrip** to go to the Knowledge Check question of slide 10.
2. Double-click the red Failure Caption and delete the text it contains.
3. Use the **Insert Variable** icon of the **Properties** inspector to insert the **v_randomFailure** User Variable in the failure message. Increase the maximum length to `150` characters to accommodate longer messages.
4. Repeat the same set of operations to insert the **v_randomSuccess** variable in the green Success Caption.

Thanks to the preceding actions, the value of the **v_randomSuccess** and **v_random failure** variables will be displayed in the feedback messages for the Knowledge Check question of slide 10. The final thing we need to do is generate those random messages using our `pickMessages()` JavaScript function when the playhead enters slide 10.

5. Still on slide 10 of the `Chapter14/takeTheTrain.cptx` file, click the scrap area to select the slide. The **Properties** inspector now displays the properties of the slide.
6. In the **Actions** tab of the **Properties** inspector, open the **On Enter** drop-down menu.
7. Select the **Execute JavaScript** action.
8. Click the **Script Window** button to open the **JavaScript** window.
9. Type `pickMessages();` in the JavaScript window.
10. Click the **OK** button to confirm these changes and close the **JavaScript** window.

Be very careful to use the correct case (a capital **M** for **Messages**, for example) and to use an empty set of parentheses after the name of the function. These parentheses are a sign that we want JavaScript to *execute* the function. Also notice that there is no space between the name of the function and the opening parenthesis. Finally, make sure that you add a semi-column (`;`) at the end of the JavaScript expression.

The preceding actions are illustrated in the following screenshot:

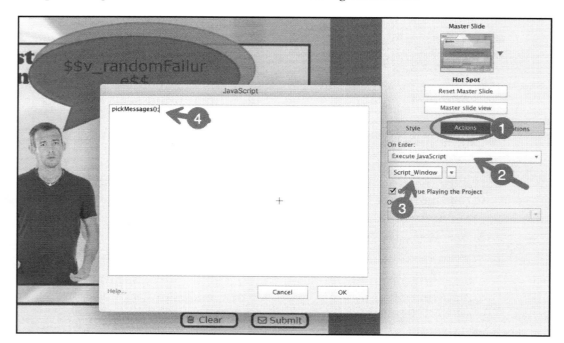

The moment of truth has arrived! It is now time to test your JavaScript function.

11. Because JavaScript is executed in a web browser, you must use the **Preview | HTML5 in Browser** icon on the Toolbar to test your JavaScript code.

When you reach slide 10 of the preview, provide the wrong answer to the question and confirm that a random feedback message from the aFailureMessages array is displayed in the red failure Caption. Then, reload the preview in the web browser. When reaching slide 10 for the second time, provide the correct answer and confirm that a random message from the aSuccessMessages array is displayed in the green Success Caption.

If everything works as expected, you can reuse the same pickMessages() function any time you need to randomize your feedback messages!

Extra Credit – Randomizing feedback messages in the Quiz

Now that you know your `pickMessages()` JavaScript function works properly, you can randomize the feedback messages of the remaining Question Slides in the project. The general steps are as follows:

- Use the **Window | Question Pool** menu item to open the **Question Pool** panel at the bottom of the screen.
- Select each Question Slide of the Question Pool one by one and change the **onEnter** action to **Execute Javascript**. Use the **Script Window** button to open the **JavaScript** window and type `pickMessages();`. Click **OK** to confirm and close the **JavaScript** window. Thanks to this step, each time a Question Slide is displayed to the Learner, the `pickMessages();` function is executed and new messages are randomly picked from the `aSuccessMessages` and `aFailureMessages` arrays.
- Replace the current feedback messages of all the Question Slides with the **v_randomSuccess** and **v_randomFailure** Captivate variables.
- Test your work in a web browser using the **Preview | HTML5 in Browser** feature of Captivate.

 Note that this technique is not limited to the Question Slides in the Quiz or to the Knowledge Check Questions in the project. You can use it anywhere Captivate displays Success and Failure Captions in response to an action.

This completes your first overview of JavaScript in Adobe Captivate. Before moving on to the next chapter, let's quickly summarize the key points of this section:

- JavaScript is the programming language of the internet. The JavaScript code is executed in a web browser when the Captivate course module is viewed by the learner.
- Captivate generates a lot of JavaScript code when the project is published.
- The Advanced Actions of Captivate allow you to leverage a small fraction of the power of JavaScript, without writing any code.
- If you are into JavaScript, Captivate lets you supply your own custom JavaScript code. To do that, use the **Execute JavaScript** action, click the **Script Window** button, and write your custom JavaScript in the **JavaScript** window that opens.

- Captivate provides a JavaScript object called the **Common JavaScript Interface for Adobe Captivate**. Use this object to link your custom JavaScript code with the Variables and functions of your Captivate modules.

- Using JavaScript gives you access to all the super powers of the JavaScript technology! But on the other hand, JavaScript is a very technical and borad topic with a steep learning curve!

Summary

Thanks to Advanced Actions and Variables, you have been able to add a whole new level of interactivity and sophistication to your projects. The good news is that you only saw the tip of the iceberg in this book. The possibilities are virtually endless, and your imagination is the ultimate limit to what can be achieved.

To implement Advanced Actions and Variables, Captivate takes advantage of the scripting capabilities included in both the HTML5 and Flash technologies. Advanced Actions and Variables can be used to create dynamic Text Captions, to turn the visibility of objects on and off, to control the course module, to access information about the course, and much, much more. If you are into JavaScript, you can even provide your own custom JavaScript and unleash the full power of the web when developing your courses!

With the completion of this chapter, your project can now be considered complete. Starting with the Captivate production workflow described at the very beginning of this book, you have now completed the second part of the process: the post-production phase. As anticipated, this has been the most time-consuming and feature-rich part of the workflow.

In the next chapter, you will finally make your work available to your learners by performing the last part of the process. The publishing step will allow you to publish your projects in various formats so that your students will be able to start watching and learning from your Captivate eLearning course!

Meet the community

In this section, we want to introduce you to Mark DuBois. Mark often provides webinars on Captivate for many different audiences. He focuses on eLearning "best practices" and always shares helpful tips and techniques. Mark tries to help faculty and staff better understand how Captivate modules can be easily incorporated into various Learning Management Systems.

Damien

When I was selected as an Adobe Education Leader, Mark was one of the first individuals I worked with. For an entire year, we worked on a project without seeing each other. We used the Adobe Connect web conferencing system to communicate and work remotely. We finally met in July 2014 in San Jose, California, during the Adobe Education Leaders summer institute. Having worked with him remotely for so many months, meeting Mark in person and having breakfast with him was a blessing. This is when I realized that no matter the technology, the human experience of an in-person conversation is priceless.

Mark DuBois

Mark DuBois has worked with web technologies since 1992. He has been developing eLearning modules for students (and faculty) since 1999 and has been using Captivate for many years. Mark recently retired as a tenured full professor at a college in Illinois, where he taught web technologies. He presently serves as Executive Director of WebProfessionals.org and still teaches on the development of eLearning modules. His main focus remains helping others become web professionals and teaching in many venues about eLearning and World Wide Web-specific topics.

During his time as a professor, Mark created the first accredited A.A.S. degree in Web Systems in the world. He also created the first accredited certificate in Rich Internet Application Development in the world.

Mark has been an Adobe Education Leader for over a decade (and often provides seminars and webinars on various aspects of Captivate to other Adobe Education Leaders and Adobe Education Trainers). Mark was awarded the AEL Impact Award by Adobe for his efforts in sharing his experience and knowledge with others (including Captivate best practices). Mark also recently authored a book for Adobe Press "Learn Adobe Dreamweaver CC for Web Authoring" with Rob Schwartz.

Working with WebProfessionals.org, Mark has personally been involved in the development and supervision of over 42 web design and development competitions throughout the world. He recently returned from one in Abu Dhabi, UAE.
You can learn more about his efforts at his personal weblog (and by following him on Twitter). Mark is also available to answer your questions about Captivate.

Contact details

- LinkedIn: www.linkedin.com/in/markduboiswebed
- Twitter: @Mark_DuBois
- Blog: http://blog.markdubois.info/
- Site: http://webprofessionals.org

15
Finishing Touches and Publishing

After working through all of the previous chapters, your time in the post-production studio is almost over. There are just a couple of things left to be done before the project can finally be published.

Most of these final changes are options and features that you will set for the entire project. These changes include checking for spelling errors, choosing how the project starts and ends, and so on. The most important of these final changes is probably the creation of a skin in the Skin Editor. A Skin allows you to customize the playback controls bar and create the Table of Contents for the project, among other things.

In the second part of this chapter, you will focus on the third and last step of the Captivate production process: publishing the project. Publishing is the process by which you make your Captivate projects available to the target audience. Most of the time, you'll publish your courses in the HTML5 format or in the Adobe Flash format so that any student can enjoy the content of your online course across different devices. However, Captivate can also publish courses in many other formats, which you will also learn about.

In this chapter, we will do the following:

- Check the spelling of the entire project
- Set the Start and End preferences of the project
- Export the properties of a project and import them into another project
- Customize the project's Skin
- Add a Table of Contents
- Publish the project in various formats

- Publish a SCORM package
- Use the Multi-SCORM packager
- Convert your HTML5 project into a native application using the Adobe PhoneGap Build service

By the end of this chapter, your work as an eLearning developer will be finished and your content will be ready to be pushed online.

Preparing your work

Before getting started with this chapter, take some time to reset the Captivate interface to its default implementation. If you are using the default interface mode, just close and restart Captivate. If you are using the advanced interface mode, use the **Window | Workspace | Reset 'Classic'** menu item to reset Captivate to its default. In this chapter, you will use the exercises that are stored in the Chapter15 folder. If you get confused by any of the step-by-step instructions, take a look at the Chapter15/final folder – which contains a copy of the files—at the end of this chapter.

Finishing touches

With the completion of Chapter 14, *Variables and Advanced Actions,* you can consider your project finished. There are, however, a few more things to do before the project can be published. In this section, you will focus on these small finishing touches.

Checking the spelling

Checking the spelling is probably one of the most fundamental finishing touches. The Spell Checker of Captivate works like any other Spell Checker that's found in any text authoring application.

In Captivate, the Spell Checker has the ability to check the text that's been typed in various locations throughout the project. This includes the text that's typed into Text Captions, Smart Shapes, Slide Notes, Text Animations, Buttons, and the Table of Contents.

Before using the Spell Checker, you will need to take a quick look at its options. You can do this by using the following steps:

1. Open the `Chapter15/encoderDemo_800.cptx` project.
2. Open the **Preferences** dialog of Captivate by using the **Edit | Preferences** (Windows) menu item or the **Adobe Captivate | Preferences** (Mac) menu item.
3. On the left-hand side of the **Preferences** dialog, click the **General Settings** category.
4. Click the **Spelling Preferences** button to open the **Spelling Options** dialog, as shown in the following screenshot:

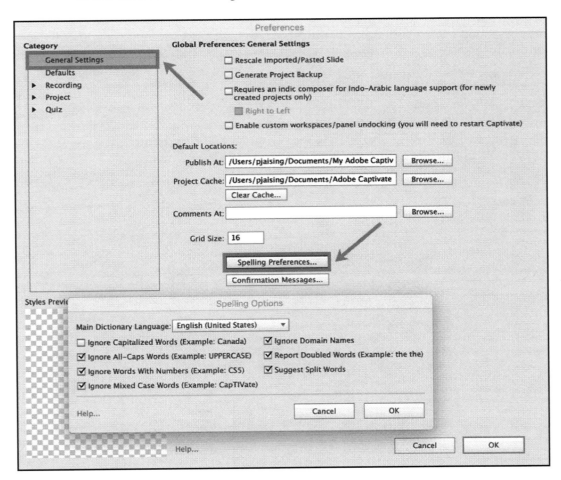

The main option of this box is the **Main Dictionary Language**. Note that, by default, most of the checkboxes of the **Spelling Options** dialog are selected.

5. Open the **Main Dictionary Language** drop-down list and take some time to inspect the available languages.
6. For this exercise, make sure you choose **English (United States)** as the **Main Dictionary Language**.
7. Take some time to inspect the other options in the dialog. They should be self-explanatory. Make sure you leave all the checkboxes at their current settings.
8. Click the **OK** button to close the **Spelling Options** dialog. Then, click **OK** again to validate these changes and close the **Preferences** dialog.

Now that you have a better idea of the available Spell Checker options, you will use this feature to check the spelling of the Encoder Demonstration.

9. Use the **Project | Check Spelling** menu item to launch the Spell Checker.

Some spelling errors have been left behind in this project. Each time a spelling mistake is found, the Spell Checker stops and proposes replacement words. Let the Spell Checker go through the whole project and handle each spelling mistake; they are detected using the dialog that's shown in the following screenshot:

At the bottom of the **Check Spelling** window are two important buttons.

10. Click the **Options** button at the end of the **Check Spelling** dialog.

The same **Spelling Options** dialog you accessed through the **Preferences** dialog will open.

11. Leave all the **Spelling Options** at their current settings and click **OK** to close the **Spelling Options** dialog.
12. In the bottom left corner of the **Check Spelling** dialog, click the **Help** link.

Such a **Help** link can be found in the bottom-left corner of many dialogs throughout Captivate. It opens the default browser and displays the **Adobe Captivate Help** page that specifically explains the options of the current dialog. The **Help** link is an easy and fast way to access specific help content.

13. Take some time to review the currently opened help page. When done, close your browser and return to Captivate.

When the spell check is finished, a message will appear, stating that the spell check is complete and that a certain number of corrections have been made.

14. Click the **OK** button to discard the information box.
15. Make sure you save the file before moving on.

Now that you've finished spell checking, you can advance to the other steps in your post-production work. Checking the spelling in Captivate is as easy as checking the spelling in any other text authoring application. Just remember that it is an essential part of any professional eLearning project.

Here's is a quick summary of what has been covered in this section:

- Captivate contains a Spell Checker that works the same way as any other Spell Checker that's found in virtually every text authoring application.
- The Spell Checker of Captivate has the ability to check the spelling of all the text that's been typed throughout the application. This includes the text that's typed into Text Captions, Slide Notes, Text Animations, Buttons, and the Table of Contents.

- The **Spelling Options** can be accessed through the **Preferences** dialog or directly from the **Check Spelling** dialog.
- The **Help** link found at the bottom left corner of many dialogs opens the default browser and displays the help page that's specifically dedicated to that dialog. It is a quick and easy way to access specific help content.
- Checking for spelling errors is an essential part of any professional eLearning project.

Exploring Start and End preferences

The next final touch you will focus on lets you decide how the course should start and how it should end. This is very important for fine-tuning a student's experience and to optimize the performance of the project when viewed over the internet.

In the following exercise, you will explore the available Start and End preferences by using the following steps:

1. If needed, return to the `Chapter15/encoderDemo_800.cptx` file.
2. Use the **Edit** | **Preferences** (Windows) menu item or **Adobe Captivate** | **Preferences** (Mac) menu item to open the **Preferences** dialog.
3. On the left-hand side of the **Preferences** dialog, select the **Start and End** category in the **Project** section.

The preferences pertaining to the **Project** section of the **Preferences** dialog are specific to the current project only. Your screen should now display the dialog that's shown in the following screenshot:

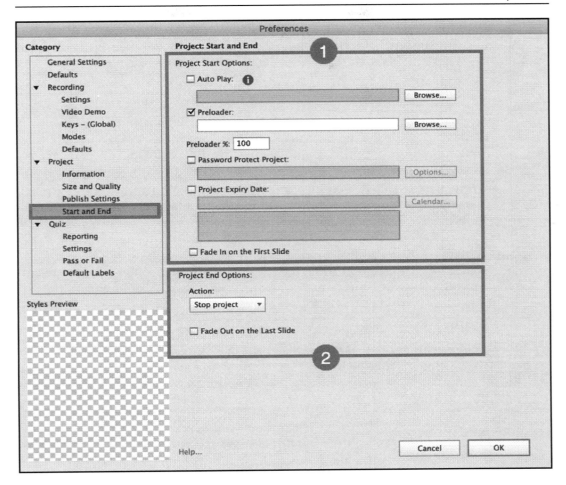

The **Start and End** preference page is divided into two sections. At the top of the page is **Project Start Options**, shown as (**1**) in the previous screenshot. At the bottom of the page is **Project End Options**, shown as (**2**) in the previous screenshot.

The following options are available under the **Project Start** section:

- **Auto Play**: If this option is selected, the project starts playing as soon as it finishes loading. If this option is not selected, the student will have to click the **Play** button to view the project. In this situation, you can use the **Browse** button to choose a static image that is displayed until the student clicks the **Play** button (such an image is often called a poster image).

Due to recent browser updates, all modern web browsers have discontinued auto-playing media in web pages. Because of that, HTML5, Responsive, and VR courses that were created using Captivate 2019 do not play automatically, even if you select the **Auto Play** option.

- **Preloader**: The **Preloader** checkbox is an image or an animation that is displayed while the movie is loading. If Preloader is selected and no preloader file is supplied, Captivate uses its default preloader. You can also create your own custom preloader or choose one from the gallery.

- **Preloader %**: This is, to us, the most important option of this **Preferences** pane. It represents the percentage of the file that has to be downloaded before the course starts playing. If it is set to 50 percent, the movie starts playing when 50 percent of the entire file has been downloaded. The remaining 50 percent is loaded while the beginning of the movie is being played. Use this option when the project is large and contains lots of audio or video; it reduces the waiting time for the student, and provides a much smoother learning experience.

There is an interesting post from the Iconlogic blog in which Kevin Siegel gives you more details about the Preloader and Preloader % options. It is available at http://iconlogic.blogs.com/weblog/2014/05/adobe-captivate -preloaders.html.

- **Password Protect Project**: This option is self-explanatory. Share the password only with those individuals who should be granted access to the project. Use this option if the project contains confidential information, or if you want to share a beta release of the project with a limited team of reviewers.

- **Project Expiry Date**: Use this option to set an expiration date for the project. The project will not be accessible if a student wants to access it after the expiration date.

- **Fade In on the First Slide**: This provides a smoother transition when the student enters the course. This option is turned off by default.

The following options are available under the **Project End Options** section:

- **Action**: The **Action** drop-down list is used to select an action that will be activated when the project is complete. By default, the **Stop project** action is selected.
- **Fade Out on the Last Slide**: This option is turned off by default, and allows the course to smoothly fade out at the end.

Now that you have had an in-depth overview of the available options, you can set the **Start and End** preferences of this particular project.

4. Set the **Preloader %** option to 50.

With the **Preloader %** option set to 50, the time spent by a student waiting for the course to download is cut in half. You will have to test what preloader percentage works best on your own projects.

5. Leave the remaining options at their default settings, and click **OK**.
6. Don't forget to save the file when done.

This concludes your overview of the **Start and End** preferences. Here's what we have learned so far:

- In the **Preferences** dialog, the pages pertaining to the **Project** section are specific to the current project only.
- In the **Start and End** category, Captivate shows options and features so that you can decide how the project should start and what happens when it has finished playing.
- Use these options to enhance the user's experience, enforce some basic security, and optimize the loading time of the movie.

Exploring other project preferences

There are some more project preferences available in Captivate that are worth exploring before publishing. Most of the time, the default settings for these particular options work just fine, so we won't modify any of these options in the Encoder Demonstration project.

In the following exercises, we will simply take a look at these preferences and briefly discuss some of them:

1. If needed, return to the `Chapter15/encoderDemo_800.cptx` file.
2. Use the **Edit | Preferences** (Windows) menu item or the **Adobe Captivate | Preferences** (Mac) menu item to open the **Preferences** dialog.
3. Open the **Size and Quality** category in the **Project** section.

This particular **Preferences** page provides options to control how the Captivate project is converted into HTML5 or Flash upon publication. If you want more information about any one of these options, don't hesitate to click the **Help** link in the bottom-left corner of the **Preferences** dialog.

4. Click the **Publish Settings** category in the **Project** section in the left column of the **Preferences** dialog.

This **Preferences** page displays additional options about how the project will be converted to HTML5 or Flash. Once again, the default options work just fine for the vast majority of projects. Let's briefly discuss some of these options:

- **Frames Per Second**: Use this option if you want to embed your Captivate project in a Flash project that has a different frame rate than 30 frames per second (FPS), or if you want to insert a video in your project that was created with a different FPS value. Otherwise, leave this option at its default value of 30 fps.
- **Publish Adobe Connect metadata**: This option adds some metadata to the project, thus producing a slightly larger file. This metadata is designed to facilitate the integration of the Captivate project in Adobe Connect. If you do not have access to an Adobe Connect server, there is no need to turn this option on.
- **Enable Accessibility**: This option makes the project 508 compliant. This was covered in detail in `Chapter 13`, *Creating Accessible eLearning*.
- **Externalize Resources**: When publishing to Flash, Captivate produces a single SWF file containing the whole project by default. Consequently, this file can be very large and hard to download based on your IT infrastructure. Externalizing resources tells Captivate to generate many smaller SWF files that reference each other. This option may help in optimizing the download time of a large project, but it makes it more difficult to push the Captivate project online once published. Note that some assets (such as inserted video files) are always externalized. Also note that when publishing to HTML5, all the resources are always externalized.

The other options on the **Preferences** page should be self-explanatory. Don't hesitate to click the **Help** link if you need more information.

> 5. Click the **Cancel** button to close the **Preferences** dialog and discard the changes you've made along the way.

This concludes our tour of project preferences. You will now export the preferences of this project and import them into another project.

Exporting project preferences

Remember that the options pertaining to the **Project** section of the **Preferences** dialog are specific to the current project only.

If you want to apply the same set of **Preferences** to another project, Captivate lets you export the preferences of the current project and re-import them in another project. In the following exercise, you will export the preferences of the Encoder demonstration and apply them to the Encoder simulation:

> 1. If needed, return to the `Chapter15/encoderDemo_800.cptx` file.
> 2. Use the **File | Export | Preferences** menu item to export the preferences of the demonstration.
> 3. Save the preferences file as `Chapter15/encoderDemo_800_Preferences.cpr`. This should be the default name that's proposed by Captivate.
> 4. Click **OK** to acknowledge the information box telling you that the export was successful.

Note that the file extension of such a preference file is `.cpr`, which stands for Captivate **PR**eferences.

You will now open the simulation and import the preferences of the demonstration. At the end of this process, both files will share the exact same project preferences.

> 5. Open the `Chapter15/encoderSim_800.cptx` file.

This is the simulation you created back in `Chapter 8`, *Capturing Onscreen Action*.

> 6. Use the **File | Import | Preferences** menu item to import a preference file in the project.
> 7. Browse to the `encoderDemo_800_Preferences.cpr` file that you created earlier in this exercise and click **Open**.

After a short while, an information box should appear on the screen telling you that the preferences were successfully imported.

8. Click **OK** to discard the information box.

9. Use the **Edit** | **Preferences** menu item (Windows) or the **Adobe Captivate** | **Preferences** menu item (Mac) to open the **Preferences** dialog of the encoderSim_800.cptx file.

10. Open the **Start and End** category in the **Project** section of the **Preferences** dialog.

11. Verify that the **Preloader %** is set to 50.

12. Click the **Cancel** button to close the **Preferences** dialog.

13. Use the **File** | **Save All** menu item to save both the Encoder demonstration and the Encoder simulation in one action.

The following list is a quick summary of what you have learned about the remaining project preferences:

- Most of the time, the default settings of the **Size and Quality** and **Publish Settings** pages of the **Preferences** dialog work just fine.
- These settings help you control the size of the published HTML5 or Flash application and optimize the download time of the project. On the other hand, they can be quite technical, and require some knowledge of Flash and HTML5 to be used efficiently.
- It is possible to export the preferences of one project and import them back into another project.

Preferences and templates

Templates offer another convenient way to share preferences across projects. Remember that the preferences that are defined in a template become the default preferences of all future projects based on this template.

Customizing the project's Skin

The Skin of a project is a collection of elements that are, for the most part, displayed around slides. This means that the elements of the Skin are not a part of the actual eLearning content. Learners use them to interact with the Captivate content, which enhances the overall user experience. A Skin is made up of three elements:

- **The Playback Controls bar**: This is the most visible element of a Skin. It contains the necessary buttons and switches that are used by the student to control the playback of the course. It also contains a progress bar that tracks the student's progression in the Captivate project.
- **The Borders**: The Skin Editor lets you create Borders around your projects. You can turn each of the four Borders on and/or off, and choose their width, color, and texture.
- **The Table of Contents**: The last element of a Skin is the Table of Contents. By default, it is turned off, but it is very easy to turn it on and generate a Table of Contents for the project.

By default, Captivate contains a handful of predefined Skins that you can apply as-is to your projects for rapid development. However, you also have the option of customizing any of the existing skins and saving that skin with your own unique Skin name.

Also remember that the color scheme of the Skin is the third element of a Theme. The other two elements are Styles and Master Slides. This has already been covered in Chapter 6, *Crafting the Graphical Experience with Styles and Themes*.

In this section, each of the three elements of the Skin will be discussed one by one. By following along, you will slowly create a unique Skin design that you will save and apply to other projects. Some more features of Captivate will be uncovered along the way.

Customizing the Playback Controls bar

The first and most visible element of the Skin is the Playback Controls bar. By default, it appears below the project and contains the necessary buttons and switches to let the student control the playback of the project.

In the following exercise, you will explore the available options and create a customized Playback Controls bar for your project:

1. Return to the `Chapter15/encoderSim_800.cptx` file.
2. Use the **Project** | **Skin Editor** menu item to open the **Skin Editor** floating pane.

The **Skin Editor** floating pane should look similar to what is shown in the following screenshot:

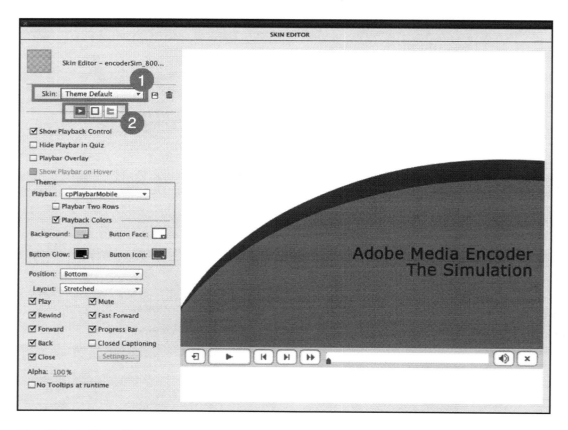

The **Skin Editor** floating pane is divided into two main areas. On the left-hand side are the switches, checkboxes, and buttons that you will use to customize the various elements of the Skin. On the right-hand side is a live preview of the first slide of the project. This area of the **Skin Editor** is automatically updated as you turn the options of the left area on and off.

Note two important controls in the upper-left area of the **Skin Editor** floating pane. The **Skin** drop-down list (marked as **(1)** in the previous screenshot) is used to choose and apply one of the predefined Skins of Captivate to the project. Right below this, there are three icons (marked as **(2)** in the preceding screenshot). Each of them represents one of the elements of the skin: the Playback Control, the Borders, and the Table of Contents.

3. Open the **Skin** drop-down list and choose any Skin you want.
4. The chosen Skin is applied to the project, and the preview area of the **Skin Editor** is updated.
5. Open the **Skin** drop-down list again and reapply the **Theme Default** Skin to the project.

The **Theme Default** Skin is the one that is stored in the Theme that's been applied to the project. As you can see, the colors of the Theme Default skin are yet to be defined given that the look and feel of the project have not yet been decided.

6. Make sure that the **Playback Colors** option is checked. Then, click the **Background Color** color picker in the **Theme** section of the left column.
7. Click the eyedropper icon in the top-center area of the color chooser.
8. Take a close look at your mouse pointer. It should look like an eyedropper. With this pointer active, click anywhere on the brown background where the **Adobe Media Encoder - The Demonstration** title is located.

The eyedropper tool takes the color of the pixel you click on and applies it to the **Background Color** property of the Playback Controls bar. This tool is an incredibly fast and easy way to make two different elements share the same color.

9. Customize the other colors of the Playback Controls bar to your taste.

Don't forget that you can import an image containing the color swatches in the Scrap area and use the Eyedropper tool to sample the colors of that image.

You will now remove the Playback Controls bar and see how the Skin updates.

10. Deselect the **Show Playback Control** checkbox.

When the preview updates, note that the playback controls are not displayed anymore, and that a border appears at the bottom of the project where the Playback Controls used to be. This is shown in the following screenshot:

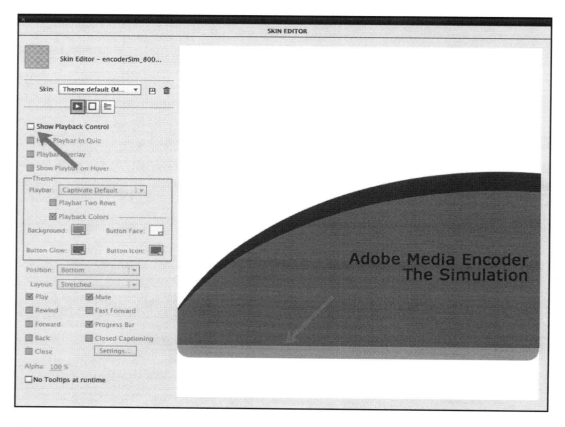

This is very interesting and deserves further investigation.

By default, when a Playback Controls bar is applied, a bottom border that has the same width as the Playback Controls bar is also automatically applied to the project. The idea is to put the Playback Controls bar on top of that bottom border so that it does not overlap with the content. This is a very good thing, and, most of the time, it works just fine. That being said, this system increases the overall height of the project. If you remember the discussion we had in Chapter 8, *Capturing Onscreen Action*, about the resolution of the movie, this can be quite a problem in some situations.

You will now set the Skin so that the Playback Controls are displayed without adding a single pixel to the height of the movie.

11. Select the **Show Playback Control** checkbox to turn the Playback Controls back on.

12. Right below the **Show Playback Control** checkbox, select the **Playbar Overlay** checkbox.

In the preview area of the **Skin Editor**, you should see that the Playback Controls bar now overlaps the slide. You can now safely turn off the border.

13. Click the **Borders** icon. It is the second of the three icons just below the **Skin** drop-down list.

14. Deselect the **Show Border** checkbox.

This is how you can accommodate Playback Controls without adding a single pixel to the height of the movie. The advantage of this is that the height of the project, as defined when creating it, is now respected. The disadvantage of this is that the Playback Controls now might sit on top of some important information that's displayed at the bottom of the slides.

15. Close the **Skin Editor** floating pane.

16. Use the **Preview | Next 5 Slides** icon on the Toolbar to test the new Playback Controls configuration.

17. When the preview is over, close the **Preview** pane.

In this example, you want the Playback Controls to be located outside the actual eLearning content. You will now return to the **Skin Editor** floating pane to revert to your latest changes before further exploring the other available options.

18. Use the **Project | Skin Editor** menu item to reopen the floating **Skin Editor** pane.

19. Deselect the **Playbar Overlay** checkbox.

20. Deselect the **Rewind, Forward, Back, Close,** and **Fast Forward** checkboxes.

21. Make sure the **Play, Mute,** and **Progress Bar** checkboxes are selected.

22. After this operation, the Playback Controls bar should contain only three buttons, along with the progress bar. Take some time to inspect the remaining options of the Playback Controls bar. Make sure that you do not change any of them before moving on to the next step.

With the completion of this exercise, you can consider the Playback Controls bar as definitive. Let's give it a try by using the **Preview** pane.

23. Close the floating **Skin Editor** pane.
24. Use the **Preview | Project** icon on the Toolbar to preview the entire project.

When the course starts to play, take a look at the Playback Controls bar below the project. It contains three buttons and the progress bar, as specified in the **Skin Editor** floating pane during the preceding exercise.

25. Close the **Preview** pane.

In the next section, you will discover the second element of a Captivate Skin: Borders.

Working with Borders

Borders are the second main element of a Captivate Skin. As discussed in the previous section, *Customizing the Playback Controls bar,* adding a Playback Controls bar automatically adds a corresponding bottom border so that the Playback Controls do not overlap with the slide elements.

 Please note that Borders are not supported in the HTML5 published output. Also, for responsive projects, the Borders option is disabled.

In the following exercise, you will further experiment with Borders and discover some more of their properties:

1. While still in the `Chapter15/encoderSim_800.cptx` file, use the **Project | Skin Editor** menu item to return to the **Skin Editor** floating pane.
2. Click the **Borders** icon below the **Skin** drop-down list.
3. Select the **Show Borders** checkbox to turn borders back on.

In the **Borders** tab of the **Skin Editor** floating pane, note that the Bottom Border is currently turned on, as shown in the following screenshot:

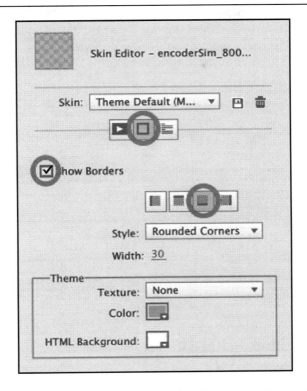

The bottom border is currently situated below the Playback Controls bar, which explains why you don't see it, even if it is turned on. You will now turn all four borders on and explore the available formatting options.

4. Click the Left border, Right border, and Top border icons to turn the corresponding borders on.
5. In the **Style** drop-down list, choose the **Square Edge** style. Note how the edges change from rounded to square.
6. Click the **Color** chooser. Use the eyedropper tool in the top right corner of the color chooser to give your border the same dark-gold color as the background of the slide.
7. Open the **Texture** drop-down list and choose any texture you want.
8. Change the **Width** option of the borders to 80.
9. Change the **HTML Background** color to a shade of gray.

The previous steps illustrate the available options of the Borders. You will now arrange these options to fit the particular needs of the Encoder simulation. Let's start with the most obvious change to be made: turning off this texture!

10. Open the **Texture** drop-down list again and choose **None** at the very top of the list.

This action turns the **Texture** off. With the **Texture** option turned off, the dark-gold border reappears.

11. Turn the Top, Left, and Right borders off. Leave only the Bottom border on.
12. Reduce the **Width** option of the border to 30 pixels.
13. Change the **HTML Background** color to white.
14. Close the floating **Skin Editor** pane and save the file.

With the completion of the preceding exercises, the first two elements of the Skin (Playback Controls and Borders) are now in place. In the next section, you will focus on the third and last element of the Skin: the Table of Contents.

Adding a Table of Contents

The Table of Contents is the third and last element of the Skin. By default, the Table of Contents is turned off.

In the following exercise, you will turn the Table of Contents on and explore the available options:

1. While still in the Chapter15/encoderSim_800.cptx file, use the **Project | Table of Contents** menu item to open the floating **Skin Editor** pane on the **Table of Contents** page.
2. Click the **Show TOC** checkbox to turn the Table of Contents on.

By default, the Table of Contents appears on the left-hand side of the project and lists every single slide. At the moment, the slides are named **Slide 1**, **Slide 2**, and so on. In the next section of this exercise, you will experiment with two ways of changing the names of the slides in the Table of Contents.

The first way is to change the name of the slide directly in the **Skin Editor** floating pane.

3. Right below the **Show TOC** checkbox, double-click the **Slide 1** title.
4. Change the name of the slide to Title and press the *Enter* key.

After a short while, the preview area will display the updated Table of Contents.

The second way of changing the slide name involves closing the **Skin Editor** floating pane and using the **Properties** inspector of each slide to specify a slide label.

5. Close the floating **Skin Editor** panel.
6. Use the **Filmstrip** panel to select slide 2. Make sure that the **Properties** inspector shows the properties of the slide and not the properties of any of the slide's elements.
7. At the top of the **Properties** inspector, type Introduction in the **Label** field.
8. Press *Enter* to confirm this change.

When you are done, take another look at the **Filmstrip** panel. The slide label should be displayed below the corresponding thumbnail.

9. Use the same technique to enter a label for other slides of the project:
   - **Slide 3**: Change the label to Beginning of the Simulation
   - **Slide 16**: Change the label to Ending slide
   - Leave the **Label** field of the other slides empty

10. Use the **Project | Table of Contents** menu item to reopen the floating **Skin Editor** pane on the **Table of Contents** page.

11. Click the **Reset TOC** icon below the list of TOC entries, as shown in the following screenshot:

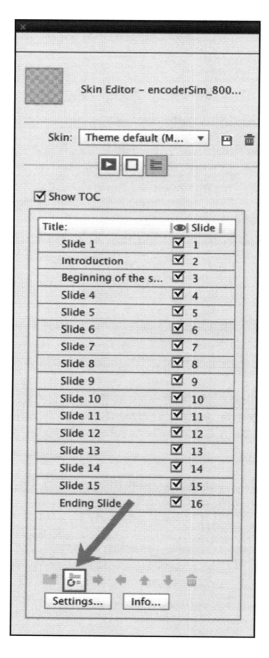

When you click on this icon, Captivate inspects the slides of the project and regenerates the entries of the Table of Contents. Note that the slide label, if any, is used as the title of the corresponding TOC entry.

Also note that there is no longer a label for slide 1. This tells you that manually changing the name of the slide in the TOC editor does *NOT* add a corresponding label to the slide.

About slide labels

In the current exercise, you are using slide labels to generate the entries of the Table of Contents, but adding labels to slides serves many other purposes as well. First of all, it makes the project easier to use and maintain, but the main benefit of a slide label is probably the enhanced accessibility it provides. The slide label is yet another piece of metadata that's used by the assistive devices of those with disabilities, and its use is mandatory to make the eLearning project 508 compliant. This option is covered in detail in Chapter 13, *Creating Accessible eLearning*.

You will now re-enter a name for slide 1 and hide the unnecessary slides from the Table of Contents.

12. In the **Skin Editor** floating pane, double-click the **Slide 1** title in the list of TOC entries. Retype Title and press the *Enter* key.
13. Uncheck the visibility checkbox for slides 4 through 15.

In the preview area of the **Skin Editor** floating pane, the corresponding slides disappear from the Table of Contents. At this point, there should be only four slides mentioned in the Table of Contents, as shown in the following screenshot:

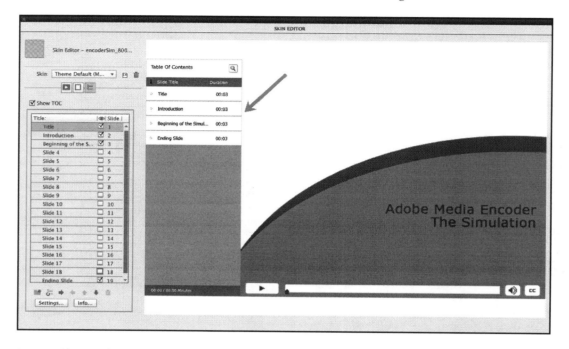

You will now finalize the look and feel of the Table of Contents.

14. Click the **Info** button at the bottom of the **Skin Editor** floating pane, below the list of TOC entries. The **TOC Information** dialog opens.
15. In the **TOC Information** dialog, click the **Project Information** button.

This last action copies the available project metadata to the corresponding fields of the **TOC Information** box.

16. Type `Adobe Media Encoder - Simulation` in the **Title** field of the **TOC Information** dialog.
17. At the bottom of the **TOC Information** dialog, open the **Font Settings** dropdown, and select **Title:**.
18. Change the Font to **Verdana**. You can also change the font color and size, if required.
19. Click the **OK** button to validate your choices and close the **TOC Information** dialog.

At this point, the Table of Contents is almost ready. One of the remaining problems is the extra space that the Table of Contents requires to be displayed properly. To address this problem, you will ask Captivate to position the Table of Contents on top of the slide and to provide a way to toggle its visibility on and off.

20. Click the **Settings** button at the bottom of the **Skin Editor** floating pane, below the list of TOC entries.
21. At the top of the **TOC Settings** dialog, change the **Style** option to **Overlay**.
22. In the **Color** section, click the **Background** color and use the eyedropper tool to apply the dark brown color from the slide.
23. Use the same technique to customize the other colors of the Table of Contents to your taste.

24. Change the **Alpha** value to 65% to create a semi-transparent Table of Contents:

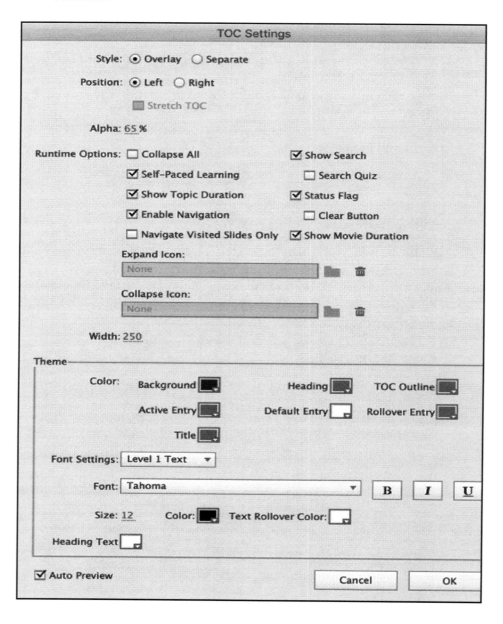

Take some time to explore the other available options, and feel free to modify them at will.

To learn more about the TOC Settings, visit the Adobe Captivate TOC Help page at `https://helpx.adobe.com/captivate/using/table-contents-toc.html`.

After performing these steps, your screen should look similar to what is shown in the following screenshot:

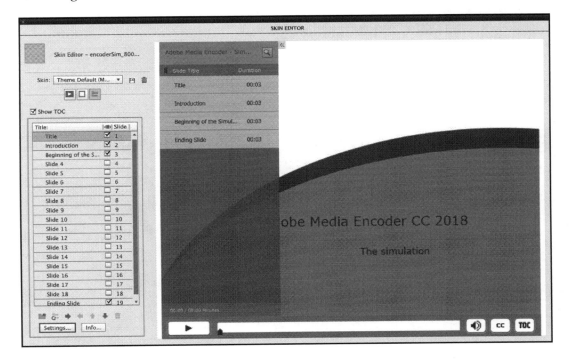

25. When you are happy with your Table of Contents, click **OK** to validate your choices and close the **TOC Settings** dialog.

26. Close the floating **Skin Editor** pane and save the file.

Your Table of Contents is now ready. It is time to give it a try in the **Preview** pane.

27. Use the **Preview | Project** icon in the toolbar to preview the entire project.

When the **Preview** pane opens, note the small double-arrow in the top-left corner of the slide.

28. Click that small double-arrow to reveal the Table of Contents.
29. Click the same icon to turn off the Table of Contents.

Note the new **TOC** button at the right edge of the Playback Controls bar.

30. Click the **TOC** icon at the right edge of the Playback Controls bar to reveal the Table of Contents.
31. Click the **TOC** icon again to turn off the visibility of the Table of Contents.
32. Close the **Preview** pane and save the file.

With the addition of the Table of Contents, the Skin of your project is now definitive. It looks so great (no kidding!) that you will want to apply it to other projects you are working on.

Applying the same Skin to other projects

To create a Skin for the Encoder simulation, you started from the **Theme Default** Skin and customized it. In this section, you will make the current Skin the **Theme Default** Skin, save the Theme, and apply it to other projects using the following steps:

1. While still in the `encoderSim_800.cptx` file, use the **Project | Skin Editor** menu item to reopen the floating **Skin Editor** pane.

The **Skin** drop-down indicates that the **Theme Default (Modified)** Skin is currently in use.

2. Next to the **Skin** drop-down list, click the **Save As** icon.
3. In the **Save As** box that pops up, leave the **Theme Default** name as it is and click **OK**.
4. Confirm that you want to replace the existing **Theme Default** Skin with a new one.
5. Close the floating **Skin Editor** pane.

The new Skin is now saved as the Default Skin of the applied Theme. You will now save the Theme in a new file and apply that theme to the Encoder demonstration.

6. Use the **Theme | Save Theme As** menu item to save the current theme as a new file.

7. Save the Theme in your exercise folder as Chapter15/encoderSim_800 Theme.cptm.

8. Switch to (or open) the Chapter15/encoderDemo_800.cptx file.

9. When in the demonstration project, click the **Themes** icon in the Toolbar to open the Themes picker.

10. Click the **Browse** link at the bottom-left corner of the Themes picker.

11. Apply the Chapter15/encoderSim_800 Theme.cptm theme that you created earlier in this exercise to the current project.

12. Click **Yes** to confirm that you want to apply the new Theme to the demonstration.

13. Go through the slides of your project, as some styles and Master Slides must be reapplied after applying the Theme to the project.

Both your demonstration and your simulation now share the very same theme. This means that they share the same set of Styles, the same Master Slides, and the very same Skin.

14. Use the **Project | Skin** menu item to open the **Skin Editor** of the Chapter15/encoderDemo_800.cptx file.

15. On the **Playback Controls** page of the **Skin Editor** floating pane, click the **TOC** icon below the **Skin** drop-down menu to jump to the **TOC** page of the Skin.

16. Click the **Show TOC** checkbox to turn the TOC on.

By default, the Table of Contents is not activated. When turned on, note that the TOC has the exact same look and feel as in the simulation project.

17. Deselect the **Show TOC** checkbox to turn the TOC off.

18. Close the floating **Skin Editor** panel.

19. Save the file when done.

Applying this Skin to future projects

If you want to apply this Skin by default to future projects, one of the possible approaches is to apply the Theme that contains the Skin to a Captivate template (a `.cptl` file). All Captivate Projects made from that template would, therefore, inherit the Skin that's been applied to that template.

Here is a quick summary of what has been covered in the Skin Editor section of this chapter:

- A Skin is a collection of three elements: Playback Controls, Borders, and a Table of Contents.
- By default, adding a Playback Controls bar to the project automatically adds a corresponding border. The idea is to place Playback Controls on top of the border to avoid overlapping between the Playback Controls and the project. You can customize the Playback Controls bar in many ways using the Skin Editor panel.
- You can also turn the Borders on and off, change their width, their color, and their texture.
- Borders are not supported in HTML5-published output and responsive projects.
- By default, the Table of Contents is turned off.
- It is possible to add labels to slides. Slide labels serve many purposes—for example, they make it easier for the developer to work with the project, they provide enhanced accessibility, and they are used to automatically generate the TOC. It is recommended that you add the slide labels before enabling the TOC.
- The **Skin Editor** floating pane provides many options to fine-tune the Table of Contents.
- Captivate contains default predefined Skins for rapid development.
- When you modify one of the predefined Skins, you actually create a new Skin that can be saved and reapplied to another project.
- The Skin of a project is one of the elements of the applied Theme. All the projects that have the same Theme inherit the same Skin.

Now that all of the *Finishing Touches* have been taken care of, you will move on to the final phase of the general Captivate production workflow and make your eLearning content available to your students.

Publishing a Captivate project

So far, you have been working with .cptx files, which is the default native file type of Captivate. The .cptx file format is great when creating and designing projects, but it has two major disadvantages:

- It can become very large. Consequently, it is difficult for you to upload the file on a website and for the student to download and view it.
- Opening a .cptx file requires Captivate to be installed on the computer system.

Publishing a Captivate project means converting (the proper word is *compiling*) the .cptx file into a format that can be easily deployed on a web server (or on an LMS), downloaded, and viewed by the students.

HTML5 and Flash are the two primary formats that you should use to publish your projects. The Flash format (also called the .swf – pronounced swiff-format) stands for ShockWave Flash. It is the file format that's used by the free Adobe Flash Player plugin. It has two advantages compared to the .cptx file:

- A .swf file is usually much smaller in size than its .cptx counterpart, making it much easier to upload and download across the internet.
- Any browser equipped with the free Adobe Flash plugin is able to open and play a .swf file. This makes it incredibly easy to deploy the courses that are made with Captivate.

That being said, the .swf format has some major disadvantages of its own:

- It requires the Adobe Flash Player plugin to be installed. If, for whatever reason, the plugin is not available, the .swf file cannot be played back.
- It cannot be modified. To modify a .swf file, you need to reopen the corresponding .cptx file, modify it in Captivate, and publish another version of the .swf file.
- The Flash Player plugin is no longer available on mobile devices. Consequently, a .swf file cannot be played back on a smartphone or on a tablet device.
- Some of the new features in Captivate such as Interactive Videos, Virtual Reality projects, and 360 Slides are not supported in .swf format.
- As per the recent announcement from Adobe Flash Player will be discontinued in 2020: see https://blogs.adobe.com/conversations/2017/07/adobe-flash-update.html for more information.

To overcome these limitations, other publishing formats are available in Captivate. The most popular alternative to the .swf format is the HTML5 format. When published in HTML5, the project can be played back in any modern browser without the need for an extra plugin. The HTML5-enabled project can also be played back on mobile devices, such as iOS and Android devices. Remember that Responsive and Virtual Reality projects can only be published in HTML5.

HTML5 also has its caveats. HTML5 cannot reproduce every single feature, animation, and interaction that Flash has made us accustomed to. That's why certain features of Captivate (such as Rollover Objects and Text Animations) are not supported when you publish your file in HTML5.

 For a complete list of unsupported features in HTML5, see the following page of the Captivate Help files: http://helpx.adobe.com/captivate/using/publish-projects-htm l5-files.html.

In this section, you will explore the various publishing options that are available in Captivate.

Publishing to Flash

In the history of Captivate, publishing to Flash has always been the primary publishing option. Even though HTML5 publishing is now taking the lead, publishing to Flash is still being used in Captivate.

In the following exercise, you will publish the Encoder Demonstration project to Flash using the default options:

1. Return to the Chapter15/encoderDemo_800.cptx file.
2. Click the **Publish | Publish to Computer** icon in the **Toolbar**. Alternatively, you can also use the **File | Publish** menu item.
3. In the **Publish to My Computer** dialog, change the **Project Title** to encoderDemo_800_swf.
4. Click the folder icon next to the **Location** field.
5. Select the Chapter15/publish folder from your exercises as the publish location.
6. Select the **Output Format** as SWF. Make sure that **HTML5** is not selected.
7. Select the **Publish to Folder** option below the Location section.

The **Publish to My Computer** dialog should now look like what's shown in the following screenshot:

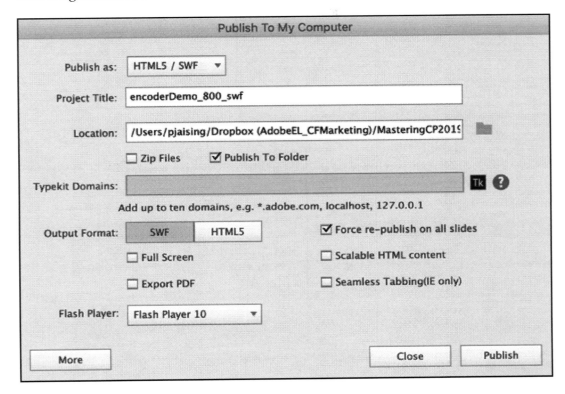

Take a quick look at the remaining options, but leave them all at their current values.

8. Click the **Publish** button in the bottom-right corner of the **Publish** dialog.

When Captivate has finished publishing the project, an information box will appear on the screen asking whether you want to view the output.

9. Click **No** to discard the information box and return to Captivate.

You will now use the Finder (Mac) or Windows Explorer (Windows) to take a look at the files Captivate has generated.

10. Use the Finder (Mac) or Windows Explorer (Window) to browse to the Chapter15/publish folder of your exercises.

Because you selected the **Publish to Folder** checkbox in the **Publish** dialog, Captivate has automatically created the `encoderDemo_800_swf` subfolder of the `Chapter15/publish` folder.

11. Open the `encoderDemo_800_swf` subfolder to inspect its contents.

There should be four files stored in this location:

- `encoderDemo_800_swf.swf`: This is the main Flash file containing the compiled version of the `.cptx` project.
- `encoderDemo_800_swf.htm`: This file is an HTML page that's used to wrap the Flash file.
- `standard.js`: This is a JavaScript file that's used to make the Flash Player work well within the HTML page.
- `captivate.css`: This file provides the necessary style rules to ensure the proper formatting of the HTML page.

If you want to embed the compiled Captivate movie in an existing HTML page, only the `.swf` file is needed. The HTML editor (such as Adobe Dreamweaver) will recreate the necessary HTML, JavaScript, and CSS files.

Captivate and Dreamweaver
Adobe Dreamweaver CC is the HTML editor of the Creative Cloud and the industry's leading solution for authoring professional web pages. Inserting a Captivate file in a Dreamweaver page is really easy! First, move or copy the main Flash file (`.swf`) as well as the required support files, if any, somewhere in the root folder of the Dreamweaver site. When done, use the Files panel of Dreamweaver to drag and drop the `.swf` file onto the HTML page. That's it! More information on Dreamweaver can be found at
`http://www.adobe.com/products/dreamweaver.html`.

You will now test the compiled project in a web browser. This is an important test as it closely recreates the conditions in which the students will experience the course once it's been uploaded onto a web server.

12. Double-click the `encoderDemo_800_swf.htm` file to open it in a web browser.

13. Enjoy the final version of the demonstration you have created!

The security settings of your Browser may prevent the Flash file from running properly. If you face any issues, refer to your Browser documents.

Now that you have experienced the workflow for publishing the project to Flash with the default options, you will explore some additional publishing options.

Using the Scalable HTML content option

Back in `Chapter 8`, *Capturing Onscreen Action*, there was a discussion about choosing the correct size for the project. One of the solutions was to use the **Scalable HTML content** option of Captivate. Thanks to this option, the eLearning content is automatically resized to fit the screen on which it is viewed. Let's experiment with this option hands-on by going through the following steps:

1. If needed, return to the `Chapter15/encoderDemo_800.cptx` file.
2. Click the **Publish | Publish to Computer** icon on the **Toolbar** to reopen the **Publish** dialog. The publishing options you defined in the previous section should have been maintained.
3. Change the **Project Title** to `encoderDemo_800_swfScalable`.
4. Ensure that the publish **Location** is still the `Chapter15/publish` folder of the exercise, that the **Publish to Folder** checkbox is still selected, and that the selected **Output Format** is still **SWF**.
5. Select the **Scalable HTML content** checkbox in the lower right area of the **Publish** dialog.
6. Leave the remaining options at their current values and click the **Publish** button at the bottom right corner of the **Publish** dialog.

When Captivate has finished publishing the project, an information box will appear on the screen, asking whether you want to view the output.

7. Click **Yes** to discard the information box and open the published project in the default web browser.

During the playback, use your mouse to resize your browser window and note how the movie is resized and always fits the available space without being distorted.

The Scalable HTML Content option also works when the project is published in HTML5 format. It is quite different from an actual Responsive Project, though. Here, the project is simply scaled up or down to fit the screen, but the layout itself is not adapted. A Responsive Project goes way beyond a simple scaling of the project as it provides a way to actually modify the layout itself based on the screen on which the content is viewed.

Publishing to HTML5

One of the main goals of HTML5 is to provide a plugin-free paradigm. This means that the interactivity and strong visual experience pioneered by the plugins (such as Adobe Flash) should be supported natively by browsers and their underlying technologies (mainly HTML, CSS, and JavaScript) without the need for an extra third-party plugin.

Because plugins are no longer necessary to deliver rich interactive content, any modern browser should be capable of rendering the interactive eLearning courses that are created by Captivate. This includes browsers that are installed on mobile devices, such as tablets and smartphones.

While this was an enormous change to deal with a few years ago, the shift from Flash to HTML5 is now almost over. Nowadays, most eLearning content is published in HTML5, which allows your students to enjoy your course modules across all their devices. Newest Captivate features, such as Responsive Projects, Interactive Videos, and Virtual Reality projects, are only supported in HTML5. Remember that in 2020, Adobe will stop supporting the Flash player. That event will conclude the shift of the entire industry from the historic Flash format toward HTML5.

Using the HTML5 Tracker panel

Because HTML5 and Flash are two different technologies, everything possible in Flash is not always possible in HTML5. Consequently, some features of Captivate that are supported in Flash are not supported in HTML5. When planning a project, it is necessary to decide up front on the format (Flash or HTML5) in which the project will be published and only use the objects that are supported by the chosen publication format.

In the following exercise, you will use the **HTML5 Tracker** to better understand what features of the Encoder demonstration are (un)supported in HTML5:

1. If needed, return to the `encoderDemo_800.cptx` file.
2. Use the **Window | HTML5 Tracker** menu item to open the **HTML5 Tracker** floating panel.

   The **HTML5 Tracker** floating panel informs you that one of the features that's used in this project is not supported in HTML5, as shown in the following screenshot:

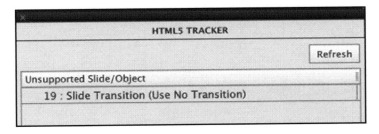

On slide 21, the slide transition is not supported, so let's remove the transition.

3. In the **HTML5 Tracker** panel, select **19 : Slide Transition (Use No Transition)**.
4. This takes you directly to slide 19. With the **HTML5 Tracker** still open, go to the **Timing** inspector.
5. Note that the current transition for this slide is set to Fade. Open the drop-down list and change it to **No Transition**.
6. In the **HTML5 Tracker**, click **Refresh** in the top right corner of the dialog. This removes slide 21 from the **Unsupported Slide/Object** list.
7. Close the **HTML5 Tracker** panel.

A comprehensive list of all the objects and features that are not supported in the HTML5 output is available in the official Captivate Help page at `http://helpx.adobe.com/captivate/using/publish-projects-htm l5-files.html`. Make sure you read this page before publishing your projects in HTML5.

In the next exercise, you will publish the Encoder demonstration in the HTML5 publishing format.

Publishing the project in HTML5

The process of publishing the project in HTML5 is very similar to the process of publishing the project in Flash. Perform the following steps to publish the project in HTML5:

1. If needed, return to the `encoderDemo_800.cptx` file.
2. Click the **Publish** | **Publish to Computer** icon in the Toolbar to reopen the **Publish** dialog.
3. Change the **Project Title** to `encoderDemo_800_HTML5`.
4. Ensure that the publish location is still the `Chapter15/publish` folder from your exercises.
5. In the **Output Format Option** section, select the **HTML5** button and then deselect the **SWF** button.
6. Deselect the **Scalable HTML content** checkbox.
7. Leave the other options at their current value and click the **Publish** button.

If you still have some unsupported slides/objects in your project, Captivate informs you that some of the features that are used in this project are not supported in HTML5.

8. Click **Yes** to discard this message and start the publication to HTML5.

When the publishing process is complete, a message appears, asking if you want to view the output.

9. Click **No** to discard the message and return to the standard Captivate interface.

You will now use Windows Explorer (Windows) or the Finder (Mac) to take a closer look at the generated files.

10. Use Windows Explorer (Windows) or the Finder (Mac) to go to the `Chapter15/publish/encoderDemo_800_HTML5` folder of the exercises.

You should find a bunch of files and folders in the `encoderDemo_800_HTML5` folder. These are as follows:

*   `index.html`: This file is the main HTML file. This is the file that the students will load into the web browser to play the course.
*   `goodbye.html`: This file is executed when the learner exits the course.

- `project.txt`: This file publishes the metadata for the course.
- `/ar`: This folder contains the required audio assets in `.mp3` format.
- `/dr`: This folder contains the required images.
- `/vr`: This folder contains the required video files in `.mp4` format.
- `/assets`: This folder contains the required CSS and JavaScript files.
- `/callees`: If your project contains a link to another Captivate project, you can copy the project to this folder.

You will now test this version of the project in a web browser.

11. Double-click the `index.html` file to open it in the default web browser.

Note that Captivate does a pretty good job of converting the demonstration to HTML5.

Publishing to Flash and HTML5

When in the **Publish** dialog, it is possible to select both the **SWF** and the **HTML5 Output Formats** at the same time. When publishing in both formats, Captivate generates the assets of both the Flash and the HTML5 application in the same folder. It also generates one extra file called `multiscreen.html`. This file is used to detect the device that's used to visit the course. If a desktop/laptop computer is detected (with Flash Player installed), it redirects the student to the Flash version of the course, but if a mobile device is detected, it redirects the student to the HTML5 version. Don't hesitate to test this out by selecting both the **SWF** and the **HTML5 Output Formats** before publishing the project.

Publishing a Responsive Project

The process of publishing a Responsive Project is quite similar to the process of publishing a standard project to HTML5. But because a Responsive Project is designed to be viewed on a mobile device right from the start, there are a few interesting options that can be fine-tuned before publication.

Using the Mobile Palette

One of the things that characterize the mobile experience (versus the desktop/laptop experience) is the touch screen. Owners of tablets and smartphones use their fingers to interact with their devices by performing various multi-touch gestures. These gestures include swipes, taps, double-taps, pinches, and so on. The Mobile Palette feature in Captivate gives you the ability to leverage the power of those mobile gestures in your projects. This is what you will examine right now using the following steps:

1. Open the `Chapter15/FluidBoxes.cptx` project. This is the Responsive Project you created in `Chapter 10`, *Creating a Responsive Project*.
2. Use the **Window | Mobile Palette** menu item to open the **Mobile Palette** floating panel.

As described in the following screenshot, the **Mobile Palette** allows you to enable mobile **Gestures** and **Geolocation** services for that project:

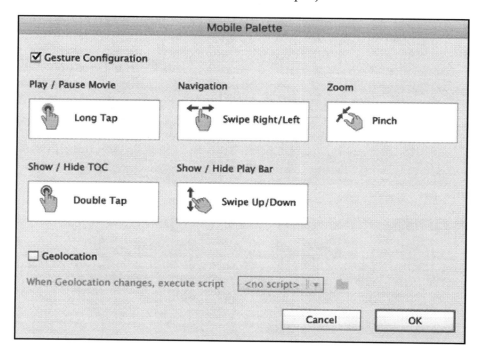

3. Make sure that the **Gesture Configuration** checkbox is selected for this project.

Since this project does not use any **Geolocation** capabilities, there is no need to select the **Geolocation** option.

4. Deselect the **Geolocation** checkbox, if needed.

Note that you can enable or disable gestures at the project level from this dialog. If you have a branched course and you wish to disable gestures for the decision screens, you can do so in the slide properties. Let's take a look at that workflow.

5. Click **OK** to validate the changes and to close the **Mobile Palette** panel.
6. To disable gestures for the first slide of this project, use the **Filmstrip** to go to the first slide.
7. Click the **Properties** icon in the Toolbar to open the **Properties** inspector.
8. In the **Properties** inspector, uncheck **Allow Gesture Navigation**.

You can follow the same steps to disable gestures for any other slide in the project.

This option in Captivate is yet another mobile-only option that has no equivalent in Flash. Note that these options are not limited to Responsive Projects. You can use Gestures and Geolocations on any standard project as well.

Publishing a Responsive Project

The actual publication process is the same as for a standard project published in HTML5. Let's check it out using the following steps:

1. Still in the `Chapter15/FluidBoxes.cptx` file, click the **Publish | Publish for Devices** icon in the Toolbar to open the **Publish** dialog.

At the top of the **Publish** dialog, note that the **Publish as** option is set to **HTML5**, without any options to turn it off or choose another publishing format.

2. If needed, change the **Project Title** to `Fluid Boxes`.
3. Use the folder icon to choose the `Chapter15/publish` folder from your exercise as the publish **Location**.
4. Make sure that the **Zip Files** checkbox is deselected.

The **Publish** dialog should now look like what's shown in the following screenshot:

Note that the bottom part of the dialog displays information about the project being published. Also note that you can use the blue hyperlinks to access various panels and preferences should you need to perform some last-minute changes before publishing.

5. Click the **Publish** button at the bottom-right corner of the dialog.

When the publishing process is complete, a second message will appear, asking you whether you want to view the output.

6. Click **Yes** to discard the message and view the published project in a web browser.

That's it! Apart from the fact that a Responsive Project can only be published in HTML5, the process is actually the same as for a standard project that's published in HTML5. Before moving on to the next section, take some time to inspect the published files on your computer. They should be in the `Chapter15/publish/Fluid Boxes` folder of your exercises.

Publishing a Virtual Reality project

Virtual Reality projects in Captivate have the same publishing options and process as those available for Responsive Projects. This is because VR projects and Responsive Projects can only be published in HTML5.

Let's check this out using the following steps:

1. Open the `Chapter15/VR_Project.cptx` project. This is the Virtual Reality project you created in `Chapter 11`, *Creating Virtual Reality Projects*.
2. Click the **Publish | Publish for Virtual Reality Devices** icon in the Toolbar to open the **Publish** dialog.

At the top of the **Publish** dialog, note that, similar to Responsive projects, the **Publish as** option is set to **HTML5**, without any options to turn it off or choose another publishing format.

3. If needed, change the **Project Title** to `VR Project`.
4. Use the folder icon to choose the `Chapter15/publish` folder from your exercise as the publish **Location**.
5. Make sure that the **Zip Files** checkbox is deselected.
6. Click the **Publish** button at the bottom right corner of the dialog.

When the publishing process is complete, a second message will appear, asking you whether you want to view the output.

7. Click **No** to discard the messagea **VR_Project.cptx** project.

The VR project is now published and ready to be deployed to a web server or an LMS.

Publishing an eLearning-enabled project

As a Captivate user, publishing an eLearning-enabled project is not very different from publishing a normal project in Flash or HTML5. Behind the scenes, however, Captivate generates a whole bunch of files to enable SCORM, AICC, or xAPI compliance. In this section, you will publish your SCORM-enabled *Take The Train* project.

Publishing the SCORM package in HTML5

In this section, you will publish your SCORM-enabled project in HTML5 format using the following steps:

1. Open the `Chapter15/takeTheTrain.cptx` project.
2. Use the **Publish | Publish to Computer** icon in the Toolbar to open the **Publish** dialog.
3. As Typekit fonts (now known as Adobe Fonts) have been used in this project, you will get a message that the fonts might look slightly different. While creating the Captivate project, you used Typekit Sync fonts, but the published files will use the corresponding web fonts, which may result in minor differences. Read the message and click **Next**.
4. In the **Publish to My Computer** dialog, change the **Project Title** to `takeTheTrain_HTML5_SCORM`.
5. Ensure that the publish **Location** is the `Chapter15/publish` folder of your exercises.
6. In the **Typekit Domains** section, type the domain name of the LMS or web server you will host your course on. You can add up to ten domains to this field.
7. Click the **More** button in the bottom-left corner of the **Publish** dialog.

Take good note of the information that's revealed by the **More** button. Note that the **eLearning Output** is set to **Disabled**. Let's change it to SCORM 1.2.

8. Click the **Disabled** link. This opens the **Preferences** dialog with the Quiz Reporting section visible.
9. Select **Enable reporting for this project**. This enables all LMS-related settings in the dialog.
10. Make sure that **Standard** is set to **SCORM 1.2**.
11. Click **OK** to confirm these changes and close the **Preferences** dialog:

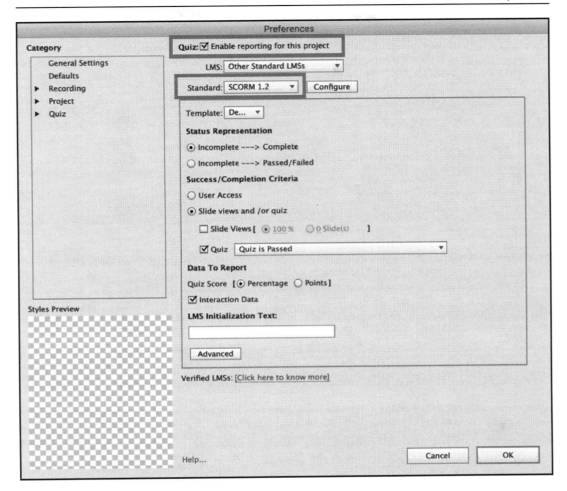

This takes you back to the **Publish To My Computer** dialog. Note that the **Zip Files** option has been automatically selected by Captivate. This is the default behavior when reporting is enabled. You should leave this checkbox selected when publishing an eLearning-enabled project. After this has been published, you have to upload that single `.zip` file to the LMS as-is. A SCORM-compliant LMS is able to unzip the package and properly deploy the files it contains.

12. In the **Output Format** section, make sure that the **HTML5** option is the only one that's selected.
13. Click the **Publish** button in the bottom-right corner of the **Publish** dialog.

A dialog should appear, warning you that negative scoring is not supported in SCORM 1.2. This means that some of the scoring properties that have been set for your quiz will not be enforced by the LMS because they are not supported in SCORM 1.2. These unsupported scoring options include negative scoring, penalties, and partial scoring.

14. Click **Yes** to acknowledge this message and move on with publishing the project anyway.
15. Acknowledge the **Publish Complete** message by clicking the **OK** button.

You will now take a look at the generated .zip file.

16. Use the Finder (Mac) or Windows Explorer (Windows) to navigate to the Chapter15/publish folder of the exercises files.

You should find the takeTheTrain_HTML5_SCORM.zip file in this folder.

17. Unzip the file to take a closer look at its content.

This is where the magic takes place! In the unzipped version of the file, you should find the same files as when you published a regular non-SCORM project in HTML5. However, because you decided to produce a SCORM-compliant package, Captivate has generated lots of extra files. These extra files are used to enable communication between the LMS and the eLearning content that's produced by Captivate.

The most important of these extra files is the imsmanifest.xml file. This file is the SCORM Manifest file. It must be stored at the root of the SCORM package. Feel free to open this file in your favorite text editor to take a look at its content (but make sure you do not modify it). The manifest file describes the course's structure to the LMS using a SCORM-compliant XML format.

Note that the actual extra files that Captivate generates depend on the standard being used (SCORM, AICC, or xAPI) and on the chosen version of SCORM.

Extra credit – Publishing the Flash version of the SCORM package

In this extra credit section, you will publish the Flash version of your eLearning-enabled project as a SCORM package. The general steps go as follows:

- Use the **Publish | Publish to Computer** icon in the Toolbar to open the **Publish** dialog.

- Make sure that the **Output Format** is set to **SWF** and that the **Location** is the `Chapter15/publish` folder of the exercises.
- Change the name of the project to `takeTheTrain_SWF_SCORM`.
- Publish the file.
- As we have added interactive video and overlay slides in this project, you will see an additional alert stating that a few objects or slides are not supported in the SWF format. Click **OK** to publish it anyway. As a result, all the other slides will be functional except the interactive video slides in this course.

Captivate should generate the `takeTheTrain_SWF_SCORM.zip` file in the `Chapter15/publish` folder. Don't hesitate to unzip that file and inspect its contents.

Working with the MultiSCO packager

In `Chapter 7`, *Working with Quizzes*, you discovered that the concept of the **Sharable Content Object (SCO)** is at the heart of the SCORM specification. As far as SCORM is concerned, the two eLearning-enabled projects you published in the previous section are both considered as SCOs. Each of these SCOs contain their own manifest file. One of the key pieces of information contained in the `imsmanifest.xml` file is the unique SCO identifier of this particular package, as entered in the **Manifest** dialog of Captivate.

One of the most interesting aspects of SCORM is the ability to take different SCOs, arrange them in a course, and publish them as a single SCORM package. This is precisely what the MultiSCO packager allows you to do.

In the next exercise, you will create one more SCO and use the MultiSCO packager to package multiple SCOs into a single package.

Creating SCOs

Captivate is not the only eLearning authoring tool that can produce valid SCORM packages. You can therefore use the MultiSCO packager to include multiple eLearning modules that have been developed by different authoring tools in a single course package.

Creating a SCORM package from the Video Demo project

A Video Demo is a project that uses the .cpvc file extension. As discussed earlier in Chapter 9, *Producing a Video Demo*, such a project can only be published as an .mp4 video file. The publishing options that are available for a Video Demo project do not allow for the creation of a SCORM package. But there is a trick! In the next exercise, you will import a .cpvc Video Demo project inside a standard Captivate project and publish it as a SCORM package using the following steps:

1. Return to Captivate and close every open file.
2. Use the **File** | **New Project** | **Blank Project** menu item to create a new Blank Captivate project.
3. In the **New Blank Project** dialog, select the size of **1280 x 720** and click **OK**.

Captivate creates a new project that is 1280 pixels in width and 720 pixels in height. The next step is to insert the Video Demo CPVC project inside this new project.

4. Use the **Insert** | **CPVC Slide** menu item to insert the Video Demo into the current project.
5. Browse to the Chapter15/encoderVideo.cpvc file and click **Open**.
6. In the **Filmstrip** panel, right-click slide 1 and delete it.
7. Save the file as Chapter15/EncoderVideo.cptx.

Thanks to the **Insert** | **CPCV Slide** menu item, you have inserted the Video Demo as a new slide in a regular project. As far as Captivate is concerned, this project is a standard project that uses the .cptx file extension. The Video Demo project can therefore be published as a SCORM package.

8. Use the **Quiz** | **Quiz Preferences** menu item to open the **Preferences** dialog on the **Quiz Reporting** page.
9. At the top of the page, select the **Enable reporting for this project** checkbox.
10. Open the **LMS** drop-down menu and choose **Moodle** as the LMS.
11. Click the **Configure** button to create a SCORM Manifest.

12. Enter the following values in the **Manifest** dialog:

Field	Content
Course Identifier	encoderVideo
Course Title	The Adobe Media Encoder Video Demo
Course Description	This video shows the student how to convert a Quick Time movie into an MP4 video
SCO Identifier	encoderVideo
SCO Title	The Adobe Media Encoder Video Demo

13. Click **OK** to validate and close the **Manifest** dialog.

There is no Quiz in this particular file, but this does not mean that you have nothing to track! In a Quizless project, SCORM can be used to track the project's completion status.

14. In the **Status Representation** section, make sure that the **Incomplete ---> Complete** option is selected.
15. In the **Success/Completion Criteria** section, select the **Slide Views** checkbox and deselect the **Quiz** checkbox.
16. Since there is no Quiz in this project, deselect the **Interaction Data** checkbox in the **Data To Report** section.
17. Click **OK** to validate and close the **Quiz Preferences** dialog.

Now that the Quiz Reporting Preferences have been correctly entered, the last step is to publish this project as a SCORM package.

18. Use the **Publish | Publish to Computer** icon in the Toolbar to open the **Publish** dialog.
19. If needed, change the **Project Title** to `encoderVideo`.
20. Use the `Chapter15/publish` folder of this exercise as the publish **Location**.
21. Select HTML5 as the only option in the **Output Format**.
22. Make sure that the **Zip Files** option is selected.
23. Leave all the other options at their default values and click **Publish**.
24. When the publication process is finished, use the Finder (Mac) or Windows Explorer (Windows) to browse to the `Chapter15/publish` folder of your exercises.

You should see another SCORM package named `encoderVideo.zip`. This ZIP file contains all the assets that are necessary to integrate the Video Demo project into a SCORM 1.2-compliant LMS, such as Moodle.

Creating a single course package from multiple SCOs

The publish folder of your exercises should now contain three separate SCORM packages: `takeTheTrain_HTML5_SCORM.zip`, `takeTheTrain_SWF_SCORM.zip` (from the *Extra Credit* section), and `encoderVideo.zip`, which you created in the previous section. Each of these packages has a unique SCO identifier that's defined in the `imsManifest.xml` file inside each package.

Using the MultiSCO packager, you will now combine these SCOs into a single SCORM course. At the end of this procedure, you will have a single `.zip` file containing all three modules. This single `.zip` file can be uploaded as-is into a SCORM-compliant LMS, such as Moodle.

Perform the following steps to create the SCORM package:

1. Return to Captivate and use the **File | New Project | Multi-SCORM Packager** menu item to open the **Adobe Multi SCO Packager** AIR application.

The **Multi SCO Packager** application is an external AIR application that is part of your Captivate installation. As shown in the following screenshot, the **Multi SCO Packager** proposes three course templates, the leftmost template being the simplest one:

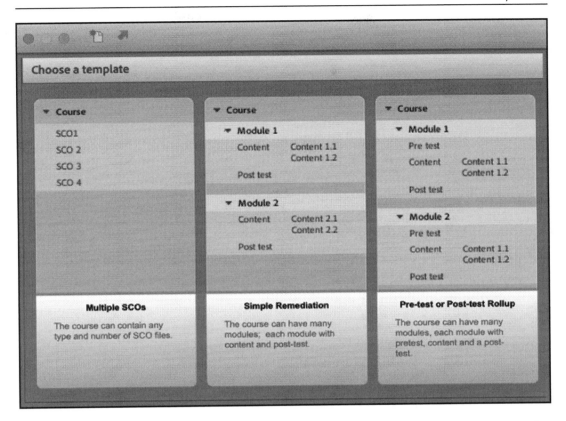

In Chapter 7, *Working with Quizzes*, you learned that the Moodle LMS is SCORM 1.2-compliant. This means that you will need to generate a SCORM 1.2-compliant package if you want to upload your course to Moodle. In the **Multi SCO Packager** application, only the simplest template is SCORM 1.2-compliant, and the other two templates are SCORM 2004-compatible.

2. Click the first (leftmost) template named **Multiple SCOs**.

3. In the **Course Manifest Details** dialog, perform the following steps:
   1. Select **1.2** in the **Version** drop-down menu under **SCORM Version**.
   2. Type `DiDaXo_bestOfSeries` in the **Identifier** field.
   3. Type `The best of DiDaXo` in the **Title** field.
   4. Type `Experience the best courses of the DiDaXo company in this sample Course package.` in the **Description** field.
   5. Type `1` in the **Version** field.

4. Click **OK** to validate these changes and close the **Course Manifest Details** dialog.

The information you just typed into the **Course Manifest Details** dialog will be merged with the Manifest files of each individual SCO contained in this course to create a single SCORM manifest for the entire course. The next step is to add multiple SCOs into the course.

5. Click the **+** icon in the top-right corner of the **Multi SCO Packager** application (identified by the tooltip).
6. Browse to the `Chapter15/publish` folder from your exercise and select the `takeTheTrain_HTML5_SCORM.zip` package. Click **Open** to add the package to the course.
7. Repeat the same operation to add the `takeTheTrain_SWF_SCORM.zip` and `encoderVideo.zip` packages of the `Chapter15/publish` folder to the course.

You can add as many SCORM packages as needed into the course. Note the icons at the bottom right corner of the **Multi SCO Packager** application. They allow you to reorder or delete the SCOs inside the course:

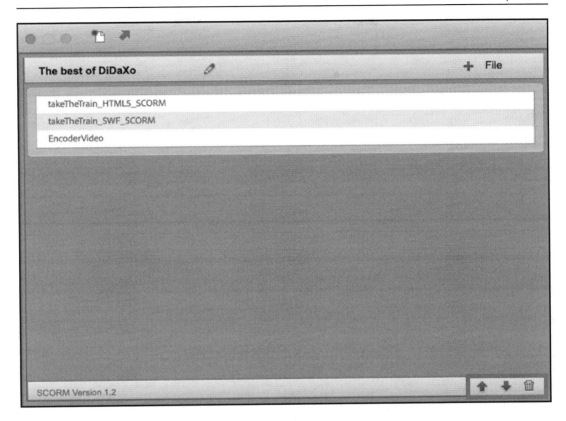

Now that every SCO has been added to the course, the last step is to publish the course as a single SCORM package that contains all three SCOs.

8. Click the **Publish Course** icon at the top left corner of the **Multi SCO Packager** application.
9. In the **Publish SCO package** dialog, use the **Publish Folder** field to choose the `Chapter15/publish` folder of the exercises as the output folder of the package.
10. Click the **Publish** button. When the process is complete, click **OK** to acknowledge the successful creation of the SCORM package.
11. Close the **Multi SCO Packager** application.
12. Use the Finder (Mac) or Windows Explorer (Windows) to browse to the `Chapter15/publish` folder of your exercises.

You should see the new `DiDaXo_bestOfSeries.zip` package that has been created by the Multi SCO Packager application. This package contains the three modules that you added in the Multi SCO Packager in the previous section. Feel free to unzip the package to check out its content. You should be able to locate a single `imsManifest.xml` file, as well as the assets pertaining to each of the three modules you added to the course.

When using the MultiSCORM Packager, remember the following points:

- Each individual component needs to be published as a SCORM package that contains a valid `imsManifest.xml` file. Such a package is called a **Sharable Content Object (SCO)**.
- A single SCO can be used in many different course packages.
- A single course can contain an unlimited number of SCOs.
- The generated course package can be uploaded as a single unit to a SCORM-compliant LMS.
- There are different versions of SCORM. Make sure you create course packages that are compliant with whatever SCORM version your LMS supports.
- The MultiSCORM Packager of Captivate proposes three course templates to choose from. Make sure the chosen Template can be used with the version of SCORM that you are targeting.

This concludes your exploration of the MultiSCORM packager of Captivate.

For more information on the MultiSCORM Packager, refer to the following Help document on the Adobe website: https://helpx.adobe.com/captivate/using/multi-scorm-packager.html.

Publishing to PDF

Another publishing option that's available in Captivate is the ability to publish the project as an Adobe PDF document. This process is tied to the Flash publishing process we covered previously. When converting to PDF, Captivate first converts the project to Flash and then embeds the resulting `.swf` file inside a PDF document. To read the Flash file that's embedded in the PDF document, the free Adobe Acrobat Reader relies on the Flash Player plugin that is installed on the student's computer. This is why this option does not work on a mobile device, even if the Adobe Reader app is installed.

Publishing the Captivate project to PDF is a great way to make the eLearning course available offline. The students can, for example, download the PDF file from a website and take the course on a train or on an airplane where no internet connection is available. However, be aware that, if the course is viewed offline or outside an LMS, quiz scores and the course completion status cannot be tracked.

In the following exercise, you will publish the Encoder Demonstration to PDF:

1. Return to the `Chapter15/encoderDemo_800.cptx` file.
2. Click the **Publish | Publish to Computer** icon on the Toolbar.
3. In the central area, change the **Project Title** to `encoderDemo_800_PDF`.
4. Make sure that the **Location** field still points to the `Chapter15/publish` folder of the exercises.
5. Choose **SWF** as the only **Output Format**.
6. Make sure that the **Publish to Folder** checkbox is selected.
7. In the bottom-left area of the **Publish** dialog, select the **Export PDF** checkbox.
8. Click the **Publish** button in the lower-right corner of the **Publish** dialog.

When the publishing process is complete, a message tells you that Acrobat 9 or higher is required to read the generated PDF file.

9. Click **OK** to acknowledge this message. A second information box will open.
10. Click **No** to discard the second message and close the **Publish** dialog.
11. Use the Finder (Mac) or Windows Explorer (Windows) to browse to the `Chapter15/publish/encoderDemo_800_PDF` folder of the exercises.

There should be five files in the `encoderDemo_800_PDF` folder. Actually, publishing to PDF is an extra option of the standard ability to publish to Flash.

12. Delete all but the PDF file from the `encoderDemo_800_PDF` folder.
13. Double-click the `encoderDemo_800_PDF.pdf` file to open it in Adobe Acrobat.
14. Note that this file plays normally in Adobe Acrobat. This proves that all the necessary files and assets have been correctly embedded into the PDF file.

In the next section, you will explore another option of Captivate: publishing the project as a standalone application.

Publishing as a standalone application

When publishing as a standalone application, Captivate generates a .exe file for playback on Windows or an .app file for playback on Mac. The .exe (Windows) or .app (Mac) file contains the compiled .swf file, plus a light version of the Flash Player.

The advantages and disadvantages of a standalone application are similar to those of a PDF file. That is, the file can be viewed offline on a train, on an airplane, or elsewhere, but features requiring an internet connection will not work.

In the following exercise, you will publish the Captivate file as a standalone application for Mac or Windows using the following steps:

1. If needed, return to the Chapter15/encoderDemo_800.cptx file.
2. Click the **Publish | Publish to Computer** icon on the Toolbar.
3. At the top of the **Publish** dialog, open the **Publish As** drop-down menu.
4. Choose the **Executable** menu item.
5. Open the **Publish Type** drop-down menu.
6. If you are on a Windows PC, choose **Windows Executable (*.exe)**. If you are using a Mac, choose **MAC Executable (*.app)**.
7. If needed, change the **Project Title** to encoderDemo_800.
8. Make sure that the Chapter15/publish folder of the exercises is still the current publish **Location**.

Take some time to inspect the other options of the **Publish** dialog. One of them allows you to choose a custom icon for the generated .exe (Windows) or .app (Mac) file.

9. Leave the other options at their current value and click the **Publish** button.

When the publish process is complete, an information box will ask whether you want to see the generated output.

10. Click **No** to clear the information message and close the **Publish** dialog.

Now that the standalone application has been generated, you will use the Finder (Mac) or Windows Explorer (Windows) to take a look at the Chapter15/publish folder and test the newly created applications.

11. Use the Finder (Mac) or Windows Explorer (Windows) to browse to the Chapter15/publish folder of the exercises.

12. Double-click the `encoderDemo_800.exe` (Windows) or `encoderDemo_800.app` (Mac) file to open the generated application.

The Captivate project opens as a standalone application in its own window. Note that no browser is necessary to play the project.

This publish format is particularly useful when you want to burn the course module to a CD-ROM. When generating a Windows executable (`.exe`), Captivate can even generate an `autorun.ini` file so that the project automatically plays when the CD-ROM is inserted into the computer.

Publishing as a .mp4 video file

When publishing a project as a video, Captivate generates an `.mp4` file and suggests various video presets for the conversion. Actually, Captivate first generates a `.swf` file and then converts it into a `.mp4` video file.

After the conversion, the video file can be played with any media player that is capable of reading the `.mp4` format. This is an ideal solution if you want to upload the resulting movie to YouTube or if you want to make it available to non-Flash devices. On the other hand, the generated `.mp4` video file permits only a linear experience—that is, no more interaction and no more branching is possible. The student experiences the video from the beginning to the end in a linear fashion, as is the case while watching a motion picture in a movie theater or on TV. Consequently, converting a Captivate project to a video file is well-suited for a demonstration, but does not work well with simulations.

In the following exercise, you will convert the Encoder Demonstration into a `.mp4` video by using the following steps:

1. If needed, return to the `Chapter15/encoderDemo_800.cptx` file.
2. Click the **Publish | Publish to Computer** icon in the Toolbar.
3. Open the **Publish As** drop-down menu and choose the **Video** item.
4. If needed, change the **Project Title** to `encoderDemo_800`.
5. Ensure that the **Location** field still points to the `Chapter15/publish` folder of the exercises.
6. Open the **Select Preset** drop-down list. Take some time to inspect the available options and choose **YouTube Widescreen HD**.
7. Click the **Publish** button in the bottom-right corner of the **Publish** dialog.

Publishing to a video file can be quite a lengthy process, so be patient. First, you will see that Captivate converts the project into a .swf file. When that first conversion is over, Captivate opens a second box named **SWF to Video Conversion** and converts the .swf file into a .mp4 video. At the end of the whole process, the **Video** dialog proposes to publish the generated video to YouTube or to open it.

8. Close the **Video** window.

9. As usual, use the Finder (Mac) or Windows Explorer (Windows) to take a look at the Chapter15/publish folder of your exercises.

10. Double-click the encoderDemo_800.mp4 file. The video will open in the default media player.

The generated video file can be uploaded to YouTube, Vimeo, DailyMotion, or any other video hosting service. You can also host the video on your own internal video streaming server (such as an Adobe Media Server) if you have one available.

Publishing to YouTube

Captivate includes a workflow that allows you to publish your Captivate movie as a video file and upload it to your YouTube account without even leaving Captivate.

In the following exercise, you will convert your file into a video and upload it to YouTube.

 This exercise requires that you have a YouTube account. If you do not have a YouTube account, you can create one for free at https://support.google.com/youtube/answer/161805 or read through the steps of this exercise.

Perform the following steps to upload the video to YouTube:

1. Return to the Chapter15/encoderDemo_800.cptx file.

2. Use the **File | Publish to YouTube** menu item to start the process.

When using this menu item, Captivate generates the slides as if you were publishing the movie in Flash format. When that first conversion is complete, Captivate opens the **SWF to Video Conversion** window and converts the `.swf` file to `.mp4`. So far, the process is exactly the same as the one you used in the previous section. At the end of the process, however, Captivate opens another window.

3. In the **Publish to YouTube** window, click **Log in**.

4. Enter your YouTube account credentials.

5. You will get a message that Adobe Captivate wants to manage your YouTube account and your YouTube videos. Click **Allow** to give access to Captivate.

6. Once logged in, enter the relevant project information:
   - Enter the title of the movie in the **Title** field
   - Enter a description in the **Description** field
   - Choose the level of **Privacy** (Public, Private, or Unlisted)
   - Select the **I have read the terms & conditions** checkbox and click the **Upload** button

Captivate will then upload the video to YouTube. When the process is complete, you will see a preview of the video in the same dialog. To go to the YouTube page and view the video, click the **YouTube** button on the bottom right corner of the video.

7. Click the **Close Window** button to close the **Publish to YouTube** window.

As you can see, Captivate makes it incredibly easy to publish a project to YouTube!

For more information on YouTube's privacy settings and the difference between a public and private video, visit `https://support.google.com/youtube/answer/157177?hl=en`.

Publishing to Microsoft Word

Another important publishing option is publishing a Captivate project as a Microsoft Word document. There are four formats available: Handout, Lesson, Step-by-Step guide, and Storyboard.

This publication option requires that both Adobe Captivate and Microsoft Word are installed on the same system. If you do not have Microsoft Word installed on your computer, just read through the steps of this exercise so that you have an idea of the workflow.

Use the following steps to publish your Captivate project as a Microsoft Word file using the Handout template:

1. Return to the `Chapter15/encoderDemo_800.cptx` file.
2. Use the **File | Print** menu item to open the **Print** dialog.
3. In the left column, change the **Project Title** to `encoderDemo_800_handout`.
4. Make sure that the **Folder** field still points to the `Chapter15/publish` folder of the exercises.
5. In the **Export Range** section, make sure that **All** is selected. You could publish a smaller selection of slides if needed.

That's it for the usual options. Before clicking on the **Publish** button, you have a few more options available in the right column of the **Print** dialog.

6. Open the **Type** drop-down list. Inspect the available options and choose the **Handouts** type.
7. In the **Handout Layout Options** section, select the **Use table in the output** option.
8. Open the **Slides Per Page** dropdown and choose to have two slides on each page of the Word document.
9. Select the **Caption Text**, **Slide Notes**, and **Include mouse Path** checkboxes.
10. Take some time to inspect the remaining options, but leave them all at their current value.
11. When ready, click the **Publish** button.

Captivate generates the Word document according to the options defined in the **Publish** dialog. When done, an information box will appear, asking whether you want to view the generated file.

12. Click **No** to discard the information box and close the **Print** dialog.
13. Use the Finder (Mac) or Windows Explorer (Windows) to browse to the `Chapter15/publish` folder of your exercises.
14. Double-click the newly created `encoderDemo_800_handout.doc` file.

The file will open in Microsoft Word. Take some time to inspect the generated Word document. Can you find the effect of each of the boxes you selected in the **Print** dialog?

Extra credit – publishing to Word

In this section, you will test the remaining Microsoft Word publishing options by generating a Lesson, Step-by-Step guide, and Storyboard. These are the general steps to follow:

1. Use the **File | Print** menu item to open the **Print** dialog.
2. Give the project a meaningful Project Title.
3. In the right area of the **Print** dialog, change **Type** to either **Lesson, Step by Step**, or **Storyboard**.
4. Experiment with the other options as well. Each Type has a specific set of options available, which are, for the most part, self-explanatory.
5. When ready, click the **Publish** button.
6. Use the Finder (Mac) or Windows Explorer (Windows) to browse to the `Chapter15/publish` folder and test your files in Microsoft Word.

Publishing for devices

When publishing an HTML5 application, you rely on the web browser that's installed on the computer (or device) of the student to render the course. That is, if the course is viewed on a tablet, your student needs to open the web browser that's installed on the tablet to see the course.

When using the **Publish for Devices (app)** feature of Captivate, you can generate a native mobile application from your eLearning content. This means that your course could be distributed by an app store (such as the Apple App Store for iOS or the Google Play store for Android) and will be installed as yet another app on the device of your learners.

To convert your course into a native application, Captivate relies on the Adobe **PhoneGap Build** service. This online service can convert any HTML5/CSS/JavaScript web application into a native mobile application. PhoneGap Build supports many mobile platforms, including iOS, Android, and Windows Phone.

 More information on the Adobe PhoneGap Build service can be found at `https://build.phonegap.com/`.

When using this option, Captivate first publishes the project in HTML5 and then uploads the HTML5 application to the PhoneGap Build service, where it is compiled into a native iOS and/or Android application. Because this system relies on HTML5, all the capabilities and limitations of regular HTML5 projects also apply to projects that are published as apps.

 Note that if you want to compile your eLearning course as an iOS application, you need to be registered as an Apple developer, pay the annual Apple Developer fee, and create an Apple-approved security certificate for your app. Android also requires a certificate, but this certificate is not mandatory for compiling the application for testing purposes.

Visit the Captivate Help page at `https://helpx.adobe.com/captivate/using/preview-publishing.html` to learn how to publish apps using PhoneGap Build.

This last section concludes your overview of the publishing options of Captivate. So, let's do a quick summary of what has been covered so far:

- Publishing is the third and last step of the Captivate workflow. The goal is to make the content available to learners in a variety of formats.
- The main publishing formats of Captivate are the HTML5 format and the Flash (SWF) format.
- When publishing in Flash format, Captivate generates a `.swf` file that can be played back by the free Adobe Flash Player plugin.
- The generated `.swf` file can be embedded in a PDF document for offline viewing. This option requires Adobe Acrobat, Adobe Reader 9, or later versions.
- A project published in HTML5 can be played back on virtually any mobile device, including iOS and Android devices.
- Not every feature of Captivate is supported in HTML5. Use the **HTML5 Tracker** to find out which slides/objects of your project are not supported.
- New features in Captivate 2019 like 360 slides, interactive videos, and VR projects are not supported for SWF format.
- It is possible to hide and show slides. A hidden slide is not part of the published project, even though it is still in the `.cptx` file.
- **Mobile Palette** allows you to enable Gestures and Geolocation services.
- When publishing as a standalone application, Captivate produces either a `.exe` file for playback on Windows or a `.app` file for playback on a Mac.

- Captivate can produce a `.mp4` video that can be optimized for YouTube and for playback on a mobile device.
- When publishing as a PDF file or standalone application, the published project can no longer connect to the internet. Consequently, some features that require an internet connection (such as communicating with an LMS) do not work.
- When the project is published as a video file, it can only be experienced as a linear video that plays from the beginning to the end. Consequently, interactivity and branching are not supported.
- Use the **File** | **Print** menu item to publish your files as Microsoft Word documents.
- It is possible to publish your eLearning content as native Android and/or iOS applications. This capability relies on the PhoneGap Build service from Adobe.

Summary

At the end of this final chapter, you can proudly turn off the lights and leave the post-production studio. You have gone through the three major steps of the production process, uncovering lots of Captivate features, tools, and objects along the way!

In this chapter, you first focused on the final fine-tuning you can apply to the project before the actual publishing phase. You checked the spelling, decided how the movie should start and end, added metadata to the project, and created a unique Skin, among other things. When all of these final changes had been taken care of, the course module was finally ready for publication.

In the second part of this chapter, you concentrated on the **Publish** dialog, where you gained experience of the main publishing features of Captivate. Publishing is the process by which the course is made available to your target audience.

Publishing to Flash is the first (and legacy) publishing option of Captivate. When published in HTML5, the project can be played back on any device that's equipped with a modern web browser. This includes the vast majority of mobile devices, such as iOS and Android smartphones and tablets.

Other publishing formats of Captivate include publishing as a standalone application, publishing as a `.mp4` video file, and publishing as a Microsoft Word document. The `.mp4` video files produced by Captivate can be easily uploaded to YouTube without even leaving the application.

Congratulations on achieving this important milestone! With the completion of this chapter comes the end of this book. We hope you have enjoyed reading these pages, and have acquired the knowledge you need to create the next generation of eLearning content with Adobe Captivate.

As for us, we would like to thank you for reading our book. We are already looking forward to your feedback or meeting you in person during an eLearning or Captivate event somewhere in the world.

Until then, have fun with Adobe Captivate!

Meet the community

Rick Zanotti is a legend in the eLearning community. Everyone knows him and he knows everyone! This is probably due to the numerous video podcasts that he makes, which have a wide number of eLearning influencers from all over the world. We strongly recommend you subscribe to his channel to get the latest and greatest from the best minds of our industry.

Rick Zanotti

Rick Zanotti is the president of RELATE, a well-known multimedia and eLearning development firm. Rick has had a long career in Information Systems and has over 20 years of experience in eLearning and media design. He's been a systems analyst, instructional designer, programmer, web developer, and voice-talent. He runs a number of technical and industry-specific internet broadcasts on the RELATECASTS channel. For 10 years, Rick was on the advisory board for RoboDemo/Adobe Captivate.

Contact details

- Website: www.relate.com
- Twitter: @rickzanotti
- Facebook: rickzanotti
- Google+: rickzanotti
- eLearnChat and other video netcasts: www.relatecasts.com
- YouTube: www.youtube.com/relatecasts

Other Books You May Enjoy

If you enjoyed this book, you may be interested in these other books by Packt:

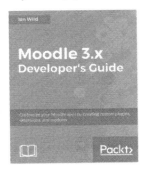

Moodle 3.x Developer's Guide
Ian Wild

ISBN: 9781786467119

- Work with the different types of custom modules that can be written for Moodle 3.x
- Understand how to author custom modules so they conform to the agreed Moodle 3.x development guidelines
- Get familiar with the Moodle 3.x architecture—its internal and external APIs
- Customize Moodle 3.x so it can integrate seamlessly with third-party applications of any kind
- Build a new course format to specify the layout of a course
- Implement third-party graphics libraries in your plugins
- Build plugins that can be themed easily
- Provide custom APIs that will provide the means to automate Moodle 3 in real time

Moodle 3 E-Learning Course Development - Fourth Edition
Susan Smith Nash, William Rice

ISBN: 9781788472197

- Know what Moodle does and how it supports your teaching strategies
- Install Moodle on your computer and navigate your way around it
- Understand all of Moodle's learning features
- Monitor how learners interact with your site using site statistics
- Add multimedia content to your site
- Allow students to enroll themselves or invite other students to join a course

Leave a review - let other readers know what you think

Please share your thoughts on this book with others by leaving a review on the site that you bought it from. If you purchased the book from Amazon, please leave us an honest review on this book's Amazon page. This is vital so that other potential readers can see and use your unbiased opinion to make purchasing decisions, we can understand what our customers think about our products, and our authors can see your feedback on the title that they have worked with Packt to create. It will only take a few minutes of your time, but is valuable to other potential customers, our authors, and Packt. Thank you!

Index

Made in the USA
Middletown, DE
02 May 2023

29899513R00426